A Gift of Fire

Social, Legal, and Ethical Issues for Computers and the Internet

2nd Edition

Sara Baase
San Diego State University

An Alan R. Apt Book

Prentice Hall

PEARSON EDUCATION, INC.
UPPER SADDLE RIVER, NJ 07458

Library of Congress Cataloging-in-Publication Data

CIP data on file

Vice President and Editorial Director, ECS: *Marcia Horton*
Publisher: *Alan R. Apt*
Associate Editor: *Toni D. Holm*
Editorial Assistant: *Patrick Lindner*
Vice President and Director of Production and Manufacturing, ESM: *David W. Riccardi*
Executive Managing Editor: *Vince O'Brien*
Assistant Managing Editor: *Camille Trentacoste*
Production Editor: *Lakshmi Balasubramanian*
Creative Director: *Carole Anson*
Art Director: *Wanda España*
Art Editor: *Gregory Dulles*
Cover Design: *Anthony Inciong*
Interior Design: *Scott Garrison*
Manufacturing Manager: *Trudy Pisciotti*
Manufacturing Buyer: *Lisa McDowell*
Marketing Manager: *Cynthia Szollose*
Marketing Assistant: *Barrie Reinhold*
Cover Credit: *Scala/Art Resource, NY*

© 2003 Pearson Education, Inc.
Pearson Education, Inc.
Upper Saddle River, NJ 07458

Printed in the United States of America
10   9   8   7

ISBN 0-13-008215-5

Pearson Education Ltd., *London*
Pearson Education Australia Pty. Ltd., *Sydney*
Pearson Education Singapore, Pte. Ltd.
Pearson Education North Asia Ltd., *Hong Kong*
Pearson Education Canada, Inc., *Toronto*
Pearson Educación de Mexico, S.A. de C.V.
Pearson Education—Japan, *Tokyo*
Pearson Education Malaysia, Pte. Ltd.
Pearson Education, Inc., *Upper Saddle River, New Jersey*

To Keith

CONTENTS

3   ENCRYPTION AND INTERCEPTION OF COMMUNICATIONS   97

4   CAN WE TRUST THE COMPUTER?   135

5   FREEDOM OF SPEECH IN CYBERSPACE   192

6   INTELLECTUAL PROPERTY   234

9   BROADER ISSUES ON THE IMPACT AND CONTROL OF COMPUTERS   364

10   PROFESSIONAL ETHICS AND RESPONSIBILITIES   400

PREFACE

This book is intended for two audiences: students preparing for careers in computer science and students in other fields who are interested in issues that arise from computer technology. The book has no technical prerequisites. It can be used at various levels, in both introductory and advanced courses about computing or technology. My students are mostly junior and senior computer science majors.

Courses on social and ethical issues

Many universities offer courses with titles such as "Ethical Issues in Computing" or "Computers and Society." These courses vary in content and focus. Some focus primarily on ethical issues (issues the student might face directly as a computer professional), whereas others address the wider social, political, and legal issues related to computers. The bulky subtitle of this book gives a hint of my preference. I believe it is useful and important for students to learn about the social, legal, philosophical, political, constitutional, and economic issues (and the historical background of those issues) related to computers—issues they might face as members of a complex technological society, not just in their professional lives. The issues are relevant to being a responsible computer user (professional or personal) and member of the public who could serve on a jury, debate social and political issues with friends, or influence legislation. Thus, for example, I think it is important to cover the implications of censorship laws for the Internet, the problems of protecting intellectual property in cyberspace, the risks of new technologies, and so on.

The last chapter focuses on ethical issues for computer professionals with discussion of case scenarios. The basic ethical principles in computing are not different from ethical principles in other professions or other aspects of life: honesty, responsibility, fairness. However, within any one profession, there are special kinds of problems that arise. Thus, we discuss "applied ethics" and guidelines for the computer profession. I include two of the main codes of ethics and professional practices for computer professionals in an Appendix. I believe students will find the discussion of ethical issues for computer professionals more interesting and useful if it has as background the discussions of the social and legal issues and controversies in the first nine chapters.

Each of the chapters in this book could easily be expanded to a whole book. I had to leave out many interesting topics and examples. In some cases, I mention an issue, example, or position with little or no discussion. I hope some of these will spark further reading and debate.

Controversies

This book presents controversies and alternative points of view: privacy vs. access to information, privacy and civil liberties vs. law enforcement, freedom of speech vs. control of content on the Net, market-based vs. regulatory solutions, and so on. Often, the discussion in the book necessarily includes political, social, and philosophical issues, but I have tried (with some difficulty because of my enthusiasm for these issues) to focus specifically on the connections between the issues and computer technology. I encourage students to explore the arguments on all sides and to be able to explain why they reject the ones they reject before they take a position. I believe this approach prepares them to tackle new controversies; they can figure out the consequences of various proposals, generate arguments for each side, and evaluate them. I encourage students to think in principles, rather than case by case, or at least to see that the same principle appears in different cases even if they choose to take different positions on them. For example, one issue that comes up several times, in different contexts throughout the book, is whether a device, a technique, or a whole technology should be banned or severely restricted because people can use it for illegal or harmful actions as well as for beneficial ones.

My point of view

Any writer on subjects such as those in this book has some personal opinions, positions, or biases. I believe strongly in the importance of the Bill of Rights. I also have a generally positive view of technology, including computer technology. Don Norman, a psychologist and technology enthusiast who writes on humanizing technology, observed that most people who have written books about technology "are opposed to it and write about how horrible it is."* I am not one of those people. I think that technology, in general, has been a major factor in bringing physical well-being, liberty, and opportunity to hundreds of millions of people. Perhaps critics of technology miss some of the most impressive and fundamental benefits because they are so used to them that they take them for granted. Think about the products we use, the food we eat, and the people we talk to in a day—and consider how different a day would be without modern communication, transportation, refrigeration, and plumbing. That does not mean technology is without problems. Most of this book focuses on problems. We must recognize and study them so that we can reduce the negative effects of computer technology and increase the positive ones.

---

* Quoted in Jeannette DeWyze, "When You Don't Know How to Turn On Your Radio, Don Norman Is On Your Side," *The San Diego Reader*, Dec. 1, 1994, p. 1.

While writing the first edition of this book, I attended a National Science Foundation-sponsored workshop on Ethical and Professional Issues in Computing. Keith Miller, one of the speakers, gave the following outline for discussing ethical issues (which he credited to a nun who had been one of his teachers years ago): "What? So what? Now what?" It struck me that this described how I wrote many sections of my book. I often begin with a description of what is happening, sometimes including a little history. Next comes a discussion of why there are concerns and what the new problems are (so what?). Finally I give some commentary or perspective and some current and potential solutions to the problems (now what?).

An early reviewer of this book objected to one of the quotations I include at the beginning of a section because he thought it was untrue. So perhaps I should make it clear that I agree with many of the quotations I have placed at the beginnings of chapters and various sections of the book—but not with all of them. I chose some to be provocative and to remind students of the variety of opinions on some of the issues.

I am a computer scientist, not an attorney. I summarize the main points of many laws and legal cases and discuss arguments about them, but I do not give a comprehensive legal analysis. Many ordinary terms have specific meanings in laws, and often a difference of one word can change the impact of a provision of a law or of a court decision. Laws have exceptions and special cases. Any reader who needs precise information about how a law applies in particular cases should consult an attorney or read the full text of laws, court decisions, and legal analysis.

Changing issues and environment

This is an extremely fast-changing field. The Y2K problem came and went between the first and second editions of the book. Spam and MP3s weren't big issues in 1996; DVDs weren't yet available. Encryption export restrictions were the subject of intense controversy for several years leading up to first edition, but now are gone. The Supreme Court ruled the Communications Decency Act unconstitutional after the first edition was published; since then, Congress has passed several more censorship laws. The changes made by the World Wide Web in just a few years are illustrated by a change I made in the exercises. In the first edition the group of exercises called "Assignments" included the instruction *These exercises require some research or activity that may need to be done during business hours or a few days before the assignment is due.* Virtually all of them can now be done at 3AM on the Web.

Some issues and examples in this book are so current that details will change before or soon after publication. I don't consider this to be a serious problem. (A few of the exercises in the book ask the reader to research the result of legal cases unsettled at the time I write this.) Specific events do not change most of the underlying issues and arguments. I encourage students to bring in current news reports about relevant issues to discuss in class. When the students begin to stay alert for relevant news, they seem impressed to find how many ties there are between the course and current events.

Class activities

The course I designed in the Computer Science Department at San Diego State University requires a book report, a term paper, and an oral presentation by each student. Students do several presentations, debates, and mock trials in class, on such topics as penalties for hackers who unintentionally cause serious damage and whether filters should be required on library terminals. The students are very enthusiastic about these activities. I include a few in the Exercises sections, marked as Class Discussion Exercises. Although I selected some exercises for this category, I find that many others in the General Exercises sections are also good for lively class discussions.

It is an extraordinary pleasure to teach this course. At the beginning of each semester, some students expect boredom or sermons. By the end, most say they have found it eye-opening and important. They've seen and appreciated new arguments, and they understand more about the risks of computer technology and their responsibilities. Many students send me e-mail with news reports about issues in the course long after the semester is over, sometimes even after they have graduated and are already working in the field.

Additional sources and Web page for this textbook

The notes at the ends of the chapters include sources for specific information in the text and, occasionally, additional information and comment. I usually put one endnote at the end of the paragraph with sources for the whole paragraph. The lists of references at the ends of the chapters provide short samplings of the material available on the topics covered in this book. I have included some references that I used, some that I think are particularly useful or interesting for various reasons, and some that are not likely to be found elsewhere. I have made no attempt to be complete, but I include references to bibliographies and Web sites, some that have extensive archives of relevant material.

The Instructor's Manual for this book is my Web site at

www-rohan.sdsu.edu/faculty/giftfire.

It contains course materials (e.g., sample assignments) and links to many documents and other sites of interest.

Feedback

This book contains a large amount of information on a large variety of subjects. I have tried to be as accurate as possible, but, inevitably, there will be errors. I appreciate corrections; please send them to me at GiftOfFire@sdsu.edu or Computer Science Department, San Diego State University, San Diego, CA 92182-7720.

Acknowledgments

The following people assisted in the preparation of this edition by providing leads and information, answering questions, and/or reading drafts: Leland Beck, John L. Carroll, Sherry Clark, Don Gotterbarn, Jeannie Martin, Alan Riggins, Carol Sanders, Jack

Sanders, Milton Sank, Deborah Simpson, Vernor Vinge. Many former students suggested relevant topics and sent me articles: Cindy Clay, John Coulombe, Lionel English, Mary Dorsey Evans, Stephen Hinkle, Sang Kang, and Philip Woodworth.

The reviewers of the manuscript provided very helpful feedback and suggestions. They are Sherry Clark (Oregon State University), Art Farley (University of Oregon), David Fields (Eastern Kentucky University), Joseph F. Fulda, Don Gotterbarn (East Tennessee State University), Stephen Leach (Florida State University), Ernst L. Leiss (University of Houston), Bruce Maxim (University of Michigan–Dearborn), Leonard Myers (California Polytechnic University–San Luis Obispo), Lee Tien (Electronic Frontier Foundation), and Jeanne Walsh (University of North Carolina).

Michael Schneider and Judy Gersting initiated my writing in this area when they asked me to contribute a chapter, "Social and Legal Issues," to their textbook *An Invitation to Computer Science*. Jerry Westby, of West Publishing Company, gave permission to reuse portions of that chapter.

I enthusiastically thank you all!

I especially thank my husband, Keith Mayers, for technical help, patience, and encouragement.

1

UNWRAPPING THE GIFT

Prometheus, according to Greek myth, brought us the gift of fire. It is an awesome gift. It gives us the power to heat our homes, cook our food, and run the machines that make our lives more comfortable, healthy, and enjoyable. It is also awesomely destructive, both by accident and by arson. The Chicago fire in 1871 left 100,000 people homeless. In 1990 the oil fields of Kuwait were intentionally set ablaze. In 2000, a fire sparked by an automobile accident burned homes and 180,000 acres in the state of Washington. In spite of the risks, in spite of these disasters, few of us would choose to return the gift of fire and live without it. We have learned, gradually, how to use it productively, how to use it safely, and how to respond more effectively to disasters, be they natural, accidental, or intentional.

Computer technology, many would agree, is the most significant new technology since the beginning of the Industrial Revolution. It is an awesome technology, with the power to make routine tasks quick, easy, and accurate, to save lives, and to create large amounts of new wealth. It helps us explore space, improve communications, and do thousands of other tasks. As with fire, the power of computers creates powerful problems: potential loss of privacy, multimillion-dollar thefts, and breakdowns of large, complex systems (such as communications networks and banking systems) on which we have come to depend. In this book, we describe some of the remarkable benefits of computer and communication technologies, some of the problems associated with them, and some of the means for reducing the problems and coping with their effects.

1.1 The Ubiquity of Computers and the Rapid Pace of Change

Everything that can be invented has been invented.

—Charles H. Duell, Director of the U.S. Patent Office, 1899[1]

In 1804, Meriwether Lewis and William Clark set out on a two-and-a-half-year voyage to explore what is now the western United States. Many more years passed before their journals were published; later explorers did not know that Lewis and Clark had been there before them. Stephen Ambrose points out in his book about the Lewis and Clark expedition, *Undaunted Courage*, that information, people, and goods moved no faster than a horse—and this limitation on speed had not changed in thousands of years.[2] In 1997, millions of people worldwide went to the World Wide Web to watch a robot cart called Sojourner roll across the surface of Mars.

Telephones, automobiles, airplanes, radio, household electrical appliances, and many other marvels we take for granted were invented in the late 19th and early 20th centuries. They led to profound changes in how we work and play, how we get information, how we interact with our neighbors (even how we define our neighborhood), and how we organize our family lives. Although fast paced when compared to earlier rates of innovation, the changes were gradual compared to those in the computer age. One of the most dramatic feats of technology in the 20th century was our entry into space. Sputnik, the first man-made satellite, was launched in 1957. Neil Armstrong walked on the moon in 1969. We still do not have personal spacecraft, vacation trips to the moon, or a large amount of commercial or research activity in space. The moon landing has had little direct effect on our daily lives.

But have you used a computer today?

When I asked my students this question, about half the class raised hands. I asked the other half if they had used an ATM machine, a CD-player, or a cell phone. More hands went up until there was only one student whose hand was not raised. As I was about to ask another question, he laughed, put his hand up, and said, "I drove my car."

The point of the question is to remind us that computers are not just PCs and Macs that sit on desks in homes and offices. Microprocessors are now in hundreds of millions of appliances and devices. They are built into microwave ovens, bread-baking machines, automobile ignition and braking systems, telephones, cameras, medical instruments, and a large number of other machines we use regularly.

When we speak of computers in this book, we include the PCs and mainframes that run application software, embedded chips that control machines, the growing variety of information, entertainment, and communications devices (like palm computers, DVD players, and game machines), and the "Net," or "cyberspace." Cyberspace is built of computers (e.g., Web servers), communications devices (wired and wireless), and storage media, but its real meaning is the vast web of communications and information—the World Wide Web, the Internet, commercial services, news and discussion groups, chat rooms, e-mail, databases, and so on—that are accessible from all over the world.

These are all recent innovations. When your grandparents were children, there were no computers, not even the old-style business mainframes. In 1994, on the 25th anniversary of the first moon landing, a television documentary reported that the lunar landing module used by the Apollo astronauts had less computing power than a 1994 automobile. Only a generation ago, computers were large machines, the size of a few refrigerators, kept in air-conditioned rooms. Library catalogs filled large rooms with racks of trays containing 3×5 index cards. There were no CD players, no VCRs, no ATMs, no cell phones, no World Wide Web. The Web is younger than college freshmen today. But now, library catalogs are databases, accessible on the Web. In 2001, Americans spent more than 3.3 billion dollars buying products online, approximately ten times the 1997 total.[3] The ubiquitousness of computers, the rapid pace of change that accompanied them, and their profound impact on daily life are dramatic aspects of the Computer Revolution.

Current research and development are producing new technologies and applications that will continue to change dramatically the way we work, play, and interact with other people. What will be the impact of *wearware*—wearable computers, displays in eye glasses or contact lenses, smart sensors in clothing? What will be the impact of tiny flying sensor/computers that communicate wirelessly and can be deployed on a military base to monitor movement of equipment and people, or in a collapsed building to search for survivors, or in homes and public places to spy on people? Genetic engineering (a biological field heavily dependent on computing technology) will eliminate or cure diseases. What else will it do? Careful thought about the issues and arguments discussed in this book should help prepare us to face issues now on the horizon.

> *Since the computer-on-a-chip was invented in 1971, the cost of computing has plunged 10 million-fold. That's like being able to buy a new Boeing 747 for the price of a large pizza.*
>
> —Michael Rothschild[4]

1.2 Examining the Gift: An Introduction to Some Issues and Themes

1.2.1 ISSUES

Analyzing and evaluating the impact of a new technology can be difficult. Some of the changes are obvious. Some are more subtle. Even when benefits are obvious, their costs and side effects might not be, and vice versa. We use the automated teller machine (ATM) in this introduction of some of the issues we discuss in more detail throughout the book. Many other examples could be used as well. While reading this discussion, try to do a similar analysis for, say, buying books on the Web.

Why do we use ATMs? Because they are convenient. They enable us to check our account balance, withdraw cash, or make other banking transactions at any time of day or night, at locations that are more accessible than our bank branch. But what are the negative aspects of ATMs?

- *Unemployment*
  The automation of the most common teller functions led to a decline in employment for bank tellers. In 1983, 480,000 people worked as bank tellers. By 1993, there were only 301,000 tellers.[5]

- *Alienation and customer service*
  Automation of teller functions removes the human contact between the customer and a live teller. Instead of talking to a smiling person, we confront a machine. The ATM can be confusing to operate. We could forget our password. We might have a question it cannot answer.

- *Crime*
  People are robbed after withdrawing cash at ATMs. Stolen and counterfeit ATM cards are used by thieves to steal millions of dollars each year. The anonymity of the machine makes ATM fraud easy. A human teller would notice if the same person made numerous withdrawals, or might know the real cardholder by sight, or might be able to identify a suspect after the theft is discovered.

- *Loss of privacy*

  Because transactions at ATMs are recorded in a database at the bank, the record of a person's transactions at various ATMs can provide information about the person's whereabouts and activities.

- *Errors*

  An error in the computer program that operates the ATMs for a large New York bank caused accounts to be debited twice the amount of the actual withdrawal. In less than one day, more than 150,000 transactions, totaling approximately $15 million, were incorrectly recorded.[6]

Unemployment, alienation, crime, loss of privacy, errors—a lot of serious problems! Are ATMs, on balance, a bad development? Are you going to stop using them? Probably not. Why? One reason is the benefit we get from them. Convenience might not at first seem like a very important thing. Later we discuss impressive life-saving and life-enhancing applications of computers. Yet, the example of ATMs suggests that many people do in fact value convenience very highly. For this one benefit, we are willing to accept several negative features. Another reason why we will not give up ATMs is that some of the problems described above are exaggerated, or would occur without ATMs, or have solutions. Let us reconsider them.

- *Unemployment*

  Compared to 15–20 years ago, there are now fewer people employed as bank tellers, but there are more people employed in computer stores. There are many jobs involving the production, sale, and use of computers that did not exist in the early 1980s. Automation causes changes in the kinds of jobs people do. Overall, have computers increased or decreased employment? In Chapter 8, we consider this question and other issues of computers and work. For example: How do computers change the work environment and the structure of businesses? How do they affect the privacy of workers?

- *Alienation and customer service*

  Anyone who wants to talk to a human teller can go into a bank during banking hours. No one is required to use an ATM machine; it is a new, additional option. In fact, banks are open more hours now than they were before ATMs existed. In the 1960s, standard bank hours were 10 AM to 3 PM, Monday through Friday. Now, many banks are open until 5 or 6 PM and have Saturday hours.

  On the other hand, many services that used to be provided by people are now handled by automatic telephone systems or Web sites. Some have the advantage of convenience; some are quite frustrating to use. Some banks now charge a fee for teller transactions that could be done at ATMs. Many banks are closing branches because services are automated. The impact of computers on customer service has been mixed.

- *Crime*

  ATM fraud is a serious problem. We discuss it, along with other forms of computer crimes (including hacking) in Chapter 7. Robberies at ATMs, while serious for the victim, are not a significant crime problem.[7] The banking industry developed many approaches to reducing fraud and ATM crime.

■ *Loss of privacy*
The records kept of ATM transactions probably are not a serious privacy problem. The time and location of transactions inside a bank could be recorded as well. But this mention of privacy serves to introduce the issues we consider in Chapter 2. A large portion of our financial transactions, including supermarket purchases, credit card purchases, loan payments, and income are recorded in computer databases. Our Web surfing can be tracked even when we are just browsing. Cameras record our movements in public places. Our governments maintain huge databases with personal information on us. Who should have access to this information, and how should it be protected from abuse and errors? How does Fourth Amendment protection against unreasonable search and seizure apply when law-enforcement agents want to search files on computers or use high-tech surveillance gear?

■ *Errors*
The bank that double-debited ATM accounts corrected the errors quickly. The error rate for ATM transactions is quite small. With billions of transactions each year, we must expect that some errors will be made, and a low error rate is tolerable. The potential for damage caused by serious errors in complex computerized systems is a significant problem. The use of computer systems leads to new kinds of errors that would not have occurred before. We need to study these and learn how to reduce them. Unfortunately, many people do not realize how easy it is for a computer system to do something wrong; they have too much confidence in these (to them) inscrutable machines. Programmers and system designers are often overconfident, too, and do not give enough thought to the potential consequences of errors or poor design. On the other hand, computers can reduce mistakes and increase safety in some cases. In Chapter 4, we look at a variety of examples and issues related to the reliability and safety of computer systems.

In general, when evaluating computer systems, we should not compare them to some ideal of perfect service or zero side effects and risk. That is impossible to achieve in most aspects of life. Instead, we should compare computer systems to the alternatives and weigh the problems against the benefits. Of course, as in any endeavor, we continue to seek cost-effective improvements and solutions to problems. The ideal shows us the direction to go.

Throughout this book, when we consider problems related to computers, we consider solutions of several kinds: technical (sometimes using computer technology itself), managerial, legal, educational, and market-based. Technical solutions involve hardware and software. For example, ATM software used by some banks has checks that would have prevented the double-debit problem we described. We include more than the computer itself as hardware; thus, improved lighting near ATMs to reduce crime is a technical solution. Management solutions are helpful business policies. Legal solutions include effective law enforcement, criminal penalties, lawsuits, legislation, and regulation. For example, there must be appropriate penalties for people who commit computer fraud and appropriate liability laws for cases where system failures occur. Market mechanisms, such as competition and consumer demand, generate many improvements. Customers and computer users must become educated about the tools they use. That includes knowing how and when to use them safely. For example, counterfeiters get account numbers by collecting receipts left at ATM machines; customers must learn to take their receipts with them. (To protect customers from theft of card numbers, some machines print only the last four digits of the number on the receipt. Some machines have a technical solution for customers who forget to take their cards after a withdrawal: The machine does not release the cash until the customer removes the card.)

The ATM example served to introduce several of the issues we study in the rest of this book, but it does not illustrate all of them. Here is a sampling of some of the others.

- *Privacy of communications (Chapter 3)*
  As new telecommunications technology and encryption methods make it possible to keep communications secret from others, how should our desire for efficiency and privacy be balanced with the need of law-enforcement agencies to intercept and monitor communications of suspected criminals?

- *Freedom of speech (Chapter 5)*
  How much freedom of speech do we have in cyberspace? How much should we have? How serious are the problems of pornography, dangerous material, and misinformation? How would censorship affect the Net? Should we have the right to be anonymous on the Net? Does freedom of speech apply to spam? How has the Internet affected freedom of speech in countries less free?

- *Intellectual property (Chapter 6)*
  It is easy to find free copies of your favorite music on the Web. Many millions of dollars worth of music and software is illegally copied each year. Storage in digital form has made intellectual property (e.g., books, software, movies, and songs) easy to copy without permission of the copyright owner. What is the extent of this problem? What can or should be done about it? What is the "free software" movement?

- *General social issues (Chapter 9)*
  How does the increasing use of computers and the Internet affect local community life? Will widespread use of computers increase the separation of rich and poor, creating a two-class society, the information "haves" and "have-nots"? Is there a need for government subsidies for people who cannot afford computers?

  Both the technological advances brought about by computers and the extraordinary pace of development can have dramatic impacts on people's lives. Individuals and businesses must adapt to the prospect that jobs and products will become obsolete. Our sense of community is changing. Traditional forms of education face competition from software and electronic classrooms. To some, this is all frightening and disruptive. They see computers as a dehumanizing tool that reduces the quality of life or as a threat to the status quo and their well-being. Others see challenging and exciting opportunities. To them the development of computer technology is a thrilling and inspiring example of human progress. Do computers have an overall positive or negative impact? We will look at this fundamental controversy.

■ *Professional ethics (Chapter 10)*
The first nine chapters of this book look at issues primarily from the perspective of any person who lives and works in a highly computerized society and is interested in the impact of computers. The final chapter looks at some of the same topics from the perspective of someone who works as a computer professional who designs or programs computer systems or as a professional in any area who must make decisions and/or set policy about the use of computers. Do system designers have a professional responsibility to develop ATM systems, for example, that print only the last four digits of the account number on receipts? What are the ethical responsibilities of the professional? The Software Engineering Code of Ethics and Professional Practice and the ACM Code of Ethics and Professional Conduct, in Appendix A, provide some guidelines.

1.2.2 THEMES

There are several themes and approaches to analysis of issues that run through this book. I introduce a few here.

OLD PROBLEMS IN A NEW CONTEXT

> Cyberspace has many of the problems, annoyances, and controversies of non-cyber life, among them crime, pornography, pedophilia, violent fiction and games, advertising, copyright infringement, gambling, and products that do not work right.

Groups that some people find offensive, be they skinheads or gay teenagers, are using the Net. Advertisements clutter our screens when we surf the Web. Our reactions to these "cyberspace issues" are likely to depend on our attitudes toward these activities themselves. Many issues and problems that arise from the development of computer technology are not fundamentally different from issues and problems we have confronted before. Thus I often draw analogies from other technologies and other aspects of life. Sometimes we can find a helpful perspective for analysis and even ideas for solutions to new problems by looking at older technologies and other contexts. The emphasis on the fact that similar problems occur in other areas is not meant to excuse problems related to computers. It suggests, however, that the root is not always the new technology, but can be human nature, ethics, politics, or other factors. We will often try to analyze how the new technology changes the context and the impact of old problems.

ADAPTING TO NEW TECHNOLOGY

> Changes in technology usually require adaptive changes in laws, social institutions, business policies, and personal skills and attitudes.

New technology makes new activities possible. Many, of course, are desirable; they are the benefits of the technology. Some are bad. Some we would naturally think of as criminal, but they were not considered when existing laws were written and, hence, are not illegal. Many new activities made possible by the new technology are so different from prior ways of doing things that we need a new set of "rules of the game" to guide people's behavior and to specify what will be permitted and what will not.

THE GLOBAL REACH OF THE NET

> The ease of communication with distant countries has profound social, economic, and political effects—some beneficial, some not.

The Net makes information and opportunities more easily available to people isolated by geography or by political system. It makes crime fighting and law enforcement more difficult, because thefts and disruption of services can be accomplished from outside the victim's country. Social behavior laws (such as antigambling laws) passed in one country may have little effect, because services can move outside the country.

TRADE-OFFS AND CONTROVERSY

> Increasing privacy and security often means reducing convenience. Privacy protection makes law enforcement more difficult. Access to vast amounts of information on the Web is accompanied by access to unpleasant, offensive, or inaccurate information.

Some of the topics we will discuss are not particularly controversial. We will sometimes address an issue more as a problem-solving exercise than as a controversy. We will look at the impact of computer technology in a particular area, observe some problems that result, and try to think of solutions. On the other hand, many of the issues are very controversial: censorship of the Internet, legislation for privacy protection, how strict copyright law should be, the impact of computers on quality of life.

We consider various viewpoints and arguments. Even if you have a strong position on one side of a controversy, it is important to know the arguments on the other side, for several reasons. Knowing that there are reasonable arguments for a different point of view, even if you do not think they are strong enough to win overall, helps make a debate more civilized. We see that the people on the other side are not necessarily evil, stupid, or ignorant; they may just put more weight on different factors. To convince others of your own viewpoint, you must counter the strongest arguments of the other side, so, of course, you first must know and understand them. Finally, you might change your own mind after considering arguments you had not thought of before.

DIFFERENCES BETWEEN PERSONAL CHOICES, BUSINESS POLICIES, AND LAW

The criteria for making personal choices, for making policies for businesses and organizations, and for writing laws are fundamentally different.

We can make a personal choice, for example, about whether to put our name on a mailing list, according to our individual values and situation. A business policy can be based on many factors, including the manager's perception of consumer preferences, what competitors are doing, the goal of making a profit, responsibilities to stockholders, and the ethics of the business owners or managers.

Laws are fundamentally different from personal choices and organizational policies because they impose decisions by force on people who did not make them. Arguments for passing a law should be qualitatively different from reasons for adopting a personal or organizational policy. It might seem odd at first, but arguments on the merits of the proposal—for example, that it is a good idea, or is efficient, or is good for business, or is helpful to consumers—are not good arguments for a law. These arguments can be used to try to convince a person or organization to (voluntarily) adopt a particular policy. Arguments for a law must show why the decision should be enforced against someone who does not agree that it is a good idea. It is better to base laws on the notion of rights rather than on personal views about their benefits or how we would like people to behave.

NEGATIVE AND POSITIVE RIGHTS, OR LIBERTIES AND CLAIM-RIGHTS

There are two quite different kinds of rights. *Negative rights*, or liberties, are rights to act peacefully without interference. *Positive rights*, or claim-rights, are rights that impose an obligation on some people to provide certain things for others.

In philosophy books, these rights are usually called negative and positive rights, but the terms liberties and claim-rights are more descriptive of the distinction.[8]

Negative rights, or liberties, are rights to act without interference. The only obligation they impose on others is not to prevent you from acting. They include the right to life (in the sense that no one may kill you), the right to be free from assault, the right to use your property, the right to use your labor, skills, and mind to create goods and services and to trade with other people in voluntary exchanges. The rights to "life, liberty, and the pursuit of happiness" described in the Declaration of Independence are liberties, or negative rights. Freedom of speech and religion, as guaranteed in the First Amendment of the U.S. Constitution, are negative rights: The government may not interfere with you, jail you, or kill you because of what you say or what your religious beliefs are. The right to work, as a liberty, or negative right, means that no one may prohibit you from working, or, for example, punish you for working without getting a government permit. The (negative) right to access the Internet is so obvious in free countries that we don't even think of it. In totalitarian countries, it is restricted or denied.

Claim-rights, or positive rights, impose an obligation on some people to provide certain things for others. A positive right to a job means that someone must hire you regardless of whether they voluntarily choose to, or that it is right, or obligatory, for the government to set up job programs for people who are out of work. A positive right to life means that some people are obligated to pay for food or medical care for others who cannot pay for them. When freedom of speech is interpreted as a claim-right, or positive right, it means that owners of shopping malls, radio stations, and online services may be required to provide space or time for content they do not wish to include. Access to the Internet, as a claim-right, could require such things as taxes on our telephone bills to provide subsidized access for poor people.

Now here is the problem: Negative rights and positive rights often conflict. Some people think that liberties are almost worthless by themselves, and that society must devise social and legal mechanisms to ensure that everyone has their claim-rights, or positive rights, satisfied, even if that means diminishing the liberties of some. Other people think that there can be no (or very few) positive rights, because it is impossible to enforce claim-rights for some people without violating the liberties of others, yet the protection of liberties, or negative rights, is essential.

This is one of the reasons for disagreement on issues like privacy protection regulations and "universal access" to computing and information services. Although we won't solve the disagreement about which kind of right is more important, we can sometimes clarify the issues in a debate by clarifying which kind of right we are discussing.

1.3 Appreciating the Benefits

Discussions of social issues related to computers often focus on problems, and indeed we discuss problems in this book. Recognizing the beneficial uses of computers is important too. Doing so is necessary to form a reasonable, balanced view of the impact and value of computer technology. In this section, I give a sampling of a variety of applications. This is not a comprehensive summary of computer applications—that would take many books. Some examples are routine things that you might use frequently; the point is to remind us that, a generation ago, those things did not exist. Some are new, perhaps still in development; the point of these is to remind us of the potential for more benefits to come.

Some of the examples described here could spark thoughts about related problems. For example, what if a database used by law enforcement to track criminals is expanded to track political dissenters? How likely is a prescription-filling robot to give a patient the wrong medicine? We look at such issues in later chapters. Here we focus on the benefits, the applications of computers that deserve appreciation.

1.3.1 THE WORLD WIDE WEB, GAMES, CRIME FIGHTING, AND MORE

Probably the first time you used a computer, it was to play a game. Computer games are hardly life-saving, awe-inspiring wonders that profoundly advance the human condition. But they sure are fun. And, if one thinks about it, entertainment and fun are valuable aspects of a happy life. In addition, the demand for computer games spurred development and improvement of many technologies, such as real-time graphics and joysticks, that have many other uses.[9]

Computers play a large role in art and entertainment. Digital technologies improved the quality of music we can listen to at home. Compression formats like MP3 made it practical to download music from the Web. The charming 1995 hit *Toy Story* was the first completely computer-generated movie. Now computerized special effects and full-length computer-generated movies seem routine.

Aside from games and other entertainment, the computer applications with which most of us are familiar are web browsers, word processors, spreadsheets, databases, and such business applications as payroll and inventory systems. All of these let us do many tasks more efficiently. Consider word processors. I wrote my first textbook the old-fashioned way: by hand, on paper. The cut-and-paste operation that most word processors provide is named for the way it was done before computers. If I wanted to rearrange paragraphs, I cut the paper into pieces and taped them together in the new order. I drove almost 20 miles to take each chapter to a good technical typist. A week later, I drove the distance again to pick up the chapter. It was expensive and awkward to make changes after a draft was typed. The typed manuscript was entirely retyped by the publisher's typesetter, a step that often introduced typographic errors.

By accomplishing business data processing more quickly and accurately, business software reduces costs to customers and improves service. A restaurant manager reported that computerized inventory and report-generating software freed him from hours of paperwork so that he could spend more time in the restaurant providing service to his customers. Business hours for many stores expanded as the accounting and inventory paperwork consumed fewer hours per transaction. A medical clinic could treat more patients when it computerized its record keeping. Customer service from mail-order companies, banks, credit-card companies, and many other businesses improved as customer-service agents became able to find a person's order or account information instantly, provide up-to-date information, and make changes. The ease of storing data on computers allows manufacturers to track the specific batches of parts that go into specific products, so that, if a flaw necessitating a recall is discovered, the products affected can be identified precisely.[10]

COMMUNICATION AND THE WORLD WIDE WEB

New York to London is only five miles further than New York to Newark via satellite.

—Nicholas Negroponte[11]

E-mail and the World Wide Web are probably the two computer applications most widely used by both technical and nontechnical people. Electronic mail has many advantages of telephone calls without the disadvantages. The mail arrives at the recipient's computer as quickly as a phone call, but it does not interrupt important work, dinner, or a shower; the message can be read at the recipient's convenience. The sender does not have the frustration of getting busy signals, nor does he or she have to consider time-zone differences when sending messages to other countries. E-mail was first used largely by computer scientists. In the 1980s, messages were short and contained only text. As more people and businesses connected to computer networks, use of e-mail expanded to scientific researchers, then to businesses, then to millions of other people. Length was no longer limited, and we began attaching digitized photos and documents. Americans sent approximately 1.4 billion e-mail messages per day in 2000. A common reason cited by older people for buying a computer is to keep in touch with grandchildren by e-mail.

Computers and the Internet and World Wide Web make the collection, searching, analysis, storage, access, and distribution of large amounts of information much easier, cheaper, and faster than before. The Web gives us access to information and access to audiences almost unimaginable a decade ago. We can type a few words into a search engine and it will then provide links to hundreds of sites around the world with information on our topic. Documents include text, graphics, video, and sound, and they are linked to related material at other sites. We hop to another site by clicking a mouse and do not need to know where the desired material actually is located.

The Web is so widely and commonly used now that we sometimes forget how new and extraordinary it is. Established in Europe in 1990 to enable high-energy physicists to share pictures and text with colleagues in other countries, it grew to more than 10,000 sites by 1993 and 33,000 in 1995. In the mid- and late 1990s, Web browsers and search engines developed, and businesses recognized the value of having a Web site. Among the earliest businesses on the Web, United Parcel Service and Federal Express allowed customers to check the status of packages they sent. This was both a novelty and a valuable service. As the Web became a tool for electronic commerce and ordinary users, it grew at an astonishing rate. In 1998, there were 320 million Web pages. By 2001, there were three billion.[12]

Individuals, organizations, and businesses provide an amazing amount of information for free. Do you need to know how to glue teak? Or when to fertilize your apple tree? Search the Web. Do you want movie schedules and reviews or weather reports? They are on the Web. Do you want to understand an illness a member of your family has? You can find the information on the Web, along with sites where other people with the same illness chat and answer questions. A Pew survey estimated that 60 million Americans sought health information on the Internet in 2000.[13] Are you thinking of buying a stereo or a camera? You can find detailed product descriptions and comments from other buyers on the Web. After you make your decision, you can order on the Web, day or night. The ease of comparison shopping on the Web has brought down the prices of a variety of products. The improved productivity generated by use of the Web, from processing forms to routing trucks, was expected to save the economy $100–230 billion between 2001 and 2005.

Web sites, Usenet news groups, and discussion groups provide forums for information and comment on thousands of subjects. These groups provide opportunities for new social and community interactions, creating *virtual communities*. They range from hobbies to political discussions to professional groups to support groups for people with personal problems.

Personal computers (and especially the Web) increase the independence and options available to people. These tools make it possible, or much easier than before, for ordinary people to make better decisions about everything from movies to medical treatments and to do things which we used to rely on experts to do for us. This is often referred to as *empowerment*. Tax software helps us fill out our tax forms without depending on (and paying) an expert. We can read the full text of government documents—bills, budgets, investigative reports, congressional testimony and debate—instead of relying on a few sentences quoted from an official news release or a sound bite from a biased spokesperson. We can read newspapers on the Web from other countries, getting different cultural and political perspectives on events. Thousands of radio stations stream over the Internet worldwide.

Web browsers make it so easy to download and print documents that relatively recent previous innovations quickly became out-of-date. For example, in the 1990s, some organizations sent faxes of articles and documents automatically to the user who selected the appropriate codes from a menu on a touch-tone phone. Before that, of course, it was much harder to locate the documents we might have wanted, and we had to go somewhere physically, perhaps a government office or library, to make a photocopy, or send a letter or make a phone call to request that a copy be mailed to us.

The Web helps us not only to find material of interest to us, but also to make available to the world whatever information we want to provide. A small business' Web site advertises to potential new customers anywhere in the world. Political activists post their views, reach like-minded people, and organize protest demonstrations. Musicians sell their music directly to the public without a contract with a major record company. Individuals set up Web sites to publicize their criticisms of specific companies. Peer-to-peer technology provides easy transfer of files by large numbers of strangers over the Internet without any centralized system or Web server.

We can access the Web and send e-mail or make telephone calls from an airplane 30,000 feet up in the sky, travelling more than 500 miles per hour. What an extraordinary feat of technology! Satellite-based international communications systems enable users of mobile telephones to send and receive voice, faxes, and data virtually anywhere. Immigrants can watch television programs from their home country via satellite TV. A group of bicyclists pedaling from Anchorage, Alaska to Argentina stopped at Internet cafés along the way to check e-mail and weather conditions and to share tips about where to sleep and eat in remote areas.

The impact of the communication and information provided by the Web is more dramatic in remote or less developed areas of the world, many of which do not have telephones. Farmers in Africa get weather forecasts and instruction in improved farming methods. Villagers in Bario, Malaysia, are separated from the next town by mountains and thick jungle, with no roads. They use a satellite connection to order supplies, to check the market price of rice to get a good deal when selling their crop, and to e-mail

DIGITAL LIBRARIES

Miles of shelves of books—hundreds of thousands of books—have been scanned and stored on electronic media, creating *digital libraries*. Library material is available to researchers and the public anywhere on the Internet. Digital libraries have many advantages, some shared with virtually all Web information systems and some unique to libraries. Books and documents are stored both in text form, to allow full text searches, and in optical images, so that the user can see an exact copy of the material on the screen.

Tasks that used to require transporting people to libraries in motor vehicles can now be done by transporting the information to people through telephone lines and optical fiber—at big savings in time and energy. The British Library owns the 11th century manuscript of *Beowulf*. Digitized images of the manuscript are now available to scholars on the Internet. The quality is so good that words erased by the original scribes, fire damage, and changes made in a 19th century restoration are visible. Scholars who used to travel to view special material like the *Beowulf* manuscript save thousands of dollars. People who could not have paid for such trips now have access.

Digital libraries reduce the demand for paper and for physical space, be it bookshelves or buildings. They provide safe access to old, unique, and fragile material. They make possible the use of sophisticated search software to find desired material from among thousands of pages, and they allow access to one document or book by many people at the same time, eliminating the problem of the desired book being checked out to someone else. They also eliminate the problem of a book's being lost, stolen, or misshelved.[14]

family photos to distant relatives. An Inuit man operates an Internet service provider (ISP) for a village in the Northwest Territories of Canada, where temperatures drop to $-40°$ F. Villagers in Nepal sell handicrafts worldwide via a Web site based in Seattle. Sales have boomed, more villagers have regular work, dying local arts are reviving, and some villagers can now afford to send their children to school. The same Web site provides a world market for crafts made by rural women's co-ops and disadvantaged urban youths.

> Today, a high-school student with a modem in Boise, Idaho has better access to federal statistics than top officials in Washington had five years ago.

—Sally Katzen, federal government administrator, 1997[15]

AUTOMOBILES AND TRUCKS

The 1991 space shuttle had a one-megahertz computer onboard. Some luxury 2001 automobiles had 100-megahertz computers. Navigation systems in cars are becoming common. Automobiles have microprocessors embedded in various components. Some chips collect information about engine behavior; mechanics use the information to diagnose and fix problems. Anti-lock braking systems (ABS) use sensors and computers to control the pressure on the brakes to prevent skids. The ABS is more expert than human drivers at safely stopping a car. To reduce trailer-truck roll-overs that killed several hundred truck drivers each year, truck makers introduced a system with sensors to detect a likely roll-over, before the driver is aware of the problem, and electronically slow the engine. "Hybrid" cars, like Honda's Insight and Toyota's Prius, use computers to alternate between burning gasoline and using battery power, reducing energy use and pollution.

Several companies and research institutes modified ordinary vehicles to drive themselves. Carnegie Mellon University's Pontiac drives with the aid of a tiny camera, image processing software, radar, artificial-intelligence software, and a personal computer in the trunk. It drove 122 miles without driver intervention. A fleet of Buicks with special equipment developed by General Motors and the University of California drove themselves only 12 feet apart in a test on a San Diego freeway. One aim of such systems is to reduce congestion and air pollution. There are many problems to solve before these vehicles can handle real traffic situations reliably and safely. A closer goal is a warning system that alerts a driver, or even takes over the steering, when the computer determines that the driver is veering off the road or into an obstacle. Such a system could prevent many of the three million accidents that occur every year in the U.S. involving a single car and a sleepy or intoxicated driver. Several companies developed radar-based and infrared systems to provide better "night vision" for drivers. The systems are especially useful for long-haul truckers who drive mostly at night. Images or diagrams of objects that might cause a collision are projected onto the windshield. Car engineers hope to reduce the bulky systems to the size of a coffee can and make them available as an option for passenger cars.[16]

EDUCATION AND TRAINING

There has been educational software almost since there have been personal computers. Early educational toys like Speak 'n Spell spoke words for a child to spell (by typing on alphabet keys). The toy corrected the child as necessary and had several difficulty levels. Now, multimedia systems, CD-ROMs, and Web sites provide more sophisticated programs and presentations to teach many subjects.

One successful education application is teaching illiterate adults to read. Traditional methods fail for many people who are embarrassed, are uninspired by the teaching techniques, or are intimidated by a teacher's impatience with their mistakes. Computer programs that teach reading, some with multimedia, are engaging and uncritical. A study at the University of Northern Arizona and observations by people who run remedial reading programs indicate that people using the programs improve dramatically faster than those using traditional methods.[17]

A variety of "distance learning" opportunities developed. Students in rural towns that cannot afford a teacher for specialized subjects take classes offered in nearby cities by interactive television. They receive and submit written assignments by e-mail or fax. Many courses and some complete college programs are offered entirely on the Web. Good courses and teachers will be available to students far from the teacher's physical location. People who work full time, have varying work schedules that conflict with normal class schedules, or have small children at home benefit from the flexibility of Web courses. People who cannot travel easily because of disabilities benefit from increased learning opportunities at home.

Speech recognition is a useful tool in many educational and training programs. Computer programs that teach foreign languages give instruction in correct pronunciation if they do not recognize what the user says. Complex simulation software with graphics and speech recognition is used for sophisticated training systems. Air-traffic controllers, for example, are trained in a mockup tower whose "windows" are projection screens. The trainee directs air traffic that is entirely simulated by computer. The computer responds when the trainee speaks to the simulated pilots. Air-traffic controllers received training before we had computers, but the simulation allows more intensive training in a safe environment. If the trainee directs two airplanes to land on the same runway at the same time, no one gets hurt.

CRIME FIGHTING

The Automated Regional Justice Information System (ARJIS) is an example of the use of computer networks and databases to aid crime fighting. It serves a county of approximately three million people, with 17 cities. The system contains crime reports, arrest reports, field-interview records (for field interviews with suspicious people where there are insufficient grounds for arrest), traffic citations, traffic accident reports, an alias file, and a variety of other kinds of records. It is used to identify suspects, clear suspects, track and identify trends and patterns of crime, and generate reports.[18]

When a crime is committed, police can enter whatever information they have about the suspect and find potential matches to investigate. With just a "street name" and a description in an attempted murder case, ARJIS helped police narrow down the suspect list to four. The perpetrator was then identified by witnesses. When a suspect with no prior record was arrested for a burglary, police searched unsolved crimes for the same MO* and found several similar burglaries in other cities. Thus ARJIS helped solve the other cases and provided evidence that the suspect was a professional burglar rather than a first-time offender. ARJIS is also used for crime analysis. It helps identify special crime problems and plan allocation of patrols. More than one million data entry and inquiry requests are processed by the system each month.

Readers of detective stories, fans of Scotland Yard, and older police officers know that ingenuity, evidence, investigation, and many scientific tools were used to solve crimes for centuries. Yet, one detective who worked with ARJIS for several years said, "I don't know how anyone could do police work before ARJIS came along."[19] Why would he make such a comment? Why is a computerized system like ARJIS indispensable now? Increased population and mobility are likely reasons. In the past, a police officer might

---

*MO is an abbreviation for the Latin *modus operandi*, or method of operating.

have personally known most of the people in the neighborhood, and neighbors were more likely to know each other. In Sherlock Holmes' day, criminals were less likely to commit crimes in several different cities.

Database searching has other applications in crime fighting. For example, insurance fraud is detected by using computers to find patients and doctors who file multiple claims. The FBI's National Crime Information Center (NCIC) is a computer database of arrest warrants and police inquiries.* It was from a query to this database that government agents learned that their suspect in the 1995 bombing of the Oklahoma City federal building had been arrested for a traffic violation shortly after the bombing.

Matching of fingerprints and photographs of suspects can now be done by computer. Many people thought that, when fingerprints were found at a crime scene, they were routinely matched against thousands of prints on file to find a suspect. This was not true. Fingerprints of a known specific suspect could be compared, but matching crime-scene fingerprints against those in a card file was slow, painstaking work performed by human specialists. Now, fingerprint information can be stored in computer databases and comparisons can be done by computer. The Automated Fingerprint Identification System (AFIS) can process millions of prints in twenty minutes. In a test of the system, prints found at the scene of an unsolved murder that occurred almost 30 years earlier led to a suspect in another state. The computer match was verified by a human fingerprint expert, and the suspect was tried and convicted for the murder. In one state, the system helped solve about 200 crimes in its first two years of operation. Wireless technology now enables police officers to check a suspect's prints on the street to verify identity. Fast processors, large data-storage capacity, and fast algorithms for processing digitized images made it possible for police to use a computer system to generate a composite photo of a suspect from a witness' description, then search databases with criminal mug shots to find a match.[20]

Specialized Internet newsgroups and Web sites help solve and deter crimes. Dealers in collectible items post information about stolen art, rare books, and even valuable baseball cards, so that a thief can be caught when trying to sell them.

1.3.2 HEALTH AND MEDICINE

Computers are used in virtually all phases of medicine, from research to the operating room to maintaining patient records. We give a brief overview of some applications and their benefits.

MEDICAL DEVICES

Physicians use machines such as CT (computer-aided tomography) scanners and MRI (magnetic resonance imaging) machines for medical imaging. MRI machines use computers to process the data generated by reflections from a magnetic field around a human body. They produce pictures of internal body organs, muscle, and other soft tissue that

---

*Because of errors and misuse, NCIC has been the subject of much controversy. We discuss some of its problems later.

X-rays cannot "see," without subjecting the patient to the risks of high-dose X-rays. These machines use a technique called *scientific visualization*: Computers process huge amounts of data and turn it into pictures that people can interpret more easily than hundreds of pages of numbers. Medical imaging was used initially mostly for diagnosis. For example, diagnosing appendicitis was not easy, and about 20% of appendectomies were found to have been unnecessary—until CT scans were used to confirm diagnoses before surgery. Now, the improved detail of medical imaging allows its use for planning of complex surgeries. Brain surgeons use images produced by MRI and other imaging machines in the operating room to reduce damage to critical parts of the brain when removing tumors. New systems process data from the scanners to produce 3-dimensional views that can be rotated for complete examination. These are used to plan surgery better and to reduce the risk and discomfort of older diagnostic procedures, in some cases reducing the time a patient must lie still from two hours to only one minute.[21]

Patient-monitoring devices of all sorts are now routinely used during and after surgery, providing more information about the patient's condition and quicker warning of complications. Microprocessors control a variety of medical instruments. One million Americans wear heart pacemakers. Pacemakers contain computer chips that fine-tune the heartbeat of a person who might otherwise die. In the mid-1980s, miniature software-controlled defibrillators were developed. They are implanted, like pacemakers, in the patient. When the device senses the start of arrhythmia, or abnormal heartbeat, it gives a low-voltage shock to the heart. Implanted defibrillators drastically reduced the mortality rates compared to surgical and drug treatments. Computer-controlled heart pumps are implanted in patients who would otherwise die while awaiting heart transplants. In Europe, the devices are used long-term, in place of transplants, for some patients.[22]

Microprocessors in medical instruments such as intravenous pumps allow patients to use sophisticated equipment at home, eliminating the expense and inconvenience of a hospital visit. Similarly, a variety of monitoring devices with data-storage capabilities can be worn at home, eliminating hospital stays for diagnosing problems that require monitoring over a long period of time.

Several companies are developing devices to measure blood glucose through the skin. Anyone with diabetes will recognize the value of such devices: They eliminate the need to prick one's finger several times a day to take blood-glucose measurements.

Physicians in France and Germany did coronary bypass surgery from a console with a 3-D monitor and joysticks that control robotic instruments. The software filters out shaky movements by the physician.[23]

Some hospitals use large robot pharmacist machines connected to the patient database. The system plucks the appropriate medications from the pharmacy shelves by reading bar codes, checks for drug interactions, and handles billing. It seems to have achieved one of its main goals, reduction of human error; in its first few years, it filled 30 million prescriptions with no errors. These machines free medical staff from tedious chores so that they can spend more time on patient care. By automating several tasks, they also reduce costs of medical care.[24]

DESIGNING NEW DRUGS[25]

Drugs to fight diseases do their job by binding to target molecules, usually proteins, and preventing, or inhibiting, them from carrying out their destructive activity. It used to be that drugs were discovered—by luck, or by tedious trial and error. Now it is more common for them to be designed—by an approach called *rational drug design*, or *structure-based drug design*. This approach, the determining of the detailed three-dimensional atomic structure of the target and the designing of specific chemical compounds to inhibit it, would be impossible without computer technology and advances in biotechnology.

In structure-based drug design, scientists grow a crystal of the protein, then use *X-ray crystallography* to map its structure. The crystal is bombarded with a powerful X-ray beam. Computers calculate the structure based on the way the X-rays diffract (i.e., scatter) after hitting the crystal. This work is heavily computational; tens of thousands of measurements of the diffracted radiation are taken and analyzed by computer. After the structure has been determined, graphical software produces a three-dimensional image of the protein.

Vertex Pharmaceuticals, Inc. used the image of an enzyme needed by the AIDS virus to develop a drug to fight AIDS. The process took two years, instead of the usual six years, and the technology allowed the company to engineer the drug with various advantages to patients. Scientists at the Memorial Sloan-Kettering Cancer Center worked out the details of the structure of a tumor-suppressor protein called *p53*. They report that mutations in p53 are "the most frequently observed genetic alterations in human cancer." Knowing p53's structure can help researchers develop drugs to counter the effects of mutated forms.

PATIENT RECORDS

Hospitals and medical centers replaced many paper patient records with computerized records. Paper files often contained illegible hand-written notes and were poorly organized. They can be read by only one person at one time, and they were unavailable nearly 50% of the time (e.g., in another doctor's office or misfiled). Computerized records solve these problems. Speed in getting medical records is especially important in emergency rooms. At a Harvard University hospital, the medical staff can get records from a computer system in about two seconds. Before the system was installed, it took an average of two hours. The improved speed reduces the wait for treatment by patients who are seriously ill or injured and in pain, and it saves hundreds of thousands of dollars in employee time. Another hospital with computerized patient records found that patients were released from the hospital almost one day earlier and had bills averaging almost $900 less than when they relied on paper records. An estimated 7000 people die each year after

Researchers at Agouron Pharmaceuticals discovered the atomic structure of an enzyme called *rhinovirus 3C protease* which is involved in replication of a class of viruses that cause the common cold.

Previously, development of new drugs involved searching databases containing thousands of compounds, then physically testing those that seemed like good candidates. Attempts to work out the structure of target molecules were made, but they took the efforts of many people over many years. The president of Agouron described the importance of computers to drug design as follows: "Through a series of computational steps which historically have sometimes involved a number of post-doctoral careers to complete, but which now move very rapidly with the advent of sophisticated algorithms and perhaps more importantly the availability of supercomputers, we are able to determine, with a very high degree of accuracy and with a net expenditure of less than a year's time, the precise architecture of a particular pharmaceutical target."[26] That was in 1989. By 2001, with improvements in computers, the time required had shrunk to months or weeks. Structural GenomiX expected to solve the structure of 5000 proteins in five years. Agouron's president continued: "In the old days when determination of the protein structure was complete..., the next step was to build a wire model of the results." He went on to say that it was difficult to overstate the advantage of using modern computer graphics software to display and manipulate the structure.

Scientists at Chiron used computerized gene mapping to develop a vaccine for a deadly form of bacterial meningitis for which no vaccine previously existed. The head of Chiron's research team said the genetic map and computer search allowed them to make "more progress in the last 18 months than in the previous 40 years."

getting the wrong medication because a pharmacist misread a doctor's handwriting on a prescription form. Typing the prescription into a computerized system can reduce this problem. Computerized records also make statistical research on diseases and treatments easier.[27]

DIAGNOSIS

Many computer-based systems aid doctors in diagnosing diseases. Some are databases that can be searched by entering symptoms. Others are specific to particular diseases. The visual-field analyzer, a device that tests for glaucoma via computer-generated images, is more accurate than its noncomputer predecessor used in the 1970s. A computer program predicts the results of biopsies for prostate cancer with 87% accuracy; doctors typically can predict the result with 35% accuracy. Several new computer systems for analyzing mammograms do a better job than radiologists; one system finds almost half the cancers they missed. An ultrasound device uses computers to analyze echoes from sound waves bounced off a lump in a woman's breast. It can determine whether the lump is benign and could eliminate the need for 40% of surgical biopsies for breast cancer. Commonly used screening tests for colon and intestinal cancer are unpleasant and hence avoided by people who may be at risk. New computed tomography scanning methods, using virtual reality techniques and 3-D displays, are being developed. Researchers developed a capsule containing a miniature camera, light, radio transmitter, and battery. When swallowed by a patient, it takes pictures of the intestines as it moves through and transmits them to a storage device. These methods reduce risk and discomfort.[28]

Strokes often strike without warning and are devastating. Engineers in Japan have developed and are testing a thin sensor that sits on a person's eyelid and analyzes vibrations caused by blood flow. It detects brain aneurysms and blood clots that can cause strokes.[29]

TELEMEDICINE, OR LONG-DISTANCE MEDICINE

Telemedicine refers to remote performance of medical exams, analyses, and procedures using specialized equipment and computer networks. Telemedicine is used on long airplane flights to help treat a sick passenger and to ascertain whether an emergency landing is needed. Prisons use telemedicine to reduce the risk of escape by dangerous criminals.

Many rural hospitals cannot afford to have a trained radiologist on staff. They send X-rays to larger hospitals for interpretation by experts. Now, the X-rays can be transmitted by telephone lines instead of being physically carried by couriers. Results are obtained more quickly, benefiting patient care, and the cost of the couriers is eliminated. Radiologists in the U.S. use similar systems to consult on cases in other countries where experts are not available. Some small-town hospitals use two-way video systems to consult with specialists at large medical centers while a local doctor is examining a patient; the specialists can see and hear and participate in the examination, eliminating the expense, time, and possible health risk of transporting the patient to the medical center.

In 2001, surgeons in New York removed a gall bladder from a patient in France. They used video and robotic devices and high-speed communication links. Such systems are being developed for emergency situations. They can save lives of soldiers wounded on battlefields far from expert surgeons. They can provide specialized surgery for remote patients, perhaps including patients who could not be moved without risks to their lives.

Researchers operate scientific instruments remotely across computer networks. Tele-microscopy is an example. High-voltage electron microscopes are very expensive, specialized instruments used for, among other things, research on Alzheimer's disease and Parkinson's disease. Researchers travel to distant microscopes with the samples they want to study. In the 1990s, researchers at the University of California in San Diego (UCSD) developed a remote-operation system allowing operation of microscopes in the U.S. from distant locations. (Samples to be studied could be sent by mail.) In 1999, the ultrahigh-voltage electron microscope at Osaka University in Japan, the only one of its power in the world, was operated remotely from the National Center for Microscopy and Imaging Research at UCSD. The system used high-speed networks, digital compression techniques for images, and other computer technologies. By eliminating the time and expense of travel and by making collaboration among distant researchers easier, telemicroscopy helps get more research done.[30]

1.3.3 TOOLS FOR DISABLED PEOPLE

One of the most heartwarming applications of computer technology is the restoration of abilities, productivity, and independence to people with physical disabilities.

There are more than 1000 computer-based devices for the disabled. Some of these devices enable disabled people to use the kinds of computer applications that other people use: e-mail, Web browsers, word processors, spreadsheets, graphics, and databases. Some enable disabled people to control household and workplace appliances that most of us operate by hand. Some improve mobility. (One company developed wheelchairs that climb stairs and support and transport a person in an upright position.[31]) Recent work focuses on using sensors and microprocessors to control artificial limbs, to detect and use brain signals, and to replace in other ways body functions that have been lost. We will describe a variety of examples.

People with poor eyesight can direct a computer display to use a large type size. For people who are blind, computers equipped with speech synthesizers read aloud what a sighted person sees on the screen. Computers can be set to echo aloud each key the user types, so that a blind user can tell if he or she makes a typing mistake. For materials that are not already stored in electronic form, a scanner, optical-character-recognition software, and a speech synthesizer combine to read aloud to a blind person. Where noise is a problem (or for a person both blind and deaf), the speech output can be replaced by a grid of buttons raised and lowered by the computer to form Braille characters. Braille printers can be substituted for regular printers to provide hard copy. For years, books have been available in large type, in Braille, or on tape, but the expense of production for a small market long kept the selection limited. Now, any book, article, e-mail message, or other document that is stored on a computer system, or can be scanned, can be read by a blind or poorly sighted person.

A system made up of a bar-code reader, a database, and a speech synthesizer helps blind people keep track of objects in their home or work environment. A blind disk jockey labels all his CDs so he can be sure he selects the one he wants to play. At home, one can scan food cans or packages and hear preparation instructions or other information stored in the database. The system can help prepare grocery shopping lists. It eliminates the need for an excellent memory and the need to know Braille and apply Braille labels. With portable equipment, a blind person can read bar codes in a supermarket and shop unassisted.[32]

The Science Institute for the Disabled at East Carolina University developed a system enabling disabled students to operate equipment in chemistry labs so that they can study college chemistry. The laboratory instruments can output their readings directly to a computer that analyzes the data and presents them in a form suitable for the user. A speech synthesizer provides output of instrument readings for a blind student. For experiments that produce a long sequence of readings, the computer produces tones of varying pitch so that the user can identify highs and lows. More complex sets of data are presented as musical patterns via a computer-controlled music synthesizer. The system includes speech recognition for students who cannot type.[33]

Researchers are developing a computer chip that will float on the retina of the eye and send visual signals to the brain, restoring some sight.

Some people, including those with degenerative nerve diseases, can use their hands, but cannot control them precisely enough to type on a keyboard. They can use specially enlarged keyboards or touch screens displaying a picture of a keyboard. Various conditions—loss of limbs, quadriplegia (paralysis in both arms and legs, often resulting from an accident), and certain diseases—eliminate all or almost all use of the hands. Speech recognition is an enormously valuable tool for such people and for deaf people. The software and hardware needed are relatively inexpensive, and speech-recognition technology has improved rapidly. One system, Dragon NaturallySpeaking, has a 230,000-word vocabulary and can distinguish words that sound alike (for example, "two," "too," and "to") from the context. IBM's system has versions for several languages besides English.[34] People without use of their hands can give commands to a computer and dictate documents to a standard word processor. Deaf people can use such a system to "hear" another speaker as the computer displays the spoken words on the monitor. (Computer chips also enormously improved hearing aids.) Without computers and speech recognition software, a quadriplegic could operate some devices with a mouth-operated control stick, a tedious process with limited applications. A deaf person would have to learn to read lips, and always face the person speaking.

Speech recognition can also be used to operate environmental control systems. "Environment" in this context means the indoor home or office environment: lighting, temperature, TV, stereo, and appliances. The system I saw demonstrated at the Disabled Opportunities Center in San Diego, called Mastervoice, operates appliances connected to a computer control box through ordinary household wiring. (The original system is in the Smithsonian Institution.) Mastervoice is programmable. For example, when the user says, "I'm home," it can respond by turning on lights (depending on the time of day), opening drapes, turning on heat or air conditioning, and turning on the stereo. "Goodnight" can direct the system to arm a security alarm, turn on hallway and bedroom lights, then turn them off after a predetermined time period. The system can be programmed to turn down the television when the phone rings, and the user can make telephone calls by simply telling the system whom to call. The system recognizes the owner's voice, so it can be used for security operations, such as locking or unlocking doors. Such a system is a boon to the safety, comfort, and independence of a person with limited mobility and use of hands. Twenty-five years ago, according to *Business Week*, voice-operated environmental-control systems would have cost $20,000 to $200,000, and the quality of speech recognition was not good. By the 1990s, the technology had improved so much that a Mastervoice system recognized the agitated and weak voice of a person whose breathing apparatus had partially failed and called for help. Now, such systems cost a few hundred to a few thousand dollars.[35]

There are several devices for people who can neither move nor speak. A person can use a wireless head mouse, a headset that detects movement of the head and moves the cursor accordingly on the screen. Other systems equipped with a small camera aimed at the user's eye can determine what the person is looking at on a computer screen. Thus someone who can move only one eye can communicate and operate a computer. Researchers in the U.S. and Europe are developing brain-computer interfaces so that severely handicapped people can operate a computer and control appliances with their thoughts. The impact of all these devices on the morale of the user is immense. Think about a person with an active mind, personality, and sense of humor—but without the ability to write, type, or speak. Imagine the difference when the person has the ability to communicate—with family and friends, and with all the people and resources available on the Internet.

Microprocessors are embedded in prosthetic devices, such as artificial arms and legs. These devices use electrodes to pick up the tiny electrical fields generated by contractions of the muscles in the upper (natural) limb. The signals are amplified and processed by the microprocessor to replace the normal complex interplay of nerves, muscles, tendons, and ligaments. The chip controls tiny motors that move the artificial limb, open and close fingers, and so on. Myoelectric limbs (artificial limbs that use electric signals from the muscles) existed before microprocessors, but they used analog motors and did not have the sensitivity and flexibility of the chip-controlled limbs. For example, the chip can make the limb move in proportion to the strength of the field generated by the muscle. Children fitted with the new arm when they are very young can learn to use the artificial hand and fingers almost as naturally as a natural limb. For some quadriplegics, a device about the size of a pacemaker, implanted in the chest, helps restore partial use of their hands.[36]

One of the results of the availability of computer technology for disabled people is that people who formerly could not work now can. Many disabled people have formed and run their own businesses. The number of disabled entrepreneurs has increased steadily.

"It is with good reason," says David Lunney, the chemist who developed special laboratory equipment for disabled students, "that the personal computer is so widely regarded as the most liberating and empowering device yet developed for people with disabilities." Jim Fruchterman, president of Arkenstone, a company that makes book readers for the blind, says simply that "PCs are the Swiss Army knife for disabled people." Fruchterman's company developed a portable system using the global positioning system (GPS), geographic information systems (detailed computerized maps), and a voice synthesizer to help blind people walk around and find their way in neighborhoods they were not previously familiar with.[37]

1.3.4 AUTOMATION

Automation in manufacturing began long ago, but computers added to the capabilities and flexibility of automated systems. Many factories and warehouses now use computer-controlled automation. An example is the sophisticated warehouse system built in 1987 by Ralphs, a southern California supermarket chain with more than 100 stores. The warehouse is ten stories high. Products are stored on more than 50,000 pallets and retrieved by huge automated cranes. The system keeps track of the location of products and the inventory. Electric eyes check the pallets and direct any with problems to the "pallet hospital." The automated system allowed the company to combine five separate facilities. The system reduced land usage and property costs, the number of employees needed, and the number of times each product had to be handled and moved. It is fast and efficient enough to allow deliveries to most of the chain's stores every day, thus improving stock management at the stores. The cost of the system was recovered from the savings it brought about in just a few years.[38]

Automation combined with vision systems produces a variety of machines that are used in production lines. For example, such systems are used to count eggs and hot dog buns on conveyer belts. The software is customized for an application and can determine the orientation of the products, count them, and inspect their quality. If this sounds easy, remember that, when we look at something, our brain does a lot of automatic processing. It is not difficult for us to count the hot dog buns even if they are scattered about and not lined up neatly. The computer processes a digital image and must distinguish the product from the background, detect edges of products that are next to each other, distinguish the product from debris on the conveyer belt (e.g., flour dust in a bakery), and so on. Unlike earlier, noncomputerized automated systems for similar applications, the vision system does not come in contact with the product, thus reducing damage. Also, the computer systems have more flexibility.[39]

Robotic arms and other robotic devices are another form of automation. Robot arms are used in factories to assemble products faster and more accurately than people can. A robotic milking machine milks cows at dairy farms while the farmhands sleep; more frequent milking boosted milk production. McDonald's and other fast food sellers installed robotic food preparation systems and self-service ordering kiosks to reduce costs and speed service. Robots are used in environments that are hazardous to people. They inspect undersea structures and communication cables; they explore volcanoes and other planets.

1.3.5 IDENTIFICATION, SENSORS, AND TRACKING SYSTEMS

Technology for identifying people and products, from bar codes to smart cards, has been getting more sophisticated and finding new applications.

Before bar codes and scanners were used on grocery products, grocery store employees put a paper price sticker on each item. The checker read the sticker and punched the amount on the cash register keyboard. With bar codes, the computer system is programmed with the price. Check-out scanners eliminate the need for the stickers and the typing of the price for each unit purchased. The computer system automatically updates inventory records and prepares purchase orders. In the highly competitive grocery industry, anything that reduces costs and provides faster service to customers is important. Many libraries use a similar system to speed the check-out of books. Each book and each customer's library card has a unique bar code. Two quick scans record the transaction in the computer system. There are numerous other applications of bar codes.

Smart cards are the size of credit cards, but they contain a microprocessor and memory. They can be read by a card-scanning machine and be used to access data in a computer network. Hundreds of applications, including uses for financial transactions, health care, credit, and telephone calls, are being developed. The cards use a variety of security techniques to protect data. Because critical medical information can be stored on the card, one advantage could be the obtaining of proper treatment during travel or in an emergency. Also, the consumer could have direct access to information not currently easily available, for example, his or her credit record.

Secure, reliable identification is clearly needed for police officers who have access to sensitive areas closed to the public and for those who may carry guns on airplanes. Federal investigators found that they could impersonate officers and get into off-limits areas at airports and in government buildings by using false ID obtained on the Internet. The Secret Service recommended that police use a smart-card ID system with encrypted information; it is much harder to counterfeit.[40]

SMART THINGS

Sensors with tiny radio transmitters are finding all sorts of applications. Here's one amusing, but useful one. Sensors implanted in chickens monitor the birds' body temperature. A computer automatically reduces the temperature in the chicken coop if the birds get too hot. This reduces disease and deaths from overheating.[41]

Sensors and microprocessors detect temperature, acceleration and stress in materials (such as airplane parts). Sandia National Laboratory developed a "chemical lab on a chip" that can detect emissions from automobiles, chemical leaks, dangerous gases in fires (reducing risk for fire fighters), and many other hazards. Such chips may be used in systems to detect chemical-warfare agents. Sensors in soil report on moisture, acidity, and so on, helping farmers to avoid waste and to use only as much chemical fertilizer as is needed.[42]

FOILING POACHERS, FOLLOWING TURTLES

Very valuable and extremely rare plants, both in the wild and in gardens, are tagged with chips and tracked by satellite so they can be located if taken by thieves. Satellite technology and microprocessors enormously improved animal tracking. Scientists attach transmitters the size of a raisin to rare birds and other animals to study their behavior and learn how to protect their food sources. Researchers learned that some animals travel much farther than previously thought: Sea turtles swam from the Caribbean to Africa; a nesting albatross flew from Hawaii to the San Francisco Bay, a weeklong round-trip, to get food for its young. To encourage interest from the public, many researchers have Web sites where we can follow the animals' movements.[43]

Many people are familiar with the tracking devices that can be installed in a car to locate it if stolen. Pets, prisoners, people with Alzheimer's disease, and children can wear, or have implanted under their skin, devices that locate them if they wander off.

New applications for identification, sensor, and tracking/locating technologies are popping up at an increasing rate. This is an area where many valuable applications will develop. But I hope the suggestion of implanting tracking chips in children made you wonder: Is that such a good idea? There are many planned and potential applications of tracking technologies that raise significant issues concerning privacy and freedom of movement; we discuss some in Chapters 2.

1.3.6 REDUCING PAPER USE AND TRASH

Electronic storage of text, and the ability to edit and update it, is reducing the need for paper in many businesses—and the amount of trash produced. A large insurance company reduced its use of paper by 100 million pages in a nine-month period by keeping its manuals on computers instead of printing them. A computerized system for recording insurance claims replaced more than 30 million index cards. A department store chain reported saving $1 million worth of paper per year by keeping sales reports on computer instead of paper.[44] Reducing paper use is of both economic and environmental value: Although release of the toxic chemicals most widely used in industry has been declining (by 46% between 1988 and 1997, according to the Environmental Protection Agency), the paper industry remains one of the highest emitters of toxic chemicals.

Electronic books have the potential to reduce use of paper drastically. We can reduce both paper use and trash when, instead of throwing away last month's issue of a magazine, we simply delete it from our disk. (The electronically distributed newsletter of the Electronic Frontier Foundation used to end with the line, "This newsletter is printed on 100% recycled electrons.")

Storage of paper records is another big expense that is being reduced by electronic media. Businesses are required by law to maintain huge amounts of paper records. In 2000, a federal law allowed some businesses to replace paper with electronic storage of insurance policies, mortgages, canceled checks, and so forth. This law allows for large savings in storage space and cost.

Fax machines and laser printers make it so easy to print things on paper that, in many situations, we use *more* paper now than we did before. Computers give us the *ability* to use less paper, but they might not give us the *incentive* to do so. Probably the increased paper use will be a temporary phenomenon. Most of us still want a paper copy of a document to read in a comfortable chair or when sprawled on the sofa or at the beach. As portable readers become more convenient and flexible, we could see a substantial decline in paper use.

1.3.7 SOME OBSERVATIONS

The life-saving and life-enhancing effects of computers are obvious in some of the applications we described. Sometimes, beneficial effects are less obvious. In Chapter 4, we describe a computer program that has been very helpful in the design of products that must withstand forceful impacts. Safety is the main goal in most of those applications.

(Reducing the amount of materials used, thus reducing waste of resources, is another goal.) By the nature of these design and development applications, the people who benefit from them may never know it. A bicycle rider who survives an accident might know that her helmet was an important factor, but she probably would not know that some detail of the design suggested by computer simulations prevented a worse injury.

For many of us, it would be hard to imagine living without computers. Yet, until very recently, we did. Tolstoy wrote *War and Peace* without a word processor. No one would design a bridge or a large building today without using computers, but the Brooklyn Bridge, built more than 100 years ago, is both a work of art and a marvelous feat of engineering. The builders of the Statue of Liberty, the Pyramids, the Roman aqueducts, magnificent cathedrals, and countless other complex structures did not wait for computers. We use computers for many tasks that used to be done without them. What are the advantages? Convenience, efficiency, options. Computers enable us to work faster and more accurately than before. For some applications, they reduce the amount of resources, including human effort, required for a task.

Efficiency is sometimes looked down upon as being simply a matter of money, an economic effect, not a social value. That is a mistaken view. If a new drug is discovered 15 years earlier than it would have been without computers, hundreds or thousands of lives might be saved or improved in those 15 years. If computers can help design a safe car that is cheaper than previous designs, more people will be able to afford to ride more safely. Any task that can be done more efficiently frees some of our time and resources for other pursuits, be they work, community, cultural, or leisure activities.

The ability to accomplish a task more efficiently is not a benefit if the task itself has negative consequences. We are ready now to begin to examine problems created or intensified by computers. In the next chapter, we consider how efficient information collection and manipulation can threaten our safety, freedom, and privacy.

> *It is precisely this unique human capacity to transcend the present, to live one's life by purposes stretching into the future—to live not at the mercy of the world, but as a builder and designer of that world—that is the distinction between human and animal behavior, or between the human being and the machine.*

—Betty Friedan[45]

EXERCISES

Review Exercises

1.1   What was the effect of automated teller machines on the employment of bank tellers?
1.2   What are some computer tools used in drug design (Section 1.3.2)?
1.3   Describe two applications of speech recognition.
1.4   List several benefits of having library materials in electronic format.
1.5   Describe one use of computers in medical care.

1.6   One of the advantages of personal computers, information systems, and the Web is personal empowerment. List three applications mentioned in this chapter that help ordinary people to do things for which we used to rely on experts.

1.7   Explain the distinction between the negative and positive right to freedom of speech.

General Exercises

1.8   Write a short essay (roughly 300 words) about some topic related to computers that interests you and has social or ethical implications. Describe the background; then identify the issues, problems, or questions that you think are important.

1.9   List two machines or devices that existed before computers, but that now have computers or microprocessors built in. (Give examples that were not mentioned in the text.)

1.10   a) Microwave ovens were first introduced without microprocessors. It is the microwaves, not the computer, that cooks the food. What benefits in microwave ovens come from the computer?
       b) Choose another device or appliance that existed before microprocessors, but now has a microprocessor in it. What is the benefit obtained from the computer?

1.11   Describe a product that has been in use for approximately 100 years or more, but that has recently become obsolete or might become obsolete in the near future because of computer technology. Explain why you think it is or will be obsolete.

1.12   List two jobs that have been made obsolete by computers. List two jobs that would not exist without computers.

1.13   Do an analysis of buying books on the Web like the analysis done for ATM machines at the beginning of Section 1.2.1. That is, briefly describe some impacts on (or of) employment, customer service, crime, privacy, and errors.

1.14   Consider the problem of making a bank deposit but not having the deposit credited to your account. Compare the likelihood of this happening with various ways of making the deposit: going to a teller in a bank, sending the deposit by mail, and using an ATM. What might go wrong? How difficult would it be in each case to convince the bank that you really made the deposit?[46]

1.15   In the following (true) cases, tell whether the people are interpreting the right being claimed as a negative right (liberty) or as a positive right (claim-right). Explain. In each case, which kind of right should it be, and why?
       a) A man sued his health insurance company because it would not pay for Viagra, the drug for treating male impotence. He argued that the insurer's refusal to pay denied his right to a happy sex life.
       b) Two legislators who lost reelection votes sued an organization that ran ads criticizing their voting records. The former legislators argued that the organization interfered with their right to hold office.

1.16   Think up some computerized device or program that does not yet exist, but that you would be very proud to help develop. Describe it.

1.17   List three applications of computer technology mentioned in this chapter that reduce the need for transportation. What are some advantages of doing so? For one of the applications you chose, describe a potential weakness or problem that might develop (relative to the old-fashioned way of accomplishing the same objective).

1.18   Describe a computer program or application with which you had experience (as a user or a programmer) in medicine, education, or crime fighting. What were its advantages?

1.19 For each of the following tasks, describe how it was probably done 20–25 years ago, before the World Wide Web. Briefly tell what the main difficulties or disadvantages of the older ways were. Tell if you think there were advantages.

a) Get a copy of a bill being debated in Congress.

b) Find out if there are new treatments for ovarian cancer and how good they are.

c) Sell a poster advertising a Beatles concert from the 1960s.

1.20 Let's start thinking about Chapter 2. Pick any two applications of computers described in Section 1.3 where the use of computers makes invasion of privacy easier or more likely. Explain how.

1.21 Thinking ahead to Chapter 4, pick any two applications of computers described in Section 1.3 where an error in the computer system could pose a serious danger to people's lives. Explain how. Describe one application that increased safety.

Assignments

These exercises require some research or activity.

1.22 Find a Web site with information relevant to any of the issues introduced in Section 1.2. Give the URL, the name of the sponsoring organization, and a brief summary of what the site contains.

1.23 Go around your home and make a list of all the appliances and devices that contain a computer chip.

1.24 Get a brochure from a car dealer for a new car. Describe the uses of computer technology in the car. For each one, tell whether its main purpose is to enhance convenience or to enhance safety.

1.25 Arrange an interview with a disabled student on your campus. Ask the student to describe or demonstrate some of the computer tools he or she uses. (If your campus has a Disabled Student Center, its staff may be able to help you find an interview subject.) Write a report of the interview and/or demonstration.

1.26 Go to your campus library and get the microfilm or microfiche for the issue of the *New York Times* published on the day you were born. (If it is not available, pick any old newspaper available in one of these media.) Read a few articles. Compare the convenience of using these media (standard for research not long ago) to reading newspaper and magazine articles on the Web.

1.27 Interview a photographer who has used both manual (film) cameras and automatic digital cameras, or interview a piano tuner who worked before and after electronic pitch-testing devices were available. Ask his or her opinions of the advantages and disadvantages of the computerized devices.

1.28 When this book was written, smart card applications were developing more slowly in the U.S. than in Europe. Find out about a current use of smart cards and describe it.

1.29 Many elderly people have trouble remembering words, people's names, and recent events. Imagine a memory-aid product. What features would it have? What technologies would you use if you were designing it?

1.30 For Computer Science majors: Read the Software Engineering Code of Ethics and Professional Practice (Appendix A.1). As you read through the rest of this book, find clauses in the Code that, if followed, might have prevented the problems being discussed.

1.31 Over the next month or two (whatever is appropriate for the length of your course), collect news articles, from print or electronic sources, on (1) benefits and valuable applications of computers and (2) failures and/or problems caused by computer systems. Collect at least five articles in each group. Mark the source and date on each article. The articles should be current, that is, published or distributed during this time period. Write a brief summary and commentary on two articles in each category, indicating how they relate to topics covered in this book.

NOTES

[1] Chris Morgan and David Langford, *Facts and Fallacies: A Book of Definitive Mistakes and Misguided Predictions*, St. Martin's Press, 1981, p. 64. Mr. Duell made his comment while urging the President to abolish the Patent Office. (Morgan and Langford refer to Duell only by his title; his name is given in Christopher Cerf and Victor Navasky, *The Definitive Compendium of Authoritative Misinformation*, Pantheon Books, 1984, p. 203.)

[2] Stephen E. Ambrose, *Undaunted Courage: Meriwether Lewis, Thomas Jefferson and the Opening of the American West*, Simon & Schuster, 1996, p. 53. Smoke signals and other visual signaling systems were exceptions.

[3] Jacqueline Klosek, *Data Privacy in the Information Age*, Quorum Books, 2000, p. 2. Erin White and Nick Wingfield, "Online Retail Spending Gained in Fourth Quarter," *Wall Street Journal*, Jan. 3, 2002, p. A3.

[4] "Beyond Repair: The Politics of the Machine Age Are Hopelessly Obsolete," *The New Democrat*, July/Aug. 1995, pp. 8–11.

[5] Joan E. Rigdon, "Technological Gains Are Cutting Costs, And Jobs, in Services," *Wall Street Journal*, Feb. 24, 1994, p. A1.

[6] Saul Hansell, "Cash Machines Getting Greedy at a Big Bank," *New York Times*, Feb. 18, 1994, p. A1, C16.

[7] The rate of attacks on customers at ATMs in the mid-1990s was one in 3.5 million transactions (and as high as one in a million in some neighborhoods). F. Barry Schreiber, "The Future of ATM Security," *Security Management*, Mar. 1994, v. 38, n. 3, p. 18A.

[8] The term "claim-rights" is used by J. L. Mackie in *Ethics: Inventing Right and Wrong*. Another term that could be used for positive rights is entitlements.

[9] Nolan Bushnell, "Relationships between fun and the computer business," *Communications of the ACM*, 39:8, Aug. 1996, pp. 31–37.

[10] The comments from the restaurant manager (of a Hungry Hunter restaurant) and the medical clinic were reported in a term paper "Automation: Friend or Foe," by my student Thomas Chhoa. The example of tracking parts (for Land Rovers) is described in Laurie Hays, "Using Computers to Divine Who Might Buy a Gas Grill," *Wall Street Journal*, Aug. 16, 1994, pp. B1, B4.

[11] "Being Digital," *Wired*, February 1995, p.182.

[12] Wade Roush, "Spinning a Better Web," *Technology Review*, April 1995, pp. 11–13. John Byczkowski, "Site Seers," *NetGuide*, June 1995, p. 28. Yahoo: A Guide to WWW. 1998 Internet and WWW data from IntelliQuest Information Group Inc., Austin TX, and the NEC Research Institute, reported in Thomas E. Weber, "Who, What, Where: Putting The Internet in Perspective," *Wall Street Journal*, Apr. 16, 1998, p. B10.

[13] S. Fox and L. Rainie, *The Online Health Care Revolution: How the Web Helps Americans Take Better Care of Themselves*, Pew Charitable Trusts, Washington, DC, 2000.

[14] The May 2001 and April 1995 issues of *Communications of the ACM* contain special sections with many articles on digital libraries.

[15] Quoted in "U.S.'s New Web Site Provides Statistics From 70 Agencies," *Wall Street Journal*, May 23, 1997, p. A20.

[16] Valerie Reitman, "Look Who's Getting a License to Drive," *Wall Street Journal*, July 25, 1997, p. A9C. Gautam Naik, "This Robot Drives and May Save Lives," *Wall Street Journal*, April 5, 1994, p. B1. Stuart F. Brown, "Trucking Gets Sophisticated," *Fortune*, July 24, 2000, pp. 270B–270R.

[17] William M. Bulkeley, "Illiterates Find Computers Are Patient Mentors," *Wall Street Journal*, Nov. 16, 1992, p. B1.

[18] The information on ARJIS is from Donald A. Woodmancy, "Spreading the Word," Police, Sept. 1989, pp. 50–52, 87–91; Kathryn Balint, "Upgrade Due for Cops' Computer System," *San Diego Union*, "ComputerLink" section, Mar. 26, 1996, p. 14; and materials provided by San Diego Data Processing Corp.

[19] Bill Knight, San Diego Police Department, quoted in Woodmancy, "Spreading the Word."

[20] Viveca Novak and Joe Davidson, "Clinton Unveils Measures To Fight U.S. Terrorism," *Wall Street Journal*, Apr. 24, 1995, pp. A3, A4. Andrea Gerlin, "New High-Tech Tools Help Solve Old Murders," *Wall Street Journal*, June 19, 1995, pp. B1, B5. Bill Richards, "Cops Nab Perps With Digitized Drawings and Databases," *Wall Street Journal*, Jan. 28, 1998, pp. B1, B2. Peter Loftus, "Police Test Wireless Fingerprint Device, As Terror Attacks May Increase Demand," *Wall Street Journal*, Nov. 26, 2001, p. B7D.

[21] "Radiologists report CT scans can reduce appendectomies," *San Diego Union–Tribune*, Dec. 4, 1996, p. A9. Carol Gentry, "Seeing the Body Electric, in 3-D," *Wall Street Journal*, Jan. 24, 2000, p. B1, B4.

[22] Joshua Cooper Ramo, "Doc in a Box," *Time*, Fall 1996, pp. 55–57. Joseph R. Garber, "Heart Software,"

Forbes, Dec. 20, 1993, p. 248. "FDA Clears Machines Aiding Heart Patients Needing Transplants," *Wall Street Journal*, Sept. 30, 1998, p. B6.

23 Antonio Regalado, "Heart Hackers," *Technology Review*, Sept./Oct. 1998, p. 28–29.

24 Stephen Sobek, "Robot pharmacist: 30 million prescriptions, zero headaches," *The San Diego Union–Tribune*, Jan. 4, 1996, p. C-3.

25 Sources include: Laura Johannes, "3-D Imaging Guides Design of AIDS Drug," *Wall Street Journal*, Apr. 15, 1999, p, B1, B12. Yunje Cho, Svetlana Gorina, Philip D. Jeffrey, and Nikola P. Pavletich, "Crystal Structure of a p53 Tumor Suppressor-DNA Complex," *Science*, July 15, 1994, 265:5170, pp. 346–355. Siegfried H. Reich and Stephen E. Webber, "Structure-based drug design," *Perspectives in Drug Discovery and Design*, v. 1, 1993, pp. 371–390. "Rational Drug Design," chapter in *Proceedings of the 2nd Annual Paine Webber Biotechnology Conference*, San Diego, CA, Oct. 1989, pp. 305–332. *Agouron Pharmaceuticals Inc. Annual Report 1989*. Michael Waldholz, "Scientists Unveil a 3-D Portrait of Cancer Gene," *Wall Street Journal*, July 15, 1994, p. B1. Richard Turner, "Agouron Pharmaceuticals Shares Soar after Discovery Linked to Common Cold," *Wall Street Journal*, March 14, 1994. Telephone interview with Dr. Steve Worland, Agouron, July 22, 1994. Penni Crabtree, "The Protein Puzzle," *San Diego Union–Tribune*, Apr. 3, 2001, p. C1. Robert Langreth, "Chiron Designs New Meningitis Vaccine That Employs Gene-Mapping Procedure," *Wall Street Journal*, Mar. 10, 2000, p. A3, A4.

26 The quotation is from *Proceedings of the 2nd Annual Paine Webber Biotechnology Conference*, p. 311.

27 Laura Landro, "Ready Access to Patient Records," *Wall Street Journal*, Nov. 13, 2000, p. R23. "Newstrack: Rx for Health Care," *Communications of the ACM*, Apr. 1993, pp. 13–14.

28 Robert Fox, "News Track," *Communications of the ACM*, Jan. 1995, 38:1, pp. 9–10. "A Neural Net to Snag Breast Cancer," *Business Week*, Mar. 13, 1995, p. 95. Rochelle Sharpe, "Computer System To Detect Cancer Gets FDA Approval," *Wall Street Journal*, June 20, 1998, p. B7. Robert Langreth, "Ultrasound That Trims Need for Biopsy In Breast Cancer Clears FDA Hurdle," *Wall Street Journal*, Dec. 12, 1995, p. B10. "Computer cuts risk, time in detecting cancer," *Cancer Researcher Weekly*, May 9, 1994, p. 5. Robert Fox, "News Track," *Communications of the ACM*, Aug. 2000, 43:8, pp. 9–10.

29 "Prototype: Stroke Sensor," *Technology Review*, July/Aug. 2001, p. 21.

30 Victoria L. Contie, "Long-Distance Microscopy," *NCRR Reporter*, May/June, 1993, 17: 3, p. 3. Telephone interview with Dr. Mark Ellisman, July 18, 1994. Akio Takaoka, Kiyokazu Yoshida, Hirotaro Mori, Soichiro Hayashi, Stephen Young, and Mark H. Ellisman, "International Telemicroscopy with a 3MV ultrahigh voltage electron microscope," *Ultramicroscopy*, v. 83, 2000, pp. 93–101.

31 John Hockenberry, "The Human Brain," *Wired*, Aug. 2001, pp. 94–105.

32 "Computer Software Makes Playing Music Easier for the Blind," *Wall Street Journal*, Dec. 20, 1999, p. B13C.

33 David Lunney, "Adapted Computers as Laboratory Aids for People With Disabilities," 1992. See also David Lunney, "Assistive Technology in the Science Laboratory: a Talking Laboratory Work Station for Visually Impaired Science Students," *Information Technology and Disabilities*, 2:1, Jan. 1995.

34 Simson L. Garfinkel, "Enter the Dragon," *Technology Review*, Sept./Oct. 1998, pp. 58–64.

35 Disabled Opportunities Center, San Diego, CA. "A Butler in the House," *Electronic House*, March/April 1990. Telephone interview with Christopher Brown, Automated Voice Systems, Inc., Yorba Linda, CA, July 27, 1994.

36 "New Technology for Artificial Arms," *Exceptional Parent*, Nov./Dec. 1993, pp. 24–26. Telephone interview with Ed Gosschalk, Southern California Orthotics and Prosthetics, Aug. 15, 1994. Robert Fox, "News Track," *Communications of the ACM*, Dec. 1995, pp. 9–10. Evan Ratliff, "Born to Run," *Wired*, July 2001, pp. 86–97. Various brain interface devices are described in John Hockenberry, "The Human Brain."

37 The quote from Lunney is in David Lunney, "Adapted Computers as Laboratory Aids for People With Disabilities," 1992. The quote from Fruchterman is from an e-mail message to me. The navigation product for the blind is described in Peter Tyson, "High-Tech Help for the Blind," *Technology Review*, April 1995, pp. 19–21.

38 "High-rise Storage System Combines with Conventional Selection Warehouse for Efficient, Productive Operation," *Grocery Distribution*, 1990. Phone interview with Rick Toneck, Operations Manager, July 12, 1994.

39 Tim Blomenberg, "Breaking New Ground in Machine Vision," *Sensors*, Aug. 1994, 11:8, pp. 28–30.

40 Gary Fields, "'Smart card' plan would help ID armed officers at airports," *USA TODAY*, June 14, 2000, p. 4.

41 Robert Fox, "News Track: The Chicken and the Chip," *Communications of the ACM*, Aug. 2000, 43:8, pp. 9–10.

42 "Sandia National Laboratory Computer to Detect Leaks," *Wall Street Journal*, Nov. 2, 1998, p. B7. Paul Saffo, "Sensors: The Next Wave of Infotech Innovation," Institute for the Future: 1997 Ten-Year Forecast, pp. 117–124.

43 John L. Eliot, "Bugging Plants to Sting Poachers," *National Geographic*, March 1996, 189:3, p. 148. Jon R. Luoma, "It's 10:00 P.M. We Know Where Your Turtles Are." *Audubon*, Sept./Oct. 1998, pp. 52–57.

[44] William M. Bulkeley, "Information Age," *Wall Street Journal*, Aug. 5, 1993, p. B1. "Newstrack" ("Claims to Fame"), *Communications of the ACM*, Feb. 1993, p. 14.

[45] Betty Friedan, *The Feminine Mystique*, W. W. Norton, 1963, p. 312.

[46] My thanks to an anonymous reviewer for the idea for this exercise.

BOOKS AND ARTICLES

Many of these references include topics that are covered throughout this book. Some of the references in Chapter 10 also include topics covered throughout this book.

- The Alliance for Technology Access, *Computer and Web Resources for People With Disabilities: A Guide to Exploring Today's Assistive Technology*, 3rd ed., Hunter House Inc., 2000. www.ataccess.org.

- Stan Augarten, *Bit by Bit: An Illustrated History of Computers*, Ticknor & Fields, 1984.

- Edward Cavazos and Gavino Morin, *Cyberspace and the Law*, MIT Press, 1994.

- Peter Denning and Robert Metcalfe, *Beyond Calculation: The Next Fifty Years of Computing*, Copernicus, 1997.

- Michael Dertouzos, *What Will Be: How the New World of Information Will Change Our Lives*, HarperEdge, 1997.

- Neil A. Gershenfeld, *When Things Start to Think*, Henry Holt & Co., 1999.

- Deborah G. Johnson and Helen Nissenbaum, eds., *Computers, Ethics & Social Values*, Prentice Hall, 1995.

- Rob Kling, ed., *Computerization and Controversy: Value Conflict and Social Choices*, 2nd ed., Academic Press, 1996.

- Duncan Langford, ed., *Internet Ethics*, St. Martin's Press, 2000.

- Richard S. Rosenberg, *The Social Impact of Computers*, Academic Press, 1997.

- Jonathan Rosenoer, *Cyberlaw: The Law of the Internet*, Springer Verlag, 1997.

- Herman T. Tavani, "CyberEthics Bibliography 2001: A Select List of Recent Works," *Computers and Society*, June 2001, pp. 30–36.

- Richard A. Spinello and Herman T. Tavani, eds., *Readings in CyberEthics*, Jones and Bartlett, 2001.

- Vernor Vinge, "Fast Times at Fairmont High," in *The Collected Stories of Vernor Vinge*, Tor, 2001. A science fiction short story, set in the near future, that imagines how computer technology may affect entertainment, communication, education, and many other facets of ordinary life.

ORGANIZATIONS AND WEBSITES

- Herman Tavani, ed., "The Tavani Bibliography of Computing, Ethics, and Social Responsibility": cyberethics.cbi.msstate.edu/biblio

2

PRIVACY AND PERSONAL INFORMATION

2.1 The Impact of Computer Technology

2.1.1 INTRODUCTION

After the fall of the communist government in East Germany, people examined the files of Stasi, the secret police. They found that the government had used spies and informers to build detailed dossiers on the opinions and activities of roughly six million people, a third of the population. The informers were neighbors, coworkers, friends, and even family members of the people they reported on. The paper files filled an estimated 125 miles of shelf space. Computers were not used at all.[1]

Medical and financial information, details of purchases, and evidence of romantic affairs can all be found by going through someone's garbage. Before the digital age, surveillance cameras watched shoppers in stores and employees at work.

Computers are not necessary for the invasion of privacy. However, we discuss privacy at length in this book because the use of computers has made new threats possible and old threats more potent. Computer technology has had a profound impact on what information is collected about us (sometimes without our permission or knowledge), who has access to it, and how they use it. Computer technology allows search and surveillance of huge numbers of people, often without our knowledge. Privacy is probably the "computer issue" that worries people most.

There are three key aspects of privacy:

- freedom from intrusion—being left alone

- control of information about oneself

- freedom from surveillance (from being followed, watched, and eavesdropped upon)

It is clear that we cannot expect complete privacy. We usually do not accuse someone who initiates a conversation of invading our privacy. Many friends and slight acquaintances know what you look like, where you work, what kind of car you drive, and whether you are a nice person. They need not get your permission to observe and talk about you. It is often said that if you live in a small town, you have no privacy; everyone knows everything about you. In a big city, you are more nearly anonymous. But if people know nothing about you, they may be taking a big risk if they rent you a place to live, hire you, lend you money, sell you automobile or medical insurance, cash your checks, accept your credit card, and so on. We give up some privacy for the benefits of dealing with strangers. We can choose to give up more in exchange for other benefits.

For the most part, in this book, we view privacy as a good thing. In this chapter and several others, we see a frequent tension between law enforcement and the privacy of innocent people. Critics of privacy argue that it gives cover to deception, hypocrisy, and wrongdoing. It allows fraud. It protects the guilty. Concern for privacy may be regarded with a suspicious "What do you have to hide?" Privacy involves a balancing act. Privacy scholar Alan Westin describes the factors to be balanced as follows:

- safeguarding personal and group privacy, in order to protect individuality and freedom against unjustified intrusions by authorities

- collecting relevant personal information essential for rational decision-making in social, commercial, and governmental life

- conducting the constitutionally limited government surveillance of people and activities necessary to protect public order and safety.[2]

In Sections 2.1.2–2.4, we look more closely at collection and use of personal information by businesses, governments, and organizations and at privacy risks and issues that result. (Although we discuss private sector and government issues in separate sections, there often is overlap.) We look at intentional, institutional uses of personal information (primarily law enforcement and tax collection in the government sector and marketing in the private sector by both businesses and non-profit organizations); unauthorized use by "insiders," the people who maintain the information; and inadvertent leakage of information through negligence or carelessness. In Section 2.2, we also consider issues of search and surveillance by governments. In Sections 2.5–2.6, we discuss a variety of approaches to protecting privacy and controversies about them.

Privacy issues arise in many different contexts. More topics with privacy implications appear in later chapters. Communications privacy is the central topic of Chapter 3. Anonymity, which can protect both privacy and freedom of speech, but makes crime easier, is discussed more fully in Chapter 5. We also discuss spam, the intrusion of online junk mail, in that chapter. We address the problem of intruders and hackers in Chapter 7; their activities can threaten privacy. In Chapter 7, we examine some methods for reducing such crimes as fraud and the release of computer viruses; we find privacy threats in some of these methods, such as the use of biometrics for identification. Privacy of employees in the workplace is discussed in Chapter 8. Privacy comes up again in Chapter 10, where we focus on the responsibilities of computer professionals.

We use the term *personal information* often in this chapter. In the context of privacy issues, it includes any information relating to or traceable to an individual person. It is not restricted solely to what we might think of as sensitive, private information, although it includes that. It also includes information associated with a particular person's "handle," user name, online nickname, identification number, or e-mail address. Nor is it restricted to text data; it extends to any information from which a living individual can be identified, including images.

> *The man who is compelled to live every minute of his life among others and whose every need, thought, desire, fancy or gratification is subject to public scrutiny, has been deprived of his individuality and human dignity. [He] merges with the mass. ... Such a being, although sentient, is fungible; he is not an individual.*

> —Edward J. Bloustein[3]

> *It's important to realize that privacy preserves not personal secrets, but a sense of safety within a circle of friends so that the individual can be more candid, more expressive, more open with "secrets."*
>
> —Robert Ellis Smith[4]

2.1.2 RISKS OF THE TECHNOLOGY

Computers and the Internet and World Wide Web make the collection, searching, analysis, storage, access, and distribution of large amounts of information much easier, cheaper, and faster than before. The sentence you just read appeared in Section 1.3.1, where the context made it clear that these were great benefits. But when the information is about our activities, opinions, and personal characteristics, the same capabilities threaten our privacy. Today there are thousands of databases, both government and private, containing personal information about us. Some of this information, such as our specific purchases in supermarkets and bookstores, was simply not recorded before. Some, including government documents like divorce and bankruptcy records, was in public records, but took a lot of time and effort to access before. In the past, conversations disappeared when people finished speaking, and personal communications were normally read by only the sender and the recipient. Now that we communicate by e-mail and electronic discussion groups, our words are recorded and can be copied, distributed, and read by others even years later. We browse in libraries and bookstores with anonymity and can buy all sorts of magazines and newspapers for cash, but, on the Web, a record can be kept of every page we visit.

INVISIBLE INFORMATION GATHERING

Invisible information gathering describes collection of personal information about someone without the person's knowledge. The important ethical issue is that, if someone is not aware that the information is being collected or of how it will be used, he or she has no opportunity to consent or withhold consent for its collection and use. Examples of invisible information gathering include satellite surveillance (discussed in more detail in Section 2.2.2) and automatic identification of a person's telephone number when he or she calls an 800 or 900 number. Invisible information gathering is common on the Web; we will describe a variety of examples shortly.

Most people who used supermarket club cards several years ago did not know that the store collected and kept a record of everything they bought when they swiped their card at the checkout stand. Now more people know, and they know that at some stores they are trading a degree of privacy for discounts. Thus, whether a particular example of personal data collection is invisible information gathering can depend on the level of public awareness and the knowledge of the particular person. Even when we know that Web sites *can* collect information, we often are not aware of just what information a particular site *is* collecting.

An Internet service provider (ISP) manages the connection between a user and the sites he or she is visiting. Thus the ISP "knows" every site we visit. Yahoo!, for example, collects four terabytes of log data daily. Logs are useful for determining customer needs, allocating resources, improving services, and advertising. ISP and Web site logs are used for tracking and collecting evidence about criminals. They include such details of our online activities as where we went, what we did, and how long we stayed at a particular page.

Cookies are files a Web site stores on each visitor's computer. The site stores in the cookie and then uses information about the visitor's activity. For example, a retail site may store the contents of our virtual "shopping cart" in a cookie. On subsequent visits, the site retrieves information from the cookie. Cookies were developed as a customer convenience; by using information in the cookie, a site avoids having to ask a user to type the same information each time he or she visits. Most big Web sites use cookies; they help companies provide personalized customer service and target advertising to the interests of each visitor. At first, cookies were controversial because the very idea that Web sites were storing files on the user's hard drive without the user's knowledge was startling and disturbing to many people. If a Web site we visit can read cookies, what else on our computers can it read? Also, cookies can be used to track our activities on many sites. A site that has our name and address can link the information together. Now more people are aware of cookies, but many Web sites do not inform visitors when they are being used.[5]

The software and sophisticated tools that Web sites use allow information about a visitor to be collected by advertisers on a site, not just the site sponsor itself. In some cases this is intentional, and the information supplied to the advertiser is limited. The complexity and obscurity of software can make it difficult to determine that information is being collected and where it is going. In some cases, personal information was sent to an advertiser as an accidental side effect of the complex design of the software that manages the information and connections between sites. Several companies discovered that such leaks, called *data spillage*, were occurring in their systems. A few examples: DoubleClick, a Web advertising company, received people's financial information from a Quicken Web site. E-Loan, an online loan business, put a lot of money and effort into ensuring privacy of the financial data entered by customers; then the company discovered that software in the systems of other companies it bought or had partnering agreements with was collecting its customer information.[6]

Some companies monitor the hard drives and search queries of people who use peer-to-peer systems to trade music and other files. The information is used for targeted marketing. QuickClick, a service of NBCi that enables the user to click on "any word, anywhere" and get information about it, collected more than just the word clicked on and transmitted a user identification number with each selected word. (NBCi said it did not use the extra information and was not interested in tracking user behavior, but the point is that information is collected invisibly—and a company's policies might not always be benign.) A company offered a free program that changed a Web browser's cursor into a cartoon character or other image; millions of people installed the program, then later discovered that the program sent to the company a report of the Web sites its users visited, along with the customer's serial number.[7] RealNetworks' program RealJukebox, which helps users manage and play digital music files, sent to RealNetworks information about the music played and copied by its users. Jukebox software provided by other companies collects similar information but informs the users and lets them turn off the data collection.[8] This last example illustrates that the data collection itself is not always sinister or dangerous. Some people don't mind giving the information; some are trading information for a free service or other benefit. The critical point is whether the user is told and thus can make an informed choice about using the software.

SECONDARY USE, COMPUTER MATCHING, AND PROFILING

The ease of copying, distributing, and analyzing data resulting from the use of computers and computer networks led to a huge increase in *secondary use* of personal information, that is, use of information for a purpose other than the one for which it was supplied. It is difficult for individuals to control their personal information if it is collected by one business, organization, or government agency and shared with or sold to others.

We will see many examples throughout this chapter. They include sale of consumer information to marketers or other businesses, use of information in various databases to deny someone a job, use of numerous databases by the Internal Revenue Service to find people with high incomes, purchase of drivers' license photographs from state motor-vehicle departments by a company providing security services, and the use of a supermarket's customer database to show alcohol purchases by a man who sued the store because he fell down.

Usenet newsgroups provide an early example of the risks of invisible information gathering and the power of storage and search technology to use information in ways utterly unanticipated at the time it was provided.* Beginning more than 20 years ago, Usenet eventually had thousands of groups, many of a technical or otherwise nonpersonal nature, but some covering sensitive political, sexual, health, and religious topics. Although participants largely knew that outsiders could log on and read any newsgroup, the likelihood was small; the presumption was that only a relatively small group of people who shared common problems or interests read the postings. The volume of postings, roughly a gigabyte a day by the mid-1990s, made it impossible for most sites to store them for longer than a few days. Participants thought their postings were as ephemeral as a conversation. But there were archives, some going back many years. The archives, especially for the technical newsgroups, form a valuable historical research source. Companies that developed some of the first search engines for the Web collected the archives and used them to demonstrate the power of their search tools. It quickly became popular for people to search for the names of their acquaintances and find all the messages they had posted. Some employers reviewed postings of job applicants. One company's software

---

*Usenet newsgroups were early discussion forums on the Internet, before the World Wide Web.

allowed creation of user profiles describing the subjects a person frequently wrote about. (In 2001, Google acquired a Usenet archive with 630 million postings from about 35,000 newsgroups.)

Computer matching means combining and comparing information from different databases (usually by using a person's Social Security number to match records). Businesses use the technique to form consumer dossiers, and government uses it primarily for detecting fraud and enforcing the law in other ways. *Computer profiling* means using data in computer files to determine characteristics of people most likely to engage in certain behavior. Businesses use profiling to find people who are likely customers for specific products and services. A few dozen federal agencies use computer profiling to identify people to watch—people who have committed no crime but might have a "propensity" to do so.[9] Computer matching and profiling are, in most cases, examples of secondary use of personal information.

LOCATION, LOCATION, LOCATION

Computer technology has increased the power and scope, while reducing the size and cost, of surveillance devices such as cameras and locating devices. In Section 1.3, we saw several benefits of tracking and location technologies. Here's the other side: Global positioning system (GPS) technology, satellites, and computer chips make it possible to track our movements and determine a person's current location. If, when you lock your keys in your car, the car company can remotely unlock it for you with a radio signal, the car company can determine your location. The cell phones and other wireless appliances many people now carry allow our location to be determined. Devices installed in rental cars, to locate them if they are stolen, can also be used to monitor or track drivers. (A rental car agency fined a man for speeding, based on information from a tracking device in the car.[10]) A company sells wireless watchband transmitters for children, so parents can monitor them. The federal government ordered that all wireless and cell phones have tracking capabilities to locate a phone making a 911 call. This is obviously useful for emergencies, but once the tracking technology is there, what else will it be used for? Some worry that we will be pestered with advertising calls as we walk or drive past a store having a sale. Some worry about abuse by government, saying that the government's ability to track and locate everyone by accessing the wireless telephone provider's system, the rental car system, and so forth, is a threat to our freedom. Will there be options for owners to turn off tracking features? It is essential that such questions be considered early in the development of new technologies and applications so that privacy concerns can influence both the technical design and the laws mandating particular features.

2.2 "Big Brother Is Watching You."

When the American Republic was founded, the framers established a libertarian equilibrium among the competing values of privacy, disclosure, and surveillance. This balance was based on the technological realities of eighteenth-century life. Since torture and inquisition were the only known means of penetrating the mind, all such measures by government were forbidden by law. Physical entry and eavesdropping were the only means of penetrating private homes and meeting rooms; the framers therefore made eavesdropping by private persons a crime and allowed government to enter private premises only for reasonable searches, under strict warrant controls. Since registration procedures and police dossiers were the means used to control the free movement of "controversial" persons, this European police practice was precluded by American governmental practice and the realities of mobile frontier life.

—Alan F. Westin, *Privacy and Freedom*, 1968[11]

In George Orwell's dystopian novel *1984*, Big Brother (the government) watched everyone virtually all the time via "telescreens" in all homes and public places. There was little crime and little political dissent—and no love and no freedom. Today, the government does not have to watch every move we make, because so many of our activities leave data trails in databases available to government agencies. The use of myriad personal-data systems to investigate or monitor people is sometimes called *dataveillance*, short for "data surveillance." When Big Brother wants to take a direct look at us and our activities, he uses sophisticated new surveillance tools. We examine some of these databases and tools and consider their compatibility with constitutional and legal protections from government intrusions.

2.2.1 DATABASES

Federal government agencies maintain thousands of databases containing personal information. As far back as 1982, it was estimated that federal agencies had approximately 3.5 billion personal files, an average of 15 for every person in the country.[12] Many are now accessible via computer networks, and other government agencies as well as private organizations use the information. Now, the federal government has access also to the huge trove of data in business databases, much of which it can get without a court order.

Government databases help government agencies perform their functions efficiently, determine eligibility for government jobs and benefits programs, detect fraud, recover payments on delinquent debts (e.g., student loans and child support payments), collect taxes, and catch criminals. Fraud in programs such as welfare, Medicare, and worker's compensation and defaults on guaranteed student loans cost billions of dollars each year. Restrictions on the government's access to and use of personal data would encourage more fraud and waste. However, because of the scope of the government's activities and the mass of data available to it, the use and misuse of personal data by government agencies pose serious threats to the liberty and personal privacy of all of us.

The Privacy Act of 1974 and the Computer Matching and Privacy Protection Act of 1988 are two of the main laws that regulate the federal government's use of personal data. Congress passed the Privacy Act of 1974 in response to abuses by the federal government

- Restricts the data in federal government records to what is "relevant and necessary" to the legal purpose for which it is collected.

- Requires federal agencies to publish a notice of their record systems in the Federal Register so that the public may learn about what databases exist.

- Allows people to access their records and correct inaccurate information.

- Requires procedures to protect the security of the information in databases.

- Prohibits disclosure of information about a person without his or her consent (with several exceptions).

Figure 2.1 Provisions of the Privacy Act of 1974

in the 1960s and early 1970s, to allay concern about the government's use of computer technology to invade citizens' privacy. In the 1960s and 1970s, the FBI secretly used its National Crime Information Center (NCIC) database to track the movements of thousands of people not wanted for any crime; many were opponents of the Vietnam war. The FBI kept files on civil rights activists, celebrities, and many other Americans. Other abuses included wiretappings, mail openings, burglaries, harassment of individuals for political purposes, and questionable use of personal records. The provisions of the Privacy Act are summarized in Figure 2.1. Although this law was an important step in attempting to protect our privacy from abuse by federal agencies, it has problems. It has, to quote one expert on privacy laws, "many loopholes, weak enforcement, and only sporadic oversight."[13]

The Computer Matching and Privacy Protection Act of 1988 requires government agencies to follow a review process before doing computer matching for various purposes. An investigation by an agency of Congress several years later found that government agencies were quite careless about following the provisions of the law.[14]

The Internal Revenue Service (IRS) uses computers to match tax data on individuals and small businesses with a variety of federal and state government records. It scans vehicle registration records for people who own expensive cars and boats; it searches professional license records for people who are likely to have large incomes. It searches a database of "suspicious" cash transactions, examining transaction information of millions of taxpayers. (Banks and other businesses are required to report all large, and suspicious small, cash transactions to the government.)[15]

In the 1990s, both the IRS and the FBI announced plans to drastically expand their databases. The IRS wanted to build a huge database of individuals, combining information from federal, state, and commercial sources, including motor-vehicle departments, credit bureaus, state and local real-estate records, newspapers, federal employment files, federal licensing data, and so on. Privacy advocates objected for several reasons, one being that the proposed system would use records that are often inaccurate. (What if the IRS matches tax returns with files of a computerized dating service that include possibly exaggerated information on income? If this example seems frivolous or unlikely, consider that the Selective Service bought the birthday list from a major ice cream parlor chain that gave free sundaes to customers on their birthdays. The list was used to find 18-year-old men who had not registered for the draft.[16]) The FBI proposed expanding NCIC to include access to many large private and government databases, including those maintained by credit bureaus, insurance companies, telephone companies, airlines, banks, the IRS, the Social Security Administration, and the Immigration and Naturalization Service (INS). The plan was scaled back because of opposition from people concerned with the potential for privacy and civil-liberties violations, but in 1996, Congress authorized millions of dollars to expand NCIC and link it to more databases.

Many government agencies, including the IRS, the FBI, and the INS, quietly found a way to access huge amounts of personal data not in their own databases: They buy personal information from private information service companies. Thus they "outsource" collection of information it would be controversial and possibly illegal for them to collect themselves. One private firm, ChoicePoint, for example, culls data from the three big credit bureaus, numerous local, state, and federal government agencies, telephone records, liens, deeds, and many other sources. ChoicePoint bought more than a dozen other personal information companies whose databases included records on drug tests, doctors' backgrounds, insurance fraud, and other areas. In 2001, the firm had more than 10 billion records in its system. ChoicePoint's clients include at least 35 government agencies. It has multimillion-dollar contracts with the Justice Department and the IRS and maintains a Web site for the use of FBI agents.* The writers of the Privacy Act and government data policies did not anticipate and explicitly cover the huge amount of information the government can buy from private information services. Some observers, including a former chief prosecutor in the Justice Department's computer crime unit, say that, if the government is not allowed to collect certain data, then it should not be allowed to buy it. The FBI and the INS argue that they are simply using a new tool to collect information and evidence they used to collect themselves before, but much less efficiently.[17]

As part of its efforts to enforce drug laws, the federal government maintains a database of people who have legally bought certain prescription medications (e.g., pain relievers containing narcotics). Does the potential value of the database in a criminal investigation justify the invasion of privacy of the vast majority of people using the medication appropriately?

BURDEN OF PROOF AND "FISHING EXPEDITIONS"

As some of our examples illustrate, computer technologies have altered the nature of tax, criminal, and other government investigations. Law-enforcement agencies obviously need to collect evidence from a large variety of sources. Traditionally, law-enforcement officials started with a crime and used a variety of techniques to look for a suspect. Now

---

*ChoicePoint won a "Big Brother" Award at the annual Computers, Freedom, and Privacy conference. The award is given to businesses and government agencies whose practices are particularly offensive to privacy advocates. The company was fined $1.37 million by the state of Pennsylvania for selling driver data in breach of a contract with the state for processing driving records.

THE U.S. CENSUS

The U.S. Constitution authorizes and requires the government to count the people in the United States every ten years, primarily for the purpose of determining the number of Congressional representatives each state will have. Between 1870 and 1880, the U.S. population increased by 26%. It took the government nine years to process all the data from the 1880 census. During the 1880s the population increased by another 25%. If the same methods were used, the government would not complete processing data from the 1890 census until after the 1900 census was to begin. Herman Hollerith, a Census employee, designed and built punch-card processing machines—tabulators, sorters, and keypunch machines—to process census data.* Hollerith's machines did the complete 1890 population count in only six weeks, an amazing feat at the time. All the rest of the processing of the 1890 census data was completed in seven years. It could have been done sooner, but the new machines allowed sophisticated and comprehensive analysis of the data, which would have been impossible before. Here is an early example of computing technology enabling increased processing of data with the potential for good and bad effects: better use of information and invasion of privacy.

The Census Bureau now requires information from everyone about their race, national origin, and housing and their relationship to people they live with. A sample of households is required to fill out the "long form," which includes questions about physical and mental health, income, household expenditures, employment, education, and so on. The information is supposed to be confidential, and federal law says that "in no case shall information furnished . . . be used to the detriment of any respondent or other person to whom such information relates."[18]

In 1942, the Census Bureau assisted the Justice Department in using data from the 1940 census to find neighborhoods with high concentrations of U.S. citizens of Japanese ancestry. Knowing how many people to look for in each block, the army rounded up Japanese-Americans and imprisoned them in internment camps. During World War I, the Census Bureau provided names and addresses of young men to the government to help find and prosecute draft resisters. There were no computers then, but now that computers are the storehouses of census data, using the data "to the detriment of any respondent" is even easier. Some cities used data from the 1980 census to find poor families who violated zoning or other regulations by doubling up in single-family housing. These people were evicted.[19]

government agencies can search through huge volumes of information, or, as we see in the surveillance examples in the next section, through huge crowds of people, seeking people who look suspicious. One result is that, in many cases, a presumption of guilt replaces the traditional presumption of innocence. The person whom a computer program considers

*The company Hollerith formed to sell his machines later became IBM.

suspicious may be detained by police, lose benefits, or be ordered to pay additional taxes. Innocent people are subject to embarrassing searches and expensive investigations and sometimes to arrest and jail.[20] Do databases and search technologies simply make the work of law-enforcement agencies more efficient, or do they fundamentally change the relationship between citizen and government?

OBEYING THE RULES

> *Quis custodiet ipsos custodes? (Who will guard the guards themselves?)*
>
> —Juvenal

Several studies have found that government agencies do not adequately protect personal information, often in violation of laws passed to protect privacy and reduce government abuse of data. The General Accounting Office (GAO) is Congress' "watchdog agency." One of its tasks is to monitor the government's privacy policies. In 1990, the GAO released a major study showing lack of compliance with the Privacy Act of 1974. In 1996 Congress investigated a "secret" database maintained by the White House on 200,000 people with more than a hundred fields of data for each person, including ethnic and political information. A 1997 study looked at privacy policies of government Web sites. It found that more than 80% of federal government Web sites linked from the White House Web page violated provisions of the Privacy Act. In response to this study, a few agencies stopped placing cookies on the hard drives of visitors to their sites. Dozens of agencies, including the White House's Office of National Drug Control Policy, the Justice Department, the Defense Department, and the Energy Department continued to use cookies, although they probably violate the Privacy Act. A GAO study of 65 government Web sites in 2000 found that only 3% of the sites fully comply with the "fair information" standards for notice, choice, access, and security established by the Federal Trade Commission for commercial Web sites. The FTC itself was one of the sites that did not comply.[21]

There are many specific cases of leakage of information from government files. According to another GAO report, abuses of the FBI's NCIC by employees of law-enforcement agencies include selling information to private investigators, snooping on political opponents, and altering or deleting information. In one case, a former law-enforcement officer used NCIC to track down his ex-girlfriend; he then murdered her. The Los Angeles Police Department found that a significant number of employees illegally snooped for criminal records on people they knew or were considering hiring for such jobs as baby-sitter. Employees of the Social Security Administration and other federal agencies have been arrested for selling data on thousands of people, both to collection agencies and to a credit-card fraud ring. A high-ranking IRS official was indicted for selling information from tax files. Year after year, hundreds of IRS employees are investigated for unauthorized snooping in people's tax files. It is likely that most such activity goes undetected. An IRS employee who was a Ku Klux Klan member read tax records of members of his Klan group, looking for income information that would indicate that someone was an undercover agent. This and other abuses led to a 1997 law with tough penalties for government employees who snoop through people's tax information without authorization. However, a 1999 GAO report found that while the IRS had made significant improvements over prior years, the tax agency still failed to adequately protect people's financial and tax information. Unauthorized IRS employees were able to alter and delete data; disks with sensitive taxpayer information were disposed of without the files being erased; and hundreds of tapes and diskettes were missing.[22]

Computers provide a new enormously powerful tool for investigation, surveillance, and intrusion into our personal lives. We should expect government to meet an especially high standard for privacy protection, because it is coercive by nature. It has the power to arrest people, jail them, and seize assets from them. We have no choice, in most cases, about providing our personal information to the government. A former director of the ACLU Privacy and Technology Project commented that, "Particularly where the government is involved, consent [to use of personal information] is coerced and meaningless."[23]

2.2.2 THE FOURTH AMENDMENT AND EXPECTATION OF PRIVACY

The right of the people to be secure in their persons, houses, papers, and effects, against unreasonable searches and seizures, shall not be violated, and no Warrants shall issue, but upon probable cause, supported by Oath or affirmation, and particularly describing the place to be searched, and the persons or things to be seized.

—Fourth Amendment, U.S. Constitution

The U.S. Constitution protects a right to privacy from intrusion by government, most explicitly in the Fourth Amendment. The Supreme Court has interpreted other parts of the Bill of Rights to provide a constitutional right to privacy from government in other areas as well. England has a similar tradition, as expressed in William Pitt's colorful statement in 1763: "The poorest man may in his cottage bid defiance to all the force of the Crown. It may be frail; its roof may shake; the wind may blow through it; the storms may enter; the rain may enter—but the King of England cannot enter . . . ."[24] Here we look at how databases and surveillance technology challenge this right.

WEAKENING THE FOURTH AMENDMENT

The Fourth Amendment sets limits on the government's rights to legally search our homes and businesses and seize documents. It requires that the government have "probable cause" for the search and seizure; that is, there must be a good reason for the specific search. The trouble is that now so much personal information is not safe in our homes or in the individual offices of our doctors and financial advisors. It is in huge databases outside of our control. Many laws allow law enforcement agencies to get information from nongovernment databases without a court order. For example, the FBI may get certain information from credit reports without a court order (though not a person's complete credit history).[25] It can get student records and many other records without a court order, in emergencies. The comprehensive federal medical privacy rules issued in 2001 allow law enforcement agencies to access medical records without court orders. The USA PATRIOT Act of 2001 lets the government collect information from financial institutions on any transactions that differ from a customer's usual pattern and eased government access to many other kinds of personal information (without a court order). What level of access should the FBI have to the logs maintained by ISPs and Web sites we visit?

As we consider all the personal information available to government agencies now, we can reflect on the worries of Supreme Court Justice William O. Douglas about the potential abuse just from government access to the records of someone's checking account. In 1968, he said:

> In a sense a person is defined by the checks he writes. By examining them agents get to know his doctors, lawyers, creditors, political allies, social connections, religious affiliation, educational interests, the papers and magazines he reads, and so on ad infinitum. These are all tied in to one's social security number, and now that we have the data banks, these other items will enrich that storehouse and make it possible for a bureaucrat—by pushing one button—to get in an instant the names of the 190 million Americans who are subversives or potential and likely candidates.[26]

Today's readers should not miss the irony of the last sentence: 190 million was the whole population of the U.S. at the time.

The next few examples illustrate more ways technology erodes Fourth Amendment protection. Courts sometimes use the notion of "expectation of privacy" to determine when the Fourth Amendment applies. We will explain this concept and its weaknesses.

SATELLITE SURVEILLANCE AND THERMAL IMAGING

Satellites use various computer technologies to take detailed photographs of the earth, detailed enough to show our homes and backyards. The federal government sells the images to state governments, which use them to catch people who are growing . . . What? Are you expecting "marijuana"? No doubt, satellites have looked for that, but they are also used to catch people growing cotton without appropriate permits. Some state government agencies use the photos to detect building or property improvements that would raise property taxes; some plan to use them to find people who have built backyard porches without all the required building permits.[27]

Is this an intrusion into our personal space, a search of our homes, that the Fourth Amendment should prohibit without a warrant? The Supreme Court has already said "maybe" in a side comment in a decision that permitted surveillance from an airplane, but so far there has been no direct legal challenge of satellite imaging. The constitutional status of searching by satellite remains open, and government agencies continue to use the images.

In 2001, the Supreme Court ruled that police could not use thermal imaging devices to search a home from the outside without a search warrant. The Court stated that where "government uses a device that is not in general public use, to explore details of the home that would previously have been unknowable without physical intrusion, the surveillance is a 'search'," and requires a search warrant.[28] This reasoning suggests that when a technology becomes more widely used, the government may use it for surveillance without a warrant. This standard may allow time for markets, public awareness, and technologies to develop to provide privacy protection against the new technology. Is it a reasonable standard, or should the government have to satisfy the requirements of the Fourth Amendment for any search of a home (in nonemergency situations)?

AUTOMATED TOLL COLLECTION AND ITEMIZED PURCHASE RECORDS

Many bridges, tunnels, and toll roads now use automated toll-collection systems. Sensors read a device in the car as it goes by without stopping, and the owner's credit card or bank account gets billed for the toll. These systems save time for drivers and reduce the costs of collection. Their flexibility also allows the implementation of variable charges for different times of the day to improve traffic flow. The database used for billing drivers contains a record of where and when a person traveled (and, in some cases, how fast). The privacy concern is that marketers and government agencies can use this information to track people. Some toll-road operators have an option allowing drivers to pay cash in advance, avoiding billing records. Currently, however, most of the systems do not provide anonymity.

Police use toll records in investigations. A bridge and tunnel authority in New York had a policy that it would not disclose a driver's travel information except when required by law or when presented with a court order by a law-enforcement agency. A judge ruled that police could get such information without a court order. The judge said that traffic movement is in public view, a person does not have a reasonable expectation that information about his or her travel is private, and therefore the Fourth Amendment does not protect it. Let's look at this reasoning and its implications.

Yes, it is true that when we drive in public, anyone might see us. Someone could stand near a bridge and write down the license plate number of each car that passes by. If the police assigned an officer to do this, there might be a fuss. In any case, it simply was not done, not at all bridges and toll roads, 24 hours a day. We expected that our travel was mostly anonymous; strangers saw but did not recognize us, and no record remained after we passed by. The automated toll systems change the situation fundamentally. They keep a detailed, computerized record, 24 hours a day, of every vehicle using the system.

When we shop in a supermarket or a bookstore, we may be observed, and someone else might occasionally remember what we bought. Before computerized checkout systems, no one recorded our specific purchases. If the judge's argument in the toll case were to apply, would the police have access, without a court order, to lists of all the books we buy? In fact, law enforcement agencies have asked bookstores and online seller Amazon.com to turn over records of books purchased by particular people, sometimes with a search warrant, sometimes without one. These requests raise First Amendment issues as much as Fourth Amendment issues. The head of the American Booksellers Association commented that "From a First Amendment perspective, having the government be able to go in and review an individual's buying or reading patterns will have an incredible chilling effect."[29]

SUPREME COURT DECISIONS AND EXPECTATION OF PRIVACY

Several Supreme Court cases addressed the impact of technology on Fourth Amendment protection in earlier contexts.[30] In *Olmstead v. United States*, in 1928, the government had used wiretaps on telephone lines without a court order. The Supreme Court used a literal interpretation of the Fourth Amendment, ruling that it applied only to physical intrusion and only to search or seizure of material things, not conversations. Justice Louis Brandeis dissented, arguing that the authors of the Fourth Amendment did all they could to protect liberty and privacy, including privacy of conversations, from intrusions by government based on the technology available at the time. He believed that the Fourth Amendment should be interpreted as requiring a court order even when new technologies give the government access to our personal papers and conversations without entering our homes.

In *Katz v. United States*, in 1967, the Supreme Court reversed its position and ruled that the Fourth Amendment does apply to conversations and that it applies in public places in some situations. In this case, law-enforcement agents had attached an electronic listening and recording device on the outside of a telephone booth to record a suspect's conversation. The court said that the Fourth Amendment "protects people, not places," and that what a person "seeks to preserve as private, even in an area accessible to the public, may be constitutionally protected." To intrude in places where a reasonable person has a reasonable expectation of privacy, government agents need a court order.

Although the Supreme Court's decision in *Katz v. United States* strengthened Fourth Amendment protection in some ways, there is significant risk in relying on reasonable "expectation of privacy" to define the areas where a court order is needed. We saw that a judge used this notion to decide that law enforcement agents have access, without a court order, to all the detailed tracking information collected by automated toll systems. We used to have a reasonable expectation of privacy while driving around in our cars or, surely, in our own backyards, but as well-informed people come to understand the capabilities of modern surveillance tools and the mass of information in databases, we might no longer expect privacy from government, in a practical sense. Does that mean we should not have it? The Court recognized this problem in *Smith v. Maryland*, in which it noted that, if law enforcement reduces actual expectation of privacy by actions "alien to well-recognized Fourth Amendment freedoms," this should *not* reduce our Fourth Amendment protection. However, the Supreme Court has interpreted "expectation of privacy" in a very restrictive way. For example, it ruled that if we share information with businesses such as our bank, then we have no reasonable expectation of privacy for that information (*United States v. Miller*, 1976). Law-enforcement agents do not need a court order to get the information. This interpretation seems absurd. We do expect privacy of the financial information we supply a bank or other financial institution, as we do for many kinds of information we share with a few, sometimes carefully selected, others.

Should the capabilities of new technology give government agencies access to formerly private or ephemeral information without the protection of the Fourth Amendment? The notion of "expectation of privacy," as now interpreted by the Supreme Court, offers weak protection. Whether we preserve the spirit, or only the words, of the Fourth Amendment remains an open question. Eternal vigilance, we have been warned, is the price of liberty. This vigilance in the context of computerized information and surveillance systems means giving careful thought to what information we allow the government to collect or access and how we allow it to be used.

2.2.3 MORE SEARCH AND SURVEILLANCE TOOLS

ELECTRONIC BODY SEARCHES

Several airports use an X-ray device that displays on a computer screen the image of a person's body without clothes. Weapons and packets of drugs hidden under clothing are visible in the image. The U.S. Customs Service first used the device to examine travelers it suspected of smuggling drugs. People singled out for search were given a choice of using the machine or undergoing a "pat-down" search. After the terrorist attacks in 2001, the Federal Aviation Administration ordered the machines for airport security.

What are the advantages and disadvantages of these devices? How does the computer technology change the impact of a search? A scan by the machine is faster, more thorough, and less physically intrusive than a pat-down search. On the other hand, the display shows the person's body in detail; a director of the American Civil Liberties Union (ACLU) described a scan by the machine as "an electronic strip search." Once the computer captures the image, it can store and copy it.[31]

There are slightly different questions to consider, depending on whether officials use the device only on people singled out as suspects for other reasons, or on all passengers. If it is used only on suspects, we might well ask how many innocent people's privacy we are willing to trade for the chance of catching a criminal. Would you consider it a reasonable trade-off if 95% of the people the Customs Service selected for drug scanning were actually carrying drugs, and only 5% were not? What if only 50% of the people scanned were carrying them? Only 10%? Is our attitude about the legitimacy of using this technology affected by our perception of how likely we are to be its innocent victims? Among the people singled out as suspected drug smugglers and scanned by the machine at Kennedy Airport in New York in 2000, only 5% were actually carrying drugs.[32]

One company that makes the airport body scanners plans for the machines to X-ray passengers as they move along on a conveyor belt—similar to the current screening method for carry-on luggage. The ease of searching people with this technology means that more people will be searched. Is routinely exposing images of our naked bodies to guards an acceptable trade-off of privacy for security?

The government is funding development of a variety of devices that can search through a person's clothing from a distance, without the person's knowledge or cooperation, to detect hidden weapons. These devices have valuable security applications, but the technology can be used for random searches, without search warrants or probable cause, on unsuspecting people. Clearly, guidelines are needed for acceptable uses of such machines.

WHO'S GOT YOUR PICTURE?

We are used to security cameras in banks and convenience stores. They deter crime and help in investigations of crimes. Prisons use video surveillance systems (sometimes called CCTV, for closed circuit television) for security; gambling casinos use them to watch for known cheaters. Video surveillance systems monitor traffic and catch traffic-law violators. Cameras alone raise some privacy issues. When combined with face-recognition systems, they raise even more. We describe some applications of face recognition and some relevant privacy and civil-liberties issues.

In 1999, a private company bought the digitized driver photos maintained by the motor-vehicle departments in several states. The company said it was buying the photos and building the database, which included other personal information such as Social Security numbers, to provide security services, for example to protect against credit fraud. Drivers had no choice about whether their photos were sold. Later it was disclosed that the U.S. Secret Service provided technical assistance and $1.46 million in funding for the project. The Secret Service supported the project to fight terrorism, illegal immigration, and "identity crimes."* Publicity about the project generated public protest, and some states decided not to sell their driver photos.[33]

The Tampa, Florida police used a computer system to scan the faces of all 100,000 fans and employees who entered the 2001 Super Bowl (causing some reporters to dub it Snooper Bowl). The system searched computer files of criminals for matches, giving results within seconds. People were not told they were being photographed. Later Tampa installed a similar system in a neighborhood of popular restaurants and nightclubs. Police in a control room zoom in on individual faces and check for matches in their database of suspects.[34] After September 11, 2001, several airports installed face-recognition systems, and police cameras in Washington, D. C. zoomed in on individuals a half mile away.

The ACLU has compared the use of the face-recognition system at the Super Bowl to a computerized police lineup, to which innocent people were subject without their knowledge or consent. Face-recognition systems had an accuracy rate of little more than 50% in the early 2000s. (Photos in databases tend to be old, and the systems do not perform well on images taken from different angles and in different lighting conditions.)

---

*The Secret Service has responsibility for investigating some kinds of financial and computer crime, in addition to its better-known role of protecting the President.

Harvard research fellow David Banisar argued that the low accuracy rate could result in the detention of many innocent people.[35] The accuracy will likely improve, but other issues will remain.

There are more than 500,000 CCTV cameras in England, many outdoors in public places to deter crime. A Londoner is likely to be recorded dozens of times a day. Government officials in a suburb of London said the CCTVs were responsible for 500 arrests in one year. Others argue that the cameras have not reduced crime. Defense lawyers complain that prosecutors sometimes destroy footage that might clear a suspect. A study by a British university found a number of abuses by operators of surveillance cameras, including collecting salacious footage, such as people having sex in a car, and showing it to colleagues.[36] A traffic monitoring system in Florida was removed after engineers were observed zooming in on individual pedestrians unrelated to traffic flow.

Is enforcing a 9 PM curfew for young people, one of the uses of public cameras in England, important enough to accept the potential abuses? Even if one thinks government curfews for young people are reasonable (and many do not), this application suggests the kind of monitoring and control of special populations made easy by the cameras. Banisar asks whether face-recognition systems would be used to track political dissidents, journalists, political opponents of powerful people—the kinds of people who were targeted for illegal or questionable surveillance in the past. More fundamentally, is this level of surveillance, with its potential for abuse, compatible with our notions of privacy and a free society? Not to 500 people who complained when the California Department of Transportation photographed their license plates and then contacted them for a survey on traffic in the area where they drove. These people objected vehemently to what they considered unacceptable surveillance by a government agency even when it was only their license plates, not their faces, being photographed for a survey, not a police action. Several city governments considered using cameras in public places, but decided not to. Toronto city officials refused to let police take over their traffic cameras to monitor a protest march and identify its organizers. In a controversial statement, the Privacy Commissioner of Canada argued that the country's Privacy Act required a "demonstrable need for each piece of personal information collected" to carry out government programs and therefore recording activities of large numbers of the general public was not a permissible means of crime prevention.[37]

Many applications of CCTV and face-recognition systems are reasonable, positive uses of the technology for security and crime prevention. But there is a clear need for controls, guidelines, and some limitations. How should we distinguish appropriate from inappropriate uses? Should international events such as the Olympics, which are sometimes terrorist targets, use such a system? Should technologies like face-recognition systems be used only to catch terrorists and suspects in serious crimes, or should they be used in public places to screen for people with unpaid parking tickets? Should people be informed about when cameras are in use? If we consider these issues early enough, we can design some privacy-protecting features into the technology and consider appropriate privacy-protecting legislation before, as the Supreme Court of Canada worries in the quote that follows, "privacy is annihilated."

To permit unrestricted video surveillance by agents of the state would seriously diminish the degree of privacy we can reasonably expect to enjoy in a free society. . . . We must always be alert to the fact that modern methods of electronic surveillance have the potential, if uncontrolled, to annihilate privacy.

—Supreme Court of Canada, 1990[38]

FIGHTING TERRORISM

For a while after the terrorist attack on the World Trade Center and the Pentagon on September 11, 2001, attitudes about surveillance technologies and policies changed drastically in the United States. Many people wanted to use all available tools to catch terrorists and prevent future terrorist attacks. In this book, we focus on the uses and abuses of technology, not all the very difficult, wider issues related to terrorism. High-tech surveillance technologies are helpful but are not a panacea. A face-recognition system will not stop a terrorist whose photo is not in the database of suspected terrorists. Airport security before the terrorist attacks could detect small knives and box cutters, but the rules permitted them. The core of the security failure in 2001 was that U.S. intelligence agencies did not know that the attack was planned.

The fundamental issues have not changed. The difficult task of choosing the right tools to use and the right trade-off between security and the privacy, freedom, and convenience of innocent people remains. We do not want to live in a "police state," nor are such places guaranteed to be safe. People in prison, the ultimate police state, manage to get weapons and illegal drugs; they rape and murder other prisoners. Security will never be complete. Certainly some high-tech security systems can help reduce terrorism, but, if used without sufficient care and protection for civil liberties and privacy, they turn us all into prisoners.

2.3 Consumer Information

2.3.1 DATABASES AND MARKETING

If you enter a contest or fill out a warranty questionnaire, information about you will be entered into a database and probably made available to direct marketers. If you buy a bicycle, you might get a solicitation from a magazine about bicycle touring. If you buy baby clothes, you will get many mailings about other baby products. Nonprofit organizations, from the Sierra Club to the National Rifle Association, use mailing lists to solicit contributions, members, and action in support of their causes. If you file a change-of-address notice with the U.S. Postal Service, your name and new address are provided to mailing-list managers who sell the lists to mass mailers. The ads you see on your computer screen while visiting certain Web sites are different from the ads seen by others; they are chosen for you by software, based on your previous activity at the site (or other sites).

Catalogs and other advertising arrive in our mailbox. Telemarketers disturb our peace with those annoying telephone sales pitches. Web pages are splattered with ads. E-mail users receive *spam*, or unsolicited, mass e-mail. The target lists and sometimes the sales pitches themselves are computer generated.

Businesses use powerful hardware and software to analyze consumer data, government records, and any other useful information to determine who might be a new customer. This is an application of a process called *data mining*, the searching of masses of data to find new information or knowledge. Marketers use thousands of criteria to decide who gets a specific catalog or promotional mailing. Long-distance telephone companies use lists of subscribers to foreign-language newspapers or Web sites to find potential customers for special telephone service deals; they send the ads in the customer's language. American Express mines hundreds of billions of bytes of data on how customers have spent hundreds of billions of dollars. They send discount coupons and special promotions for the specific stores where customers shop. Online book and music sellers make recommendations to you that are based on prior purchases by you and other people with similar buying patterns. Some supermarket chains store a year's worth of data on the details of customer purchases. Airlines send incentives to frequent flyers who are flying less frequently. Cruise lines send ads to people who have gone on cruises before. A pasta company sends coupons to people who buy its competitor's products. A company sells lists of e-mail addresses of people who post to newsgroups on the Internet; the lists are organized by interest areas, including general interests, hobbies, religion and "adult." This kind of marketing was not possible without computers and was not possible even with the technology of about 15 years ago. Marketers were limited to studying buying habits of people in broad categories, such as women from 25 to 49.

DoubleClick, an online advertising service that sells ads on 1500 Web sites, caused a highly publicized controversy in 2000 by planning to combine its huge database of Web-surfing activity with a huge database of offline purchases and real names and addresses. Faced with strong criticism by angry privacy advocates and investigations by government agencies, DoubleClick dropped the plan. However, some other ad companies mix online and offline data to target ads.[39] Most people do not distinguish between mailings generated by sophisticated computer mining of databases and mailings addressed to "occupant." Both infringe on the first aspect of privacy: being free from intrusion. The sale of personal data and the building of detailed profiles of a consumer's opinions, preferences, and activities infringe on the second aspect of privacy: control of information about oneself (if the person has not given permission). As one journalist said, it "gives some people the creeps."[40] We now consider some potential problems and some perspectives.

A purchase of pasta or the fact that someone reads weather reports on the Web is not particularly personal or sensitive. An immigrant may appreciate getting ads in his or her native language. But would a customer be happy being on a list of people considered likely to buy a product for adults who are incontinent? One company compiled such a list and made it available through a commercial list broker. Would a customer be happy that a store has a record of how many packs of cigarettes, bottles of brandy, or contraceptives he or she buys? A person might not want to be on a list of participants in an online discussion group about computer hacking or neo-Nazism.

Many companies that maintain huge consumer databases have bought (or merged with) others, combining data to build more detailed databases and dossiers. The 1998 purchase of Metromail by Great Universal Stores, a British company, is an example. Metromail maintained a huge database of consumer information (with files on roughly half the people in the United States) and sold targeted marketing lists. A few years earlier, Great Universal bought Experian, formerly the TRW consumer credit bureau, one of the three major U.S. credit reporting companies. In 1998, the Experian database had information on 780 million consumers in 17 countries. When a consumer buys a product from a company owned by Great Universal and consents to company use of his or her customer information, the person probably has no idea how extensive the parent company is and how far the data could travel.

Marketers argue that finely targeted marketing is likely to be useful to the consumer and that it reduces overhead and, ultimately, the cost of products. L.L. Bean, a big mail-order business, says it sends out fewer catalogs as it does a better job of targeting customers. A Web ad company said users clicked on 16% of ads displayed based on the user's activity profile—many more than the 1% typical for untargeted Web ads. Another firm says that 20–50% of people used the personalized coupons it provided on screen or by e-mail, compared with the 1–5% redemption rate for newspaper inserts. The companies say targeting ads based on personal consumer information reduces the number of ads overall that people will see and provides ads that people are more likely to want.[41]

A statement from the Audubon Society, a nature organization, explains why it exchanges its mailing list with other groups and does mass mailings. Its arguments are similar to the arguments given by commercial direct marketers: These practices help in recruiting new members, reducing costs, and funding Audubon programs. "It's only 'junk mail' if it goes to the wrong person," the statement says. "Direct mail is one of the most cost effective ways to educate the public, effect social change, and attract new funders."[42] In spite of the clear arguments, the tone of the statement is almost apologetic. They know that some members do not approve of direct mail and the exchange of lists. (The Audubon Society, like many other organizations and businesses, allows members to exclude their names from the distributed list.)

To many consumers, the "intrusion" of advertisements is a welcome intrusion. Ninety-two million Americans respond by purchasing products or sending contributions.[43] They purchase enough of the products and services offered, and donate enough money, to make the mailings worthwhile to the businesses and organizations that send them. On the other hand, some people refer to such mailings as "junk mail" and dislike them intensely.* A

---

*Newspapers invented the term "junk mail" to disparage direct mail because they feared it would reduce their revenue from advertising flyers included in newspapers.[44]

PRISONERS PROCESSING PERSONAL DATA

A woman, along with more than two million other consumers, filled out a detailed consumer profile form for Metromail, expecting to receive discount coupons and free sample products. The form included hobbies, income, buying habits, health information, investments, and much other personal information. Later, she received a frightening 12-page letter, containing graphic sexual fantasies, from a convicted rapist in a Texas prison who knew everything about her. Prisoners had been contracted to enter the questionnaire data into computers. Several state governments also use prisoners to process personal data, including vehicle registrations, property records, and unemployment records.

In 2000, the woman won a lawsuit against Metromail. She received a monetary award and a court order prohibiting Metromail and its subcontractors from using prisoners to input data. The order required Metromail to inform the other people who filled out the survey; they were eligible for monetary awards. The settlement included establishing a million-dollar fund to promote consumer privacy.[45]

direct marketing expert says catalog companies expect that nine out of 10 of their catalogs are thrown away. The recipient has the burden of disposing of the volume of paper received.[46] Some critics of direct marketing point out that some people, often elderly, have little self-control; they respond to the ads and spend thousands of dollars they do not have.

When people lived in small communities and shopped at local stores, merchants knew the customers and their preferences, and could tell them about new products or special deals that would interest them. Some marketers say that collecting consumer data allows them to provide personalized service that was lost as society and shopping became more anonymous.

Most objections to consumer data collection arise from its intended uses by businesses. Another problem is that consumer data can leak in ways that can threaten people's safety. The example in the nearby box and the risks to children that we discuss later illustrate the importance of thinking about possible dangerous uses of personal information and the consequences of making it available to the wrong people.

We must take care when assigning blame for problems caused by direct mailings. For example, as an illustration of bad effects of computerized marketing lists, several writers mention the case of a woman who had a miscarriage and continued to receive mailings about baby products.[47] If a woman does not consent to her name being on the lists, she may object to being sent ads, regardless of whether she has a miscarriage. However, many expectant mothers happily and willingly put their names on mailing lists for baby products and services. A miscarriage can cause profound emotional pain. Baby catalogs arriving in the mail—or the sight of another mother with an infant—are reminders of the pain, but it is unreasonable to blame marketers or computerized mailing lists if the woman gave consent to the distribution of her name. Is there anything about computerization of marketing lists that contributes to the woman's pain in such a case? Yes. The ease of copying computer files means that a large number of businesses could have bought her name. It might take a huge effort to track down every company that now has her name and ask each to stop sending mail. Consent to distribution of our names and addresses for marketing purposes is a decision that is difficult to revoke.

2.3.2 CHILDREN ON THE WEB

There are two main privacy issues related to children on the Web, one of which is linked to safety: Child molesters use the Web to find children, win their confidence via e-mail and chat, then arrange meetings. The second issue is the collection of personal information by the many Web sites designed for children. Adults can make decisions about what information they want to give out, or what degree of tracking they want to allow in exchange for discounts or access to certain sites. Young children are not likely to understand the risks and trade-offs. Children give out family income data and other personal family information on the Web. Aside from the general problems of consumer data and the activity profiles we have already mentioned, detailed profiles about children, including their hobbies, nicknames, names of friends, and so forth, are a treasure for child predators. Parents and privacy advocates, concerned about the safety of children, criticized Metromail for providing a service, intended for marketers but available to others, that included names, addresses, and ages of children.[48]

In 1998, a Federal Trade Commission (FTC) study found that 89% of Web sites aimed at children collected personal information, and only 23% of the sites asked children to get consent from their parents before providing the information. Later that year, Congress passed the Children's Online Privacy Protection Act (COPPA) ordering the FTC to set up rules for protecting children under age 13. The rules (which went into effect in 2000) prohibit Web sites from collecting personal information from children under 13 without "verifiable parental consent." The sites must prominently post their policy telling what information they collect and how it is used.

2.3.3 CREDIT BUREAUS

Credit-bureau databases are one of the best examples of the observation that data collected for one purpose almost inevitably will be used for other, unexpected purposes.

The three major credit-reporting companies, Experian, Equifax, and Trans Union, receive and process millions of records daily. In addition to bill-paying history, a credit report may contain information from public records, such as lawsuits, bankruptcies, and liens. The primary purpose of the credit bureaus is to provide a central storehouse of information for evaluating applicants for credit. Some employers (including the federal government) also use credit bureaus as part of a background check on job applicants.

The Fair Credit Reporting Act of 1970 (FCRA) was, according to *Privacy Journal*, the first law, anywhere in the world, to establish regulations for use of consumer information by private businesses.[49] It restricts credit bureaus to disclosing credit information only to employers, the government, insurance companies, and others who need it for legitimate business purposes involving the consumer.[50] That last category is vague and easy to circumvent. It was relatively easy to get someone's credit report for other purposes. Credit reports have embarrassed political candidates and undermined spouses in divorce cases. In 1996, Congress amended the FCRA, setting stronger standards to reduce access to credit records and making access under false pretenses a felony.

Credit information is of concern to privacy advocates because a bad credit report can prevent someone from getting a mortgage, a car loan, a job, or other services. (Privacy advocates and business people tend to disagree on the weight given to credit information when making decisions.) Sometimes an applicant is unaware that a credit report is the basis for a negative decision. The FCRA places limits on old negative information, about, for example, bankruptcies, criminal convictions, and civil judgments. Some see this as a privacy protection, whereas others see it as an unreasonable restriction on the flow of relevant information.

Some critics have strongly rebuked credit bureaus for selling mailing lists to marketers. The bureaus used their databases and other sources to produce and sell lists of "elite retail shoppers," "highly affluent consumers," people in financial difficulties, and other specially targeted groups. Credit bureaus had catalogs describing and promoting the variety of lists that were available.[51] As a result of public criticism and pressure, Equifax terminated its marketing mailing-list business in 1991. The Federal Trade Commission ruled that the practice violated the FCRA. Experian (then called TRW) agreed to stop. Trans Union fought in court, and eventually lost in 2001.[52]

For many years, credit bureaus sold "header" information from credit files, including name, address, phone number, Social Security number, and so on. Marketers, lawyers, and many others made many uses of this information. In 2001, a federal judge ruled that the law restricting sale of personally identifiable financial information included the headers on credit reports, and the credit bureaus could no longer sell header information without consumer consent.[53] This ruling was a significant change in privacy protection.

2.3.4 PRINCIPLES FOR DATA COLLECTION AND USE

The first principle for ethical treatment of personal information is *informed consent*: Businesses and organizations must inform consumers* about what information they are collecting and how they will use it. We have seen that people can trade information

---

*When I use the term "consumers," I include members, contributors, Web-site visitors, and others who would be in the databases of various businesses and organizations.

for many benefits, from borrowing a large amount of money for a home mortgage to convenient shopping on the Web. People vary in how much they value their privacy, how desirable or annoying they find advertising, and so forth. When people are informed about the data collection and use policies of a business or organization, they can decide whether or not to interact with that business or organization.

After informing people about what an organization does with personal information, the next simplest and most desirable policy is to give people a choice about whether data collected about them is distributed to other businesses or organizations and is used to send advertisements. The two most common forms for providing such choice are called *opt out* and *opt in*. Under an opt-out policy, one must check a box on a contract, membership form, or agreement, or call or write to the organization to request removal from distribution lists. If the consumer does not take action, the presumption is that his or her information may be used. Under an opt-in policy, personal information is not distributed to other businesses or organizations unless the consumer has explicitly checked a box or signed a form permitting disclosure. (Be careful not to confuse the two. Under an opt-out policy, more people are likely to be "in," that is, on the lists, and under an opt-in policy, more people are likely to be "out," because the default presumption is the opposite of the policy name.)

Until the late 1990s, neither policy was widely used. Many businesses indicated in small print in their customer agreements that they might use consumer data in various ways and exchange it with other businesses. Now, it is common for such agreements to have an opt-out box. (For some kinds of businesses, for example financial institutions, this is required by law.[54])

Some libraries have a policy of destroying the checkout record when a book is returned—the best protection against disclosure. Most databases cannot use this technique, but it is a good reminder of a goal. There is a tendency among people not to throw anything away, including information. A policy of destroying records that are old or no longer needed protects privacy.

Both the public and private sectors need to have strong sanctions against employees who release information without authorization. A vice president of Bell Atlantic (now Verizon) stated one example of a good policy: Someone who gives out information on a consumer is fired.[55]

Figure 2.2 summarizes privacy principles for personal data. Many government statements and laws, recommendations from many privacy organizations, and many business policies include various versions of these principles. There is wide variation in interpretation and implementation of the principles. For example, businesses and privacy advocates disagree about what information businesses "need" for customer service, marketing, and decision making. Thus these are very reasonable as principles or guidelines, but attempts to enforce them in laws are controversial. We discuss some of the controversy in Section 2.6.

1. Collect only the data needed.
2. Inform people when data about them are being collected, what is collected, and how it will be used. (Do not use invisible information gathering techniques without informing people.)
3. Offer a way for people to opt out from mailing lists and from transfer of their data to other parties.
4. Provide stronger protection for sensitive data. For example, use an opt-in policy for disclosure of medical data.
5. Keep data only as long as needed.
6. Maintain accuracy and security of data.
7. Provide a way for people to access and correct data stored about them.

Figure 2.2 Privacy Principles for Personal Data

2.4 More Privacy Risks

2.4.1 SOCIAL SECURITY NUMBERS AND NATIONAL ID SYSTEMS

The real danger is the gradual erosion of individual liberties through automation, integration, and interconnection of many small, separate record-keeping systems, each of which alone may seem innocuous, even benevolent, and wholly justifiable.

—U.S. Privacy Protection Study Commission, 1977[56]

With the advent of smart cards (cards containing a microprocessor and memory), there are increasing proposals for establishment of a computerized national identification card system. In one year alone, there were reports that the U.S. Postal Service, the IRS, the Defense Department, the National Security Agency, and NASA were among the agencies working on ID card plans. We review the background of Social Security cards and some problems with them, then consider national ID cards.

SOCIAL SECURITY NUMBERS[57]

We use our Social Security number (SSN) for identification for numerous services, yet its insecurity compromises our privacy and exposes us to fraud. Because the SSN is an identifier in so many databases, someone who knows your name and has your SSN can, with varying degrees of ease, get access to your work and earnings history, credit report, driving record, bank account, and other personal data. The potential for both privacy invasion and fraud (particularly identity theft, which we discuss in Chapter 7) is clear. SSNs appear on public documents and other openly available forms. Property deeds, which are public records, often require SSNs. SSNs are the ID numbers for students and faculty at many universities; the numbers appear on the face of the ID cards. The state of Virginia included SSNs on published lists of voters until a federal court ruled in 1993 that its policy of requiring the SSN for voter registration was unconstitutional.[58] Some states use the SSN as the driver's license number. (In 1999, Congress repealed an earlier law *requiring* that SSNs be included on drivers' licenses. However, it requires that states collect the SSN on driver-license applications and renewals.) Some employers use the SSN as an identifier and put it on badges or give it out on request. Many companies, hospitals, and other organizations to which we might owe a bill request our SSN to run a credit check. Some routinely ask for an SSN and record it in their files, although they do not actually need it. Although the risks of careless treatment of SSNs is high, government and businesses have only recently begun to treat them with appropriate security.

The history of the SSN illustrates how the use of a national identification system grows. When SSNs first appeared in 1936, they were for the exclusive use of the Social Security program. The government assured the public at the time that it would not use the numbers for other purposes. Only a few years later, in 1943, President Roosevelt signed an executive order requiring federal agencies to use the SSN for new record systems. In 1961, the IRS began using it as the taxpayer ID. So now employers and others who must report to the IRS require it. In 1976, state and local tax, welfare, and motor-vehicle departments received authority to use the SSN. A 1988 federal law requires that parents provide their SSN to get a birth certificate for a child. The IRS requires taxpayers to report the SSN for each child over one year old claimed as a dependent (or provide other proof of the existence of the child). A 1996 law authorized use of SSNs for occupational licenses and marriage licenses.[59] Although we were promised otherwise, the SSN has become a general identification number.

SSNs have little-known but serious flaws for their role as a person's ID number in many databases: They are not unique, and they do not identify people. In some cases, Social Security Administration offices in different areas issued the same numbers to different people. In some cases, the same number was issued to different people with the same name. There are a few numbers used by thousands of people because the numbers were on sample cards in new wallets. The Social Security Administration estimates that 10 million people have more than one number. Social security cards are made of paper. They are easy to forge, but that hardly matters, because people are rarely asked for the card, and numbers are rarely verified. The Social Security Administration itself used to issue cards without verification of the information provided by the applicant. In 1991, the agency's commissioner told Congress that more than 60% of SSNs were based on unverified information. While criminals have little trouble creating false identities, innocent, honest people suffer arrest, fraud, destruction of credit rating, and so on, because of problems with the SSN.

Because of the security and identity problems with Social Security numbers, designers of databases with personal information should not use the SSN as the record identifier unless there is a compelling reason to do so. There are techniques for designing more secure ID number systems that distinguish between valid and invalid numbers, thus reducing fraud and errors.

NATIONAL ID SYSTEMS

Proposed national ID cards would contain (on a magnetic strip or in smart-card memory) a person's name, photo, Social Security number, other identifying information, and health, tax, financial, citizenship, employment, or other data, depending on the specific proposal and the government agency advocating it. It might include biometric information such as fingerprints or a retina scan. In many proposals, the cards would also access a variety of databases containing such information. The cards would allow accurate verification of a person's identity when interacting with government agencies and for transactions such as credit card purchases, government payments, medical treatment, and banking transactions.[60]

Advocates of a national ID card describe several benefits. You would need the actual card, not just a number, to verify identity. The cards would be harder to forge than Social Security cards. A person would need to carry only one card, rather than separate cards for various services, as we do now. The authentication of identity would help reduce fraud both in private credit card transactions and in government benefit programs. Use of ID cards for verifying work eligibility would prevent people from working in the U.S. illegally. Criminals and terrorists would be easier to track and identify.

Opponents to these proposals argue that national ID cards are profound threats to freedom and privacy. "Your papers, please" is a demand associated with police states and dictatorships. In Germany under the Nazis, identification papers included the person's religion, making it easy to enforce restrictions on and imprisonment of Jews. Under the infamous pass laws of South Africa, people carried passes, or identification papers, that categorized them by race and controlled where they could live and work. Smart cards, with the large amount of personal information they can carry or access in national databases, have even more potential for abuse. Most people might not have access to the machinery that reads the cards; thus they would not always know what information they are giving others about themselves.

For several years in the 1990s, anti-immigration sentiment in the U.S. provided the most support for a national ID card. Consider the program to prevent illegal immigrants (or legal immigrants without work permits) from working in the United States. Every time any person applied for a job, the prospective employer would have to verify the person's right to work by checking with the Immigration and Naturalization Service (INS) database. For the scheme to succeed, each person would need a "fraud-proof" ID card. The immediate threat of such a system is the loss of liberty to work. "It is absolutely unprecedented," said congressman Steve Chabot, "to say that the government must grant affirmative permission every time any employee is hired."[61] In a country with an active economy and as large and mobile a population as the U.S., such centralized power over people's freedom to work would not be possible without modern computer and communications networks. In addition to the reduction of freedom, a serious flaw in the INS database illustrates potential practical problems with any ID card linked to a national database: It is riddled with errors. In experiments with the system, approval for 19% of (legal) workers was delayed for several weeks. Approximately 65 million people in the U.S. change jobs or enter the workforce every year, so a 1% error rate would mean denial of work for 650,000 people each year.[62]

After the terrorist attacks on the World Trade Center and the Pentagon in 2001, proposals arose again for requiring everyone in the U.S. to carry a national ID card. Many of the terrorist hijackers in 2001 had government-issued ID cards, some valid, some fake. There is no indication that accurate identification would have stopped them. Of course, there are many circumstances in which a secure ID card system would help catch criminals and terrorists. It would not stop anthrax attacks by mail or many kinds of terrorist attacks in public places. As usual, we must consider the trade-offs and not expect an ID card to accomplish things it cannot do.

Peter Neumann and Lauren Weinstein warned of the many risks that arise from the databases and communication complexes that would support a national ID card system: "card readers, real-time networking, monitoring, data mining, aggregation, and probably artificially intelligent inference engines of questionable reliability. The opportunities for overzealous surveillance and serious privacy abuses are almost limitless, as are opportunities for masquerading, identity theft, and draconian social engineering on a grand scale."[63]

In Chapter 4 we will see that a woman could not get her tax refund after records mistakenly indicated she had died. She would still have been able to get a new job, withdraw money from her bank account, pay her rent, send e-mail, and go to her doctor while she was resolving the problem with the tax agency. What if the worker verification database had used the tax records? Or what if a mistake cancelled the one ID card required for all these transactions? A critic of a proposal for a national identification card in Australia described the card as a "license to exist."[64] Is that description literal or a metaphor?

2.4.2 PERSONAL HEALTH AND MEDICAL INFORMATION

> *Whatsoever things I see or hear concerning the life of men, in my attendance on the sick or even apart therefrom, which ought not to be noised about, I will keep silence thereon, counting such things to be as sacred secrets.*
>
> —From the Hippocratic Oath

Our health and medical information is personal. Some is very sensitive: information about alcoholism, sexually transmitted diseases, psychiatric treatment, and suicide attempts. We might strongly desire to keep other health problems private even if they do not have negative social connotations.

Large medical care providers and hospitals are replacing paper medical records with computer databases. In Chapter 1, we mentioned that computerized records can improve medical care and cut costs. They can help protect privacy too. Studies have shown that, when a person is in a hospital, approximately 75–80 people may read his or her record (doctors, nurses, lab technicians, billing clerks, etc.). In such an environment, it is easy for unauthorized people to see a paper record, and it is easy for people to read parts of it that they do not need to see. Various database-access controls for computerized records (some described in Section 2.5) increase a patient's privacy. On the other hand, many kinds of medical information in databases and on the Web face the same privacy risks as other personal data.

Marketers love medical information. Metromail, the mailing-list broker, sold lists of people with specific diseases, such as diabetes and angina, to the pharmaceutical industry. Metromail said it had obtained the health information it sold from voluntary responses to ads and questionnaires. Large drug companies have bought other companies that sell prescription drugs to consumers mainly to gain access to the customer lists.[65] The huge burst in growth of the World Wide Web included medical Web sites sponsored by a variety of organizations and businesses. According to a critical review of such sites, some do not follow their stated privacy policies and some provide customer information, including e-mail addresses, to advertisers.

Patients refill prescriptions and check results of lab tests on the Web. Patients correspond with doctors by e-mail. These are great conveniences that can lower medical costs and improve medical care, but they open up new risks of leaks. For example, it is very easy to send e-mail to the wrong place, and one HMO did. It accidentally sent several hundred doctor-to-patient e-mail messages to 17 patients who were not supposed to get them. Some of the messages discussed personal medical details and included patients' addresses and telephone numbers.

Aside from marketing and technology, two economic factors diminish our control over our medical records: Most of us do not pay directly for our medical care, and we get care from large medical organizations rather than individual, private doctors. We waive confidentiality of our medical records for insurance payments. The insurer needs access to the records to verify eligibility and amounts of payments and to check for fraud (by patients or doctors). The anonymity and impersonal nature of a system of third-party payers (e.g., insurance companies or government) make it an inviting target for fraud. (One father/son team collected $16 million in Medicaid claims for nearly 400,000 phony medical visits.[66]) Preventing and detecting fraud requires access to medical and personal information about patients.

Because medical records can be available to insurance companies, employers, and government agencies, many people take measures to keep information out of their records. Some pay for certain medical services themselves, even if the treatment would be covered by insurance. They go to a different physician to keep the record entirely separate from insurance-paid medical care.[67] Psychiatric patients often pay cash and ask doctors not to keep notes of their sessions. When patients worry about the privacy of medical

PRIVACY VS. PUBLIC HEALTH

The San Francisco Department of Public Health determined that several men who contracted syphilis had met through an AOL gay chat room. The department asked AOL for the real names and contact information of others who visited the chat room, so that it could inform them about possible exposure to the disease. AOL followed its policy of not releasing information that links screen names with real names; it declined the request.[68]

What do you think of AOL's response? What alternate methods would disseminate information to potentially affected people? How do you weigh the trade-off between the possibility of an infected person's not being informed and the loss of privacy to all visitors to the chat room? How important is it that AOL abide by its posted privacy policy? Why?

information, the quality of care they receive can suffer. (Of course, the ethical consumer must distinguish between keeping medical information "off the record" to protect privacy and hiding information about relevant health conditions or risky behavior from insurance companies. *Informed* consent is as important a principle for sellers of insurance as it is for consumers. Hiding relevant data can also be fraud.)

In 2001, after years of controversy, the federal government issued comprehensive medical privacy regulations, effective in 2003, covering both electronic and paper records. Before that, various legal and privacy writers described medical-confidentiality laws, passed by the individual states, as "a dizzying array," a "patchwork," and "ambiguous, confusing." Congress' Office of Technology Assessment described the legal situation in the early 1990s as "inadequate to guide the health care industry with respect to obligations to protect the privacy of medical information in a computerized environment. It fails to confront the reality that, in a computerized system, information will regularly cross state lines and will therefore be subject to inconsistent legal standards with respect to privacy."[69] Some aspects of the new federal regulations are big steps forward in medical privacy. For example, medical insurers now must not disclose patient medical information to lenders, employers, and marketers without the patient's consent. Given the enormous variety of kinds of medical information and potential uses of the information, any regulations are bound to have problems. Some medical organizations described the rules, presented and explained in 1500 pages, as "an operational nightmare." Written consent is required for most disclosures of medical information, and health care providers must not disclose more than the minimum amount of information needed for each purpose. Some feared that the heavy civil and criminal penalties for serious violations might cause medical groups to adopt policies that are too restrictive, inhibiting the flow of necessary medical information among the practitioners treating a patient and leading to less-than-optimal patient care. Until the government issued additional clarifying explanations, pharmacists worried that they might not be allowed to give prescription medicines to family members or friends who came to pick them up for a sick person. Privacy advocates objected to exceptions to the consent requirement. The rules allow law-enforcement agencies and various other government agencies access to patient medical records without patient consent or a court order. Some privacy advocates object that the rules do not prohibit medical organizations from using generalized consent forms; they prefer a requirement that the patient must give written permission for each individual disclosure.[70]

There is debate about various other proposals related to medical privacy and computer technology. We discuss two.

- Creation of a government or quasi-government national database containing health and personal information on virtually all Americans.

- Requirement for everyone to have a national electronic health ID card. The card would be used to verify a person's eligibility for health care, to store data, and to access medical records.

The benefits of a national database containing everyone's medical record include accessibility when one is traveling or moves to a new area and the ease with which government and medical researchers can get complete data on diseases and health issues they are studying. However, a national database and medical ID cards have significant privacy risks. Some of the risks, we have seen, already exist. Centralization, lack of options for consumers, and access by more people distant from the actual health care provider increase those risks. Access by law enforcement and other government agencies is easier in such a system. Errors in a huge, centralized system are more likely and could prevent someone from getting medical care. On the other hand, critics of the health-care industry and some privacy advocates argue that broad public-sector medical-record systems will be cheaper and will provide better privacy protection than private health-care providers.

Privacy is threatened by the possibility that the Social Security number (SSN) will be used as the health identification number or that a health ID card will become a *de facto* national ID card. If the government requires a national medical ID system, it would be desirable to have a prohibition against using it for any other purpose. Unfortunately, the history of the SSN (described in Section 2.4.1) suggests that such a prohibition is not likely to be effective. In fact, because many government agencies are aware of the weaknesses of the SSN, if a secure, unique, universal identification system is developed for health care, it would be hard for the government to resist using it as a replacement for the SSN.

> *Patient medical information is confidential. It should not be discussed in a public place.*
>
> —A sign, directed at doctors and staff, in an elevator in a medical office building, a reminder to prevent low-tech privacy leaks.

2.4.3 PUBLIC RECORDS: ACCESS VS. PRIVACY

The Web makes it easier for ordinary people to obtain information. That's one of its major benefits. At the same time, it exposes some information to the whole world that we might prefer be kept more restricted. Many government databases contain "public records," that is, records that are available to the general public. Examples include bankruptcy records, arrest records, marriage-license applications, divorce proceedings, property-ownership records (including mortgage information), salaries of government employees, and wills. These have long been public, but available on paper in government offices. Lawyers, investigators, real-estate brokers, and others use the records. Some state governments made millions of dollars selling personal information about drivers from motor-vehicle-department records. The murder of an actress by a man who allegedly obtained her address from the motor-vehicle department led to stricter rules about release of driver information. The federal Driver's Privacy Protection Act of 1994 prohibits unauthorized disclosure of state motor-vehicle-department records, but it has numerous exceptions; for example, it allows disclosure to any government agency and to licensed private investigators.

Now that it is so easy to search and browse through files on the Web, more people access public records for fun, for research, for valid personal purposes—and for purposes that can threaten the peace, safety, and personal secrets of others. In a few cases, courts approved restrictions on the form in which information from government files is provided, allowing access to paper records but not electronic ones. This solution is clearly temporary. Most records are now created and stored on computer systems instead of on paper, and scanners coupled with character-recognition systems make it easy to convert older, printed records to digital formats. Attempts to solve problems generated by a new technology by preventing its use are not likely to succeed.

To illustrate some problems and potential solutions, we consider two cases of specialized information: flight information for private airplanes and the financial statements of judges.

The pilots of the roughly 10,000 company airplanes in the U.S. file a flight plan when they fly. A few businesses have combined this flight information, obtained from government databases, with aircraft registration records, also public government records, to provide a service telling where a particular plane is, where it's going, when it will arrive, and so on. Who wants this information? Competitors can use it to determine with whom top executives of another company are meeting. Terrorists could use it to track movements of a high-profile target. The information was available before, but not so easily and anonymously.

The Ethics in Government Act requires federal judges (about 1600 of them) to file financial disclosure reports. The public can review these reports to determine whether a particular judge might have a conflict of interest in a particular case. An online news agency sued the government to make the records available online.[71] Judges object that information in the records can disclose where family members work or go to school, putting them at risk from defendants who are angry at a judge.

How should access to sensitive public information be controlled? Under the old rules, people requesting access to a judge's financial statement had to sign a form disclosing their identity. This is a sensible rule; the information is available to the public, but the record of who accessed it could deter most people intent on doing harm. Can we implement a similar system online? Technologies for digital signatures (discussed in Chapter 3) are gaining increased use for e-commerce, but are not yet widespread enough for use by everyone accessing sensitive public data on the Web. They might be routinely used in the future, but that raises another issue: How will we distinguish data that requires identification and a signature for access from data the public should be free to view anonymously, to protect the viewer's privacy?[72]

2.5 Protecting Privacy: Education, Technology, and Markets

2.5.1 AWARENESS

Most people have figured out by now you can't do anything on the Web without leaving a record.

—Holman W. Jenkins Jr., 2000[73]

The first step in protecting privacy from the risks of computer technology is awareness of how the technology works, how it is being used, what the risks are, and what tools are available to reduce exposure and unwanted uses of personal data. No one would have made the statement in the quotation at the beginning of this section a few years earlier; people did not know. (And Jenkins was somewhat optimistic; in 2000, most people probably still did not.) Since the mid 1990s, however, television programs, newspapers, magazines, pro-privacy Web sites, and many organizations have informed the public about risks to privacy from marketing and government databases and the World Wide Web. Articles and books with titles like "The Death of Privacy," can help prevent the death of privacy. The demand for privacy is being met, to some degree, by individual programmers who post free privacy-protecting software on the Web, entrepreneurs who have built new companies to provide technology-based privacy protections, large businesses that are responding to consumer demand, organized efforts of privacy advocates such as the Electronic Privacy Information Center (EPIC), and threats of regulation by government.

As consumers, once we are aware of the problems and potential solutions, we can decide to what extent we wish to use privacy-protecting tools, be more careful about the information we give out, and consider the privacy policies of businesses and Web sites we use or visit. As business managers, we can learn and implement techniques to respond to the privacy demands of customers. As computer professionals, we can design database systems and Web software that make it easier to build in privacy protection and reduce the risks of unauthorized leaks.

2.5.2 PRIVACY TECHNOLOGIES AND MARKET RESPONSES

The market responds to consumer desire for privacy by producing tools that individuals and organizations can use to protect privacy and by encouraging businesses to adopt policies consumers prefer. We consider several examples in this section.

PRIVACY-ENHANCING TECHNOLOGIES

Often problems that arise as side effects of a new technology can be solved with new applications of the technology. Soon after "techies" became aware of the use of cookies by Web sites, they wrote cookie disablers and posted them on the Web. Netscape's and Microsoft's Web browsers have options to alert the user whenever a Web site is about to store a cookie and allow the user to reject it. Magazine articles and online newsletters tell people how to set this option.

Companies like Anonymizer.com and Zero-Knowledge Systems, Inc., provide services with which people can surf the Web anonymously, leaving no record of the sites they visit. Zero-Knowledge is developing digital cash, so that people can make purchases online that are not linked to their names by a credit card. Similar techniques can be used with smart cards for purchasing physical things in the offline world. (Some early attempts to implement digital cash online failed, in part because they were not convenient to use.) Extensions of these techniques have the potential for providing an unprecedented amount of privacy and solving many of the privacy problems we are discussing.

Companies are developing technologies like the Platform for Privacy Preferences (P3P) that "automatically" protect people's privacy when they use the Web. Such systems include software in Web browsers and on Web sites. An individual user specifies his or her privacy requirements. For example, a user can choose not to accept cookies, or not to visit sites unless they allow users to opt out of mailing lists. Web sites include special code that the browser reads, describing their privacy policies. The browser mediates with Web sites. A participating Web site can adapt its actions to meet the user's preferences (e.g., not send a cookie or not collect certain information). The browser can alert the user if he or she attempts to visit a site whose policies do not meet the user's privacy preferences.

A well-designed database for sensitive information includes several features to protect against leaks, intruders, and unauthorized access by employees. Each person with authorized access to the system should have a unique identifier and a password. Users can be restricted from performing certain operations, such as writing or deleting, on some files. User IDs can be coded so that they give access to only specific parts of a record. For example, a billing clerk in a hospital does not need access to the results of a patient's lab tests. The computer system keeps track of information about each access, including the ID of the person looking at a record and the particular information viewed or modified. This is called an *audit trail*. It can be used later to trace unauthorized activity. The knowledge that a system contains such provisions will discourage many privacy violations. Storing information in encrypted form reduces some abuses by unauthorized employees and intruders from the outside.

It is the responsibility of computer-system designers and managers to be familiar with privacy-enhancing technologies and to design systems so that such methods are easy to implement.

TRUSTED THIRD PARTIES

Mailing lists and databases with consumer-purchase histories or Web-activity records are valuable assets that give businesses a competitive advantage. The owners of such lists and databases, as much as the people in them, have an interest in preventing unlimited distribution. Thus, for example, mailing lists are not actually sold; they are "rented." When a list is rented to another organization or business, the renter does not receive a copy (electronic or otherwise); a specialized firm does the mailing. The risk of unauthorized copying is thus restricted to a small number of firms whose reputation for honesty is important to their business. This idea of using trusted third parties to process confidential data can be used in other applications too. In some states, car-rental agencies access a computer service to check the driving record of potential customers. The service examines the motor-vehicle-department records for the rental company's criteria (say, a specific number of traffic tickets or accidents) and reports a simple yes or no. The car rental company does not see the driver's record.[74]

PAYING FOR CONSUMER INFORMATION

Consumer information is very valuable to marketers. In the 1990s, some privacy advocates argued that consumers should be paid for its use. In many circumstances, we are paid indirectly. For example, when we fill out a contest entry form, we trade data for the opportunity to win prizes. Many stores give discounts to shoppers who use cards that enable tracking of their purchases. A business that sells customer information might be able to charge less for its services than a competitor that does not. Many new businesses offered to trade free computers, free Internet connections, or other services (e.g., personalized product-discount coupons) for permission to send advertising messages to people or to track their Web surfing. These offers are very popular. Free-PC started the trend in 1999 with its offer of 10,000 free PCs in exchange for providing personal information and watching advertising messages. It was swamped with applications from hundreds of thousands of people in the first day. ComScore Networks, Inc., in its first few months of operation, attracted about two million people in the U.S. and other countries with its program to track Internet use. Its incentives included contests and special software that provided faster Web access. By 2000, more than a dozen companies paid people to view ads on the Web. When one such company, AllAdvantage, with millions of members, reduced the number of hours of ad reading it would pay for, many members were disappointed at the reduced earnings opportunity. The success of these businesses shows that many people do not consider the intrusion of online ads to be extremely bothersome, nor their Web surfing to be particularly sensitive. They are willing to trade some privacy for other things. People who value their privacy more highly do not sign up.

Some people view such programs as more options for consumers in general and, particularly, options for low-income people to obtain Internet service or product discounts. Some privacy advocates vehemently oppose these programs. For example, Lauren Weinstein, founder of Privacy Forum, argues that less affluent people, to whom the attraction of free services may be strong, will be "coerced" into giving up their privacy.[75]

ARE BUSINESSES GETTING THE MESSAGE?

In 1998, the Federal Trade Commission examined 674 commercial Web sites and found that 92% of them collected personal information but only 14% informed people of what they did with the information. A year later, Georgetown University examined 364 of the most popular sites, those that get about 99% of Web traffic, and found that two-thirds of the sites post their policy about information use and more than three-quarters of those offer a choice about how a person's data are used.[76]

It has become common for credit card companies, Web sites, Internet service providers, cable companies, health companies, magazines, retail chains, and so on to have explicit policy statements about how they use the information collected from their subscribers and customers. The statements vary in clarity, completeness, and prominence. The policies vary in content and have improved over time. In the early 1990s, America Online's policy stated that "AOL, Inc. may use or disclose information regarding Member for any purpose" (with a few exceptions, and with an opt-out option).[77] By 2000, however, AOL had an 8-page privacy policy stating, among other things, that it did not use or disclose any information about where a member goes in AOL or on the Web and did not give out telephone numbers or information that links screen names with real names.[78]

Web-site operators pay thousands, sometimes millions, of dollars to companies that do *privacy audits*. Privacy auditors check for leaks of information, review the company's privacy policy and its compliance with its policy, evaluate warnings on its Web site to alert visitors when sensitive data are requested and how they will be used, and so forth. Hundreds of large businesses established a new position called *chief privacy officer*; this person guides company privacy policy. DoubleClick, after its colossal blunder in trying to combine its database of consumer activity online with a database of offline personal information, hired a chief privacy officer and hired PricewaterhouseCoopers to do regular privacy audits. Just as the Automobile Association of America rates hotels, the Better Business Bureau and new organizations like TRUSTe offer their seal of approval to be posted on Web sites of companies that comply with their privacy standards.*[79]

Large companies use their economic influence to improve consumer privacy on the Web. IBM and Microsoft decided to remove their Internet advertising from Web sites that do not post clear privacy policies. Walt Disney Company and Infoseek Corporation did the same and, in addition, stopped accepting advertising on their Web sites from sites that don't post privacy policies. The Direct Marketing Association adopted a policy

---

*TRUSTe was criticized for sometimes weak standards, but it was a beginning.

requiring its member companies to inform consumers when personal information will be shared with other marketers and to give people an opt-out option.

More than a dozen credit-information companies, the three major credit bureaus among them, agreed to limit availability of sensitive consumer information, including unlisted telephone numbers, driving histories, medical records, and all information about children. In 2000, a group of major online advertising companies, led by DoubleClick, agreed to give consumers "robust notice and choice" about how marketers use their information collected online. The companies also agreed to ban the use of sensitive information, including medical information and sexual orientation, for marketing. They agreed to give consumers access to the information collected about them and to give consumers an opportunity to opt out before information collected online is combined with offline information.

There continue, of course, to be many businesses without strong privacy policies and many abuses, such as various forms of invisible information collection. The examples described here represent a strong trend, not a privacy utopia.

2.6 Protecting Privacy: Law and Regulation

In Section 2.2, especially in Section 2.2.2, we considered some aspects of law and constitutional principles related to protection of privacy from government. The privacy right protected by the Fourth Amendment is the negative right against intrusion and interference by government. The main application for the discussion in this section is legal remedies for privacy problems related to personal data collected or used by other people, businesses, and organizations.

We separate legal remedies from technical, management, and market solutions because they are fundamentally different. The tools and policies described in Section 2.5 are voluntary and varied. Different people or businesses can choose from among them. Law, on the other hand, is enforced by fines, imprisonment, or other penalties. Thus we should examine uses of law more carefully. Privacy is a condition or state we can be in, like good health or financial security. To what extent should we have a legal right to it? Is it a negative right or a positive right (in the sense of Section 1.2.2)? How far should law go, and what should be left to the voluntary interplay of markets, educational efforts of public interest groups, consumer choices and responsibilities, and so forth?

2.6.1 PHILOSOPHICAL VIEWS

Until the late 19th century, legal decisions supporting privacy in social and business activities were based on property rights and contracts. An independent right to privacy was not recognized. In 1890, a crucial article called "The Right of Privacy," by Samuel Warren and Louis Brandeis[80] (later a Supreme Court Justice), argued that privacy was distinct from other rights and needed more protection. Judith Jarvis Thomson, an MIT philosopher, argued in a 1975 essay that the old view was more accurate, that in all cases where a violation of privacy is a violation of someone's rights, another right has been violated.[81] We present some of the claims and arguments of these papers.

One purpose of this section is to show the kinds of analyses that are done by philosophers, legal scholars, and economists in trying to elucidate underlying principles. Another is to emphasize the importance of principles, of working out a theoretical framework in which to make decisions about particular issues and cases.

WARREN AND BRANDEIS: THE INVIOLATE PERSONALITY

The main target of criticism in the Warren and Brandeis article is newspapers, especially the gossip columns. They vehemently criticize the press for "overstepping . . . obvious bounds of propriety and decency." The kinds of information of most concern to them are personal appearance, statements, acts, and interpersonal relationships (marital, family, and others).[82] Warren and Brandeis take the position that people have the right to prohibit publication of facts about themselves and photographs of themselves. Warren and Brandeis argue that, for example, if someone writes a letter in which he says he had a fierce argument with his wife, that fact is protected and the recipient of the letter cannot publish it. This claim is not based on any property right or other rights besides privacy; rather, it is part of the right to be left alone. Warren and Brandeis base their defense of privacy rights on, in their often-quoted phrase, the principle of "an inviolate personality."

Privacy violations can be addressed by laws against other wrongs, such as slander, libel, defamation, copyright infringement, violation of property rights, and breach of contract, but Warren and Brandeis argue that there remain many privacy violations that those other laws do not cover. For example, publication of personal or business information could constitute a violation of a contract (explicit or implied), but not if someone has no contract or relationship of trust with the victim. Libel, slander, and defamation laws protect us when someone spreads false or damaging rumors about us, but they do not apply to true personal information whose exposure makes us uncomfortable. According to Warren and Brandeis, privacy is distinct and needs its own protection. They allow exceptions for publication of information of general interest (news), use in limited situations when the information concerns another person's interests, and oral publication. (They were writing before radio and television, so oral publication meant a quite limited audience.)

JUDITH JARVIS THOMSON: IS THERE A RIGHT TO PRIVACY?

Judith Jarvis Thomson argues the opposite point of view. She gets to her point after examining a few scenarios.

Suppose you own a copy of a magazine. Your property rights include the right to refuse to allow others to read, destroy, or even see your magazine. If someone does anything to your magazine that you did not allow, that person is violating your property rights. For example, if someone uses binoculars to see your magazine from a neighboring building, that person is violating your right to exclude others from seeing it. It does not matter whether the magazine is an ordinary news magazine (not a privacy issue), or a pornographic magazine, or any other magazine you do not want others to know you read (a privacy issue). The right violated is your property right.

You may waive your property rights, intentionally or inadvertently. If you absent-mindedly leave the magazine on a park bench, someone could take it. If you leave it on the coffee table when you have guests at your home, someone could see it. If you read the magazine on a bus, and someone sees you and tells other people that you read dirty magazines, your rights are not violated. The person might be doing something impolite, unfriendly, or cruel, but not something that violates a right.

Our rights to our person and our bodies include the right to decide to whom to show various parts of our bodies. By walking around in public, most of us waive our rights to prevent others from seeing our faces. (Some Muslim women cover their faces, exercising their right to keep others from viewing them.) If someone uses binoculars to spy on us at home in the shower, they are violating our rights to our person. Similarly, according to Thomson, our right to our person includes the right to decide who may listen to us. Someone who eavesdrops on our intimate conversations at home violates our right to our person. If we speak in public, we waive the right, and people may listen.

If someone beats on you to get some information, the beater is violating your right to be free from physical harm done by others. If the information is the time of day, privacy is not at issue. If the information is more personal, then your privacy is compromised, but the right violated is your right to be free from attack. On the other hand, if a person peacefully asks whom you live with or what your political views are, then no rights are violated. If you choose to answer and do not make a confidentiality agreement, the person is not violating your rights by repeating the information to someone else, though it could be inconsiderate to do so. However, if the person agreed not to repeat the information, but then does, it does not matter whether or not the information was sensitive; the confidentiality agreement has been violated.

In these examples, whether or not privacy is compromised depends on the kind of information. In each case, there is no violation of privacy without violation of some other right, such as the right to control our property or our person, the right to be free from violent attack, or the right to form contracts (and expect them to be enforced). Thomson concludes, "I suggest it is a useful heuristic device in the case of any purported violation of the right to privacy to ask whether or not the act is a violation of any other right, and if not whether the act really violates a right at all."[83]

CRITICISMS OF WARREN AND BRANDEIS AND OF THOMSON

Critics of the Warren and Brandeis position argue that their arguments do not provide a workable principle or definition from which to conclude that a privacy-right violation occurs. Their notion of privacy is too broad; it conflicts with freedom of the press; it appears to make any unauthorized mention of a person a violation of the person's right. Some critics present theories and examples, in addition to Thomson's, to show that existing legal wrongs encompass privacy violations; for example, trespass and appropriation of a person's likeness.[84]

Critics of Thomson present examples in which a right to privacy (not just a desire for privacy), but no other right, is violated. Thomson's notion of the right to our person can be seen as vague or too broad. Her examples might (or might not) be a convincing argument for the thesis that considering other rights can resolve privacy rights questions, but no finite number of examples can prove such a thesis.

Neither article directly refutes the other. Their emphases are different. Warren and Brandeis focus on how information is used (publication); Thomson focuses on how it is obtained. This distinction sometimes underlies differences in arguments by those who advocate strong legal regulations on use of personal data and those who advocate more reliance on technical and market solutions.

APPLYING THE THEORIES

How do the theoretical arguments apply to the privacy issues related to the vast amount of personal data in computerized databases and the practice of tracking our activities on the Web?

Throughout Warren and Brandeis, the objectionable action is publication of personal information—its widespread, public distribution. Many court decisions since the appearance of their article have taken this point of view.[85] If information in consumer databases were published (in print or electronically, say on the Web), that would violate the Warren and Brandeis notion of privacy. A plaintiff might well win a case if his or her consumer profile were published or if he or she were on a published list of people who bought condoms or did not pay their debts. But publication is not the main concern in the current context of consumer databases and Web tracking. Warren and Brandeis and various court decisions allow disclosure of personal information to people who have an interest in it. By implication, they do not preclude, for example, disclosure of a person's driving record to a car rental company from which he or she wants to rent a car or disclosure of information about whether someone smokes cigarettes to a life insurance company from whom the person is trying to buy insurance. They do not preclude use of consumer information to generate targeted mailing lists if the lists are not published. (If disclosure of the information violates a trust or confidence or contract, then it is not permissible.)

An important aspect of both the Warren and Brandeis paper and the Thomson paper is that of consent. There is no privacy violation if information is obtained or published with the person's consent.

TRANSACTIONS

No matter which of the views presented so far in this section you find convincing or weak, we have another puzzle to consider: how to apply philosophical and legal notions of privacy to transactions, which automatically involve more than one person. The following scenario will illustrate the problem.

One day in the small farm community of Friendlyville, Joe buys five pounds of potatoes from Maria, and Maria sells five pounds of potatoes to Joe. (I describe the transaction in this repetitious manner to emphasize that there are two people involved and two sides to the transaction.)

Either Maria or Joe might prefer the transaction to remain secret. Joe might be embarrassed that his own potato crop failed. Or Joe might be unpopular in Friendlyville, and Maria fears the townspeople will be angry at her for selling to him. Either way, we are not likely to consider it a violation of the other's rights if Maria or Joe talks about the purchase or sale of the potatoes to other people in town. But suppose Joe asks for confidentiality as part of the transaction. Maria has three options. (1) She can say OK. (2) She can say no; she might want to tell people she sold potatoes to Joe. (3) She can agree to keep the sale confidential if Joe pays a higher price. In the latter two cases, Joe can decide whether to buy the potatoes. On the other hand, if Maria asks for confidentiality as part of the transaction, Joe has three options. (1) He can say OK. (2) He can say no; he might want to tell people he bought potatoes from Maria. (3) He can agree to keep the purchase confidential if Maria charges a lower price. In the latter two cases, Maria can decide whether to sell the potatoes.

Privacy includes control of information about oneself, but the point here is that there is no clear reason for either party to the transaction to have more right than the other to control information about the transaction. If a confidentiality agreement is made, then the parties are obliged to respect it.

If control of the information about the transaction is to be assigned to one of the parties, we need a firm philosophical foundation for choosing which party gets it. Warren and Brandeis are not of much help. They say we should have control of publication of facts about ourselves. Even if we consider discussion of the transaction in the town square to be publication, we still have the question: Is the transaction a fact about Maria or a fact about Joe? There does not appear to be a convincing reason to favor one over the other, yet this problem is critical to legal policy decisions about consumer information in computer databases.

Philosophers and economists often use simple two-person transactions or relationships, like the Maria/Joe scenario, to try to clarify the principles involved in an issue. Do the observations and conclusions about Maria and Joe generalize to large, complex societies and a global economy, where one party to a transaction is often a business? All transactions are really between people, even if indirectly. So if a property right or a privacy right in the information about a transaction is to be assigned to one of the parties, we need an argument showing how the transaction in a modern economy is different from the one in Friendlyville. In the next section, we will discuss two viewpoints on the regulation of information about consumer transactions: the free-market view and the consumer-protection view. The free-market view treats both parties equally, whereas the consumer-protection view includes arguments for treating the parties differently.

1. *Truth in information gathering.* Organizations collecting personal data (including government agencies and businesses) should clearly inform the person providing the information if it will not be kept confidential (from other businesses, individuals, and government agencies) and how it will be used. They should be liable for violations.

2. *Freedom in information contracting.* People should be free to enter agreements (or not enter agreements) to disclose personal information in exchange for a fee or for services according to their own judgment.

3. *Freedom of speech and commerce.* People (as well as businesses and organizations) should not be prevented by law from disclosing facts independently and unintrusively discovered (e.g., without theft, trespass, or violation of contractual obligations).

Figure 2.3 Freedom of Information Use Guidelines

2.6.2 CONTRASTING VIEWPOINTS

When asked "If someone sues you and loses, should they have to pay your legal expenses?" more than 80% of people surveyed said "yes." When asked the same question from the opposite perspective: "If you sue someone and lose, should you have to pay their legal expenses?" about 40% said "yes."

The political, philosophical, and economic views of many scholars and advocates who write about privacy differ. As a result, their interpretations of various privacy problems and their approaches to solutions often differ, particularly when they are considering regulation of personal information collected and used by businesses.* We will contrast two perspectives; I call them the free-market view and the consumer-protection view.

THE FREE-MARKET VIEW

People who prefer market and contractual solutions for privacy problems tend to emphasize the diversity of individual tastes and values, the flexibility of technological and market solutions, the response of markets to consumer preferences, and the flaws of detailed or restrictive legislation and regulatory solutions.

Figure 2.3 shows a set of guidelines that express a free-market viewpoint for use of personal information.[86] It incorporates informed consent, freedom of contract, and free flow of information acquired without violating rights or agreements. The market viewpoint respects the right and ability of consumers to make choices for themselves that are based on their own values. Market supporters expect consumers to take the responsibility that goes with freedom, for example, to read contracts or to understand that desirable services have costs.

---

*There tends to be more agreement when considering privacy threats and intrusions by government.

Market supporters prefer to avoid restrictive legislation and detailed regulation for several reasons. They argue that the political system is a worse system than the free market for determining what consumers want in the real world of trade-offs and costs. It is impossible for legislators to know in advance how much money, convenience, or other benefits people will want to trade for more or less privacy. Businesses respond over time to the preferences of millions of consumers expressed through their purchases. Different companies can offer different levels of privacy, satisfying different consumers. In response to the desire for privacy expressed by many people, the market provides a variety of privacy-protection tools.

Market supporters argue that laws requiring specific policies or prohibiting certain kinds of contracts violate the freedom of choice of both consumers and businesses. Private firms are owned by individuals or groups of individuals who have invested their own resources in the business. They should be free to offer the selection of products, services, and terms that they choose. Consumers should have the freedom to sell personal data if they choose.

We cannot always expect to get exactly the mix of attributes we want in any product, service, or job; it could be that no seller or employer chooses to offer that combination. Just as we might not get cheeseless pizza in every pizza restaurant or find a car with the exact set of features we want, we might not be able to get both privacy and special discounts. We might not be able to get certain Web sites—or magazines—without advertising, or a specific job without agreeing to provide certain personal information to the employer. These compromises are not unusual or unreasonable when interacting with other people.

There is an extraordinary range in the amount of privacy different people want. Some tell details of their personal lives on television shows. Some set up personal Web pages describing their lives and families to the world. Some gladly sign up for free services in exchange for allowing their activity to be tracked. Others use cash to avoid leaving a record of their purchases, encrypt all their e-mail and use anonymizers when surfing the Web, never give personal information on warranty cards, and are appalled and angry when information is collected about them. The free-market viewpoint sees privacy as a "good," both in the sense that it is desirable and that it is something we can obtain varying amounts of by buying or trading in the economy, like food, entertainment, and safety. Just as some people choose to trade some safety for excitement (bungee jumping, motorcycle riding), money (buying a cheaper, but less safe product), or convenience, some choose different levels of privacy. As with safety, law can provide minimum standards, but should allow the market to provide a wide range of options to meet the range of personal preferences.

THE CONSUMER-PROTECTION VIEW

Advocates of strong privacy regulation emphasize all the unsettling business uses of personal information we have mentioned throughout this chapter. They argue for more stringent consent requirements, strong limitations on secondary uses, legal restrictions on consumer profiling, and prohibitions on certain types of contracts or agreements to disclose data. They urge, for example, that companies be required by law to have opt-in policies because the opt-out option may not be obvious or easy enough for consumers who would prefer it. As we mentioned earlier, many privacy advocates are very critical of contracts to trade free computers and Web services for either personal information, or consent to the monitoring of Web activity.

The focus of this viewpoint is to protect consumers against abuses by businesses and against their own lack of knowledge, judgment, or interest. Advocates of the consumer-protection viewpoint argue that people do not understand the risks of agreeing to disclose personal data and that business privacy policies are vague, in small print, or hard to find. (Thus, many privacy advocates support bans on generalized consent forms or waivers.) Consumer advocate and privacy "absolutist" Mary Gardiner Jones does not accept the idea of consumers consenting to dissemination of personal data. She said, "You can't expect an ordinary consumer who is very busy trying to earn a living to sit down and understand what [consent] means. They don't understand the implications of what use of their data can mean to them." She said the idea that some consumers like having their names on mailing lists is a myth created by the industry.[87] The view that informed consent is not sufficient protection was expressed by a former director of the ACLU's Privacy and Technology Project who urged a Senate committee studying confidentiality of health records to "re-examine the traditional reliance on individual consent as the linchpin of privacy laws."[88]

Consumer and privacy protection groups argue for banning various kinds of contracts and transactions. For example, they supported the laws that stopped merchants from asking for a telephone number when a customer uses a credit card. Some advocate bans on all sales of personal medical data even if the person consents.

These advocates would argue that the Joe/Maria scenario in Friendlyville, described in Section 2.6.1, is not relevant in a complex society. The imbalance of power between the individual and a large corporation is one reason. Another is that, in Friendlyville, the information about the transaction circulates to only a small group of people, whom Joe and Maria know. If someone draws inaccurate or unfair conclusions, Joe or Maria can talk to the person and present his or her explanations. In a larger society, information circulates among many strangers, and we often do not know who has it and what decisions about us are being based on it.

A consumer cannot realistically negotiate contract terms with a business; at any specific time, the consumer can only accept or reject what the business offers. And the consumer is often not in a position to reject it. If we want a loan for a house or car, we have to accept whatever terms lenders currently offer. If we need a job, we are likely to agree to disclose personal information against our true preference because of the economic necessity of working.

The business-policy improvements that have occurred resulted from government action or the threat of it, not from business response to consumer preferences. Self-regulation by business does not work. Businesses sometimes don't follow their stated policies. Consumer pressure is sometimes effective, but some companies ignore it. Instead, all businesses must be required to adopt pro-privacy policies. Privacy-enhancing technologies are far from perfect, hence not good enough to protect privacy.

The consumer-protection viewpoint sees privacy as a right rather than something to be bargained about. For example, a Web site jointly sponsored by the Electronic Privacy Information Center and Privacy International flashes the slogans "Privacy is a right, not a preference" and "Notice is not enough."[89] The latter indicates that they see privacy as a positive right, or claim-right (in the terminology of Section 1.2.2). As a negative right, privacy allows us to use anonymizing technologies and to refrain from interacting with those who request information we do not wish to supply. As a positive right, it means we can stop others from communicating about us. A spokesperson for the Committee for Democracy and Technology expressed that view in a statement to Congress, saying that we must incorporate into law the principle that people should be able to "determine for themselves when, how and to what extent information about them is shared."[90]

2.6.3 CONTRACTS AND REGULATIONS

A BASIC LEGAL FRAMEWORK

A good basic legal framework that defines and enforces legal rights and responsibilities is essential to a complex, robust society and economy. One of its tasks is enforcement of agreements and contracts. Contracts—including freedom to form them and enforcement of their terms by the legal system—are a mechanism for implementing flexible and diverse economic transactions that take place over time and between people who do not know each other well or at all.

We can apply the idea of contract enforcement to the published privacy policies of businesses, organizations, and Web sites. The Toysmart case is an example. Toysmart, a Web-based seller of educational toys, collected extensive information on about 250,000 visitors to its Web site, including family profiles, shopping preferences, and names and ages of children. Toysmart had promised not to release this personal information. When the company filed for bankruptcy in 2000, it had a large amount of debt and virtually no assets—except its customer database, which was valued highly. Toysmart's creditors wanted the database sold to raise funds to repay them. Toysmart offered the database for sale, causing a storm of protest. Consistent with the interpretation that Toysmart's policy was a contract with the people in the database, the bankruptcy-court settlement reached in 2001 included destruction of the customer database.

A second task of a legal system is to set defaults for situations that are not explicitly covered in contracts. Suppose a Web site posts no policy about what it does with the information it collects. What should the site be legally permitted to do with the information? Many sites and offline businesses act as though the default is that they can do anything they choose. A privacy-protecting default would be that the information could be used only for the direct and obvious purpose for which it was supplied. The legal system can (and should) set special confidentiality defaults for sensitive information, such as medical and financial information, that tradition and most people consider private. If a business or organization wants to use information for purposes beyond the default, it would have to specify those uses in its policies, agreements, or contracts or request consent for its uses. Many business interactions do not have written contracts, so the default provisions established by law are very influential (hence controversial).

REQUIRING SPECIFIC CONSENT POLICIES

When we go beyond the basic framework, there is more controversy. We consider consent policies as an example of privacy-protecting regulation. The principle of informed consent can be incorporated into law in a variety of ways differing in their levels of control. Here are four levels:

1. Businesses and organizations must clearly state their policy for use of personal information. If a person proceeds and makes a purchase, explores the Web site, provides information, and so on, consent to the policy is assumed.
2. Businesses and organizations must provide an opt-out option.
3. Businesses and organizations must use an opt-in policy.
4. Businesses and organizations must obtain consumer consent for each individual secondary use, disclosure, or transfer of their personal information.

What level should the law enforce? The first is the least intrusive, but provides the least privacy protection. The strictest level of regulation above provides the most privacy protection. Privacy advocates who think blanket consent agreements are too broad recommend this regulation; consumers do not realize all the ways others may use the information. This option has an attribute economists call "high transaction cost." It could be so expensive and difficult to implement that it would eliminate most secondary uses of information, including those many consumers find desirable. Market supporters oppose it for this reason and because it violates freedom to offer and form contracts with broader consent provisions.

REGULATION

Technical tools for privacy protection (like those described in Section 2.5.2), market mechanisms, and self-regulation by businesses are not perfect. Some privacy advocates consider this a strong argument for regulatory laws. Regulation is not perfect either. We must evaluate regulatory solutions by considering effectiveness, costs and benefits, side effects, and ease of use (clarity), just as we do throughout this book for computer technology itself and for other kinds of potential solutions to problems caused by technology. Whole books can be written on the pros and cons of regulation. We briefly point out some of its weaknesses in the next four paragraphs.

The actual laws that get passed often depend more on the current focus of media attention and special-interest pressure than on well thought-out principles and true cost/benefit trade-offs.[91]

It is extremely difficult to write reasonable regulations for complex situations. General statements of principle are not precise enough in a context where people may be fined or jailed. When laws are not written carefully, they often have unintended effects or interpretations.[92] They could apply where they do not make sense or where people simply do not want them.

Regulations often have high costs, both direct dollar costs to businesses (and, ultimately consumers) and hidden or unexpected costs, such as loss of services or increased inconvenience. Consider the response to the Children's Online Privacy Protection Act (COPPA) which required that Web sites get parental permission before collecting personal information from children under 13 (Section 2.3.2). Some sites deleted online profiles of all children under 13, some canceled their free e-mail and home pages for kids, and some banned children under 13 entirely. (The *New York Times* does not allow children under 13 to register to use its Web site.) An attorney who helps sites meet COPPA's requirements estimated the cost of compliance at $60,000–100,000 per year, a lot for a small business, not a burden for large ones like AOL and Disney.[93] (Regulations often provide a relative benefit to large businesses and organizations over smaller ones because they have the legal department to deal with the rules and the revenue to absorb the added costs.) Even laws like COPPA, one of the less controversial privacy regulatory laws, must be examined carefully to determine whether they are effective and whether the increased cost or loss of some services is a reasonable price for the increased protection.

Laws that include very specific regulations prevent other options from being tried.

OWNERSHIP OF PERSONAL DATA

Some economists, legal scholars, and privacy advocates propose giving people property rights in information about themselves. The concept of property rights can be very useful even when applied to intangible property (intellectual property, for example), but there are problems in using this concept for personal information. First, as we have seen, activities and transactions often involve at least two people, each of whom would have reasonable but conflicting claims to own the information about the transaction. Some personal information does not appear to be about a transaction, but there still may be problems in assigning ownership. For example, your birthday is recorded in some databases. Do you own your birthday? Or does your mother own it? After all, she was a more active participant in the event!

The second problem with assigning ownership of personal information arises from the notion of owning facts. (Copyright, the main topic of Chapter 6, protects intangible property such as computer programs and music, but facts cannot be copyrighted.) Ownership of facts would severely impair the flow of information in society. Information is stored on computers, but it is also stored in our minds. Can we own facts about ourselves without violating the freedom of thought and freedom of speech of others?

Some of the information of most concern to privacy advocates is information that can lead to denial of a job or some kind of service or contract (e.g., a loan). Federal

Judge Richard Posner offered a different perspective when he considered how to allocate property rights to information. He argued that a person should not have a property right to "discreditable" personal information (e.g., one's criminal history or credit history) or other information whose concealment aids people in misrepresentation, fraud, or manipulation.[94]

Although it may be unreasonable to assign ownership in individual facts, another issue is whether we can own our "profiles," that is, a collection of data describing our activities, purchases, interests, and so on. We cannot own the fact that our eyes are blue, but we do have the legal right to control some uses of our photographic image. In almost all states, a person's photograph cannot be used for commercial purposes without the person's consent. Should our consumer profiles be treated the same way? How can we distinguish between a few facts about a person and a "profile"?

CONFLICTS WITH FREEDOM OF SPEECH

Law professors Eugene Volokh and Tom W. Bell argue that laws that prohibit communicating information about people's transactions violate freedom of speech. (Contractual agreements not to transfer data do not violate free speech.) Courts have made some exceptions to the First Amendment, for example, for libel and for some advertising, but not for transfer of commercially valuable information. Volokh argues that it would be unwise to create such an exception for facts about people's transactions and activities. Advocates of strict laws regulating transfer of such information argue that it does not have the social value and significance of political speech and hence should not have First Amendment protection. Volokh points out that a similar argument is used by supporters of laws to censor speech with sexual content. It is risky to chip away at the First Amendment by designating more categories of speech not worthy of protection.[95]

Some groups advocate restrictions on sharing of information that might facilitate negative decisions about people, for example, landlords sharing a database with information about tenant payment histories. Should landlords have as much right to communicate to each other about bad tenants as tenants have to communicate about bad landlords?

One of the main arguments that led the Supreme Court to rule Internet censorship laws unconstitutional was that people could use filtering software to avoid pornography and other undesirable material. (We discuss these laws and arguments in Chapter 5.) Bell points out that the same reasoning applies to laws that would restrict freedom of speech by businesses about Internet users.[96] Web surfers can use a variety of tools such as cookie disablers and anonymizers. Many of the same organizations that successfully fought censorship laws, partly on the grounds that self-help technologies were available, support laws that restrict business speech, partly on the grounds that privacy enhancing technologies are not perfect. Bell sees these positions as inconsistent; he says both kinds of laws restrict speech that some people argue can be harmful, but that both kinds of laws are unnecessary and have similar constitutional problems.

PRIVACY REGULATIONS IN THE EUROPEAN UNION

The European Union (EU) passed a comprehensive privacy directive covering processing of personal data.[97] It defines "processing" to include collection, use, storage, retrieval, transmission, destruction, and other actions. The 30-page directive sets forth general principles that the 15 EU member nations were required to implement in their own laws. The principles, similar to the privacy principles in Figure 2.2, include the following:

1. Personal data may be collected only for specified, explicit purposes and must not be processed for incompatible purposes.

2. Data must be accurate and up to date. Data must not be kept longer than necessary.

3. Processing of data is permitted only if the person consented unambiguously, or if the processing is necessary to fulfill contractual or legal obligations, or if the processing is needed for tasks in the public interest or by official authorities to accomplish their tasks (or a few other reasons).

4. Special categories of data, including ethnic and racial origin, political and religious beliefs, health and sex life, and union membership, must not be processed without the subject's explicit consent. Member nations may outlaw processing of such data even if the subject does consent.

5. People must be notified of the collection and use of data about them. They must have access to the data stored about them and a way to correct incorrect data.

6. Processing of data about criminal convictions is severely restricted.

While the European Union has much stricter regulations than the U.S. on collection and use of personal information by the private sector, some civil libertarians believe that the European Directive does not provide enough protection from use of personal data by government agencies.

The EU Data Privacy Directive prohibits transfer of personal data to countries outside the European Union that do not have an adequate system of privacy protection. This part of the Directive caused significant problems for companies that do business both in and outside of Europe and might normally process customer and employee data outside the EU. In 2001, the EU determined that Australia, for example, did not have adequate privacy protection. Australia allows businesses to create their own privacy codes consistent with the government's National Privacy Principles. The Australian government argued that it had adequate protection. The U.S. has privacy laws covering specific areas such as medical information, video rentals, driver license records, and so on, but does not have comprehensive privacy laws covering all personal data. Business and government officials worked to develop standards other than national laws that could be accepted as meeting the requirement for adequate privacy protection. Possibilities include business privacy policies (enforceable by law in some cases) and certifications by independent organizations such as TRUSTe and the Better Business Bureau's BBLOnLine Privacy Seal Program. In

2000, the EU agreed to the "Safe Harbor" plan, under which companies outside the EU that agree to abide by a set of privacy requirements similar to the principles in the Data Protection Directive may receive personal data from the EU.[98]

Many privacy advocates describe U.S. privacy policy as "behind Europe" because the U.S. does not have comprehensive federal legislation regulating personal data collection and use. Others point out that the U.S. and Europe have different cultures and traditions. European countries tend to put more emphasis on regulation and centralization, especially concerning commerce,* whereas the U.S. tradition puts more emphasis on contracts, consumer pressure, and the flexibility and freedom of the market.

When the EU Directive was passed, in 1995, member nations were required to implement its principles in their own laws within three years. In 2000, the European Commission determined that many countries had not yet complied. In 2001, a study done by Consumers International found that 80% of European Web sites did not comply with the Privacy Directive requirement that Web sites provide an opt-out option, while almost 60% of the most popular sites in the U.S. offered an opt-out option. The study also found that about a third of EU sites that collected data on users posted their privacy policies, and 62% of U.S. sites did. The study, while critical of privacy policies on both U.S. and EU sites, concluded that "despite tight EU legislation . . . U.S.-based sites tend to set the standard for decent privacy policies."[100] Consumer and privacy advocates argued that in the EU, even though enforcement was weak, people have legal recourse, whereas in the U.S. they often do not.

EXERCISES

Review Exercises

2.1   What does the term *personal information* mean?

2.2   What does the term *invisible information gathering* mean? Give an example.

2.3   What does the term *secondary use* mean? Give an example.

2.4   Give an example of computer technology being used to collect personal information that existed before computer technology, but wasn't collected at all before.

2.5   Give one example in which release of someone's personal information threatened the person's safety.

2.6   Describe two tools people can use to protect their privacy on the Web.

2.7   Explain the difference between *opt in* and *opt out* policies for distribution of a customer's name and address (and other personal information) to other businesses.

---

*For example, German laws prohibit or severely restrict discounts, rebates, and sales; store hours are limited by law; and businesses could not advertise unconditional-return policies or that they give a contribution to charity for each sale. Some of these laws, in force for 90 years, are now being repealed because of globalization and competition from the Internet. They were defended on the grounds that discounts and guarantees confuse or trick consumers.[99]

General Exercises

2.8　List two government databases that probably have information about you. For each one, tell what service or benefit, if any, you got in exchange for providing information about yourself.

2.9　List two private databases that probably have information about you. For each one, tell what service or benefit, if any, you got in exchange for providing information about yourself.

2.10　A company that supplies filtering software to schools (to block access by children to Web sites with violence or pornography) sold statistical data about the sites visited by school children. The data did not identify the children or individual schools. Was this a privacy violation? Why or why not?

2.11　Many telephone directories on the Web do not provide a reverse directory feature. That is, they do not allow a user to type in a telephone number and find out to whom it belongs.
　　a) Give some arguments for and against this policy. Do you think it is a good policy?
　　b) Printed reverse directories existed in book form before the Internet. How might making them available on the Web change their use and impact?

2.12　A confidential file containing the names of about 4000 AIDS patients was sent from a county health department to a newspaper, presumably by a disgruntled employee.
　　a) Would this have been more or less likely to have happened if the names were in paper files, not electronic files? Why?
　　b) What are some ways this leakage of sensitive data could have been prevented?

2.13　A city government wants to track down people who run small businesses and do not pay the city's $125 business-license fee. The city hired a private detective to obtain IRS tax records of city residents and determine who has reported small-business income to the IRS but not paid for a license.[101]
　　a) What arguments might the city government give in support of this action? What arguments might privacy advocates give against it?
　　b) Do you think this application of computer matching should be permitted or prohibited? Give your reasons.

2.14　Suppose a small political party strongly opposes an existing law, for example, the income tax or the law against smoking marijuana. Consider the possibility of allowing government agencies like the IRS and the FBI to use the voter-registration database (which includes a person's party affiliation in some states) to initiate investigations of party members to see whether they comply with the existing laws. Give arguments in favor of this; give arguments in opposition. Which side do you think is stronger? Why?

2.15　The National Insurance Crime Bureau maintained a big database of suspicious insurance claims to be checked for fraud. Federal, state, and local law enforcement agencies had direct, almost unlimited access to the database. When the NICB announced plans in 1997 to expand the database to include *all* insurance claims, privacy advocates objected. What are some advantages of the expanded database? What are some privacy concerns?

2.16　The Federal Aviation Administration has proposed that airlines be required to collect the Social Security number of each passenger. Discuss some possible reasons for this and some possible risks. Evaluate them. Is the proposal a good idea?

2.17　Give an example of a database whose access by law-enforcement agents without a court order seems inconsistent with the spirit of the Fourth Amendment to the U.S. Constitution. (Use an example not discussed in Section 2.2.2.)

2.18　Describe some uses of satellite surveillance that you think are acceptable extensions of traditional law enforcement activities and capabilities. Describe some uses where the technology makes a fundamental change that is not acceptable. Explain your reasoning.

2.19 Police used to search manually through mug shots (photos of people who have been arrested) to find one that matched a witness' description of a person who committed a crime. Modern computer techniques allow police to search large databases of digitized photos. What are some benefits and some risks of expanding the search to include all driver's-license photos?

2.20 A member of the Tampa, Florida, City Council described the camera and face-recognition system installed in a Tampa neighborhood (Section 2.2.3) as "a public safety tool, no different from having a cop walking around with a mug shot."[102] Is he right? What are some similarities and differences, relevant to privacy, between the camera system and a cop walking around?

2.21 An individual set up a 24-hour-a-day webcam, on an island on the Atlantic coast, aimed at a ferry dock used by local people and tourists. People could visit his Web site to check on weather conditions, to determine if ferry service were likely to be canceled. But some people complained that the webcam violated their privacy. Suppose you are asked to help settle the dispute. What solution would you suggest? What arguments would you give?[103]

2.22 Computer chips are implanted into pets and farm animals so they can be identified if they get lost. Some people suggest using the same technology for children. Discuss the privacy implications of such proposals. What are the risks? Do the benefits outweigh the risks? If there were a bill in Congress to require ID chips in children, would you support it? Why?

2.23 Consumers Union, publisher of *Consumer Reports*, uses a huge mailing-list broker to find potential customers, but *Consumer Reports* does not give information on its subscribers to the list broker.[104] First take the position that their behavior is inconsistent and hypocritical. Give arguments for this position. Then take the position that the policy is reasonable. Give arguments for this position. Which side you think is more persuasive? Which principles or points are most important?

2.24 When formulating a policy on whether certain government records should be open to the public, we must anticipate a broad range of uses. Consider motor-vehicle records. Formulate a policy about access to the database by the news media. (News media could include both a newspaper trying to get home addresses from vehicle license-plate numbers for cars parked at an abortion clinic and a newspaper trying to get home addresses from vehicle license-plate numbers for cars parked at a Ku Klux Klan rally).

2.25 Give arguments in favor of and opposed to a law to require that credit bureaus send a copy of each person's credit report to the person once a year (without charge).

2.26 A business maintains a database containing the names of shoplifters. It distributes the list to stores that subscribe.
   a) Should such a service be illegal as a violation of privacy? (Give reasons.)
   b) Describe the likely position of each of Warren and Brandeis, Judith Thomson (Section 2.6.1), Richard Posner (Section 2.6.3), and Eugene Volokh (Section 2.6.3), with their reasons, on this question.
   c) Would your answer to part (a) differ if the question were about a database of tenant history available to landlords? How and why?

2.27 "Caller ID" is the feature that displays the telephone number of the caller on the telephone of the recipient of a telephone call.
   a) What aspect of privacy (in the sense of Section 2.1.1) does Caller ID protect for the recipient of the call? What aspect of privacy does Caller ID violate for the caller?
   b) What are some good reasons why a nonbusiness, noncriminal caller might not want his or her number displayed?

c) What are some positive and negative business uses of caller ID?

d) In your state, what options are available for using or blocking Caller ID? Do you consider them reasonable?

2.28 Suppose students who live in a dormitory on a college campus are given cards with a magnetic strip that opens the front door of the dorm. Students are not told that each card contains the individual student identifier and that a record of each use of the card is kept. What are possible good purposes of such record keeping? What are some problems with it? Is it right? Is it okay if students are told? Give arguments and examples to support your answers.

2.29 A company called, say, Digitizer provides a service for many other companies by converting their paper documents to digital files on CDs. The documents include employee information, medical records, business records, and many others. Digitizer hires relatively unskilled employees to organize the documents and get them ready to scan.

a) What are some potential risks here? Describe at least two actual examples with some similarity to this situation.

b) Describe some actions Digitizer can take or policies it can adopt to reduce the risks.

2.30 Suppose you want to borrow $200,000 to buy a house. List all the kinds of information you think a mortgage lender might ask for and a likely reason for each. Which, if any, of the items do you think is not needed? Why?

2.31 One writer defines privacy as "freedom from the inappropriate judgement of others."[105]

a) Is this a good definition of privacy? Why or why not?

b) Suppose we use this definition. Should people have a positive right (claim-right) for this kind of privacy? Why or why not? Should people have a negative right (liberty) for this kind of privacy? Why or why not? (See Section 1.2.2 for explanations of negative and positive rights.)

2.32 a) Consider a company that specializes in information services or manages databases with personal information (e.g., a popular Web site, a large retailing chain, a credit-card company). The vice president for privacy policy in the company recommends that the staff prepare a privacy-impact study for any new information service or database the company develops and that the study be used in deciding whether to proceed with the new service and how to design it. Give factors or arguments the president of the company should consider for and against this policy. Should the policy be adopted? Why?

b) A privacy-advocacy group recommends that privacy impact studies be required by law, as are environmental-impact studies, to assess the implications of new information systems on consumer privacy. The study would have to be prepared by a licensed privacy analyst and submitted to a government agency for approval before a company could use or market the new system. Give arguments for and against such a law. Should the law be passed? Why?

2.33 Give an explanation, with examples and/or analogies, to describe what it would mean for privacy to be a negative right (liberty). Do the same for considering privacy a positive right (claim-right). (See Section 1.2.2 for explanations of negative and positive rights.) Which kind of right, if either, seems more appropriate for privacy? Why?

2.34 Many privacy activists propose that the United States establish an office or position at the federal government level to oversee and regulate privacy issues. (Several European countries have such an office.) Give arguments for and against this proposal.

Assignments

These exercises require some research or activity.

2.35 Find out what policy your university has about releasing the names, addresses, and telephone numbers of students either individually or as a list. Is there an online student directory?

2.36 Get a warranty form or an application from a local supermarket, discount store, or video rental store for a check-cashing card or store club membership card. Does it say anything about how information about the applicant will be used? If so, summarize the statement.

2.37 Find a Web site at which people can buy something online with a credit card. Look for the privacy policy that tells how the site uses the customer information it collects. Write a brief summary of the privacy policy. Include the URL, the business name, and the type of product. Also, tell how many sites you looked at before finding one with a privacy policy.

2.38 The Telephone Consumer Protection Act of 1991 regulates telemarketing. Find this law and summarize its main provisions.

2.39 Find a recent application of smart cards. Discuss its privacy implications and protections.

Class Discussion Exercises

These exercises are for class discussion, perhaps with short presentations prepared in advance by small groups of students.

2.40 Are businesses that provide free Internet services or PCs in exchange for tracking Web activity offering a fair option for consumers, or are they unfairly taking advantage of low-income people who must give up some privacy for these services?

2.41 A health-information Web site has many articles on health and medical issues, a chat room where people can discuss health issues with other users, and provisions for people to send questions by e-mail to be answered by doctors. You have been hired to do a privacy audit. In other words, you are to examine the site, find privacy risks (or good privacy protection practices), and make recommendations for changes as needed. Describe at least three things you would look for, explain their significance, and tell what your recommendations would be if you do or don't find them.

2.42 Your town is considering setting up a camera and face-recognition system in the downtown area and in a neighborhood with a high crime rate. You are hired as a consultant to help design policies for use of the system. Consider a variety of aspects, for example, who will have access to the system, what databases of photos will be used for matching, how long video will be stored, and other factors you consider important. Describe some of your most important recommendations to the city with your reasons for them.

2.43 A company planned to sell a laser device a person can wear around his or her neck that makes photographs taken of the person come out streaked and useless. It was marketed to celebrities who are hounded by photographers. Suppose the device works well against CCTV cameras and many people begin to use it routinely in public places. Law-enforcement agencies will almost certainly try to ban it. Give arguments for and against such a ban.

2.44 Consider the kinds of search and surveillance tools described in Section 2.2.3. Choose several of them and discuss whether they would (singly or in combination) likely have prevented the terrorist attack on September 11, 2001. What other computer-related technology might prevent such attacks in the future?

NOTES

1. James O. Jackson, "Fear and Betrayal in the Stasi State," *Time*, Feb. 3, 1992, pp. 32–33.

2. Alan F. Westin, "Consumer Privacy Issues in the Nineties," from *The Equifax Report on Consumers in the Information Age*, Harris survey, 1990.

3. "Privacy as an Aspect of Human Dignity," in Ferdinand David Schoeman, ed., *Philosophical Dimensions of Privacy: An Anthology*, Cambridge University Press, 1984, pp. 156–203, quote on p. 188.

4. "Reading *Privacy Journal*'s Mail," *Privacy Journal*, May 2001, p. 2.

5. The history of cookies is presented in John Schwartz, "Giving Web a Memory Cost Its Users Privacy," *New York Times*, Sept. 4, 2001, pp. A1, C10.

6. Glenn R. Simpson, "Intuit Acts To Curb Leaks on Web Site," *Wall Street Journal*, Mar. 2, 2000, pp. A3, A8. Michael Moss, "A Web CEO's Elusive Goal: Privacy," *Wall Street Journal*, Feb. 7, 2000, pp. B1, B6.

7. Associated Press, "Popular Software for Computer Cursors Logs Web Visits, Raising Privacy Issue," *Wall Street Journal*, Nov. 30, 1999, p. B6.

8. Steven Levy, "Is It Software? or Spyware?" *Newsweek*, Feb. 19, 2001, p. 54. Associated Press, "Popular Software Secretly Sends Music Preferences," *CNN.com*, Nov. 1, 2001.

9. Jeffrey Rothfeder, *Privacy for Sale*, Simon & Schuster, 1992, p. 25. Rothfeder mentions specifically the Social Security Administration, the IRS, and the Secret Service.

10. Jeffrey Selingo, "It's the Cars, Not the Tires, That Squeal," *New York Times*, Oct. 25, 2001, p. D1.

11. Alan F. Westin, *Privacy and Freedom*, Atheneum, 1968, p. 67.

12. David F. Linowes, *Privacy in America*, University of Illinois Press, 1989, p. 82.

13. Steven A. Bercu, "Smart Card Privacy Issues: An Overview," *BOD-T-001*, July 1994, Smart Card Forum.

14. *Computer Matching: Quality of Decisions and Supporting Analysis Little Affected by 1988 Act*, Oct. 18, 1993, (GAO/PEMD-94-2).

15. Janet Novack, "'You Know Who You Are, and So Do We'," *Forbes*, April 11, 1994, 153:8, pp. 88–92.

16. Rothfeder, *Privacy for Sale*, p. 142.

17. Glenn R. Simpson, "If the FBI Hopes to Get the Goods on You, It May Ask ChoicePoint," *Wall Street Journal*, Apr. 13, 2001, pp. A1, A6. "ChoicePoint—Still With us After All These Years," *Privacy Journal*, Jan. 2001, pp. 5–6.

18. U.S. Code, Title 13.

19. Letter from Vincent Barabba, director of Census Bureau under Presidents Nixon and Carter, and comments from Tom Clark, Justice Department coordinator of alien control, quoted in David Burnham, *The Rise of the Computer State*, Random House, 1983, pp. 23–26.

Margo Anderson, *The American Census: A Social History*, Yale University Press, 1988. James Bovard, "Honesty May Not Be Your Best Census Policy," *Wall Street Journal*, Aug. 8, 1989.

20. These observations were made in John Shattuck, "Computer Matching Is a Serious Threat to Individual Rights," *Communications of the ACM*, June, 1984, 27:6, pp. 537–545, and in "A Review of NCIC 2000," Computer Professionals for Social Responsibility.

21. *Computers and Privacy: How the Government Obtains, Verifies, Uses, and Protects Personal Data*, U.S. General Accounting Office, 1990 (GAO/IMTEC-90-70BR). "House Panel Probes White House Database," *EPIC Alert*, Sept. 12, 1996. OMB Watch study, reported in "U.S. Government Web Sites Fail to Protect Privacy," *EPIC Alert*, Sept. 4, 1997. washingtonpost.com/wp-dyn/articles/A38715-2000Jun21.html. www.wired.com/news/politics/0,1283,37314,00.html. *Internet Privacy: Comparison of Federal Agency Practices with FTC's Fair Information Principles*, U.S. General Accounting Office, Sept. 11, 2000 (GAO/AIMD-00-296R).

22. The GAO report on NCIC abuses is reported in John Hanchette, "Some Computer Data Bases Dangerous to Your Privacy," *Gannett News Service*, Sept. 1, 1994, and Winn Schwartau, "AFIS and the NCIC—Privacy Please!" *Security Technology News*, June 17, 1994. Other cases are from the following sources: Rothfeder, *Privacy for Sale*, p. 25. *Privacy Journal*, May 1992, p. 3, and Jan. 1992, p. 1. "Tax Report," *Wall Street Journal*, p. A1, Sept. 8, 1993 and April 28, 1999. Saul Hansell, "U.S. Workers Stole Data On 11,000, Agency Says," *New York Times*, Apr. 6, 1996, p. 6. "Other Executive Branch Activity," *Privacy and American Business*, 1:4, 1994, p. 14. *Privacy Journal*, Dec. 1992, p. 2. "GAO Finds IRS Security Lacking," *EPIC Alert*, Jan. 20, 1999; the GAO report is *IRS Systems Security*, Dec. 1998 (AIMD-99-38).

23. Janlori Goldman, statement to the Senate Judiciary Subcommittee on Technology and the Law, Jan. 27, 1994.

24. Quoted in David Banisar, *Privacy and Human Rights 2000: An International Survey of Privacy Laws and Developments*, EPIC and Privacy International, 2000.

25. Intelligence Authorization Act of 1996, reported in Vanessa O'Connell, "Wider FBI Access To Credit Files Stirs Privacy Concerns," *Wall Street Journal*, Mar. 21, 1996, p. A4.

26. *Marchetti v. United States* 390 U.S. 39 (1968), quoted in Steven A. Bercu, "Smart Card Privacy Issues: An Overview," *BOD-T-001*, July 1994, Smart Card Forum.

27. Ross Kerber, "When Is a Satellite Photo An Unreasonable Search?" *Wall Street Journal*, Jan. 27, 1998, pp. B1, B7.

28 *Kyllo v. United States*, 99-8508 (2001).

29 Alvin Mark Domnitz, quoted in Felicity Barringerhen, "Using Books as Evidence Against Their Readers," *New York Times*, WeekinReview section, Apr. 8, 2001.

30 The citations for the cases mentioned in this section are *Olmstead v. United States*, 277 U.S. 438(1928), *Katz v. United States*, 389 U.S. 347(1967), *Smith v. Maryland*, 442 U.S. 735(1979), and *United States v. Miller*, 425 U.S. 435(1976).

31 Michael Allen, "Are These X-Rays Too Revealing?" *Wall Street Journal*, March 2, 2000, pp. B1, B4 (includes the ACLU director's quote).

32 Allen, *ibid.*

33 "Feds Funded Private Drivers' Photo Database," *EPIC Alert*, Feb. 19, 1999. "Documents Reveal Secret Service Role in Identity Database," *EPIC Alert*, Sept. 9, 1999.

34 Dana Canedy, "TV Cameras Seek Criminals in Tampa's Crowds," *New York Times*, July 4, 2001, pp. A1, A11.

35 An accuracy rate of 57% was reported by the National Institute of Standards and Technology, a federal government agency. Jesse Drucker and Nancy Keates, "The Airport of the Future," *Wall Street Journal*, Nov. 23, 2001, pp. W1, W12. David Banisar, "A Review of New Surveillance Technologies," *Privacy Journal*, Nov. 2001, p. 1.

36 Marc Champion and others, "Tuesday's Attack Forces an Agonizing Decision on Americans," *Wall Street Journal*, Sept. 14, 2001, p. A8.

37 Thomas C. Greene, "Feds Use Biometrics Against Super Bowl Fans," *The Register*, Feb. 1, 2001, www.theregister.co.uk/content/6/16561.html, viewed Apr. 18, 2001. Ross Kerber, "Privacy Concerns Are Roadblocks on 'Smart' Highways," *Wall Street Journal*, Dec. 4, 1996, pp. B1, B7. Michael Spencer, "One Major City's Restrictions on TV Surveillance," *Privacy Journal*, Mar. 2001, p. 3. Murray Long, "Canadian Commissioner Puts a Hold on Video Cameras," *Privacy Journal*, Nov. 2001, pp. 3–4.

38 Quoted in Murray Long, "Canadian Commissioner Puts a Hold on Video Cameras," *Privacy Journal*, Nov. 2001, pp. 3–4.

39 Andrea Petersen, "A Privacy Firestorm at DoubleClick," *Wall Street Journal*, Feb. 23, 2000, pp. B1, B4.

40 Jonathan Berry *et al.*, "Database Marketing," pp. 56–62, *Business Week*, Sept. 5, 1994.

41 Julia Angwin, "A Plan to Track Web Use Stirs Privacy Concern," *Wall Street Journal*, May 1, 2000, pp. B1, B18. Paulette Thomas, "'Clicking' Coupons On-Line Has a Cost: Privacy," *Wall Street Journal*, June 18, 1998, pp. B1, B8.

42 Statement provided by the Audubon Society.

43 Anne Wells Branscomb, *Who Owns Information?*, Basic Books, 1994, p. 11.

44 Branscomb, *Who Owns Information?*, p. 187.

45 The case is *Dennis v. Metromail*. "The Quintessential Abuse of Privacy," *Privacy Journal*, May 1996, 22:7, pp. 1,4. Lee Drutman, "Should Prisoners Be Processing Personal Information?" *Privacy Journal*, July 1998, 24:9, p. 1. "There's $1 Million Available for Privacy Activism," *Privacy Journal*, Feb. 2001, 27:4, p. 1.

46 One popular argument against mass mailings, that they destroy forests, seems to be weak. Most paper is made from recycled ingredients or from trees grown specifically for that purpose, as a crop. Using less paper to save trees is like eating less bread to save wheat. But there is no good reason to buy a loaf of bread if you are just going to throw it in the trash.

47 *Second Annual Report of the Privacy Rights Clearinghouse*, p. 24. Branscomb, *Who Owns Information?* p. 20.

48 Jill Goldsmith, "Donnelley Under Attack on Child Data," *Wall Street Journal*, June 14, 1996, p. B7D.

49 "Privacy and Surveillance in the 20th Century," *Privacy Journal*, Dec. 1999, p. 3. "ChoicePoint—Still With us After All These Years," *Privacy Journal*, Jan. 2001, p. 5.

50 Fair Credit Reporting Act of 1970, 15 U.S. Code Section 1681.

51 Some marketers used income data available from credit bureaus by ZIP code to choose neighborhoods in which to advertise or distribute discount coupons. Privacy advocates objected to these practices because the consumers did not consent to the use of their credit information for marketing purposes. Interestingly, people in less affluent neighborhoods objected because they did *not* receive the notices and special offers.

52 *Trans Union Corporation v. Federal Trade Commission*, DC Circuit Court No. 00-1141, Apr. 13, 2001; laws.lp.findlaw.com/dc/001141a.html.

53 Judge Ellen Segal Huvelle, in *Individual References Services Group, Inc. v. Federal Trade Commission, et al.*

54 By regulations established under the Gramm–Leach–Bliley Act of 1999, which were responsible for the millions of privacy notices and opt-out forms mailed out by credit card companies in 2001.

55 Ed Young, vice president of Bell Atlantic, at Privacy and American Business conference, Washington, DC, Oct. 5, 1994.

56 Quoted in a Privacy Rights Clearinghouse flyer.

57 Most of the information in this section is from Chris Hibbert, "What to do when they ask for your Social Security Number," www.cpsr.org/cpsr/privacy/ssn/ssn.faq.html. Data from the Social Security Administration is reported in "ID Cards to Cost $10 Billion," *EPIC Alert*, Sept. 26, 1997, and in Glenn Garvin, "Bringing the Border War Home," *Reason*, Oct. 1995, pp. 18–28.

58 *Greidinger v. Davis*, U.S. Court of Appeals, Fourth Circuit.

59 Hibbert, "What to do when they ask for your Social Security Number." Simson Garfinkel, *Database Nation: The Death of Privacy in the 21st Century*, O'Reilly, 2000, pp. 33–34.

60 Mitch Ratcliffe, "Feel Like You're Being Watched? You Will . . . ," *EFFector Online*, May 6, 1994.

61 Quoted in Joe Davidson, "House Panel Backs Telephone Process To Verify Authorization of New Hires," *Wall Street Journal*, Sept. 22, 1995, pp. A2, A14.

62 The figures are from Glenn Garvin, "Bringing the Border War Home."

63 Peter G. Neumann and Lauren Weinstein, "Inside Risks," *Communications of the ACM*, Dec. 2001, p. 176.

64 Quoted in Jane Howard, "ID Card Signals 'End of Democracy'," *The Australian*, Sept. 7, 1987, p. 3.

65 "Who's Reading Your Medical Records?" *Consumer Reports*, Oct. 1994, pp. 628–632.

66 Branscomb, *Who Owns Information?* p. 71.

67 The Privacy Rights Clearinghouse makes these suggestions in its Fact Sheet No. 8, "How Private Is My Medical Information?"

68 "AOL Refuses Request For User Information Amid Syphilis Scare," *Wall Street Journal*, Aug. 26, 1999, p. B2.

69 Branscomb, *Who Owns Information?* p. 65. U. S. Congress, Office of Technology Assessment, "Protecting Privacy in Computerized Medical Information," Sept. 1993, p. 15.

70 Robert Pear, "Bush Accepts Rules to Guard Privacy of Medical Records," *New York Times*,. Apr. 13, 2001, pp. A1, A12. "New Federal Rule Protects Medical Records—Or Does It?" *Privacy Journal*, Jan. 2001, p. 3.

71 APBnews.com filed the suit in Dec. 1999.

72 The article "Can Privacy and Open Access to Records be Reconciled?" *Privacy Journal*, May 2000, p. 6, outlines principles and guidelines devised by Robert Ellis Smith for access to public records.

73 "On Web Privacy, What Are We *Really* Afraid Of?" *Wall Street Journal*, Aug. 2, 2000, p. A23.

74 R. J. Ignelzi, "Road Blocks," *The San Diego Union–Tribune*, July 19, 1994, pp. E1, E3.

75 Angwin, "A Plan to Track to Track Web Use Stirs Privacy Concern."

76 Nick Wingfield, "A Marketer's Dream," *Wall Street Journal*, Dec. 7, 1998, p. R20. John Simons, "New Internet Privacy Laws Appear Less Likely With Release of New Survey," *Wall Street Journal*, May 13, 1999, p. B9.

77 Handbook of Company Privacy Codes, *Privacy and American Business*, Oct. 1994, pp. 81, 86.

78 "The AOL Privacy Policy," accessed Jan. 19, 2001.

79 Andrea Petersen, "Private Matters," *Wall Street Journal*, Feb. 12, 2001, p. R24. Petersen, "A Privacy Firestorm at DoubleClick."

80 Samuel D. Warren and Louis D. Brandeis, "The Right to Privacy," *Harvard Law Review*, 1890, v. 4, p. 193.

81 Judith Jarvis Thomson, "The Right to Privacy," in Schoeman, *Philosophical Dimensions of Privacy: An Anthology*, pp. 272–289.

82 The inspiration for the Warren and Brandeis article, not mentioned in it, was gossip columnists writing about extravagant parties in Warren's home and particularly, newspaper coverage of his daughter's wedding. The background of the article is described in a biography of Brandeis and summarized in the critical response to the Warren and Brandeis article by William L. Prosser ("Privacy," in Schoeman, *Philosophical Dimensions of Privacy: An Anthology*, pp. 104–155).

83 Thomson, "The Right to Privacy," p. 287.

84 See, for example, Schoeman, *Philosophical Dimensions of Privacy: An Anthology*, p. 15, and Prosser, "Privacy," pp. 104–155.

85 Cases are cited in Prosser, ibid.

86 These guidelines show up in some form in the writings of various market-oriented writers. The presentation here closely follows Phil Salin, "Notes on Freedom of Electronic Assembly and Privacy," Nov. 27, 1990.

87 Dan Freedman, "Privacy Profile: Mary Gardiner Jones," *Privacy and American Business*, 1:4, 1994, pp. 15, 17.

88 Janlori Goldman, statement to the Senate Judiciary Subcommittee on Technology and the Law, Jan. 27, 1994.

89 www.privacy.org.

90 Deirdre Mulligan, May 18, 2000, www.cdt.org/testimony/000518mulligan.shtml.

91 For example, Congress passed the Video Privacy Protection Act of 1988 after reporters obtained a list of video rentals by the family of Judge Robert Bork, who was being considered for appointment to the Supreme Court.

92 Recall that the Privacy Act of 1974 prohibits disclosure of government files about a person without his or her consent, a sensible rule in many cases. A news reporter who was held hostage in the Middle East for more than a year decided to write a book about his ordeal. His requests for relevant government files were denied by several federal agencies; he was told that to protect the privacy of his captors, he would need their permission to see the files. ("Held Hostage Again," *Privacy Journal*, Dec. 1992, p. 6. "In the Courts," *Privacy Journal*, Nov. 1994, p. 7.)

93 John Simons, "New FTC Rules Aim to Protect Kid Web Privacy," *Wall Street Journal*, Apr. 21, 1999, p. B1. "FTC Proposes Rules for Kids' Privacy Protection," *EPIC Alert*, Apr. 22, 1999, 6:06. "New Children's Privacy Rules Pose Obstacles for Some Sites," *Wall Street Journal*, Apr. 24, 2000, p. B8.

94 Richard Posner, "An Economic Theory of Privacy," *Regulation*, American Enterprise Institute for Public Policy Research, May/June 1978, pp. 19–26. (Appears in several anthologies including Schoeman, *Philosophical Dimensions of Privacy*, listed at the end of the chapter, pp. 333–345, and Johnson and Nissenbaum, *Computers, Ethics & Social Values*, listed at the end of Chapter 1.)

95 Eugene Volokh, "Personalization and Privacy," *Communications of the ACM*, 43:8, Aug. 2000, pp. 84–88. See

also Volokh's article and the article by Solveig Singleton listed at the end of the chapter.

96 Tom W. Bell, "Internet Privacy and Self-Regulation: Lessons from the Porn Wars," Cato Institute Briefing Paper No. 65, Cato Institute, Aug. 9, 2001.

97 Directive 95/46/EC of the European Parliament and of the Council of 24 October 1995 on the protection of individuals with regard to the processing of personal data and on the free movement of such data. Appears as Appendix 2 in Jacqueline Klosek, *Data Privacy in the Information Age*, Quorum Books, 2000.

98 Klosek, *Data Privacy in the Information Age*, pp. 169–193. "Australia: We're 'Adequate!'" *Privacy Journal*, May 2001, p. 4.

99 Neal E. Boudette, "German Shoppers May Get 'Sale Freedom'," *Wall Street Journal*, Jan. 23, 2002, p. B7D.

100 "Privacy@net," Consumers International, Jan. 2001, www.consumersinternational.org/news/press-releases/fprivreport.pdf

101 Melinda Powelson, "Faced with Cash Crunch, City Turns to Allegedly Big-brother Tactics," *San Diego Reader*, Jan. 21, 1993, p. 4.

102 Robert F. Buckhorn Jr., quoted in Dana Canedy, "TV Cameras Seek Criminals in Tampa's Crowds."

103 Based on an actual case described in "Webcams in Public Called Intrusive," *Privacy Journal*, May 2001, p. 3.

104 "Who's Reading Your Medical Records?" *Consumer Reports*, Oct. 1994, pp. 628–632.

105 L. D. Introna, "Workplace Surveillance, Privacy and Distributive Justice," *Proceedings for Computer Ethics: Philosophical Enquiry (CEPE2000)*, Dartmouth College, July 14–16, 2000, pp. 188–199.

BOOKS AND ARTICLES

■ Catherine A. Allen and William J. Barr, eds., *Smart Cards: Seizing Strategic Business Opportunities*, Irwin Professional Publishing, 1997. A collection of articles on applications, from an industry perspective.

■ Tom W. Bell, "Internet Privacy and Self-Regulation: Lessons from the Porn Wars," Cato Institute Briefing Paper No. 65, Cato Institute, Aug. 9, 2001.

■ Anne Wells Branscomb, *Who Owns Information?*, Basic Books, 1994.

■ Simson Garfinkel, *Database Nation: The Death of Privacy in the 21st Century*, O'Reilly, 2000.

■ Jacqueline Klosek, *Data Privacy in the Information Age*, Quorum Books, 2000. Describes the European Union data privacy directive, privacy laws in many European countries, and major U.S. privacy laws.

■ Richard P. Kusserow, "The Government Needs Computer Matching to Root Out Waste and Fraud," *Communications of the ACM*, June 1984, 27:6, pp. 446–452. The government's side of the computer-matching controversy. See the Shattuck entry for the opposing side.

■ National Research Council, *Protecting Electronic Health Information*, National Academy Press, 1997.

■ James Rachels, "Why Privacy Is Important," in *Philosophy and Public Affairs*, 4–4, Princeton University Press, 1975. (Appears in several anthologies including Schoeman, *Philosophical Dimensions of Privacy*, listed below, and Johnson and Nissenbaum, *Computers, Ethics & Social Values*, listed at the end of Chapter 1.)

■ Jeffrey Rosen, *The Unwanted Gaze: The Destruction of Privacy in America*, Random House, 2000.

■ Jeffrey Rothfeder, *Privacy for Sale*, Simon & Schuster, 1992.

■ Ferdinand David Schoeman, *Philosophical Dimensions of Privacy: An Anthology*, Cambridge University Press, 1984.

■ John Shattuck, "Computer Matching Is a Serious Threat to Individual Rights," *Communications of the ACM*, June 1984, 27:6, pp. 537–545. See the Kusserow entry for the government's arguments in favor of computer matching.

- Solveig Singleton, "Privacy As Censorship: A Skeptical View of Proposals to Regulate Privacy in the Private Sector," Cato Institute Policy Analysis No. 295, Jan. 22, 1998.

- Robert Ellis Smith, *Ben Franklin's Web Site: Privacy and Curiosity from Plymouth Rock to the Internet*, Privacy Journal, 2000.

- Robert Ellis Smith, publisher, *Privacy Journal*. A monthly newsletter covering news on many aspects of privacy.

- Jacob Sullum, "Secrets for Sale," *Reason*, April 1992 (www.reason.com/9204/fe.sullum.html). Criticizes many regulatory approaches to solving privacy problems; argues for use of contracts.

- Charles Sykes, *The End of Privacy: Personal Rights in the Surveillance Society*, St. Martin's Press, 1999.

- Eugene Volokh, "Freedom of Speech and Information Privacy: The Troubling Implications of a Right to Stop People From Speaking About You," *Stanford Law Review*, (52 Stanford L. Rev. 1049), 2000. Also at www.law.ucla.edu/faculty/volokh/privacy.htm.

- Alan F. Westin, *Privacy and Freedom*, Atheneum, 1968.

ORGANIZATIONS AND WEBSITES

- Cato Institute: www.cato.org/tech

- Electronic Frontier Foundation: www.eff.org

- Electronic Frontiers Australia: www.efa.org.au

- Electronic Privacy Information Center: www.epic.org. See also www.privacy.org, jointly sponsored by EPIC and Privacy International

- Federal Trade Commission: www.ftc.gov

- Junkbusters: www.junkbusters.com

- The Library of Congress site for U.S. laws and bills currently going through Congress: thomas.loc.gov

- Privacilla: www.privacilla.org. A site on privacy policy from a free-market, pro-technology perspective

- Privacy & American Business (Center for Social and Legal Research): www.pandab.org

- Privacy Commission of Australia: www.privacy.gov.au

- Privacy Commissioner of Canada: www.privcom.gc.ca

- Privacy Forum: www.vortex.com/privacy

- Privacy International: www.privacyinternational.org. Privacy International's page on video surveillance: www.privacy.org/pi/issues/cctv/index.html. Privacy International's Frequently Asked Questions page on identity cards: www.privacy.org/pi/activities/idcard/idcard_faq.html

- Privacy Rights Clearinghouse: www.privacyrights.org

- TRUSTe: www.truste.org

3

ENCRYPTION AND INTERCEPTION OF COMMUNICATIONS

3.1 Overview of the Controversies

In this chapter, we study two closely related issues that profoundly affect communications privacy: interception of communications (via telephone, e-mail, and the Internet) by government agencies and government attempts to restrict the use of secure encryption. We consider how new technologies and government policies affect the ability of law-enforcement agencies to intercept and read or listen to the communications of criminals and law-abiding citizens. We also describe some intriguing applications of cryptography that have the potential for making personal and business activities on computer networks both secure and anonymous, thus avoiding many of the privacy problems we discussed in the previous chapter.

At the same time that computer technology created new risks to privacy by increasing the amount and sensitivity of information available over telecommunications systems, some aspects of the technology (such as use of optical fiber) and new features it enabled made wiretapping more difficult. The increased use of encryption meant that law-enforcement agents could not read some communications they intercepted. Privacy advocates and civil libertarians argued for strong protection for communications using new technologies, to regain the level of privacy we had had before, while the FBI argued for increased control over telecommunications technology and restrictions on the use of encryption to regain the level of access to communications and documents it had had before.

In 1991, the following statement appeared in a bill in the U.S. Senate. It expresses the goal pursued by the FBI and other government agencies since then.

> It is the sense of Congress that providers of electronic communications services and manufacturers of electronic communications service equipment shall ensure that communications systems permit the government to obtain the plain text contents of voice, data, and other communications when appropriately authorized by law.[1]

The phrase "plain text" in the statement means unencrypted, that is, in a form such that the government can read or hear the contents. In this statement, the government attempted to give telecommunications service and equipment providers the responsibility to ensure that the government could both intercept any message and decrypt (decode) it if it were encrypted. One critic compared this to requiring building contractors to provide the government with master keys for all buildings in the U.S.[2] The statement of intent did not pass in 1991, but the government has undertaken an intensive campaign to implement it. Congress passed the Communications Assistance for Law Enforcement Act (CALEA) in 1994 requiring that the technology used in communications systems be redesigned, and existing equipment modified, to ensure the ability of law-enforcement agencies to intercept communications. The law itself was controversial, and, because many of the details were still being worked out many years later, the dispute continued.

Carnivore and Echelon are surveillance systems. The FBI's Carnivore system sifts through millions of e-mails, looking for those of a suspect for whom the FBI has a court order. The constitutionality and necessity of Carnivore are under question. Virtually everything about Echelon is under question because it is a secret system. It appears that Echelon is a system of satellites and computers that monitors communications worldwide. It is jointly operated by the U.S. National Security Agency (NSA) and the governments of several other countries. Some claim that it is conducting industrial espionage and spying on political organizations.

Interception tools address only one part of the government's problem. Since 1993, the government has proposed a variety of schemes for government agents to be able to decrypt encrypted communications. All met with intense opposition. The government's prohibition on export of secure encryption software was another source of intense controversy. Intended to keep strong encryption from terrorists, the export restrictions caused use of less secure encryption in legitimate applications and threats of arrest of researchers and others who discussed secure encryption on the Web. In 1997, the government proposed banning encryption that could not be immediately decrypted at its request. The bill failed, but the idea resurfaced in 2001 after the terrorist attacks on the World Trade Center and the Pentagon.

The essential argument in favor of CALEA, Carnivore, Echelon, and encryption controls—and of any new systems and proposals to guarantee access to communications by law-enforcement agencies—is to maintain the ability of those agencies to protect us from drug dealers, organized crime, other criminals, and terrorists. The problems with them, according to critics, include threats to privacy and civil liberties, the large potential for abuse by government, and side effects that threaten the security of electronic commerce and the global competitiveness of U.S. industry.

In Section 3.2, we look at interception of communications: wiretapping, CALEA, Carnivore, and Echelon. In Section 3.3, we provide some explanation of encryption and its uses; in Section 3.4, we look at the government's efforts to control encryption; in Section 3.5, we consider some arguments and issues that apply to all the various laws, systems, proposals, and restrictions.

3.2 Intercepting Communications

3.2.1 WIRETAPPING

TELEPHONE

Within ten years of the invention of the telephone, people (in and out of government) were wiretapping them.[3] Before that, people intercepted telegraph communications. Throughout the years when telephone connections were made by human operators and most people had party lines (one telephone line shared by several households), operators and nosy neighbors sometimes listened in on telephone conversations.

Increased wealth and new technology eliminated party lines and human operators, but telephones were still vulnerable to wiretapping. The legal status of wiretapping was debated throughout most of the 20th century. Wiretapping was used widely by federal and state law-enforcement agencies, businesses, private detectives, political candidates, and others. In 1928, the Supreme Court ruled that wiretapping by law-enforcement agencies was not unconstitutional, but that it could be banned by Congress. In 1934, Congress passed the Federal Communications Act. This law states that no person not authorized by the sender could intercept and divulge a message; there is no exception for law-enforcement agencies. A 1937 Supreme Court decision ruled that wiretapping violated the law.[4] Federal and state law-enforcement agencies and local police ignored the ruling and continued to wiretap regularly for decades, sometimes with the approval of the Attorney General. In one well-publicized case, the FBI monitored the telephone calls between a defendant and her attorneys during her trial. Evidence obtained by illegal wiretapping could not be used in court, so the FBI kept a separate, secret file system. The FBI bugged and wiretapped members of Congress and the Supreme Court. Most states had their own laws prohibiting wiretapping, but although there was publicity about extensive use of wiretapping by police, none was prosecuted. In many cases, of course, law-enforcement agencies were wiretapping people suspected of crimes, but, in many other cases, they tapped people with unconventional views, members of civil rights groups, and political opponents of powerful government officials. The wiretap issue continued to be debated fiercely in Congress, state legislatures, the courts, books, and the news media. Congress repeatedly rejected proposals to allow wiretapping and electronic surveillance. In 1967 (in *Katz v. United States*, discussed in Section 2.2.2), the Supreme Court ruled that intercepting telephone conversations without a court order violated the Fourth Amendment to the U.S. Constitution. In 1968, as part of the Omnibus Crime Control and Safe Streets Act, Congress explicitly allowed wiretapping and electronic surveillance by law-enforcement agencies, with a court order, for the first time in U.S. history. The main argument given for this change was the necessity to combat organized crime. (The riots over race issues, the assassinations of President John F. Kennedy, Martin Luther King, Jr., and Robert Kennedy, and the antiwar demonstrations in the five years leading up to passage of the crime law probably contributed to its passage.)

The government needs a court order to (legally) intercept or record the content of a telephone call for a criminal investigation. Law-enforcement agents must justify the request; it is granted for a limited time period. The government can intercept communications without a court order in some emergencies. A device called a *pen register* and a *trap and trace* can be used to determine the telephone numbers called or the number from which a call was made, respectively. These do not require as much court scrutiny and justification as intercepting the contents of a call.

Senator Sam Ervin commented in 1968, "The mere fact of passing a law never resolves a controversy as fierce as this one."[5] He was right. Debate continued about whether the privacy protections in the Omnibus Crime Act were strong enough to be constitutional; Supreme Court justices disagreed. Wiretapping by government and politicians that was illegal or of questionable legality continued, most notably during the Vietnam war, the Watergate scandal, and the Pentagon Papers case. Journalists and government employees were victims of unconstitutional wiretaps during the Nixon administration. In 1998, Los Angeles police officers admitted using wiretaps improperly in a large number of cases.

Most other countries have constitutional and legal protections for communications privacy. The U.S. State Department reported that, in the late 1990s, the police and intelligence agencies of more than 90 countries routinely performed illegal monitoring of political opponents, human rights workers, and journalists.[6]

NEW TECHNOLOGIES

E-mail and cellular phone conversations were not explicitly covered by old laws, and interception was common. Driving around Silicon Valley eavesdropping on cell phone conversations was, reportedly, a popular form of industrial spying in the 1980s. Cellphone conversations of politicians and celebrities were intercepted. The Electronic Communications Privacy Act of 1986 (ECPA), with amendments in 1994, extended the 1968 wiretapping restrictions to electronic communication, including electronic mail, cordless and cellular telephones, and paging devices. This was a significant step toward protecting privacy in cyberspace from private and governmental snooping. It required that the government get a court order to legally intercept e-mail or read stored e-mail.* The USA PATRIOT Act of 2001 reversed direction and loosened restrictions on government surveillance and wiretapping activities after the terrorist attacks.[†]

3.2.2 DESIGNING COMMUNICATIONS SYSTEMS FOR INTERCEPTION AND TRACKING

The Internet and the World Wide Web have drastically altered the nature and scope of information the government can collect by intercepting our communications. Computer networks carry a vast amount of personal and business information. In addition to sending e-mail, we shop, read news, do research, visit myriad Web sites, and send Web sites a variety of personal information. The government can learn a lot more about our habits, activities, and interests than it could from tapping telephone calls before the growth of the Web.

In some ways, on the other hand, new communications technologies make access to information and the content of calls more difficult for law-enforcement agencies than it was before. When people use toll-free long-distance services or call forwarding, the first number called—the number law-enforcement agents can legally get fairly easily—does not give information about the actual recipient of the call. On the Internet, e-mail, files, and Internet telephone calls are broken into pieces called packets that might travel, mingled with others, along different routes to the destination where they are reassembled.

---

*The ECPA allows businesses to read the e-mail of employees on the business system. We discuss this issue related to employee privacy in Chapter 8.

†The law is very long and details are complex. Some provisions were written to expire in a few years if not renewed by Congress.

STEVE JACKSON GAMES AND THE SECRET SERVICE [7]

The Electronic Communications Privacy Act of 1986 (ECPA) faced its first major test in the Steve Jackson Games case. Steve Jackson Games is a company that publishes role-playing games. It was raided by the Secret Service in 1990. The raid occurred at a time when law-enforcement agents knew very little about computers and many were suspicious of virtually any young people who were computer literate and discussed hacking or computer crime. Agents seized computers, printers, disks, business records, and other material. The government claimed that an employee of the company had a copy of a document stolen by hackers from BellSouth; they thought he had put it on the company's computer bulletin board system (BBS). The document was not on the system, and no charges were ever filed against the company, its owner, or the employee. However, the seizure and long delay in returning the seized material caused disruption of business, financial loss, and the layoff of some employees.

The ECPA prohibits the government from seizing electronic mail without a court order. The Secret Service seized the Steve Jackson Games Illuminati BBS, which contained private e-mail of several hundred people who were not suspects. The government argued that BBS users had no "reasonable expectation of privacy" for their e-mail and that the ECPA did not prohibit the government from seizing and reading e-mail on the BBS because they had a search warrant for Jackson's computers. The judge concluded that e-mail stored on the BBS was protected by the ECPA, and government agents violated the law when they seized, read, and destroyed the mail.

(This is called packet-mode communication.) Intercepting Internet phone calls is more difficult than attaching a clip to an old analog telephone wire.

The FBI, arguing that new telephone technology was interfering with its ability to intercept phone calls, helped draft (and lobbied for) the Communications Assistance for Law Enforcement Act of 1994 (CALEA). This law requires that telecommunications equipment be designed (and existing equipment modified) to ensure that the government[‡] can intercept telephone calls (with a court order or other authorization). In the past, communications equipment was designed for its communications purpose; the FBI developed its tools for interception, and communications providers were required to assist. The significance of CALEA is that, previously, the government could not require that communications equipment be designed and modified to meet the interception needs of law enforcement.

Opposition to CALEA came from computer and telecommunications companies, industry organizations, privacy advocates, civil libertarians, and such professional organizations as Computer Professionals for Social Responsibility. CALEA was a compromise.

[‡]In this context "government" includes the federal government and its agencies, state governments, and various other government subdivisions.

Congress made it clear that the law was not intended to extend law-enforcement's surveillance power. The law contains a few limitations on government activity; for example, it limits authority to obtain tracking and location information for mobile-phone users.

CALEA specified that the actual details of standards and requirements were to be determined by consultation between the FBI and representatives of the telecommunications industry. The FBI wanted requirements that all equipment be designed so that it could

- intercept all wire and electronic communications originating from or coming to a particular subscriber in real time, at any time (in ways not detectable by the parties to the communication)

- perform a large number of interceptions simultaneously

- receive intercepted communications and call-identifying information at a location specified by the government

- receive numbers entered after the initial number dialed, with the looser justification standard that applies to pen registers

- intercept conference calls

- determine the physical location of cell-phone users

- intercept packet-mode communications on the Internet.

There was intense disagreement about what standards were reasonable. Because the two sides could not agree, the deadline for implementing the law was extended. The Federal Communications Commission (FCC) issued rules in 1999. Privacy and civil liberties organizations sued to block the rules. They argued that some of them, in particular requirements for determining the physical location of cell-phone users and ensuring that the government could intercept packet-mode communications on the Internet, went beyond the scope of the law and extended the government's surveillance power. They objected to increased authority for law enforcement to get numbers entered after the initial phone number called. Such numbers could include account numbers, passwords, PINs, and so forth. A federal appeals court ordered the FCC to rewrite many of the rules. The court found that some were not adequately justified and that the FCC had not addressed privacy issues.

The many years of controversy and the court challenges indicate the huge gulf separating the FBI and other law-enforcement agencies, on one side, from the telecommunications industry and privacy and civil-liberties groups on the other.

COSTS: DOLLARS, SECURITY, COMPETITIVENESS, CIVIL LIBERTIES

CALEA authorized $500,000,000 for hardware and software modifications to existing telecommunications equipment to meet the demands of law enforcement. The communications industry estimated that the actual cost would be in the billions. Whether half a billion or several billion, and whether we pay on our telephone bill or our tax bill, it is clear that the changes are expensive.

Economists point out that anything subsidized is likely to be overused, thus wasting resources. Rather than requiring taxpayers to spend billions to subsidize wiretapping, one economist recommended that law-enforcement agencies be given a reasonable budget and then be permitted to decide on the most effective means of using it. Just as police departments weigh the costs and benefits of patrol cars versus helicopters, investigators can weigh increased expenditures to improve their wiretapping and decryption capabilities against spending on other techniques, such as informers, bugs, undercover agents, and so on.[8]

Aside from the direct implementation expenses, legal requirements for specific technological capabilities have indirect costs. They prevent potential improvements in communications technology from being implemented. A system with a designed-in capability for wiretapping is more vulnerable to criminals, industrial spies, and foreign governments. It threatens the growth and security of the World Wide Web.

Most of the several hundred federal wiretaps authorized by federal courts each year were conducted in the New York City/New Jersey area, and most were for drug suspects. (State agencies obtained a total of several hundred wiretap orders each year also.) Interceptions in cases related to foreign intelligence or terrorism are approved by a separate, secret federal court. Government officials and other supporters of the government's proposals argued that, in the cases where wiretaps are used, they are essential for catching and/or convicting dangerous criminals. Wiretaps were used in 90% of terrorism cases that went to trial in the 1990s. Especially after September 11, 2001, the terrorist threat is a compelling argument to many people.[9]

Critics claim that wiretaps are a less useful law-enforcement tool than informants, detective work, witnesses, and so on. The relatively small number of legal wiretaps, their geographic concentration, and the focus on drug crimes raises the question of whether the government really needs such extreme, system-wide controls on the communications systems used by nearly 300 million Americans. If drug prohibition were to end, as alcohol prohibition did in the 1930s, would we find ourselves with a costly infrastructure of intrusion and relatively little legitimate need for it?

New technologies, competition, and varied customer needs generated extraordinary growth in the development and diversity of new telecommunications services, equipment, protocols, algorithms, and companies. There are approximately 2000 service providers. New innovations keep changing the technology. This change and diversity is frustrating to the FBI. "The prospect of trying to enforce laws without a nationwide standard for surveillance would turn enforcement into a nightmare," according to the FBI.[10] The idea of communications technology designed for a "nationwide standard for surveillance" is a nightmare to those who place high value on privacy and civil liberties.

3.2.3 CARNIVORE

Carnivore is the FBI's system for intercepting e-mail.* When the FBI gets a court order to intercept someone's e-mail, a computer containing the Carnivore system is installed at the suspect's Internet service provider (ISP). It filters all the e-mail from that ISP, examining the headers to find and copy the suspect's e-mail. The system can also collect files downloaded by a suspect and conversations in chat rooms. Congress and the public learned of the system in 2000 (after it had been in use about a year). The main concern is that once the system is installed, the FBI can extract anyone's mail (and other communications), not just that of the suspect for whom the FBI has the court order.

Supporters of Carnivore argue that the system is necessary because of differences in the technology of old-time analog telephones and modern e-mail. It was easy to tap a specific telephone line and, thus, intercept only the calls to or from the target of the court order. All e-mail from subscribers of an ISP go through the ISP's lines; there is no way to tap one person's e-mail stream alone. Thus intercepting e-mail is more difficult than tapping telephones was. Supporters compare Carnivore's review of all the e-mail headers passing through the ISP to reading the addresses on envelopes.

Critics of Carnivore respond that ISPs can collect the e-mail of a particular subscriber and turn it over to the FBI when presented with a court order. There is no need to allow the FBI to install its own system and sift through everyone's mail. There is insufficient protection to prevent violation of the Fourth Amendment and the Electronic Communications Privacy Act. Procedures are needed to prevent tampering with the collected evidence (e.g., editing files). Also, as a practical matter, because of incompatibilities, the Carnivore system can cause service disruptions at ISPs.

Members of Congress, privacy advocates, and ISPs requested more detail about how Carnivore works, so that they could discover what privacy safeguards it contains and ascertain that it would not disrupt service. The FBI refused, claiming that, if more information about Carnivore were made public, criminals could find ways to evade it. The FBI said it collects only the communications for which it has legal authorization, and the speed and storage capacity of Carnivore make it impossible to collect all the traffic at any but a tiny ISP. Under pressure from Congress and privacy groups, the FBI allowed a small group of experts from a university to review the Carnivore software. Several universities declined because of the conditions the FBI placed on the review—including its right to edit the report of the review committee before it was released. The group that did the review said it found that the system does what the FBI claimed it did (and did not collect communications it was not supposed to), but that there were many weaknesses in the design that could easily allow collection of innocent people's communications by accident or intent. The panel recommended several changes. The Electronic Privacy Information Center found, via a Freedom of Information Act request, that Carnivore can capture and archive unfiltered traffic.[12]

---

*The FBI apparently has a talent for choosing names that don't inspire public confidence. *Privacy Journal* reported that the FBI's internal name for the proposals that led to CALEA was "Operation Root Canal."[11] In 2001, the FBI changed the name of Carnivore to DCS1000.

CARNIVORE'S COUSINS[13]

A 1995 law in Russia allows law-enforcement agencies to tap telephones, read mail, and intercept e-mail. The government required Internet service providers to install SORM, the government's system for intercepting e-mail. SORM routes communications to the local Federal Security Service offices. Nail Murzakhanov, the operator of a small ISP, was asked to install the system when he began operation in 1998. He refused, saying he had signed a confidentiality agreement with his customers. He agreed to cooperate only if shown a court order confirming that one of his customers was under a criminal investigation. The government put him out of business for a few months by turning off his satellite dish; it threatened to revoke his license to operate. Mr. Murzakhanov sued, and, in 2000, the government backed down, admitting it did not have legal grounds for its actions. However, it might seek changes in the law.

When the Russian public learned of the government's e-mail interception program in 1998, visits to a Russian Web site that provides the e-mail encryption program PGP increased about ten-fold. The legal status of PGP is unclear; it had been banned in Russia unless the user had permission to use it from the Russian national security agency.

The Treaty on Cybercrime, written by the Council of Europe, has provisions requiring member nations to pass legislation that authorizes Carnivore-like systems in each country or requires ISPs to intercept and store communications for law-enforcement agencies. Privacy advocates, civil liberties groups, and businesses criticized the treaty, saying that it entrenches government surveillance of the Internet and that the storage requirements could impose huge costs on ISPs.

The Carnivore controversy illustrates how new technology requires reevaluation, and sometimes clarification and updating of existing laws. Does the FBI's sifting through millions of e-mail headers violate the wiretapping laws and the Electronic Communications Privacy Act? Is collection of e-mail headers (not contents) analogous to using a pen register to obtain telephone numbers called? The FBI's general counsel argued that it is. However, an e-mail header contains more information than a telephone number. An e-mail address usually identifies a particular person, not just a household or office, as many phone numbers do. An e-mail header contains a subject line, which is more like content information. Should the FBI have access to that under the lower standards for pen registers? An FBI internal memo (obtained under the Freedom of Information Act) indicated that an FBI attorney believed that pen registers could be used legally only to obtain the phone number called by a modem. If that were the case, Carnivore's reading of all e-mail headers would be illegal. The FBI agent who sent the memo (in 2000) stated that "I don't think we in the field have a grasp of how the existing telecommunications laws apply to computer communications."[14]

Privacy advocates remained concerned about whether the system, whose operation is under complete control of the government agency using it, has enough safeguards to prevent illegal uses and abuses. They continued to argue that Carnivore's source code be made public so that computer security experts could monitor it.

In 2001, the USA PATRIOT Act allowed law-enforcement agents to use pen-register authority to get destination and time information for e-mail. (It also allowed them to get a variety of other information about people's e-mail and Internet use from ISPs, including payment information such as credit-card numbers, without a court order.)

3.2.4 THE NATIONAL SECURITY AGENCY AND ECHELON

THE NSA

The National Security Agency (NSA) was formed in 1952 by a secret presidential order. Its budget is still unpublished, although it was estimated at approximately $4 billion in 2001. The NSA owns and uses the most powerful computers available. *Newsweek* said it had nearly half the computing power in the world.[15] As part of its responsibility for national security, the NSA monitors communications between the U.S. and other countries and a lot of communications within other countries. Because of the secrecy of most of its activities, little is publicly known about its successes and abuses.

In 1920, the federal government's Black Chamber, a secret group of code experts and a precursor to the NSA, successfully pressured the main cable (telegram) companies to let the government routinely see foreign cables, in violation of the federal Radio Communication Act of 1912 which made it illegal for a cable company employee to divulge a message to anyone except the addressee without a court order. In the 1970s, a Congressional committee chaired by Senator Church found that the NSA had been secretly and illegally collecting international telegrams, including telegrams sent by American citizens, since the 1950s and searching them for foreign intelligence information. As a result, Congress passed the Foreign Intelligence Surveillance Act establishing oversight rules for the NSA. The Agency was prohibited from collecting masses of telegrams without a warrant and from compiling lists of Americans to be watched without a warrant. The law set up a secret federal court to issue warrants to the NSA to intercept communications of people it could show were agents of foreign powers or involved in terrorism or espionage.[16]

In the past several decades, increased wealth, travel, and trade generated more business communication—cluttering international communications media and making it harder for the NSA to detect messages of interest. At the same time, communications of ordinary people became more vulnerable as we sent messages, files, and Web requests through the same media used by international businesses and terrorists. Satellite communications were a boon to the NSA; it could pick messages out of the air. The vastly increased processing power of computer systems enabled law enforcement and spy agencies to filter and analyze huge quantities of communications of innocent people instead of targeting only specific suspects. The mass of communications available to the NSA may be getting larger. Undersea fiber-optic cables carry millions of phone calls, e-mails, faxes, and files translated into beams of light. Both the physical conditions and the huge number of messages make interception of international communications in fiber optic cables extremely difficult. While some people in the communications industry believe tapping the cables is technically infeasible, former intelligence officials said the NSA did an experimental tap in the mid-1990s. Intelligence agencies are spending $1 billion to outfit a ship with state-of-the-art technology to perform undersea fiber-optic taps.[17]

WHAT IS ECHELON?

Beginning in 1998, several reports about the NSA's "Echelon" system caused a furor in Europe and the U.S.[18]

Echelon raises issues similar to issues about Carnivore, but on an international scale. The NSA, in partnership with intelligence agencies of Canada, Britain, Australia, and New Zealand, operates a huge system of listening stations to intercept satellite communications, which are then searched for targeted people or subjects. It is uncertain exactly what aspect of the system the name "Echelon" refers to, because the system is secret; the NSA declined to confirm or deny its existence. The government of Australia confirmed an agreement for cooperation among the intelligence agencies of the five countries. James Bamford, in his book *Body of Secrets*, about the NSA's post-Cold War activities, says that the partnership grew out of the UKUSA Communications Intelligence Agreement signed in 1946. Echelon, he says, is the code name for the software system that allows the intelligence agencies of any of the member countries to specify targets (keywords, names, phone numbers, etc.) and access information intercepted by any of the others. It works like a search engine—searching through everyone's communications instead of through Web sites.[19] As the controversy about Echelon grew, Michael Hayden, the director of the NSA, made a statement at a congressional hearing about the NSA's electronic surveillance activities but did not use the word "Echelon."[20] Hayden said that the NSA collects information related to international terrorism, narcotics trafficking, and proliferation of weapons of mass destruction. He said the NSA also gathers economic intelligence for the purpose of tracking money laundering and corporate corruption.

Echelon, apparently, uses voice recognition to select telephone conversations of targeted suspects. It uses artificial intelligence programs to find messages of interest. It filters huge numbers of communications each day, including telephone calls, e-mail, and Internet downloads. The NSA does not need a court order to monitor foreign communications. The NSA's eavesdropping provided important information in the Gulf War, the Kosovo conflict, and in preparation for terrorist "Y2K" activity at the beginning of 2000. By intercepting messages from Iran trying to buy parts for nuclear missiles from France and phone calls of complaint from Iran to China, Echelon helped confirm that China kept an agreement to stop selling nuclear missiles to Iran.[21]

WHAT IS CONTROVERSIAL ABOUT ECHELON?

Echelon's targets include more than terrorist and military activities. Echelon's scope includes friendly countries and political and economic topics. The NSA collects information to help the U.S. economy and U.S. business. For example, the Agency intercepted telephone conversations between executives of Japanese automobile companies when they met with U.S. trade officials in Geneva to discuss high tariffs imposed by the U.S. on Japanese luxury cars. When the European Parliament began investigating Echelon, it expressed strong concern and anger that Echelon appeared to be collecting economic and corporate information, perhaps at a level amounting to industrial espionage on behalf of member countries. NSA Director Hayden said in his Congressional testimony that the NSA provides information on foreign corporations only to government agencies. He said the NSA does not do foreign economic espionage for U.S. corporations. A former director of the U.S. Central Intelligence Agency said the U.S. spied on some European companies because they use bribes to get big government contracts for which U.S. companies are also bidding.[22] Critics believe some government agencies pass information to U.S. businesses. A European Parliament report said there were no confirmed cases of industrial espionage.

Echelon might be violating the laws of several countries and infringing on the privacy of people in the Echelon member countries and other countries. This too angered European countries that are not part of the system. Bamford describes how a salesperson or a business can mistakenly be put on watch lists and international blacklists because of misinterpretation of snippets of communications extracted by Echelon. There is evidence that Echelon secretly monitors political organizations, including human rights groups such as Amnesty International.

The U.S. and some Echelon partners prohibit national security organizations from monitoring their own citizens except under extremely strict limitations. A former employee of the Canadian system reported that, when an Echelon member agency wants information on a citizen of its country, it gets around the prohibition by asking one of the other partner agencies to intercept the person's communications. Someone who worked at the British facility said she heard telephone conversations of a U.S. senator.[23] Hayden stated, in his congressional testimony, that the NSA is not permitted to ask other countries to spy on people in the U.S., and denied that it is done.

Should we worry about monitoring by agencies of the U.S. government whose role is to protect us from criminals and terrorists? Some say only dishonest people and irrationally paranoid people would be so suspicious and critical of the U.S. government's intelligence gathering. The reaction of the European countries to Echelon suggests otherwise. The governments and people of Europe were furious that other governments—even those of democratic, free societies—were monitoring their communications. A European Parliament report encouraged their people and businesses to use secure encryption to protect their communications. No one likes to be spied on. Many do not trust the NSA.*

The terrorist attacks of 2001 and the ensuing efforts to track down terrorist leaders illustrate the importance of intelligence gathering. Because of the secrecy necessarily associated with international intelligence, we may never know why the NSA's sophisticated

---

*European (and other) governments engage in similar communications monitoring on a scale smaller than Echelon. Some have been accused of, and some have admitted, spying on American business people.[24]

surveillance system failed to detect plans of the attacks. Perhaps al Qaeda leaders knew enough about Echelon to send significant communications by means Echelon could not detect. Perhaps they used encryption the NSA could not break. Perhaps overconfidence in high-tech "Sigint" (signals intelligence) systems caused insufficient emphasis on "Humint" (human intelligence), such as informants. Political influences may have shifted focus toward drug dealers and economic spying. Whatever the reason, we observe that, while a system like Echelon can be of enormous benefit for learning of the plans and activities of terrorists, success is not automatic, and the many purposes to which it can be applied may distort its effectiveness.

THE IMPACT OF TECHNOLOGY ON THE POLITICAL ISSUES

The most serious issues related to Echelon are political ones. How much privacy should we be expected to give up in exchange for protection from the "bad guys"? (This question is at the core of all the controversies we discuss in this chapter.) How much information about a government's activities should be kept secret from its people in exchange for such protection? How much spying is appropriate for the U.S. government and its Echelon partners to do in free countries that are allies and friends? How reliable are the assurances of NSA officials that the NSA obeys existing legal standards for its activities? These questions are beyond the scope of this book, but awareness of the technical tools used in intelligence gathering could contribute toward the development of informed answers.

3.3 Cryptography and Its Uses

3.3.1 CRYPTOGRAPHY AND PUBLIC-KEY CRYPTOGRAPHY

Simply put, cryptography is the making and breaking of secret codes. More elegantly, it is "the art and science of hiding data in plain sight."[25] The point is to transform a message or data, called the *plaintext*, into a form that is meaningless to anyone who might intercept it. The message could be battle plans carried by a runner through territory occupied by an opposition army, or it could be business plans or medical records sent by e-mail over a computer network. The coded text is called *ciphertext*. The recipient of the ciphertext decodes it (this process is called *decryption*) and reads the plaintext message.

Encryption generally includes a coding scheme, or cryptographic algorithm, and a specific sequence of characters (e.g., digits or letters), called a *key*, used by the algorithm. For example, a coding scheme many children learn is one where each letter of the alphabet is replaced by another specific letter. A key would be a scrambled alphabet, for example, qwertyuiopasdfghjklzxcvbnm. With this key, each *a* in the message is replaced by *q*, each *b* is replaced by *w*, each *c* by an *e*, and so on. (This is not a good encryption scheme; it is easy to break.)

Encryption is used because someone else wants the information in the message. Thus, while some people are busy trying to develop good encryption algorithms, others are busy trying to develop methods to decode ciphertext. The latter endeavor is called *cryptanalysis*.

For all encryption methods used until recently, both the sender and the recipient of an encrypted message must know the key—and keep it secret from everyone else. This presents a problem. If the key could be safely sent by the same communication method as the message, encryption would not be needed. Generally, the key must be transmitted by a more secure, hence more expensive or difficult, method, perhaps an in-person meeting of the parties. The military can afford the expense of couriers, armed guards, and other means of getting keys to a relatively small number of officers, but, for individuals and most businesses that communicate with a large number of people and other businesses, this is impractical.

In the 1970s, a revolution in cryptography occurred. Whitfield Diffie and Martin Hellman developed an encryption scheme called *public key cryptography* that eliminates the need for secure transmission of keys and has a variety of other fascinating applications. Soon after, Ronald Rivest, Adi Shamir, and Leonard Adleman developed RSA, a practical implementation of the Diffie and Hellman method.* In this scheme, there are two mathematically related keys. One is used to encrypt a message, the other to decrypt it. The feature that makes public-key cryptography so remarkable is that knowing the key used to encrypt the message provides no help at all in decrypting it. Thus, each person can have his or her own key pair, and the encrypting key can be public; it is called the person's *public key*. The decrypting key is the person's *private key*. Public keys can be made widely available in directories. Anyone who wants to send someone a secret message can encrypt the message with the recipient's public key. Even if the ciphertext and the recipient's public key are known by an outsider, the outsider cannot decrypt the message. Only the recipient, using the private key, can do that.

One major advantage of public-key cryptography is that it eliminates the need to transmit a secret encryption key between the two parties. Indeed, it eliminates the need for any prior planning or communication between the parties. All that is needed is the recipient's public key. Thus, public-key cryptography provided encryption for e-mail and for economic transactions on the Internet.

Encryption schemes commonly used now for protecting data and communications are based on mathematical computations. The keys, strings of bits (zeros and ones), can vary in size. The strength, or security, provided by an encryption scheme depends on both the cryptographic algorithm and the length of the key. One can try to decode a message without the key by exploiting tricks based on weaknesses in the algorithm or by brute force—that is, by trying every possible key. If a 40-bit key is used, there are 2^{40}, or more than a trillion, possible keys (because there are two choices for each bit). Several decades ago, that was enough to make a brute-force attack worthless; with the computing power then available, it took too much time to try all the keys. In the 1990s, the 40-bit-key encryption standard of the 1970s could be cracked quickly, and RSA was used with 512-bit keys. With current encryption methods and key sizes, it is extremely difficult to decode a message without the proper key, even with the government's fastest computers.

---

*An engineer and two mathematicians working for a British intelligence agency developed a similar method several years earlier, but their work was classified and kept secret until 1997.[26]

3.3.2 USES OF ENCRYPTION

> *The technologies of anonymity and cryptography may be the only way to protect privacy.*
>
> —Nadine Strossen, president of the American Civil Liberties Union[27]

Church officials, lovers, and merchants have used codes in the past, but, for centuries, the most serious users were governments, their military agencies, and their spies. Most people never used encryption, except perhaps to play with codes on cereal boxes and cryptograms and similar puzzles in magazines and newspapers.

That has changed. Data transmitted by satellite can be "seen" by anyone with a satellite dish. E-mail that goes through several computers on its way to its destination may be read on any of those intermediate systems. Messages and data in transit can be read by wiretaps. Information sent to and from Web sites can be intercepted. Industrial espionage has a whole bag of new techniques. The Internet and e-commerce have enormously increased the need for security and secrecy of communications. Encryption is one of the main tools for providing them. A few examples of private-sector applications of encryption are listed in Figure 3.1. With the huge number of financial transactions that occur over computer networks, the second item alone shows the importance of encryption. By the mid-1990s, the Clearinghouse Interbank Payment System transmitted approximately one trillion dollars per day over wire and by satellite.[28] Encryption is essential to the integrity of the financial system. Note that, in addition to communications applications, encryption of stored material protects it from unauthorized access, modification, or theft by outsiders. Surveys of businesses show a high rate of unauthorized access to their computer systems; intruders include competing businesses and hackers. There have been numerous incidents of hackers stealing lists of customer credit-card numbers from Internet service providers and Web sites. The numbers are useless to a thief if they are encrypted. It may come

---

- Protecting communications from unauthorized access.
  Examples: e-mail, telephone.

- Protecting data in transit from unauthorized access (and manipulation for fraudulent purposes).
  Examples: credit-card numbers, for purchases on the Internet; Social Security numbers or personal financial data sent to a Web site; electronic transfer of funds between financial institutions.

- Protecting stored data from unauthorized access (and alteration).
  Examples: passwords and personal identification numbers stored on computer systems; bank records and other financial data (to protect against theft as well as to protect privacy); medical records; research and product-development files; personal files on home computers.

Figure 3.1 Uses of Encryption

- Authentication.
     Examples: digital signatures; techniques for verifying that documents have not been altered.

- Digital cash and micropayment systems (for buying services on the Web).

- Protection of intellectual property in electronic form from copyright infringement (unauthorized access and copying).
     Examples: electronic books, songs, and movies sold on the Web; cable-television signals. (We discuss problems and issues related to intellectual property in Chapter 6.)

Figure 3.2 More Uses of Encryption

to be expected as a routine security measure that sensitive information be encrypted in storage as well as during transmission, to protect against leaks and intruders.

A company that provided encryption for cellular phone calls reported that the biggest and fastest-growing segment of its customers consisted of lawyers. Lawyers are concerned about the ease with which they can be overheard, perhaps compromising attorney-client confidentiality and leaking information about negotiations or courtroom strategies. Football teams use radio helmets to transmit instructions to quarterbacks on the field; the transmissions are encrypted to protect them from the opposing team. Researchers and writers who collaborate over computer networks can encrypt their discussions and drafts of papers to protect their ideas before publication. Often, people are not even aware that they are using encryption; it is handled by the software on personal computers and Web sites. Some wireless telephones have built-in encryption.

Eavesdropping by private citizens and unauthorized access to computer systems are prohibited by law, but that is not sufficient protection. Burglary is illegal, but we put deadbolt locks on our doors, and some people install alarm systems in their homes. The law provides for punishment of offenders who are caught and convicted, but we use technology to protect ourselves. And we have seen that laws are sometimes ignored even by the people who are supposed to enforce them. Encryption is widely viewed as the most important technical method for ensuring the privacy of messages and data sent through computer networks.

Figure 3.2 lists applications of encryption whose purpose is not to keep something secret. The encryption techniques developed in recent years have a flexibility and variety of applications not previously associated with encryption. For example, they assure authenticity as well as privacy. We describe a few of these applications.

PROTECTION FROM THE "DOSSIER SOCIETY"

Money is coined liberty.

—Fyodor Dostoevsky[29]

Several companies are marketing systems that generate a unique credit-card number for each online transaction, providing both security and privacy. The credit card issuer generates the numbers and bills all of one person's charges to one account, so transactions are not totally private, but merchants cannot link transactions by credit-card number, and the number is useless to any hacker who steals it. Computer scientist David Chaum devised techniques using cryptography that make possible "digital cash" and other privacy-protected transactions.[30] Several companies are developing digital cash schemes. They can let us do secure financial transactions electronically without the seller acquiring a credit-card or checking-account number from the buyer. The techniques also ensure that bank records contain no information linking the payer and recipient of the funds. They combine the convenience of credit-card purchases with the anonymity of cash. Because a unit of digital cash is simply a file, it can be stored on one's hard disk at home and used for transactions on the Internet, or it can be stored on a Smart Card and used for shopping in stores. Digital cash carried on a card can be backed up at home, so, if the card is lost or stolen, the owner does not lose the cash. There are ways to prevent the same file from being spent twice, so duplicating a digital cash file is not a problem.

With such schemes, records of different transactions cannot be easily linked to form a consumer profile or dossier. These techniques provide both privacy protection for the consumer with respect to the organizations he or she interacts with and protection for organizations against forgery, bad checks, and credit-card fraud. They can help us keep our names off marketing lists, if we choose, and provide more control over personal information than many proposed laws for privacy protection. Cash transactions make it harder for governments to detect and prosecute people who are "laundering" money earned in illegal activities, earning money they are not reporting to tax authorities, or transferring or spending money for criminal purposes. Thus a truly anonymous digital cash system would be opposed and probably prohibited by most governments. Some people have speculated that, while the government emphasizes its concern about use of secure encryption by kidnappers, drug dealers, and terrorists, it might be equally concerned about the potential loss of tax revenue that could occur if most economic transactions and records were truly private. Some digital cash systems include provisions for law enforcement and tax collection. The potential illegal uses of digital cash have long been possible with real cash. It is only in recent decades, as we have increased our use of checks and credit cards, that we have lost the privacy we had from marketers and government when we used cash for most transactions.

DIGITAL SIGNATURES

For centuries, people put their signatures (or their mark) on such paper documents as contracts and checks to formalize a legal agreement or transaction. The signature binds us to a contract, authorizes sale of property, releases assets or funds to others, and so on. Of course, signatures can be forged, but our financial and legal systems rely on them. Now, we can review a deal, negotiate terms, and discuss drafts of contracts all by e-mail, but, in most cases, we still sign a paper copy. That practice is on the verge of a major change. One of the remarkable features of some public-key cryptography schemes lets us "sign" an electronic copy: The roles of the two keys can be reversed. That is, if a message is encrypted with the private key, it can be decrypted with the public key from that key pair (and by no other key). This feature provides *digital signatures*. A person who wishes to sign an electronic document can add a statement of acceptance to it and then encrypt it with his or her private key. The ciphertext can be decrypted with the person's public key. Applying any other key to the ciphertext produces gibberish. The document can be decrypted and read by the other parties to the contract, or by a court. The encrypted version is a signed contract because it could not have been encrypted except by using the signer's private key. (The actual techniques used for digital signatures are more complicated; this simplified description in intended to illustrate the basic idea.) By 2000, both the European Union and the U.S. had passed laws giving documents signed with digital signatures the same legal enforceability as those signed on paper. These laws, an example of the legal system adapting to a new technology, enabled huge growth in business and consumer transactions on the Web.

Suppose we want to send a private (secret), signed message. The digital-signature technique described so far has the flaw that the message can be read by anyone who has a copy of it, because it can be decrypted with a public key. To send a private, signed message, the sender can first encrypt the message with his or her own private key, thus "signing" it, then encrypt the ciphertext with the recipient's public key, generating ciphertext of the ciphertext. The recipient first applies his or her private key, then the sender's public key, and recovers the original plaintext message. Because the first stage of recovery requires the recipient's private key, no one else can decrypt the message.

Many computer science students and hackers know that, on some computer systems, it is easy to fake e-mail return addresses. One can send a message purporting to be from someone else, causing mischief or worse problems. Digital signatures can be used in applications where authentication of the sender is important. In another application of digital-signature technology, aimed at reducing the risk of unauthorized access to medical information online, the American Medical Association issues digital credentials to doctors that can be verified when a doctor, say, visits a laboratory Web site to get patient test results. There are likely to be thousands of applications of this technology.

CRIMINAL USE OF ENCRYPTION

> *Unfortunately, the same encryption technology that can help Americans protect business secrets and personal privacy can also be used by terrorists, drug dealers, and other criminals.*

> —Dee Dee Myers, White House Press Secretary, 1994[31]

Some pedophiles and child molesters encrypt child pornography and information about victims on their computers. A group of neo-Nazis in Germany encrypted messages on their bulletin board network, used to plan illegal activities. The Japanese organization

Aum Supreme Truth, which killed several people by releasing Sarin nerve gas in a subway, encrypted records. In some cases, law-enforcement officials were able to decrypt the files; in others, they could not. By 1997, there had been 500 criminal cases worldwide involving encryption; the number has likely grown significantly since then.[32] The U.S. Intelligence services learned much about the activities of al Qaeda by decrypting encrypted files on computers captured in Afganistan in 2001. In several other incidents, law-enforcement agencies decrypted files on computers seized from terrorists.

3.3.3 STEGANOGRAPHY

Steganography is the art and science of hiding a message. The message itself might or might not be encrypted, but the point of steganography is to hide the fact that the message exists. Early forms of steganography included physically hiding a message inside an object or writing messages in invisible ink. A message could be hidden in a book by making tiny marks over selected letters. Modern steganographic methods include hiding messages within digitized documents and images. For example, the spacing between lines of a document can be varied by a tiny, not obvious amount; the line numbers of the shifted lines can encode a message. The least significant bits of a digitized image or audio file can be changed without making a visible or audible difference; those bits can encode a message.

The Web provides new opportunities for use of steganography. Images and other files that hide messages can be posted to Web sites. The intended recipients of the hidden messages are effectively anonymous among the many people who visit the site. After the terrorist attacks in 2001, there was speculation that Osama bin Laden used such methods to communicate plans and orders for more terrorist attacks.

There are techniques to analyze digital files to detect steganographic alterations, but, if one does not know where to look, the message is safe. One research group analyzed two million files from eBay auctions in 2001 and found no hidden messages.[33] It is not feasible to search everything.

3.4 Encryption Policy: Access to Software, Keys, and Plaintext

3.4.1 SECRECY AND EXPORT CONTROLS

SECRECY

For decades, the main characteristic of U.S. government policy about cryptography was secrecy. Most of the cryptographers in the country worked for the National Security Agency (NSA). It reportedly is still the world's largest employer of mathematicians. One apparent goal of the NSA has been to design codes for the government that no other governments could break; another is to break everyone else's codes. The NSA almost certainly could break virtually any codes that were in use before the mid-1970s.[34] (An exception is a method called one-time pads, but it is inconvenient to use and is not significant in the issues discussed here.)

In an attempt to keep secure encryption methods out of the hands of enemies, terrorists, and private citizens, the government classified much information about cryptography as secret or confidential. It is a crime to give classified material to anyone who does not have government authorization to receive it. In the late 1970s, researchers in universities were developing public-key cryptography, and inventors were inventing scrambling devices. George Davida, an electrical engineer and computer scientist specializing in data security and cryptography, applied for a patent and instead received a "secrecy order" in the mail telling him he would be breaking the law if he told anyone about his work. The NSA tried to discourage cryptography researchers from publishing their work, threatening to classify it. The inventors and researchers fought back, and the NSA backed down. Next the NSA argued for a law either prohibiting distribution of cryptographic information completely or requiring that all such work be submitted to a government agency (presumably NSA) for approval prior to dissemination. An advisory group of academics approved a voluntary scheme whereby the NSA would ask that a specific work not be published. George Davida, the only member of the advisory group to vote against the plan, argued that such censorship was a dangerous precedent allowing the government to control the publication of scientific research. He said:

> It would be only too easy for us to lose our constitutional freedoms in bits and pieces. ... One gets the impression that the NSA is struggling to stand still, and to keep American research standing still with it, while the rest of the world races ahead. ... The NSA can best perform its mission in the old-fashioned way: Stay ahead of others.

Another tactic tried by the NSA was to take over funding for cryptography research from the National Science Foundation so that it could control the researchers.[35]

EXPORT RESTRICTIONS

Throughout the 1990s, the government maintained a costly and ultimately futile policy of prohibiting export of powerful encryption software. The government implemented the policy by classifying encryption software as "munitions," like tanks and bombs, which are subject to export control. Secure encryption (often called "strong crypto") was not approved for export.* The government argued that the export prohibition was necessary to keep strong encryption from terrorists and enemy governments.

The case of Philip Zimmermann illustrates the broad reach of the export restrictions. Zimmermann, a computer programmer, developed a program using public key cryptography for e-mail. He called it PGP (for Pretty Good Privacy). Believing that it was essential

---

*The terms "strong crypto" and "strong encryption" mean encryption that is so difficult and expensive to crack that it cannot, in practice, be done. The difficulty usually depends on the key size.

to provide people with a secure means of protecting their privacy, Zimmermann gave away his program for free. In 1991, copies of PGP appeared on numerous Internet sites in the U.S. from which it could be, and was, downloaded in other countries. The government began an investigation of Zimmermann; for more than two years he was under threat of indictment for exporting encryption and could have been sent to jail for several years. The government's position was that anything posted on the Internet was effectively exported. Zimmermann said that the investigation repressed his political speaking. PGP was widely distributed on the Internet and became the most popular program for e-mail encryption around the world.* Ironically, a law-enforcement expert recommended PGP to police departments and estimated that hundreds of law-enforcement officers were using it.[36] Eventually, the government closed the investigation without bringing charges, but it continued to interpret posting on the Internet as a form of export, hence illegal without a government license.

Encryption products produced by U.S. companies for export were less competitive than those of foreign companies that used the better encryption techniques. One data security expert reported that a $100 million contract for financial computer terminals went to a European company after U.S. companies were prohibited by the government from exporting a truly secure system. A survey in 1998 estimated that U.S. industry would lose 200,000 jobs and $60 billion in the next four years because of the export controls.[37]

U.S. software makers who included encryption software in their products had to go to the extra expense of making two versions of each product, one for the domestic market and one for export, or sell one weak version in both markets, or give up their export business. Many could not efficiently distribute two versions of the products, so they used the weaker, exportable version for all customers. International businesses with domestic and foreign offices had to use weak encryption that could be exported to overseas offices. The vulnerability of exportable encryption was highlighted in 1995 when a French student decoded a message encrypted by the foreign version of Netscape's Internet navigation software. Internet businesses complained that the export restrictions were slowing the growth of international electronic commerce.

The U.S. policy was strangely outdated, long before the government modified it. The stronger encryption schemes, including implementations of RSA and PGP, were available on Internet sites all over the world. In 1994, the federal government's Computer Systems Security and Privacy Advisory Board, made up of government and industry representatives, stated that "controls are negatively impacting U.S. competitiveness in the world market and are not inhibiting the foreign production and use of cryptography."[38] By 1997, there were almost 2000 strong-encryption software packages available outside the United States. Even the strong U.S. products were widely available—in illegal, pirated copies, for which the U.S. programmers and publishers received no income. In one case,

---

*RSA Data Security, the company founded by the developers of RSA, accused Zimmermann of violating its patents. Zimmermann signed an agreement to stop distributing PGP. PGP is still available on the Internet for free, but it is also sold by a company that licensed RSA's technology.

the government banned export of diskettes containing source code for cryptographic algorithms after allowing export of a book containing the identical algorithms. Many of the algorithms were in the public domain and had been published in other places; some originated outside the United States. The government's reason for distinguishing between the book and the diskettes was that providing the code on disks made it easier for someone to use it to provide encryption in a product. Critics of the decision pointed out that it was already quite easy to use optical character scanners to scan printed information such as the book and produce files identical to those on the disks.[39]

U.S. companies tried several tactics to legally get around the export restrictions. Some companies set up subsidiaries or formed partnerships with companies in other countries to develop and sell strong encryption systems from outside the United States. Some exported software designed so that encryption programs like PGP could be used with it, even though the software did not actually include the encryption programs. Although these actions did not violate the export restrictions, the government, determined to thwart the use of strong encryption, threatened investigations and prosecution.[40] Government officials continued to argue that the export restrictions kept strong encryption from many international terrorists, criminals, and unfriendly foreign powers.

During the 1990s, the encryption policies of other countries varied. France prohibited its citizens from using encryption; some countries had looser export restrictions than the United States. The U.S. government continually tried to convince European governments to impose strict restrictions on encryption. In various policy documents in the late 1990s, especially after publicity about the Echelon system (Section 3.2.4), the European Union and other governments rejected the U.S. approach and adopted rules supporting secure encryption and loose export controls.

Under intense pressure from major companies in the computer industry, civil libertarians, privacy advocates, and activist users of the Internet, the U.S. government finally, at the end of the 1990s, began to relax the export restrictions. It was a step-by-grudging-step process. The government agreed to approve export of systems with built-in techniques to allow the government to obtain the encryption keys. It allowed export of strong encryption systems to large financial institutions in other countries. It allowed export to a select list of countries. The pressure from opponents to the export controls continued.

During this time, the courts were considering legal challenges to the export restrictions, ones based on the First Amendment. The question is whether cryptography algorithms, and computer programs in general, are speech and hence protected by the First Amendment. Cryptography researcher Daniel Bernstein filed suit against the government in 1993. He wanted to publish his work, including encryption algorithms, on the Internet and discuss it at technical conferences and other public meetings. The rules required that he obtain a license from the State Department and report to the government everyone who received a copy of his work. Penalties for failure to comply included a large fine and a long jail sentence. The requirement that each recipient of the work be tracked and reported made distribution or discussion of the work on the Internet impossible. Bernstein's suit argued that the export restrictions, intended for military equipment, violated the First Amendment when applied to publications. It claimed that by denying the right to publish, the government's regulations abridged the constitutional freedom to speak, publish, associate with others, and engage in academic inquiry.[41] The government argued that software is not speech and that control of cryptography is a national-security issue, not a freedom-of-speech issue; the restrictions were necessary to keep strong cryptography from potential foreign enemies and terrorists. The federal judge who heard the case stated in 1996 that

> This court can find no meaningful difference between computer language . . . and German or French. . . . Like music and mathematical equations, computer language is just that, language, and it communicates information either to a computer or to those who can read it. . . . For the purposes of First Amendment analysis, this court finds that source code is speech.[42]

The Bernstein case and others continued for several more years, but in 1999 and 2000, two federal appeals courts ruled that the export restrictions violate freedom of speech. One court praised cryptography as a means of protecting privacy.

In 2000, the U.S. government removed almost all export restrictions on encryption.

People devised many theories about why the U.S. government insisted on maintaining strict limits on export and tried hard and long to convince other countries to do the same when strong crypto was already so widespread, so easily available to terrorists, and so important for security and electronic commerce. Some speculated that the government wanted to reduce the use of strong crypto by ordinary citizens so it could spy on anyone. Some speculated that the purpose was to ensure its ability to monitor all economic transactions and collect taxes, some that the government did not want development of e-cash systems to threaten its control of the money supply and monetary policy.[43] In their book *Privacy on the Line*, Whitfield Diffie and Susan Landau offered three very plausible explanations.[44] Although other agencies had the official role of deciding what exports to approve, it was generally believed that the NSA made the decisions. The NSA sifts through huge amounts of communications. If all communications were encrypted, the task of determining which messages to capture and read would be more difficult. Diffie and Landau suggest that the main goal of the export rules was to restrict encryption to what the NSA could routinely crack in "real time," that is, as the messages are scanned. Another goal, they suggest, was to prevent adoption of standard cryptography systems. Standards would encourage more use of encryption and make it harder for the NSA to distinguish the messages it wants to read. Finally, they point out that the export rules required that companies that wanted to export encryption systems had to disclose the details of their products to the government, ensuring that the NSA had full knowledge of the technologies in use.

The combination of the court decisions on publication of crypto research, the obvious need for strong encryption in electronic commerce, and the continuing complaints from industry about lost business might be enough to explain the government's policy change after years of fighting to maintain the export restrictions. However, there is another intriguing factor to consider. The early rules allowed export of encryption using the Data Encryption Standard (DES), developed by IBM and the NSA, with 40-bit keys, but not 56-bit keys. The government allowed export of 56-bit DES at about the time that researchers were cracking it. RSA encryption with 512-bit keys was considered uncrackable for a long time. It was widely used in Web browsers and commercial applications, e.g., for transmitting credit-card numbers on the Web. In 1999, researchers, including Adi Shamir, one of the developers of RSA, showed that 512-bit RSA could be cracked. Shamir said the special-purpose computer he designed for the job probably could be built for only $5000.[45] The question is: If researchers could discover and develop the methods to crack once highly secure codes, what about the NSA? With its huge budget and powerful computer systems, by 2000, the NSA had possibly regained the lead; it might be able to decrypt messages fast enough to scan encrypted traffic and read most of the communications it wants to read.

3.4.2 DOMESTIC ENCRYPTION CONTROLS?

There have never been legal restrictions on the use of encryption in the United States.

In 1992, AT&T was about to sell telephones equipped with encryption to the public. Everyone—individuals, businesses, and criminals and terrorists—could, if they chose, encode their messages and telephone conversations so that the government could not understand them. A journalist described this situation as "the NSA's worst nightmare." We review attempts by the U.S. government to control use of encryption within the U.S.

KEY ESCROW AND THE CLIPPER CHIP

In 1993, the government announced the Clipper Chip, its first attempt to ensure its access to encryption keys, and thereby created a blistering public controversy.

The opposition ranged across the political spectrum, including civil libertarians, conservative talk-show host Rush Limbaugh, industry groups, privacy advocates, and a colorful group of people called cypherpunks. One writer describes the cypherpunks as a "loose-knit band of scrappy, libertarian-leaning computer jockeys who have dedicated themselves to perfecting and promoting the art of disappearing into the virtual hinterlands."[46] Some wear long hair and sandals and earned millions of dollars from their pioneering work in computer technologies, and all of them believe that privacy from government and large business institutions must be protected.

The Clipper Chip, designed for telephones, used an encryption algorithm, called Skipjack, developed by the NSA. Skipjack was also implemented on chips for computers.[47] The Clipper Chip and several of the government's later proposals used a form of *key escrow*. That means that a copy of the encryption keys is kept by some organization other than the user of the encryption. The organization is called an *escrow agent*. Law-enforcement agents, with a court order, could get a key from an escrow agent. The government designated two government agencies as escrow agents for the Clipper Chip and made it clear that it wanted the system to become standard for all telephone and computer communications. The fact that the government itself would keep the keys was one of the many aspects of the plan that drew opposition. We have seen that government employees in the IRS and Social Security Administration illegally sold data from government records. How confident should we be that the keys would be well protected?

The algorithm used in the government-designed chips was secret. It was kept secret so that people (in the U.S. and in other countries) could not use it in other devices without providing the keys to the government's escrow agents. The NSA, quite sensibly, does not want the results of its work in developing a strong encryption algorithm to be available to foreign individuals and foreign governments—the very people whose communications the NSA monitors. However, many problems arise from the use of secrecy. We discuss some in Section 3.5.1.

The government dropped its goal of widespread use of the Clipper Chip because of technical flaws and political opposition. It began a series of alternative proposals for key-escrow and key-recovery plans, in which other encryption methods could be used yet the government would still have access to the keys (with an appropriate court order). An assistant to then-President Clinton explained the government support of encryption controls by saying:

> The Government was concerned that the widespread use of this [encryption] technology could make lawfully authorized electronic surveillance much more difficult. Historically, law enforcement encountered very little encryption, owing largely to the expense and difficulty in using such technology. With growing availability of lower-cost, commercial encryption technology for use by U.S. industry and private citizens, it became clear that a strategy was needed that could accommodate the needs of the private sector for top-notch communications security; of U.S. industry to remain competitive in the world's secure communications market; and of U.S. law enforcement to conduct lawfully-authorized electronic surveillance.[48]

KEY RECOVERY

There are good business and personal reasons for using some sort of key-recovery system. If a company employee is not available and someone else in the company must read files that were encrypted by the employee, there is a problem. If someone loses an encryption key, encrypted files cannot be decrypted. A number of businesses developed key recovery plans. There are many possibilities. Large companies and organizations can establish their own escrow office for their employees. Bonded companies, like escrow companies that process real estate purchases, can offer key escrow service to businesses and individuals.

With commercial key-escrow and key-recovery services, law-enforcement agencies would be able to obtain messages and have them decoded by escrow agents by using search warrants and court orders without any fundamental change in its older powers or procedures. When commercial key escrow and key recovery develop as services available in the market, there are no major political issues. The government, however, used the advantages described above to argue for compulsory key-recovery plans. There was constant opposition, and none was adopted.

VOLUNTARY OR COMPULSORY?

One of the big weaknesses of key-escrow and key-recovery schemes was that, even if they were widely adopted, drug dealers and terrorists could use other devices and software to encrypt their messages. Government officials argued that, even if criminals and terrorists used another form of encryption when communicating among themselves, they would be using escrowed encryption when communicating with legitimate businesses, and those communications would be helpful to law enforcement. However, the obvious "loophole" in any voluntary scheme led many observers to believe the government's goal was to outlaw other encryption methods. The government frequently claimed that use of key-escrow encryption would be voluntary. For example, in 1994, an administration official told a Congressional committee:

> As the Administration has made clear on a number of occasions, the key escrow encryption initiative is a voluntary one; we have absolutely no intention of mandating private use of a particular kind of cryptography, nor of criminalizing the private use of certain kinds of cryptography.[49]

However, in a 1993 document obtained by the Electronic Privacy Information Center from the FBI under the Freedom of Information Act, the FBI, NSA and Department of Justice had already concluded that

> Technical solutions, such as they are, will only work if they are incorporated into all encryption products. To ensure that this occurs, legislation mandating the use of Government-approved encryption products or adherence to Government encryption criteria is required.[50]

Another FBI document advocated legislation prohibiting cryptography that did not meet the government standard.[51]

THE NATIONAL RESEARCH COUNCIL REPORT

In the midst of the encryption controversies, Congress requested that the National Research Council (NRC), the research affiliate of the National Academy of Sciences, do a thorough study of U.S. encryption policy and make recommendations. The NRC report, prepared by a panel of experts from business, government, and academia, was completed in 1996. It strongly supported the use of powerful encryption and loosening of export controls. The report stated that there should be no law barring manufacture, sale, or use of any form of encryption in the United States. It argued that strong encryption provides increased protection against hackers, thieves, and terrorists who threaten our economic, electric-power, and transportation infrastructures. It argued that the free market and business needs for data protection would do a better job than the National

WARTIME METHODS—BANNING FLOWER ARRANGEMENTS

When trying to measure the depth of the government's concern about information passed secretly to or among enemies, it may help to consider some of the restrictions placed on communications in wartime. During World War II, the government employed almost 15,000 people to open mail going overseas to eliminate any that contained military information of use to Germany or Japan. The censors read a million pieces of mail per day. They also listened to telephone conversations and read magazines and movie scripts. The drawings of children were suspect; they could mask a map of some sort. Crossword puzzles could contain hidden messages. And so could knitting instructions, moves in a chess game played by mail, orders of flowers that specified the particular types of flowers to be included, and phoned-in requests to radio stations to play specific songs. Any of these normally innocent things could be a form of code, giving vital information to an enemy. Many of these activities were simply banned during the war. During the Persian Gulf War, military censors refused to allow Navajos at home to broadcast greetings on Armed Forces Radio to their relatives and friends stationed overseas. They feared that the Navajos could be transmitting secret information. (During World War II, the Marines used Navajos to do exactly that; a military code was developed using the spoken Navajo language. Because of the Navajo contribution to that war, public attention shamed the censors into lifting the ban in the Gulf War.)[52]

In wartime, the highest priority of the government is to win the war. The fear that there might be one secret enemy message hidden in the thousands of innocent drawings, songs, flower arrangements, or Navajo greetings was enough to restrict the freedom and peaceful activities of everyone. Two questions arise from this history. Were these actions paranoia on the government's part or a reasonable precaution to protect the lives and freedom of Americans? How relevant are such restrictions to times of peace, or wars on drugs, or wars against terrorists?

Security Agency and the FBI. It said that plans that rely on government escrow of keys would have security and liability risks.[53]

The government ignored the NRC report. It considered such compulsory controls as licensing of escrow agents, requiring that all users of encryption use a licensed agent, and banning nonescrowed encryption. From the Clipper Chip onward, the proposals evolved, becoming less specific about the particular technology to be used, but broader in coverage and more clear in providing compulsory access by government to plaintext. Various bills were drafted to implement some of these proposals, but none passed. At the same time, opponents of the government's position introduced bills to protect the right of Americans to use any encryption they chose and to end export controls. None of these passed either.

IMMEDIATE ACCESS TO PLAINTEXT

In 1997, the following statement was inserted in a bill under consideration in Congress:

> After January 31, 2000, all encryption products manufactured or imported for sale or use in the United States must include features that permit immediate decryption of the encrypted data upon the receipt of a valid court order.[54]

This bill went well beyond the various key-escrow and key-recovery schemes. The requirement for immediate decryption was new. Like CALEA, it set standards for the technology itself. The decryption requirement would cover encryption that protects communications in transit and data stored on computer disks. Wording in other amendments introduced at about the same time made it clear that the decryption was to be accomplished without the knowledge or cooperation of the person whose information was requested by the government.

To opponents, the statement was an extreme and shocking extension of government power. An immediate decryption feature would drastically weaken encryption systems, threatening privacy and security of electronic commerce. To supporters, it simply implemented the statement of purpose we quoted at the beginning of Section 3.1 and would allow law-enforcement agencies to do their job. The bill generated enormous opposition; it did not pass. Although some law-enforcement officials continued to argue for such a law, there was no serious discussion about it for a few years. Immediately after the terrorist attacks in 2001, support revived for a law requiring that all encryption have a "back door" for law enforcement. Many technical experts argued that such a law would be extraordinarily difficult to implement because encryption is now embedded in Web browsers and many other common computing tools. They also argued that terrorists would simply use encryption methods that did not comply with the law. No requirement for a "back door" for law enforcement was included in the USA PATRIOT Act, the law that increased government surveillance and wiretapping authority after the attacks.

IS THE GENIE OUT OF THE BOTTLE?

Cypherpunks and others who support our right to use whatever technical means we choose to protect our privacy are fond of saying, "The genie is out of the bottle." They mean that strong encryption is so widely available that governments cannot stop its use. This argument misses some serious consequences of proposals to ban encryption without an immediate decryption feature for law enforcement. Consider the analogy of drug laws. They have not stopped the use of drugs, but the drug laws force users into criminal society, contribute to corruption of law-enforcement personnel, and allow violations of standard principles of justice (e.g., seizure of property of people suspected, but not convicted, of violating the law). Forcing secure encryption underground would jeopardize the freedom of noncriminal, honest people who simply believe in protecting privacy. If the mere distribution or use of secure encryption is a crime, the government can put its critics, or people with unpopular views, in jail without proving that they have done anything that is otherwise illegal.

In addition, increases in computer power make older encryption schemes almost worthless. In the same year that Adi Shamir described a system to crack RSA encryption with 512-bit keys, he also cracked the code used in millions of cell phones worldwide.[55] If encryption without law-enforcement access were outlawed, software companies would not continue to develop and sell new, updated versions. Secure encryption might be developed and distributed in the cyberspace underground—and by well-funded terrorists, organized crime groups, and other governments—but would not be available for e-commerce and for most people's e-mail and personal privacy.

3.5 Fundamental Issues

3.5.1 THE ROLE OF SECRECY

To maintain its control over cryptography and access to communications, the government has regularly used secrecy—of cryptographic research, its wiretapping difficulties caused by new technology (in the CALEA debate), its algorithms (in the Clipper Chip), its software (Carnivore), and everything about Echelon. During the CALEA debate, when several organizations used the Freedom of Information Act (FOIA) to obtain internal government memos about wiretapping difficulties, the FBI stalled until after the law passed. There is an excellent reason for the government to try to keep the details of its algorithms, software, and wiretapping capabilities secret: Disclosing information can help criminals and terrorists.

There are, however, problems with secrecy.

Consider secret algorithms and software. Computer scientists cannot evaluate the protection secret algorithms provide from hackers or industrial spies. The quality of an encryption algorithm is quite important. More than one expert has suggested that the security of our vast communications and financial systems, and the economic health of our technology export business, may be more important to our national security than being able to read secret messages of potential enemies.[56] To reassure the technical community and the public that the algorithm used in the Clipper Chip was secure, the government allowed a panel of cryptography experts to examine the algorithm after agreeing not to disclose any details. They concluded that there was no significant risk that it could be broken. A few months later a scientist at AT&T found a flaw in the design. Although the flaw was not one that compromised the encryption itself, the finding illustrates that a small panel of experts can miss something. New techniques and technologies are more robust and reliable if they are exposed to testing and experimentation by many researchers, engineers, and customers.

When an encryption algorithm designed by the NSA for public use is kept secret, there is the possibility, or the concern about the possibility, that the NSA has built in a back door that lets government agencies decrypt messages without getting a court order. Secrecy of software such as that in Carnivore similarly leaves open the possibility that the software can be used to intercept e-mail from people for whom the FBI does not have a court order or can be used to copy more information than the order permits.

The involvement of the secretive NSA is yet another issue. In the discussions about encryption standards in the 1970s and 80s, the National Institute of Standards and Technology (NIST) was the public participant, although people in the industry and others believed that the NSA was directing the government's positions and decisions. With the Clipper Chip, the NSA apparently gave up its attempts to stay in the background. Documents released to Computer Professionals for Social Responsibility under the FOIA indicate that the NSA was also involved in devising the FBI's wiretap bills that led to CALEA.[57] Some people see the involvement of the NSA in domestic communications policy as sinister in and of itself. Spy agencies are not known for their adherence to constitutional rights. Spokesmen for the Electronic Frontier Foundation wrote:

> Inasmuch as digital privacy policy has broad implications for constitutional rights of free speech and privacy, these issues must be explored and resolved in an open, civilian policy context. This principle is clearly articulated in the Computer Security Act of 1987. ... The structure of the Act arose, in significant part, from the concern that the national security establishment was exercising undue control over the flow of public information and the use of information technology. When considering the law in 1986, the Congress asked the question, 'Whether it is proper for a super-secret agency [the NSA] that operates without public scrutiny to involve itself in domestic activities...?' The answer was a clear no. ...[58]

3.5.2 THE EVER-CHANGING STATUS QUO

In defending its efforts to obtain the plaintext of communications, from Clipper Chip to key escrow to CALEA to Carnivore, the FBI argued repeatedly that it was not asking for any new powers; it was just maintaining the status quo. To the FBI, the status quo was the fact that they could intercept and read any communication they wanted. Opponents argue that CALEA and Carnivore include significant changes from the previous thirty years (not to mention the long history of opposition to wiretapping that preceded the 1968 law): CALEA mandated that telecommunications equipment be designed for interception, and Carnivore lets the FBI sift through thousands of people's e-mail rather than just having a tap on the line of the target of a court order.

Arguments about the status quo, on either side of the debate, are rather silly. The "status quo" is the existing state of affairs at any particular time. What time shall we choose? Technology is always changing the status quo. Before the telephone and telegraph, any two people—honest or criminal—who wanted to have a private conversation could walk some distance from other people and converse. No neighbor or police officer could intercept the conversation. The telegraph, telephone, and radio allowed people to communicate over distance—quite a change in the status quo, but they allowed easy interception. Codes and ciphers have been used for a few thousand years. For centuries, people did not know how to break simple codes we now consider trivial; encrypted messages could not be read by those who intercepted them. Then methods were discovered to break those codes, and for centuries, many governments, employing the best cryptanalysts, could decode any message they intercepted. In the 16th century, a new scheme for making codes was developed. It was unbreakable until the 19th century. During World War I, many new codes were generated, but they were quickly broken. The pace of research and technological change has speeded up. Public-key cryptography gave us unbreakable codes—for a while. The "unbreakable" 512-bit RSA of the 1990s is now threatened, and longer keys are used. A new technique under development, called quantum computing, could threaten the secure codes of today. A new technique, called quantum cryptography, might lead to new unbreakable codes.[59] There is no good reason why the status of privacy or the government's ability to intercept and decode communications at a particular time should be adopted as a moral or political standard just because it is the status quo.

3.5.3 TRUST IN GOVERNMENT

We have seen abuses of wiretapping by the FBI and local police agencies throughout the 20th century. We have seen abuses by the NSA. We have seen that the government was not completely honest in its early claims that it did not intend to impose any restrictions on the encryption American citizens could use. In addition, some of its arguments were disingenuous. For example, the government presented the Clipper Chip and key escrow as tools to improve privacy. In 1993, few telephone conversations and e-mail messages were encrypted at all; the government compared the level of privacy using key escrow with the level that was current at the time. The motivation for the government's proposals came from worries about the likely future of private, fully secure encryption. They were trying to reduce the level of privacy that would otherwise become available.

Throughout the wiretapping and encryption controversies, the government emphasized that it could wiretap and obtain encryption keys only with a court order. It insisted it was not trying to expand its power; it agreed not to insist on tracking people's location. Throughout the same time, the FBI continually tried to expand its wiretapping authority, for example to allow emergency wiretaps without court orders in more situations, to reduce the requirements for roving wiretaps (tapping phones used near a target individual without having to get authorization for the specific phones), and to allow tracking the location of a cell-phone user—without a court order in emergencies. (Roving wiretaps were authorized in 1999.) The FBI secretly installed a key logger system (a system that records every key a person types) on a gambling suspect's personal computer to obtain his encryption key. It also collected e-mail he typed, without a court order for a wiretap. Secret access to everything typed on one's keyboard, including e-mail, seems to go well beyond a constitutional search.

Secure encryption can hide terrorist messages, but it can also protect *against* terrorists, especially when the terrorists are in power. Philip Zimmermann, author of PGP, widely publicized a message he received from Latvia telling him that PGP was very popular among the anti-Soviet underground. International human-rights organizations routinely use

PGP to protect dissidents and informers. The CryptoRights Foundation promotes the use of cryptographic communications tools to protect human-rights workers. Zimmermann said Americans do not understand why he is so paranoid about the government, "but people in police states, you don't have to explain it to them. They already get it, and they don't understand why we don't."[60]

What law-enforcement surveillance and interception policies are appropriate when we use computer networks for casual e-mail, purchases, access to discussion groups and information services, and sensitive business and financial communications? Should communications systems be designed to meet "a nationwide standard for surveillance," or should they use the best technology available for achieving speed, convenience, low cost, and privacy? How much should the freedom and privacy of honest and peaceful people be weakened to aid the government's law-enforcement activities? How far can we trust the government not to abuse its power?

There are very strong emotions on both sides of the debates about access to communications. To some people it seems so obvious that legitimate law-enforcement needs require that the government have access to any communication (with a court order). To others the potential for abuse is the overriding concern. I have puzzled over the question of why "gut reactions" differ so much. Perhaps it is because the same agency that deals with the horrors of kidnapped children and terrorist bombings also infiltrates and wiretaps groups whose religious or political views differ from the mainstream or are simply opponents of powerful people. Tension about the powers of law enforcement arises from laws that are unpopular with large segments of the peaceful, normally law-abiding public, both on the left and right (e.g., laws against use of marijuana and laws against ownership of certain guns). This tension will probably not diminish as long as the same law-enforcement agencies protect us from violent criminals and terrorists and also suppress contrary ideas and unconventional activities.

HOW MUCH DOES TECHNOLOGY MATTER?

The quote that follows is from a paper by one of my students. Like the example of Stasi, with which we opened Chapter 2, he reminds us that many governments around the world oppress their people, denying privacy and freedom of speech, and they do it without advanced technology. It reminds us too, I hope, of the importance of protecting freedom and privacy, whatever the level of technology.

> *In western countries, with the development of ingenious electronic devices, Big Ears and Big Eyes hide in the deep blue sky. Satellites see us in action in our backyard, and if needed, our conversations are wiretapped by some powerful agencies. . . . In less developed countries, surveillance is realized by human eyes and ears. In Vietnam where the freedom of speech is "legally" banned, I remember being taught to listen to family members and report conversations having some specific keywords, such as "communism," "United States," "old government" . . . and I would have done it for the good of my country. I'd*

witnessed kid-heroes sending their families to concentration camps. Without freedom of speech, with fear of speaking, we listened with resignation.

—Thuc Luu[61]

EXERCISES

Review Exercises

3.1   Describe at least three different kinds of uses of encryption that have social value. (Indicate why they are valuable.)

3.2   What is an important difference between public-key cryptography and secret-key cryptography?

3.3   What is the main difference between the Communications Assistance for Law Enforcement Act of 1994 and the wiretapping capability the government had before?

3.4   What kinds of information does Echelon collect?

3.5   Give two reasons why the U.S. government eventually dropped most encryption-export controls.

3.6   What are some reasons why a business might choose to use a private system to escrow encryption keys?

3.7   What were some of the communications censored by the U.S. government during World War II?

3.8   Give an example of the use of secrecy in an attempt to protect an encryption algorithm.

General Exercises

3.9   An online bookseller that provided e-mail service for a large number of book stores saved copies of thousands of e-mail messages and analyzed them to collect data on sales trends. Was this legal? Explain.

3.10 Among the threats from which the Communications Assistance for Law Enforcement Act is designed to protect us, which do you think is the most serious? Which arguments against the Communications Assistance for Law Enforcement Act do you think are the strongest?

3.11 According to the FBI, why is Carnivore needed? According to its critics, what are the main risks or privacy threats from Carnivore?

3.12 Explain how public-key cryptography provides a mechanism for digitally "signing" a document.

3.13 You are trying to decode an encrypted message without the key. Suppose it takes five minutes of computing time to try every 40-bit key. You are given a message encoded by the same algorithm, but using 41-bit keys.

a) Roughly how much computer time would it take to try all possible keys?

b) Suppose computers become a million times faster, but the encryption scheme uses 512-bit keys. How much time would it take to try all possible keys?

3.14 Two examples of use of PGP are (1) neo-Nazi bulletin boards with information about illegal activities, and (2) interviews with victims and/or witnesses of death-squad activities, presumably sanctioned by the government, in a Third World country. Do these examples balance each other out when one is considering whether the government should have access to encrypted communications and files, or does one case give a more compelling argument for one side?

3.15 Give similarities and differences between requirements to register our cars and requirements to register our encryption keys.

3.16 Explain what the right to send e-mail in encrypted form means as a negative right and what it means as a positive right. Be specific; give an example of what might violate the right or what might be necessary to implement it.

3.17 Give two examples from the box in Section 3.4.2 that are examples of steganography.

3.18 Digital cash can be designed to allow transactions to be made securely and anonymously. Considering the privacy benefits and the potential for use by tax evaders and criminals, do you think fully anonymous digital cash should be made illegal? Give your reasons.

3.19 Consider commercial key recovery, described in Section 3.4.2. Give some arguments in favor of requiring by law that all business users of encryption use a key-recovery system approved by the government. Give some arguments against such a requirement.

3.20 In 2001, the FBI held closed meetings with telecommunications industry representatives and attempted to keep secret the technical standards being developed to aid the FBI in intercepting communications. Technical standards are normally developed openly by engineers and others in the appropriate fields. Discuss arguments for and against keeping telecommunications standards secret.

Assignments

These exercises require some research or activity.

3.21 Contact police departments in your area and ask whether they can describe a case where they used wiretapping or e-mail interception to catch or convict a criminal. Write a summary of such a case.

3.22 Find information from a company making software for digital cash and report on any one of its products. What are some advantages and some disadvantages of using the product?

3.23 Has important new legislation about encryption been passed since this book was published?

3.24 What has been the impact so far of changes in government policies for interception of telephone and e-mail communications after the terrorist attack on the World Trade Center and Pentagon in 2001?

Class Discussion Exercises

These exercises are for class discussion, perhaps with short presentations prepared in advance by small groups of students.

3.25 Hold a debate in class on the question of whether the FBI should be permitted to continue to use Carnivore.

3.26 James Bidzos, president of RSA Data Security, offered an analogy to the concern about criminal use of secure encryption. He suggested that law-enforcement agencies could have made similar arguments against the building of the interstate highway system. Criminals could flee to different states or transport stolen goods across state lines. We recognize that, yes, these are indeed problems, but the economic and personal benefits from a safe, convenient, efficient transportation system outweigh the problems.[62]

Is this a good analogy? Develop other analogies where we use a tool that can be seriously misused by criminals, but we accept the risk because of the benefits. How well do the arguments about trade-offs in these analogies apply to the use of secure encryption? Do the benefits of secure encryption outweigh the risks?

NOTES

1. Senate Bill 266, Senators Biden and DeConcini.

2. John Perry Barlow, in "Decrypting the Puzzle Palace," *Communications of the ACM*, July 1992, 35:7, p. 25–31.

3. The historic information in this section is from Alan F. Westin, *Privacy and Freedom*, Atheneum, 1968, Alexander Charns, *Cloak and Gavel: FBI Wiretaps, Bugs, Informers, and the Supreme Court*, University of Illinois Press, 1992 (Chapter 8); Edith Lapidus, *Eavesdropping on Trial*, Hayden Book Co., 1974; and Walter Isaacson, *Kissinger: A Biography*, Simon and Schuster, 1992.

4. *Nardone v. U.S.* 302 U.S. 379(1937).

5. The quote is in the foreword of Lapidus, *Eavesdropping on Trial*.

6. For example: U.S. Department of State, "Country Reports for Human Rights Practices for 1996," Jan. 30, 1997. www.state.gov/www/global/human_rights/hrp_reports_mainhp.html.

7. Mark Leccese, "Telecomputing and the U.S. Constitution: Steve Jackson Games Goes to Trial," *Connect*, May/June 1993, pp. 38–43. "Electronic Publishing, Bulletin Board E-Mail, and the Steve Jackson Games Case," *Legal Bytes*, published by George, Donaldson & Ford, Winter 1992–93, 1:1, p. 5. Dorothy Denning, "The United States vs. Craig Neidorf," *Communications of the ACM*, March 1991, 34:3, pp. 23–32. www.sjgames.com/SS. "10th Anniversary of USSS Raid on Steve Jackson Games & Illuminati BBS," *EFFector*, Mar. 1, 2000, 13:2 (www.eff.org).

8. Robin Hanson, "Can Wiretaps Remain Cost Effective?" *Communications of the ACM*, Dec. 1994, 37:12, pp. 13–15.

9. "Just Published," *Privacy Journal*, June 2000, p. 7. "Federal Wiretaps Stay at High Level," *Privacy Journal*, June 1996, p. 6. Robert Fox, "Newstrack," *Communications of the ACM*, July 1994, 37:7, p. 9. "In Congress: FBI Wiretapping Proposal on a Fast Track," *Privacy Journal*, Sept. 1994, p. 3. Hoffman *et al.*, p. 115. Dorothy E. Denning and William E. Baugh, Jr., "Encryption and Evolving Technologies As Tools of Organized Crime and Terrorism," National Strategy Information Center, 1997.

10. John Schwartz, "Industry Fights Wiretap Proposal," *Washington Post*, March 12, 1994, p. C1, C7.

11. "Overkill By the FBI For New Tapping Authority," *Privacy Journal*, Dec. 1993, p. 3.

12. "Independent Technical Review of the Carnivore System," Illinois Institute of Technology Research Institute, Nov. 17, 2000, www.usdoj.gov/jmd/publications/carniv_entry.htm. David Banisar, "A Review of New Surveillance Technologies," *Privacy Journal*, Nov. 2001, pp. 1, 5–7. www.epic.org/privacy/carnivore/foia_documents.html

13. Guy Chazan, "A High-Tech Folk Hero Challenges Russia's Right to Snoop," *Wall Street Journal*, Nov. 27, 2000, p. A28. Christopher Hamilton, "Russians Fight for Net Privacy," *ABCNEWS.com*, June 12, 1999. The treaty is at http://conventions.coe.int/treaty/EN/projets/cybercrime27.htm. Will Rodger, "Trans-Atlantic Treaty Would Authorize Close Monitoring of Internet Usage," *Privacy Journal*, June 2001, 27:8, pp. 1, 4.

14. Ted Bridis, "FBI's E-Mail Suggests Divisions On Legality of Web Surveillance," *Wall Street Journal*, Dec. 7, 2000, p. B9.

15. Gregory Vistica, "Inside the Secret Cyberwar," *Newsweek*, Feb. 21, 2000, p. 48. The 2001 budget estimate is from the Federation of American Scientists (www.fas.org).

16. James Bamford, *The Puzzle Palace: A Report on NSA, America's Most Secret Agency*, Houghton Mifflin, 1982, p. 12. Testimony of Gen. Hayden. Bamford, *Body of Secrets*, pp. 435–440.

17. Neil King Jr., "As Technology Evolves, Spy Agency Struggles To Preserve Its Hearing," *Wall Street Journal*, May 23, 2001, p. A1, A10.

18. European Parliament, "An Appraisal of Technologies of Political Control," Jan. 6, 1998, and European Parliament, "Interception Capabilities 2000," Apr. 1999. These documents (and others about Echelon) are available at www.privacy.org/pi/activities/tapping. Report of the Temporary Committee on the Echelon Interception System, May 2001, www.europarl.eu.int/tempcom/echelon/pdf/prechelon_en.pdf. Echelonwatch FAQ, www.aclu.org/echelonwatch/faq.html, visited Feb. 7, 2001.

19. James Bamford, *Body of Secrets: Anatomy of the Ultra-Secret National Security Agency, from the Cold War Through the Dawn of a New Century*, Doubleday, 2001, pp. 404, 409.

20. Statement for the Record of NSA Director Lt. General Michael V. Hayden, USAF; House Permanent Select Committee on Intelligence, Apr. 12, 2000. www.nsa.gov/releases/DIR_HPSCI_12APR.HTML.

21. Neil King Jr., "Security Agency Defends Eavesdrop Use," *Wall Street Journal*, Apr. 13, 2000, p. A4. Bamford, *Body of Secrets*, pp. 414–418.

22. R. James Woolsey, quoted in Bamford, *Body of Secrets*, p. 425.

23. Patrick Poole, "'Echelon' Spells Trouble for Global Communications," *Privacy Journal*, Sept. 1999, pp. 3–4.

24. The French government admitted eavesdropping on the communications of American business people and providing valuable commercial information to French companies (Mary Eisenhart, "Encryption, Privacy & Data Security," *MicroTimes*, March 8, 1993, pp. 111–122.)

25 Larry Loen, "Hiding Data in Plain Sight," *EFFector Online*, Jan. 7, 1993, 4.05.

26 Steven Levy, "The Open Secret," *Wired*, April 1999, pp. 108–115; Simon Singh, *The Code Book: The Evolution of Secrecy From Mary Queen of Scots to Quantum Cryptography*, Doubleday, 1999, pp. 279–292.

27 Quoted in Steve Lohr, "Privacy on Internet Poses Legal Puzzle," *New York Times*, Apr. 19, 1999, p. C4.

28 Lance J. Hoffman, Faraz A. Ali, Steven L. Heckler, Ann Huybrechts, "Cryptography Policy," *Communications of the ACM*, Sept. 1994, 37:9, pp. 109–117.

29 Fyodor Dostoevsky, *The House of the Dead*, 1862; translation by Constance Garnett, 1915.

30 David Chaum, "Achieving Electronic Privacy," *Scientific American*, Aug. 1992, pp. 96–101. David Chaum, "A New Paradigm for Individuals Living in the Information Age," in Deborah G. Johnson and Helen Nissenbaum, *Computers, Ethics & Social Values*, Prentice Hall, 1995, pp. 366–373. Julian Dibbell, "Building a Better Monkey Wrench," *Village Voice*, Aug. 3, 1993, p. 34.

31 Quoted in *EFFector Online*, 7:3, Feb. 9, 1994

32 Eric Dexheimer, "Police Uneasy with This Cure for the Common Code," *San Diego Union–Tribune*, Computer Link section, March 1, 1994, p. 1ff. Steven Levy, "Battle of the Clipper Chip," *New York Times Magazine*, June 12, 1994, pp. 44–70 (p. 49). Dorothy E. Denning and William E. Baugh, Jr., "Encryption and Evolving Technologies As Tools of Organized Crime and Terrorism," National Strategy Information Center's U.S. Working Group on Organized Crime, 1997. Dorothy E. Denning and William E. Baugh, Jr., "Cases Involving Encryption in Crime and Terrorism," www.cosc.georgetown.edu/~denning/crypto/cases.html.

33 Niels Provos and Peter Honeyman, University of Michigan Center for Information Technology Integration.

34 Philip Elmer-Dewitt, "Who Should Keep the Keys?" *Time*, March 14, 1994, pp. 90–91. Julian Dibbell, "Code Warriors Battling for the Keys to Privacy in the Info Age," *Village Voice*, Aug. 3, 1993, pp. 33–37. Singh, *The Code Book*, p. 318. Bamford, *The Puzzle Palace*, p. 4.

35 Bamford, *The Puzzle Palace*, pp. 356–357, 361–362. The Davida quote is on p. 361.

36 William Sternow, quoted in Dexheimer, "Police Uneasy with This Cure for the Common Code."

37 James Bidzos, president of RSA Data Security, quoted in John Perry Barlow, "Decrypting the Puzzle Palace," p. 27. Kimberley A. Strassel, "U.S. Limits on Encryption Exports Create Fans Overseas, *Wall Street Journal*, July 7, 1998, p. B5.

38 Hoffman et al, "Cryptography Policy," pg. 113.

39 Paul Wallich, "Cracking the U.S. Code," *Scientific American*, Apr. 1997, p. 42. The book containing the code that could not be exported on disk is *Applied Cryptography: Protocols, Algorithms, and Source Code*

in C, by Bruce Schneier, published in 1994. "State Dept: 1st Amendment Doesn't Apply to Disks," *EPIC Alert*, Oct. 28, 1994, v. 1.06. Telephone interview with Philip Karn, March 17, 1995.

40 Loring Wirbel, "State Dept. Tries to Quash APIs for PGP Cryptography," *Electronic Engineering Times*, Apr. 29, 1996, p. 4. Don Clark, "Sun Holding Off On Plans to Market Encryption Systems," *Wall Street Journal*, Mar. 9, 1998, p. B3.

41 "EFF Sues to Overturn Cryptography Restrictions," *EFFector Online*, Feb. 23, 1995, 8:2.

42 Judge Marilyn Patel, quoted in Jared Sandberg, "Judge Rules Encryption Software Is Speech in Case on Export Curbs," *Wall Street Journal*, Apr. 18, 1996, p. B7.

43 Josh McHugh, "Politics for the Really Cool," *Forbes*, Sept. 8, 1997, pp. 172–179.

44 Whitfield Diffie and Susan Landau, *Privacy on the Line: The Politics of Wiretapping and Encryption*, MIT Press 1998, pp. 107–108.

45 Michael J. Martinez, "New Computer Could Foil Encryption Schemes," *ABCNEWS.com*, May 7, 1999.

46 Julian Dibbell, "Tale From the Crypto Wars," *Village Voice*, Aug. 3, 1993, p. 36.

47 Whitfield Diffie and Susan Landau, *Privacy on the Line*, pp. 207–217. See also S. Kent et al, "Codes, Keys and Conflicts: Issues in US Crypto Policy, Report of a Special Panel of the ACM US Public Policy Committee," June 1994 (http://info.acm.org/reports/acm_crypto_study.html).

48 John Podesta, quoted in "Answers to Clipper Questions," *EFFector Online*, 5:14, Aug. 5, 1993.

49 Assistant Attorney General Jo Ann Harris, before a Senate Judiciary Subcommittee, May 3, 1994.

50 The report is titled "Encryption: The Threat, Applications and Potential Solutions." It is quoted in "Documents: FBI & NSA Want to Ban Non-Escrowed Encryption," *EPIC Alert*, Aug. 21, 1995, v. 2.09.

51 "Impact of Emerging Telecommunications Technologies on Law Enforcement," also quoted in *EPIC Alert*, ibid.

52 David Kahn, *The Codebreakers*, Macmillan, 1967, pp. 515–517. Dibbell, "Tale From the Crypto Wars." Nathan Aaseng, *Navajo Code Talkers*, Walker & Co., 1992.

53 Kenneth W. Dam and Herbert S. Lin, eds., National Research Council, *Cryptography's Role in Securing the Information Society*, National Academy Press, 1996 (books.nap.edu/html/crisis).

54 From the Security and Freedom through Encryption Act (SAFE), as amended by the House Intelligence Committee, Sept. 11, 1997.

55 Martinez, "New Computer Could Foil Encryption Schemes," Will Rodger, "Cell phone encryption code cracked," *USATODAY.com*, Dec. 8, 1999.

56 James Bidzos, in Eisenhart, "Encryption, Privacy & Data Security." James Chandler, George Washington University National Law Center, mentioned in Hoffman *et al.*, "Cryptography Policy," p. 115.

[57] "Overkill by the FBI for New Tapping Authority," *Privacy Journal*, Dec. 1993, p. 3.

[58] Jerry Berman and Daniel J. Weitzner, *EFFector Online*, 5:5, April 2, 1993.

[59] Simon Singh, *The Code Book*, pp. 45–78, 317–350.

[60] www.cryptorights.org. Zimmermann quotes from Dexheimer, "Police Uneasy with This Cure for the Common Code," p. 12.

[61] Book report on *1984* written for my course, CS 440, Fall 2000; used with permission.

[62] Eisenhart, "Encryption, Privacy & Data Security," p. 118.

BOOKS AND ARTICLES

- James Bamford, *Body of Secrets: Anatomy of the Ultra-Secret National Security Agency, from the Cold War Through the Dawn of a New Century*, Doubleday, 2001. Includes a description of Echelon.

- James Bamford, *The Puzzle Palace: A Report on NSA, America's Most Secret Agency*, Houghton Mifflin, 1982.

- John Perry Barlow, "A Plain Text on Crypto Policy," *Communications of the ACM*, Nov. 1993, 36:11, pp. 21–26.

- Duncan Campbell, "Interception Capabilities 2000," www.cyber-rights.org/interception/stoa/interception_capabilities_2000.htm. A report on Echelon to the European Parliament.

- Alexander Charns, *Cloak and Gavel: FBI Wiretaps, Bugs, Informers, and the Supreme Court*, University of Illinois Press, 1992.

- David Chaum, "Achieving Electronic Privacy," *Scientific American*, Aug. 1992, pp. 96–101.

- Robert Corn-Revere, "The Fourth Amendment and the Internet," Testimony before the Subcommittee on the Constitution of the House Committee on the Judiciary, Apr. 6, 2000, www.house.gov/judiciary/corn0406.htm.

- Dorothy E. Denning, *Information Warfare and Security*, Addison Wesley, 1999.

- Dorothy E. Denning, "The Case for 'Clipper'," *Technology Review*, July 1995, pp. 48–55.

- Dorothy E. Denning et al., "To Tap or Not To Tap," *Communications of the ACM*, March 1993, 36:3, pp. 25–44. This debate on wiretapping and encryption policy includes an article by Denning and responses from a variety of points of view.

- Dorothy E. Denning and William E. Baugh, Jr., "Encryption and Evolving Technologies As Tools of Organized Crime and Terrorism," National Strategy Information Center's U.S. Working Group on Organized Crime, 1997.

- Dorothy E. Denning and William E. Baugh, Jr., "Cases Involving Encryption in Crime and Terrorism," www.cosc.georgetown.edu/~denning/crypto/cases.html.

- Whitfield Diffie and Susan Landau, *Privacy on the Line: The Politics of Wiretapping and Encryption*, MIT Press 1998.

- Dorn, James A., ed., *The Future of Money in the Information Age*, Cato Institute, 1997.

- David Flaherty, *Protecting Privacy in Surveillance Societies*, University of North Carolina Press, 1989.

- Robin Hanson, "Can Wiretaps Remain Cost Effective?" *Communications of the ACM*, Dec. 1994, 37:12, pp. 13–15.

- Lance J. Hoffman, ed., *Building In Big Brother: The Cryptographic Policy Debate*, Springer Verlag, 1995.

- S. Kent *et al.* "Codes, Keys and Conflicts: Issues in US Crypto Policy, Report of a Special Panel of the ACM US Public Policy Committee," June 1994, http://info.acm.org/reports/acm_crypto_study.html.

- Edith Lapidus, *Eavesdropping on Trial*, Hayden Book Co., 1974. Contains history of wiretapping and the relevant sections of the Omnibus Crime Control and Safe Streets Act of 1968.

- Steven Levy, *Crypto: How the Code Rebels Beat the Government—Saving Privacy in the Digital Age*, Viking Press, 2001.

- Wayne Madsen and David Banisar, *Cryptography and Liberty 2000: An International Survey of Encryption Policy*, Electronic Privacy Information Center, 2000.

- National Research Council, *Cryptography's Role in Securing the Information Society*, National Academy Press, 1996, books.nap.edu/html/crisis.

- Bruce Schneier, *Secrets and Lies: Digital Security in a Networked World*, John Wiley & Sons, Inc., 2000.

- Solveig Singleton, *Encryption Policy for the 21st Century: A Future without Government-Prescribed Key Recovery*, Cato Institute Policy Analysis, No. 325, Nov. 19, 1998.

- Simon Singh, *The Code Book: The Evolution of Secrecy From Mary Queen of Scots to Quantum Cryptography*, Doubleday, 1999. A history of codes and cryptography.

- Alan F. Westin, *Privacy and Freedom*, Atheneum, 1968. Contains history of wiretapping and other means of surveillance.

- Philip R. Zimmermann, *The Official PGP User's Guide*, MIT Press, 1995. Includes discussion of legal, ethical, and political issues surrounding PGP.

ORGANIZATIONS AND WEBSITES

- The CryptoRights Foundation: www.cryptorights.org

- Echelonwatch, sponsored by the American Civil Liberties Union, the Electronic Privacy Information Center, and other organizations: www.echelonwatch.org

- The EFF and EPIC sites, listed at the end of Chapter 2 contain a lot of material about the controversies in this chapter. For example, www.epic.org/crypto

- The Federal Bureau of Investigation: www.fbi.gov

- The National Security Agency: www.nsa.gov

4

CAN WE TRUST THE COMPUTER?

4.1 What Can Go Wrong?

4.1.1 QUESTIONS ABOUT RELIABILITY AND SAFETY

> *"Data Entry Typo Mutes Millions of U.S. Pagers"*
> *"Software Errors Cause Radiation Overdose"*
> *"IRS Computer Sends Bill For $68 Billion in Penalties"*
> *"Robot Kills Worker"*
> *"California Junks $100 Million Child Support System"*
> *"Man Arrested Five Times Due to Faulty FBI Computer Data"*
> *"High-Tech Baggage System 'Eats' Luggage"*
> *"Computer Predicts We Will Run Out of Copper by 1985"*

What can go wrong when we use computers? Almost anything. Most computer applications, from consumer software to systems that control airplanes and telephone networks, are so complex that it is virtually impossible to produce a program with no errors. In this chapter, we will describe a variety of mistakes, problems, and failures involving computers—and some of the factors responsible for them. Some errors are minor; for example, a word processor might incorrectly hyphenate a word that does not fit at the end of a line. Some incidents are funny; some are tragic; some cost millions of dollars. All of the examples can teach us something.

Are computer-controlled medical devices, factory automation systems, and airplanes too unsafe to use? Are we too dependent on computers? Or, like many stories on the evening news, do the headlines and horror stories emphasize the bad news—the dramatic and unusual events? Car crashes are reported on the news, but we do not hear that 200,000 car trips were completed safely in our city today. Although most car trips are safe, there is a good purpose for reporting crashes on the news: It teaches us what the risks are (e.g., driving in heavy fog) and it reminds us to be responsible and careful drivers. Just as car crashes can be caused by many factors (faulty design, sloppy manufacturing or servicing, bad road conditions, a careless or poorly trained driver, confusing road signs, etc.), computer glitches and system failures also have myriad causes, including faulty design, sloppy implementation, careless or insufficiently trained users, and poor user interfaces. Often, more than one factor is involved. Because of the complexity of computer systems, it is essential to follow good procedures and professional practices for their development and use. (The ACM/IEEE-CS Software Engineering Code of Ethics and Professional Practice and the ACM Code of Ethics and Professional Conduct, in Appendix A, are two important sets of guidelines for such practices.) Sometimes, no one does anything clearly wrong, but an accident occurs anyway. Occasionally, the irresponsibility of software developers is comparable to driving while very drunk.

Although millions of computers and software programs are working fine every day, it is crucial that we understand the risks and reasons for computer failures. How much risk must or should we accept? If the inherent complexity of computer systems means they will not be perfect, how can we distinguish between errors to be accepted as trade-offs for the benefits of the system and errors that are due to inexcusable carelessness, incompetence, or dishonesty? How good is good enough? When should we, or the government, or a business decide that a computer is too risky to use? We cannot answer these questions completely, but this chapter provides some background and discussion that can help us in forming conclusions. It should help us understand computer-related problems from the perspective of several of the roles we play:

- *A computer user.* Whether we use a personal computer at home or a sophisticated, specialized system at work, we should understand the limitations of computers and the need for proper training and responsible use. We must recognize that, as in other areas, there are good products and bad products.

- *A computer professional.* Studying computer failures should help you become a better computer professional (system designer, programmer, or quality assurance manager, for example) if that is your career direction. Understanding the source and consequences of computer failures is also valuable if you will be responsible for buying, developing, or managing a complex system for a hospital, airport, or business. The discussions of the examples in this chapter include many implicit and explicit lessons about how you can avoid similar problems.

- *An educated member of society.* There are many personal decisions and social, legal, and political decisions that depend on our understanding of the risks of computer system failures. We could be on a jury. We could be an active member of an organization lobbying for legislation. We could be deciding whether to try an experimental computer-controlled medical device or whether to fly in a new computer-controlled airplane.

    Your reaction to some examples in this chapter may be frustration and a feeling of helplessness. You might think, "How could those people make such stupid, incompetent errors? How can I protect myself?" I hope that Section 4.4 provides some perspective on the reliability and safety of various computer applications and of computer technology in general.

Computer errors and failures can be categorized in several ways, for example, by the cause, by the seriousness of the effects, or by the application area. In any scheme to organize the discussion, there will be overlap in some categories and mixing of diverse examples in some. For the remainder of this section, I use three categories: problems for individuals, usually in their roles as consumers; system failures that affect large numbers of people and/or cost large amounts of money; and problems in safety-critical applications where people may be injured or killed. We will look at one case in depth (in Section 4.2): the Therac-25. This computer-controlled radiation treatment machine had a large number of flaws that resulted in the deaths of several patients. In Sections 4.3 and 4.4, we try to make some sense of the jumble of examples we will have seen. Section 4.3 looks at underlying causes in more depth and describes some approaches to reducing problems. Section 4.4 puts the risks of computer systems into perspective in various ways, including considering risks in other systems and risks due to not using computers. In Section 4.5, we consider a somewhat different aspect of trusting computers: the reliability of analysis and predictions made by complex mathematical models run on computers.

The incidents described here are a sampling of the many that occur. In most cases, by mentioning specific companies or products, I do not mean to single those out as unusual offenders. One can find many similar stories in newspapers and magazines—and especially in The Risks Digest organized by Peter Neumann.[1] Neumann has collected thousands of reports describing a wide range of computer-related problems.

4.1.2 PROBLEMS FOR INDIVIDUALS

Many people are inconvenienced and/or suffer losses from errors in billing systems and databases containing personal data. Users of home computers confront frustrating bugs in operating systems and applications software.

BILLING ERRORS

The first few errors we look at are relatively simple ones whose negative consequences were relatively easily undone.[2]

- A woman was billed $6.3 million for electricity; the correct amount was $63. The cause was an input error made by someone using a new computer system.

- The IRS is a constant source of major bloopers. In 1993, it modified its programs with the intent of not billing Midwest flood victims. Instead, the computer generated erroneous bills for almost 5000 people. One Illinois couple received a bill for a few thousand dollars in taxes—and $68 billion in penalties. In 1998, the IRS sent 3000 people bills for slightly more than $300 million. One woman received a tax bill for $40,000,001,541.13.

- The auto insurance rate of a 101-year-old man suddenly tripled. Rates depend on age, but the program was written to handle ages only up to 100. It mistakenly classified the man as a teenager.

- Hundreds of Chicago cat owners were billed by the city for failure to register dachshunds, which they did not own. The city was using computer matching with two databases to try to find unlicensed pets. One database used DHC as the code for domestic house cat, and the other used the same code for dachshund.

Some of these errors could have been avoided with more care. Programs could have included tests to determine whether the amount was outside some reasonable range or changed significantly from previous bills. In other words, because programs could contain errors, good systems have provisions for checking their results. If you have some programming experience, you know how easy it would be to include such tests and make a list of cases for someone to review. These errors are perhaps more humorous than serious. When mistakes are as big as these, they are obvious, and the bills are corrected. They are still worth studying because the same kinds of design and programming errors can have more serious consequences in different applications. In the Therac-25 case (Section 4.2) we will see that including tests for inconsistent or inappropriate input could have saved lives.

DATABASE ACCURACY PROBLEMS

Credit bureaus have been strongly criticized for incidents where incorrect information caused people to lose their homes, cars, jobs, or insurance. Thousands of residents of New England were listed incorrectly in the TRW credit bureau* records as not having paid their local property taxes. The problem was attributed to an input error. People were denied loans before the scope of the problem was identified and it was corrected. (TRW paid damages to many of the people affected.) Like $40-billion tax bills, credit-record errors that result from a systematic error affecting thousands of people are likely to be recognized and corrected. More serious perhaps are all the small errors in individual people's records. It is difficult to get accurate and meaningful error rates. We need to distinguish between a spelling error in someone's address and an incorrect report that someone bounced several checks. By reviewing numerous surveys and figures, including some provided by the credit bureaus, *Privacy Journal* estimated that 25% of credit records have serious errors. Many people battle for years to get the credit bureaus to correct information in their records, and a few have won large settlements in lawsuits.[3]

A county agency used the wrong middle name in a report to a credit bureau about a father who did not make his child-support payments. Another man in the same county had the exact name reported; he could not get credit to buy a car or a house. A woman in Canada could not get her tax refund because the tax agency insisted she was dead. Her identification number had been mistakenly reported in place of her mother's when her mother died. Although computerized records were used in these cases, computers did not cause the problem. The source of the problems was the entry of incorrect data into records; they might have been as likely to occur with paper forms.

Federal law requires states to maintain databases of people convicted of sex crimes against children and to release information about them to the public. A family was harassed, threatened, and physically attacked after their state posted an online list of addresses where sex offenders live. The state did not know the offender had moved away before the family moved in. Others have also suffered because of these databases. A man convicted of statutory rape for having sex with his 17-year-old girlfriend, and now married to her for many years, was in a sex-offender database. While technically not an error in the database, this case illustrates the need for careful thought about what a database includes and how it is presented to the public, especially if it involves such a highly charged subject.

Many people were mistakenly purged from the Florida voting rolls and could not vote in the close 2000 U.S. presidential election because their names matched names of convicted felons (who are not permitted to vote). The state had hired a division of ChoicePoint, a huge database company, to supply lists of convicted felons. Apparently, the election officials used the lists without the extra verification step the company warned was needed.[4]

---

*TRW's credit bureau was later sold and is now Experian.

THE EXCLUSIONARY RULE AND COMPUTER ERRORS

The exclusionary rule prohibits the use of evidence in court if it was obtained by law-enforcement agents illegally. Law-enforcement agents often argue for loosening or elimination of this rule.

In an Arizona case, based on a computer check showing an arrest warrant, police conducted a search of a man's car after a routine traffic stop—a search that would be illegal if there was no warrant for the driver. And there was none; the computer was wrong. However, the Supreme Court ruled that evidence of a (nonviolent) crime found in the car during the search could be used against the man.[5]

An important issue here is how such a ruling affects the incentive of law-enforcement officials to improve the accuracy of their records. The Arizona Supreme Court argued that

> It is repugnant to the principles of a free society that a person should ever be taken into police custody because of a computer error precipitated by government carelessness. As automation increasingly invades modern life, the potential for Orwellian mischief grows. Under such circumstances, the exclusionary rule is a "cost" we cannot afford to be without.[6]

A 14-year-old boy in his first year of high school was excluded from football and some classes without explanation. He eventually learned that school officials thought he had been using drugs while in junior high school. The two schools used different disciplinary codes in their computerized records. The boy had been guilty of chewing gum and being late.[7] This case is very similar to the case of the dachshund/cat confusion described earlier—except that the consequences were more significant. Both cases illustrate the problems of relying on computer systems without taking the responsibility of learning enough about them to use them properly.

When errors occur in databases used by law-enforcement agencies, the consequences can include arrest at gunpoint, strip-searches, and being jailed with violent criminals. Studies of the FBI's National Crime Information Center (NCIC) database in the 1980s found that roughly 11% of the arrest warrants listed in it were inaccurate or no longer valid. People are arrested when a check of the database shows a warrant for them—or for someone with a similar name. I will mention a few NCIC cases; the news media and government studies reported many more. An adoption agency ran a routine check on an applicant and found that he had been convicted of grand larceny. In fact, he had been involved in a college prank—stealing a restaurant sign—years before, and the charges had been dropped after he apologized and paid for the damage. The error could have caused the agency to deny the adoption. A Michigan man was arrested for several crimes, including murders, committed in Los Angeles. Another man had assumed his

The Supreme Court reversed the Arizona court ruling, saying that the error was made by a court employee, not a law-enforcement official, and therefore excluding the evidence would not deter future errors by law enforcement. In a dissenting opinion, Justice Ginsburg argued that it was artificial to distinguish between court employees and police employees. In practice, it can be difficult to determine who made the error. "Applying an exclusionary rule as the Arizona court did may well supply a powerful incentive to the State to promote the prompt updating of computer records."

People are understandably concerned and angry that sometimes clearly guilty, violent criminals are set free because of violations of proper procedure. The purpose of the Bill of Rights is to protect innocent people from intrusions and abuse by the government and to provide a set of rules that will protect the guilty from unreasonable treatment. There will always be a tension between aggressive criminal investigation and protection of the rights of both innocent and guilty people. The problem is to balance the need to investigate and punish crime with the need to prevent abuse by law-enforcement agents. At issue here (and in many other topics throughout this book) is whether and how rules adopted for the use of databases (and other computer technology) by law-enforcement agencies will tilt the balance.

identity after finding his lost wallet (or a discarded birth certificate; reports varied). It is understandable that the innocent man was listed in NCIC as wanted. However, he was arrested four more times within 14 months. (After repeatedly asking the city of Los Angeles to correct the records, he sued and won a judgment against the city.) A man was imprisoned at a military base for five months because NCIC mistakenly reported that he was AWOL.* A college professor returning from London was arrested and jailed for two days after a routine check with NCIC at Customs showed that he was a wanted fugitive. NCIC was wrong—for the third time about this particular man. NCIC now includes digitized photographs and fingerprints. This should help reduce the number of incidents in which an innocent person is detained because his or her name, Social Security number, or car is similar to that of a criminal in the database.[8]

The FBI maintains another database, the Interstate Identification Index (III), containing arrest and conviction files on major offenders from participating states and available to police throughout most of the country. In some states, it is also used by licensing boards and employers. *Privacy Journal* reported that about half the records do not indicate whether a suspect was convicted or exonerated and that there was a high inaccuracy rate. Similar problems occur with local police systems: An innocent driver was stopped by police and frisked because his license-plate number was incorrectly listed as the license

---

*AWOL means "absent without leave."

number of a man who had killed a state trooper. The computer record did not include a description of the car.[9]

Several factors contribute to the frequency and severity of the problems people suffer because of errors in databases:

- a large population (Many people have identical or similar names, and most of our interactions are with strangers)

- automated processing without human common sense or the power to recognize special cases

- overconfidence in the accuracy of data stored on computers

- errors (some due to carelessness) in data entry

- failure to update information and correct errors

- lack of accountability for errors.

The first item is unlikely to change; it is the context in which we live. The second is partly a side effect of the increased speed and processing ability of computer technology, but its negative impacts can be reduced with better system specifications and training of users. When information is entered automatically by other computer systems, mistakes that might be obvious to a human can be overlooked. Even if an error is corrected, the problems may not be over for the person affected. Computer records are copied easily and often; copies of the incorrect data may remain in other systems. The remaining factors are all within our control as individuals, professionals, and policy makers. We discuss some solutions in Section 4.3.

4.1.3 SYSTEM FAILURES

Modern communications, power, medical, financial, retail, and transportation systems depend heavily on computers. The computers do not always function as planned.

COMMUNICATIONS

Nationwide AT&T telephone service for voice and data was disrupted for nine hours in January 1990 because of a software error in a four-million line program. The disruption prevented roughly 50 million calls from getting through. AT&T's official report stated, "While the software had been rigorously tested in laboratory environments before it was introduced, the unique combination of events that led to this problem couldn't be predicted." In June and July of 1991, telephone networks in several major East Coast and West Coast cities failed. The cause was a three-line change in a two-million line telecommunications switching program. The program had been tested for 13 weeks, but was not retested after the change—which contained a typo. In November 1991, a four-hour telephone outage in New England occurred when a technician changed a piece of disk equipment. Flights at Logan Airport in Boston were delayed or canceled because the communication systems used by air-traffic controllers and pilots was connected to the AT&T system that failed. In 1996, Bell Atlantic's directory assistance system failed when an upgrade was installed; hundreds of thousands of people in the Northeast could not get through.[10]

A glitch in a routine software upgrade at America Online prevented subscribers from logging in all over the U.S. for several hours in 1997. A major AT&T system for business data communications failed for a day in 1998. Thousands of businesses were affected; 1200 Wells Fargo ATM machines shut down; credit cards could not be used. Millions of pagers failed when someone typing codes into a database forgot to hit the enter key in a line of data.[11]

Satellites are a fundamental part of our communications systems. When a Galaxy IV satellite computer failed in 1998, many systems we take for granted stopped working. Pager service stopped for an estimated 85% of users in the U.S., including hospitals and police departments. Some radio and television broadcasts were interrupted. Airplane flights were delayed for airlines that get their weather information via the satellite. Credit cards could not be verified from the gas stations of a major chain. Some services were quickly switched to other satellites or backup systems; some were not restored for days.[12]

BUSINESS, FINANCIAL, AND TRANSPORTATION SYSTEMS

Every few years, the computer system of one of the world's large stock exchanges or brokerages fails. The NASDAQ stock exchange was virtually shut down for two and a half hours in July 1994 by a problem with new communications software that had been installed earlier in the week. Another computer failure caused an hour-long shutdown a year later. At various times, large investment firms and newspapers reported incorrect or out-of-date stock prices; they blamed computer errors. A glitch in an upgrade in the computer system at Charles Schwab Corporation crashed the system for more than two hours and caused intermittent problems for several days. Customers could not access their accounts or trade online. In 2000, a computer malfunction froze the London Stock Exchange for almost eight hours—on the last day of the tax year, affecting many people's tax bills.[13]

A failure of Amtrak's reservation and ticketing system during Thanksgiving weekend in 1996 caused delays because agents had no printed schedules or fare lists. Two large travel reservations systems that handle reservations for airlines, car rental companies, and hotels shut down for many hours because of computer problems. Two hundred American Airlines flights were delayed; electronic tickets could not be verified. Thousands of passengers were delayed by a failure of the computer that prepares flight plans for America West Airlines.

American Express Company's credit card verification system failed during the Christmas shopping season in 1999. Merchants had to call in for verification, overwhelming the call center.

DESTROYING BUSINESSES

A few dozen companies that bought an inventory system called Warehouse Manager blamed the system for disastrous losses; one previously successful company saw its income decline by about half and laid off half its employees. The specific complaints were numerous. One company could not get the system to place a purchase order for several weeks; the company claimed the backlog in orders cost $2000 per day. Processes that were supposed to take seconds, such as printing invoices, took several minutes while customers waited in long lines. The system gave incorrect information about inventory. Clerks were told that products were in stock when they were not, and vice versa. According to users of Warehouse Manager, the system reported incorrect prices to clerks. A part that cost $114 was listed for sale at 54 cents. A $17 part was listed for sale at $30. The first error means lost money for the company; the second means lost customers who find a better price elsewhere. When two clerks tried to access the computer from their terminals simultaneously, the terminals locked up. Some companies said the system erased information needed for accounting and tax reports.[14]

What was responsible for the problems in Warehouse Manager? The program was sold by NCR Corporation, but it was developed by another company. It was originally designed for and implemented on a different computer and operating system. It appears that there were unexpected problems when the program was rewritten for NCR's machines and its ITX operating system. According to the *Wall Street Journal*, internal memos at NCR reported that the system had been inadequately tested and was performing badly in real business settings. NCR salespeople told prospective customers that Warehouse Manager was running successfully at 200 installations, but most of those were installations using the machine for which the program was originally designed. Several users claimed that although NCR was receiving complaints of serious problems from many customers, the company told them the problems they were having were unique. NCR blamed the problems on the company that wrote Warehouse Manager and modified it for ITX. Eventually NCR agreed it "did not service customers well" and the program should have been tested more. The company settled most of the few dozen lawsuits out of court, with confidentiality agreements about the terms. The sources of the problems in this case included technical difficulties (converting software to a different system), poor management decisions (inadequate testing), and, according to the customers, dishonesty in promoting the system and responding to the problems.

STALLED AIRPORTS: DENVER, HONG KONG, AND MALAYSIA

In 1994, I flew over the huge Denver International Airport and the miles of wide highway leading to it. The airport covers 53 square miles, roughly twice the size of Manhattan. It was an eerie sight—nothing was moving. There were no airplanes or people at the

DESTROYING CAREERS AND SUMMER VACATIONS[15]

CTB/McGraw-Hill develops and scores standardized tests for schools; about nine million students take its tests each year. An error in CTB's software caused it to report test results incorrectly—substantially lower than the correct scores—in several states. In New York City, school principals and superintendents were fired because their schools appeared to be doing a poor job of teaching students to read. Educators were personally and professionally disgraced. One man said he applied for 30 other superintendent jobs in the state, but did not get one. Parents were upset. Nearly 9000 students were mistakenly required to attend summer school because of the incorrect scores. Eventually, the error was corrected; New York City's reading scores had actually risen five percentage points.

Why was the problem not detected sooner, soon enough to avoid firings and summer school? School testing officials in several states were skeptical of the scores showing sudden, unexpected drops. They questioned CTB but were told nothing was wrong; none were told that other states experienced similar problems and also complained. When CTB discovered the software error, the company did not inform the schools for another seven weeks, even though the president of CTB met with school officials about the problem during those weeks.

What lessons can we learn from this case? Software errors happen, of course. Significant mistakes are usually noticed, and they were here. But the company did not take seriously enough the questions about the accuracy of the results and was reluctant to admit the possibility—and later certainty—of errors. It is this behavior that must be overcome. The damage from a computer error can be reduced if it is found and corrected quickly.

CTB recommended that scores on its standardized tests not be used as the sole factor in deciding which students should attend summer school. But New York City did so. We saw earlier that Florida state officials relied on computer-generated lists to prevent some people from voting, even though the database company supplying the lists said they needed additional verification. Relying solely on results produced by computers is temptingly easy. It is a temptation that people responsible for critical decisions in many situations should resist.

airport and no cars on the highway—10 months after the $3.2 billion airport was to have opened. The opening was rescheduled at least four times. The delay cost more than $30 million per month in bond interest and operating costs. Most of the delay was attributed to the computer-controlled baggage-handling system, which cost $193 million.[16]

The plan for the baggage system was quite ambitious. Outbound luggage checked at ticket counters or curbside counters was to be delivered to any part of the airport in less than 10 minutes via an automated system of carts traveling at up to 19 miles per hour on 22 miles of underground tracks. Similarly, inbound luggage was to be delivered to terminals or transferred directly to connecting flights anywhere in the airport. Each bag was to be put into a cart bar-coded for its destination. Laser scanners throughout the system tracked the 4000 carts and sent information about their locations to computers. The computers used a database of flights, gates, and routing information to control motors and track switches to route the carts to their destinations.

The system did not work as planned. During tests over several months, carts crashed into each other at track intersections; luggage was misrouted, dumped, and flung about; and carts that were needed to move luggage were mistakenly routed to waiting pens. Both the specific problems and the general underlying causes are instructive. Some of the specific problems were

- *Real-world problems.* Some scanners got dirty or were knocked out of alignment and could not detect carts going by. This was related to the cart crashes.

- *Problems in other systems.* The airport's electrical system could not handle the power surges associated with the baggage system; the first full-scale test blew so many circuits that the test had to be halted. Faulty latches on the carts caused luggage to be dumped on the tracks between stops.

- *Software errors.* The routing of carts to waiting pens when they were actually needed was attributed to a software error.

No one expects software and hardware of this complexity to work perfectly the first time it is tested. In real-time systems,* especially, there are numerous interactions and conditions that might not be anticipated. It is not surprising that problems would be encountered during development. Mangling a suitcase is not embarrassing if it occurs during an early test and if the problem is fixed. It is embarrassing if it occurs after the system is in operation or if it takes a year to fix. What led to the extraordinary delay in the Denver baggage system? There seem to have been two main causes:

- *The time allowed for development and testing of the system was insufficient.* The only other baggage system of comparable size was at Frankfurt Airport in Germany. The company that built that system spent six years on development and two years testing and debugging. BAE Automated Systems, the company that built the Denver system, was asked to do it in two years. Some reports indicate that, because of the electrical problems at the airport, there were only six weeks for testing.

- *Significant changes in specifications were made after the project began.* Originally, the automated system was to serve United Airlines, but Denver officials decided to expand it to include the entire airport, making the system 14 times as large as the automated baggage system BAE had installed for United at San Francisco International Airport.

PC Week's reporter said, "The bottom-line lesson is that system designers must build in plenty of test and debugging time when scaling up proven technology into a much more

---

* Real-time systems are systems that must detect and control activities of objects in the real world within time constraints.

complicated environment."[17] Some observers criticized BAE for taking on the job when the company should have known that there was not enough time to complete it. Others blamed the city government for poor management, politically motivated decisions, and proceeding with a grandiose but unrealistic plan.

A few years later, opening day at the new airports in Hong Kong and Kuala Lumpur took the headlines and the Denver Airport fiasco faded into the background. The ambitious and complex computer systems at these airports were to manage *everything*: moving 20,000 pieces of luggage per hour and coordinating and scheduling crews, gate assignments for flights, and so on. Both systems failed spectacularly. At Hong Kong's Chek Lap Kok airport, cleaning crews and fuel trucks, baggage, passengers, and cargo were directed to the wrong gates, sometimes far from where their airplanes were. Airplanes scheduled to take off were empty. At Kuala Lumpur, airport employees had to write boarding passes by hand and carry luggage. Flights, of course, were delayed; food cargo rotted in the heat in Malaysia.

At both airports, the failures were blamed on people typing in incorrect information. In Hong Kong, it was perhaps a wrong gate or arrival time that was dutifully sent throughout the system. In Kuala Lumpur, mistakes by check-in agents unfamiliar with the system paralyzed it. "There's nothing wrong with the system," said a spokesman at Malaysia's airport. A spokesman at Hong Kong made a similar statement. They are deeply mistaken. One incorrect gate number would not have caused the problems experienced at Hong Kong. Any system that has a large number of users and a lot of user input must be designed and tested to handle incorrect input. The "system" includes more than the software and hardware; it includes the people who operate it. They were not adequately trained. As in the case of the Denver airport, there were questions about whether the scheduled time for the opening of the airports was determined by political considerations rather than by the need for adequate training.

ABANDONED SYSTEMS

Many systems are so fundamentally flawed that they are junked after wasting millions, or even billions, of dollars. The California Department of Motor Vehicles, for example, abandoned a $44 million computer system that never worked properly. A consortium of hotels and a rental car business spent $125 million on a comprehensive travel-industry reservation system, then canceled the project because it did not work. The state of California spent more than $100 million to develop one of the largest and most expensive state computer systems in the country: a system for tracking parents who owe child support payments. After five years, the state abandoned the system because it didn't work. It lost data, miscalculated payments, and couldn't communicate with other government agencies. After spending $4 billion, the IRS abandoned a tax-system modernization plan; a General Accounting Office report blamed mismanagement.[18] There are many more such examples.

4.1.4 SAFETY-CRITICAL APPLICATIONS

There are many examples of problems in safety-critical computer systems in military applications, power plants, aircraft, trains, automated factories, medical applications, and so on. Most of the deaths that have occurred because of computer-related problems were in aviation and medical applications.[19] We look briefly at a few aviation cases, then at one medical-instrument case in depth in the next section.

COMPUTERS IN THE AIR

The A320 Airbus airplane was the first fully "fly-by-wire" airplane. The pilots do not directly control the plane; their actions are inputs to computers that control the aircraft systems. Between 1988 and 1993, four A320s crashed. Although the official cause for some of the crashes was ruled "pilot error," pilots and some observers blamed the fly-by-wire system. Pilots complained that the airplane does not respond as expected, that it seems to have "a mind of its own" and may suddenly behave in unexpected and inappropriate ways. In the 1992 crash, the pilots specified a rate of descent of 3300 feet per minute instead of the normal 800 feet per minute. The official report on the crash indicated that reasons for the error probably included the pilots' lack of familiarity with the A320 automation equipment and confusing design of the controls and displays. The crew left the "vertical navigation" entirely to the automatic systems although there were indications that the descent rate was too high. Perhaps they had too much confidence in the computer's ability to detect and correct mistakes. In the 1993 crash, the computer did not recognize that the plane had landed; it prevented the pilot from reversing engine thrust to brake the airplane. Pilots and human-factors specialists emphasized the need for an easy way to override the computer and easy transfer between automatic and manual control.[20]

The Traffic Collision Avoidance System (TCAS) detects a potential in-air collision and directs the airplanes to avoid each other. It is a great advance in safety, according to the head of the Airline Pilots Association's safety committee. But the first version of the system had so many false alarms that it was unusable. In some incidents, the system directed pilots to fly toward each other rather than away, potentially causing a collision instead of avoiding one.[21]

In 1999 and 2000, the Federal Aviation Administration (FAA) installed a $1 billion system at major airports for tracking high-altitude, long-distance flights. It worked well in some of the airports where it was tested, but problems at other airports occurred within a day of modifications, causing hundreds of flights to be canceled. When the FAA installed its upgraded radar system at its traffic control center in southern California in 2000, the system crashed, and flights had to be grounded nationwide. Twice in June 2000, the computer that controls flights that enter British airspace broke down. Controllers used manual backup systems; flights were delayed three hours on average.[22] Air-traffic control is extremely complex. The systems that manage it include computers on the ground at airports, devices in thousands of airplanes, radar, databases, communications, and so on—all of which must work in real time, tracking airplanes moving very fast. The inherent difficulty of the task is perhaps compounded by the bureaucratic and political decision-making and funding processes.

We discuss more incidents of failures of aircraft systems in Sections 4.3 and 4.4, where we look at solutions (including better computer systems) and put the failures in perspective.

4.2 Case Study: The Therac-25

4.2.1 THERAC-25 RADIATION OVERDOSES

The Therac-25 was a software-controlled radiation-therapy machine used to treat people with cancer. Between 1985 and 1987, Therac-25 machines at four medical centers gave massive overdoses of radiation to six patients. In some cases, the operator repeated an overdose because the machine's display said that no dose had been given. Medical personnel later estimated that some patients received between 13,000 and 25,000 rads,* where the intended dose was in the 100–200 rad range. These incidents caused severe and painful injuries and the deaths of three patients.

What went wrong?

Studies of the Therac-25 incidents showed that many factors were involved in causing the injuries and deaths. The factors include lapses in good safety design, insufficient testing, bugs in the software that controlled the machines, and an inadequate system of reporting and investigating the accidents. (Articles by computer scientists Nancy Leveson and Clark Turner and by Jonathan Jacky are the main sources for this discussion.[23])

To understand the discussion of the problems, it will help to know a little about the machine. The Therac-25 is a dual-mode machine; that is, it can generate an electron beam or an X-ray photon beam. The type of beam to be used depends on the tumor being treated. The machine's linear accelerator produces a high-energy electron beam (25 million electron volts) that is dangerous. Patients are not to be exposed to the raw beam. The computer monitors and controls movement of a turntable on which three sets of devices are mounted. Depending on whether the treatment is electron or X-ray, a different set of devices is rotated in front of the beam to spread it and make it safe. It is essential that the proper protective device be in place when the electron beam is on. A third position of the turntable may be used with the electron beam off, and a light beam on instead, to help the operator position the beam in precisely the correct place on the patient's body.

---

*A rad is the unit used to quantify radiation doses. It stands for "radiation absorbed dose."

4.2.2 SOFTWARE AND DESIGN PROBLEMS

DESIGN FLAWS

The Therac-25, developed in the late 1970s, followed earlier machines called the Therac-6 and Therac-20. It differed from them in that it was designed to be fully computer controlled. The older machines had hardware safety interlock mechanisms, independent of the computer, that prevented the beam from firing in unsafe conditions. Many of these hardware safety features were eliminated in the design of the Therac-25. Some software from the Therac-20 and Therac-6 was reused in the Therac-25. The software was apparently assumed to be functioning correctly. This assumption was wrong. When new operators used the Therac-20, there were frequent shutdowns and blown fuses, but no overdoses. The Therac-20 software had bugs, but the hardware safety mechanisms were doing their job. Either the manufacturers did not know of the problems with the Therac-20, or they completely missed their serious implication.

The Therac-25 malfunctioned frequently. One facility said there were sometimes 40 dose-rate malfunctions in a day, generally underdoses. Thus operators became used to error messages appearing often, with no indication that there might be safety hazards.

There were a number of weaknesses in the design of the operator interface. The error messages that appeared on the display were simply error numbers or obscure messages ("Malfunction 54" or "H-tilt"). This was not unusual for computer programs in the 1970s, when computers had much less memory and mass storage than they have now. One had to look up each error number in a manual for more explanation. The operator's manual for the Therac-25, however, did not include any explanation of the error messages. Even the maintenance manual did not explain them. The machine distinguished between the severity of errors by the amount of effort needed to continue operation. For certain error conditions, the machine paused, and the operator could proceed (turn on the electron beam) by pressing one key. For other kinds of errors the machine suspended operation and had to be completely reset. One would presume that the one-key resumption would be allowed only after minor, not safety-related, errors. Yet this was the situation that occurred in some of the accidents in which patients received multiple overdoses.

Investigators studying the accidents found that there was very little documentation produced during development of the program concerning the software specifications or the testing plan. Although the manufacturer of the machine, Atomic Energy of Canada, Ltd. (AECL), a Canadian government corporation, claimed that it was tested extensively, it appeared that the test plan was inadequate.

BUGS

Investigators were able to trace some of the overdoses to two specific software errors. Because many readers of this book are computer-science students, I will describe the bugs.

These descriptions illustrate the importance of using good programming techniques. However, some readers have little or no programming knowledge, so I will simplify the descriptions.

After treatment parameters are entered by the operator at a control console, a software procedure called Set-Up Test is run to perform a variety of checks to be sure the machine is positioned correctly, and so on. If anything is not ready, this procedure schedules itself to be run again so that the checks are all done again. (The system might simply have to wait for the turntable to move into place.) The Set-Up Test procedure can run several hundred times while setting up for one treatment. A flag variable is used to indicate whether a specific device on the machine is positioned correctly. A zero value means the device is ready; a nonzero value means it must be checked. To ensure that the device is checked, each time the Set-Up Test procedure runs, it increments the variable to make it nonzero. The problem was that the flag variable was stored in one byte. When the routine was called the 256th time, the flag overflowed and showed a value of zero. (If you are not familiar with programming, think of this as an automobile's odometer rolling over to zero after reaching the highest number it can show.) If everything else happened to be ready at that point, the device position was not checked, and the treatment could proceed. Investigators believe that in some of the accidents, this bug allowed the electron beam to be turned on when the turntable was positioned for use of the light beam, and there was no protective device in place to attenuate the beam.

Part of the tragedy in this case is that the error was such a simple one, with a simple correction. No good student programmer should have made this error. The solution is to set the flag variable to a fixed value, say 1, rather than incrementing it, to indicate that it must be checked.

Other bugs caused the machine to ignore changes or corrections made by the operator at the console. When the operator typed in all the necessary information for a treatment, the program began moving various devices into place. This process could take several seconds. The software was written to check for editing of the input by the operator during this time and to restart the set-up if editing was detected. However, because of bugs in this section of the program, some parts of the program learned of the edited information while others did not. This led to machine settings that were incorrect and inconsistent with safe treatment. According to the later investigation by the Food and Drug Administration (FDA), there appeared to be no consistency checks in the program. The error was most likely to occur if the operator was experienced and quick at editing input.

In a real-time, multitasking system where physical machinery is controlled and an operator enters—and may modify—input, there are many complex factors that can contribute to subtle, intermittent, and hard-to-detect bugs. Programmers working on such systems must learn to be aware of the potential problems and to use good programming practices to avoid them.

4.2.3 WHY SO MANY INCIDENTS?

There were six known Therac-25 overdoses. You may wonder why the machine continued to be used after the first one.

The Therac-25 had been in service for up to two years at some clinics. It was not immediately pulled from service after the first few accidents because it was not known immediately that it was the cause of the injuries. Medical staff members considered various other explanations. The staff at the site of the first incident said that one reason they were not certain of the source of the patient's injuries was that they had never seen such a massive radiation overdose before. The manufacturer was questioned about the possibility of overdoses, but responded (after the first, third, and fourth accidents) that the patient injuries could not have been caused by the machine. According to the Leveson and Turner investigative report, they also told the facilities that there had been no similar cases of injuries.

After the second accident, AECL investigated and found several problems related to the turntable (not including any of the ones we described). They made some changes in the system and recommended operational changes. They declared that the safety of the machine had been improved by five orders of magnitude, although they told the FDA that they were not certain of the exact cause of the accident; that is, they did not know whether they had found the problem that caused the accident or just other problems. In making decisions about continued use of the machines, the hospitals and clinics had to consider the costs of removing the expensive machine from service (in lost income and loss of treatment for patients who needed it), the uncertainty about whether the machine was the cause of the injuries, and, later, when that was clear, the manufacturer's assurances that the problem had been solved.

A Canadian government agency and some hospitals using the Therac-25 made recommendations for many more changes to enhance safety; they were not implemented. After the fifth accident, the FDA declared the machine defective and ordered AECL to inform users of the problems. The FDA and AECL spent about a year (during which the sixth accident occurred) negotiating about changes to be made in the machine. The final plan included more than two dozen changes. The critical hardware safety interlocks were eventually installed, and most of the machines remained in use with no new incidents of overdoses after 1987.[24]

OVERCONFIDENCE

In the first overdose incident, when the patient told the machine operator that she had been "burned," the operator told her that was impossible. This was one of many indications that the makers and some users of the Therac-25 were overconfident about the safety of the system. The most obvious and critical indication of overconfidence in the software was the decision to eliminate the hardware safety mechanisms. A safety analysis of the machine done by AECL years before the accidents suggests that they did not expect significant problems from software errors. In one case where a clinic added its own hardware safety features to the machine, AECL told them it was not necessary. (None of the accidents occurred at that facility.)

The hospitals using the machine assumed that it worked safely, an understandable assumption. Some of their actions, though, suggest overconfidence, or at least practices that should be avoided, for example, ignoring error messages because the machine produced so many of them. A camera in the treatment room and an intercom system enabled the operator to monitor the treatment and communicate with the patient. (The treatment room is shielded, and the console used by the operator is outside the room.) On the day of an accident at one facility, neither the video monitor nor the intercom was functioning. The operator did not see or hear the patient try to get up after an overdose; he received a second overdose before he reached the door and pounded on it. This facility had successfully treated more than 500 patients with the machine before the accident.

4.2.4 OBSERVATIONS AND PERSPECTIVE

From design decisions all the way to responding to the overdose accidents, the manufacturer of the Therac-25 did a poor job. Minor design and implementation errors might be expected in a complex system, but the number and pattern of problems in this case, and the way they were handled, suggest serious irresponsibility. This case illustrates many of the things that a responsible, ethical software developer should not do. It illustrates the importance of following good procedures in software development. It is a stark reminder of the consequences of carelessness, cutting corners, unprofessional work, and attempts to avoid responsibility. It reminds us that a complex system can work correctly hundreds of times with a bug that shows up only in unusual circumstances—hence the importance of always following good safety procedures in operation of potentially dangerous equipment. This case also illustrates the importance of individual initiative and responsibility. Recall that some facilities installed hardware safety devices on their Therac-25 machines. They recognized the risks and took action to reduce them. The hospital physicist at one of the facilities where the Therac-25 overdosed patients spent many hours working with the machine to try to reproduce the conditions under which the overdoses occurred. With little support or information from the manufacturer, he was able to figure out the cause of some of the malfunctions.

Even if the Therac-25 case was unusual,* we must deal with the fact that the machine was built and used, and it killed people. There have been enough accidents in safety-critical applications to indicate that significant improvement is needed. Should we not trust computers for such applications at all? Or, if we continue to use computers for safety-critical applications, what can be done to reduce the incidence of failures? We discuss some approaches in the next section.

To put the Therac-25 in perspective, it is helpful to remember that failures and other accidents have always occurred and continue to occur in systems that do not use computers. Two other linear-accelerator radiation-treatment machines seriously overdosed

---

*Sadly, some software safety experts say the poor design and lack of attention to safety in this case are not unusual.

patients. Three patients received overdoses in one day at a London hospital in 1966 when safety controls failed. Twenty-four patients received overdoses from a malfunctioning machine at a Spanish hospital in 1991; three patients died. Neither of these machines had computer controls. Two news reporters reviewed more than 4000 cases of radiation overdoses reported to the U.S. government. Most of the cases did not involve computers. Here are a few of the overdose incidents they describe. A technician started a treatment, then left the patient for 10–15 minutes to attend an office party. A technician failed to carefully check the prescribed treatment time. A technician failed to measure the radioactive drugs administered; she just used what looked like the right amount. In at least two cases, technicians confused microcuries and millicuries.* The underlying problems were carelessness, lack of appreciation for the risk involved, poor training, and lack of sufficient penalty to encourage better practices. In most cases, the medical facilities paid small fines or were not fined at all. (One radiation oncologist severely injured five women. He was eventually sued.)[25] Some of these problems might have been prevented by good computer systems. Many could have occurred even if a computer were in use. None excuse the Therac-25. They suggest, however, that individual and management responsibility, good training, and accountability are factors more important than whether or not a computer is used.

4.3 Increasing Reliability and Safety

Success actually requires avoiding many separate possible causes of failure.

—Jared Diamond, in *Guns, Germs, and Steel: The Fates of Human Societies*[26]

4.3.1 WHAT GOES WRONG?

Computer systems fail for two general reasons: The job they are doing is inherently difficult, and the job is often done poorly. Several factors combine to make the task difficult. Early computer programs were fed some numbers, did mathematical computations, and provided some answers. Errors were sometimes made, but the task was not extremely complex. Computer systems now interact with the real world (including both machinery and unpredictable humans) have numerous features and interconnected subsystems, and are extremely large. Computer programs have tens of thousands, hundreds of thousands, or millions of lines of code. (Microsoft's Windows 2000 has about 40 million lines.) Computer software is "non-linear" in the sense that, whereas a small error in an engineering project may cause a small degradation in performance, a single typo in a computer program can cause a dramatic difference in behavior.

The job can be done poorly at any of many stages, from system design and implementation to system management and use. (This characteristic is not unique to computer

---

*A curie is a measure of radioactivity. A millicurie is one thousand times as much as a microcurie.

- Interaction with physical devices that do not work as expected.

- Incompatibility of software and hardware, or of application software and the operating system.

- Management problems, including business and/or political pressure to get a product out quickly.

- Inadequate attention to potential safety risks.

- Not planning and designing for unexpected inputs or circumstances.

- Insufficient testing.

- Reuse of software from another system without adequate checking.

- Overconfidence in software.

- Carelessness.

- Misrepresentation; hiding problems; inadequate response when problems are reported.

- Problems with management of the use of a system:
    Data-entry errors.
    Inadequate training of users.
    Errors in interpreting results or output.
    Overconfidence in software by users.
    Insufficient planning for failures; no backup systems or procedures.

- Lack of market or legal incentives to do a better job.

Figure 4.1 Some Factors in Computer System Errors and Failures

systems, of course; the same can be said about building a bridge, a space shuttle, or a car, or about a medical-care system or any complex system in the modern world.) Figure 4.1 lists common factors in computer errors and system failures. Most of them are illustrated in examples we described. Some are technical issues, and some are managerial, social, legal, and ethical issues.

OVERCONFIDENCE

Overconfidence, or an unrealistic or inadequate understanding of the risks in a complex computer system, is a core issue. When system developers and users appreciate the risks, they are more motivated to use the techniques that are available to build more reliable and safer systems and to be responsible users. How many PC users never backed up their files until after they had a disk crash and lost critical data or months of work?

Some safety-critical systems that failed (e.g., systems that control airplanes and trains) had supposedly "fail-safe" computer controls. In some cases the logic of the program was fine, but the failure resulted from not considering how the system interacts with real users (such as pilots) or real-world problems (such as loose wires or fallen leaves on train tracks).

Can the risks of failure in a system be analyzed and quantified? Yes, but the techniques for developing estimates of failure rates must be used carefully. For example, the computers on the A320 airplane each have redundant software systems designed by separate teams of programmers. The redundancy is a safety feature, but how much safety does it provide? The failure rate was supposed to be less than one failure per billion flight hours. It was calculated by multiplying the estimated failure rates of the two systems, one in 100,000 hours. The calculation is reasonable if the systems are independent. But safety experts say that even when programmers work separately, they tend to make the same kinds of errors, especially if there is an error, ambiguity, or omission in the program specifications.[27]

Unrealistic reliability or safety estimates can come from genuine lack of understanding, from carelessness, or from intentional misrepresentation. People without a high regard for honesty sometimes give in to business or political pressure to exaggerate safety, to hide flaws, to avoid unfavorable publicity, or to avoid the expense of corrections or lawsuits. The manufacturer of the Therac-25 declared that changes in the system increased safety by five orders of magnitude (a factor of 100,000). It is hard to guess how the company arrived at that figure.

Political pressure to produce inflated safety predictions is not restricted to computer systems. In 1986, the Challenger space shuttle broke apart, killing the seven people aboard. The investigation by Nobel Prize winner Richard Feynman sheds interesting light on how some risk estimates are made. Feynman found that NASA engineers estimated the chance that an engine failure would terminate a flight to be about one in 200–300. Their boss gave the official NASA estimate of the risk: one in 100,000. The document that justified this unbelievable (in Feynman's judgment) estimate calculated it from failure estimates for various components. Feynman concluded that the failure rates for the components were chosen to yield the prechosen result of one in 100,000.[28] One lesson from the Therac-25 and Challenger is to be skeptical about numbers whose magnitudes seem unreasonable to common sense.

REUSE OF SOFTWARE: THE ARIANE 5 ROCKET

Less than 40 seconds after the first Ariane 5 rocket was launched in 1996, it veered off course and was destroyed as a safety precaution. The rocket and the satellites it was carrying cost approximately $500 million. The failure was caused by a software error.[29]

The Ariane 5 used some software designed for the earlier, successful Ariane 4. The software included a module that ran for about a minute after initiation of a launch on the Ariane 4. It did not have to run after takeoff of the Ariane 5, but a decision was made to avoid introducing new errors by making changes in a module that was known to operate fine in Ariane 4. This module did calculations related to velocity. The Ariane 5 travels faster than the Ariane 4 after takeoff. The calculations produced numbers bigger than the program was designed to handle (an "overflow" in the technical jargon), causing the system to halt.

Does something about this sound familiar? In the Therac-25 (Section 4.2), software from earlier machines, the Therac-6 and Therac-20, was used. The software seemed to function acceptably in those systems, but was not appropriate or safe for the Therac-25. Should we not reuse software? One of the goals of programming paradigms like object-oriented code is to make software elements that can be widely used, thus saving time and effort. Reuse of software should also increase safety. After all, it has been tested in the field, in a real, operational environment; we know it is working. At least, we think it is working. The critical point is that it is working in a different environment. Especially for safety-critical applications, it is essential to reexamine the specifications and design of the software, and to retest it, when it is to be used in a new environment.

4.3.2 PROFESSIONAL TECHNIQUES

SOFTWARE ENGINEERING AND PROFESSIONAL RESPONSIBILITY

The many examples of computer-system errors and failures suggest the importance of using good software engineering techniques at all stages of development, including specifications, design, implementation, documentation, and testing. There is a wide range between poor work and good work, as there is in virtually any field. Professionals, both programmers and managers, have the responsibility to study and use the techniques and tools that are available and to follow the procedures and guidelines established in the various relevant codes of ethics and professional practices. Professional responsibility includes knowing or learning enough about the application field and the software or systems being used to understand potential problems and to do a good job. Obviously, this is especially important in safety-critical applications.

A subfield of computer science focusing on design and development of safety-critical software is growing. Safety specialists emphasize that safety must be "designed in" from the start. There are techniques of hazard analysis that help system designers identify risks and protect against them. Software engineers who work on safety-critical applications should have special training. Software safety expert Nancy Leveson emphasizes that we can learn much from the experience of engineers in building safe electromechanical systems. "One lesson is that most accidents are not the result of unknown scientific principles but rather of a failure to apply well-known, standard engineering practices. A second lesson is that accidents will not be prevented by technological fixes alone, but will require control of all aspects of the development and operation of the system."[30]

Software developers need to recognize the limitations of software. As computers have become more capable, software monitoring and control of machinery have become more common. In Chapter 1, we mentioned computer systems now being developed to take over some of the tasks involved in driving a car. The risks of turning control over to computers must be weighed carefully. Most software today is simply not safe enough for safety-critical applications. Hardware safety mechanisms, as used by engineers in pre-computer systems, still have an important role.

USER INTERFACES AND HUMAN FACTORS

If you are using a word processor or editing program to edit a document and you try to quit without saving your changes, what happens? Most programs will remind you that you have not saved your changes and give you a chance to do so. The designers of the programs know that people forget or sometimes click or type the wrong command. This is a simple and common example of considering human factors in designing software—one that has avoided personal calamities for millions of people.

Well-designed user interfaces can help avoid many computer-related problems. Principles and practices for doing a good job are known.* System designers and programmers need to learn from psychologists and human-factors experts. User interfaces should provide clear instructions and error messages; they should be consistent; and they should include appropriate checking of input to reduce major system failures caused by typos or other errors a person can be reasonably expected to make.

The importance of consistency (and other aspects of good user interfaces) is illustrated by the crash of American Airlines Flight 965 near Cali, Columbia in 1995. While approaching the airport, the pilot intended to lock the autopilot onto the beacon, called Rozo, that would lead the plane to the airport. The pilot typed "R," and the computer system displayed six beacons beginning with "R." Normally, the closest beacon is at the top of the list. The pilot selected it without checking carefully. The beacon at the top of the list was called Romeo and was more than 100 miles away, near Bogota. The plane turned more than 90 degrees and headed for Romeo. In the dark, it crashed into a mountain, killing 159 people.[31]

In the lawsuits that followed, the crash was attributed mostly to pilot error. The pilot chose the wrong beacon without checking and continued to descend at night after the plane made a large, unexpected turn. A jury assigned some of the responsibility to the companies that provided the computer system. While it is clear that the pilot could have and should have avoided the crash, it is also clear that the inconsistency in the display—not putting the nearest beacon at the top of the list—created the dangerous situation.

As an illustration of more principles that can help build safer systems, we consider other aspects of automated flight systems. An expert in this area emphasizes the following points:[32]

- *The pilot needs feedback to understand what the automated system is doing at any time.* This is critical when the pilot must suddenly take over if the automation fails or must be turned off for any reason. One example is having the throttle move as a manually operated throttle would, even though movement is not necessary when the automated system is operating.

- *The system should behave as the pilot (or, in general, experienced user) expects.* Pilots tend to reduce their rate of climb as they get close to their desired altitude. On the

---

* See, for example, the Shneiderman, Tufte, Nielsen, and Norman books in the list of references at the end of the chapter.

McDonnell Douglas MD-80, the automated system maintains a climb rate that is up to eight times as fast as pilots typically choose. Pilots, concerned that the plane might overshoot its target altitude, made adjustments, not realizing that their intervention turned off the automated function that caused the plane to level out when it reached the desired altitude. Thus, because the automation behaved in an unexpected way, the airplane climbed too high—exactly what the pilot was trying to prevent. (The incidence of the problem was reduced with more training, but the human-factors approach is to design the automation to suit the human, not vice versa.)

■ *A workload that is too low can be dangerous.* Clearly, if an operator is overworked, mistakes are more likely. One of the goals of automation is to reduce the human workload. However, a workload that is too low can lead to boredom, inattention, or lack of awareness of current status information that might be needed in a hurry when the pilot must take over.

Good user interfaces are essential in safety-critical applications. They are important also in ordinary business applications. Customers do not return to Web pages that are confusing or cause problems for their Web browsers. It is not a coincidence that some of the most popular Web sites are, according to design experts, some of the best designed.

REDUNDANCY AND SELF-CHECKING

Redundancy and self-checking are two techniques important in systems on which lives and fortunes depend. The space shuttles in the 1980s used four identical but independent computer systems that received input from multiple sensors and checked their results against each other. If one computer disagreed with the other three, it was taken out of service. If one of the three remaining was judged by the other two to be faulty, it was taken out of service, and the rest of the flight was canceled. In case of a more serious problem, perhaps caused by a common flaw in the software, there was a fifth computer, made by another manufacturer and programmed by different programmers, that could control the descent of the shuttle.[33] This degree of redundancy is expensive and is not used in many applications, but it illustrates the kinds of precautions that can be taken for systems that operate in dangerous physical environments where human lives are at stake.

Complex systems can collect information on their own activity for use in diagnosing and correcting errors. AT&T's telephone system handles roughly 100 million calls a day. The system is designed to constantly monitor itself and correct problems automatically. Half of the computing power of the system is devoted to checking the rest for errors. When a problem is detected in a switching component, the component automatically suspends use of the switch, informs the rest of the network that it is out of service temporarily and should not receive calls, activates recovery routines that take a few seconds to correct the problem, then informs the network that the component is functioning again. But wait a minute! This is the same system that failed several years ago, disrupting phone service for hours. In fact, it was this very part of the system that caused the breakdown. There was a bug in the routine that processed recovery messages from switches that had failed and recovered. The same software operated in each switch. Thus, each switch that received the message failed, then recovered and sent a recovery message. A chain reaction of failures occurred. The bug was in a software upgrade that had been running for about a month.[34] Even when the best professional practices are followed, even with extensive testing, we cannot be guaranteed that such complex systems do not have bugs.

TESTING

It is difficult to overemphasize the importance of adequate, well-planned testing of software. Testing is not arbitrary; there are principles and techniques for doing a good job. Unfortunately, many programmers and software developers see testing as a dispensable luxury, a step to be skimped on to meet a deadline or to save money. This is a common, but foolish, risky, and often irresponsible attitude.

In his Challenger investigation, Richard Feynman concluded that the computer systems used on board the space shuttle were developed with good safety criteria and testing plans.* Ironically, he was told that, because the shuttle software usually passed its tests, NASA management planned to reduce testing to save money. Fortunately, instead, as a result of studies after the loss of the Challenger, NASA instituted a practice called independent verification and validation (IV&V). That means that the software is tested and validated by a company other than the one that developed the program and other than the customer. (Testing and verification by an independent organization is not practical for all projects, but many software developers have their own testing teams that are independent of the programmers who develop a system.) The IV&V team acts as "adversaries" and tries to find flaws. After a few years, NASA planned to eliminate IV&V, but switched direction again. In response to several studies, including an extensive one done by software safety experts, NASA decided to make IV&V a permanent part of the program.[35] This example illustrates a common ambivalence about testing.

4.3.3 LAW AND REGULATION

CRIMINAL AND CIVIL PENALTIES

Legal remedies for faulty systems include suits against the company that developed or sold the system and criminal charges when fraud or criminal negligence occurs. Families of Therac-25 victims sued; the suits were settled out of court. A bank won an $818,000 judgment against a software company for a faulty financial system that caused problems described as "catastrophic" by a user.[36] Several people have won large judgments against credit bureaus for incorrect data in credit reports that caused havoc in their lives.

Many contracts for business computer systems limit the amount the customer can recover to the actual amount spent on the computer system. Customers know, when

---

*The destruction of the Challenger was caused by seals that failed in cold weather, not by a software error. Studies were done on many aspects of safety afterwards.

they sign the contract, that losses incurred because the system did not meet their needs for any reason are generally not covered. Such contract limitations have been upheld in court. If people and businesses cannot count on the terms of a contract being upheld by the legal system, contracts would be almost useless; millions of business interactions that take place daily would become more risky and therefore more expensive. Because fraud and misrepresentation are not, of course, part of a contract, some companies that suffer large losses allege fraud and misrepresentation by the seller in an attempt to recover some of the losses, regardless of whether the allegations are firmly grounded.

Well-designed liability laws and criminal laws—not so extreme that they discourage innovation, but clear and strong enough to provide incentives to produce good systems—are important legal tools for increasing reliability and safety of computer systems, as they are for other industries. After-the-fact penalties do not undo the injuries that occurred, but the prospect of paying for mistakes and sloppiness is incentive to be responsible and careful. Fines compensate the victim and provide some justice. An individual, business, or government that does not have to pay for its mistakes and irresponsible actions will make more of them.

Unfortunately, liability law in the U.S. is very flawed. Multimillion-dollar suits are often won when there is no scientific evidence or sensible reason to hold the manufacturer or seller of a product responsible for accidents. Abuse of the liability lawsuit system virtually shut down the small-airplane manufacturing industry in the United States. The newness and complexity of large computer systems make designing liability standards difficult, but this task needs to be done.

WARRANTIES FOR CONSUMER SOFTWARE

Most mass, retail consumer software, from word processors to games, comes packaged with "shrink-wrap" licensing agreements or online with "click-wrap" agreements that indicate the software is sold "as-is;" there is no guarantee that it works correctly. Consumer advocates and the software industry disagree on the extent to which these agreements should be upheld by law. At one extreme, a model law proposed for adoption by the states, the Uniform Computer Information Transactions Act (UCITA), would accept the agreements as binding contracts, letting software sellers continue to sell products with known bugs. (UCITA is more than 300 pages long, covering contracts for development, sale, and licensing of software and many forms of electronic information. There is much controversy about its potential impact on software quality, intellectual property, and the ability of software vendors to exercise broad control over customers' use of their products.) At the other extreme, some consumer advocates argue for mandatory warranties on software, for making software companies pay for bugs.

Supporters of strict legal requirements for warranties argue that such requirements would encourage responsibility on the part of software sellers and produce better software. Consumers would have legal protection against large, indifferent companies. Consumers are paying for a product that works, and fairness dictates that they get one that does.

Opponents point out that such requirements would raise prices. The additional cost of development, testing, and insurance would hurt small companies most, putting them out of business and leading to concentration of the industry in large companies. The costs would also reduce innovation and development of new software. The inherent complexity of software makes production of error-free software infeasible; actual use by consumers is an important part of the testing that leads to corrections and upgrades. Some companies pay users a few dollars for each bug they find.

Supporters of stricter laws might respond that we would not accept these arguments if we were discussing, say, microwave ovens. If we buy one, we expect it to work. A basic issue in this debate is whether legal standards and requirements for quality and warranties should be the same for software as for physical products. Some related questions: How well did the first microwave ovens, the first cars, the first record players work? Are we in the early stages of software as a product? Are consumers willing to trade having bugs in software for other benefits? Would a warranty law speed up the process of improving software?

Having different liability standards for software and physical products raises some problems. A microwave oven has embedded software. Can the sellers of microwave ovens claim that their product should be covered by the weaker standards for software? Would companies making various devices and appliances add software to their products unnecessarily, just to bring the products under the lower software standards? Would this lead to a serious decline in product quality? Although there are good arguments for treating consumer software differently from physical products, laws would have to define carefully the category of products to which they apply.[37]

REGULATION AND SAFETY-CRITICAL APPLICATIONS

Is there legislation or regulation that can prevent life-threatening computer failures? A law saying that a radiation machine should not overdose a patient would be silly. We know that it should not do that. No legislator or regulator knew in advance that that particular computer application would cause harm. We could ban the use of computer control for applications where an error could be fatal, but such a ban is ill advised. In many applications the benefits of using computers are well worth the risks.

A widely accepted option is regulation, possibly including specific testing requirements and requirement for approval by a government agency before a new product can be sold. The FDA has regulated drugs and medical devices for decades. Extensive testing, huge quantities of documentation, and government approval are required before new drugs and some medical devices can be sold. Arguments in favor of such regulation, both for drugs and for safety-critical computer systems, are the following:

- The profit motive might encourage businesses to skimp on safety; the government has a responsibility to prevent that from happening.

- It is better to prevent a bad product from being used than to rely on after-the-calamity remedies.

- Most potential customers and people who would be at risk (patients, airplane passengers) do not have the expertise to judge the safety or reliability of a system.

■ It is too difficult and expensive for ordinary people to sue large companies successfully.

If the FDA had thoroughly examined the Therac-25 before it was put into operation, the flaws might have been found before any patients were injured. However, the weaknesses and trade-offs in the regulatory approach should be noted.[38]

■ The approval process is extremely expensive and time-consuming. The delays caused by the regulation and requirements for government review cost many lives. Companies sometimes abandon useful products because the expense of meeting FDA requirements is too high.

■ Regulations that require specific procedures or materials discourage or prevent the use of newer and better ones that were not thought of by the people who wrote the rules.

■ The goal of the regulation, be it safety, privacy, accuracy, reduction of pollution, or whatever, tends to get lost in the details of the paperwork required. One writer on software safety commented, "The whole purpose of [following good software development techniques and documenting the steps] is to ensure that the necessary planning and design is performed, but regulatory agencies tend to focus on the visible products of the effort: the documents."[39]

■ The approval process is affected by political concerns, including influence by competitors and the incentive to be overcautious. (Damage caused by an approved product results in bad publicity and possible firing for the regulator who approved it. Deaths or losses caused by the delay or failure to approve a good new product are usually not obvious and get little publicity.)

Leveson and Turner, in their Therac-25 article, summarize some of these dilemmas:

> The issues involved in regulation of risky technology are complex. Overly strict standards can inhibit progress, require techniques behind the state of the art, and transfer responsibility from the manufacturer to the government. The fixing of responsibility requires a delicate balance. Someone must represent the public's needs, which may be subsumed by a company's desire for profits. On the other hand, standards can have the undesirable effect of limiting the safety efforts and investment of companies that feel their legal and moral responsibilities are fulfilled if they follow the standards. Some of the most effective standards and efforts for safety come from users. Manufacturers have more incentive to satisfy customers than to satisfy government agencies.[40]

DATABASE ACCURACY

We have focused mainly on business-system failures and on dangers in safety-critical applications. What about the problem of accuracy of information in databases maintained by businesses and government agencies? Most of the discussion above about liability and regulation applies as well to accuracy of private (business) databases. Achieving and maintaining accuracy in government databases is made difficult by the lack of market incentives for accuracy and the fact that the government can refuse to be sued. Outside of government, we pay for accidents and carelessness.

PROFESSIONAL LICENSING

Another controversial approach to improving software quality is mandatory licensing of software development professionals. Licenses are required by law for hundreds of trades and professions. Licensing requirements typically include specific training, the passing of competency exams, ethical requirements, and continuing education. The desired effect is to protect the public from poor quality and unethical behavior. The history of mandatory licensing in many fields shows that the actual goals and the effects were and are not always very noble. In some trades, particularly plumbing, the licensing requirements were devised to keep black people out. Requirements for specific degrees and training programs, as opposed to learning on one's own or on the job, tend to keep poorer people from qualifying for licenses. Economic analyses have shown that the effect of licensing is to reduce the number of practitioners in the field and keep prices and income for licensees higher than they would otherwise be, in some cases without any improvement in quality.[41] A legal prohibition on working for pay without a government-approved license is seen by some as a fundamental violation of the freedom to work (that is, of the negative right, or liberty, to work, in the terms of Section 1.2.2).

These objections do not apply to the many valuable *voluntary* approaches to measuring or certifying qualifications of software personnel, for example, a diploma from a respected school and certification programs by professional organizations, particularly for advanced training in specialized areas.

4.3.4 TAKING RESPONSIBILITY

In some of the cases we mentioned, businesses made large payments to customers in compensation for problems or damages caused by computer programs. For example, Intuit offered to pay interest and penalties that resulted from errors in flawed income-tax programs. When United Airlines mistakenly posted ticket prices on its Web site as low as about $25 for flights between the U.S. and Europe, it honored tickets purchased before the error was corrected. United, at first, charged the buyers the correct fare and probably had the legal right not to honor the incorrect low price, but the airline concluded that having angry customers would cost more than the tickets.

We noted that business pressures are often a reason for cutting corners and releasing defective products. Business pressure can also be a cause for insistence on quality and maintaining good customer relations. Good business managers recognize the importance of customer satisfaction and the reputation of the business. Also, some businesses have an ethical policy of behaving responsibly and paying for mistakes, just as a person would pay for accidentally breaking a neighbor's window with a misdirected softball.

Other market mechanisms besides consumer backlash encourage a quality job. Insurance companies have an incentive to evaluate the systems they insure. The insurer for the company that operated several faulty communications satellites commented that the lapse in testing and quality control would be taken into account in the future. Satellite-failure incidents illustrate another market mechanism for dealing with the risk of computer failures: Some businesses paid a higher rate for "uninterrupted" service, meaning that their communications would be switched quickly to other satellites in case of a failure. Businesses that can withstand a few hours of interruption need not pay for that extra protection. Organizations whose communications are critical to public safety, such as police departments and hospitals, should take the responsibility of paying for appropriate backup service.

How can customers protect themselves from faulty software? How can a business avoid buying a seriously flawed program? For high-volume, consumer software, one can consult the many magazines and Web sites that review new programs. Specialized systems with a small market are more difficult to evaluate before purchase. We can use a hint from another field where there seem to be some reliable and some questionable practitioners: home remodeling. We can check the company's reputation with the Better Business Bureau. We can get references (i.e., names of previous customers) and ask them how well the job was done. Online user groups for specific software products are excellent sources of information for prospective customers. In the case of the Therac-25, the users eventually spread information among themselves. If the World Wide Web had existed at the time of the accidents, it is likely that the problems would have been identified sooner and that some of the accidents would thereby have been avoided.

4.4 Perspectives on Failures, Dependence, Risk, and Progress

4.4.1 PUTTING FAILURES IN PERSPECTIVE

BILLING AND BANKING

How close to perfection should we expect billing systems to be? A water-utility company sent a customer an incorrect bill for $22,000. A spokesman for the company pointed out that one incorrect bill out of 275,000 monthly bills is a good error rate. Is that reasonable? How accurate should the software for ATMs be? The double-withdrawal incident mentioned in Chapter 1 affected roughly 150,000 transactions. With approximately eight billion ATM transactions each year, that is one error in roughly 45,000. Is that an acceptable rate? (There were probably other ATM errors in that year, but the publicity given this case suggests that it affected far more transactions than others.) How accurate should software for check processing be? 99%? 99.9%? Banks process tens of millions of checks per day. Even if they made errors on 1000 checks every day, that would be an accuracy rate of better than 99.99%.[42] (How high would the accuracy rate be if checks and bills were processed without computers?) At some point, the expense of improving a system is not worth the gain, especially for applications where errors can be detected and corrected at lower cost than it would take to try to eliminate them.

COMPLEX SYSTEMS

On October 28, 1997, 1.2 billion shares of stock were traded on the New York Stock Exchange—76% more than the previous record. The Stock Exchange computers handled the sales without errors or delays. The Exchange managers had planned in advance, spending $2 billion on a system with 450 refrigerator-size computers, 200 miles of fiber-optic cable, 8000 telephone circuits, and 300 data routers. They had spent weekends testing the system on triple and quadruple the normal trading volume. Similarly, over one weekend, Barclays Bank replaced three incompatible computer systems with a new system to handle 25 million accounts. The transition, estimated to cost more than £100 million, was successful.[43]

Many large, complex, expensive computer systems work. We described a variety of problems related to aircraft computer systems in Sections 4.1.4 and 4.3.2, so we continue here with examples and discussion of aircraft systems. The same points apply to almost any other application area. The enhanced ground-proximity warning system (GPWS) was designed to prevent airplanes from crashing into mountains. Older radar-based systems sometimes gave warning only 10 seconds before a potential impact. The new system contains a digital map of the world's topography. It can give a pilot up to a minute of warning if a plane is too close to a mountain and automatically displays a map of nearby mountains. Dangerous peaks are shown in red. The system combines ground-detection technology and a graphical user interface. In addition, it works where the older system did not: The radar-based system could not distinguish between approaching the ground for landing and a potential crash, so it did not give warnings during a landing approach. The digital maps enable the computer system to make the distinction, and the new GWPS is credited with helping avoid a crash into a mountain by an Air France plane attempting to land in conditions of poor visibility.[44]

There is controversy about how much control should be given to a flight computer. The computers in newer Airbus planes are programmed to prevent certain actions even if the pilot tries them (for example, banking at a very steep angle). Some people object, arguing that the pilot should have ultimate control in case unusual action is needed in an emergency. Some airlines (and private pilots) disable parts of the computer systems because they don't trust the computer or because they believe the pilot should be more actively engaged in flying the plane. However, there are circumstances where the computer can do better than most people. Like anti-lock braking systems (ABS) in automobiles that control braking to avoid skidding, new computer systems in airplanes control sudden sharp climbs to avoid stalling. Based on accident statistics, some airlines agree that more lives can be saved by preventing pilots from doing something "stupid" than by letting them do something outside the program limitations in the rare cases where that might be needed. According to an FAA official, computer automation has reduced or eliminated some types of pilot errors while introducing new ones. As population and travel increase, computer systems are essential. Overall, computers and other technologies have made air travel safer. During the 1970s and 1980s, the death rate from commercial airplane accidents declined from 0.8 per 100,000 people to 0.4 per 100,000. In the 1990s, the rate of fatal crashes per million miles flown by the major U.S. airliners dropped about 85%, from roughly 0.13 to under 0.02 (in 1998).[45]

4.4.2 ARE WE TOO DEPENDENT ON COMPUTERS?

A fire at a telephone switching facility in Los Angeles disrupted telephone service for half a day. A newspaper article reported the impact.[46] More than 150,000 customers could barely function without their phones and modem-equipped computers. Drivers could not buy gasoline with their credit cards. "Customers were really angry," said a gas station manager. Stockbrokers could not connect to New York by phone or computer. More than 1000 automated teller machines did not function; they used phone lines to connect to central computers. A travel agent could not make reservations for clients. 1200 out of 22,000 California state lottery terminals were down; people couldn't buy tickets or collect winnings.

The incident serves as a good reminder about how many ordinary daily activities are dependent on communications and computer networks. People have come to take reliable operation of these systems for granted. Echoing the gas station manager: When an AT&T system used by banks failed, a supermarket manager reported "Customers are yelling and screaming because they can't get their money, and they can't use the ATM to pay for groceries."[47] A physician commented that modern hospitals and clinics cannot function efficiently without medical-information systems. Modern crime fighting depends on computers. Some military jets cannot fly without the assistance of computers.

Comments about our dependence on computers appear in many discussions of the social impact of computers. Because of their usefulness and flexibility, computers are now virtually everywhere. Is this good? or bad? or neutral? Often the word "dependence" has a negative connotation. "Dependence on computers" suggests a criticism of our society or of our use of computers. Is it appropriate? Several aspects of these criticisms are wrong, but some are valid. Some misconceptions about dependence on computers come from a poor understanding of the role of risk, confusion of "dependence" with "use," and blaming computers for failures where they were only innocent bystanders. On the other hand, abdication of responsibility that comes from overconfidence or ignorance is a serious problem. Also, there are valid technical criticisms of dependence when a system is designed so that a failure in one component can cause a major breakdown.

"DEPENDENCE" OR "USE"?

> *Electricity lets us heat our homes, cook our food, and enjoy security and entertainment. It also can kill you if you're not careful.*
>
> —"Energy Notes," May 1994. (Flyer sent with SDG&E utility bills)

Hospitals and clinics cannot operate without electricity. We use electricity for lighting, entertainment, manufacturing—just about everything. In the early 1990s, there were several disruptions of telephone systems and air traffic because of computer problems. In those same years, there were several disruptions of telephone systems and air traffic because of electric-power problems. In 2001, rolling power blackouts severely disrupted normal activity in California.

Is our "dependence" on computers different from our dependence on electricity? Is it different from a farmer's dependence on a plow? The Sioux people's dependence on their bows and arrows? Modern surgery's dependence on anesthesia? Computers and plows are tools. We use tools because we are better off with them than without them. They reduce the need for hard physical labor and tedious routine mental labor; they help us be more productive, or safer, or more comfortable. When we have a good tool, we can forget, or no longer even learn, the older method of performing a task. If the tool breaks down, we are stuck; we cannot perform the task until the tool is fixed. That can mean that no telephone calls get through for several hours. It can mean that a large amount of money is lost, and it can mean that people are endangered or die. But the negative effects of a breakdown do not condemn the tool. To the contrary, for many computer applications (not all), the inconveniences or dangers of a breakdown are a reminder of the convenience and productivity provided by the tool when it is working, for example, of the billions of telephone calls (carrying voice, e-mail, files, and data) that are completed—that are made possible or more convenient or cheaper because of computers.

We could avoid the risk of a broken plow by plowing with our hands. We could avoid the risk of losing a document file on a disk by doing all our writing by hand on paper. Even ignoring the possibility of a fire destroying our paper records, it should be clear that we reject the "safe" (nondependent) option because, most of the time, it is less convenient and less productive. If one enjoys wilderness camping, as I do, one can observe how "dependent" we normally are on electric lights, refrigeration, and plumbing. That does not mean we should cook on camp stoves and read by firelight at home.

RISK AND PROGRESS

We trust our lives to technology every day. We trust older, noncomputer technologies every time we step into an elevator, a car, or a building. As the tools and technologies we use become larger, more complex, and more interconnected, the amount of damage that results from an individual disruption or failure increases, and the costs may be paid in dramatic and tragic events. If a person out for a walk bumps into another person, neither is likely to be hurt. If both are driving cars at 60 miles per hour, they could be killed. If two jets collide, or one loses an engine, several hundred people could be killed. However, the death rate per mile traveled is not higher for air travel than for cars.

Most new technologies were not very safe when they were first developed. If the death rate from commercial airline accidents in the U.S. were the same now as it was 50 years ago, 8,000 people would die in plane crashes each year (instead of fewer than 200). Some early polio vaccines, in which the virus was not totally inactivated, caused polio in some children. We learn how to make improvements; problems are discovered and solved; scientists and engineers study disasters and learn how to prevent them and how to recover from them.

While reading about GPWS, the system that warns pilots if they are headed toward a mountain, it occurred to me that many lives could have been saved if it had been installed on the American Airlines plane that crashed near Cali, Columbia. Then I read that this crash triggered adoption of the new system, and no U.S. airliner has crashed into a mountain since then. Similarly, a disastrous fire led to the development of fire hydrants—a way to get water at the scene from the water pipes under the street. Automobile engineers used to design the front of an automobile to be extremely rigid, to protect passengers in a crash. But people died and suffered serious injuries because the force of a crash was transmitted through the car frame to the people—and the engineers learned it was better to build cars with "crumple zones" to absorb the force of impact.[48] The Cali crash is used as an example in software engineering textbooks, so that future software specialists will not repeat the mistakes in the plane's computer system. We learn.

What has happened to the safety record in other technologies? The number of deaths from automobile accidents declined from 54,633 in 1970 to fewer than 42,000 in 1999 (while population, of course, increased). Why? Some significant reasons are increased education about responsible use (i.e., the campaign against drunk driving), devices that protect people when the system fails (seat belts and airbags), and improvements in technology, many of which use computers. As use of technology, automation, and computer systems has increased in virtually all work places, the risk of dying in an on-the-job accident dropped from 390 in one million (in 1934) to 40 in one million (in 1994).[49]

Risk is not restricted to technology and machines. It is a part of life. Sharp tools are risky. Someone living in a jungle faces danger from animals. A desert hiker faces rattlesnakes. We are safer if we know the risks and take reasonable precautions. We are never 100% safe.

Software safety expert Nancy Leveson says that the mistakes made in software are the same as those that used to be common in engineering. Over many years engineers developed techniques and procedures to increase safety. Software developers need to learn from engineers and adapt their methods to software.

There are some important differences between computers and other technologies. Computers make decisions; electricity does not. The power and flexibility of computers encourages us to build more complex systems—where failures have more serious consequences. The pace of change in computer technology is much higher than that in other technologies. Software is not built from standard, trusted parts as is the case in many engineering fields. The software industry is still going through its "growing pains;" it has not yet developed into a mature, fully developed discipline.

FALSE CHARGES—OR, BLAMING THE STOVE FOR A POORLY COOKED MEAL

As we have said several times already, computers are virtually everywhere. That means that, when anything goes wrong, there is probably a computer that can be blamed, sometimes unfairly. I will mention just a few such examples that have appeared in other books.

In Holland, the body of a reclusive, elderly man who died in his apartment was not discovered until six months after his death, when someone noticed that he had a large accumulation of mail. This incident was described as a "particularly disturbing example of computer dependency." Many of the man's bills, including rent and utilities, were paid automatically, and his pension check was automatically deposited in his bank account. Thus "all the relevant authorities assumed that he was still alive."[50] But who expects the local gas company or other "relevant authorities" to discover a death? The problem here clearly was the lack of concerned family, friends, and neighbors. I happened to be present in a similar situation. An elderly, reclusive woman died in her home. Within two days, not six months, the mailman noticed that she had not taken in her mail. He informed a neighbor, and together they checked the house. I do not know if her utility bills were paid by computer; it is irrelevant.

Published collections of computer-related risks involving trains include cases of faulty brakes, operators disabling safety controls, a loose wire, and a confused driver who drove his train in the wrong direction during rush hour. Many of the cases involved human errors. We have seen that some human errors are the result of confusing or poorly designed computer systems, but that was not apparently the case in several of the reported incidents. An incident where a computer reportedly fell on a man's foot was listed as a health risk of computers.[51]

I mention these cases because accurate identification of the source of a problem is an important step to solving it. Including such incidents as risks of computers obscures the distinction between them and cases where computer systems *are* at fault—it is on the latter that we must focus our attention to make improvements.

4.4.3 OBSERVATIONS

We have made several points:

1. Many of the issues related to reliability for computers have arisen before with other technologies.
2. Perfection is not an option. The complexity of computer systems makes errors, oversights, and so on likely.
3. There is a "learning curve" for new technologies. By studying failures, we can reduce their occurrence.
4. Risks of using computers should be compared with risks of other methods and with benefits obtained.

This does not mean that computer errors and failures should be excused or ignored because failures occur in other technologies. It does not mean that carelessness or negligence should be tolerated because perfection is not possible. It does not mean that accidents should be excused as part of the learning process, and it does not mean that accidents should be excused because, on balance, the contribution of computers is positive.

The potential for serious disruption of normal activities and danger to people's lives and health because of flaws in computer systems should always remind the computer professional of the importance of doing his or her job responsibly. Computer system developers and other professionals responsible for planning and choosing systems must assess risks carefully and honestly, include safety protections, and make appropriate plans for shutdown of a system when it fails, for backup systems where appropriate, and for recovery.

Knowing that one will be liable for the damages one causes is strong incentive to find improvements and increase safety. When evaluating a specific instance of a failure, we can look for those responsible and try to ensure that they bear the costs of the damage they caused. It is when evaluating computer use in a particular application area or when evaluating the technology as a whole that we should look at the balance between risks and benefits and compare the risks and benefits with those of noncomputerized alternatives.

4.5 Computer Models

4.5.1 EVALUATING MODELS

Computer-generated predictions and conclusions about subjects with important social impact frequently appear in the news. Figure 4.2 lists a few examples.

A mathematical model is a collection of data and equations describing, or simulating, characteristics and behavior of the thing being studied. The models and simulations of interest to us here require so much data and/or computation that they must be run on computers. Computers are used extensively to model and simulate both physical systems, such as the design for a new car or the flow of water in a river, and intangible systems, such

---

- Population growth.

- The cost of a proposed government program.

- The effects of second-hand smoke.

- When we will run out of a critical natural resource.

- The effects of a tax cut on the economy.

- The threat of global warming.

- When a big earthquake is likely to occur.

Figure 4.2 Some Problems Studied with Computer Models

as parts of the economy. Models allow us to simulate and investigate the possible effects of different designs, scenarios, and policies. They have obvious social and economic benefits: They help train operators of power plants, submarines, and airplanes. They enable us to consider alternatives and make better decisions, reducing waste, cost, and risk. They enable us to project trends and plan better for the future.

Although the models we consider are abstract (i.e., mathematical), the meaning of the word "model" here is similar to its meaning in "model airplane." Models are simplifications. Model airplanes generally do not have an engine, and the wing flaps might not move. In a chemistry class, we could use sticks and balls to build models of molecules, to help us understand their properties. The molecule models might not show the components of the individual atoms. Similarly, mathematical models do not include equations for every factor that could influence the outcome, or they can include equations that are simplified because the correct ones are unknown or too complicated. For example, a constant known as the acceleration of gravity can be used in equations to determine when an object dropped from a high place will hit the ground. The effect of wind might not be included in the equations, but, on some days, wind could make a difference.

Physical models are usually not the same size as the real thing. Model planes are smaller; the molecule model is larger. In mathematical models, it is time rather than physical size that often differs from reality. Computations done on a computer to model a complex physical process in detail often take more time than the actual process takes. For models of long-range social phenomena, such as population growth, the computation must take less time than the real phenomenon for the results to be useful.

Predictions from expensive computers and complex computer programs impress people, but models vary enormously in quality. Some are worthless; others are very reliable. Predictions about problems like those in Figure 4.2 are used to justify multibillion-dollar government programs, restrictions on people's freedom, and regulations with significant impact on the economy and the standard of living of hundreds of millions of people. It is important for both computer professionals and the general public to have some idea of what is in such computer programs, where their uncertainties and weaknesses might lie, and how to evaluate their claims. It is the professional and ethical responsibility of those who design and develop models for public issues to describe honestly and accurately the results, assumptions, and limitations of their models.

Among three models developed to predict the change in health care costs that would result if the U.S. adopted a Canadian-style national health plan, the predictions varied by $279 billion. Two of the models predicted large increases and one predicted a drastic decrease.[52] Why was there such a difference? There are both political and technical reasons why models may not be accurate. Political reasons, especially for this example, are probably obvious. Among the technical reasons:

■ We might not have complete knowledge of the system being modeled. In other words, the basic physical or social science involved might not be fully understood.

- The data describing current conditions or characteristics might be incomplete or inaccurate.

- Computing power could be inadequate for the number of computations that would be needed if the full complexity of the system were modeled.

- It is difficult, if not impossible, to numerically quantify variables that represent human values and choices.

The people who design models decide what simplifications and assumptions to make.

Are reusable (washable cloth) diapers better for the environment than disposable diapers? When bans and taxes on disposable diapers were proposed, this controversy consumed almost as much energy as diaper manufacturing. Several computer models were developed to study the question. This particular kind of model is called a life-cycle analysis; it attempts to consider the resource use and environmental effects of all aspects of the product, including manufacture, use, and disposal. To illustrate how difficult such a study may be, Figure 4.3 lists a few of the questions about which the modelers made assumptions. Depending on the assumptions, the conclusions differed.[53]

The TAPPS computer model for nuclear winter, popularized by Carl Sagan in the 1980s, predicted that millions of tons of smoke from a nuclear war would stay in the sky for months, blocking sunlight, causing temperatures on earth to drop 15°C–25°C, and causing crops and people to freeze. One critic of the model pointed out that it represented the earth as a smooth, oceanless ball, did not distinguish day from night, and did not include effects of wind. Another observed that the model was a brilliant "tour de force," combining knowledge of physics, pyrology, nuclear strategy, and meteorology, but that most of its assumptions were very unlikely. One of the ethical issues raised about this model was its presentation to the public as a scientific prediction of what was likely, rather than as a simplified model using worst-case assumptions.[54]

- How many times is a cloth diaper used before it is discarded? (Values ranged from 90 to 167.)

- Should credit be given for energy recovered when waste is incinerated, or does pollution from incineration counterbalance the benefit?

- What value should be assigned for the labor cost of washing diapers?

- How many cloth diapers are used each time a baby is changed? (Many parents use two at once for increased protection.) The models used values ranging from 1.72 to 1.9.

- How should the pesticides used in growing cotton be counted?

Figure 4.3 Factors in Diaper Life-Cycle Modeling

The following questions help us determine the validity and accuracy of a model.

1. How well do the modelers understand the underlying science or theory (be it physics, chemistry, economics, or whatever) of the system being studied? How well understood are the relevant properties of the materials involved? How accurate and complete are the data?
2. Models necessarily involve assumptions and simplifications of reality. What are the assumptions and simplifications in the model?
3. How closely do the results or predictions of the model correspond with results from physical experiments or real experience?

The examples in the next two sections illustrate our discussion of evaluating computer models and simulations. They also illustrate the distinction between applications where modeling results are highly reliable and applications where modeling is very difficult and the results controversial.

Likeness to truth is not the same thing as truth.

—Peter L. Bernstein[55]

4.5.2 CAR CRASH-ANALYSIS PROGRAMS*

Car crash-analysis programs had gained wide usage by the late 1980s. One of the major programs, DYNA3D, was developed at Lawrence Livermore National Laboratory for military applications, but is now used in product design. The program models the interactions of physical objects on impact, especially in high-speed collisions. It uses a technique called the finite-element method. A grid is superimposed on the frame of a car, dividing the car into a finite number of small pieces, or elements. The grid is entered into the program, along with data describing the specifications of the materials making up each element (e.g., density, strength, and elasticity). Suppose we are studying the effects on the structure of the car from a head-on collision. Data can be initialized to represent a crash into a wall at a specified speed. The program computes the force, acceleration, and displacement at each grid point and the stress and strain within each element. These calculations are repeated to show what happens as time passes in small increments. Using graphics programs, the simulation produces a picture of the car at intervals after impact, as illustrated in Figure 4.4. These programs require intensive computation. To simulate 40–100 milliseconds of real time from the impact took up to 35 hours of computer time on a supercomputer in the early 1990s.[56]

The cost of a real crash test can range from $50,000 to $800,000. The high figure is for building and testing a unique prototype for a new car design. The crash-analysis programs allow engineers to consider alternatives, for example, to vary the thickness of steel for selected components, or change materials altogether, and discover the effect without building another prototype for each alternative. But how good are the programs?

---

*An earlier version of this section appeared in my chapter, "Social and Legal Issues," in *An Invitation to Computer Science* by G. Michael Schneider and Judith L. Gersting, West Publishing Co., 1995. (Used with permission.)

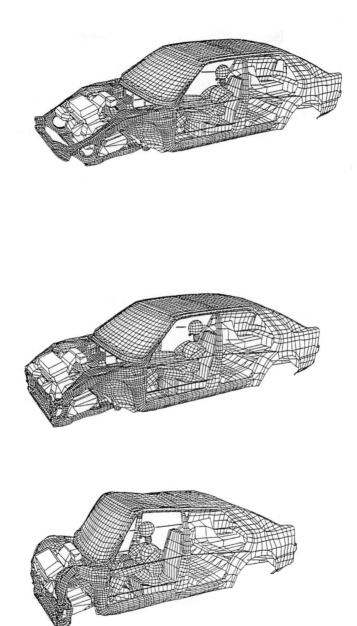

Figure 4.4 LS-DYNA3D Simulation of a Frontal Crash (35 mph before impact; 20 and 70 milliseconds after). (Reproduced by the permission of Livermore Software Technology Corporation.)

How well is the physics of car crashes understood? How accurate and complete are the data? Force and acceleration are basic principles; the physics involved in these programs is very straightforward. The relevant properties of steel, plastics, aluminum, glass, and other materials in a car are fairly well known. However, although the behavior of the materials when force is applied gradually is well known, the behavior of some materials under abrupt acceleration, as in a high-speed impact, and their behavior near or at breaking point are less understood. There are good data on the density, elasticity, and other characteristics of materials used in the model.

What simplifications are made in the programs? The grid pattern is the most obvious; a car is smooth, not made up of little blocks. Also, time is continuous; it does not occur in steps. The accuracy of the simulation will depend in part on how fine the grid is and how small the time intervals are. As computer speeds increase, we can do more precise computation. The programs described here had roughly 10,000–50,000 d updated the calculations for time intervals of one millionth of a second.

How do the computed results compare to actual crash tests on real cars? The real tests are recorded by high-speed cameras. Various kinds of sensors are attached to the car, and reference points are marked on the frame. The values recorded by the sensors are compared with values computed by the program, and the distortion or displacement of the reference points can be physically measured and compared to the computed positions. From the results of the physical crash, elementary physics can be used to calculate backward and determine the deceleration and other forces acting on the car. These can be compared to the values computed in the simulation. The conclusion? The crash-analysis programs do an extremely good job. Results from the program correspond very closely to data collected in actual test crashes.[57]

Car crash-analysis programs are replacing physical crash testing as a design tool for new cars. Engineers who work with the crash-analysis programs do not believe that physical crashes will or should be eliminated. They remind us that the simulation is an implementation of theory. The program might give poor results if it is used by someone who does not understand it well. Results could be poor if something happens that the program simply was not designed to consider. The crash-analysis programs are excellent design tools that enable increases in safety with far less development cost. The physical crash test is confirmation.

In part because of the confidence that has developed over time in the validity of the results, crash-analysis programs are used in a large variety of other impact applications. We list some in Figure 4.5.

4.5.3 CLIMATE MODELS AND GLOBAL WARMING

BACKGROUND

In the 1970s, after global temperatures had been dropping for about 30 years, some scientists warned that we faced serious problems from global cooling, including the possibility of a new Ice Age. Then temperatures began to rise again. By the late 1980s, the threat of excess global warming, possibly caused by human-induced increase of carbon dioxide

- Predict damage to a hazardous waste container if dropped.

- Predict damage to an airplane windshield or nacelle (engine covering) if hit by a bird.

- Determine whether beer cans would get dented if an assembly line were speeded up.

- Simulate a medical procedure called balloon angioplasty, where a balloon is inserted in a blocked artery and inflated to open the artery. The computer program helps researchers determine how to perform the procedure with less damage to the arterial wall.

- Predict the action of airbags and the proper location for sensors that inflate them.

- Design interior parts of cars to reduce injuries during crashes (e.g., from the impact of a steering wheel on a human chest).

- Design bicycle and motorcycle helmets to reduce head injuries.

- Design cameras to reduce damage if dropped.

- Forecast effects of earthquakes on bridges and buildings.

Figure 4.5 Other Uses of Crash-Analysis Programs

(CO_2) and other greenhouse gases in the atmosphere, replaced global cooling in the headlines and scientific journals. Global warming predictions are based on computer models of climate. In this section, we consider these models, but first we need a little background.

The earth is warmed by solar radiation. Some of the heat is reflected back; some is trapped by gases in the atmosphere. The latter phenomenon is known as the greenhouse effect. Without it, the temperature on the earth would be too cold to support life. The main "greenhouse gases" are water vapor, carbon dioxide (CO_2), methane, chlorofluorocarbons (CFCs), and ozone. Water vapor is the most significant, but, among those whose concentration has been increased by human activity, CO_2 is most important.

The concentrations of CO_2 and methane in the atmosphere are substantially higher than they were for most of the past 160,000 years.* An upward trend for both CO_2 and methane, from near their lowest values, began roughly 16,000 years ago. However, since the beginning of the Industrial Revolution, concentrations have been increasing at a faster rate. Since 1950, the climb has been steeper than before. The main human-generated source of increased CO_2 is the burning of fossil fuels (e.g., oil and coal). The top three sources of methane are thought to be natural wetlands, animals (e.g., cattle), and industry (coal, natural gas, and petroleum).

---

*The past data come from measurements of gases trapped in ice cores drilled in Antarctica and Greenland. Concentrations were likely higher than current levels millions of years ago.

Between the late 19th century and the end of the 20th, the average temperature near the surface of the earth rose by about $0.4°C–0.8°C$. It is unknown how much of the rise resulted from the end of the roughly three-century Little Ice Age, how much from other natural climate variability, and how much from human activity.

The computer climate models are called general circulation models (GCMs). GCMs were developed from atmospheric models for weather prediction. They are quite complex. They contain information about the sun's energy output; the orbit, inclination, and rotation of the earth; geography (a map of land masses); topography (mountains, etc.); clouds; sea and polar ice; soil and air moisture; and a large number of other factors. The equations simulate atmospheric pressure, temperature, incoming solar energy, outgoing radiant energy, wind speed and direction, moisture, precipitation, and so forth. For global-warming studies, the atmospheric models are combined with models of the oceans that include temperature, currents, and other factors. The combined models are called coupled models.

Researchers use climate models to study several aspects of future climate. They try, for example, to determine the effect of doubling CO_2 concentration in the atmosphere. (Current trends suggest the concentration will have doubled, from its approximate level at the beginning of the 20th century, by some time in the 21st century.*) The models try to project the likely increase in global temperature, sea level, and other climate characteristics over the next century, in various scenarios with assumptions about population, industrial and economic activity, energy use, and so on. Another task for the models is to attempt to distinguish how much warming is caused by human activity and how much is natural. The results of the models for all three problems (and what to do about them politically and socially) remain controversial.

The Intergovernmental Panel on Climate Change (IPCC), sponsored by the United Nations and the World Meteorological Organization, publishes major reports on the science of climate change roughly every five years. The reports are prepared and reviewed by several hundred scientists worldwide. They are considered an authoritative review of the state of scientific knowledge about climate change, although scientists who support the view that human activity is causing significant warming tend to be more involved in the IPCC reports than scientists who are more skeptical. The IPCC reports are among the main references used for this discussion.[58]

EVALUATING THE MODELS

How well is the science of climate activity understood? How accurate and complete are the data?

Climatologists know an enormous amount about climate. The models are based on a huge amount of good science and data. But the amount not known is also huge. We briefly describe a few areas of uncertainty.

---

*Other greenhouse gases are included too by converting their amount and effect to the equivalent number of units of CO_2.

According to the 2001 IPCC report, the level of scientific understanding for the impact of the major greenhouse gases is high; they have been studied most. The level of understanding for the impact of ozone is "medium," and the level for a variety of other factors listed (including dust particles in the air, some aspects of land use, and solar variability) is "very low." (Some have warming effects, and some have cooling effects.)[59]

Clouds are extremely important to climate. Many processes involved with the formation, effects, and dissipation of clouds are not particularly well understood. The IPCC 2001 report summarizes: "As has been the case since the first IPCC Assessment Report in 1990, probably the greatest uncertainty in future projections of climate arise from clouds.... Clouds represent a significant source of potential error in climate simulations."[60]

If temperatures rise, natural wetlands give off more methane, contributing to more warming. This is called positive, or destabilizing, feedback: An output or side effect of the process amplifies the original effect. There are negative, or stabilizing, feedbacks too. For example, when the earth warms, more water evaporates and forms clouds; the clouds reflect some of the sun's heat back up away from the earth. (Clouds have positive feedback effects also.) Many such feedback mechanisms affect climate. For some, it is not known whether the feedback is positive or negative. Many uncertainties in the models are attributed to lack of knowledge and to incomplete representation of feedback mechanisms.

In the 1980s and 1990s, for reasons scientists do not understand, methane concentration grew much more slowly than expected and assumed in the models. More research is needed on the relation between emissions of some greenhouse gases and their concentration and lifetime in the atmosphere.

Each of the IPCC reports lists several areas where more fundamental understanding of climate processes is needed and where more data are needed.

What simplifications and assumptions are made in the models?

Like the crash-analysis models, the climate models use a grid. The grid circles the earth, rises through the atmosphere, and goes down into the ocean. The computer programs solve equations for each grid point and element (grid box) for specified time intervals. Grid sizes vary among models; generally, grid points are roughly 200 kilometers apart. The grids are coarse because the computing time required to run the programs depends on the number of points. (Recall that it took hours of computer time to simulate 40–100 milliseconds of a car crash. Climate models simulate roughly 100 years over a much bigger space.) Because of the grid limitations, small storms, clouds, and other small phenomena that fall between the grid points are not accurately represented.

Some models in the late 1980s and early 1990s did not distinguish between day and night. This simplification was significant because temperature records for large areas of the northern hemisphere show increases in the nighttime winter lows and decreases (or in some areas, smaller increases) in the daytime summer highs, which could be a benign or even beneficial form for an average warming to take.[61] The newer models distinguish day from night; they predict more warming at night than during the day.

The computation requirements for ocean models are about a thousand times as large as those for atmospheric modeling, because of the grid sizes and time scales necessary for good results. Early models represented only the top layer of the oceans. The ocean models used now represent more layers and are more sophisticated than those used in the 1980s. Because of the enormous computational expense, however, coupled models (those that include both atmosphere and sophisticated ocean models) are not used for many model studies; older or simpler models are used instead.

Ideally, all of the processes that affect climate would be represented in the models by equations derived from the underlying science (generally, physics and chemistry). This is not possible, because it would require too much computation time and because all the underlying science is not known. Many processes are represented by simplified equations, called parametrizations, that seem to give realistic results but are not derived from scientific theory. The specific parametrizations vary among the models, reflecting the choices of the modelers. Values for estimated variables are chosen to make the models predict present and past conditions with reasonable accuracy. The process of modifying the values until the desired result is achieved is called "tuning" the model. Although models can be tuned by balancing the values for several variables so that the model accurately describes present conditions, it is not known whether that choice of values will predict future conditions accurately.

The model projections based on scenarios (rather than a specific increase in greenhouse gas concentration) include numerous assumptions about technological development, political control of emissions, population, economic development, energy use, and so on, throughout a century.

How closely do the results of the computer programs correspond to results from physical experiments?

We cannot do physical experiments for global warming; thus, we consider other ways to assess the results of the computer simulations.

The models predict seasonal variations and other actual broad-scale phenomena. The general patterns of predictions by different models are similar. For example, they all predict warming, and they all predict that more of the warming would take place near the poles and in winter. The models project that doubling CO_2 concentration in the atmosphere will cause a global temperature increase within the range $1.5°–4.5°C$. The wide variation suggests weaknesses in understanding of climate behavior and/or limitations of the models. For a well-understood phenomenon, the predictions of good models would show more agreement. Models still differ in their responses to a variety of factors that are not yet well understood.

One way to evaluate the models is to run them for conditions of the past to see whether their projections match the actual temperature record. Some of the climate models of the 1980s predicted temperature increases three to five times as high as what actually occurred over the previous century. The newer models are better at matching past data, but discrepancies remain. Satellite data (available since 1979), weather-balloon data, and other data show very little or no warming in the troposphere for the last two decades of the 20th century.* However, the models say that the troposphere should have warmed more than the surface. Some critics interpreted this discrepancy as indicating a serious flaw. Although the models indicate more warming near the poles, temperatures in major areas of Antarctica have been decreasing significantly.

CONCLUSIONS AND ETHICAL ISSUES

We focused on uncertainties and weaknesses in the climate models. As we said earlier, there is a huge amount of good science and data in the models, too. Projecting climate change is an extraordinarily difficult task. The models have become more detailed and complex in the few decades that scientists have been developing and working with them. Increased computer power allows more experiments, better calibration, and increased resolution (smaller grid size). Increased data collection and basic science research improve our understanding of the behavior and interactions of climate system components. The models are a tool for understanding climate change, but are not yet at a stage where we can rely on the precision of their results. Certainly they have not achieved the level of reliability of the car-crash-analysis models.

The IPCC 2001 report says that the coupled models (the complex models that include both atmosphere and oceans) provide "credible" simulations of climate. They are "suitable tools to provide useful projections of future climate."[62] The wording is careful: "credible," "suitable," "useful," and "projections," instead of "accurate," "reliable," and "predictions." Scientific papers about climate models (in the IPCC reports and in research journals) routinely describe the uncertainties and limitations of their results. News headlines, and even the policy summaries provided with the IPCC reports, sometimes do not.

The impression this discussion of climate models gives of the certainty, magnitude, and causes of global warming is probably quite different from the impression most people get from the news media. The entertainment industry dramatizes and shows cities underwater in movies like *Waterworld* and *A.I.* Scientists and computer programmers have an ethical responsibility to be more accurate. I saw a science-museum exhibit on global warming showing water up to the middle of the Statue of Liberty (about 200 feet above sea level). The projections of the climate models for sea level vary with different assumptions, but most are in the range of a 4 to 30-inch rise (between 1990 and 2100). If we hope to solve real potential problems (e.g., possible flooding in low-lying areas), we must first identify them accurately.

Some of the reasons why people exaggerate both the certainty and negative impacts of a potential problem are expressed in the following quotation from a scientist at one of the climate modeling centers.

---

*The troposphere is the lower atmosphere, roughly 5000–30,000 feet above the earth's surface.

We need to get some broad-based support, to capture the public's imagination. That, of course, entails getting loads of media coverage. So, we have to offer up scary scenarios, make simplified dramatic statements, and make little mention of any doubts we may have. . . . Each of us has to decide what the right balance is between being effective and being honest.[63]

Although he said he hoped climate scientists could be both effective and honest, there is clearly an ethical problem when we trade honesty for something else.

EXERCISES

Review Exercises

4.1   List several cases described in this chapter where insufficient testing was a factor in a program error or failure.

4.2   List several cases described in this chapter where the provider did an inadequate job of informing customers about flaws in the system.

4.3   The Therac-25 radiation machine involved errors in software, overall design, and management or operations. Describe one error of each type.

4.4   Describe one principle of human-interface design that is particularly important in safety-critical applications.

4.5   What questions were used to evaluate computer models?

4.6   What is one simplification in the car-crash models? In the climate models?

General Exercises

4.7   a) Suppose you write a program to add two integers. Assume that each integer and their sum will fit in the standard memory unit used by the computer for integers. How likely do you think it is that the sum will be correct? (If you used the program a million times on different pairs of integers, how many times do you think it would give the correct answer?)

b) Suppose a utility company has a million customers and it runs a program to determine whether any customers have overdue bills. How likely do you think it is that the results of the program will be correct?

c) Probably your answers to parts (a) and (b) were different. Give some reasons why the likely number of errors would be different in these two examples.

4.8   Consider the case described in Section 4.1.2, in which a boy was assumed to be a drug abuser because two schools used different disciplinary codes in their computerized records.

a) Is this kind of problem more likely to occur with computerized records than with paper records? Why, or why not?

b) Describe some policies or practices that can help prevent such problems.

4.9   A man was turned down by all the retail stores to which he applied for jobs. Eventually he learned that he was listed as a shoplifter in a database used by the stores to screen applicants. A real shoplifter had given the police the innocent man's identification from a lost wallet.

Is this incident a consequence of computerization? Would it have been as likely to happen 30 years ago? The innocent man sued the company that maintains the database and the store where the real shoplifter was arrested. Should he win? Give reasons.

4.10 Consider the standardized-test score-reporting error discussed in the box in Section 4.1.3. Suppose the scores had been reported to the schools as significantly higher, rather than lower, than the correct scores. Do you think the schools would have questioned the scores? Do you think the error would have been discovered? If so, how? Give a few examples of situations where you think computer errors would not be reported. For each example, give your reason (e.g., optimism, ignorance, gullibility, dishonesty).

4.11 It was possible for many years to make airplane reservations by phone; tickets were mailed to the customer. Now, we can buy electronic tickets. We can make a reservation by phone or on the Web, get a confirmation number, and show a picture ID, such as a driver's license, at the airport gate to board the plane.
a) What is the role of computers in making e-ticket service possible?
b) What is one advantage of this service to the customer? To the airline? To society in general?
c) Describe two potential problems that could occur with e-tickets.

4.12 Suppose you are on a consulting team to design a computerized voting system for your state. People will vote on computers at the voting place (not over the Internet; we consider Web-based voting in an exercise in Chapter 7). What are some important design considerations?

4.13 Find several provisions of the Software Engineering Code of Ethics and Professional Practice (Appendix A.1) that were violated in the Therac-25 case.

4.14 Suppose you are responsible for the design and development of a computer system to control an amusement-park ride. Sensors in the seats will determine which seats are occupied, so the software can consider weight and balance. The system will control the speed and time of the ride. The amusement park wants a system where, once the ride starts, a person is not needed to operate it.

List some important things that can or should be done to ensure the safety of the system. Consider all aspects of development, technical issues, operating instructions, and so on.

4.15 After making a programming change in a major bank's computer system, an employee forgot to enter certain commands. As a result, approximately 800,000 direct deposits received by the bank were not posted to the customer accounts until the next day. In what way is this a "computer error"? What are some potential consequences of the error? If you were the bank president, what would you say in a statement to the news media or your customers?

4.16 Who are the "good guys"? Pick two people or organizations mentioned in this chapter whose work helped make systems safer or reduced the negative consequences of errors. Tell why you picked them.

4.17 The Strategic Defense Initiative of the 1980s was a proposal for a computer system to detect a nuclear attack and automatically launch weapons to destroy the incoming missiles. The idea was revived in 2001 by President Bush. Discuss some potential risks of such a system.

4.18 A technician on a Navy guided-missile ship entered a zero in the wrong place in a computer program calibrating a fuel valve. The program, designed to divide by the entered number, crashed because division by zero is an invalid operation. The program failure caused the ship's entire Local Area Network to fail, leaving the ship dead in the water for almost three hours. (This is a true incident.)

To what degree is each of the following people responsible: the technician, the person who wrote the fuel-valve calibration program, the person who selected and purchased the ship's Local Area Network, the software company that sells the network software, the captain of the ship? What, if anything, did each do wrong, and what could be done to reduce the chance of such a problem in the future? Are there any other people who bear some of the responsibility? (You can't give a full and definite answer without more detailed information. Where necessary, indicate what additional information would be needed and how it would affect your answer.)

4.19 Do you think it is likely that throttles will disappear from airplanes and steering wheels and gas pedals will disappear from automobiles as more control is given to computer systems operated by the pilot or driver on a console or by voice? How soon do you think it might happen?

4.20 There is a story that a major retail company "lost" a warehouse from its inventory computer system for three years. No goods were shipped to or from the warehouse. Payroll was handled by a separate system, so the employees continued to be paid. To what extent is this a computer failure? What other important factors are involved? Why would such an incident be less likely without computers? Is this incident a strong argument against using computerized inventory systems?

4.21 During the Gulf War, a commander in the Royal Air Force left disks containing military plans for Desert Storm in his car. They were stolen—apparently by ordinary thieves who took his computer, not by spies. One book describes this as a "particularly disturbing example of computer dependency."[64] The point of this exercise is to analyze how much difference it would have made if the plans were in a paper file folder. Give reasons for your answers to each of the questions.

Do you think the commander would have been more likely or less likely to leave paper files in his car? Would the thieves have been more or less likely to recognize what the files contained if they had been on paper? Would the thieves have been likely to panic and discard the files, return them, or sell them to Iraq? Was the commander more or less likely to face a court-martial if the files were on paper? Overall, how much do you think computers have to do with the essential issues in this case?

4.22 Choose some noncomputer activity that you are familiar with and that has some risks (e.g., skateboarding, scuba diving, working in a restaurant). Describe some of the risks and some safety practices. Describe analogies with risks related to computer systems.

4.23 Software developers are sometimes advised to "design for failure." Give some examples of what this might mean.

4.24 Write five questions whose answers would be needed in a life-cycle-analysis model comparing the environmental impact of juice boxes with the environmental impact of juice in bottles. (Use the questions for diapers in Figure 4.3 as a guide.) Consider manufacture, transportation, use, and disposal.

4.25 Fire departments often do "controlled burns;" that is, they carefully burn areas of brush to prevent a destructive wildfire from starting later. Some departments use a computer model to tell when it is safe to do a burn (e.g., not too windy). A fire department official with 25 years experience believed the computer model was not very good. He ignored the model, used his own judgment, and did a burn safely with no problems. But he was reprimanded by his boss for ignoring the computer. Give an argument in his defense. Give an argument in support of his boss.

4.26 Suppose there are three companies that make a similar product. One does physical tests to check the safety of the product. One uses only computer simulations. The third will not disclose the testing methods it uses. Suppose you are on a jury for a case where someone is suing one of the companies because of an injury received from the product.

a) Would your decision about awarding money to the plaintiff be affected by the company's policy about testing? If so, how? If not, what factors are more important to you?

b) Suppose reliable data show that the injury rate for the product is almost identical for all three companies. With that additional information, would your decision be affected by the company's testing policy?

4.27 An article in the magazine *Audubon* in 1993[65] stated that "Since the 1960s more than 100 separate studies have confirmed that a doubling of the CO_2 concentration would raise average surface temperatures by one to four degrees centigrade." Was this an accurate statement? Explain your answer.

4.28 Which of the following models do you think would produce very accurate results? Which do you think would be less reliable? Give your reasons.

- Models that predict the effect of an income tax change on government revenue.

- Models that predict the position of the moon in relation to the earth, 30 years from now.

- Models that predict how much optical fiber will be needed in a major city 30 years from now.

- Models that predict how much CO_2 will be emitted worldwide by burning fossil fuel for energy 50 years from now.

- Models that predict the speed of a new racing boat hull design under specified wind conditions.

4.29 Suppose you have the following data:

- The number of tons in the known reserves of an important natural resource, say, copper.

- The average amount of the resource used per person (worldwide) per year.

- The total population of the world.

  Suppose a computer program uses these data to determine in how many years the resource will run out. It also uses an estimate of the rate of population increase for the next few decades.

  a) List all the reasons you can think of why this program is really not a good predictor of when we will run out of the resource.

  b) In 1972, a group called the Club of Rome received a lot of attention when it published a study using computer models that implied that the world would run out of several important natural resources in the 1980s. Today, many of those resources are cheaper than they were then, indicating that they are now less scarce. Why do you think so many people accepted the predictions in the study?

Assignments

These exercises require some research or activity.

4.30 Read a few items in the current issue of the Risks Forum (www.csl.sri.com/~risko/risks.txt). Write a summary of two items.

4.31 Find newspaper or magazine articles about the drop by more than 500-points in the stock market that occurred in October 1987. What was the role of computer programs in this incident?

4.32 Find two articles about the TAPPS nuclear winter model from newspapers or magazines in the mid-1980s (try 1984–1986). (Do not use those in the endnotes for Section 4.5.) What information, if any, do they provide about the assumptions, simplifications, and limitations of the model?

4.33 Many records stored on computers include a date, and older software systems often used two digits to represent the year (e.g., 78, 95). As expected, many computer systems experienced problems in the late 1990s when they began using dates in or after the year 2000. For example, credit cards with expiration dates in 2000 would not work. Businesses and governments around the world spent many billions of dollars on the "Y2K problem," tracking down two-digit dates in their software and making modifications before January 1, 2000.

Find out what some people expected to happen on Jan. 1, 2000. Report on some of the actual software failures that occurred.

Class Discussion Exercises

These exercises are for class discussion, perhaps with short presentations prepared in advance by small groups of students.

4.34 Assume that the family of one of the victims of the Therac-25 is suing the hospital where the machine was used, AECL (the maker of the machine), and the programmer who wrote the Therac-25 software. Divide students into six groups: attorneys for the family against each of the three respondents and attorneys for each of the three respondents. Each group is to present a five-minute summation of arguments for its case. Then, let the class discuss all aspects of the case and vote on which, if any, of the respondents should pay the family and whether any should be charged with a criminal offense.

4.35 Consider the following scenario. A state's highway patrol keeps records of stolen cars in its computer system. A car can be checked by typing in the license-plate number. The records are not routinely updated when stolen cars are recovered. A car was still listed as stolen a few years after it had been recovered and later sold. The new owner of the car was shot and killed by a police officer during a traffic stop; the officer thought the car was stolen and that the driver was acting suspiciously. An investigation concluded that the officer "acted in good faith." The family filed a wrongful death suit against the highway patrol.*

To what extent should the highway patrol be held responsible?

4.36 A factory contains an area where all the work is done by robots. The area is fenced and human workers are not supposed to enter while the robots are working. When the fence is opened, it automatically cuts off power to the robots. A worker jumped over the fence to repair a robot that was malfunctioning. Another robot, bringing parts to the malfunctioning robot, pinned the worker against a machine, killing him.

Suppose your class is a consulting team hired (by a neutral party) to investigate this case and write a report. Consider several factors relevant in safety-critical software. What was done right? What was done wrong? Is there important information not included in this summary of the case that you would ask about? If so, what? What degree of blame should be assigned to the software company that designed the robot system, the company that operates the factory, and the worker? Why? What changes, if any, should the factory operators make to reduce the likelihood of more deaths?

4.37 Poll the class and find out how many students have tried hang-gliding or bungee-jumping. How many say "No way!"? How many would ride on a computer-controlled train that had no human driver? How many would like to be one of the first people to have a computer chip implanted in his or her head to, say, aid memory, or do calculations?

Generate a discussion of personal differences in risk-taking. Is there one correct level of risk?

---

*I have changed some details, but this scenario was suggested by a real case.

N O T E S

1   *The Risks Digest: Forum on Risks to the Public In Computers and Related Systems* (formerly the comp.risks newsgroup on Usenet). Archived at cat-less.ncl.ac.uk/Risks; current issue at www.csl.sri.com/~risko/risks.txt.

2   Philip E. Ross, "The Day the Software Crashed," *Forbes*, April 25, 1994, 153:9, pp. 142–156. Peter G. Neumann, "Inside Risks," *Communications of the ACM*, July 1992, p. 122.

3   Jeffrey Rothfeder, *Privacy For Sale*, Simon & Schuster, 1992, p. 34 and pp. 130–131; "A Case of Mistaken Identity," *Privacy Journal*, Dec. 1992, p. 7; "In the States," *Privacy Journal*, Jan. 1993, p. 3; Neumann, "Inside Risks," *Communications of the ACM*, Jan. 1992, p. 186, and July 1992, p. 122. "Reading Privacy Journal's Mail," *Privacy Journal*, Aug. 1998, pp. 1, 3, 5.

4   Andrea Robinson, "Firm: State Told Felon Voter List May Cause Errors," *Miami Herald*, Feb. 17, 2001.

5   Paul M. Barrett, "Aiding Prosecutions, Justices Allow Use Of Some Improperly Obtained Evidence," *Wall Street Journal*, March 2, 1995, p. B4.

6   *Arizona v. Evans*, reported in "Supreme Court Rules on Use of Inaccurate Computer Records," *EPIC Alert*, March 9, 1995, v. 2.04.

7   Associated Press, "Teen 'Convicted' by Computer," *San Jose Mercury*, Mar. 7, 1996, p. 3B.

8   Dan Joyce, e-mail correspondence, May 17, 1996 (the adoption case). Study by the Office of Technology Assessment, reported in Rothfeder, *Privacy For Sale*. "Jailing the Wrong Man," *Time*, Feb. 25, 1985, p. 25. David Burnham, "Tales of a Computer State," *The Nation*, April 1983, p. 527. Evelyn Richards, "Proposed FBI Crime Computer System Raises Questions on Accuracy, Privacy," *Washington Post*, Feb. 13, 1989, p. A6. "Wrong Suspect Settles His Case of $55,000," *New York Times*, Mar. 6, 1998, p. 30. Peter G. Neumann, "Risks to the Public in Computer and Related Systems," *Software Engineering Notes*, Apr. 1988, 13:2, p. 11. Several similar cases are reported by Peter G. Neumann in "Inside Risks," *Communications of the ACM*, Jan. 1992, p. 186.

9   *Privacy Journal*, Aug. 1998, p. 4.

10 "AT&T Crash, 15 Jan 90: The Official Report," in "Subsection on Telephone Systems," *Software Engineering Notes*, April 1990, 15:2, p. 11–14. Ross, "The Day the Software Crashed." Ann Lindstrom, "Outage Hits AT&T in New England," *Telephony*, Nov. 11, 1991, 221:20, p. 10. "Bell Atlantic Customers Put on Hold by Directory Assistance," Nov. 26, 1996, PGN Abstracting.

11 Penni Crabtree, "AT&T system crash is wake-up call for business," *San Diego Union–Tribune*, Apr. 15, 1998, p. C1. "Data Entry Typo Mutes Millions of U.S. Pagers," *Wall Street Journal*, Sep. 27, 1995, p. A11.

12 Frederic M. Biddle, John Lippman, and Stephanie N. Mehta, "One Satellite Fails, and the World Goes Awry," *Wall Street Journal*, May 21, 1998, p. B1.

13 David Craig, "NASDAQ Blackout Rattles Investors," *USA Today*, July 18, 1994, p. 2B. Associated Press, "NASDAQ Defends Its System after Stock-Pricing Errors," *New York Times*, Sept. 13, 1994, p. D19. "Note to Readers," *Boston Globe*, Oct. 25, 1994, p. 52. Julia Flynn, Sara Calian, and Michael R. Sesit, "Computer Snag Halts London Market 8 Hours," *Wall Street Journal*, Apr. 6, 2000, p. A14.

14 Thomas Hoffman, "NCR Users Cry Foul Over I Series Glitch," *Computerworld*, Feb. 15, 1993, p. 72. Milo Geyelin, "Faulty Software Means Business for Litigators," *Wall Street Journal*, Jan. 21, 1994, p. B1. Milo Geyelin, "How an NCR System for Inventory Control Turned into a Virtual Saboteur," *Wall Street Journal*, Aug. 8, 1994, p. A1, A5. Mary Brandel and Thomas Hoffman, "User Lawsuits Drag On for NCR," *Computerworld*, Aug. 15, 1994, p. 1.

15 Jacques Steinberg and Diana B. Henriques, "When a Test Fails the Schools, Careers and Reputations Suffer," *New York Times*, May 21, 2001, pp. A1, A10–A11.

16 The DIA delay was widely reported in the news media. A few of the articles used as sources for the discussion here are W. Wayt Gibbs, "Software's Chronic Crisis," *Scientific American*, Sept. 1994, 271:3, pp. 86–95. Robert L. Scheier, "Software Snafu Grounds Denver's High-tech Airport," *PC Week*, 11:19, May 16, 1994, p. 1. Price Colman, "Software Glitch Could Be the Hitch. Misplaced Comma Might Dull Baggage System's Cutting Edge," *Rocky Mountain News*, April 30, 1994, p. 9A. Steve Higgins, "Denver Airport: Another Tale of Government High-Tech Run Amok" *Investor's Business Daily*, May 23, 1994, p. A4. Julie Schmit, "Tiny Company Is Blamed for Denver Delays," *USA Today*, May 5, 1994, pp. 1B, 2B.

17 Scheier, "Software Snafu Grounds Denver's High-tech Airport."

18 Carl Ingram, "DMV Spent $44 Million on Failed Project," *Los Angeles Times*, April 27, 1994, p. A3. Effy Oz, "When Professional Standards Are Lax: The CONFIRM Failure and its Lessons," *Communications of the ACM*, Oct. 1994, 37:10, pp. 29–36. Virginia Ellis, "Snarled Child Support Computer Project Dies," *Los Angeles Times*, Nov. 21, 1997, p. A1, A28. Peter G. Neumann, "System Development Woes," *Communications of the ACM*, Dec. 1997, p. 160.

19 Data compiled by Peter Mellor, Centre for Software Reliability, England, reprinted in Peter G. Neumann, *Computer-Related Risks*, Addison Wesley, 1995, p. 309.

20 "Airbus Safety Claim 'Cannot Be Proved'," *New Scientist*, Sept. 7, 1991, 131:1785, p. 30. Robert Morrell

Jr., *Risks Forum Digest*, July 6, 1994, 16:20. "Training 'Inadequate' Says A320 Crash Report," *Flight International*, Dec. 22, 1993, p. 11 (on the Jan. 1992 Strasbourg A320 crash, excerpted by Peter B. Ladkin in *Risks Forum Digest*, Jan. 2, 1994). Ross, "The Day the Software Crashed," p. 156, on the 1993 Warsaw crash. David Learmont, "Lessons from the Cockpit," *Flight International*, Jan. 11, 1994.

21 William M. Carley, "New Cockpit Systems Broaden the Margin of Safety for Pilots," *Wall Street Journal*, Mar. 1, 2000, pp. A1, A10. Barry H. Kantowitz, "Pilot Workload and Flightdeck Automation," in M. Mouloua and R. Parasuraman, eds., *Human Performance in Automated Systems: Current Research and Trends*, pp. 212–223 (TCAS problems on p. 214).

22 Alan Levin, "FAA finally unveils new radar system," *USA Today*, Jan. 20, 1999, p. 01.A. Anna Wilde Mathews and Susan Carey, "Airports have delays, cancellations due to problems in air-traffic control," *Wall Street Journal*, May 7, 1999, p. A20. "Software Glitch" (editorial), *San Diego Union–Tribune*, Oct. 23, 2000, p. B8. Robert Fox, "News Track: Air Communication Breakdown," *Communications of the ACM*, Aug. 2000, 43:8, p. 10.

23 Nancy G. Leveson and Clark S. Turner, "An Investigation of the Therac-25 Accidents," *IEEE Computer*, July 1993, 26:7, pp. 18–41. Jonathan Jacky, "Safety-Critical Computing: Hazards, Practices, Standards, and Regulation," in Charles Dunlop and Rob Kling, eds., *Computerization and Controversy*, Academic Press, 1991, pp. 612–631. Most of the factual information about the Therac-25 incidents in this chapter is from Leveson and Turner.

24 Conversation with Nancy Leveson, Jan. 19, 1995.

25 Jonathan Jacky, "Safety-Critical Computing," p. 615. Peter G. Neumann, "Risks to the Public in Computers and Related Systems," *Software Engineering Notes*, April 1991, 16:2, p. 4. Ted Wendling, "Lethal Doses: Radiation That Kills," *Cleveland Plain Dealer*, Dec. 16, 1992, p. 12A. (I thank my student Irene Radomyshelsky for bringing the last reference to my attention.)

26 W. W. Norton, 1997, p. 157.

27 "Airbus Safety Claim 'Cannot Be Proved'," p. 30.

28 Richard P. Feynman, *What Do You Care What Other People Think?*, W. W. Norton & Co., 1988.

29 The report of the inquiry into the explosion is at www.esrin.esa.it/htdocs/tidc/Press/Press96/ariane5rep.html.

30 From an e-mail advertisement for Nancy G. Leveson, *Safeware: System Safety and Computers*, Addison Wesley, 1995.

31 A particularly good article discussing human factors and the causes of the crash is Stephen Manes, "A Fatal Outcome From Misplaced Trust in 'Data'," *New York Times*, Sept. 17, 1996, p. B11.

32 Kantowitz, "Pilot Workload and Flightdeck Automation."

33 Feynman, *What Do You Care What Other People Think?* The shuttle was not immune to problems. The Risks Forum includes reports of computer failures caused by a loose piece of solder, subtle timing errors, and other factors.

34 "AT&T Crash, 15 Jan 90: The Official Report."

35 Feynman, *What Do You Care What Other People Think?*, pp. 190–194 and 232–236. Aeronautics and Space Engineering Board, National Research Council, *An Assessment of Space Shuttle Flight Software Development Processes*, National Academy Press, 1993.

36 Mary Brandel and Thomas Hoffman, "User Lawsuits Drag On for NCR," *Computerworld*, Aug. 15, 1994, p. 1.

37 This issue is raised by Professor Philip Koopman of Carnegie Mellon University. See his Web site, www-2.cs.cmu.edu/-koopman/ucita/ for more on UCITA.

38 These problems and trade-offs occur often with regulation of new drugs and medical devices, regulation of pollution, and various kinds of safety regulation. They are discussed primarily in journals on the economics of regulation.

39 Jacky, "Safety-Critical Computing," p. 624.

40 Leveson and Turner, "An Investigation of the Therac-25 Accidents," p. 40.

41 See, for example, Walter Williams, *The State Against Blacks*, McGraw-Hill, 1982, Chapters 5–7. One year during a construction lull, a state failed everyone who took the building contractor's license exam. It is illegal in 48 states for most software engineers to call themselves software engineers because of licensing laws for engineers. One company was forced to spend thousands of dollars changing job titles, business cards, and marketing literature to remove the word "engineer." (Julia King, "Engineers to IS: Drop That Title!" *Computerworld*, May 30, 1994, 28:22, pp. 1, 119.)

42 "More Risks of Computer Billing—$22,000 Water Bill," *Software Engineering Notes*, Oct. 1991, 16:4, p. 6. Richard M. Rosenberg, "Success Components for the 21st Century," *The Magazine of Bank Management*, Jan/Feb. 1994.

43 Raju Narisetti, Thomas E. Weber, and Rebecca Quick, "How Computers Calmly Handled Stock Frenzy," *Wall Street Journal*, Oct. 30, 1997, p. B1, B7. Peter G. Neumann, "System Development Woes," *Communications of the ACM*, Dec. 1997, p. 160.

44 William M. Carley, "New Cockpit Systems Broaden the Margin of Safety for Pilots," *Wall Street Journal*, Mar. 1, 2000, p. A1.

45 Holman W. Jenkins Jr., "Look Ma, No Hands!" *Wall Street Journal*, Oct. 20, 1999, p. A27. William M. Carley, "Could a Minor Change in Design Have Saved American Flight 965?" *Wall Street Journal*, Jan. 8, 1995, pp. A1, A8. National Air Transportation Safety Board and the U. S. Bureau of the Census, *Statistical Abstract of the United States: 1994*, Tables 134

and 996. Air Transport Association, reported in "Safer Skies," *Wall Street Journal*, July 9, 1999, p. W4.

46 Miles Corwin and John L. Mitchell, "Fire Disrupts L.A. Phones, Services," *Los Angeles Times*, March 16, 1994, p. A1.

47 Heather Bryant, an Albertson's manager, quoted in Penni Crabtree, "Glitch fouls up nation's business," *San Diego Union–Tribune*, Apr. 14, 1998, p. C1.

48 An excellent "Nova" series, "Escape! Because Accidents Happen," aired Feb. 16 and 17, 1999, shows examples from 2000 years of history of inventing ways to reduce the injuries and deaths from fires and from boat, car, and airplane accidents.

49 "A Fistful of Risks," *Discover*, May 1996, p. 82.

50 Tom Forester and Perry Morrison, *Computer Ethics: Cautionary Tales and Ethical Dilemmas in Computing*, second edition, MIT Press, 1994, p. 4.

51 Peter G. Neumann, "Inside Risks: Risks on the Rails," *Communications of the ACM*, July 1993, 36:7, p. 130, and *Computer-Related Risks*, p. 71. Although I take issue with some particulars, Neumann's Risks Forum, articles, and book are invaluable sources of information and analysis about risks in computer systems.

52 Amanda Bennett, "Strange 'Science': Predicting Health-Care Costs," *Wall Street Journal*, Feb. 7, 1994, p. B1.

53 Cynthia Crossen, "How 'Tactical Research' Muddied Diaper Debate," *Wall Street Journal*, May 17, 1994, pp. B1, B9.

54 Richard P. Turco, Owen Toon, Thomas Ackerman, James Pollack, and Carl Sagan, "Nuclear Winter: Global Consequences of Multiple Nuclear Explosions," *Science*, Dec. 23, 1984, p. 1284. Russell Seitz, "In From the Cold: 'Nuclear Winter' Melts Down," *The National Interest*, Fall 1986, pp. 3–17. Howard Maccabee, "Nuclear Winter: How Much Do We Really Know?" *Reason*, May 1985, pp. 26ff.

55 *Against the Gods: The Remarkable Story of Risk*, John Wiley & Sons, 1996, p. 16.

56 The main sources for this section include J. O. Hallquist and D. J. Benson, "DYNA3D–An Explicit Finite Element Program for Impact Calculations," in *Crashworthiness and Occupant Protection in Transportation Systems*, T. B. Khalil and A. I. King, eds., American Society of Mechanical Engineers, v. 106, p. 1. William H. Allen, "How To Build a Better Beer Can," pp.

32–36, and "DYNA Gets to the Heart of the Matter," p. 36, both in *Supercomputing Review*, March 1991. Steve Wampler, "DYNA3D: This Computer Code Seems to Offer Something for Everyone," *The Quarterly*, Lawrence Livermore National Laboratory, Sept. 1989, 20:2, pp. 7–11. "Motorists, Pedestrians May Find LLNL Computer Code a Life-Saver" and "LLNL Computer Code Makes the Jump from Modeling Machines to Man," news releases from Lawrence Livermore National Laboratories, March 7, 1991 (NR-91-03-01 and NR-91-03-02).

57 Thomas Frank And Karl Gruber, "Numerical Simulation of Frontal Impact and Frontal Offset Collisions," *Cray Channels*, Winter 1992.

58 J. T. Houghton *et al.*, eds., *Climate Change 2001: The Scientific Basis*, 2001; J. T. Houghton *et al.*, eds., *Climate Change 1995: The Science of Climate Change*, 1996; J. T. Houghton, B. A. Callander, and S. K. Varney, eds., *Climate Change 1992: The Supplementary Report to the IPCC Scientific Assessment*, 1992; J. T. Houghton, G. J. Jenkins, and J. J. Ephraums, eds., *Climate Change: The IPCC Scientific Assessment*, 1990; all published by Cambridge University Press. I also used a large variety of other books and articles for background. A book by climatologists critical of the models is included in the references at the end of the chapter.

59 D. L. Albritton and L. G. Meira Filho *et al.*, "Technical Summary," in J. T. Houghton *et al.*, eds., *Climate Change 2001*, pp. 21–83; see p. 37.

60 Albritton and Meira Filho *et al.*, "Technical Summary," p. 49.

61 Houghton *et al.*, *Climate Change 1992*, pp. 17, 139. Patrick J. Michaels, *Sound and Fury: The Science and Politics of Global Warming*, Cato Institute, 1992, pp. 114–118. "Technical Summary," *Climate Change 1995*, p. 27.

62 B. J. McAvaney *et al.*, "Model Evaluation," in J. T. Houghton *et al.*, eds., *Climate Change 2001*, pp. 471–523; see p. 473.

63 Stephen Schneider, quoted in Jonathan Schell, "Our Fragile Earth," *Discover*, Oct. 1989, pp. 44–50.

64 Forester and Morrison, *Computer Ethics*, pp. 4–5.

65 Bruce Stutz, "The Landscape of Hunger," *Audubon*, March/April 1993, pp. 54–63; see p. 62.

BOOKS AND ARTICLES

■ W. Robert Collins, Keith W. Miller, Bethany J. Spielman, and Phillip Wherry, "How Good Is Good Enough?" *Communications of the ACM*, Jan. 1994, 37:1, pp. 81–91. A discussion of ethical issues about quality for software developers.

- Richard Epstein, *The Case of the Killer Robot*, John Wiley and Sons, 1996.

- Richard P. Feynman, *What Do You Care What Other People Think?*, W. W. Norton & Co., 1988. Includes Feynman's report on the investigation of the explosion of the Challenger space shuttle, with many insights about how to, and how not to, investigate a system failure.

- Jonathan Jacky, "Safety-Critical Computing: Hazards, Practices, Standards, and Regulation," in Charles Dunlop and Rob Kling, eds., *Computerization and Controversy*, Academic Press, 1991.

- Thomas K. Landauer, *The Trouble With Computers: Usefulness, Usability, and Productivity*, MIT Press, 1995.

- Nancy G. Leveson, *Safeware: System Safety and the Computer Age*, Addison Wesley, 1995.

- Nancy G. Leveson and Clark S. Turner, "An Investigation of the Therac-25 Accidents," *IEEE Computer*, July 1993, 26:7, pp. 18–41.

- Patrick J. Michaels and Robert C. Balling Jr., *The Satanic Gases: Clearing the Air about Global Warming*, Cato Institute, 2000. Michaels and Balling are climatologists critical of the climate models.

- Peter G. Neumann, *Computer-Related Risks*, Addison–Wesley, 1995.

- Peter G. Neumann *et al.*, "Inside Risks," *Communications of the ACM*, regular column, on the last page of each issue.

- Jakob Nielsen, *Designing Web Usability: The Practice of Simplicity*, New Riders Publishing, 2000.

- Donald Norman, *The Invisible Computer: Why Good Products Can Fail, the Personal Computer Is So Complex, and Information Appliances Are the Solution*, MIT Press, 1998.

- Donald Norman, *The Psychology of Everyday Things*, Basic Books, 1988. A study of good and bad user interfaces on many everyday devices and appliances.

- Effy Oz, "When Professional Standards Are Lax: The CONFIRM Failure and its Lessons," *Communications of the ACM*, Oct. 1994, 37:10, pp. 29–36. A study of a $125 million project that was canceled.

- David Parnas, "SDI: Violation of Professional Responsibility," *Abacus*, Winter 1987, pp. 46–52.

- Ivars Peterson, *Fatal Defect: Chasing Killer Computer Bugs*, Times Books (Random House), 1995.

- Henry Petroski, *To Engineer Is Human: The Role of Failure in Successful Design*, St. Martin's Press, 1985.

- Shari L. Pfleeger, *Software Engineering: Theory and Practice*, second edition, Prentice Hall, 2001.

- Jeffrey Rothfeder, *Privacy for Sale*, Simon & Schuster, 1992. Although the main focus of this book is privacy, it contains many examples of problems that resulted from errors in databases.

- Ben Shneiderman, *Designing the User Interface: Strategies for Effective Human–Computer Interaction*, third edition, Addison Wesley Longman, 1998.

- Edward Tufte, *Envisioning Information*, Graphics Press, 1990.

- Edward Tufte, *Visual Explanations*, Graphics Press, 1997.

- Aaron Wildavsky, *Searching for Safety*, Transaction Books, 1988. On the role of risk in making us safer.

ORGANIZATIONS AND WEBSITES

- Peter G. Neumann, moderator, *The Risks Digest: Forum on Risks to the Public In Computers and Related Systems*, archived at catless.ncl.ac.uk/Risks; current issue at www.csl.sri.com/~risko/risks.txt

5

FREEDOM OF SPEECH IN CYBERSPACE

5.1 Changing Communications Paradigms

Congress shall make no law . . . abridging the freedom of speech, or of the press. . . .

—First Amendment, U.S. Constitution

In this chapter, we consider several issues that relate to freedom of speech—for example, pornography on the Web and attempts to restrict it or to restrict access by children; anonymity as a protection for speakers; and spam (mass, unsolicited e-mail). We examine how the protection of the First Amendment to the U.S. Constitution affects, and is affected by, computer systems and the World Wide Web. We describe various incidents and cases and discuss issues they raise. We examine how the global nature of the Web interacts with different laws and levels of freedom of speech in different countries. Although much of our discussion is in the context of the U.S. Constitution's First Amendment and we use U.S. laws and court decisions as examples, similar issues arise in other free countries.

In this section, we introduce the traditional three-part framework for regulation and First Amendment protection of communications media. As we will see, this framework does not fit cyberspace.

REGULATORY PARADIGMS

It is by now almost a cliché to say that the Internet lets us all be publishers. We do not need expensive printing presses or complex distribution systems. We need only a computer and a modem. Any business, organization, or individual can set up a home page on the World Wide Web. We can "publish" whatever we wish; it is available to be read by anyone who chooses. In 1994, shortly before the Web was widely used, Mike Godwin, then an attorney with the Electronic Frontier Foundation, described the dramatic change brought about by computer communications as follows:

> It is a medium far different from the telephone, which is only a one-to-one medium, ill-suited for reaching large numbers of people. It is a medium far different from the newspaper or TV station, which are one-to-many media, ill-suited for feedback from the audience. For the first time in history, we have a many-to-many medium, in which you don't have to be rich to have access, and in which you don't have to win the approval of an editor or publisher to speak your mind. Usenet and the Internet, as part of this new medium, hold the promise of guaranteeing, for the first time in history, that the First Amendment's protection of freedom of the press means as much to each individual as it does to Time Warner, or to Gannett, or to the *New York Times*.[1]

The new computer communications technologies *might* guarantee freedom of the press for all of us, but the guarantee is not certain. Telephone, movies, radio, television, cable, satellites, and, of course, computer networks did not exist when the Constitution was written. Freedom of the press applied to publishers who printed newspapers and books and to "the lonely pamphleteer" who printed and distributed pamphlets expressing unconventional ideas. One might think the First Amendment should be applied to each new communications technology according to its spirit and intention: to protect our freedom to say what we wish. Governments, however, regularly try to restrict freedom of speech and the press for new technologies. Law professor Eric M. Freedman sums up: "Historical experience—with the printing press, secular dramatic troupes, photographs, movies, rock music, broadcasting, sexually explicit telephone services, video games, and other media—shows that each new medium is viewed at first by governments as uniquely threatening, because it is uniquely influential, and therefore a uniquely appropriate target of censorship."[2]

Historically in the U.S., communications technologies were divided into three categories with respect to the degree of First Amendment protection and government regulation:

- Print media (newspapers, books, magazines, pamphlets).

- Broadcast (television, radio).

- Common carriers (telephone, telegraph, and the postal system).

The first category has the strongest First Amendment protection. Although books have been banned in the U.S. and people were arrested for publishing information on certain topics such as contraception, the trend has been toward fewer government restraints on the printed word.

Television and radio are similar to newspapers in their role of providing news and entertainment, but both the structure of the broadcasting industry and the content have been highly regulated. Broadcasting licensees are selected by the government and must meet government standards of merit, a requirement that would not be tolerated for publishers because of the obvious threat to freedom of expression. The government has used threats of license revocation to get stations to cancel sexually oriented talk shows or to censor them. Cigarette ads are legal in magazines, but they are banned from radio, television, and all electronic media under the control of the Federal Communications Commission. Some words may appear in print but must not be said on the radio. The federal government frequently proposes requirements to reduce violence on television or increase programming for children, but the government cannot impose such requirements on print publishers. Whether you favor or oppose any of these particular regulations, the point is that the government has more control over television and radio content than it has over communication methods that existed at the time the Bill of Rights was written. The main argument used to deny full First Amendment treatment to broadcasters was scarcity of broadcast frequencies, that is, that broadcasters had a monopoly. With cable, satellites, and hundreds of channels, the monopoly argument is irrelevant now, but the precedent of government control remains. The argument now used to justify government-imposed restrictions on content is that broadcast material comes into the home and is difficult to keep from children.

Common carriers provide a medium of communication (not content) and must make their service available to everyone. In some cases, as with telephone service, they are required to provide "universal access" (i.e., to subsidize service for people with low incomes). Based on the argument that common carriers are a monopoly, they have been prohibited from controlling the content of material that passes through their system. Telephone companies were prohibited from providing content or information services on the grounds that they might discriminate against competing content providers who must also use their telephone lines. Common carriers had no control over content, so they had no responsibility for it. (As new technologies blurred the technical boundaries between cable, telephone, computer networks, and content providers, the law began to adapt. The Telecommunications Act of 1996 changed the regulatory structure. It removed many artificial legal divisions of service areas and many restrictions on services that may be provided by telecommunications companies.)

The Internet, computer bulletin-board systems, commercial services like CompuServe, Prodigy, and America Online (AOL), and ultimately the World Wide Web became major arenas for distribution of news, information, and opinion. Various political forces are fighting over the issue of control versus freedom. There are always people who want to restrict or prevent the distribution of certain kinds of information; each new communications technology provides a new battleground for battles that have been fought before. Because of the immense flexibility of computer communications systems, they do not fit neatly into the publishing, broadcasting, and common carriage paradigms. Cable television strained these categories previously. In commenting on a law requiring cable stations to carry certain broadcasts, the Supreme Court said cable operators have more freedom of speech than television and radio broadcasters, but less than print publishers.[3] But the Web does not fit between the existing categories any better than it fits within them. It has similarities to all three, and, in addition, to bookstores, libraries, and rented meeting rooms—which are all treated differently in law. It remains uncertain what degree of censorship and regulation of speech will apply to the Internet and the Web. In 1996, the main parts of the first major Internet censorship law, the Communications Decency Act (CDA), were ruled unconstitutional. In this decision, a federal judge commented that "as the most participatory form of mass speech yet developed, the Internet deserves the highest protection from government intrusion."[4] However, efforts to censor the Net continued after the CDA decision. Also, censorship decisions in other countries will have an impact on Internet content.

As we proceed with our discussion of free speech issues, it is helpful to remember several important points. The First Amendment was written precisely for offensive and/or controversial speech and ideas; it would not be needed to protect speech and publication that no one objected to. The First Amendment covers spoken and written words, pictures, art, and other forms of expression of ideas and opinions (including, for example, wearing armbands to express support of a political cause). The First Amendment is a restriction on the power of government, not individuals or private businesses. Although some laws and court decisions take the opposite position, it would seem that, for individuals and organizations, freedom of speech inherently includes freedom not to promote ideas they do not agree with.[5] Publishers are not required to publish material they consider offensive, poorly written, or unlikely to appeal to their customers for any reason. Rejection or editing by a publisher is not a violation of a writer's First Amendment rights.

Over the course of many years and many cases, the Supreme Court developed principles and guidelines about protected expression. Advocating illegal acts is (usually) legal; a listener has the opportunity and responsibility to weigh the arguments and decide whether or not to commit the illegal act. There are some restrictions on speech.* Libel (making false and damaging statements) and direct, specific threats are not protected by the First Amendment. Inciting violence, in certain circumstances, is illegal. Although the First Amendment makes no distinctions among categories of speech, the courts have had a tradition of treating advertising as "second class" speech and allowing restrictions that would not be acceptable for other kinds of speech. However, a large number of cases in the past several years have gone against that trend; courts have begun to rule that restrictions on truthful advertising do indeed violate the First Amendment.[6] Anonymous speech has been protected in many court decisions, but there are serious attempts to limit or prohibit anonymity on the Internet.

There is a censorship issue when the government owns or substantially subsidizes communications systems or networks (or controversial services). For example, in the 1980s, federally subsidized family-planning clinics were not permitted to discuss abortion. In the past, the government has made it illegal to send information through the mail that was otherwise protected by the First Amendment. A federal agency that provides funds for public radio stations rejected the application of a university because it broadcasts one hour a week of religious programming. In Section 5.2.3, we will see an attempt by Congress to use its funding power to require censorship of the Internet in public libraries and schools. No matter what side of these issues you are on, no matter how the policy changes with different presidents or Congresses, the point is that, in many circumstances, when the government pays, it can choose to restrict speech that would otherwise be constitutionally protected.

The issues in this chapter have far-reaching implications for freedom. As Ithiel de Sola Pool wrote, in his important book *Technologies of Freedom*,

> Networked computers will be the printing presses of the twenty-first century. If they are not free of public [i.e., government] control, the continued application of constitutional immunities to nonelectronic mechanical presses, lecture halls, and man-carried sheets of paper may become no more than a quaint archaism.
>
> The onus is on us to determine whether free societies in the twenty-first century will conduct electronic communication under the conditions of freedom established for the domain of print through centuries of struggle, or whether that great achievement will become lost in a confusion about new technologies.[7]

---

*The specific laws, court decisions, and guidelines are complex in some cases. The discussion here is general and simplified.

5.2 Offensive Speech and Censorship in Cyberspace

I disapprove of what you say, but I will defend to the death your right to say it.

—Voltaire's biographer, describing his view of freedom of speech[8]

5.2.1 WHAT IS THERE? WHAT IS ILLEGAL?

What is offensive speech? What should be prohibited or restricted by law in cyberspace? The answer depends on who you are. It could be political or religious speech, pornography, sexual or racial slurs, Nazi materials, libelous statements, abortion information, anti-abortion information, advertising of alcoholic beverages, advertising in general, depictions of violence, or information about how to build bombs. There are vehement advocates for banning each of these—and more. The state of Georgia tried to ban pictures of marijuana from the Internet. A doctor argued for regulating medical discussion on the Net so that people would not get bad advice.

Most of the efforts to censor the Internet focus on pornographic, or sexually explicit, material, so we use pornography as the main example. Many of the same constitutional principles apply to efforts to censor other kinds of material.

Pornography online is a multibillion-dollar business with sites worldwide. Some people are shocked that pornography is common in cyberspace, especially on the Internet, which began as a forum for research and scientific discussion. It is not, however, a surprising development. The same kind of material was already available in adult magazines, bookstores, and movie theaters. As a writer for *Wired* contends, sexual material quickly invades all new technologies and art forms.[9] He points out that, from cave paintings to frescos in Pompeii to stone carvings at Angkor Wat, erotica have flourished. The printing press produced Bibles and porn. Photography produced *Playboy*. Many of the first videocassettes were pornographic. When handheld computers grew in popularity, "adult" content providers offered simpler images and erotic stories for the small screens. Whether all this is good or bad, whether it is a natural part of human nature or a sign of degeneracy and evil, whether it should be tolerated or stamped out, are moral and political issues beyond the scope of this book. Pornography is debated endlessly. In addressing the issue of pornography and other kinds of speech that offend people, we try to focus specifically on new problems and issues related to computer systems and cyberspace. Anyone can sit in a library or a bookstore and read about sex or bombs, make photocopies of pages, and send them by mail without a return address. Many of the targets of censorship on the Net are legal in other media. But inappropriate material can be easier for children to get on the Web, and problematic material spreads more easily and anonymously. We consider how existing laws, precedents, and the First Amendment guide solutions to new problems.

STRAINING OLD LEGAL STANDARDS

On the Internet, communities have no physical locations. Instead, they are defined by the people who choose to associate in chat rooms and on Web sites because of common interests. The definition of "community" proved critical in an early Internet case. A couple in California operated a computer bulletin board system (BBS) called Amateur Action that made sexually explicit images available to members. Legal observers generally agreed that the Amateur Action BBS operators would not be found guilty of a crime in California. But the federal government apparently wanted to shut it down. A postal inspector in Memphis, Tennessee, working with a U.S. attorney there, became a member of the BBS (the only member in Tennessee[10]) and downloaded sexually oriented images in Memphis. The couple, who lived and worked in California, were prosecuted in Tennessee and found guilty in 1994 of distributing obscenity under the local community standards. Both received jail sentences. A spokesman for the ACLU commented that prosecutions like this one meant that "nothing can be put on the Internet that is more racy than would be tolerated in the most conservative community in the U.S."[11]

The Net also changed the meaning of "distribution." Did the BBS operators send obscene files to Tennessee? BBSs were accessed by the telephone system; anyone, from anywhere, could call in if they chose. The postal inspector in Tennessee initiated the telephone call to the BBS and initiated the transfer of the files. He selected and downloaded them. Critics of the prosecution of the BBS operators argued that it is as if the postal inspector went to California, bought pornographic pictures, and brought them home to Memphis—then had the seller prosecuted under Memphis community standards.[12]

WHAT WAS ALREADY ILLEGAL?

In 1973, the Supreme Court, in *Miller v. California*, established a three-part guideline for determining whether material is obscene under the law. Obscene material is not protected by the First Amendment. The criteria are that (1) it depicts sexual (or excretory) acts whose depiction is specifically prohibited by state law, (2) it depicts these acts in a patently offensive manner, appealing to prurient interest as judged by a reasonable person using community standards, and (3) it has no serious literary, artistic, social, political, or scientific value. The second point—the application of community standards—was a compromise intended to avoid the problem of setting a national standard of obscenity in so large and diverse a country. Thus, small conservative or religious towns could restrict pornography to a greater extent than cosmopolitan urban areas.

Child pornography includes pictures or movies of actual minors (children under 18) in sexual positions or engaged in sexual acts. It has long been illegal to create, possess, or distribute child pornography, primarily because its production is considered abuse of the actual children, not because of the impact of the content on a viewer. It is not automatically illegal to make such movies or photos where a minor character is played by an adult actor. In other words, child pornography laws prohibited using (abusing and exploiting) children, not portraying them. (Similarly, crime reports or crime fiction describing a rape of a child, for example, would not generally be illegal.) In 1996, Congress passed the Child Pornography Prevention Act to extend the law against child pornography to include "virtual" children, that is computer-generated images that appear to be minors, as well as other images where real adults appear to be minors. After conflicting federal appeals court decisions about whether the law violated the First Amendment, the Supreme Court ruled, in 2002, that it did.[13]

5.2.2 MATERIAL INAPPROPRIATE FOR CHILDREN

The distinctions between categories such as erotica, art, and pornography are not always clear, and different people have very different personal standards. But there is no doubt that there is material on the Web that most people would consider inappropriate for children. Many parents do not want their children to view hate material or sites promoting racism, anti-Semitism, and sexism. Some parents do not want their children to see violence on the Web in stories, images, games, and video. People discuss sexual activity, of conventional and unconventional sorts, including pedophilia, in graphic detail in cyberspace. Child molesters can easily talk to children in chat rooms. There is much on the Web that is extremely offensive to adults. It is not surprising that some people see the Internet as a scary place for children.

The worst of the material is already illegal in any medium. It is the attempts to restrict access to adult material by new censorship laws and other means that have created major controversies. Before we discuss the controversies, we look at how cyberspace has changed the risks to children.

HOW THE TECHNOLOGY CHANGES THE CONTEXT

If a young child tried to buy a ticket for an X-rated movie or to buy an adult magazine, a cashier would see the child and refuse (at least, most of the time). On the Web, a child can access pornography without an adult observer. The Web site operator or e-mailer supplying the material does not see that the customer is a child.

In a supermarket or a playground, a parent or other observer might see a "stranger" talking to a child. A potential child molester in a chat room is not visible. The anonymity of the Net makes it easier for people to prey on children. On the other hand, the anonymity also makes it easier for an undercover officer to pretend to be a 12-year-old girl online.

In the early days of the Web, one had to know how to find pornography and invoke special software to view it. Young children were not likely to come upon pornography by accident. Search engines and Web browsers changed that. Porn arrives in e-mail, and porn sites turn up in lists found by search engines for many innocent topics. A click displays images and video.

Schools and libraries used to be relatively safe havens from pornography and violent or hateful materials. The introduction of Internet terminals allows entrance of the undesirable material. Indeed, the home used to be a safe haven from such material; parents could relax when a child was playing in his or her bedroom. Now they might wonder what the child is looking at or with whom he or she is chatting.

PROTECTING CHILDREN

The first attempts to protect children from sexually explicit material on the Net came in the form of federal censorship laws. The first few major laws were rejected by the Supreme Court or other federal courts as unconstitutional restrictions on freedom of speech, but the final status of some is still undetermined. We discuss the laws in Section 5.2.3.

Child pornography is illegal, and it is illegal to lure children into sexual acts. Federal agents regularly conduct raids and make many arrests for these crimes where suspects use e-mail and chat rooms. Highly publicized arrests were used by some as an argument in support of stronger laws to censor the Net. Others argued that the arrests illustrate that law enforcement has the tools to fight these crimes. Federal agents use surveillance, court orders to read e-mail (as required by the Electronic Communications Privacy Act), search warrants, sting operations, and undercover investigations to build their cases and make the arrests.

Are new restrictions on freedom of speech needed to protect children on the Internet (and to protect adults from material that is offensive to them)? Are there other solutions that do not threaten to diminish free discussion of serious subjects or deny sexually explicit material to adults who want it? As we have seen for many problems, there are a variety of solutions based on the market, technology, responsibility, and education, as well as on enforcement of existing laws.

Commercial services cooperate with investigations of child pornography. America Online, for example, warns that, when subscribers notify the company of illegal activity, AOL reports it to the FBI and complies with subpoenas. It expelled subscribers who e-mailed child pornography to others. Its customer agreement gives it the right to remove anything it considers offensive. In response to market demand, companies offer online services and Web sites targeted to families and children. Some allow subscribers to lock children out of certain areas. AOL lets parents set up accounts for their children without e-mail, or with a specified list of addresses from which e-mail will be accepted. Many online services distribute information with tips on how to control what children can view. The Web sites of the FBI and organizations such as the National Center for Missing and Exploited Children provide information about risks to children and guidelines for reducing them. (One simple recommendation is to place the computer in the living room or family room where the child using it can easily be occasionally observed by a parent.)

Software filtering products with names such as Cyber Patrol, X-Stop, SurfWatch, and Net Nanny block access to sites that contain material that might be inappropriate for a child. Many products allow parents to choose categories to filter (e.g., sex or violence), add their own list of banned sites, and review a log of the sites their child visits. Many organizations are working on voluntary rating systems for Web sites; software filters can block sites according to ratings. When used by parents at home, filters are one tool available for controlling what children are exposed to on the Web. When mandated for schools and libraries, filters are much more controversial. We discuss the controversy in Section 5.2.4.

Parents have a responsibility to supervise their children and to teach them how to deal with inappropriate material and threats. Parents cannot always be present, of course, nor should they be watching over older children constantly, but good communication and instruction in expected behavior can avoid many problems. One of the best ways to protect children is good parenting.

> *Two-point-five million use America Online. That's like a city. Parents wouldn't let their kids go wandering in a city of 2.5 million people without them, or without knowing what they're going to be doing.*
>
> —Pam McGraw, America Online, 1995[14] [By 2001, the AOL "city" had about 33 million members.]

5.2.3 CENSORSHIP LAWS

In the 1990s, as more nontechnical people began using the Internet, a variety of religious organizations, anti-pornography groups, and groups that objected to other kinds of material began a campaign to pass federal legislation to censor the Net. Other people and organizations, including librarians, publishers, Internet companies, and civil liberties groups, opposed such legislation. Congress passed new laws when earlier ones were found unconstitutional. We examine the arguments, the standards for freedom of speech established by court decisions, and the continuing attempts to criminalize certain material on the Net or restrict access to it.

THE COMMUNICATIONS DECENCY ACT

In 1995, the FBI reported that "utilization of online services or bulletin-board systems is rapidly becoming one of the most prevalent techniques for individuals to share pornographic pictures of minors, as well as to identify and recruit children into sexually illicit relationships."[15] Popular news magazines shocked the public with dramatic cover stories on "Cyberporn." Increasing publicity and political pressure led Congress to pass the Communications Decency Act of 1996 (CDA).* The law attempted to avoid an obvious conflict with the First Amendment by focusing on material available to children. It provided that anyone who made available to anyone under 18 any communication that is obscene or indecent would be subject to a fine of $100,000 and two years in prison.

Opponents saw the CDA as a profound threat to freedom of expression. A broad collection of organizations, businesses, and individuals sued to block it. Two federal courts and the Supreme Court (in 1997) ruled unanimously, in *American Civil Liberties Union et al. v. Janet Reno*, that the censorship provisions of the CDA were unconstitutional. The courts made strong statements about the importance of protecting freedom of expression in general and on the Internet. The decisions against the CDA established that "the

---

*Passed as part of the Telecommunications Act of 1996.

Internet deserves the highest protection from government intrusion." The courts accepted two main arguments against the CDA: that it was too vague and broad, and that it did not use the least restrictive means of accomplishing the goal of protecting children. We elaborate on these arguments.

The law refers to "obscene, lewd, lascivious, filthy, or indecent" material. Some of these terms have legal definitions; some are vague. An enthusiastic love letter or an adult joke sent by e-mail might qualify. Opponents of the CDA gave examples of information that is legal in print but might be cause for prosecution if available online: the Bible, some of Shakespeare's plays, and serious discussions of sexual behavior and health problems like AIDS. The difficulty in determining what to censor is illustrated by America Online's action in response to government pressure to prohibit obscene or vulgar language. AOL included the word "breast" in its list of words banned from subscriber profiles. A week later the ban was reversed after protest, ridicule, and outrage from breast-cancer patients.[16]

Supporters of the CDA argued that this was over-reaction; no one would be prosecuted for transmitting Shakespeare or the Bible online or for discussing health problems online. The lack of clear standards, however, can lead to uneven and unfair prosecutions. When a government action or law causes people to avoid legal speech and publication out of fear of prosecution, the action or law is said to have a "chilling effect" on First Amendment rights. Courts generally rule against laws or government actions that have such effects.

Although there is disagreement over the standards for what material adults have the right to view, most people agree that a tighter standard is appropriate for children. It is sometimes difficult to design a law that keeps inappropriate material from children while allowing access for adults. The Supreme Court ruled on this problem in *Butler v. Michigan*, a significant 1957 case striking down a Michigan law that made it illegal to sell material that might be damaging to children. Justice Frankfurter wrote that the state must not "reduce the adult population of Michigan to reading only what is fit for children."[17] The CDA restricted indecent material accessible by children, but a child can access almost anything on the Net. Thus, opponents said, it would have violated Justice Frankfurter's dictum, not just in Michigan, but throughout the country. Judges quoted from *Butler v. Michigan* in their decisions rejecting the CDA.

When the government is pursuing a legitimate goal that might infringe on free speech (in this case, the protection of children), it must use the least restrictive means of accomplishing the goal. The courts found that the then newly developing filtering software was less restrictive and more desirable than censorship. The judges also commented, "The government can continue to protect children from pornography on the Internet through vigorous enforcement of existing laws criminalizing obscenity and child pornography."[18]

THE CHILD ONLINE PROTECTION ACT

Congress tried again, with the Child Online Protection Act (COPA), passed in 1998. This law was more limited than the CDA. COPA made it a federal crime for commercial Web sites to make available to minors material "harmful to minors," as judged by community standards. Offenses would be punishable by a $50,000 fine and six months in jail. Sites with potentially "harmful" material would have to get proof of age from site visitors. Once again, First Amendment supporters argued that the law was too broad and would threaten art, news, and health sites. A federal appeals court agreed, in 2000, that the censorship provisions of the law were unconstitutional. It specifically noted that, because the Web is accessible everywhere, the community-standards provision would restrict the entire country to the standards of the most conservative community. The Supreme Court heard the government's appeal in late 2001 and has not yet ruled.

Another provision of COPA set up the Child Online Protection Commission to study and report on ways to protect children. The commission included representatives from family organizations, government, universities, and industry. Its report, issued in 2000, said that most of the material of serious concern on the Internet was already illegal. It encouraged educational efforts and the use of technological protections (including filtering software). It encouraged improvements in efforts to enforce existing law, but proposed no new laws.[19]

THE CHILDREN'S INTERNET PROTECTION ACT

Pressure continued from organizations like the Family Research Council[20] for laws to prevent minors from obtaining sexually explicit material on the Internet. Rejection of COPA by a federal appeals court meant that advocates of censorship laws had to try a different approach. In 2000, Congress passed the Children's Internet Protection Act (CIPA). This law targets Internet terminals in schools and libraries. It applies only to schools and libraries that participate in certain federal programs (receiving federal money for technology). It requires that such schools and libraries install filtering software on all Internet terminals to block access to sites with child pornography, obscene material, and material "harmful to minors." We discuss arguments about the use of filters and attempts to mandate them in the next section.

> *Perhaps we do the minors of this country harm if First Amendment protections, which they will with age inherit fully, are chipped away in the name of their protection.*
>
> —Judge Lowell A. Reed Jr., when granting an injunction against COPA

5.2.4 INTERNET ACCESS IN LIBRARIES AND SCHOOLS

PROBLEMS WITH FILTERS

The development of software filters to block access to inappropriate material on the Internet was used by free-speech proponents and the courts as a major argument against censorship laws. Quickly, however, the filters themselves became the topic of intense controversy.

Software filters work in a variety of ways. They can block sites with specific words or phrases. They can block sites according to various rating systems. They can contain long lists of specific sites to block. Some companies that make filters hire people to spend hours surfing the Web, reviewing sites, and classifying them according to their level of violence, sexually explicit material, and so on. Customers can get updated lists frequently.[21]

It should be obvious that filters cannot do a perfect job. In fact, many do a very poor job. They screen out both too much and too little. Subjectivity and drastically different personal values influence decisions about what is too sexual or too violent or too critical of a religion, what medical information is appropriate for children of what age, what is acceptable to say about homosexuality, and so on. Various studies have shown that filters block numerous innocent, legal sites for no apparent reason. One study found that a filter blocked 99% of sites found by an unblocked search engine when given search phrases "American Red Cross," and "Thomas Edison." The editor of an online technology law journal intentionally misspells words like "sex" and "pornography" in his journal's articles so that filters will not block his subscribers from receiving their copies.[22] Figure 5.1 lists Web pages blocked by some filters. Clearly, some contain political discussion and educational material.

On the other hand, filters cannot block all Web pages with pornography or other material that some parents or legislators want to exclude. New sites appear regularly. Some objectionable material may be buried in documents or low-level Web pages that are not obvious to a person reviewing the site. Files transferred with peer-to-peer systems are not filtered.

The weaknesses of filters should not be a big surprise, nor do they mean that filters should be rejected totally. Filters will improve as new techniques are used to consider the context of "banned" keywords, but errors and subjectivity about what to block cannot be completely eliminated. None of the solutions we describe in this book for problems generated by new technologies are perfect. They have strengths and weaknesses and are useful in some circumstances and not others. Parents (or administrators of private schools) can carefully review the characteristics of competing products and make a choice about whether to use one. More significant social issues and controversies arise when public institutions like libraries and schools use filters and when legislators mandate them.

Another potential concern is that filters could be incorporated into popular, widely-used search engines, thus substituting the standards of the companies that provide search engines for the judgment of individual adult users. Social pressure from organizations that support freedom of speech might prevent this from happening.

PROBLEMS IN LIBRARIES

As soon as Internet terminals were installed in public libraries, some people used the terminals to view "X-rated" pictures, in view of children or other library users who were offended. Some people tied up terminals for hours viewing such material while others waited to use the terminals. Children accessed adult sexual material. Children and adults accessed extremist political sites and racist and Nazi material. All of this activity caused problems for library staff.

- Sites about Middlesex and Essex.

- Pages at sites of advocacy organizations such as the American Civil Liberties Union, the Electronic Privacy Information Center, and the Electronic Frontier Foundation.

- The court decision about the Communications Decency Act.

- All student organizations at Carnegie Mellon University.

- A page with Robert Frost's poem "Stopping by Woods on a Snowy Evening" (with the lines "My little horse must think it queer/ to stop without a farmhouse near").

- The Beaver College site (The college changed its name to Arcadia University in 2001, in part because some filters blocked its Web site.)

- The National Institutes of Health's Spanish-language site about diabetes (The word "hora," meaning "hour," appears often on the site; it refers to a prostitute in Swedish.)

- Sites with information about sex education, breast cancer, feminism, or gay and lesbian rights.

- The home page of Yale University's biology department.

- A wrestling site and a motorcycle sport magazine site.

- The Web site of a candidate for Congress (containing statements about abortion and gun control).

- A map of Disney World (I don't know why.)

- The Heritage Foundation (a conservative think tank) and a Quaker site.

Figure 5.1 What Gets Filtered

Librarians, confronted with new situations created by new technology, tried to satisfy library users, parents, community organizations, civil libertarians, and their own Library Bill of Rights (which opposes restricting access to library materials because of age). Libraries around the country responded in different ways. Some installed polarizing filters on terminals or walls around terminals so that the screens were visible only from directly in front (both to protect the privacy of the user and to shield other users and employees from material they find objectionable). Most set time limits on use of terminals. Some librarians asked patrons to stop viewing pornography, just as they would ask someone to stop making noise. Some revoked borrowing privileges of people viewing pornography. Some installed filtering software on all terminals, some on only terminals in the children's section. Some required parental supervision for children using the Internet, and some required written parental permission.

The efforts of the librarians did not prevent lawsuits. In a California city whose library did not use filtering software, a 12-year-old boy downloaded pornographic images and printed copies for his friends. His mother sued, arguing that the library harmed her son by exposing him to pornography. (A judge dismissed this suit.) A Virginia county adopted a policy requiring filters on all terminals. A group of citizens sued, arguing that the policy treated them like children and violated their First Amendment rights. (We discuss this case below.) Library staff members in Minneapolis and Chicago filed complaints with the federal Equal Employment Opportunity Commission (EEOC) arguing that they are subjected to a "hostile work environment" in unfiltered libraries because they are forced to view offensive material on the screens of library users and pornographic printouts left on library printers. The EEOC agreed in the Minneapolis case, a reminder of the frequent conflict between sexual harassment laws and freedom of speech.

Voters and legislators showed no consistency either. Voters in a Michigan town, for example, rejected a proposition to require filters in their libraries. In the same month, the Utah state senate unanimously passed a bill to deny funding for libraries unless they install filters.[23]

THE LOUDOUN, VIRGINIA LIBRARY CASE AND THE CHILDREN'S INTERNET PROTECTION ACT

The Loudoun County, Virginia library board of trustees established a policy that its libraries must install filters on Internet terminals to block child pornography, obscene material, and material harmful to juveniles (under standards set by Virginia law). The Children's Internet Protection Act, mentioned earlier, required schools and libraries receiving certain federal funds to install filtering software to block child pornography, obscene material and material "harmful to minors." The first two categories indicated in both Loudoun County and the CIPA are illegal, so blocking might seem uncontroversial, but there are many problems:

1. Who makes the determination that specific material is obscene? Is filtering software produced in one state customized for the community standards of all communities? (Generally not.) Civil libertarians argue that only the courts can decide what is obscene under the standards set by *Miller v. California*.

2. Companies that sell filtering software treat their lists of blocked Web sites as secret, proprietary information. Thus, libraries using the filters might not even know what sites they are blocking.

3. Public libraries and public schools are government institutions and, hence, subject to the First Amendment. The fact that filters block a huge amount of legal information is crucial when they are used in government institutions.

4. Filters block access by adults as well as children, violating the principle established in *Butler v. Michigan* (mentioned in Section 5.2.3).

5. People who cannot afford their own computers or Internet services are more likely to use libraries. Thus, poorer and less educated people will be the ones most affected by reduced access to information.

A group of citizens of Loudoun County sued to overturn the library policy. They won. As in the cases of the other Internet censorship laws we described, the judge in the Loudoun case made strong statements supporting the application of the First Amendment. She rejected the filtering policy because it was not necessary to accomplish a compelling government purpose, it was too broad, and it restricted access by adults to legal material.[24]

The authors of CIPA attempted to avoid the courts' rejection of the CDA and COPA by using the federal government's funding power rather than imposing a filtering requirement on all schools and libraries. Of course, the difference is minor in practice; many schools and libraries rely on those funds. Civil liberties organizations and the American Library Association sued to block this law; the Supreme Court had not yet ruled when this book was being written.[25]

5.2.5 TALKING ABOUT BOMBS—OR FARMING

Within a few weeks of the bombing of the Oklahoma City federal building in 1995, the Senate's terrorism and technology subcommittee held hearings on "The Availability of Bomb Making Information on the Internet." There are many similarities between the controversy about bomb-making information on the Net and the controversy about pornography. As with pornography, bomb-making information is already widely available in traditional media, protected by the First Amendment. It also has legitimate uses. Information about how to make bombs can be found in the *Encyclopedia Britannica* (which describes how to make an ammonium nitrate and fuel oil bomb, the kind reportedly used in Oklahoma City) and in books in libraries and bookstores. Such information, again including the ammonium nitrate and fuel oil bomb, is available to the public in a booklet called the "Blaster's Handbook"; it is published by the U.S. Department of Agriculture. Farmers use explosives to remove tree stumps.[26]

Arguing to censor information about bombs on the Internet after the Oklahoma City bombing, Senator Dianne Feinstein said, "there is a difference between free speech and teaching someone to kill."[27] Arguing against censorship, a former U.S. attorney said that "information-plus," (i.e., information used in the commission of a criminal act) is what should be regulated. Senator Patrick Leahy emphasized that it is "harmful and dangerous *conduct*, not speech, that justifies adverse legal consequences." This is more or less established legal principle outside of cyberspace. There are, of course, existing laws against the actual acts of using bombs to kill people or destroy property and laws against making bombs or conspiring to make them for such purposes.

Because of the conflict with the First Amendment, there was no federal law against bomb information on the Internet until 1999—after the shootings at Columbine High School in Littleton, Colorado. The two students who killed several others were reported to have used information obtained on the Internet to make bombs they carried. Congress passed a law mandating 20 years in prison for anyone who distributes bomb-making information knowing or intending that it will be used to commit a crime. Although there have been several incidents since then in which young people have built and used bombs made with information from the Internet, no one has been prosecuted under this law. It is too difficult to determine (and prove) what a person posting the information knows and intends about its uses. Much of the information about bombs is posted by people who do not intend it to be used for a crime.[28]

AOL and various companies that host Web sites have policies against allowing bomb-making information on their sites, but they note that, because of the large number of members and the huge amount of new material posted regularly, it is very difficult to keep such material out.

5.2.6 CHALLENGING OLD REGULATORY PARADIGMS AND SPECIAL INTERESTS

> *The beauty of it all is that the Internet puts my little farm on a par with a multinational company.*
>
> —Andrew Freemantles, pig farmer, whose Web site includes video clips of his pigs[29]

Quicken and Nolo Press sell self-help legal software to assist people in writing wills, premarital agreements, and many other documents. The software includes legal forms and instructions for filling them out. It is a typical example of empowering ordinary people and reducing our dependence on expensive experts—and, in a typical example of the backlash of special interests who see threats to their income and influence, a Texas judge banned Quicken legal software from Texas in 1999. Texas authorities pursued a similar case against Nolo Press. The judge decided the software amounted to the practicing of law without a Texas license. (The Texas legislature later changed its law to exempt software publishers.)

Several similar cases illustrate how the Web challenges existing interests by providing new options. Some of the cases have free-speech implications. Several involve regulatory laws that restrict advertising and sales on the Web. Such regulations have some noble purposes, such as protecting the public from fraud, but they also have the effect of entrenching large, established businesses, making it more difficult for new and small businesses to flourish, and of keeping prices high. We describe cases related to investment newsletters and wine sales.

The Web is a popular forum for discussing investments. In 1997, publishers of online newsletters and Web sites about commodities and futures investments discovered that they were violating 25-year-old regulations requiring government licenses. License requirements included fees, fingerprinting, a background check, and presenting a list of subscribers on demand to the Commodity Futures Trading Commission (CFTC), the federal agency that administers the regulations. Publishers who did not register with the CFTC could be fined up to $500,000 and jailed up to five years. The regulations were designed for traders who handle other people's money, but the CFTC applied them to people selling investment newsletters or software to analyze commodity-futures markets. The Institute for Justice represented several clients arguing that the licensing requirement violated the First Amendment. A federal judge ruled that the CFTC regulations were a prior restraint on speech and violated the First Amendment both for Internet publishers and for traditional newsletter publishers. In 2000, the CFTC revised its rules to exempt newsletter publishers, software developers, and Web site operators from the licensing requirements. The decision was important in avoiding a precedent of needing government approval to discuss certain subjects on the Net or via software. Also, by raising an issue of free speech on the Web, this case led to termination of a long-standing unconstitutional restraint of free speech in traditional media as well.[30]

The Web provides the potential for reducing prices of many products by eliminating the "middleman." Small producers who cannot afford expensive distributors or whole-salers can set up a Web site and sell directly to consumers nationwide—but not if they operate a small winery. Twenty-nine states in the U.S. have laws restricting the shipping of out-of-state wines directly to consumers. The laws protect large wholesaling businesses that typically get 18%–25% of the price and buy mostly from large wineries or those that sell expensive wines. They also protect state revenue; state governments cannot collect sales taxes on many out-of-state sales. State governments argue that the laws are needed to prevent sales to minors. However, a federal judge who struck down a New York law that banned cigarette sales by mail or on the Internet said that a state could require Internet sellers to get proof of age. Lawsuits in several states are challenging the laws against out-of-state wine shipments. New York law also bans *advertising* out-of-state wines directly to consumers in the state. A winery that advertises its wines on a Web site runs a risk because the Web site is accessible in New York. A lawsuit filed by the Institute for Justice challenging the New York wine law argues that it unconstitutionally restricts freedom of speech, interferes with interstate commerce, and discriminates against out-of-state businesses.[31] If these suits are successful, this will be another instance where the Web leads to removal of longstanding restrictions on freedom of speech and commerce.

5.2.7 CENSORSHIP ON THE GLOBAL NET

> The coffee houses emerged as the primary source of news and rumor. In 1675, Charles II, suspicious as many rulers are of places where the public trades information, shut the coffee houses down.
>
> —Peter L. Bernstein[32]

THE GLOBAL IMPACT OF CENSORSHIP

For a long time, the "conventional wisdom" among most users and observers of the Net (if anything about the Net can be called conventional) was that the global nature of the Net is a protection against censorship. Web sites with content that is illegal in one country can be set up in some other country. Online gambling casinos, for example, are established offshore to get around U.S. anti-gambling laws. The U.S. export restrictions for encryption software did not keep strong encryption from foreigners, because the software was available on hundreds of Web sites outside the United States. People in countries that censor news can access information over the Net from other countries and send information out by e-mail. E-mail and fax machines played a significant role during the collapse of the Soviet Union and the democracy demonstrations in China's Tiananmen Square. Both countries had far fewer computers and fax machines than the U.S., and totalitarian governments restrict ownership of publishing and communication equipment, but there were enough such machines available to provide a steady flow of information. By the time of the war in Kosovo, the Web was a major tool for informing (and sometimes misinforming) the world about what was happening.

In general, access to information and communications decreases a government's ability to abuse its people. Arthur C. Clarke commented, "No government will be able to conceal, at least for very long, evidence of crimes or atrocities—even from its own people. The very existence of the myriads of new information channels, operating in real time and across all frontiers, will be a powerful influence for civilized behavior."[33]

In some ways however, the globalness of the Net makes it easier for one nation to impose restrictive standards on others, wiping out not only the notion of community standards, as we saw in the Amateur Action BBS case (Section 5.2.1), but also the notion of different national standards. Also, governments are finding ways to use new technology to prevent their citizens from accessing prohibited material.

The first case to indicate the problem of one nation's restrictive laws affecting content outside that country occurred in 1995, when German prosecutors told CompuServe to block access by German subscribers to newsgroups with indecent and offensive material. The German government also said CompuServe violated German law because it was possible to access a neo-Nazi site in Canada by using CompuServe's Internet connection. CompuServe responded by cutting off access to more than 200 newsgroups—not only for its German subscribers, but for everyone. (It later restored access to all but five.) Similarly, when the government of China objected to a particular program of the British Broadcasting Corporation (BBC) that was critical of Mao Tse-tung, the satellite provider cut the BBC completely out of its transmission to China. The area affected by the cut also included Taiwan and Hong Kong.[34]

In 2000, a French court ordered Yahoo! to block access by French people to Yahoo!'s U.S.-based auction sites where Nazi memorabilia was sold. (Display and sale of Nazi memorabilia are illegal in France and Germany, with some exceptions for historical purposes.) The order raised several technical and legal issues; it was widely viewed as a threat to freedom of speech.[35]

Yahoo! and other critics of the order cited two technical issues. First, it was technically infeasible to block access by all French people because they could access Yahoo!'s sites from outside France or use anonymizing services that obscured their location. One of the basic characteristics of the Net is that one's physical location is almost irrelevant; it is also difficult to determine. Second, the use of filters to screen out Nazi material has the problems we discussed earlier (Section 5.2.4). Yahoo! said filters would be less than 50% effective and could not distinguish references to Nazis in hate material from references in *The Diary of Anne Frank* or Holocaust memorials.[36]

Technology solves problems—even problems some people would prefer not be solved. At the time of the Yahoo! case, advertisers were beginning to use software to try to determine the location of Web site visitors so that localized advertising could be better targeted. Companies providing the software adapted it for use by Web sites to comply with such restrictions as in the Yahoo! case. The software is far from perfect, but it can enable blocking of some visitors according to their location.

Shortly after the French court issued its order, Yahoo! announced that it would ban "hate material," including Nazi and Ku Klux Klan memorabilia, from its auction sites (though not all material that is illegal in France). EBay, the huge online auction site, also announced a ban on memorabilia about Nazis, the Ku Klux Klan, and other hate groups. It cited the complex of regulations and different cultural standards of other countries in which it was expanding its business. Free-speech advocates worried that the policy changes demonstrate the power of one government to impose its censorship standards on other countries. Others see it as adoption of a responsible policy, discouraging the spread of such material. But what about other material that is illegal in some countries? Germany, for example, has extremely restrictive laws about advertising; it prohibits direct price comparisons.[37] Would commercial Web sites with price comparisons have to screen out German shoppers? Should online services bar people in totalitarian countries from news and political discussion that is banned in those countries? If Web sites must comply with the laws of 180 countries, what would happen to the openness and global information flow of the Web? In 2001, a U.S. court said the U.S. government would not enforce the French court ruling against Yahoo! However, other countries could seize foreign assets or arrest visiting executives of companies that do not comply with their censorship orders.

CENSORSHIP IN OTHER NATIONS

The office of communications is ordered to find ways to ensure that the use of the Internet becomes impossible. The Ministry for the Promotion of Virtue and Prevention of Vice is obliged to monitor the order and punish violators.

—Excerpt from the Taliban edict banning all Internet use in Afghanistan, 2001[38]

The vibrant communication made possible by the Internet threatens governments in countries that lack political and cultural freedom. Many governments took steps to cut, or seriously reduce, the flow of information and opinion on the Net (as they had done earlier with other communications media). We give a sampling of such restrictions.

Governments make use of excellent text-searching tools to scan electronic newsletters and discussion groups to identify their critics. In 1994, the administrators of Singapore's Technet, a government-funded service, examined 80,000 files belonging to users in a search for "countersocial activity." In this case, they were looking for pornography, but, clearly, in countries where criticism of the government is illegal or not tolerated, searches for "countersocial activity" have ominous implications.[39]

In 1996, Pakistan banned Internet telephony. In 2000, Burma (Myanmar) banned use of the Internet or creation of Web pages without official permission, posting of material about politics, and posting of any material deemed by the government to be harmful to its policies. Under an earlier law, possession of an unauthorized modem or satellite dish was punishable by a jail term of up to 15 years. Internet access was prohibited in Eritrea. Many countries in the Middle East limited access. Vietnam uses filtering software to find and block anticommunist messages coming from other countries. The government of Iran made people dismantle satellite dishes to avoid "cultural contamination" from U.S. television. The legality of satellite dishes in many parts of Asia and the Middle East is fuzzy.[40]

In some long-unfree countries, the governments are struggling with the dilemma of modernizing their economy and technology while trying to maintain tight control over information. China channeled all foreign Internet traffic through a small number of gateways under its control. The Chinese government filters online international economic news through its news agency and blocked access to some Web sites in the West and to sites with news and commentary from Taiwan. It blocks sites about the Falun Dafa religious group. A Chinese Internet entrepreneur was sentenced to two years in jail for sharing e-mail addresses with a pro-democracy Internet journal based in the United States. Users of the Internet and other international computer networks are required to register with the police (even to use terminals in Internet cafes). Sale of satellite dishes was banned (just as residential telephones were banned in China in the past). Regulations prohibit "producing, retrieving, duplicating and spreading information that may hinder public order." Some observers point out that the regulations are better than blocking Internet access totally, and that, in practice, the government cannot monitor all users, so the regulation is actually a step toward more freedom and information access than was previously available.[41]

Singapore required that online political and religious groups register with the government. Content providers were prohibited from distributing material that could "undermine public morals, political stability or religious harmony." In 1996, the government of Singapore justified its censorship attempts in part by citing the censorship efforts in the United States. In 1999, Singapore, which made a great effort to build a high-tech economy, relaxed enforcement of Internet censorship laws but did not change them.[42]

Knowledge is liberty's greatest ally.

—David F. Nolan, co-founder, Libertarian Party

5.3 Anonymity

The Colonial press was characterized by irregular appearance, pseudonymous invective, and a boisterous lack of respect for any form of government.

—"Science, Technology, and the First Amendment," U.S. Office of Technology Assessment

5.3.1 *COMMON SENSE* AND THE INTERNET

From the description in the Office of Technology Assessment's report, quoted above, the Colonial press—the press the authors of the First Amendment to the U.S. Constitution found it so important to protect—had a lot in common with the Internet, including its controversial anonymous e-mail and anonymous postings to chat rooms and discussion groups.

Jonathan Swift published his humorous and biting political satire *Gulliver's Travels* anonymously. Thomas Paine's name did not appear on the first printings of *Common Sense*, the book that roused support for the American Revolution. The Federalist Papers, published in newspapers in 1787 and 1788, argued for adoption of the new U.S. Constitution. The authors, Alexander Hamilton, James Madison, and John Jay, had already served the newly free confederation of states in important roles. Jay later became chief justice of the Supreme Court, and Madison later became president. But when they wrote the Federalist Papers, they used a pseudonym, Publius. Opponents of the Constitution, those who believed it gave far too much power to the federal government, used pseudonyms as well. In the nineteenth century, when it was not considered proper for women to write books, women writers such as Mary Ann Evans and Amantine Lucile Aurore Dupin published under male pseudonyms, or pen names (George Eliot and George Sand). Prominent professional and academic people use pseudonyms to publish murder mysteries, science fiction, or other nonscholarly work, and some writers—for example, the iconoclastic H. L. Mencken—used pseudonyms for the fun of it.

On the Internet, people talk about personal things in chat rooms and discussion forums devoted to topics such as health, gambling habits, problems with teenage children, religion, and so on. Many people use pseudonyms ("handles," aliases, or screen names) to keep their real identity private. Victims of rape and of other kinds of violence and abuse and users of illegal drugs who are trying to quit are among those who benefit from a forum where they can talk candidly without giving away their identity. (In traditional in-person support groups and group counseling sessions, only first names are used, to protect privacy.) Whistleblowers, reporting on unethical or illegal activities within the government agency or business where they work, may choose to release information via anonymous postings (although, depending on whether the information is verifiable, credibility for such anonymous postings may be low). In wartime, anonymity can be a life-or-death issue; people in Kosovo used anonymous remailers in 1999 to prevent detection by the Serbian military.[43]

To send anonymous e-mail, one sends the message to a remailer service, where the return address is stripped off and the message is resent to the intended recipient. Messages can be routed through many intermediate destinations to more thoroughly obscure their origins. If someone wants to remain anonymous but receive replies, he or she can use a service where a coded ID number is attached to the message when it is sent by the remailer. The ID assigned by the remailer is a pseudonym for the sender, maintained by the remailer. Replies go to the remailer site, where the message is forwarded to the original person. Thus people can have conversations where neither knows the identity of the other.

Johan Helsingius set up the first well-known "anonymous" remailer in Finland in 1993, originally for users in the Scandinavian countries. (Users were not entirely anonymous; the system retained identifying information.) It was extremely popular and grew to an estimated 500,000 users worldwide. Helsingius became a hero to dissidents in totalitarian countries and to free speech and privacy supporters everywhere. He closed his remailer in 1996 after the Church of Scientology and the government of Singapore took action to obtain the names of people using it. By then, he said, it was no longer needed, because many other similar services had become available.

Several businesses, like Anonymizer.com and Zero-Knowledge Systems, provide a variety of sophisticated tools and services that enable us to send e-mail and surf the Web anonymously. Some of the anonymity services are designed, using encryption schemes, so that even the company that operates them cannot identify the user. Many people use anonymous Web browsers to thwart the efforts of businesses to collect information about their Web activity and build dossiers for marketing purposes. The founder of SafeWeb, which provides anonymous Web-surfing services, said the company develops tools to help people in Iran, China, and Saudi Arabia get around their governments' restrictions on Internet access.[44]*

> *Introducing anonymity online from American Express. Don't leave home-pages without it.*[TM]
>
> —Newspaper advertisement for American Express[45]

5.3.2 IS ANONYMITY PROTECTED?

For those not using true anonymity services, secrecy of our identity online depends both on the privacy policies of ISPs and services like AOL and MSN and on the laws and court decisions about granting subpoenas for disclosure. What happens when someone wants to know the real identity of a person who posted something? How well protected are our real identities? How strongly should they be protected? In this section, we consider political speech, controlled by state and federal laws, and attempts of corporations to learn the identities of their online critics. In the next section, we look at arguments against complete anonymity.

POLITICAL SPEECH

Political speech is protected under the First Amendment in the U.S, but there are still many ways in which the government can retaliate against its critics. There are also many

---

*The U.S. Central Intelligence Agency is a major SafeWeb customer. A senior CIA official commented "We want to operate anywhere on the Internet in a way that no one knows the CIA is looking at them."[46]

AOL AND THE SAILOR

AOL's terms-of-service agreement states that their policy is "not to disclose identity information to third parties that would link a Member's screen name(s) with a Member's actual name, unless required to do so by law or legal process served on AOL, Inc. (e.g., a subpoena)." AOL reserves the right to make exceptions in special circumstances, such as a suicide threat or suspected illegal activity. An AOL employee violated the policy in a widely publicized case in 1997. The employee gave a caller—pretending to be a friend, but actually a Navy investigator—the real name of a sailor who described himself as gay in an online profile. This incident illustrates several points. First, AOL has a very good identity-protecting policy. Second, a company must train its employees well to follow the policy and to understand that someone who calls requesting information might not be who he claims to be. Finally, this incident illustrates the risks. The sailor might be gay—or, like many other people, he might have created a fictitious persona online—but the Navy tried to discharge him after 17 years of service with an excellent record.[47]

personal reasons why someone might not want to be identified as holding certain views. Anonymity provides protection against retaliation and embarrassment.

The Web enables anyone to express political opinions to a wide audience inexpensively. Some individuals prefer to express their opinions anonymously. Can they do so? The Supreme Court has repeatedly ruled that the right to speak anonymously (in print) is included in the freedom of speech guaranteed by the First Amendment. In 1995, the Supreme Court invalidated an Ohio state law under which a woman was fined for distributing pamphlets against a proposed school tax without putting her name on them. The Court ruled that distribution of anonymous political leaflets (by an individual) is an exercise of freedom of speech protected by the First Amendment. The court said "anonymous pamphleteering is not a pernicious, fraudulent practice, but an honorable tradition of advocacy and of dissent. Anonymity is a shield from the tyranny of the majority."[48] A federal court threw out Georgia's 1996 law against using a false identity on the Internet, citing the Supreme Court decision in the Ohio case.

Regulations of the Federal Election Commission (FEC) restrict anonymity. Disclosure and financial filing requirements were established, before the Web, to monitor campaign spending of large corporations and other large organizations. How do they apply to the Web? A man set up a Web page to express his opposition to reelection of a member of Congress. Another man had a Web page satirizing the governor of his state. These appear to be clear examples of speech protected by the First Amendment, speech that should be permitted anonymously. But the FEC told the first man that he might have to comply with federal campaign laws requiring that he identify himself on the Web site and file financial statements. The governor filed a complaint against the second man, suggesting that he be required to do the same. The overhead of the reporting paperwork, the low spending threshold ($250 in some cases), and fear of inadvertently breaking the law could discourage ordinary people from expressing their views on their Web sites. The FEC regulations seem to conflict with the First Amendment and the court decisions mentioned above. The Web reopens the issue of conflicts between campaign regulations and freedom of speech.

CRITICIZING CORPORATIONS

> *Internet stock message boards are to Wall Street what talk radio is to current events: Occasionally crude, often wrong, frequently useless but nonetheless a vital and widely used forum where people can speak their minds.*
>
> —Aaron Elstein, *Wall Street Journal* reporter[49]

Yahoo! has several thousand discussion forums devoted to individual companies where investors, employees, and others discuss the company. AOL and other services have similar forums. Much of the discussion centers on investment issues, which include how well the company is run and its future financial prospects. Businesses have two areas of legitimate complaints: postings that spread false and damaging rumors (libel or defamation), and postings that include confidential business documents or other proprietary information. People post false comments stating that a business is near bankruptcy or that its managers are committing fraud. They post personal accusations, for example that the executives of the business engage in wife swapping. In one case, a former employee posted particularly nasty comments about a company and its executives, including charges of adultery. When sued, he apologized and said he made it all up.[50] We are not exempt from ordinary ethics and defamation laws merely because we are using the Internet or signing comments with an alias rather than a real name. On the other hand, many postings are simply strong criticism, which is free speech even when expressed in the flaming style common in some online forums. Should businesses be able to get real names of people posting messages they object to? If a service gives out someone's real name, should the person be informed?

By 2000, businesses had filed more than 100 libel lawsuits against people who posted critical comments. After a lawsuit is filed, the business normally gets a subpoena ordering the service to disclose the person's real name and address. Often, the person is not informed that the information has been disclosed. A popular stock chat site said it received roughly one subpoena per day and did not have the staff to notify everyone. AOL gives members 14 days notice before turning over their information, so a member has an opportunity to fight a subpoena in court. Yahoo! did not notify people when they were the target of a subpoena—until one person sued Yahoo! for disclosing his identity to his employer (who fired him). Other people have been fired for posting comments critical of their employer. It is widely believed that businesses use the libel lawsuits as a tool to obtain the identities of people who are expressing their opinions (legally) and to intimidate them into being quiet.

Free-speech advocates developed legal defenses to use in fighting subpoenas for the names of people who are exercising freedom of speech and not committing libel or posting proprietary company material. Lawyers argued that judges should examine the individual case and determine if the evidence for defamation is strong enough that the company is likely to win—and only then issue a subpoena for the real name of the defendant. Some suggested using the same standards for requiring journalists to disclose their sources. Some recommended that ISPs be required by law to notify a member when the ISP receives a subpoena for the member's identity. Gradually, as more attention focused on the threats to free speech, some courts rejected some subpoenas for real names. A federal judge ruled for a defendant saying that Internet postings are almost always opinions, which are protected speech; they are "full of hyperbole, invective, . . . and language not generally found in fact-based documents."[51] Some lawyers proposed a general defense to defamation suits for message board comments: These forums are full of exaggeration and shrillness. Sensible people do not take the comments seriously; thus, no one's reputation can truly be damaged in such a forum, and there is no defamation.[52] Which of these standards or policies is reasonable?

5.3.3 AGAINST ANONYMITY

ANONYMITY VS. COMMUNITY

In some contexts, anonymity is seen as unneighborly or risky. The WELL,* for example, takes the position that people should take responsibility for their opinions and statements by letting their identities be known. Esther Dyson, editor of *Release 1.0* and a frequent writer on the computing environment, commented that "anonymity is the opposite of community" (while also commenting that there are situations where anonymity is okay).[53] Dyson was careful to make the distinction that many overlook: People might object to something, choose not to use it, and discourage its use in certain environments, without advocating the imposition of the force of the government to stop its use. Commenting on a lawsuit challenging Georgia's anti-anonymity law, Dyson said "Anonymity shouldn't be a crime. Committing crimes should be a crime."[54]

Because of its potential to shield criminal activity or because they consider it incompatible with politeness and netiquette (online etiquette), some services choose to discourage or prohibit anonymity. Some require identification of all members and users. Some do not accept any e-mail from known anonymous remailer sites. On the other hand, Web sites that emphasize debate on controversial issues or have discussion groups on socially sensitive topics often consider anonymity to be a reasonable way to protect privacy and encourage open, honest discussion. If policy decisions about anonymity are made by those responsible for individual services and Web sites, the policies can be flexible and diverse enough to be adapted to a particular service and clientele.

---

*The WELL is the Whole Earth 'Lectronic Link, one of the earliest online communities.

LAWS AGAINST ANONYMITY

Anonymity on the Internet is used for criminal and antisocial purposes. It is used for fraud, harassment, and extortion. It is used to distribute child pornography, to libel or threaten others with impunity, and to infringe copyrights by posting and downloading copyrighted material without authorization. It can be used to plan terrorist attacks. Like encryption, anonymity technology poses strong challenges to law enforcement. Anonymity makes it difficult to track criminals and terrorists.

Law-enforcement agencies argue for laws that require ISPs to maintain records of the true identity of each user and to maintain records of online activity for a specified period of time for potential use in criminal investigations. Such laws would prevent true anonymity and ban some services provided by companies such as Anonymizer.com and Zero-Knowledge. Civil libertarians, privacy advocates, and ISPs object that any such requirements conflict with the First Amendment and privacy and that the record keeping would place an expensive burden on the ISPs. The potential for illegal access to the records by government agencies and other (e.g., hackers) would also compromise freedom of speech and privacy.

Many of the core issues are the same as those in the law-enforcement controversies we discussed in Chapters 2 and 3. Does the potential for harm by criminals who use anonymity to hide from law enforcement outweigh the loss of privacy and restraint on freedom of speech for honest people who use anonymity responsibly? Is anonymity an important protection against possible abuse of power by government? Should people have the right to use available tools, including strong encryption or anonymity, to protect their privacy? We can send hardcopy mail without a return address; should there be more restrictions on anonymity on the Net than in other contexts?

5.4 Spam

5.4.1 WHAT'S THE PROBLEM?

Defining spam, as we will see, is not a simple task, especially if one is defining it in a law to restrict it. We will loosely describe spam as unsolicited mass e-mail.* Spam has infuriated users of the Internet since the mid-1990s, and in 2001 it invaded cellphones. Most, but not all, spam is commercial advertising. Spam developed because e-mail is extremely cheap compared to printed direct-mail advertising. Some businesses and organizations compile or buy huge lists of e-mail addresses and send their unsolicited messages. Some build lists, using automated software that surfs the Web and collects anything that looks like an e-mail address.

---
*Spam is the name of a spiced lunch-meat product sold in cans by Hormel Foods. The use of the word in the context of e-mail comes from a Monty Python skit in which some characters repeatedly shouted "Spam, spam, spam," drowning out other conversation.

Spam angers people because of both the content and the way it is sent. Content can be ordinary commercial advertising, political advertising (for candidates or issues), solicitations for funds from nonprofit organizations, pornography and advertisements for it, and fraudulent "get rich quick" schemes. Many people just do not want any unsolicited ads and announcements. Some spammers disguise their e-mail return address so that they are not bothered with bounced mail from closed or invalid accounts. ISPs filter out e-mail from known spammers, so some disguise their return address and use other schemes to avoid filters.

How much spam travels through the Internet? The first case that created an anti-spam furor involved advertising messages sent by a law firm to 6000 bulletin boards or news groups in 1994. At that time, any advertising or postings not directly related to the topic of the group raised the ire of Net users. Within a few years, as e-mail use grew, one notorious spammer alone was estimated to be sending 25 million e-mails per day.[55]

Why is spam a problem? "Junk mail" is one form of violation of privacy: unwanted intrusion. The recipient has the annoyance of receiving junk mail, wasting time reading enough to determine what it is, and deleting it. In addition, spam has costs for the recipient. Early e-mail accounts allowed limited space for e-mail, possibly causing some to be lost when one's inbox filled with spam. Some users paid fees depending on how long they were online or how much disk space they used. Spam costs service providers who need a system large and fast enough to handle the load and who must deal with the clog of undeliverable mail. In many cellphone systems, the owner of the phone pays for incoming messages.

5.4.2 CASES AND FREE-SPEECH ISSUES

AOL VERSUS CYBER PROMOTIONS AND OTHER SPAMMERS

In 1996, about half of the e-mail received at AOL was spam,* and a lot of it came from a company called Cyber Promotions, an e-mail advertising service founded by Sanford Wallace. AOL installed filters to block mail from Cyber Promotions. Cyber Promotions changed its return address to avoid the filters and obtained an injunction against AOL's use of filters, claiming its First Amendment rights were being violated. Thus began the battle over the legal status of spam.

Cyber Promotions' case was weak, and the injunction was soon removed. Why did AOL have the right to block incoming spam? The spam used AOL's computers, imposing a cost on AOL. AOL's property rights allow it to decide what it accepts on its system. AOL is a membership organization; it can implement policies to provide the kind of environment it believes its members want. Finally, AOL is a private company, not a government institution. The First Amendment prohibits government from restricting freedom of speech; it does not require anyone to listen. On the other side, some civil liberties organizations were uneasy about allowing AOL to filter e-mail because AOL

---

*A 1997 study reported typical rates of 2%–10% on corporate networks and at ISPs. Some aspects of AOL's system made spam more common there.

decided what e-mail to block from its members. They argued that because AOL is large, it is a lot like the Post Office, and it should not be allowed to block mail.

Over the next few years, AOL filed several lawsuits and sought injunctions to stop spammers from sending unsolicited mass mailings to members. Notice the subtle shift: Cyber Promotions sought an injunction to stop AOL from filtering out its e-mail. AOL sought injunctions to stop spammers from sending e-mail. Filters do not violate a spammer's freedom of speech, but does an order not to send the mail violate freedom of speech? We listed several arguments why a company like AOL should be free to filter incoming mail. Do any of the arguments support injunctions against the spammers? One does: the argument that the spam uses the recipient company's property (computer system) against its wishes and imposes a cost on the recipient. AOL and other services won multimillion-dollar settlements from Cyber Promotions and other spammers.[56]

AN INTEL EMPLOYEE

Over a period of less than two years, a former Intel employee, Ken Hamidi, who maintained a Web site critical of the company, sent six mass e-mailings to more than 30,000 Intel employees. He disguised his return address, making it difficult for Intel to block his e-mail with a filter. Intel sought a court order prohibiting him from sending more e-mail to its employees (at work). Note that, in this case, the spam was not commercial. Should the judge have granted the order? Would it infringe Hamidi's freedom of speech? Intel argued that freedom of speech gave him the right to operate his own Web site, but did not give him the right to intrude in Intel's property and use its equipment to deliver his messages. The judge granted the order.[57]

HUMAN RIGHTS AND POLITICAL ORGANIZATIONS

Amnesty International has long used its network of thousands of volunteers to flood government officials in various countries with mail when a political prisoner was being tortured or was in imminent danger of execution. Now, volunteers can log on to its Web site and send a prewritten e-mail letter. This is not commercial mail, and it differs from most spam in that a small number of recipients receive a large amount of similar mail, but it is intended to be of large volume and it is certainly unsolicited by the recipient.

Various political and advocacy organizations use the same kinds of systems. People can click to send prewritten e-mail to politicians or other organizations and businesses. Will we have different points of view about whether this is free speech or spam, depending on how sympathetic we are to the specific organization's message? These examples illustrate how careful we must be when designing legal restrictions on spam.

5.4.3 SOLUTIONS

As usual, we discuss solutions drawn from technology, market pressure, business policies, and law.[58]

MARKETS, TECHNOLOGY, AND BUSINESS POLICY

Filters were used early to screen out spam at the recipient's site, by blocking e-mail from specified addresses and by more sophisticated methods. ISPs can block certain e-mail from their systems entirely and also let individual members establish their own lists and criteria for mail to block.

Many businesses subscribe to services that provide lists of spammers to block. The Mail Abuse Prevention System (MAPS), for example, had 20,000 subscribers in 2000, including small companies and large ISPs. Aggressive anti-spam services list not only spammers, but also ISPs that do not take sufficient action to stop members from sending spam. For example, MAPS put some ISPs and Microsoft Network on its list. Such action encourages managers to do something, for example, limiting the number of outbound e-mail messages sent from one account. (Early in the spam wars, most ISPs refused accounts to Cyber Promotions.)

How much discretion should an anti-spam listing service have in deciding whom to include on its list of spammers? Harris Interactive, which conducts public opinion surveys by e-mail ("Harris polls"), sued MAPS for including Harris on its blacklist. Harris claimed that the people receiving its e-mail signed up to receive it; MAPS claimed Harris did not meet its standards for assuring the recipients' consent. Harris claimed it was recommended for the spammer list by a competing polling company.[59] MAPS publicizes its criteria and offers its list to ISPs, who can decide whether or not to use it. Harris claimed inclusion on the list cut it off from about half of its survey participants and harmed its business; it wanted to collect for damages. A business might sue services like MAPS, arguing that inclusion on the list amounts to defamation. In this case, Harris dropped the suit not long after filing it, so no legal issues were settled. The case had the effect of making users more aware of MAPS' criteria and the differences of opinion that can arise about who is a spammer.

Spam is cheap. Thus one idea for reducing it is to increase its cost. Proposals include schemes in which e-mail senders pay a tiny charge to the recipient for each e-mail message sent. Such plans depend on the development of micropayment systems (that have many other uses too). For most users of e-mail, the charge would be insignificant, but, for spammers who send a million messages a day, it would be a disincentive. Some proposals make the payment an option to the recipient, with the idea that most people would not invoke the charge for most personal e-mail, but would click to charge when e-mail comes from an advertiser.

ANTI-SPAM LAWS

Several anti-spam laws have been introduced in Congress, but none had passed by the time this book was being written. As we observed earlier, a key problem with any government actions, injunctions, or laws to restrict or prohibit spam is that they might conflict with freedom of speech. The basis for the legality of filtering and blocking is that freedom of speech does not require the intended listener, or e-mail recipient, to listen. But how far can the law go in restricting the sender?

AN ISSUE FOR DESIGNERS AND USERS OF FILTERS

We saw that filters are not perfect; they block more or less than the material one wants blocked, and often they block both more and less. If the filter is intended to block sexually explicit material from young children, it might be acceptable to err on the side of blocking some inoffensive material to be sure of preventing the undesirable material from getting through. On the other hand, if the filter is for spam, most people would not mind a few spam messages getting through, but would be quite unhappy if some of their nonspam e-mail was thrown away.

Provisions in proposed laws include the following:

- Unsolicited commercial e-mail must be labeled so that it can easily be filtered out.
- ISPs must provide filters for members to block spam.
- Spam must identify the sender and include instructions for opting out.
- Senders must honor opt-out requests from recipients and send them no additional mail.
- Spam must include a valid e-mail reply address.
- False or misleading subject lines are prohibited.
- All unsolicited commercial e-mail is banned.

Definitions in a spam law are critical. Many proposed anti-spam laws focus on commercial e-mail. One reason is that most offensive spam is commercial. Another is that restrictions on commercial messages have a better chance of being accepted by the Supreme Court as not violating the First Amendment. Although we usually think of spam as mass e-mail, some define it as *one* or more unsolicited (commercial) messages. How will "unsolicited" be defined? How much of the e-mail you received today did you solicit? What are your criteria? We saw that Harris Interactive and MAPS disagreed on the definition. Is unsolicited mail always unwelcome mail? If it were illegal to send someone mail without the recipient's consent, how would someone contact the recipient to get consent?

More than a dozen states have laws regulating spam sent to people in the state. As we saw in the French case against Yahoo! (Section 5.2.7), it is not always feasible to determine the location of the recipient. Some state laws have been challenged on the grounds that they interfere with interstate commerce. The globalness of the Net adds another problem: If laws are passed in one country, but not in most others, many spammers will set up shop on computers outside the country.

Spam that includes fraudulent "get rich quick" schemes or ads for child pornography is sent by people who clearly do not care about what is legal. They are not likely to obey laws to identify themselves, and so forth. Such laws may make it easier to fine or jail them by convicting them of violating anti-spam regulations in cases where there is insufficient evidence for convictions based on the content of the messages. (This is a little like sending gangster Al Capone to jail for income-tax evasion.) But such laws can be applied selectively and abusively. It is not good policy to rely on government officials to use broader laws only against the true "bad guys." Laws restricting speech (from the Alien and Sedition Acts of 1798 to regulation of Political Action Committees) have been used against newspaper editors who disagreed with the political party in power and against ad hoc groups of people speaking out on issues, though proponents of the laws said they were designed for traitors or special-interest groups.

5.5 Ensuring Valuable and Diverse Content

Most of this chapter has been about censorship and other attempts to restrict information available on the Net. The political right, or social conservatives, tends to favor that kind of governmental control, censoring sexual and other material on the Net. The kind of control we discuss in this section tends to be favored by the political left, or liberals. Some organizations and people, including Computer Professionals for Social Responsibility (CPSR); Lawrence Grossman, former president of the Public Broadcasting System (PBS) and NBC News; and philosophers who write about computer ethics, advocate a variety of legal regulations, taxes and subsidies, and other mechanisms to ensure that content they consider desirable is available on the Web. They want to create a balance between commercial and educational information and to ensure that there will be material to benefit children.

The particular kinds of content advocated by these groups changed as the Web developed. In the early 1990s, advocates of efforts to ensure socially valuable content worried that, if it were left to the decisions of profit-seeking businesses, cyberspace would be all shopping malls, advertisements, and movies and a few large companies would dominate the market for information on the Net, reducing diversity of opinion. Grossman argued that large media corporations would not provide the civic, educational, and cultural programming the public needs. He advocated the establishment of a public telecommunications trust fund to provide free online forums for labor unions, civic organizations, community-action groups, public-interest groups, citizen's organizations, political candidates, and political parties. As the Web bloomed and many of these organizations set up their own Web sites, the focus of the proposals changed. In 2001, Grossman and others in an organization called Digital Promise advocated spending $18 billion for educational material, civic information, and arts and cultural sites on the Web.[60]

Given the enormous quantity and diversity of material already on the Net by the mid-1990s and the even larger quantity and diversity on the Web now, the continued concern about ensuring valuable content might seem surprising. Nonetheless, it is worth examining the arguments for subsidizing or requiring certain content that some people deem desirable and not sufficiently available.

Content in an information technology depends in part on how it is funded (e.g., via government subsidies, advertising, donations, or payment by consumers) and in part on whether there are explicit legal licensing and content requirements (e.g., the Fairness Doctrine or requirements for a certain percentage of news coverage or public-service announcements). Government funding for television and radio via the Public Broadcasting System (PBS) is seen by many as a model for providing socially valuable programming within a mostly privately funded communications industry.* CPSR suggested the establishment of "public spaces" on the Net. Public areas might be set up by the government or established by online service providers in exchange for tax deductions. The idea is somewhat similar to public-access cable television channels, or to PBS. The purpose is to provide both access to information and a place for anyone to post messages with a guarantee of freedom of speech.[61]

Objections to tax-funded or mandated content are based on free-speech and practical issues. There are serious controversies over government funding for the Public Broadcasting System, art shows sponsored by the National Endowment for the Humanities, and exhibits at the Smithsonian Institution and the Library of Congress. These controversies indicate that there is not strong agreement among the public about what constitutes socially valuable—or offensive—content. Subsidized programs might promote particular political, social, or aesthetic views that some taxpayers oppose; a freedom-of-speech issue arises whenever governments subsidize content. Also, opponents view subsidies and regulations as unnecessary, given the extraordinary variety on the Web.

EXPERIENCES WITH OTHER INFORMATION MEDIA

Why should it not surprise us that labor unions and community, ethnic, religious, and environmental organizations, to name just a few noncommercial groups, have Web sites now? or that the goals of content diversity and opportunities to speak are being met and will continue to be met without special government mandates? We can approach this question by observing some analogies with other information and entertainment media.

There are many parallels between the Internet and publishing. In the first few decades after the invention of the printing press, we might have worried that it would be used almost exclusively for printing junk fiction and government propaganda, that magazines and newspapers would be full of advertising, and that there would be no good books for children. In fact, we did get junk fiction and magazines and newspapers full of advertising. We also got books, magazines, and newsletters on science, philosophy, astrology, communism, capitalism, Christianity, Islam, gay rights, cooking (from beef to vegetarian), and an enormous number of other subjects and points of view. Excellent children's books are plentiful. We have expensive, beautifully bound books and inexpensive paperbacks. There are numerous content providers: large and small publishers who hope to make profits and writers or foundations who publish without regard to commercial success. The printing press provides tremendous diversity. The development of enormous diversity of information and opinion on the Web has been similar, though enormously quicker.

---

*PBS stations receive support from members and donors, as well as from government.

Who controls the printing press to ensure diversity and socially valuable content? Publishers? Consumers? Publishers decide what books their company will publish, but they choose those they think the public will buy. No one publisher or one consumer decides what will or will not be published. We do not have majority votes about what should be published. (What implications would *that* have for publication of material on minority viewpoints and lifestyles?) Who is in control? Nobody and everybody.

Television and radio have been more regulated and less diverse than print media. When radio was new, there was much discussion about how to fund high-quality programming. Many people strongly opposed advertising on the radio. An alternative suggestion was for the government to subsidize programming. The negative implications for freedom of speech were widely recognized, and this idea was dropped. Soon after the Federal Communications Commission was formed, the number of television networks dropped from four to three and remained there for decades, although spectrum was available for a much larger number of stations.[62]

Although there are some very large publishing companies, they do not dominate publishing as much as the television networks dominated television. (That domination lessened somewhat with the competition from cable.) There are numerous small publishers filling special niches, as there are many small Web sites. Advocates of mandated or subsidized public spaces on the Net see the experience of television rather than publishing as the more likely model for cyberspace, perhaps without realizing that television was the more regulated paradigm.

What could prevent diversity of content on the Web from continuing? With mergers between large companies like AOL and Time Warner, there is still concern that, as large news and entertainment conglomerates move into cyberspace, only a few points of view will be presented. Commercial interests could dominate over honest and fair reporting and debate. Another potential threat is that large companies will use laws and regulations to restrict their competition, as established businesses have often done. The television networks used laws to delay cable for more than a decade. In Argentina, there are more than 2000 low-power radio stations in rural areas and poor shantytowns; they provide community-oriented programming and a wide range of political views. Low-power radio stations (called "micro radio") were until recently virtually illegal in the United States; in the early years of radio, the larger, established broadcasting companies encouraged the federal government to ban them.* A jazz radio station in Missouri was staffed by volunteer music lovers who had other paying jobs. The government fined the station and ordered it to pay the volunteers minimum wage, which the station could not afford.[63] Volunteers maintain many Web sites. The analogies from radio and television suggest the importance, when considering any proposed regulation of the Internet, service providers, or Web sites, of looking carefully at direct and indirect effects that threaten the survival of small operators who fill specialized niches and provide a diversity of topics and opinions. If they are not hindered by law, they are likely to flourish.

---

*In 2000, the FCC authorized 1000 micro radio stations, with fierce opposition from the National Association of Broadcasters.

Review Exercises

5.1   Briefly explain the differences between common carriers, broadcasters, and publishers with respect to freedom of speech and control of content.

5.2   Describe two methods parents can use to restrict access by their children to inappropriate material on the Web.

5.3   What was one of the main reasons why the censorship provisions of the Communications Decency Act were ruled in violation of the First Amendment?

5.4   What are two Web sites (or kinds of sites) blocked by filters that are not the kinds of sites filters are intended to block?

5.5   Mention two methods used by some governments to control access to information.

5.6   Give an example of an anonymous publication more than 100 years ago.

5.7   Give two reasons people object to spam.

General Exercises

5.8   Considering all the services available on the Internet, describe a service or feature that is similar to each of the following.
   a) A magazine publisher
   b) A library
   c) The post office
   d) A telephone company
   e) A television station
   f) A landlord who rents office space to a club

5.9   How has the Internet changed the notion of community standards for determining if material is legally obscene? Do you think the community-standards criterion can be preserved on the Internet? If so, explain how. If not, explain why.

5.10 In many cities, one can buy both ordinary newspapers and sexually oriented publications from coin-operated machines on sidewalks. College campuses often have newspaper machines, but not the machines for sexually oriented publications. Should colleges restrict access to sexually oriented Web sites from campus computers? List several similarities and differences between coin-operated machines and Web sites that might be relevant to a college's decision.

5.11 What policy for Internet access and use of filter software do you think is appropriate for elementary schools? What policy for Internet access and use of filter software do you think is appropriate for high schools? Give your reasons.

5.12 The Children's Internet Protection Act (CIPA, Section 5.2.3) allows that people doing "bona fide research" can request unfiltered access to the Internet in a library. What are some problems with this provision? Is this a sufficient exception to the CIPA's filtering requirement?

5.13 Canada and France have laws that restrict the number of U.S. movies, television programs, and magazines allowed into their countries. The reason given is to protect their culture. Another reason is to protect their domestic movie, TV, and magazine companies from foreign competition. How do you think the Web will affect such policies or be affected by them?

5.14 Four high school students found instructions for making a bomb on a Web site. They built the bomb and set it off in the hallway of their school. One of the students, an 18-year-old, said they had no idea how powerful the bomb would be and they had no intention of hurting anyone. He commented "These are really dangerous sites. . . . I'm not a troublemaker or anything. I'm just a regular kid."[64] Evaluate his comments.

5.15 Suppose that, near Christmas time, many Web sites and religious discussion groups carry a large amount of material about the religious meaning of Christmas and the religious importance of Jesus Christ. To the majority of Americans, this is not only acceptable, but valuable and positive. To members of non-Christian religions and to atheists, it may be offensive; they may not want their children to view this material. What would be your reaction to a law restricting availability of such material on the Internet? In what ways do the issues about restricting religious material, sexual material, sexist or racist comments, or bomb-making material on the Internet differ? In what ways are these issues similar?

5.16 In 2001, Yahoo! expanded its online store for adult material (erotica, sex videos, and so forth—all legal). Many users and advertisers complained, and Yahoo! quickly reversed policy and removed ads for adult material. Some described Yahoo!'s reversal as an unprincipled cave-in to pressure for censorship. Others saw it as a reasonable response to customer preferences. Give arguments people with each point of view might make. Which side do you agree with? Does the legal right of adults to purchase adult entertainment (a negative right, to be free from arrest) impose an ethical obligation on a Web site to sell it?

5.17 Amateur astronomers around the world have been locating and tracking satellites—both commercial and spy satellites—and posting their orbits on the Web.[65] Some intelligence officials argue that, if enemies and terrorists know when U.S. spy satellites are overhead, they can hide their activities. What issues are raised by this problem? Should posting satellite orbits be illegal? Give arguments on both sides. Which are stronger? Why?

5.18 Suppose Harris Interactive had not dropped its suit against the Mail Abuse Prevention System for listing Harris on its spammer list (Section 5.4.3). Give arguments on both sides of the case. What side do you think should win? Why?

5.19 One of the arguments used to justify increased government control of television content is that television is "invasive." It comes into the home and is more difficult to keep from children. Do you think this argument is strong enough to outweigh the First Amendment? Give reasons. Is this argument more valid for the Internet than for television, or less valid for the Internet than for television? Give reasons.

5.20 A bill was introduced in Congress to require that Web sites with pornography get proof of age (at least 17) from anyone who tries to visit the site, possibly by requiring a credit card number or some other adult identification number. Discuss some arguments for and against such a law.

5.21 An anti-abortion Web site posts lists of doctors who perform abortions and judges and politicians who support abortion rights. It includes addresses, Social Security numbers, and other personal information about some of the people. When doctors on the list were injured or murdered, the site reported the results. A suit to shut the site for inciting violence failed; a controversial appeals court decision found it to be a legal exercise of freedom of speech. The essential issue is the fine line between threats and protected speech, a difficult issue that predates the Internet. Does the fact that this is a Web site rather than a printed and mailed newsletter make a difference? What, if any, issues are raised by this case that relate to the impact of the Internet?

5.22 Suppose you are setting up an online dating service. Members will post a description of themselves and their interests, and other members may respond. Discuss the pros and cons of setting up pseudonyms for your customers. Do traditional dating services or personal advertisements in your area's newspapers use real names or codes to identify people? If you consider use of pseudonyms acceptable for a dating service, but not in certain other circumstances, try to identify the principles or characteristics that could be used to distinguish where they are okay and where they are not.

5.23 Secret voting is an important part of a free and democratic political system. Give arguments on both sides of the following proposition: If we can vote anonymously, we should be free to argue anonymously for or against political candidates on the Web.

5.24 Suppose you are writing an anti-spam law. What do you think is a reasonable definition of spam in this context? Indicate the number of messages and how the law would determine whether a message was unsolicited.

5.25 When answering the questions in this exercise, consider how your answers apply to these examples.

> A man set up a Web site called "Babes on the Web" with links to women's personal and professional home pages that included their photo. "Babes on the Web" included ratings of the women's appearance.

> Microsoft's Seattle Sidewalk, an entertainment site, included links to Web pages at Ticketmaster, where people could purchase tickets for local events. These links bypassed Ticketmaster's home page (a practice called *deep linking*). Ticketmaster sued, claiming Microsoft needed its permission to link.

> Some Web sites link to sites that sell illegal drugs or contain software or music available for copying without authorization of the copyright holder.

a) Suppose someone puts on his or her Web site a description of another site and its URL (as plain text, not a link). Is that an exercise of freedom of speech that should not be restricted by law?

b) Suppose the URL is a clickable link to the other site. Should that change whether putting it on one's Web site is protected as freedom of speech?

5.26 The Web sites of many tax-exempt charitable organizations have links to sites of organizations that do political lobbying, an activity illegal for tax-exempt groups. For example, a think tank has links to Handgun Control, Inc. and the National Rifle Association, so visitors can find relevant research materials. The Internal Revenue Service (IRS) announced an investigation into the issue of whether such links violate the rules for tax-exempt status. What do you think they should conclude? How would various possible decisions by the IRS affect the Web?

Assignments

These exercises require some research or activity.

5.27 Find out whether your college restricts access to any Web sites from its computer systems. What is its policy for determining which sites to restrict? What do you think of the policy?

5.28 Find out whether the Supreme Court has ruled on the constitutionality of the Child Online Protection Act or the Children's Internet Protection Act (Section 5.2.3). If so, summarize the results. If not, describe what you think the decisions should be and why.

5.29 Find a few sites on the Web with a large amount of some type of "hate speech." Describe the kind of material on the sites. Is it protected by the First Amendment? How does dissemination of such speech on the Web differ from previous media? Pick one of the sites or topics and find other sites on the Web that present the other side. Briefly describe what you found.

5.30 Interview a librarian in a public library to find out what problems, if any, the library is having with people misusing Internet access. Find out how the library handles problems. Does it use filters?

5.31 Keep a log of the e-mail you receive for one week. For each message, indicate whether it is commercial or some other form of spam (describe your criteria) and whether it was solicited by you.

Class Discussion Exercises

These exercises are for class discussion, perhaps with short presentations prepared in advance by small groups of students.

5.32 To what extent is violence on the Web and in computer games responsible for shootings in schools? What should be done about it, without violating the First Amendment?

5.33 *Background.* A computer system manager at a public university noticed that the number of Web accesses to the system jumped dramatically. In one day, there were 13,000 accesses to one student's home page. The system manager discovered that his home page contained several sexually oriented pictures. The pictures were similar to those published in many magazines available legally. The system manager told the student to remove the pictures.

The grievance cases. A female student who accessed the pictures before they were removed filed a grievance against the university for sexual harassment. The student who set up the home page filed a grievance against the university for violation of his First Amendment rights.

The hearings. Divide the class into four groups: representatives for the female student, the male student, and the university (a separate group for each grievance). A spokesperson for each group presents arguments. After open discussion of the arguments, take a vote of the class on each grievance.

5.34 Should ISPs be required by law to keep records on the real identity of all users? (Should true anonymity on the Internet be banned?)

5.35 What rules or standards should be applied when an individual, business, or government agency asks a court for a subpoena to get the real name of a person who has posted messages online?

5.36 Should spam be considered a form of trespass? Restaurants are open to the public but can exclude rowdy people. What rules or laws does that analogy suggest about sending spam to subscribers of an ISP? Is the First Amendment more relevant in one case than in the other?

5.37 Consider the following quotation from Edward R. Murrow, a renowned radio (and later TV) journalist in the 1930s–1950s. Do you agree with it? Why? Are there some aspects of different kinds of communication systems that influence the kind and quality of content they are likely to have?

> A communication system is totally neutral. It has no conscience, no principle, no morality. It has only a history. It will broadcast filth or inspiration with equal facility. It will speak the truth as loudly as it will speak a falsehood. It is, in sum, no more or no less than the men and women who use it.[66]

NOTES

1 From a speech by Mike Godwin at Carnegie Mellon University, Nov. 1994, quoted with permission. (The speech is excerpted, including part of the quotation used here, in Mike Godwin, "alt.sex.academic.freedom," *Wired*, Feb. 1995, p. 72.)

2 Eric M. Freedman, "Pondering Pixelized Pixies," *Communications of the ACM*, Aug. 2001, 44:8, pp. 27–29.

3 "High Court Rules Cable Industry Rights Greater Than Broadcast's," *Investors Business Daily*, June 28, 1994.

4 Adjudication on Motions for Preliminary Injunction, *American Civil Liberties Union et al. v. Janet Reno* (No. 96-963) and *American Library Association et al. v. United States Dept. of Justice* (No. 96-1458).

5 In a 1995 Supreme Court case, Justice David Souter wrote, "One important manifestation of the principle of free speech is that one who chooses to speak may also decide what not to say." (The case concerned the right of organizers of privately sponsored parades to exclude groups from participation. The quote is in *Time*, July 3, 1995, p. 12.) Other court decisions have upheld requirements that owners of property such as shopping centers allow distribution of leaflets on their property even if they disagree with the content.

6 Cases concerned advertising of tobacco, legal gambling, vitamin supplements, alcohol content of beer, prices of prescription drugs, and Nike's claim that it did not use sweatshop labor. Robert S. Greenberger, "More Courts Are Granting Advertisements First Amendment Protection," *Wall Street Journal*, July 3, 2001, pp. B1, B3.

7 Ithiel de Sola Pool, *Technologies of Freedom*, Harvard University Press, 1983, pp. 224–225 and p. 10.

8 The quotation is often incorrectly attributed to Voltaire himself. See Paul F. Boller, Jr. and John George, *They Never Said It: A Book of Fake Quotes, Misquotes, and Misleading Attributions*, Oxford University Press, 1989, for the history.

9 Gerard van der Leun, "This Is a Naked Lady," *Wired*, Premiere Issue, 1993, pp. 74, 109.

10 Mike Godwin, "Sex, Cyberspace, and the First Amendment," *Cato Policy Report*, Jan/Feb 1995, 17:1, p. 10.

11 Robert Peck, quoted in Daniel Pearl, "Government Tackles a Surge of Smut on the Internet," *Wall Street Journal*, Feb. 8, 1995, p. B1.

12 For a commentary on the many issues in this case, see Mike Godwin, "Virtual Community Standards," *Reason*, Nov. 1994, pp. 48–50.

13 Arguments against the law are in Eric M. Freedman, "Pondering Pixelized Pixies," *Communications of the ACM*, Aug. 2001, 44:8, pp. 27–29. Arguments on the other side appear in Foster Robberson, "'Virtual' child porn on net no less evil than real thing," *Arizona Republic*, Apr. 28, 2000, p. B11.

14 Quoted in David Foster, "Children Lured from Home by Internet Acquaintances," Associated Press, Jun. 13, 1995.

15 FBI statement, reported in "On-line Child-porn Probe Yields Searches, Arrests" (Associated Press), *San Diego Union-Tribune*, Sept. 14, 1995, p. A10.

16 Associated Press and New York Times News Service, "Cybercensors Reverse Ban on 'Breast'," Dec. 2, 1995.

17 *Butler v. Michigan*, 352 U.S. 380(1957).

18 Adjudication on Motions for Preliminary Injunction, *American Civil Liberties Union et al. v. Janet Reno* (No. 96-963) and *American Library Association et al. v. United States Dept. of Justice* (No. 96-1458).

19 "Final Report of the COPA Commission," Oct. 20, 2000, www.copacommission.org/report.

20 www.frc.org. On the other side, see for example, the National Coalition Against Censorship, www.ncac.org.

21 For a good overview of issues and legal cases about filters, see Richard S. Rosenberg, "Controlling Access to the Internet: The Role of Filters," *Proceedings for Computer Ethics: Philosophical Enquiry*, eds. Deborah G. Johnson, James H. Moor, and Herman T. Tavani, July 14–16, 2000, at Dartmouth College, pp. 232–261.

22 Electronic Privacy Information Center, "Faulty Filters," www2.epic.org/reports/filter_report.html, 1997. See also Rosenberg, ibid. Pamela LiCalzi O'Connell, "Law Newsletter Has to Sneak Past Filters," *New York Times*, Apr. 2, 2001, p. C4.

23 "Current State of Internet Content Filtering," *EPIC Alert*, Mar. 2, 2000.

24 Judge Leonie M. Brinkema, *Mainstream Loudoun, et al. v. Board of Trustees of the Loudoun County Library, et al.*

25 *ALA v. United States.*

26 Brock Meeks, "Internet As Terrorist," *Cyberwire Dispatch* (an electronic newsletter), May 11, 1995. Brock Meeks, "Target: Internet," *Communications of the ACM*, Aug. 1995, 38:8, pp. 23–25.

27 The quotations in this paragraph are from Meeks, "Internet As Terrorist."

28 David Armstrong, "Bomb Recipes Flourish Online Despite New Law," *Wall Street Journal*, Jan. 18, 2001, pp. B1, B8.

29 Tamzin Booth, "The Web Work," *Wall Street Journal*, Nov. 20, 2000, p. B6. The site is www.pigbrother.uk.com.

30 John Simons, "CFTC Regulations On Publishing Are Struck Down," *Wall Street Journal*, June 22, 1999, p. A8. Scott Bullock, "CFTC Surrenders on Licensing Speech," *Liberty and Law*, Institute for Justice, Apr. 2000, 9:2, p. 2.

31 *Swedenburg v. Kelly.*

32 *Against the Gods: The Remarkable Story of Risk*, John Wiley & Sons, 1996, p. 89.

[33] Arthur C. Clarke, "Beyond the Global Village," *1984 Spring: A Choice of Futures*, Ballantine/Dell, 1984, p. 7.

[34] Stewart Baker, "The Net Escape Censorship? Ha!" *Wired*, Sept. 1995, pp. 125–126.

[35] For a review of this case and its implications, see Lisa Guernsey, "Welcome to the Web. Passport, Please?" *New York Times*, Mar. 15, 2001, pp. D1, D8.

[36] Mylene Mangalindan and Kevin Delaney, "Yahoo! Ordered To Bar the French From Nazi Items," *Wall Street Journal*, Nov. 21, 2000, pp. B1, B4.

[37] Guernsey, "Welcome to the Web," *op. cit.*

[38] Barry Bearak, "Taliban Will Allow Access to Jailed Christian Aid Workers," *New York Times*, Aug. 26, 2001, p. 8.

[39] David P. Hamilton, "Asians Taste Free Speech on Internet," *Wall Street Journal*, Dec. 8, 1994, pp. B1, B10.

[40] *Wired*, Sept. 1996, p. 42. James Miles, "Burmese Ban on Political Websites," Jan. 20, 2000, news.bbc.co.uk/hi/english/world/asia-pacific/news-id_611000/611836.stm, viewed Aug. 27, 2001. "State Department Releases World Human Rights Report," *EPIC Alert*, 5.02, Feb. 10, 1998. Robert Fox, "Newstracks," *Communications of the ACM*, Dec. 1996, pp. 9–10.

[41] Zixiang Tan, Milton Mueller, and Will Foster, "China's New Internet Regulations: Two Steps Forward, One Step Back," *Communications of the ACM*, Dec. 1997, 40:12, pp. 11–16. Marcus W. Brauchli, "China Requires Computer Networks to Get Registered," *Wall Street Journal*, Feb. 5, 1996, p. C15.

[42] Darren McDermott, "Singapore Unveils Sweeping Measures to Control Words, Images on Internet," *Wall Street Journal*, Mar. 6, 1996, p. B6. Michele Levander, "Singapore to Relax Censorship Laws As It Seeks to Expand Internet Access," *Wall Street Journal*, Sept. 1, 1999, p. A18.

[43] Steve Lohr, "Privacy on Internet Poses Legal Puzzle," *New York Times*, Apr. 19, 1999, p. C4.

[44] Jeffrey M. O'Brien, "Free Agent," *Wired*, May 2001, p. 74.

[45] *Wall Street Journal*, Nov. 14, 2000, p. A11

[46] Neil King, "Small Start-Up Helps CIA Mask Its Moves on Web," *Wall Street Journal*, Feb. 12, 2001, pp. B1, B6.

[47] Numerous articles in the *Washington Post, New York Times, Honolulu Star-Bulletin*, and others, Dec. 1997–May 1998, some collected at www.gaymilitary.org/mcveigh2.htm.

[48] *McIntyre v. Ohio Elections Commission*, 514 U.S. 334, 115 S.Ct. 1511 (1995).

[49] "Defending Right To Post Message: 'CEO Is a Dodo'," Sept. 28, 2000, pp. B1, B12.

[50] *HealthSouth v. Krum.*

[51] Judge David O. Carter, *Global Telemedia International, Inc. v. Doe 1*, 00-1155 (C.D. Cal. Feb 23).

[52] For an in-depth discussion of cases and legal background and recommendations, see Lyrissa Barnett Lidsky, "Silencing John Doe: Defamation and Disclosure in Cyberspace," *Duke Law Journal*, 49:4, Feb. 2000, pp. 855–946. (Available at www.law.duke.edu.)

[53] In a speech at the Computers, Freedom, and Privacy Conference, San Francisco, March 1995.

[54] Quoted in Jared Sandberg, "Suit Challenges State's Restraint of the Internet," *Wall Street Journal*, Sept. 25, 1996, pp. B1, B4.

[55] Sanford Wallace, founder of CyberPromotions and other e-mail advertising companies, as reported in Thomas E. Weber, "The Spam King Is Back, and His New Recipe Clicks On Changing Net," *Wall Street Journal*, Dec. 13, 1999, p. B1.

[56] In 1998, Cyber Promotions announced that it was quitting the spam business. Sanford Wallace later formed a new business that sent e-mail advertising for its client companies only to people who requested it.

[57] Some of the case documents for *Intel Corporation v. Hamidi* are available at www.intelhamidi.com. Or see appellatecases.courtinfo.ca.gov, case no. C033076.

[58] See Laurie Faith Cranor and Brian A. LaMacchia, "Spam!" *Communications of the ACM*, Aug. 1998, 41:8, pp. 74–83, for a longer discussion of spam cases and potential solutions.

[59] Jayson Matthews, "Harris Interactive Continues Spam Battle with MAPS," siliconvalley.internet.com/news/article/0,2198,3531_434061,00.html, Aug. 9, 2000. Viewed Apr. 9, 2001.

[60] Lawrence K. Grossman, "Maintaining Diversity in the Electronic Republic," *Technology Review*, Nov./Dec. 1995, pp. 23–26. "Groups Urge a 'Digital Gift' to the Nation," news release, Apr. 5, 2001, www.digitalpromise.org/pressrelease1.asp.

[61] CPSR, "Serving the Community: A Public Interest Vision of the National Information Infrastructure," p. 23.

[62] Todd Lappin, "Déjà Vu All Over Again," *Wired*, May 1995, pp. 175–177, 218–222. Thomas W. Hazlett, "The Rationality of U.S. Regulation of the Broadcast Spectrum," *Journal of Law & Economics*, Apr. 1990, pp. 133–175.

[63] Jesse Walker, "Don't Touch That Dial," *Reason*, Oct. 1995, pp. 30–35. Charles Oliver, "Brickbats," *Reason*, Nov. 1995, p. 17.

[64] Armstrong, "Bomb Recipes Flourish Online Despite New Law."

[65] Massimo Calabresi, "Quick, Hide the Tanks!" *Time*, May 15, 2000, p. 60.

[66] Quoted in David Dary, *TV News Handbook*, Tab Books, 1971, p. 7. I thank my student Lee Ellen Merchant for finding this quote.

BOOKS AND ARTICLES

- Laurie Faith Cranor and Brian A. LaMacchia, "Spam!" *Communications of the ACM*, Aug. 1998, 41:8, pp. 74–83.

- Alan Dershowitz, "The Right to Transmit Hate Anonymously," United Feature Syndicate, 1995.

- Electronic Privacy Information Center, *Filters and Freedom 2.0: Free Speech Perspectives on Internet Content Controls*, www.epic.org, 2000.

- Jonathan Emord, *Freedom, Technology, and the First Amendment*, Pacific Research Institute, 1991.

- Mike Godwin, *Cyber Rights: Defending Free Speech in the Digital Age*, Times Books, Random House, 1998.

- Lawrence K. Grossman, "Maintaining Diversity in the Electronic Republic," *Technology Review*, Nov./Dec. 1995, pp. 23–26.

- Thomas W. Hazlett, "The Rationality of U.S. Regulation of the Broadcast Spectrum," *Journal of Law & Economics*, Apr. 1990, pp. 133–175.

- Heins, Marjorie, *Not In Front of the Children: "Indecency," Censorship, and the Innocence of Youth*, Hill & Wang, 2001.

- Nat Hentoff, *Free Speech for Me—But Not for Thee: How the American Left and Right Relentlessly Censor Each Other*, Harper Collins, 1992.

- Peter Huber, *Law and Disorder in Cyberspace* Oxford Univ. Press, 1997. Criticizes FCC regulation of telecommunications, showing examples where regulations have delayed introduction of new technologies.

- Mitchell Kapor, "Civil Liberties in Cyberspace," *Scientific American*, Sept., 1991, pp. 159–164.

- Lyrissa Barnett Lidsky, "Silencing John Doe: Defamation and Disclosure in Cyberspace," *Duke Law Journal*, 49:4, Feb. 2000, pp. 855–946. (Available at www.law.duke.edu.)

- A. Lin Neumann, "The Resistance Network," *Wired*, Jan. 1996, 4:1, pp. 108–114. Use of computer networks by human rights organizations, many in countries with oppressive governments.

- "Science, Technology, and the First Amendment, Special Report," Office of Technology Assessment, U.S. Dept. of Commerce, Washington, DC, Jan. 1988 (Report NO. OTA-CIT-369).

- George Orwell, *1984*, 1948. Orwell's dystopian novel in which the totalitarian government controlled the people via ubiquitous telescreens. (Orwell introduced the term "Big Brother" for the government.)

- Charles Platt, "Americans Are Not As Free As We Think We Are," *Wired*, Apr. 1996, pp. 82–91.

- Richard S. Rosenberg, "Controlling Access to the Internet: The Role of Filters," *Proceedings for Computer Ethics: Philosophical Enquiry*, eds. Deborah G. Johnson, James H. Moor, and Herman T. Tavani, July 14–16, 2000, at Dartmouth College, pp. 232–261.

- Scott Shane, *Dismantling Utopia: How Information Ended the Soviet Union*, I. R. Dee, 1994.

- Ithiel de Sola Pool, *Technologies of Freedom*, Harvard University Press, 1983. This book describes the history, rights, restrictions, and responsibilities of the various communications technologies in depth.

- Eugene Volokh, "Freedom of Speech in Cyberspace from the Listener's Perspective:

Private Speech Restrictions, Libel, State Action, Harassment, and Sex," *Univ. of Chicago Legal Forum*, 1996, pp. 377–436.

■ Jesse Walker, *Rebels On the Air: An Alternative History of Radio in American*, New York University Press, 2001.

■ Jonathan D. Wallace, "Nameless in Cyberspace: Anonymity on the Internet," Cato Institute Briefing Papers, No. 54, Dec. 8, 1999.

6

INTELLECTUAL PROPERTY

The Congress shall have Power To . . . promote the Progress of Science and useful Arts, by securing for limited Times to Authors and Inventors the exclusive Right to their respective Writings and Discoveries . . .

—U.S. Constitution, Article I, Section 8

6.1 Intellectual Property and Changing Technology

6.1.1 WHAT IS INTELLECTUAL PROPERTY?

Have you ever given a CD to a friend that contained a copy of a computer game or a program? Have you ever recorded a televised movie to watch later in the week? Have you downloaded music or a movie from the Web without paying for it? Have you e-mailed a copy of an online newspaper or magazine article to a dozen friends? Have you set up a Web site about your favorite band or actor, with short videos from performances? Do you know which of these actions are legal and which are illegal, and why?

Books, articles, plays, songs (both music and lyrics), works of art, movies, and software are protected by copyright, a legal concept that defines rights to intellectual property. Some software is protected by patent, another legal concept that defines rights to intellectual property.

Why is intellectual property given legal protection? The value of a book or a song or a computer program is much more than the cost of printing it, putting it on disk, or uploading it to the Web. The value of a painting is higher than the cost of the canvas and paint used to create it. The value of intellectual and artistic works comes from the creativity, ideas, research, skills, labor, and other nonmaterial efforts and attributes provided by their creators. Designing and developing a computer program can take months or years of work and cost thousands or millions of dollars. Our property rights to the physical property we create or buy include the rights to use it, to prevent others from using it, and to set the (asking) price for selling it. We would be reluctant to make the effort to buy or produce physical things if anyone else could just take them away. If anyone could copy a novel, a computer program, or a movie for the small price of the copying, the creator of the work would receive very little income from the creative effort, and some of the incentive for producing it would be gone. Protection of intellectual property has both individual and social benefits: It protects the right of the creator of something of value to be compensated for what he or she has created, and, by so doing, it encourages production of valuable, intangible, easily copied, creative work.

The key to understanding intellectual property protection is to understand that the thing protected is the intangible creative work—not the particular physical form in which it is embodied. When we buy a novel, we are buying the physical collection of paper and ink, or an e-book file, that contains a copy of the book's contents, but we are not buying the intellectual property—that is, the plot, the organization of ideas, the presentation, the characters and events that form the abstraction that is the intangible "book."[1] The owner of a physical book may give away, lend, or resell the one physical book he or she bought, but not make copies (with some exceptions). The right to make copies belongs to the owner of the intangible "book," that is, the owner of the copyright. The principle is similar for software, music, movies, and so on. The buyer of a software package is buying only a copy of it or a license to use the software. When we buy a movie on DVD, we are buying one copy with the right to watch it, but not to play it in a public venue or charge a fee. When we pay to hear music online, we might be buying the right to listen to it a specific number of times, but not the right to copy it. The copyright owner owns the intangible program or movie or music.

The author of a particular piece of intellectual property, or his or her employer (e.g., a newspaper or a software company), may hold the copyright or may transfer it to a publisher, a music recording company, a movie studio, or some other entity. Copyrights are granted for a limited, but long, time—for example, the lifetime of the author plus 70 years. U.S. copyright law (Title 17 of the U.S. Code) gives the copyright holder the following exclusive rights, with some very important exceptions that we will describe:

- to make copies of the work;

- to produce derivative works, such as translations into other languages or movies based on books;

- to distribute copies;

- to perform the work in public (e.g., music, plays); and

- to display the work in public (e.g., artwork, movies, computer games).

Intellectual property differs from physical property in that the making of a copy does not deprive anyone else of the work's use. Thus, taking intellectual property by copying is quite different from theft of physical property, and intellectual property law does not prohibit *all* unauthorized copying, distribution, and so on. A very important exception is the "fair use" doctrine, which we discuss in Section 6.2.2. A specific exception for software allows the owner of a copy of a program to make a backup ("archival") copy. Uses of copyrighted material that are not authorized by the copyright owner or permitted by one of the exceptions in the law are infringements of the copyright and are subject to civil or criminal penalties.

Facts, ideas, concepts, processes, and methods of operation are not copyrightable.* Copyright protects creative expression, that is, the expression, selection, and arrangement of ideas. The boundary between an idea and the expression of an idea is often not clear. Hence, many cases of alleged copyright infringement involving similar, but not identical, works go to court.

The government grants patents (covered in Title 35 of the U.S. Code) for inventions of new things or processes. They protect new ideas by giving the inventor a monopoly

---

* Recall, from Chapter 2, that some privacy advocates suggest giving people property rights in facts about themselves, whereas copyright law has always recognized that copyrighting facts would be an unreasonable infringement on the flow of information.

on the invention for a specified period of time (e.g., 20 years). The purposes of patents are similar to those of copyrights: to reward the inventor and encourage new invention. Patents differ from copyrights in that they protect the invention, not just a particular expression or implementation of it, and they prohibit anyone else from using the idea without authorization of the patent holder, even if another person independently came up with the same idea or invention. Thus, if the invention of a word processor or Web search engine were patentable, all companies that sell these products would have to make agreements with, and pay royalties to, the patent holders. In addition to copyright and patent, there are other forms of intellectual property that various laws protect. They include trademarks and trade secrets. This chapter concentrates mostly on copyright.

Intellectual property protection is well-established in Western countries, but not in all areas of the world. Most of the issues in this chapter are within a context that accepts the legitimacy of intellectual property protection, but revolve around its extent, how new technology challenges it, and how it can or should evolve. Some people argue that there should be no copyright protection for software, that we should all be permitted to copy software freely. We elaborate on these views in Section 6.6.*

6.1.2 PROBLEMS FROM NEW TECHNOLOGIES

Electronic media, microprocessors, computer networks, and the World Wide Web created new challenges for protection of literary, artistic, and musical works and computer software. They also created new controversies about how intellectual property law should apply. Previous technologies raised such challenges in the past. For example, photocopiers, by making copying of printed material easy, threatened copyright protection, but earlier technologies were not nearly as serious a threat as modern digital technology. A complete photocopy of a book is bulky, sometimes of lower print quality, awkward to read, and more expensive than a paperback. Computers and communications technologies made high-quality copying and high-quantity distribution extremely easy and cheap. Some of the technological factors are the following:

- storage of all sorts of information (text, sound, graphics) in standard digitized formats;

- high-volume, relatively inexpensive digital storage media, such as hard disks, CD-ROMs, and DVDs (digital versatile disks, also called digital video disks);

- character scanners and image scanners, which simplify converting printed text, photos, and artwork to digitized electronic form;

- compression formats, such as MP3 and DivX, that make music and movie files small enough to download, copy, and store;

---

* Some people reject the whole notion of copyrights and patents. They see these mechanisms as providing government-granted monopolies, violating freedom of speech, and limiting productive efforts. This issue is independent of computer technology, so we do not directly cover it in this book. However, some arguments about free software, in Section 6.6, overlap arguments about the legitimacy of copyright.

- the ease of copying digitized material and the fact that each copy is a "perfect" copy;

- the ease of distributing digitized material over computer networks;

- the World Wide Web, which makes it easy to find and download material; and

- peer-to-peer technology, which permits easy transfer of files by large numbers of strangers over the Internet without any centralized system or service.

Prices of new digital gadgets, like prices of computers, keep falling, making them available to the general public and spurring more copyright infringement. For example, CD recording drives (also called CD burners) sold for about $1000 when they were introduced in 1996. Prices dropped to $99 within about three years, and millions were sold. They became a standard feature with many new PCs. More than 30 million DVD players were sold between 1997, when they were introduced, and mid-2001; the price dropped below $100.

Software publishers have long used the colorful term "software piracy" for high-volume unauthorized copying of software. Copying of many kinds of intellectual property flourished with the advent of the technologies of the Web. Although estimates from industry organizations tend to be exaggerated (for example, by counting the retail cost of all unauthorized copies), it is reasonable to estimate losses for the entertainment and software industries in the billions of dollars per year. Fearing that widespread copying would severely reduce their income, the software and entertainment industries fought back aggressively with lawsuits and lobbying for bans or severe restrictions on services, devices, and technologies that make copying—and therefore copyright infringement—easy.

The initial impact of digital technology tended to weaken copyright protection, but one aspect of the technology has the potential to give copyright holders much more control than they had previously. We have long taken for granted our right to browse (e.g., read part of a book in a bookstore or library) and lend, rent, and resell a purchased copy of a copyrighted work. These activities do not require making a copy. If we could not lend, rent, or resell a book to a friend, the friend might buy a copy, providing income to the publisher. But courts and law established the principle that the publisher has the right only to the "first sale" of a copy. The buyer of the book must not make additional copies, but may transfer the purchased copy. Publishers, especially of textbooks, which are resold often, lobbied for legislation requiring that a royalty be paid to the publisher on each resale; they were unsuccessful. But browsing and transferring a copy on a computer network require the *making of another copy* of the digital work. Viewing a Web site, reading an e-book, and listening to music online require making copies. A strict focus on copying as an infringing action would fundamentally change the effect of copyright law in cyberspace and restrict long-accepted activities.

Restriction on copying has been the key element of copyright law for literary work, music, software, and so on, but the clause in the Constitution on which copyright is based makes no mention of "copies" or "copyright." The focus on the making of copies has always caused some seemingly odd distinctions, but in the past they were not significant.

Why, for example, is it okay to pass a magazine around among 12 friends so they can read a particular article, but of questionable legality to make 12 copies and mail them to friends who do not live nearby? Cyberspace provides new examples: Why is it okay for a college professor to clip out and post a newspaper or magazine article on the bulletin board outside her office for any member of the campus community to read, but of questionable legality to scan the article and post a copy of it on a Web page?[2]

As an MIT computer science professor points out "control of reproduction is a means, not the goal."[3] It may be necessary to develop a new legal paradigm to protect the first-sale principle, browsing, and other long-established public uses of information.

In the rest of this chapter, we discuss issues introduced in this section and many others. We consider a variety of approaches to resolving the new problems that arise from computer and information-sharing technologies. We discuss the Napster music-sharing case (Section 6.3.2) and the controversial Digital Millennium Copyright Act (Section 6.4.2) in depth because they illustrate many issues that arise in dealing with copyrighted material in cyberspace.

6.2 Copyright Law

6.2.1 A BIT OF HISTORY

A brief history of copyright law will provide necessary background and help illustrate how new technologies require changes or clarifications in law.[4]

The first U.S. copyright law, passed in 1790, covered books, maps, and charts. The law was later extended to cover new technologies: photography, sound recording, and movies. The definition of an unauthorized copy in the Copyright Act of 1909 specified that it had to be in a form that could be seen and read visually. Even with the technologies of the early 20th century, this requirement was a problem. It was based on a court decision in a 1908 case about copying a song onto a perforated piano-music roll. (Automatic pianos played such rolls.) A person could not read the music visually from the piano roll, so the copy was not judged a violation of the song's copyright, even though it violated the spirit and purpose of copyright.[5] In the 1960s, the government began recognizing copyrights for software and databases, although copyright law at the time did not mention them. In the 1970s, a company sued for protection of its chess program, which was implemented on a read-only-memory (ROM) chip in its hand-held computer chess game. Another company sold a game with the identical program; it was assumed they copied the ROM. But because the ROM could not be read visually, a court held that the copy was not an infringement of the program's copyright.[6] Again, the purpose of copyright was not served well. This decision did not protect the creative work of the programmers; they received no compensation from a competitor's sales of their work.

In 1976 and 1980, copyright law was revised to cover software. "Literary works" protected by copyright include computer databases and computer programs that exhibit "authorship," that is, contain original expression of ideas. Recognizing that technology was changing rapidly, the revised law specifies that appropriate literary works could be copyrighted "regardless of the nature of the material objects . . . in which they are embodied." A copy is in violation of a copyright if the original can be "perceived, reproduced, or otherwise communicated by or from the copy, directly or indirectly." Film, tapes, discs, and cards are examples of forms in which protected material can be embodied. During the 1980s, many other countries extended their copyright laws to cover software; the details vary.

One significant goal in the development of copyright law, illustrated by the examples above, has been the devising of good definitions to broaden the scope of protection to new technologies. As copying technologies improved, another problem arose: A lot of people will break a law if it is easy to do so and the penalties are weak. In the 1960s, high growth in illegal sales of unauthorized copies of recorded music (e.g., tapes) accompanied the growth of the music industry. In 1982, high-volume copying of records and movies became a felony. In the 1980s, a large amount of copying of software accompanied the enormous growth of the software industry. The industry responded by pressing for explicit legal limitations on copying and for stiffer penalties for software copyright infringement. In 1992, making multiple copies of copyrighted work "willfully and for purposes of commercial advantage or private gain" became a felony offense. Making or distributing ten or more copies with retail value of more than $2500 within six months became punishable by up to five years in jail. The copies could be of different programs (e.g., one copy each of ten programs). Fines under some circumstances could be as high as $250,000.[7] Companies could be sued or prosecuted if ten employees out of hundreds or thousands have an illegal copy of a program on their computers. Many software users and attorneys believed that the 1992 law went too far, that making ten copies worth $2500 is too small an offense to merit such severe penalties.

The No Electronic Theft Act, passed in 1997, is stricter. It was a response to the 1994 David LaMacchia case. LaMacchia, an MIT student, was accused of running a bulletin board on a university computer on which, according to prosecutors, users copied over a million dollars' worth of copyrighted software, including popular applications packages and games, all during less than two months of operation. The indictment against LaMacchia was dropped because he did not charge anyone to use the bulletin board; there was no "commercial advantage or private gain." The No Electronic Theft Act made it a criminal offense to willfully infringe copyright by reproducing or distributing one or more copies of copyrighted works with total value of more than $1000 within a six-month period.

Continuing the trend toward stricter laws, Congress passed the Digital Millennium Copyright Act (DMCA) in 1998.[8] This law prohibits the making, distributing, or using of tools (devices, software, or services) to circumvent technological copyright protection systems used by copyright holders. (There are limited exceptions.) The law provides for penalties of up to 5 years in prison or a $500,000 fine for a first offense. The anti-circumvention provisions are extremely controversial, because they outlaw devices and software that have legitimate purposes, criminalize actions that do not infringe any copyrights, and (many argue) conflict with freedom of speech. We discuss them in Section 6.4.2.

Why did copyright laws get more restrictive and punishing? Generally, creators and publishers of copyrighted works, including print publishers, movie companies, music publishers and sound recording companies (record labels), and the software industry support stronger copyright protection. Congress often delegates the drafting of laws in complex areas to the industries involved. For most of the 20th century, the intellectual property industries drafted laws heavily weighted toward protecting their assets. On the other side, libraries and academic and scientific organizations opposed strict rules reducing the public's access to information. Most people were unaware of or indifferent to copyright issues. Digital media, and especially widespread public use of the Web and file sharing, focused attention on issues about how much control copyright owners should have. In the 1990s, cybercitizens and organizations such as the Electronic Frontier Foundation joined librarians and others to fight what they view as overly restrictive copyright law. The challenge is to maintain the benefits of easily available material on the Web while protecting the rights and investment of the owners of the intellectual property.

6.2.2 THE FAIR-USE DOCTRINE

As the Constitution indicates, the purpose of copyright is to encourage production of useful work. Copyright law and court decisions have attempted to define the rights of authors and publishers consistent with this goal and the goal of encouraging the use and flow of information. The fair use doctrine allows uses of copyrighted material that contribute to the creation of new work (such as reviews that quote part of a copyrighted work) and uses that are not likely to deprive authors or publishers of income for their work. Fair uses do not require the permission of the copyright holder.

The notion of fair use (for literary and artistic works) grew from judicial decisions. In 1976 U.S. copyright law explicitly included it; it applies to software also. (Fair-use policies differ in other countries.) The 1976 copyright law was written before the widespread use of personal computers. The software issues addressed pertained mainly to large business systems, and the law did not address issues related to the Web at all. Thus, the law did not take into account many situations where questions of fair use now arise. The law mentions possible fair uses, such as "criticism, comment, news reporting, teaching (including multiple copies for classroom use), scholarship, or research."[9] The law lists four factors to consider in determining whether a particular use is a "fair use." They are

1. The purpose and nature of the use, including whether it is for commercial purposes or nonprofit educational purposes. (Copying for commercial purposes is less likely to be fair use.)

2. The nature of the copyrighted work. (Creative work, such as a novel, has more protection than factual work.)

3. The amount and significance of the portion used.
4. The effect of the use on the potential market for or value of the copyrighted work. (Uses that reduce sales of the original work are less likely to be considered fair.)

No one of the factors alone determines whether a particular use is fair, but the last one gets more weight than the others. It is often not obvious what constitutes a "fair use" of a copyrighted work; courts interpret and apply the guidelines in specific cases. Law scholars say that results of fair-use cases are notoriously difficult to predict. The guidelines would benefit from revision to clarify fair use for modern digital technology.

6.2.3 FAIR-USE CASES

The fair-use doctrine is important for two quite different contexts. First, it helps us figure out under what circumstances we as consumers can legally copy software, music, movies, and so on. Second, software developers often must copy some or all of another company's program as part of the process of developing their own products, which might compete with the other company's work. Is such copying a fair use? We look at a few cases here to cover both situations. We consider fair use again in the Napster case (Section 6.3.2), in the discussion of the Digital Millennium Copyright Act—the law banning methods to thwart copy protection—(Section 6.4.2), and in some other cases that have freedom-of-speech implications (Section 6.5).

SONY VS. UNIVERSAL CITY STUDIOS

The Sony case was the first case about private, noncommercial copying of copyrighted work that the Supreme Court decided.[10] It is not about software or the Web, but the decision has implications for fair use involving new technologies; it is cited in Web-based entertainment cases, as well as in cases about new kinds of digital recording devices.

Two movie studios sued Sony for contributing to copyright infringement because some customers used its Betamax video cassette recording machines to record copyrighted movies shown on television. Thus, one important issue raised in this case is whether makers of copying equipment can be sued because some users will use the equipment to infringe copyrights. First we focus on the other issue the Supreme Court decided in the Sony case: whether recording a movie for personal use was a copyright infringement or a fair use. The entire movie was copied, and movies are creative, not factual, works. Thus factors (2) and (3) of the fair-use guidelines argue against the taping. The main purpose of recording the movie was to view it at a later time. Normally the consumer reused the tape after viewing the movie, making it an "ephemeral copy." The copy was for a private, noncommercial purpose, and the movie studios could not demonstrate that they suffered any harm. The Court interpreted factor (2), the nature of the copyrighted work, to include not simply whether it was creative or factual, but also the fact that the studios receive a large fee for broadcasting movies on television, and the fee depends on having a large audience that views the movies for free. So factors (1), (2), and (4) argue for fair use. The Court ruled in 1984, in a 5–4 decision, that recording a movie for viewing at a later time was a fair use.

The fact that people copied the entire work did not necessitate a ruling against fair use, although many examples of fair use apply only to small excerpts. The fact that the copying was a private, noncommercial use was significant. The Court said that private, noncommercial uses should be presumed fair unless there was realistic likelihood of economic harm to the copyright holder. Publishers generally are not happy with this presumption.

On the issue of the legitimacy of the Betamax machine, the Court said makers of a device with substantial legal uses should not be penalized because some people use it to infringe copyright. This is a very important principle, but the Digital Millennium Copyright Act has eroded it. Before and since the DMCA, some publishers advocated outlawing or restricting various copying technology, for example, digital tapes and CD writers. We return to this issue in Sections 6.3 and 6.4.

REVERSE ENGINEERING: GAME MACHINES

In the Sony case, the Supreme Court ruled that noncommercial copying of an entire movie was fair use. In several cases involving game machines, the courts ruled that copying an entire computer program for a *commercial* use was fair, largely because the purpose was to create a new product, not to sell copies of another company's product. A federal appeals court decided *Sega Enterprises, Ltd. v. Accolade, Inc.* in 1992. Accolade made videogames to run on Sega machines. To make their games run properly, Accolade needed to figure out how part of Sega's game-machine software worked. Accolade copied Sega's program and decompiled it (i.e., translated it from machine code to a form in which they could read and understand it). This is called *reverse engineering*. Sega sued; Accolade won. Accolade was making new games. The court viewed Accolade's activities as fitting the purpose of fair use, that is, to encourage production of new creative work. The fact that Accolade was a commercial entity was not critical. Although Accolade's games might reduce the market for Sega's games, that was fair competition; Accolade was not selling copies of Sega's games.[11]

In another 1992 case, *Atari Games v. Nintendo*, the court also ruled that making copies of a program for reverse engineering (to learn how it works so that a company can make a compatible product) was not copyright infringement. It is a fair "research" use.

The court applied the same arguments in 2000 in deciding in favor of Connectix Corporation in a suit by Sony Computer Entertainment, Inc. Connectix copied Sony's PlayStation BIOS (the basic input–output system) and reverse-engineered it to develop software that emulates the PlayStation console. Game players could then buy the Connectix program and play PlayStation games on their computers without buying the PlayStation console. Connectix's program did not contain any of Sony's code, and it was a new product, different from the PlayStation console. The copying of the BIOS was fair use.[12]

These decisions show how the courts have interpreted fair use to apply to situations not imagined when the guidelines were written. Many software products must interact with hardware and other software. These important decisions make it easier to develop new products.

6.3 Copying Music, Movies, Software, and Books

6.3.1 FROM FLOPPIES TO THE WEB

The first category of intellectual property to face significant threats from digital media was computer software itself. People gave copies to friends on floppy disks, and businesses copied business software. Only about a decade ago, "cyberspace" meant the pre-Web Internet, Usenet newsgroups, and bulletin-board systems. Music and graphics were complicated; the files were too large to transfer conveniently, and tools for listening to music or viewing images were unavailable or awkward to use. But already then the problem of copyright-infringing material in cyberspace had begun to get attention. One could find and download popular humor columns (copied from newspapers), scenes from Walt Disney Co. movies, Playboy pinups, and myriad Star Trek items. Early Web sites provided lyrics of popular songs.

The technology improved. More computer memory and gigabytes of disk space, faster computers, new compression formats for files, new storage media, and, of course, the World Wide Web combined to make copying easy, fast, cheap, and ubiquitous. The new technology spawned many new services to provide music, television programs, and other entertainment to the public in convenient ways, some that violated copyrights. We look at a few examples—and the response from the industry.

MP3 is a file-compression format that reduces the size of files by a factor of about 10–12, so that you can download a song in a few minutes.* In 1997 and 1998, college students and other music hobbyists set up hundreds of MP3 sites, making thousands of songs available. Where there is no issue of copyright infringement, speed and ease of transferring files is a great benefit. Many songwriters and bands considered MP3 to be a marvelous tool for promoting their work without the need for a contract with a large record company. But MP3 has no mechanism for preventing unlimited or unauthorized copying. It was an ideal tool for copyright infringement; most trading of MP3 files on the Net was unauthorized. For the Recording Industry Association of America (RIAA), the main record-company trade organization, MP3 created a nightmare and an enforcement problem. The RIAA shut down many of the MP3 sites by threatening legal action. They also tried to ban devices that play MP3 songs. From the RIAA's perspective, the nightmare got worse when mp3.com and Napster (and many other, less well-known sites)

---

*In the early 1990s, without MP3 and with the slower modems used then, it would have taken roughly a day to download one three-minute song.

opened for business. Mp3.com provided a service whereby members could store copies of their music CDs on mp3.com's computers, then listen to the music from anywhere (with a computer) without having to carry their CDs with them. The company modified the service to eliminate the step of copying the member's CD to mp3.com; without authorization from the copyright holders, mp3.com created a huge database of songs that members could download. Several record labels filed copyright infringement lawsuits. In 2000, mp3.com was found to have infringed copyrights and paid (according to estimates) more than $100 million to settle the suits.

RecordTV.com set up a free service allowing users to record television programs and store them on its Web site for later viewing. The company believed the Sony case (Section 6.2.3) made it clear that the service was legal, but a dozen entertainment companies sued in 2000 for copyright infringement. Scour Inc. operated a search engine and sharing service for music and movies. Scour offered to remove any material whose owners requested it, and promised to remove users who repeatedly violated copyrights, but two dozen major record and movie companies sued, asking for $150,000 in damages for each copyright infringement. Neither company could get new funding, in part because of the suits. RecordTV agreed to stop recording copyrighted movies. Scour laid off most employees and filed for bankruptcy protection.

6.3.2 THE NAPSTER CASE

When Big Steel and the auto industry were under pressure during the '70s from low-cost imports, their first instinct was not to change their outmoded manufacturing plants but to beseech the courts to bar the outlanders. The record industry has taken a similar tack.

—Karl Taro Greenfeld[13]

Napster opened on the Web in 1999 as a service allowing users to copy songs in MP3 files from the hard disks of other users. It was wildly popular and had more than 50 million users by little more than a year later. By late 2000, an average of 98 million MP3 files were available on the service. More than 40% of U.S. colleges blocked access to Napster because users were clogging the college Internet connections. A survey by Webnoize of more than 4000 college students found that almost 75% of them used Napster at least once a month. Some new bands, singers, and songwriters willingly made their music available to promote their work, but it was well known that Napster users copied and distributed most of the songs they traded without authorization. In late 1999, eighteen record companies sued for copyright infringement and asked for thousands of dollars in damages for each song traded on Napster. After more than a year in the courts, Napster lost.[14]

The Napster case is important for many reasons. The fact that so many people participated in an activity that courts decided was illegal is an indication of how new technology challenges existing law and attitudes about what is acceptable. Many people thought the success of Napster meant the end of copyright. Instead, the court decision showed that the legal system can still have a powerful impact. The arguments in the case apply to many other Internet cases.

Why was Napster so popular? When I asked my college students (while Napster was thriving), many shouted out "It's free!" That's the obvious reason, but it is not the only one. My students quickly generated a list of other desirable features of Napster. They could get individual songs, without having to buy a whole CD to get the few songs they wanted. They could sample songs to see if they really wanted them. Through Napster, they had access to a huge "inventory" and were not limited to one particular music label. They could get songs that were not commercially available. They liked the convenience of getting their music online. They could download and play a song from anywhere; they didn't need to have their physical CD with them. They could get information on the site about singers and musicians, and they could chat online with other users while they downloaded songs in the background. Thus, Napster used a variety of new technologies to provide flexibility, convenience, and services, in addition to free music. Many of the students acknowledged they would not mind paying a small fee for Napster-like service. A majority of Napster users in the Webnoize survey said they would be willing to pay $15 per month. The record companies did not embrace the new technologies. They expected their customers to continue to buy CDs (complete with some less desirable songs) from a store or order on the Web and wait a few days for shipping. But did the stodgy attitude of the industry legally (or ethically) justify Napster?

THE LEGAL ARGUMENTS

The issues in the lawsuit against Napster were the following:

- Was the copying and distribution of music by Napster users legal under the fair-use guidelines?

- If not, was Napster responsible for the actions of its users?

We look at a variety of arguments made by Napster and the record companies.

FAIR USE?

Napster argued that the sharing of songs by its users was a legal fair use. Let's review the fair-use guidelines and how they apply.

Copying songs via Napster does not fit any of the general categories of purposes covered by fair use (e.g., education, research, news), but neither does copying movies or music on tapes. The *Sony v. Universal City Studios* case and a copyright law change in 1992 (which lets buyers of CDs make copies for personal use to play, for example, in their cars) showed that the Supreme Court and Congress are willing to include entertainment.

Napster argued that sharing songs via its service was fair use because people were making copies for personal, not commercial, use. Copyright experts said "personal" meant very limited use, say within a household, not trading with thousands of strangers.

Songs (lyrics and music) are creative material, and users were copying complete songs. Thus fair-use guidelines (2) and (3) argue against fair use, but, as the Sony case indicated, they do not necessarily outweigh other factors.

The final, and perhaps most important, point is the impact on the market for the songs, that is, the impact on the income of the artists and music companies that hold the copyrights. Napster argued that it did not hurt record industry sales; users sampled music on Napster and bought the CDs they liked. One survey said that people who listened to music online were likely to increase their purchases, but survey and sales data did not unequivocally support either side. One of my students said he had not bought a single CD since Napster opened. How typical was that? Sales data for music albums, CDs, and tapes are reported in different ways with varying numbers, but most showed sales rising significantly during most years in the 1990s, and dropping or rising only slightly in 2000. For example, music sales in the U.S. (the largest market) dropped 1.5% in 2000. Sales of singles were down 46%, while CD album sales were up 2.5%.[15] We do not know if Napster was the only reason for the declines, but it is reasonable to conclude that the huge volume of copying on Napster had an impact and that the impact on sales would increase if services like Napster were determined to be legal.

Many legal observers thought the large-scale copying on Napster was illegal copyright infringement, not fair use, and that is how the court ruled.

NAPSTER'S RESPONSIBILITY

Napster did not keep copies of songs on its computers. It provided lists of available songs and lists of users logged on at any time; users transferred songs from each other's hard disks using peer-to-peer software downloaded from Napster. Napster argued that it was similar to a search engine, and the Digital Millennium Copyright Act protects search engines from responsibility for copyright violations by its users. The record companies argued that the law requires search-engine companies to make an effort to prevent copyright violations, but Napster did not take sufficient steps to eliminate unauthorized songs or users who committed violations.

Napster cited the Sony Betamax case, in which the Supreme Court said the maker of devices with substantial legitimate uses are not liable for users of the device who infringe copyrights, even if the maker knows some will. Napster had substantial legitimate uses in promoting new bands and artists who were willing to let users copy their songs. The recording industry argued that Napster was not a device or new technology, and it was not asking to ban a technology or shut Napster down. The record companies objected to how Napster *used* widely available technology to aid copyright infringement; it wanted Napster to stop listing unauthorized songs.

Sony's relationship with a customer ended when the customer bought the Betamax machine; Napster interacted with its members in providing access to songs to be copied. The court said Napster was liable because it had the right and ability to supervise its system, including the copyright infringing activities, and it had a financial interest in those activities. Napster was a business. Although it did not charge for copying songs, it expected the free copying to attract users so that it would make money in other ways.

The court ruled that Napster "knowingly encourages and assists in the infringement of copyrights."[16] Napster was ordered to remove from its listings song titles provided by the record companies. It faced civil suits that could require payments of billions of dollars in damages. After some ineffective attempts to manage the lists, Napster shut down.

AFTER THE NAPSTER DECISION

Some technology advocates, such as the Electronic Frontier Foundation (EFF), argued that the decision against Napster went too far, that it severely narrowed the Sony decision by ruling that even though Napster had substantial noninfringing uses, it was liable for the infringing uses. The decision, according to its critics, threatened development of new peer-to-peer technology and applications by requiring that technology providers police their systems. An attorney for EFF concluded that "the copyright industry continues to secure dangerously broad legal precedents against innovative technologies whose full ramifications have not yet been thoroughly considered . . . ."[17]

High-volume unauthorized copying of music on the Web will not stop just because it is illegal, just as pirating of software and the sale of illegal drugs will not stop because they are illegal. Many Napster clones—other Web sites offering free music trading—appeared while the lawsuit went through the legal system. Within a few months of the court decision, several million users switched to a handful of other free music services. Many music sharing services are in other countries. Peer-to-peer systems, such as Gnutella and Morpheus, present another challenge for the entertainment industry. They enable copying of files among users on the Internet without a central service like Napster. Peer-to-peer programs have huge potential for productive, legal uses, but there is no central service or company to sue when they are used to infringe copyrights. Within months of Gnutella's creation, there were more than a million files available; many were unauthorized MP3 music files and pirated software. Early Gnutella users thought its decentralization made enforcement virtually impossible, as action against each individual user was unlikely. However, the entertainment industry targeted ISPs. Industry organizations sent notices threatening legal action against ISPs whose subscribers operate Napster-like services or trade unauthorized files via Gnutella. The service providers can be held liable if they do not cut service to known violators. In 2001, a group of more than two dozen entertainment companies sued MusicCity (and others) for providing the infrastructure and services (including Morpheus and anonymity) that enable massive copyright infringement.

The entertainment industry had another option for responding to technologies that make copying easier—meeting consumer demand and providing services like Napster's for a reasonable fee. Consumers made it clear they do not want to have to visit each record label's Web site to get music; they prefer a central location like Napster. When companies began to work together to set up such services, they ran into another old legal institution that may need some updating for the electronic era: antitrust. The U.S. Department of Justice began antitrust investigations of joint music-label services and joint online movie services. Various other questions and lawsuits arose. For example, are Web sites that stream music more like radio programs or music sellers, which are treated differently in copyright law?

> *The smart people in music are already working on ways to make a single playing too cheap to be worth stealing.*
>
> —Holman W. Jenkins, Jr.[18]

6.3.3 SOFTWARE PIRACY

Billions of dollars worth of software is copied illegally worldwide every year. "Software piracy" includes the copying of software (and documentation) in large quantities for resale, illegal copying by businesses and organizations for their own use, and large-scale unauthorized distribution of software on the Web. Many businesses, organizations, and schools buy one or a few copies of a software package and install it on dozens or hundreds of computers. People intentionally put copyrighted software on Web sites (and previously, on computer bulletin boards) for others to download. Some sites are set up for the sole purpose of trading *warez*, a term for illegal copies of software (typically after its copy-protection has been "cracked," or defeated, by "underground" groups of programmers).

Before the Web made it easier for people to set up their own sites, pirated software showed up in surprising places. Hackers broke into the National High Magnetic Field Laboratory at Florida State University and set up a hidden cache of copyrighted software. In one day about 200 people, most with overseas Internet addresses, logged on to download the programs. Someone broke into a restricted computer system at Lawrence Berkeley Laboratory and loaded stolen software worth thousands of dollars. The locations and access methods for these secret depositories of software on legitimate systems were disclosed in online chat sessions for users who wanted to acquire the programs without paying for them. Pirated software includes word processors, spreadsheet programs, operating systems, utilities, and games—just about anything one might find in a large software store. Some, such as new versions of popular games, are pirated before they are available in stores.[19]

The Software and Information Industry Association (SIIA, a merger of the former Software Publishers Association, SPA, and the Information Industry Association) and the Business Software Alliance (BSA), the two main industry organizations, estimated that the value of software pirated worldwide has been roughly $11–13 billion per year for many years.* Obviously, it is difficult to get accurate figures for illegal activities. To make its estimates, the SIIA estimated the average number of software applications likely to be installed on each computer, then used sales information to calculate the average number of applications purchased for each. The gap between the number purchased and

---

*Some reports describe these figures as "losses to the software industry" from piracy. It is impossible to estimate accurately how many people using pirated software would buy full-price legal copies if the pirated copies were not available. It is reasonable to say that many would not, so the loss to publishers is significantly smaller than the total value of pirated software.

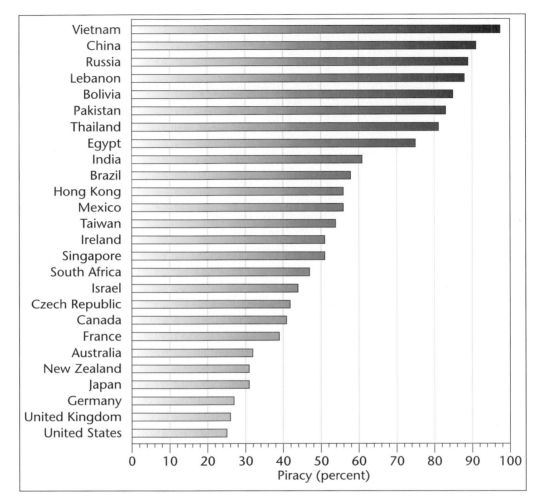

Figure 6.1 Estimated Software Piracy Percentage Rates for 1999

the number installed is attributed to piracy. Piracy rates are higher than 90% in some countries. The piracy percentage in the U.S. is lower than in most other countries, but the total amount of software used is high. The SIIA estimated that $2.8 billion of software was pirated in the U.S. in 1998.[20] Figure 6.1 shows the SIIA estimates of software piracy rates in various countries.

Whole illegal businesses exist to produce, transport, and sell copies of the disks, documentation, and sometimes identical packaging for popular business and personal computer software. This form of software piracy is called counterfeiting. Raids by law enforcement agencies in the U.S. and other countries uncovered millions of unauthorized copies of software. In China, more than two dozen factories allegedly produced millions of pirated compact disks (both software and music CDs), mostly for export to other countries (including the U.S.). Armed robbers stole about 200,000 certificates of authenticity for Microsoft software (which could be attached to pirated copies). In 2000, Microsoft found that 90% of Microsoft products offered for sale on auction sites in Europe, the Middle East, and Africa were illegal copies. Also in 2000, enforcement agents seized five million units of pirated Microsoft products. Pirated copies of Windows XP, like earlier version of Windows before it, appeared in other countries before its official release.[21]

Counterfeiters sell software for lower prices than legal copies, but they profit because they do not pay the designers, developers, programmers, managers, clerical staff, and other employees of the companies that developed the software. The difference between the legal and the pirate price can be extreme. In China, for example, one could buy a software package with a legal value of $6000 for just $105.[22] Some businesses produce copies of software packages "to order." In some countries, one can walk into a store, request a particular program, and wait while the storekeeper goes into the back room to make a copy. Hardware vendors sometimes load unauthorized copies of software onto a machine they are selling and charge the buyer a price far below the price of legal copies. Some software resellers sell unlicensed copies of expensive business packages to business customers. Sometimes the customer is unaware that the software is not legitimate.

Some countries traditionally have not recognized or protected intellectual property, including copyrights, patents, and trademarks. Ignoring foreign copyrights has long been common practice, especially in Asia. I have on my bookshelf a copy of the first edition of my *Computer Algorithms* textbook—in Chinese. It was produced in China without permission from (or payment to) the publisher or me. Counterfeiting of brand name products, from blue jeans to expensive watches, is also common in Asia. Thus, software piracy is a variant of an old phenomenon.

Under pressure from the U.S. in 1991, China passed laws to protect intellectual property rights, and particularly rights for foreign works, but the laws were not enforced. Some of the copying of software was reportedly done in government factories. In 1995, with encouragement from the software and entertainment industries, the U.S. government again pressured the Chinese government to enforce copyrights. The form of the pressure applied by the U.S. government was a threat of high tariffs on Chinese products. Unfortunately, in international negotiations, the offenders are not necessarily those who are threatened with punishment. In this case, punishment falls on legitimate Chinese businesses that produce export products, and on American consumers who buy them. In 1996 the Chinese government took a number of significant steps toward reducing piracy. However, some involve controls that would be unacceptable threats to freedom of expression in the U.S., for example, prohibiting import of CD production equipment without government approval and requiring registration with the government of all CDs produced.[23] Most countries now are parties to international agreements to respect intellectual property and enforce laws to do so, but enforcement is weak.

Why is software piracy (and other product piracy) more common outside the U.S.? We mentioned the general lack of a tradition of legal recognition and protection of intellectual property in some countries. There are other factors as well. Many countries with high piracy rates do not have a significant software industry. Thus they do not have domestic programmers and software companies to lobby for protection of software. (The lack of a domestic software industry may be an effect, as well as a contributing cause; it is difficult for such an industry to develop when it cannot recover its investment in software development.) The fact that the victims of piracy are from another country, and a rich one, may make both the people and the governments less inclined to take action to reduce software theft. In the U.S., where in most cities there are legitimate software stores with aisles full of fancy boxed software, a customer is likely to know that back-room copying is illegal. In countries with few legitimate dealers and where it is not unusual to purchase food unpackaged in outdoor markets, customers may not think there is anything unusual (or wrong) about the way vendors sell software. Another possible reason for software piracy in other countries is that the people are poorer; they cannot afford the high legal price of software. However, although some countries with high piracy rates are poor, others are not. Many individuals and businesses who buy pirated software would probably not steal clothes, food, or office furniture. Thus, although the economic savings are a factor, the cultural and political factors, and the lack of enforcement, are probably more important.

6.3.4 ETHICAL ARGUMENTS ABOUT COPYING

There is intrinsic "fuzziness" about the ethics of copying. The border between what is and what is not ethical is often unclear. Many people who downloaded large numbers of copyrighted songs via Napster and similar services realize they got "something for nothing." They benefited from the creativity and effort of others without paying for it. To most people, that seems wrong. On the other hand, even though we benefit in some way from any copying (or we would not have done it), much copying does not seem wrong. We explore some of the reasons and distinctions.

Copying a song or computer program does not decrease the use and enjoyment any other person gets from his or her copy. This fundamental distinction between intellectual property and physical property explains why some copying is ethical. However, most people who create intellectual property in entertainment, software, and so on, are doing so to earn income, not for the benefit of using their product themselves. If movie theaters could show copies of movies without paying for them, almost no one would invest money, time, energy, and creative effort in making movies. Thus the value of intellectual property is not just the direct use and enjoyment one gets from a copy. Its value is also as a product offered to consumers to earn money. That is an aspect of the property that can be stolen from the copyright holder. And that is why a lot of copying is wrong.

People trade copyrighted music, movies, and software for personal use, not charging for it, not profiting financially. Personal use is, reasonably, more likely to be considered fair use than is commercial use, but is personal use always fair? Is financial gain always relevant? In some contexts, a profit motive, or financial gain, is essential to concluding that an activity is a crime. In other contexts, it is irrelevant. A profit motive is not a significant factor in determining where to protect freedom of speech; virtually all book, magazine, and newspaper publishers are in business to make a profit, yet they have strong freedom-of-speech protection. Vandals do not profit financially from their action, but vandalism is a crime because it destroys—or reduces the value of—someone's property. When people widely copy intellectual property without permission, they diminish the value of the work as an asset to the owner.

Supporters of music-sharing services and people who advocate loose restrictions on copying other intellectual property argue that permitting copying for, say, sampling music or trying out a computer program benefits the copyright owner because it encourages sales. Some people sample music, then buy what they like. Such uses seem ethical, and indeed, since a lot of the "wrong" in unauthorized copying stems from depriving owners of income from their product, the fourth of the fair use guidelines considers the impact on the market for the product. However, we should be careful not to go too far in usurping a copyright holder's decisions. Many businesses give free samples and low-priced introductory offers to encourage sales, but that is a business decision. The investors and employees of the business take the risk for such choices. A business normally makes its own decisions about how it markets its product, not consumers who want free samples, nor even the courts.

Many people make copies of software for friends who do not want to pay the price of buying one. Many people accept copies from friends. Although these activities, in most cases, are copyright infringement, the people involved are not likely to be caught or prosecuted. Thus the issue to deal with here is the ethical one. Should people do this? Would you do this? Here are some arguments people make in support of personal copying (in situations that are not fair use) and some counterpoints to consider.

- *I cannot afford to buy the product.* There are many things we cannot afford; not being able to afford something is not an excuse for taking it.

- *The company is a large, wealthy corporation.* The size and success of the company do not justify taking from it. Programmers, writers, and performing artists lose income too when copying is common.

- *I wouldn't buy it at the retail price anyway. The company is not really losing a sale.* The person is taking something of value, getting "something for nothing," even if the something is less than the retail price. There are times when we get something for nothing. Our neighborhood looks better when our neighbors paint their houses. People do us favors. It can be easy to ignore a crucial distinction: Who makes the decision?

- *Making a copy for a friend is just an act of generosity.* Philosopher Helen Nissenbaum argues that someone who copies software for a friend has a countervailing claim against the programmer's right to prohibit making the copy: the "freedom to pursue the virtue of generosity."[24] Surely we have a liberty (i.e., a negative right) to be generous, and we can exercise it by buying a copy of the program for the friend. It is less clear that we have a claim-right (a positive right) to be generous. Is copying the software an act of generosity on our part or an act that compels involuntary generosity from the programmer?

■ *This violation is insignificant compared to the billions of dollars lost to piracy by dishonest resellers making big profits.* Yes, large-scale commercial piracy is worse. That does not imply that individual copying is ethical. And, if the practice is widespread, the losses become significant.

■ *Everyone does it. You would be foolish not to.* The number of people doing something does not determine whether it is right. A large number of people in one peer group could share similar incentives and experience (or lack thereof) that affect their point of view.

Laws are rarely good guides for ethical decisions, but the fair-use guidelines do a respectable job of identifying criteria to help distinguish fair and unfair copying. Because of the complexity of the issues, there will always be uncertainty in the application of the guidelines, both ethically and legally. The guidelines need expansion and clarification to cover new media and issues computer technology raises, but they give us a good framework that corresponds to sensible ethical criteria.

6.4 Solutions (Good and Bad)

What problem are we seeking solutions for? To writers, singers, artists, actors—and to the people who work in production, marketing, and management—the problem is to ensure that they are paid for the time and effort they put in to create the intangible intellectual property products we enjoy. To the entertainment industry, to publishers and software companies, the problem is to protect their investment and expected, or hoped-for, revenues. The methods of the industry include a mix of reasonable protection measures, unreasonable restrictions on new technologies, and lobbying for laws that benefit them, fair or not.* To scholars, policy makers, and various advocates, the problem is how to apply existing laws, rules, and/or guidelines, or develop new ones, to protect copyright owners, but also to protect fair use, reasonable public access, and the opportunity to use new technologies to the fullest to provide new services.

6.4.1 TECHNOLOGY, MARKETS, AND LAW

Many technical, managerial, and legal solutions address the problems of copyright infringement. They include technologies to prevent or deter copying, technologies for micropayments on the Web, marketing and contractual changes that reduce the incentive

---

*An example of the latter is the extension of the copyright protection period from 75 years to 95 years obtained by the movie industry when the first Mickey Mouse cartoon was about to enter public domain.

to copy illegally, education about the reasons for copyright protection, and enforcement and revision of copyright law.

TECHNOLOGY

Software was the first digital product to be widely copied, so a variety of techniques for protecting software were developed early, with varying success. We describe a few. Encoding an expiration date in free sample versions of software allowed the software to destroy itself after that date. Some business software included a hardware *dongle*, a device that the purchaser had to plug into a port on the computer so that the software would run, thus ensuring that the software ran on only one machine at a time. Consumer software publishers used "copy protection" on diskettes to ensure that you could not copy a diskette or, if you could, the copy could not run. Companies dropped those techniques, largely because consumers rejected them. Customers did not like the inconvenience of replacing a diskette if something went wrong. Some customers refused to buy copy-protected software if there was a nonprotected competitor. Some of these systems were "cracked;" that is, programmers found ways to thwart the protection mechanisms. Some companies sold programs that deactivated the built-in copy protection on other programs. The principle of the Sony Betamax case applied in a case where a software vendor sued a company selling a program to thwart its copy protection: The court ruled that, because the program had lawful applications (e.g., enabling someone to make backup copies), it could be sold.[25] In 2001, Microsoft irritated customers with its "activation" feature in Windows XP. The feature might prevent some unauthorized copying, but it inconveniences people who want to move their software when they replace an old computer. (Instructions for disabling this feature appeared on the Internet soon after Microsoft released Windows XP.)

Now, a variety of hardware and software schemes use encryption to protect intellectual property. *Digital rights management* technologies are a collection of techniques using encryption that allow prevention of copying or viewing without appropriate authorization, or allow the producer of a file to specify what may be done with it, for example, make a limited number of copies or view once on a digital television. The software prevents other actions such as saving, printing, making additional copies, or distributing the file. Music companies, movie studios, and book publishers hesitated to deliver digital copies of their products on the Web because they could not prevent mass copying. As the technology was developed to build in limits on the life or uses of digitized works, record companies began offering subscription services where customers could listen to a specified number of songs each month for a fixed fee. The technology encourages more flexibility, including free demos and low-priced, limited-use options. Such options may eliminate a lot of unauthorized copying; most people are willing to pay for what they use if the price is reasonable and the purchase is convenient. However, there are many criticisms of digital rights management. While it can prevent some copying made easy by digital technologies, it can cause a variety of new problems.

SALE VS. LICENSE

As we explained earlier, when we buy a book, CD, or DVD, we are buying just one copy, not the abstract work—the intellectual property. Copyright law prohibits some uses, but we do own the purchased copy, and we may keep it forever, read or play it as often as we like, lend it, rent it, or resell it. Many companies license their software rather than selling copies. In an attempt to reduce unauthorized copying, the publishing and entertainment industries are shifting toward the licensing paradigm. Licensing has a variety of pros and cons, some with potentially significant consequences.

A license is a contract that specifies permissible uses and places some restrictions on uses. Licenses are usually for a term; that is, they have a time limit. Licenses have the many advantages of contracts. They permit flexibility; the owner can negotiate and tailor terms for particular customers and situations. The flexibility makes possible lower-priced options than does outright sale.

If licensing becomes the standard paradigm for digital intellectual property, the buyer loses the existing copy when he or she no longer wants to pay the license fee. The impact on individuals and libraries would be quite different from the sale paradigm. On the other hand, many of us have books on our shelves that we read once and will never look at again. The market could provide options at different prices for short-term licenses and permanent sales.

License agreements could include provisions prohibiting licensees from telling others of flaws in a computer program or prohibiting uses that are fair uses under copyright law. For example, Network Associates, a major seller of anti-virus and firewall software, stated on disks for some of its programs and on its Web site that customers are prohibited from publishing reviews of the products without the company's approval. In this case, New York State sued the company on the grounds that the statement was deceptive, because the prohibition was not in the license agreement on the software. What if it were? UCITA, the proposed law discussed in Section 4.3.3, would allow such license provisions. Another concern is that business software customers that invest huge amounts of money in the systems, training, and so on, associated with their software would be in a weak bargaining position if the software vendor made unfavorable changes in the license provisions when the term expired.

Although such "strong-arm" tactics are possible, it is not clear that they would survive in the market; libraries negotiate contract terms that protect fair use, and businesses negotiate terms that do not leave them exposed. Some see the potential for unfavorable license terms as a significant concern and advocate laws regulating what may be in a license. As usual with regulation, we must be careful to avoid rules that eliminate valuable flexibility and interfere with voluntary contract formation.

Digital rights-management technologies prevent fair uses as well as infringing uses. Publishers will likely release new songs, books, and movies only in protected formats.

Several companies, including Microsoft, planned to design their systems so that music in unprotected formats such as MP3 files would not play with good quality. You cannot play or view protected works on old or incompatible machines. (When record companies began selling CDs with technology to prevent copying, the CDs failed to play on a variety of devices, angering consumers.) Some critics see digital rights management as a significant tool for implementing licensing agreements with restrictive provisions, as described in the box nearby, "Sale vs. license." We return to the problem of the interference of digital-rights management technology with fair use in Section 6.4.2, when we discuss the Digital Millennium Copyright Act's prohibition on circumventing copyright-protection schemes. Some critics of digital rights-management technologies see a future with all information locked up and tagged with a price.

MARKETS AND MANAGEMENT

Business groups developed management solutions for copyright problems in the past, both for nonelectronic media and for earlier electronic media. Organizations representing copyright holders for music, journals, and magazines made arrangements with users of such works to collect fees. For example, the American Society for Composers, Authors, and Publishers (ASCAP) and Broadcast Music, Inc. (BMI) collect hundreds of millions of dollars a year in fees for live performances and recordings of copyrighted songs played in commercial places. After photocopying machines gained widespread use in the 1960s, making the copying of books and magazines easier and resulting in increased copyright infringement, journal publishers formed the Copyright Clearance Center. The Center negotiates yearly fees with large companies whose employees frequently make copies of journal articles or other material. There are now services that do the same for digitized photographs. These organizations make it feasible for the users of copyrighted material to pay reasonable fees without having to go to the large expense of finding the copyright holder for each item they wish to copy and negotiating with each one individually. The organizations distribute the collected fees to authors and publishers either in accordance with the number of times a particular author's work is used, or, where that is difficult to determine, by other formulas worked out by the organizations and members.

Similar schemes for paying copyright fees developed for the use of creative work online. The National Writers Union established the Publication Rights Clearinghouse to provide for collection of license fees for freelance writers whose articles are distributed by UnCover, a large database of magazines and academic journals, and by other Web sites.[26]

Solutions to some problems concerning licensing of software for businesses need cooperation, flexibility, and innovative contracting terms from software vendors. Publishers of printed scientific journals have long set subscription rates for libraries higher than for individuals because more people use library copies. Software publishers experiment with different pricing policies that might more accurately reflect the usage of a program. For software on networks, metering technology allows a business to pay for usage instead of for users. Academic discounts are a good public relations and anti-theft tool for educational users. Quantity discounts can reduce infringement in large businesses.

ENFORCEMENT

People ignore laws they consider unreasonable, especially if many others do so as well, if it is socially acceptable, and if enforcement is weak. Copying software used to be common practice. As one writer said, it was "once considered a standard and acceptable practice (if it were considered at all)."[27] In 1994, Richard Kenadek became the first computer bulletin board system (BBS) operator indicted for criminal copyright infringement. Subscribers paid $99 a year to copy from approximately 200 commercial programs on his BBS, called Davy Jones Locker. The government claimed he received approximately $40,000. Kenadek pleaded guilty and received a sentence of six months of home confinement and two years' probation.[28]

Publishers, movie studios, software industry organizations, and other copyright owners aggressively monitor cyberspace. The RIAA and BMI use customized software, called Web crawlers and robot programs, to search for unlicensed music files. Similarly, software-publisher organizations search for keywords like "warez" and "cheap software." Staff members examine sites to determine whether their clients' and members' products are being used without authorization. In several countries, the BSA pays large rewards for tips leading to successful legal action against software pirates. Individual software companies, including Microsoft, have offered large rewards for information leading to the arrest and conviction of people who put the companies' programs on the Internet. Companies obtain court orders to shut down Web sites, pressure Internet service providers to cancel accounts of offenders, and file civil suits. In England in 1994, an estimated 45% of all videos sold were pirate copies; by 2000, the rate was below 5%, after an aggressive campaign by an industry group to track down violators, raid swap meets, and prosecute sellers.[29] After a 15-month undercover investigation of global groups alleged to be responsible for cracking copy-protection and distributing pirated software, movies, and other intellectual property, law-enforcement agents in the U.S., England, Australia, Norway, and Finland identified dozens of suspects and raided homes, businesses, and universities. In 2002, a leader of the group DrinkOrDie pled guilty to copyright infringement causing more than $2.5 million in damages and faced a jail sentence of up to five years.

Employees of many businesses and organizations made unauthorized copies of software for large numbers of computers, and they allowed an unauthorized number of users to share software on networks. Large newspaper companies, architectural firms, consulting firms, manufacturing companies, government agencies, and schools and universities have done this. The industry's "software police" (SPA, SIIA, BSA) were active in business offices before they began trawling cyberspace. Since 1988, these groups have conducted both an educational and an enforcement campaign to reduce software theft. They encourage tips about business violators; tips come from current or former employees of the offending organizations—or competitors. Ethical and legal concerns, spite, and, in the case of competitors who pay for their software, dislike of unfair competition motivate them. The SIIA responds by sending warning letters and arranging to conduct voluntary audits of the organization's software. In some cases, they get a court order and conduct a surprise raid accompanied by law-enforcement officers. In most cases, the violation of the law and volume of copying are so clear that the business or organization agrees to pay for the copied software and to pay fines rather than go to trial. Some examples of violators and the fines they paid include an environmental and engineering firm ($350,000), a junior college in Florida ($135,000), a rental car company ($403,000), and an Internet business ($480,000). The raids and fines are highly publicized to remind other businesses and organizations that software copyrights will be enforced.[30]

Some information service managers have criticized the industry's high-profile attack on software piracy. A column in *PC Week* argued that "the idea of using embarrassment, negative publicity and CIA-like covert tactics to get end users and their employers to 'comply' with license agreements is petty, childish and counterproductive." A service bureau manager commented that "what the SPA does is like a mob shakedown."[31] Others accept the enforcement as legitimate. It appears to work. An executive at a large publishing company said, "We are proactive in ensuring compliance, especially since SPA actively seeks out folks who aren't in compliance."[32] Reasons for increased compliance among businesses include both a better understanding of the ethical issues involved and a fear of fines and exposure in a business climate that gradually came to view large-scale copyright violation as not acceptable.

6.4.2 RESTRICTIONS AND BANS ON TECHNOLOGY

In its campaign to protect its intellectual property, the entertainment industry has made many attempts to ban, restrict, or tax technologies, devices, and computer programs that make copying easy and have legal uses but are likely to be used widely in ways that infringe copyrights. We describe examples and cases and discuss critical conflicts with fair use and freedom of speech.

LAWSUITS AND TAXES

The technology for consumer CD-recording devices for music was available from 1988, but lawsuits filed by record companies delayed its introduction. Similarly, the record industry sued to block digital audio tape (DAT) and DAT recorders and lobbied for a law banning DAT machines without built-in copy protection. A group of companies, including a television network and Walt Disney Corp., sued the makers of digital-video recorder machines that store TV programs on a hard disk and can skip commercials. The movie and record industries delayed introduction of DVD players by threatening to sue the companies that make them if consumers could copy movies on the devices. The Rio machine, sold by Diamond Multimedia Systems, is a portable device that plays MP3 music files. The RIAA sued in 1998 and obtained a restraining order stopping Diamond from shipping the devices. (Diamond eventually won the case on a technical point: The Rio did not make copies; it merely played them. The user's computer copied the files to the Rio.)

As an alternative to banning digital media that increase the likelihood of copyright infringement, several governments (including the U.S. and some European countries) tax manufacturers of digital media and equipment (for example, audio tape and CD recorders) to pay copyright holders for losses expected from unauthorized copying. In 2001, France and Germany added taxes on manufacturers of personal computers, printers, scanners, and CD recorders (more than $25 on some equipment). Advocates of these taxes argue that makers of copying equipment are responsible for losses their equipment causes for intellectual-property owners, and the schemes are a reasonable compromise in a situation where it is difficult to catch each infringer. Critics argue that the taxes make equipment more expensive, penalize equipment makers unfairly, charge honest users unfairly, and politicize the difficult job of fairly distributing the money collected.

More recently, the U.S. entertainment industry has been lobbying heavily for laws and industry agreements to require that makers of personal computers and digital recorders and players for music, television programs, and movies build copy-protection mechanisms into their products. Such requirements could help reduce the high levels of illegal copying and encourage the industry to make more entertainment available to consumers in digital form. However, requirements building in copy protection and other digital rights management enable the industry to severely restrict legal copying for personal use and other fair uses. They could complicate sharing of material in the public domain. They interfere with development of new technologies that enable innovative ways to arrange and deliver entertainment, and they violate the freedom of manufacturers to develop and sell products they deem appropriate.

THE DMCA VS. FAIR USE AND FREEDOM OF SPEECH

Every time a 42-year-old figures out how to lock something up, a 14-year-old is going to figure out a new program.

—Jim Griffin, music-industry consultant[33]

Digital rights-management and copy-protection schemes control uses of movies, e-books, music, and so forth. When researchers and programmers studied these schemes and found ways to thwart them, they were arrested or threatened with lawsuits for violating the Digital Millennium Copyright Act (DMCA). The DMCA prohibits the making, distributing, or using of tools (devices, software, or services) to circumvent technological copyright protection systems used by copyright holders. The law provides for heavy penalties and fines for violators. We describe several cases in which the DMCA's anti-circumvention provisions conflict with fair use and freedom of speech and raise other issues as well. Note that in none of these cases was the person accused of violating any copyrights. Some of these cases were not settled as of this writing.

The Content Scrambling System, or CSS, is a protection scheme for movies. A 15-year-old programmer in Norway wrote a program, called DeCSS, that defeated the scrambling. DeCSS became the focus of the first major legal cases based on the DMCA. Several Hollywood studios sued Web-site operators who posted DeCSS on their sites. The studios sued to force Eric Corley, the operator of 2600.com, to remove DeCSS and also to remove links to other sites with DeCSS.[34] Attorneys for Corley argued that

DeCSS could be used for fair uses, that banning DeCSS violated freedom of speech, and that programmers need to discuss computer code and techniques. None of these arguments mattered much; the judge ruled that DeCSS was illegal under the DMCA. The judge ordered Corley to remove links to other sites that contained DeCSS as well. Soon after the decision, descriptions of DeCSS appeared on the Web in haiku, bar code, short movies, a song, a computer game, and art[35]—demonstrating how difficult it is to distinguish between computer code and forms of expression that the First Amendment protects. The movie studios argued that DeCSS was a "digital crowbar," not speech.[36] In the same month that an appeals court upheld the decision ordering removal of DeCSS—and links to it—from the Web, another court reversed an injunction against publication of DeCSS, as an unconstitutional restraint on free speech.[37] The encryption export rules (discussed in Chapter 3), like the DMCA, restricted publication of research and software, but eventually a judge ruled that the First Amendment protects software. The inconsistent rulings about DeCSS show how unsettled these issues are.

In another case, a team of researchers responded to a challenge by the Secure Digital Music Initiative (SDMI), an industry consortium, to test its digital watermarking schemes (a form of digital copyright protection) for music files. The researchers quickly found ways to thwart several of the techniques and planned to present a paper on the flaws in the protection schemes at a conference. The head of the research group, Princeton University computer science professor Edward Felten, said SDMI threatened lawsuits based on the DMCA; he decided not to present the paper. (The paper leaked and appeared on the Web. It was eventually published at a computer security conference.)[38] The DMCA has exceptions for actions necessary for encryption research and computer security, but the scope of the exceptions is unclear. The Felton case showed that the DMCA and the industry's threats of lawsuits have a chilling effect on publication of research. Felton and a group of other researchers filed a suit asking a federal court to rule that the anti-circumvention provisions of the DMCA (when applied to software and research) violated the First Amendment. The ACM, one of the main organizations for professional and academic people in computer science, submitted a statement in support of Felton. The ACM argued that open publication of research evaluating strengths and weaknesses of computer systems is essential to development of effective security and that the fear of prosecution under the DMCA could cause researchers and conferences to leave the U.S., eroding its leadership in the field.[39] The case ended after the recording industry and the government issued statements that lawsuits under the DMCA against scientists and researchers studying access control technologies were not appropriate.

A company in Russia developed and sold a program that circumvents controls embedded in electronic books using Adobe Systems' control software. The program is legal in Russia and most of the world, but, when the program's author, Dmitry Sklyarov, was in the U.S. to present a talk on the weaknesses in control software used in e-books, he was arrested on criminal charges of violating the DMCA. Programmers, researchers, computer science students and professors at major universities joined protests of Sklyarov's arrest. (The government eventually suspended prosecution of Sklyarov and allowed him to return home, but continued to press a criminal case against his employer.)

These cases raise several basic issues. Should we ban or restrict software, a technology, a device, or research because it has the potential for illegal use, or should we ban only the illegal *uses*? Do bans on publishing software violate freedom of speech? Should a Web-site operator be liable for what is on other sites his or her site links to? Are links a form of speech, protected by the First Amendment?

The movie industry argued that DeCSS would be used mostly in ways that infringe copyright. Adobe argued that the e-book program was a threat to copyright. Both programs could, of course, be used to infringe copyrights and create numerous unauthorized copies, and that might well be their main use. But they, and other circumvention techniques, have many legitimate uses. DeCSS enables users of the Linux operating system to view (legally purchased) DVDs on their computers. CSS is implemented differently in the U.S. and Europe, so disks sold in one place cannot be viewed on machines sold in the other. DeCSS allows the legal owner of a DVD to view the disk anywhere in the world. It allows someone to fast-forward through commercials if the fast-forward feature is locked out on a DVD. Similarly, the program to circumvent e-book protection allows the owner of an e-book to read it on more than one machine, print a copy for more comfortable reading, and so forth—which would be legal fair uses.

Librarians, universities, and many organizations and individuals oppose the DMCA's ban on circumvention methods because it criminalizes tools that make possible fair use of copyrighted material for research, education, and ordinary consumer uses of information and entertainment. Researchers oppose the ban because it hinders open discussion of the relevant technologies. Many computer science professors use DeCSS in their classes as an example of a vulnerable encryption scheme.

Before the DMCA, court decisions protected machines and software that have significant legitimate, noninfringing uses. (Examples are the Sony Betamax case and the case about software to defeat copy protection for computer programs sold on floppy disks, mentioned in Section 6.4.1). The DMCA changed that for circumvention software.

In previous chapters, we examined the issue of banning technology that has criminal uses. In Chapter 3, we described the FBI's and NSA's pressure for banning telephone technology that is difficult to tap and encryption schemes that were difficult for them to crack. We saw that law-enforcement agencies advocate banning anonymous Web browsing and e-mail, because they can hide criminal activity. We saw that the entertainment industry tries to ban, delay, and tax electronic devices and media that make copyright infringement easier than it was before. The issue of banning or restricting tools that have criminal uses has also arisen in numerous areas unrelated to computing. Some U.S. cities prohibit sale of spray paint to minors, because they might paint graffiti on walls. Of course, they could also paint a bookcase. Chewing gum is not inherently terrible, but some cities ban it because some people discard the gum on the street, making a mess. Many countries restrict or deny the freedom of ordinary people to own guns to protect their homes because some people misuse guns. Laws ban drug paraphernalia because people might use it with illegal drugs. Some of these laws make prevention of specific crimes easier. For example, it might be hard to find the person who painted graffiti, but it is easy to reduce the sale of spray paint by threatening shop owners with fines. But, in a free society, which should win: the freedom of people to develop, discuss, and use tools for legal purposes—or prevention of potential crimes? Those who reject the policy of banning a tool that has some legitimate uses and some illegal ones show its absurdity by taking it to its extreme: arguing that we should ban matches because arsonists use them. Others argue that we should look at each application individually, considering the risks of harm. Proponents and lobbyists for bans on tools usually rank the damage they could cause (in general or to the interests of their clients) more highly than the loss of freedom and convenience to those who would use the tool honestly and productively. We can rarely predict all the creative and innovative (legal) uses of a new technology. Bans, delays, and expensive restrictions often cost all of society the unforeseen benefits. It is well worth remembering that the technologies listed in Section 6.1.2 as causes of problems for intellectual-property protection are technologies that are the foundation of the incredible, marvelous benefits of the computer and communications revolution.

6.4.3 THE FUTURE OF COPYRIGHT

> *Copyright law will disintegrate.*
>
> —Nicholas Negroponte[40]

> *New technologies have been disrupting existing equilibria for centuries, yet balanced solutions have been found before.*
>
> —Pamela Samuelson[41]

Users and observers of digital media and of the Internet debate whether copyright can survive the enormously increased ease of copying and the habits and expectations that have developed about access to information and entertainment online. Opinions vary widely about the future of copyright and about whether technology or law will be the most significant factor in determining its future.

Attorney Lance Rose has argued that copyright will survive for several reasons, mostly related to enforcement. The "cops," including providers of software and literary and artistic work, are patrolling cyberspace, as we indicated. Large Web sites, ISPs, and services like AOL will police their own subscribers to avoid suits; they will, as Rose puts it, be "scared straight." Rose points out that illegal activities have extra costs that most people do not want to pay. If trading in unauthorized copies is kept "underground," most people will pay the legal price rather than make the effort to find an illicit site that supplies what they want, learn how to access it, make the extra effort to avoid detection, and risk prosecution for copyright infringement. Copyright infringement will continue, but that does not matter. There are always some lawbreakers. The amount will be small enough not to put publishers out of business, Rose argued.[42]

Esther Dyson, editor of *Release 1.0* (a newsletter that covers computer-related issues), takes a different point of view.[43] She has said the ease of copying will win out over attempts to protect copyright. Most content will be free or almost free. Software producers, for example, will have to earn their income by providing support services, such as training, custom work, and upgrades—as movie companies earn millions of dollars from toys, tee-shirts, and other paraphernalia based on their movies.* Writers and other creators of traditionally copyrighted work will have to develop appropriate services to offer for pay in conjunction with their works. It is not clear that Dyson's view is a good change for all authors and publishers, many of whom may have expertise in authorship, but not in ancillary services. Movie makers earn the majority of their income from the movie itself.

The comments from Rose and Dyson and the quotations at the beginning of this section are from 1994 and 1995, yet they still reflect the different points of view extant, many years later. The decisions in the mp3.com and Napster cases suggest that digital technology and the Web have not killed copyright. The courts are ruling that the basic principles of the law remain in force in cyberspace as well as outside of it. At the time Rose and Dyson wrote, the encryption-based protection schemes for intellectual property did not exist or were in early stages of development. They might have a significant impact in reducing the trend toward easy copying. But programmers keep cracking protection schemes, and new technologies come along, like peer-to-peer file transfer, that challenge copyright. Some predict the end of copyright once again. For example, a technology columnist for the *Wall Street Journal*, describing peer-to-peer technology, said in 2000, "A new technology sweeping through cyberspace promises to unleash an entirely new wave of anarchy onto the Web, making it impossible for anyone to protect intellectual property online or shut down a rogue Web service." A programmer working on a version of Gnutella said "This is unstoppable."[44] Given the continuing development of new technologies in response to perceived problems with previous technologies, both such fears and such hopes are almost certainly exaggerated.

6.5 Free-Speech Issues

We saw that the Digital Millennium Copyright Act's restrictions on publication of circumvention software may be unconstitutional. Here, we briefly describe a few other examples of conflicts between freedom of speech and intellectual-property laws.

DOMAIN NAMES

Some businesses and organizations use trademark infringement claims to sue or threaten suits against people who register domain names (Web addresses) that express criticism of the company or organization. For example, if XYZ were the name of a big consumer products maker, they might sue someone with the Internet domain name XYZIsJunk.com. The Pacifica Foundation, an operator of radio stations that, ironically, used to call itself "free speech radio," threatened suits against operators of several Web sites critical of Pacifica management. They used domain names that include the call letters of the stations, for

---

* Some companies that give away software already do many of the things Dyson mentioned.

example, freewpwf.org. A company name is a protected trademark, but many observers believe its use in a domain name is a form of comment, or protected free speech.

In many cases, the company or product name is not used in a negative or critical way. For example, Ford Motor Company sued the operator of ClassicVolvo.com, a business that sells old Volvos and spare parts. (Ford owns Volvo.) Ford also sued the operator of jaguarcenter.com, a site about jaguars (the animal), not Jaguars (the car brand owned by Ford). At issue is how far control of a product name extends. A court dismissed many of these trademark suits, but other actions continue. Some companies buy hundreds of domain names that include names of their products, not to use the names themselves, but to prevent others from using them.

POSTING DOCUMENTS FOR CRITICISM

In 1995 and 1996, the Church of Scientology in effect filed suits against critics of the Church, including several former members, charging that they had posted copyrighted documents containing sacred teachings of the church on the Internet.*

The people who posted the documents argued that the postings were fair use. They made copies of entire documents, but not for commercial gain. The postings were part of discussions of alleged abuses by the church. What are the arguments against accepting the postings as fair use? The copying was not commercial, but it was not for a limited, private use. Copies were posted publicly where many people could see and easily copy them again. This, of course, is true of anything posted to the Internet. The Church considered some of the documents "secret" and would show them only to high-ranking members, who pay fees to move up the ranks in the Church.[45]

The Church pressured BBS operators and Internet-access providers to discontinue carrying newsgroups that discussed the church and its teachings. It sued the *Washington Post* and Netcom, an Internet service provider. A BBS operator was ordered to prevent a former Scientology minister from posting messages and to screen postings for Church material. The BBS operator said that monitoring all the traffic was impossible, and that small operators like him do not have the insurance or deep pockets to fight copyright-infringement litigation. He said he would have to shut down.[46]

Many Net observers considered the fair-use argument to be strong and the freedom of speech implications of the cases to be significant. One judge, in a ruling against the Church, said "the dispute was presented as a straightforward one under copyright and trade secret law. However, the court is now convinced that the primary motivation of [the Church] . . . is to stifle criticism of Scientology in general and to harass its critics."[47] However, in two cases, the men who posted material were found to have infringed the Church's copyright. A judge fined one defendant, found him in contempt of court for posting the transcript of his trial (which included some of the Church material), and prohibited him from posting a list of Web sites containing Church material.

---

*Auxiliary organizations, the Religious Technology Center and Bridge Publications, took the actual legal actions.

There are several issues here. Fair use permits quoting copyrighted material for research, discussion, review, and comment, but how much of a document may someone copy without infringing the copyright? When, if ever, should the law prohibit people from posting links to other Web sites? We considered some aspects of this question in Exercise 5.25 and in the discussion of the DeCSS case; we consider it again in Exercise 6.19.

The Ford Motor Company tried to shut down a Web site that posted some internal Ford documents that Ford claimed contained trade secrets. A court denied Ford's request for an injunction, citing the First Amendment. Other companies have used similar methods, suing or threatening suits for copyright or trade-secret violations, to stop criticism.

6.6 Free Software

6.6.1 WHAT IS FREE SOFTWARE?

Free software is an idea, an ethic, advocated and supported by a large loose-knit group of computer programmers who let people copy and modify their software, often without charge, and encourage others to do so. The *free* in free software means freedom, not necessarily lack of cost, though often there is no charge. Free-software enthusiasts advocate allowing unrestricted copying of programs and making the source code (the human-readable form of a program) available to everyone. Software distributed or made public in source code is called *open source*, and the open-source movement is closely related to the free-software movement. (Commercial software, often called *proprietary software*, is normally sold in object code, the code run by the computer, but not intelligible to people. The source code is kept secret.)

Richard Stallman is the best-known founder and advocate of the free-software movement. In 1983, Stallman began the GNU project, which includes a UNIX-like operating system, Emacs (a sophisticated text editor), and many compilers and utilities; GNU programs are freely available and very popular.* To develop and distribute GNU and other free software and to promote his ideas, Stallman founded the Free Software Foundation and the League for Programming Freedom. With freely distributed software, more people can use and benefit from a program. With source code available, any of thousands of programmers can find and fix bugs quickly. Users and programmers can adapt and improve programs. Programmers can use existing programs to create new and better ones. Stallman compares software to a recipe; we can all decide to add a little garlic or take out some salt without paying a royalty to the person who developed the recipe.

How are free-software developers paid when there are no restrictions on copying and distributing their software? Contributions, some from computer manufacturers, support Stallman's foundation. A lot of free software is developed by programmers who donate their work because they believe in the sharing ethic of free software. They enjoy doing

---

* "GNU" is an acronym for "GNU's Not UNIX."

what they do. Stallman believes that many good programmers would work like artists for low pay because they are committed to their craft. Stallman suggested government grants to universities as another way of funding software.

For a long time, technically savvy programmers and hobbyists were the principal users of free software. Commercial software companies were hostile to the idea. That view changed gradually, then more dramatically, with the Linux operating system.[†] Linus Torvalds wrote the Linux kernel in 1991. Torvalds distributed it for free on the Internet, and a global network of free-software enthusiasts continued development, generally on their own time after work. At first, Linux was difficult to use, not well suited as a consumer or business product. Businesses referred to it as "cult software." Two early users were the company that did the special effects for the movie *Titanic* and the NASA Goddard Space Flight Center. Gradually, some small companies began selling a version of Linux along with manuals and technical support, and, by 1999, major computer companies, including IBM, Oracle, Hewlett-Packard, and Silicon Graphics, used, supported, and marketed it. Large businesses like Royal Dutch/Shell and Home Depot adopted Linux. Several movie studios adopted Linux for their special effects and digital animations. Apache, the most widely used program to run Web sites, is another example of free software. IBM supports and distributes Apache, using it to sell more Web software, hardware, and services.

Major companies began to appreciate the benefits of open source, and several made source code for their own products public (though with restrictions on free uses). Sun Microsystems, for example, made source code for its Solaris operating system public, allowing it to be used for free in noncommercial applications. Repeating some of the arguments of the free-software movement, Sun expected that programmers would trust the software more if they could see how it operates; they might be more likely to use it and to improve it. In 2000, IBM placed full-page ads in major newspapers announcing that it "embraced Linux and the open-source movement as a pillar of e-business."[48] Free software became a significant competitor for Microsoft and so was seen as a considerable social benefit by those who are very critical of Microsoft's products and influence.

Critics (and some supporters) of free software point out some of its weaknesses. Much free software is not easy for ordinary consumers to use. There is no technical support number to call for help. (Programmers and users share information about problems and fixes on very active Web sites.) Because anyone can modify free software, there are many versions and few standards, creating a difficult and confusing environment for nontechnical consumers and businesses. Many businesses want to deal with a specific vendor from whom they can request enhancements and assistance; they are uncomfortable with the loose structure of the free-software movement. Some of these weaknesses are fading as businesses learn how to work with a new paradigm, new businesses develop to support and enhance free software (like Red Hat for Linux), and established businesses embrace the movement.

[†] Technically, Linux is the kernel, or core part, of the operating system. Other parts are from the GNU project, but the whole operating system is often referred to as Linux.

6.6.2 SHOULD ALL SOFTWARE BE FREE?

Some people in the free-software movement do not believe that software should be copyrighted at all. They argue that all software should be open-source, free software. Thus, here we consider not the question "Is free software a good thing?" but "Should free software be the only thing?" When considering this question, we must take care to clarify the context of the question. Are we looking at it from the point of view of a programmer or business deciding how to release software? Are we developing our personal opinion about what would be good for society? Or are we advocating that we change the legal structure to eliminate copyright for software, to eliminate proprietary software? We will focus on the last two: Would it be good if all software were free software? and should we change the legal structure to require it?

Free software is undoubtedly valuable, but does it provide sufficient incentives to produce the huge quantity of consumer software available now? A lot of free software consists of free variants of popular proprietary software, such as Linux as an alternative for the UNIX system. Some critics (and proponents) of free software believe it is better at this role, but it probably would not innovate major new projects. (Apache is an exception; its creators wrote it because there was nothing available as good and with the features they wanted.)

Would the current funding methods for free software be sufficient? Most programmers work for a salary, even if they write free software on their own time. Would the extra services for which a business could charge bring in enough revenue to support all software development? Would the free-software paradigm support the kinds of consumer software sold in millions of copies? What other funding methods could developers use? Some writers have suggested that software is a "public good," like public schools and national defense, that we should allow anyone to copy it, and that the federal government subsidize it. They suggest basing the amount of the subsidy to software companies on how many people use their software and how much the users think it is worth, with these amounts determined by surveys.[49] Would this work?

A supporter of free software used the analogy of listener-supported radio and television. It is a good analogy for free software, but not one for eliminating proprietary software, because most communities have one listener-supported station and numerous proprietary ones.

Stallman believes that proprietary software—particularly, the aspect that prohibits people from making copies and changes in programs without the software publisher's approval—is ethically wrong. He argues that copying a program does not deprive the programmer, or anyone else, of use of the program. (We saw some counterarguments to this viewpoint in Section 6.3.4.) He emphasizes the distinction between physical property and intellectual property. He also points out that the primary purpose of copyright, as stated in the U.S. Constitution, is to promote progress in arts and sciences, not to compensate writers.[50]

To enforce the openness and sharing of free software within the current legal framework that provides copyright protection, the GNU project developed the concept of *copyleft*.[51] Under copyleft, the developer copyrights the program and releases it under an agreement that allows people to use, modify, and distribute it, or any program developed from it, but only if they require the same agreement. In other words, no one may develop a new program from a copylefted program and add restrictions that limit its use and free distribution. The widely used GNU General Public License implements copyleft. For those who oppose copyright and proprietary software completely, this is an excellent device for protecting the freedom of free software within the current legal framework. For those who believe there are important roles for both free and proprietary software, this is an excellent example of how the two can coexist.

6.7 Issues for Software Developers

There are many issues about copyright and patent that are of particular interest to software developers. Legal scholars and software industry commentators emphasize that we need clear rules so that companies can do their work without the threat of changing law and unforeseen suits. Unfortunately, complex questions about how similar one software developer's program may legally be to another's are still unresolved. Software companies sue other software companies whose products are similar.

6.7.1 COPYRIGHT OR PATENT?

There is disagreement about whether copyright is the appropriate protection mechanism for software. Some argue for patents, some for completely new rules designed specifically for software. There are two aspects to the debate. First, what is the nature of a new program, or a new kind of program? Is it an invention, a new idea? Or is it a "writing," an expression of ideas, algorithms, techniques? Second, what are the practical consequences of each choice in terms of encouraging innovation and production of new products?

Software is so broad a field and so varied that specific programs can fit in either category—invention or writing. The first spreadsheet program, VisiCalc, introduced in 1979, was a remarkable innovation that had enormous impact on ways of doing business planning and on the sales of computer software and hardware. If the government had been willing to grant patents on software at that time, VisiCalc would likely have qualified for one. Similarly, the first hypertext system or peer-to-peer system might be seen as a patentable invention. On the other hand, a particular computer game may have more in common with a literary work, like a novel.

The Supreme Court said, in 1972, that software could not be patented because it was abstract. In 1981, it changed position and specified some conditions for patenting software. In the 1980s and 1990s, the U.S. Patent Office began to issue software patents and courts upheld them, sometimes interpreting the Supreme Court guidelines loosely.[52] The Patent Office made mistakes. It granted some patents for techniques that were obvious and/or were already in wide use. In one such case, the Patent Office reversed itself and withdrew a patent it had granted to Compton's New Media for a search system for multimedia databases. Commerce on the Web introduced many new tools, such as online shopping baskets and one-click shopping. Which of these are basic processes that any e-commerce site may use, and which are patentable inventions? Amazon.com generated a lot of criticism when it sued barnesandnoble.com for violating its patent on one-click shopping. Many in the industry objected that the government should not have granted the patent in the first place.

6.7.2 SIMILAR SOFTWARE PRODUCTS

Subtle problems about defining and identifying copyright violations are involved in decisions about whether one software company's product resembles another's. If another work is similar, we have to determine whether it copies only ideas and functions or the copyrighted expression of the ideas and functions. This is difficult for literary works and even more difficult for software. Some principles about software copyright infringement emerged from court cases, but the boundaries of permissible uses are not certain.

CRITERIA

In a 1986 case, *Whelan Associates v. Jaslow Dental Laboratory*, the court ruled that a program that was very similar to another in structure and performance, although written in a different programming language for a different computer, infringed the copyright on the first program.[53] The ruling treated programs somewhat like novels and movies, which can infringe copyrights if they are too similar, even if they are not literal copies. That much is reasonable, and in a case where a program is simply translated to a new language for another computer system, it makes sense to treat it like an infringing translation of a book. A serious problem with the *Whelan* decision, though, was the court's interpretation of what the "idea" in a program is: the purpose of the program. Anything else in the program not essential to the purpose was copyrightable. This meant that a program that simply used well-known and widely used techniques and routines could infringe another program's copyright. Later decisions by other courts indicate that they agree the *Whelan* decision went too far.

A 1987 decision took an extreme position in the other direction. A court ruled in *Plains Cotton Co-op Association v. Goodpasture Computer Service* that only literal copying of code was infringement. This is a far narrower protection than is given literary work. Any programmer knows that there is a lot of creative expression in the organization and structure of a program, as there is in the plot and characters in a novel, but if this ruling were interpreted for novels, it would mean that anyone else could use the plot and characters if they changed the words.

A reasonable interpretation of the boundaries for infringement lies somewhere between these two decisions. Such an in-between position is likely to be complicated, like the 1992 decision in *Computer Associates International v. Altai*. The court specified a complex process for deciding whether a program infringed a copyright. A brief and simplified summary is: First, identify the purpose of the program, remove from consideration the parts that are in the public domain, are common practice, or are the only efficient way of accomplishing some part; copyright does not protect them. Then compare the remaining parts of the two programs to see how similar they are. Any particular case would need expert witnesses and a complex analysis of the programs. Several subsequent court decisions used this approach.

"LOOK AND FEEL"

The term "look and feel" of a program refers to the user interface: the use of pull-down menus, windows, and icons, as well as the specific commands, menus, icons, and so on used to select actions. Two programs that have similar user interfaces are sometimes called "workalike" programs. The internal structure and programming could be entirely different. One program might be faster or have other advantages. Should the look and feel of a program be copyrightable? Does a workalike program infringe the copyright of the earlier program it resembles? Rulings by different courts have been inconsistent, but clarified some points.

In the 1986 *Whelan* decision mentioned earlier, the court found that a user interface designed for the dental profession was copyrightable.[54] In the early 1990s, Lotus Development Corp., producer of the Lotus 1-2-3 spreadsheet program, won significant copyright infringement suits against Paperback Software International and Borland International Inc. for using its menus and commands. Borland deleted the infringing features from its Quattro Pro spreadsheet and faced a huge damages penalty, but the *Lotus v. Borland* decision was reversed on appeal in 1995. In the meantime, Apple sued Microsoft and Hewlett-Packard for user interfaces that Apple claimed were too similar to its Macintosh window and icon interface. Apple lost. Other factors complicated the Apple cases, so although many in the industry welcomed the decision, its implications for future cases were not entirely clear. In overturning the *Lotus v. Borland* decision, the federal appeals court ruled that menu commands are "a method of operation," explicitly excluded from copyright protection. They are, the court said, like the controls of a car, or the buttons on a VCR.[55] Other analogies offered by opponents of user-interface copyright are the arrangement of the keys on a piano—or the keys on a typewriter or computer keyboard. Lotus appealed to the Supreme Court. The Supreme Court deadlocked and let the appeals court ruling stand without setting a precedent. One court said the status of "look and feel" cases is "in a state of creative ferment."[56]

The main argument in favor of protecting a user interface is that it is a major creative effort. Thus, the usual arguments for copyright and patent apply: protect the programmers who create an interface so that they profit from their effort. Without protection, companies will be reluctant to make the large investment necessary to develop innovative new systems. On the other side, there are arguments about social benefits. Standard user interfaces increase productivity of users and programmers. We do not have to learn new interfaces for each program. Programmers do not have to "reinvent the wheel," that is, design a new interface just to be different; they can concentrate on developing the truly new aspects of their programs. They can reduce development costs for new programs, keeping prices down.

The trend of various court decisions is against copyright protection for "look and feel." Courts recognized the value of compatibility. Various courts ruled that features like overlapping windows, pull-down menus, and common operations like cut and paste are outside the scope of copyright.

EXERCISES

Review Exercises

6.1 What is the main difference between copyright and patent?

6.2 What is one noncomputer technology that made copyright infringement easier than it had been before?

6.3 What are two computer technologies that made copyright infringement easier than it had been before?

6.4 What are the four factors to be used in deciding whether a use of copyrighted material is a fair use?

6.5 Summarize the main reasons why the court in the Sony Betamax case ruled that videotaping a movie from television to watch later was not an infringement of copyright.

6.6 Describe two technical means of protecting copyright of intellectual property on the Web.

6.7 List some benefits of free software (in the sense of Section 6.6).

General Exercises

6.8 Describe two things the entertainment industry has done to protect its copyrights. For each, tell whether you think it is justified. Give reasons.

6.9 In a 1996 case, a swap-meet owner was sued because a vendor sold pirated CDs at the swap meet. The owner was found liable for "contributory copyright infringement." Was Napster like a swap meet? Describe some similarities and differences between a swap meet and Napster.

6.10 Your uncle owns a sandwich shop. He asks you to write an inventory program for him. You are glad to help him and do not charge for the program. The program works pretty well, and you discover later that your uncle has given copies to several friends who also operate small food shops. Do you believe your uncle should have asked your permission to give away your program? Do you believe you should be paid for the copies?

6.11 This book, like many others, includes short quotations from other people's work at the beginning of many sections. Such quotes are almost always used without explicit permission. Explain why they are fair uses.

6.12 One criterion that could be added to the fair-use guidelines is the difficulty of obtaining authorization to copy, compared to the value of the product.

   a) One example where this criterion might apply is if you want to e-mail a copyrighted article from the *The New York Times Online* to your list of 20 friends. Even if you are willing to pay a small fee, how would you get permission? Give another example where the suggested criterion might apply. Are my example and your example already covered under the fair-use guidelines?

   b) Do you think the suggested criterion is a good fair-use criterion? Why?

   c) Suppose this criterion were part of the fair-use guidelines. Analyze its application to unauthorized online music-sharing services.

6.13 A political group organized a forum on its Web site where people were encouraged to post and comment on individual newspaper articles relevant to political issues of concern to the group. Other participants added their comments, and debate and discussion of the articles continued. Two newspapers sued, arguing that posting the articles violated their copyrights. Analyze the case. How do the fair-use guidelines apply? Who should win?[57]

6.14 You are a teacher. You would like your students to use a software package, but the school's budget does not include enough money to buy copies for all the students. Your school is in a poor neighborhood, and you know most of the parents cannot afford to buy the software for their children.

    a) List some ways you could try to obtain the software without making unauthorized copies.

    b) Suppose none of the methods you try work. Will you copy the software or decide not to use it? Give some arguments for and against your position. Explain why you think the arguments on your side are stronger.[58]

6.15 Which of the following activities do you think should be a fair use? Give reasons using copyright law and/or court cases.

    a) Making a copy of a friend's spreadsheet software to try out for two weeks, then either deleting it or buying your own copy.

    b) Making a copy of a computer game, and playing it for two weeks, then deleting it.

    c) Your printer is not working. You install your word processor on a friend's computer to use the friend's printer, then delete it when you are done.

6.16 Think up and describe a situation, other than those in Exercise 6.15, where there is a question about whether copying a computer program is a fair use.

6.17 Mr. J wrote the first serious book on the problem of stuttering about 35 years ago. The book is out of print, and Mr. J is dead. Mr. J's son wants to make this classic work available to speech pathologists by scanning it and putting it on his Web page. The copyright (still in effect) was held by the publisher, but the original publishing company was merged or bought out by another company; the son does not know who has the copyright now.

    a) Analyze this case according to the fair-use guidelines. Consider each of the criteria and tell how it applies. Do you think Mr. J's son should post the book?

    b) Suppose Mr. J's son does put the book on the Web, and the publishing company that holds the copyright asks a judge to issue an order for Mr. J to remove it. You're the judge. How would you rule? Why?

6.18 A software service company, Service Consultants, copied a software vendor's program as part of its business of providing software maintenance service to customers of the vendor. Service Consultants did not make the copy to resell the software; it needed it to provide service. The vendor sued, and the service company argued that the copying was a fair use. Give arguments for each side. Which side do you think should have won? Why?[59]

6.19 a) Suppose the movie industry asks a court to order a Web site to remove links to other sites that have pirated DivX movie files. Give arguments for each side. What do you think the decision should be? Why?

    b) Suppose the Church of Scientology asks a court to order a Web site to remove links to discussion forums that have copies of Church religious documents. Give arguments for each side. What do you think the decision should be? Why?

    c) If your decisions are the same for both cases, explain what similarity or principle led you to that conclusion. If your decisions differ for the two cases, explain the distinction between the cases.

6.20 A company sells a digital video recorder called ReplayTV that can automatically skip commercials and transmit copies to other people with the same device. The entertainment industry sued to prevent sale of the device. How does this case compare to the Sony Betamax case? Are the differences significant enough that the decision should be different from the decision in the Betamax case? Justify your answer.

6.21 Performix Inc. sold an expensive business software package that secretly sent e-mail to Performix when the program was installed. By receiving one such message, Performix discovered that a competing company had installed an unauthorized copy of the program on its computers.[60] Suppose this practice of sending e-mail upon installation became common for software and other intellectual property. Discuss its benefits and some objections to it.

6.22 Compare the following statements. Are they equally valid (or invalid)? Why or why not? Is home burglary a good analogy for disabling copy protection? Why or why not?

> One side effect of the DMCA's anti-circumvention provision is to reduce incentive for the entertainment and publishing industries to develop truly strong protection schemes. The DMCA allows them to use weak schemes, then threaten anyone who cracks them with legal action.
>
> One side effect of laws against burglary is to reduce incentive for homeowners to use sturdy locks. The law allows people to use weak locks, then take legal action against anyone who breaks in.

6.23 Which of the arguments for free software apply to music? What differences between music and software make some of the arguments weaker for music?

6.24 Thomas Jefferson and several modern writers used fire as an analogy for copying intellectual property: We can light many candles from one without diminishing the light or heat obtained from the first candle. Suppose a group of people go camping in the wilderness using primitive methods. One person gets a fire started. Others want to start their fire from hers. Can you think of any ethical or practical reasons why they should be expected to trade something, perhaps some wild fruit they found, for the use of the fire?

6.25 Suppose the "public good" solution to creating software without copyright protection, described in Section 6.6.2 were adopted. How do you think it would affect the quantity and quality of software that would be produced? Give reasons, perhaps including analogies with other federally subsidized goods and services.

6.26 Suppose you operate a Web site for backpackers with a few thousand paid members. Members discuss equipment, trip locations, safety, and related subjects. They also use the site to plan specific trips and find compatible trip companions. Discuss what policies and procedures you would implement to deal with the problem of members posting the following kinds of material.

   a) Copyrighted material (e.g., a first aid manual) without authorization of the copyright holder.
   b) Sexually harassing messages.
   c) Discussions about how to sneak into legally closed natural areas.

6.27 Just as software was a new form of intellectual property requiring new thinking about copyright and patent, other new forms of intellectual works are created in electronic media. What copyright or patent protection, if any, do you think the following should have?[61]

   a) A collection of links to Web sites on a specialized topic.
   b) Virtual realities.

6.28 Which of the actions mentioned in the first paragraph of this chapter are illegal? Why? If there is not enough information given, explain what your answer would depend on.

6.29 Describe one kind of software or technique used in software that you think is innovative, like an invention, for which patent protection might be appropriate.

Assignments

These exercises require some research or activity.

6.30   Read a license agreement for a software package. It could be a spreadsheet, word processor, game, operating system, utility, or so on, on a package you bought for your own computer or one in a store or on a Web site that sells software.

   a) What does the license agreement say about the number of copies that can be made?

   b) Does it specify penalties for making unauthorized copies?

   c) Was the agreement easy to read before purchase (e.g., on the outside of the package or available on the Web site)?

   d) Do you consider the license agreement to be clearly stated? Reasonable?

6.31   After pressure from the U.S. movie industry, in 2002, the government of Norway charged Jon Johansen, author of DeCSS, with breaking a Norwegian law. Report on the status of this case and the relevant arguments.

6.32   Read the articles by Esther Dyson and Lance Rose from *Wired* (listed in the references below). Write a short essay telling which author's views about the future of intellectual property in the "digital age" are more convincing to you and why.

Class Discussion Exercises

These exercises are for class discussion, perhaps with short presentations prepared in advance by small groups of students.

6.33   Digital rights-management techniques prevent the viewing, copying, and distribution of works of intellectual property without authorization. The controls can prevent fair uses. Some people argue that such use of digital rights management violates the public's right to fair uses.

   a) Should a person or company that creates intellectual property have the legal right to offer it for sale (or license) in a form protected by their choice of digital rights-management technology (assuming the restrictions are made clear to potential customers)? Give reasons.

   b) Should people have a legal right to develop, sell, buy, and use devices and software to remove digital rights-management restrictions for fair uses? Give reasons.

   c) Considering your answers for the questions above, do you interpret fair use as a negative or positive right (in the terminology of Section 1.2.2)? Explain.

6.34   Debate whether the Digital Millennium Copyright Act's anti-circumvention provisions should be repealed.

6.35   Suppose an employee of Yahoo!'s U.S. auction system visits France to meet with Yahoo! employees there. Suppose he or she is arrested because U.S.-based Yahoo! auction sites include material illegal in France. (See Section 5.2.7.) Would such an arrest be more or less justified than the U.S. government's arrest of Dimitry Sklyarov? Why?

6.36   Which factor will be more important for protection of digital intellectual property: strict copyright laws or technology-based protections (or neither)? Why?

6.37   Debate whether software should be copyrightable or should be freely available for copying.

NOTES

1   The philosophical issue of the nature of the "intangible book" is addressed in Jorge J.E. Garcia, "Textual Identity," *Sorites*, July 1995, pp. 57–75.

2   These examples were suggested by Carol H. Sanders, who made a number of helpful suggestions for this chapter.

3   Randall Davis, "The Digital Dilemma," *Communications of the ACM*, 44:2, Feb. 2001, pp. 77–83.

4   Several sources were used for the history in this section. National Research Council, *Intellectual Property Issues in Software*, National Academy Press, 1991. Neil Boorstyn and Martin C. Fliesler, "Copyrights, Computers, and Confusion," *California State Bar Journal*, April 1981, pp. 148–152. Judge Richard Stearns, *United States of America v. David LaMacchia*, 1994. Robert A. Spanner, "Copyright Infringement Goes Big Time," *Microtimes*, March 8, 1993, p. 36.

5   The piano roll case is *White-Smith Publishing Co. v. Apollo*, reported in Boorstyn and Fliesler, "Copyrights, Computers, and Confusion."

6   *Data Cash Systems v. JS & A Group*, reported in Neil Boorstyn and Martin C. Fliesler, "Copyrights, Computers, and Confusion."

7   Criminal penalties for copyright infringement are in Title 18 of the U.S. Code.

8   Pub. L. No. 105-304 §100; 112 Stat. 2860 (Oct. 28, 1998).

9   U.S. Code Title 17, Section 107.

10   *Sony Corporation of America v. Universal City Studios, Inc.*, 464 U.S. 417(1984). Pamela Samuelson, "Computer Programs and Copyright's Fair Use Doctrine," *Communications of the ACM*, Sept. 1993, 36:9, pp. 19–25.

11   "9th Circuit Allows Disassembly in Sega vs. Accolade," *Computer Law Strategist*, Nov. 1992, 9:7, pp. 1, 3–5. "Can You Infringe a Copyright While Analyzing a Competitor's Program?" *Legal Bytes*, George, Donaldson & Ford, L.L.P., publisher, Winter 1992–93, 1:1, p. 3. Pamela Samuelson, "Copyright's Fair Use Doctrine and Digital Data," *Communications of the ACM*, Jan. 1994, 37:1, pp. 21–27.

12   *Sony Computer Entertainment, Inc. v. Connectix Corporation*, U.S. 9th Circuit Court of Appeal, No. 99-15852, Feb. 10, 2000.

13   "The Digital Reckoning," *Time*, May 22, 2000, p. 56.

14   Stuart Luman and Jason Cook, "Knocking Off Napster," *Wired*, Jan. 2001, p. 89. Karl Taro Greenfeld, "Meet the Napster," *Time*, Oct. 2, 2000, pp. 60–68. "Napster University: From File Swapping to the Future of Entertainment," June 1, 2000, www.webnoize.com/research.

15   Charles Goldsmith, "Sharp Slowdown in U.S. Singles Sales Helps to Depress Global Music Business," *Wall Street Journal*, Apr. 20, 2001, p. B8.

16   *A&M Records v. Napster*, No. 0016401, Feb. 12, 2001, DC No. CV-99-05183-MHP.

17   Robin D. Gross, "9th Circuit Napster Ruling Requires P2P Developers to Ensure No One Misuses Their Systems," *EFFector*, 14:4, Mar. 5, 2001.

18   "Let's Give It Up for Metallica," *Wall Street Journal*, May 10, 2000, p. A27.

19   Jared Sandberg, "Pirated Copies of the Latest Software From IBM, Others Posted on the Internet," *Wall Street Journal*, Oct. 31, 1994, p. B6. "Netwatch," *Time*, July 25, 1994, p. 18.

20   Trevor Moores and Gurpreet Dhillon, "Software Piracy: A View from Hong Kong," *Communications of the ACM*, Dec. 2000, 43:12, pp. 88–93.

21   Russell Watson *et al.*, "A Little Fight Music," *Newsweek*, Feb. 13, 1995, pp. 38–39. Estimates of the number of counterfeit CDs produced in China were in the range of 45–75 million per year in the mid-1990s. "Asides," *Wall Street Journal*, Aug. 25, 1995, p. A8. Craig S. Smith, "Microsoft Finds Pirated Software in Raid in China," *Wall Street Journal*, May 1, 1996, p. A13. "Microsoft Gear Is Stolen From Scottish Plant," *Wall Street Journal*, Nov. 19, 1997, p. B4. Rebecca Buckman, "Microsoft Steps Up Software-Piracy War," *Wall Street Journal*, Aug. 2, 2000, p. B6. Glenn Simpson, "Microsoft Urges Global Attack Against Piracy," *Wall Street Journal*, Apr. 2, 2001, p. A3.

22   Watson et al., "A Little Fight Music."

23   Watson et al, "A Little Fight Music." Helene Cooper and Kathy Chen, "China Averts Trade War with the U.S., Promising a Campaign Against Piracy," *Wall Street Journal*, Feb. 27, 1995, p. A3. R. W. Bradford pointed out the unfairness of the tactic used to pressure the Chinese to enforce copyright in "Whose Ox is Xeroxed," *Liberty*, May 1995, 8:5, pp. 8–9. William P. Alford, "A Piracy Deal Doesn't Make a China Policy," *Wall Street Journal*, July 17, 1996, p. A14.

24   Helen Nissenbaum, "Should I Copy My Neighbor's Software?" in Deborah G. Johnson and Helen Nissenbaum, *Computers, Ethics & Social Values*, Prentice Hall, 1995, pp. 201–213.

25   Pamela Samuelson, "The Copyright Grab," *Wired*, Jan. 1996, pp. 134–138, 188–191. The companies were Vault and Quaid.

26   Junda Woo, "Case Reveals Flaws in Royalty System," *Wall Street Journal*, Jan. 3, 1995, p. 18. *Frank Music Corp., et al. v. CompuServe*. "Publication Rights Clearinghouse," news release from the National Writers Union, Dec. 27, 1995 (www.nwu.org).

27   Laura Didio, "Crackdown on Software Bootleggers Hits Home," *LAN Times*, Nov. 1, 1993, 10:22.

28   "Millbury Man Pleads Guilty in 'Davey Jones' Computer Case," *Worcester Telegram & Gazette* (MA), Dec. 16, 1994.

29 Robert Fox, "News Track: Music Copyright Bot," *Communications of the ACM*, Dec. 1997, 40:12, p. 10. Robina Gibb, "Bounty to Trap Software Pirates," *The Sunday Telegraph*, Oct. 9, 1994, p. 1. Jared Sandberg, "Pirated Copies of the Latest Software From IBM, Others Posted on the Internet," *Wall Street Journal*, Oct. 31, 1994, p. B6. Brandon Michener, "Video Industry In Britain has Pirates at Bay," *Wall Street Journal*, Aug. 16, 2000, pp. B1, B4.

30 Software Publishers Association, "Settlement Announced In Copyright Infringement Case," (news release), May 16, 1996. Jonathan Groner, "Swatting Back at Software Pirates," *Legal Times*, May 18, 1992, p. 7. "Budget Rent a Car to Pay $403,000 in Settlement," *Wall Street Journal*, June 29, 1998, p. A10. Glenn R. Simpson, "ThoughtWorks Made Illegal Use Of Others' Software," *Wall Street Journal*, Jan. 31, 2001, p. B9.

31 Aaron Goldberg, "Let's say 'bye-bye' to the SPA," *PC Week*, Jan. 18, 1993, 10:2, p. 126. Mitzi Waltz, "Making Piracy a Management Issue," *MacWeek*, June 22, 1992, 6:24, p. 10.

32 Karl Peterson of McGraw-Hill, quoted in Didio, "Crackdown on Software Bootleggers Hits Home."

33 Quoted in Karl Taro Greenfeld, "The Free Juke Box," *Time*, Mar. 27, 2000, p. 82.

34 *Universal City Studios, Inc. v. Reimerdes*, 111 F.Supp.2d 294 (S.D.N.Y. 2000).

35 David S. Touretzky, a computer science professor at Carnegie Mellon University, collected many forms of expressing DeCSS on his Web site, "Gallery of CSS Descramblers," www.cs.cmu.edu/~dst/DeCSS/Gallery; viewed Apr. 12, 2001.

36 "Court of Appeals Asks: Is Computer Code Speech?" *EPIC Alert*, June 15, 2001.

37 *DVDCCA v. Bunner.*

38 Scott A. Craver et al, "Reading Between the Lines: Lessons From the SDMI Challenge," www.usenix.org/events/sec01/craver.pdf.

39 *Felton et al. v. RIAA, SDMI, et al.*. The ACM statement is at www.acm.org/usacm/copyright/felten_declaration.html.

40 Nicholas Negroponte, "Being Digital," *Wired*, February 1995, p. 182.

41 Pamela Samuelson, "Copyright and Digital Libraries," *Communications of the ACM*, Apr. 1995, 38:3, pp. 15–21, 110.

42 Lance Rose, "The Emperor's Clothes Still Fit Just Fine," *Wired*, Feb. 1995, pp. 103–106.

43 Esther Dyson, "Intellectual Value," *Wired*, July 1995, pp. 136–141, 182–184. Excerpted from Release 1.0, Dec. 1994.

44 Thomas E. Weber, "Maverick Programmers Prepare to Unleash Anarchy on the Web," *Wall Street Journal*, Mar. 27, 2000, p. B1. The programmer quoted by Weber is Bryan Mayland.

45 David G. Post, "New World War," *Reason*, Apr. 1996, pp. 28–33. *EFFector Online*, Oct. 7, 1995, 8:16.

46 Tom Klemesrud, reported in *EFFector Online*, Feb. 23, 1995, 8:2.

47 Judge Leonie Brinkema, quoted in Jason L. Riley, "The Internet vs. the First Amendment," *Wall Street Journal*, Oct. 25, 1999, p. A53.

48 For example in the *Wall Street Journal*, May 11, 2000, p. A7.

49 Barbara R. Bergmann and Mary W. Gray, "Viewpoint: Software As a Public Good," *Communications of the ACM*, Oct. 1993, 36:10, pp. 13–14.

50 This is a brief summary of Stallman's views. See his article "Why Software Should Be Free" and many others at the GNU Web site, www.gnu.org/philosophy.

51 "What Is Copyleft?" www.gnu.org/philosophy.

52 *Gottshalk v. Bensen*, 409 U.S. 175 (1972) and *Diamond v. Diehr*, 450 U.S. 175 (1981). Dan L. Burk, "Copyrightable Functions and Patentable Speech," *Communications of the ACM*, 44:2, Feb. 2001, pp. 69–75.

53 The source for information about the cases in this section is "When Is a Computer Program a Copy?" *Legal Bytes*, George, Donaldson & Ford, L.L.P., Winter 1992–93, 1:1, pp. 1,2,4.

54 Anne Wells Branscomb, *Who Owns Information?*, Basic Books, 1994, p. 147.

55 David L. Hayes, "A Comprehensive Current Analysis of Software 'Look and Feel' Protection," Fenwick & West LLP, 2000, at www.fenwick.com/pub/ip_pubs.

56 Fifth Circuit Court of Appeals, quoted in Hayes, "A Comprehensive Current Analysis of Software 'Look and Feel' Protection."

57 This exercise is based on the *Los Angeles Times v. Free Republic* case. The court's decision in favor of the newspapers seems inconsistent with the reasoning in the reverse-engineering cases described in Section 6.2.3 and was criticized by some scholars.

58 This exercise was sparked by a brief note in Helen Nissenbaum, "Should I Copy My Neighbor's Software?" in Deborah G. Johnson and Helen Nissenbaum, *Computers, Ethics & Social Values*, Prentice Hall, 1995, p 213.

59 *Southeastern Express Co. v. Triad Systems Corp.*, reported in "Software Copyrights," *Wall Street Journal*, Feb. 27, 1996, p. A2. The court ruled that copying the program infringed the copyright.

60 Glenn R. Simpson, "A '90s Espionage Tale Stars Software Rivals, E-Mail Spy," *Wall Street Journal*, Oct. 25, 1995, pp. B1, B5.

61 The idea for this exercise comes from Samuelson, "Copyright's Fair Use Doctrine and Digital Data" and Jack Russo and Michael Risch, "Copyright Protection For Virtual Realities," *Computer Law Strategist*, Oct. 1992, pp. 1, 3, 4, and Nov. 1992, pp. 2–3.

BOOKS AND ARTICLES

- John Perry Barlow, "The Economy of Ideas: A Framework for Rethinking Patents and Copyrights in the Digital Age," *Wired*, March 1994, pp. 84–90, 126–129.

- Anne Wells Branscomb, *Who Owns Information?*, Chapter 8: Who Owns Computer Software?, Basic Books, 1994.

- Randall Davis, Pamela Samuelson, Mitchell Kapor, and Jerome Reichman, "A New View of Intellectual Property Rights," *Communications of the ACM*, March 1996, 39:3, pp. 21–30.

- Esther Dyson, "Intellectual Value," *Wired*, July 1995, pp. 136–141, 182–185.

- David D. Friedman, *Law's Order: What Economics Has to Do With Law and Why It Matters*, Princeton University Press, 2000, Chapter 11: Clouds and Barbed Wire: The Economics of Intellectual Property. Economic pros and cons for intellectual property rights.

- Derrick Grover, ed., *The Protection of Computer Software—Its Technology and Applications*, second edition, British Computer Society Monographs in Informatics, Cambridge University Press, 1992.

- David L. Hayes, "A Comprehensive Current Analysis of Software "Look and Feel" Protection," Fenwick & West LLP, 2000, at www.fenwick.com/pub/ip_pubs.

- Stan J. Liebowitz and Stephen E. Margolis, *Winners, Losers, & Microsoft: Competition and Antitrust in High Technology*, revised edition, The Independent Institute, 2001.

- Jessica Littman, *Digital Copyright: Protecting Intellectual Property on the Internet*, Prometheus Books, 2001.

- Glyn Moody, *Rebel Code: Inside Linux and the Open Source Revolution*, Perseus, 2001.

- National Research Council, *The Digital Dilemma: Intellectual Property in the Information Age*, National Academy Press, 2000; books.nap.edu/html/digital_dilemma/notice.html.

- Andrew Oram *et al.*, *Peer-to-Peer: Harnessing the Power of Disruptive Technologies*, O'Reilly, 2001.

- L. R. Patterson, *Copyright In Historical Perspective*, Vanderbilt University Press, 1968.

- David G. Post, "New World War," *Reason*, Apr. 1996, pp. 28–33. Covers the Church of Scientology cases and aspects of the Internet that affect the flow of information and protection of intellectual property.

- Eric S. Raymond, *The Cathedral and the Bazaar*, O'Reilly, 1999.

- Lance Rose, "The Emperor's Clothes Still Fit Just Fine," *Wired*, Feb. 1995, pp. 103–106.

- Pamela Samuelson, "Computer Programs and Copyright's Fair Use Doctrine," *Communications of the ACM*, Sept. 1993, 36:9, pp. 19–25.

- Pamela Samuelson, "Why the Anticircumvention Regulations Need Revision," *Communications of the ACM*, Sept. 1999, 42:9, pp. 17–21.

- Linus Torvalds and David Diamond, *Just for Fun: The Story of an Accidental Revolutionary*, HarperBusiness, 2001.

- Jesse Walker, "Copy Catfight: How Intellectual Property Laws Stifle Popular Culture," *Reason*, Mar. 2000, pp. 44–51.

ORGANIZATIONS AND WEBSITES

- The Electronic Frontier Foundation's site about the Digital Millennium Copyright Act: www.eff.org/IP/DMCA

- The GNU project and free software: www.gnu.org/philosophy

- News about file sharing: www.gnutellanews.com

- UCLA's Cyberspace Law and Policy Institute: www.gseis.ucla.edu/iclp

- Many articles and legal documents: www.mp3.com/my/news/yourmusic.html

- The Recording Industry Association of America: www.riaa.com

- The Software & Information Industry Association: www.siia.net

7

COMPUTER CRIME

7.1 Introduction

Computers and the Internet make many activities easier for us. They also make many illegal activities easier for criminals—such as the distribution of child pornography, copyright infringement (as we saw in Chapters 5 and 6), stock manipulation and various other scams. Computers and the Web provide a new environment for fraud, embezzlement, theft, forgery, and industrial espionage. Hacking, or intentional unauthorized access to computer systems, is a whole new category that includes a wide range of illegal activities from harmless pranks to huge thefts and shutdowns of important services on which lives and livelihoods depend.

People reacted with shock and consternation when the Internet, initially used for research, collaboration, and science, was invaded by criminals. But it should not be surprising. Computers are tools, like telephones and cars. When telephones became available, criminals used them too.* Nineteenth-century bank robbers fled the scenes of their crimes on horseback; in the 20th century, they drove get-away cars. Employees used to embezzle funds from their employers by "doctoring" the books. Now they do it by modifying or misusing the company's software. Teenagers have committed pranks and minor crimes for generations; now they hack.

Crimes committed with computers and on the Web are more devastating and harder to detect than similar crimes committed without computers. A robber who enters a bank and uses a gun gets $2,500–$5000 on average. The average loss from a computer fraud is more than $100,000.[1] A thief who steals a credit card gains access to a much larger amount of money than the thief who stole a wallet in the past with only cash. A hacker who breaks into an e-commerce Web site might steal not one or a dozen, but hundreds or thousands of credit-card numbers. Identity theft can disrupt a victim's life for years. Computer vandalism by teenagers brings business operations of major companies to a halt. Terrorists could sabotage power and communications systems and other critical infrastructure.

Computers present new challenges for prevention, detection, and prosecution of crimes. Criminals can steal, commit fraud, or destroy data from miles away or from another country, by modem. Global business networks and the Web extend the criminal's reach and make arrests and prosecutions more difficult. Some tools that aid law enforcement conflict with privacy and civil liberties. Detecting and protecting against the large number of hacking attacks is expensive. Deciding on punishments appropriate for young hackers is difficult.

In this chapter, we will see how computers are used in a variety of crimes and consider some steps taken to reduce the problem. We discuss many aspects of hacking. The example cases described here are representative of dozens or hundreds more.

---

*A 1907 magazine called telephone companies "allies of the criminal pool-rooms."

7.2 Hacking

7.2.1 WHAT IS "HACKING"?

From news headlines, it is easy to conclude that hackers are irresponsible, destructive criminals. They intentionally release computer viruses; steal sensitive personal, business, and government information; steal money; crash Web sites; destroy files; and disrupt businesses. But other people who call themselves hackers do none of these things. So our first problem is to figure out what "hacker" means.

To organize the discussion, we describe three phases of hacking:

Phase 1—the early years (1960s and 1970s), when hacking was a positive term;

Phase 2—the period from the 1970s to the 1990s, when hacking took on its more negative meanings;

Phase 3—beginning in the mid-1990s with the growth of the Web and of e-commerce and the participation of a large portion of the general public online.

The boundaries are not sharp, and each phase includes most of the kinds of hacking common in the earlier phases.

PHASE 1: THE JOY OF PROGRAMMING

In the early days of computing, a "hacker" was a creative programmer who wrote very elegant or clever programs. A "good hack" was an especially clever piece of code. Hackers were called "computer virtuosos." They created many of the first computer games and operating systems. They tended to be outside the social mainstream, spending many hours learning as much as they could about computer systems and making them do new things. Many hackers were high-school and college students who "hacked" the computers at their schools. If they found a way into systems where they were not invited, the early hackers were interested primarily in learning and in intellectual challenges—and, sometimes, the thrill of going where they did not belong. Most had no intention of disrupting services; they frowned on doing damage. The *New Hacker's Dictionary* describes a hacker as a person "who enjoys exploring the details of programmable systems and how to stretch their capabilities; . . . one who programs enthusiastically (even obsessively)."[2] Jude Milhon, one of the relatively few women hackers, described hacking as "clever circumvention of imposed limits."[3] The limits can be technical limits of the system one is using, limits imposed by someone else's security system, legal limits, or the limits of one's own skills. Her definition is a good one in that it stretches over many of the uses of the term. Steven Levy captured some of the spirit of the early hackers in his book *Hackers: Heroes of the Computer Revolution*, when he said "Art, science, and play had merged into the magical activity of programming."

Nowadays, one use of "hacking" with the old meaning of clever programming that reflects a high level of skill describes the writing of software that circumvents the limits of digital protection schemes for intellectual property (for example, movies on DVDs and electronic books, discussed in Section 6.4.2). Hacking often has a whiff of challenge to powerful institutions.

PHASE 2: FROM THE 1970S TO THE MID-1990S

The meaning, and especially the connotations, of the word "hacker" changed as more people began using computers and more people began abusing them. Computers were and still are a mystery to most people, and it was easy for the public and the news media to lump all young people who can work magic with these machines in the same category, not seeing the distinction between good magic and bad. The word "hacking" took on its most common meaning today: breaking into computers on which the hacker does not have authorized access. By the 1980s, hacking also included spreading computer viruses, then mostly in software traded on floppy disks. Hacking behavior included pranks, thefts (of information, software, and sometimes money), and *phone phreaking* (manipulating the telephone system).

Hacking a computer at a big research center, corporation, or government agency was a challenge that brought a sense of accomplishment, a lot of files to explore, and respect from one's peers. In 1986, one hacker broke into at least 30–60 computers on the Stanford University campus, several other universities, 15 Silicon Valley companies, three government laboratories, and several other sites. It appeared that his goal was simply to get into as many computers as he could. This case was typical of the "trophy" hacking often associated with young hackers.[4] Clifford Stoll described a more serious case in his book *The Cuckoo's Egg*: A German hacker broke into dozens of U.S. computers, including military systems, in the 1980s, looking for information to sell to the Soviet Union.

Hackers committed pranks and small crimes. They spoofed e-mail from the premier of Ontario, Canada, sending out unflattering comments about Ontario's parliament. The Secret Service reported that a 15-year-old hacked a credit-reporting service and the telephone system in a scheme to get Western Union to wire money to him from other people's accounts. He is also believed to have hacked a McDonald's payroll computer and given raises to his friends. Some hackers became a serious threat to security and privacy. Using programs called "sniffers," they read information traveling over the Internet and extracted passwords. Security analysts estimated that one million passwords might have been compromised in 1994.[5]

Adult criminals began to recognize the possibilities of hacking; thus, business espionage and significant thefts and frauds joined the list of hacking activities in the 1980s and 1990s. For example, a Russian man, with accomplices in several countries, used stolen passwords to steal $400,000 from Citicorp. While unknowingly under computer surveillance by authorities, he transferred another $11 million to bank accounts in other countries.

HACKING THE PHONE COMPANY

Since the 1970s, when John Draper (who called himself Captain Crunch) discovered that a whistle in a cereal box fooled the telephone system into giving free access to long-distance telephone lines, phone phreaking (hacking the phone system) has been a popular pastime of young hackers and serious criminals. Hackers infiltrated the BellSouth system for years, exploring and creating new phone numbers with no bills, until they did something overt enough to be noticed (redirecting calls for a probation office to a phone-sex line). A man manipulated telephone connections so that he would win thousands of dollars in prizes in a radio station contest. Hackers cracked private business networks and voice-mail systems, then switched to outside lines and made calls that were billed to the company. They eavesdropped on voice mail or erased it. Hacker groups set up their own voice mailboxes in the cracked system to communicate with each other with less chance of being traced. They shut down companies by taking control of a company's phone system and preventing legitimate calls from getting through. A prosecutor who handled several hacker cases reported a revenge prank: Hackers rigged the system to think her home telephone was a pay phone; when she picked it up to make a call, a recording told her to deposit coins. A group of hackers routed FBI telephone numbers to phone-sex chat lines in Germany, Hong Kong, and Moldavia; the FBI was billed about $200,000 for the calls.[6]

BellSouth, the telephone company whose computers were broken into by members of a hacker group called the Legion Of Doom in the late 1980s, described the group as "a severe threat to U.S. financial and telecommunications industries." A U.S. attorney said "The Legion of Doom had the power to jeopardize the entire phone network." There is, of course, a difference between having the power to do something and having the intent. Anyone with a match has the power to burn a house down. Frank Darden, one of the members of the Legion of Doom, agreed that "If we'd wanted to, we could have knocked out service across the Southeastern U.S." Darden seemed as surprised as any other telephone customer might be at the vulnerability of the BellSouth computers: "The fact that I could get into the system amazed me."[7]

Kevin Mitnick is one of the more notorious hackers of the 1980s. He was tracked down and arrested in 1995 after stealing thousands of files from the home computer of Tsutomu Shimomura, a computer security expert at the San Diego Supercomputer Center. At that time he was a fugitive who had gone into hiding while on probation for a 1988 hacking conviction. He was charged with hacking into computers of universities, cell-phone manufacturers, and Internet-service providers. He hacked into major companies, such as Digital Equipment Corporation, Sun Microsystems, Nokia, and Motorola and stole proprietary software. In their book *Cyberpunk*, Katie Hafner and John Markoff describe Mitnick's hacking career before his 1988 arrest. They describe how he took

FINDING THE RIGHT WORDS

Some hackers of the 1960s and their intellectual heirs, who still like to use the term with its earlier respect, try to preserve the old meaning of "hacker" by using the term "cracker" for those who break into systems without authorization, or for those who break in with intent to do damage. "Hacking is art. Cracking is revolution," said a hacker who is a professional software engineer.[8] One writer describes crackers as "mean-spirited hackers."[9] The news media and the public use the word "hacker" so commonly now that trying to replace it with a different word, like "cracker," is almost futile.

In old cowboy movies, the good guys wore white hats and the bad guys wore black hats. So people began using the terms "white-hat hacker" and "black-hat hacker" for the cowboys of the computer frontier. White-hat hackers, for the most part, use their skills to demonstrate system vulnerabilities and improve security; many are computer security professionals. Some spent time in jail or on probation for hacking when teens, but later changed hats. Some hackers wear different hats on different days.

revenge on people he disliked, for example, by switching telephone records to send large bills to the victim.[10] The damage done by Mitnick was estimated at several million dollars.* However, for all Mitnick's notoriety, his exploits had relatively limited effects compared to the e-mail viruses and major hacking attacks on the Web that began in the 1990s.

The vulnerability of the Internet as a whole was demonstrated by the Internet Worm in 1988. Robert T. Morris, a graduate student at Cornell University, wrote a worm program and released it onto the Internet.† The worm did not destroy files or steal passwords, and there was disagreement about whether Morris intended or expected it to cause the degree of disruption that it did. However, the worm spread quickly to computers running particular versions of the UNIX operating system, jamming them up and preventing normal processing. It was estimated that a few thousand computers on the Internet were affected (a large portion of the Net at the time).[11] It took a few days for systems programmers to discover, decode, and rid their systems of the worm. Some infected sites were not functioning normally until several days later. The worm disrupted research and other activities and inconvenienced a large number of people. This incident raised concern about the potential to disrupt critical computer services and cause social disruption. It could happen by accident or be caused by a terrorist, extortionist, or teenager.

---

*Damage figures that include the retail value of software copied or telephone and computer services used by hackers are usually overestimates (similar to the overestimates of the cost of software piracy, as we mentioned in Chapter 6).

†A worm is a program that copies itself to other computers. The concept was developed to make use of idle resources, but was adopted by people using it maliciously. A worm might destroy files or just use resources.

PHASE 3: THE WEB ERA

In the era of the Web, hacking includes "all of the above" plus a variety of new threats. Beginning roughly in the mid-1990s, the intricate interconnectedness of the Web and the increased use of the Internet for e-mail and other communications, for sensitive information, and for economic transactions made hacking more dangerous and damaging—and more attractive to criminal gangs and military organizations. Hacking now affects almost everyone. With basic infrastructure systems (for example, water and power, hospitals, transportation, emergency services, in addition to the telephone system) accessible on the Net, the risk increased. Hacking for political motives increased. As the Web spread globally, so did hacking. We describe examples ranging from new pranks to serious disruptions.

Even before Windows 98 was shipped, a hacker wrote a virus for it. The virus caused screens, including the Windows logo, to appear reversed, as mirror images. Hackers modified the programming at an online gambling site so that everyone won; the site lost $1.9 million.

When businesses and government agencies began to set up Web sites, Internet security expert Dan Farmer ran a program to probe 1700 sites of banks, newspapers, government agencies, and pornography sellers for software loopholes that made it easy for hackers to invade and disable or damage the sites. He found that about two-thirds of the sites had such security weaknesses—and only four sites apparently noticed that someone was probing their security. Farmer's warnings had little effect. In the next few years, actual attacks on Web sites skyrocketed. By mid-2001, attrition.org's online archive had copies of more than 15,000 defaced Web pages. In the U.S., hackers modified or defaced the Web pages of the White House, the Bureau of Labor Statistics, and the FBI. They revised the Department of Justice page to read "Department of Injustice" in protest of the Communications Decency Act. They changed the CIA's site to read "Central Stupidity Agency" and added links to pornography sites. A member of the Global Hell hacker group* hacked the U.S. Army's Web site and tried to make it look like the work of the Chinese government. As the FBI investigated, questioned, and searched the homes of members of Global Hell in 1999, hackers responded by defacing numerous government Web sites and taunting the FBI.[12]

In many cases, hackers obtain information that can threaten other people's financial assets or privacy. According to the FBI, hacker groups in Russia and the Ukraine broke into more than 40 online businesses and stole more than a million credit-card numbers. In some cases, they demanded extortion payments, for example, from CDUniverse and Creditcards.com. After Creditcards.com refused to pay for 55,000 stolen card numbers, hackers posted the numbers on Web sites in three countries. Some hackers who steal credit-card numbers are members of organized-crime groups; others sell the numbers to organized-crime groups. In several hacking incidents, medical records were copied. Two

---

*We mentioned in Chapter 3 that the FBI had a knack for choosing names to arouse public concern, such as Carnivore for its e-mail collecting program. Hacker groups, too, have a penchant for colorfully threatening names.

men were convicted of cracking into property records in Israel and selling land owned by elderly Israelis living abroad.[13]

A teenager crippled a computer system that handled communications between the airport tower and incoming planes at a small airport. The same boy obtained confidential patient information from a drugstore database and shut down telephone service to several hundred homes. Hackers in England impersonated air-traffic controllers and gave false instructions to pilots. In 1998, the U.S. Deputy Defense Secretary described a series of attacks on numerous U.S. military computers as "the most organized and systematic attack the Pentagon has seen to date."[14] Two boys, aged 16 and 17, were caught and pleaded guilty. They had also hacked computers at top universities, national laboratories, and two sites in Mexico.

A decade after the Internet Worm, several computer viruses showed that the Internet, by then much bigger, was still vulnerable. The Melissa virus of 1999 mailed copies of itself to the first 50 people in a computer's e-mail address book on systems using popular Microsoft software. Each new copy sent 50 more copies, and the virus quickly infected approximately a million computers worldwide, including those of individuals, govern- ment and military agencies (e.g., the U.S. Marines), and hundreds of businesses. Many of the clogged systems shut down. In 2000, the "Love Bug," or "ILOVEYOU" virus, spread around the world in a few hours, propagating among computers using Microsoft's Windows and Outlook programs by mailing itself to people in the infected computer's address book and by other means. It also destroyed digital image and music files, modi- fied the computer's operating system and Internet browser, and collected passwords. The destruction of image files alone was devastating to individuals who lost personal photos. The virus was expensive for businesses that lost valuable resources or time restoring sys- tems from backups. The virus infected major corporations like Ford and Siemens and 80% of U.S. federal agencies, including the State Department, the Pentagon, and NASA, along with members of the British Parliament and the U.S. Congress. Many businesses and government agencies had to shut down their e-mail servers. The virus hit tens of millions of computers worldwide and did an estimated $10 billion in damage.[15]*

Within about a week in 2000, almost a dozen major Web sites were shut down, some for several hours, by *denial-of-service attacks*. Victims included Yahoo!, eBay, Amazon, E*Trade, Buy.com, CNN, and others. In this kind of attack, hackers overload the target site with hundreds of thousands of requests for Web pages and other information. The requests were generated by programs planted on numerous other systems (many at universities) to disguise their origin; thus it is also called a *distributed denial-of-service attack*. The attack was traced to a 15-year-old Canadian who used the name mafiaboy; he pleaded guilty to a long list of charges. The U.S. government estimated the cost of this incident at $1.7 billion. One disturbing aspect of this case is that mafiaboy apparently did not write the destructive programs himself; he found them on the Net, where other 15-year-olds can find them too. Availability of hacking programs on the Web

---

*Damages from such virus attacks are difficult to value precisely; estimates may be rough.

is a growing problem. Kids who are not especially clever or technically skilled themselves use these easily obtained programs (called scripts) and are derisively called *script kiddies* by more knowledgeable hackers. Denial-of-service attacks against individual Web sites are frequent. They are difficult to avoid. In one case in 2001, a 13-year-old repeatedly shut down a site over several days because he thought, mistakenly, that the site operator had called him a script kiddy.[16]

In 2001, the Code Red worm program quickly spread to 300,000 server computers at thousands of businesses worldwide. It exploited a flaw in Microsoft server software discovered a month earlier and caused infected servers to flood the White House Web site with huge numbers of messages, clogging the Internet. A variant of Code Red set up a "back door" on infected computers that allowed anyone to access infected servers and copy sensitive information such as credit card numbers.

THE FUTURE

The future is full of surprises. Most of the current uses of the Web were unplanned and unexpected. But, using indications from current developments, I suggest two areas where hacking will increase, with potentially dangerous and destructive impact.

Before the denial-of-service attacks that shut down popular Web sites were traced to a 15-year-old, some people speculated that the attacks were the work of terrorists. They could have been. Hacking by terrorists and by government-sponsored military organizations is likely to increase. The governments of the U.S., China, and other countries are using or planning such attacks (and working on defenses against attacks by others). The Japanese Defense Agency said it is developing computer viruses for military uses. China and Singapore are believed to be doing the same, for both military and civilian computer networks in other countries. Early incidents included attacks apparently by the Chinese government against Web sites of the religious group Falun Dafa and attacks by China and Taiwan against each other.[17]

We already have "things that think," that is, appliances with embedded computer chips—from microwave ovens to cars to factory machinery to heart monitors. Many such appliances are going online, that is, connecting to the Internet. So, while driving home from work, you can tell your stove to start cooking dinner or tell your garden sprinklers to water the lawn. Doctors will access and control medical devices over the Net. Automated fleets of cars will communicate with each other to drive safely on highways. We have already seen that some hackers think misdirecting airplane pilots is fun. The potential for havoc will increase when hackers can control devices, not just information.

HARMLESS HACKING?

In many cases, particularly with young hackers, it is the excitement and challenge of breaking in and copying files as trophies that motivates them. Some hackers claim that such hacking is harmless. Is it?

When a system administrator for a computer system at a university, a corporation, or the military detects an intruder, he or she cannot immediately distinguish a nonmalicious hacker from a thief, terrorist, or spy. The intrusion must be stopped. The administrator's responsibility is to protect the system and its data. Thus, at a minimum, time and effort will be expended to track down the intruder and shut off his or her means of access. In many cases, companies shut down their Internet connection, at great inconvenience, while investigating and defending against an intruder. The large number of young people hacking into sensitive systems just for fun help to mask the people hacking with malicious intent. Nonmalicious, prank hacking also uses up resources that could be needed to respond to serious threats. When hackers deface Web pages or bring down business sites, the cost includes lost business, the cost of investigating and responding to the attack, and inconvenience to the public who use the site.

Uncertainty about the intruder's intent and activities has additional costs for systems that contain sensitive data. According to the head of the computer crime unit at the Department of Justice, after a hacker accessed a Boeing computer, apparently just to hop to another system, Boeing spent $75,000 to verify that no files had been changed. Would we be comfortable flying a new Boeing airplane if this were *not* done? A group of young Danes broke into the National Weather Service computers and computers of numerous other government agencies, businesses, and universities in the U.S., Japan, Brazil, Israel, and Denmark. The efforts to track the Danish hackers cost time, effort, and computer resources of the Weather Service, the FBI, MIT, and the Danish police. They were eventually caught, and it appeared they had done little damage to the systems they cracked. But consider the risks. If the hackers had damaged Weather Service files, for example, they could have halted air traffic that is dependent on weather reports. In fact, their activities did cause the Weather Service computers to slow down. There was the potential that serious weather conditions, such as tornadoes, could have gone undetected and unreported.[18] Similarly, if unauthorized access is detected in a medical records system, a credit database, a computer containing design plans for a new product, payroll data, and others, responsible administrators must stop the intruders and verify that no changes have been made to the records. Uncertainty causes harm, or expense, even if hackers have no destructive intent.

Another problem, of course, is that a hacker with good intentions could make a mistake; significant damage can be done accidentally. Almost all hacking is a form of trespass. Hackers with nonmalicious intentions must understand that they will often not be viewed kindly.

7.2.2 HACKTIVISM, OR POLITICAL HACKING

Hacktivism is the use of hacking to promote a political cause. What new problems are raised by hacktivism? Is such hacking ethically justified? Should hacktivists be treated differently from other hackers when they are caught?

Some academic writers and political groups argue that hacktivism is ethical, that it is a modern form of civil disobedience. Others argue that the political motive is irrelevant, or at the other extreme, that political hacking is a form of cyberterrorism. Of course, just as hacking in general ranges from mild to highly destructive activities, so can political hacking. We consider some examples.

A hacker posted anti-Israeli messages on the site of a pro-Israel lobbying organization. (He also posted personal information about a few hundred of the group's members, including their credit-card numbers.) Three teenagers hacked into the network of an atomic-research center in India and downloaded files to protest India's tests of nuclear weapons. The governments of Indonesia and China were targeted for their anti-democratic policies. Pro-Zapatista hackers hit Mexican government sites. Someone posted a pro-drug message on a U.S. police department anti-drug Web site. Earlier, we mentioned numerous cases of defacement of U.S. government Web sites; many make political statements. Before mafiaboy was caught, people speculated that the denial-of-service attacks against many major Web sites in 2000 was a political act—a statement against commercialization of the Web.

One problem with hacktivism is that it quickly became a cover for ordinary pranks and serious mischief. In several cases, hackers posted political messages on Web pages they hacked to direct suspicion at others or to divert attention from their true motives, including theft of credit-card numbers or other data.

A more fundamental problem with evaluating political hacking is that it can be hard to identify. People who agree with the political or social position of the hackers will tend to see an act as "activism" while those who disagree will tend to see it as ordinary crime (or worse). Is posting a pro-drug message on a police Web site a political statement against the futility, dishonesty, expense, and international intrusions of U.S. drug policy, or is it the act of a kid showing off? Were a pair of Arab men who defrauded elderly Israelis committing a political act or robbing vulnerable people? To some political activists, any act that shuts down or steals from a large corporation is a political act. To the customers and owners, it is vandalism and theft.

Suppose we know that the hackers are motivated by a political cause. How can we begin to evaluate the ethics of their hacktivism? Suppose a religious group, to protest homosexuality, disables a Web site for gay people, and a environmentalist group, to protest a new housing development, disables a real-estate developer's site. Many of the people who might argue that one of these acts is justifiable hacktivism would argue that the other is not. Yet it would be extremely difficult to develop a sound ethical basis for distinguishing them.

Some writers argue that hacktivism should be considered a legitimate form of civil disobedience and not subject to felony prosecution.[19] Civil disobedience has a respected, nonviolent tradition. Henry David Thoreau, Mahatma Gandhi, and Martin Luther King, Jr., refused to cooperate with rules that violated their freedom. Peaceful protestors have marched, rallied, and boycotted to promote their goals. Burning down ski resorts and homes because one would prefer to see the land undeveloped is quite another category of activity. To evaluate incidents of hacktivism, it is helpful to fit them into such a scale from peaceful resistance to destruction of other people's property and actions that risk serious harm to innocent people. Denial-of-service attacks, for example, can interfere with health and emergency services.

Freedom of speech does not include the right to hang a political sign in a neighbor's window or paint one's slogans on someone else's fence, even if that "someone else" is a group of people organized as a business or corporation. We have the freedom to speak, but not the right to compel others to listen. Crashing a Web site or defacing a Web page is comparable to shouting down a speaker with whom one disagrees or burning newspapers with articles one does not like. The latter activities occur on college campuses and are defended by some who believe that the specific content or cause is more important than the principle of freedom of speech. It is common for people involved in political causes to see their side as unquestionably morally right, and anyone on the other side as morally evil, not simply someone with a different point of view. This often leads to the view that the freedom of speech, freedom of choice, and property rights of the other side deserve no respect. Peace, freedom, and civil society require that we respect such basic rights and not impose our views on those we disagree with.

Another factor to consider when evaluating hactivism is the political system under which the hacktivists live. From both an ethical and social perspective, in free countries where almost anyone can post messages to numerous online forums, set up a Web page, and stream their video of police brutality at international protests, it is hard to justify hacking someone else's site to promote a political cause. Activists use the Internet to organize opposition to oil exploration in Alaska that they fear will harm a caribou herd. Activists use the Internet to organize mass demonstrations against international meetings of government leaders. Human rights groups like Amnesty International use the Web effectively. Groups supporting all kinds of nonmainstream causes, from animal rights to anarchism to odd religions, have Web sites. None of this activism requires hacktivism.

In countries with oppressive governments that control the means of communications and prohibit open political discussion, that have secret police who kill dissenters, that ban some religions, that jail people who express opposition views—in such countries, where sponsoring one's own Web site is impossible or dangerous, political hacking, to get one's message out to the public and, in some cases, to sabotage government activities, might be justified. Unfortunately, the nations in which hacktivism is likely to be most ethically justified are those most likely to impose harsh penalties on anyone who expresses opposing views and especially on anyone who interferes with or embarrasses the government. Those nations are least likely to respect acts of civil disobedience.

How should defacing government Web pages be treated in relatively free countries like the U.S.? Defacing government sites embarrasses governments because it demonstrates weak security at sites the public expects to be best protected. Some people smile when they hear of pompous or powerful agencies being embarrassed. Some consider such hacking a juvenile act of minor vandalism, while others see it as a serious symbolic attack on the authority of the government. We have many laws authorizing stronger penalties for crimes committed against government employees or agencies than for the same crime against ordinary citizens or businesses. In a free society, where the government serves the people, it is reasonable to question this double standard. Perhaps the just approach is to treat defacing a government Web page the same as defacing a Web page belonging to any business, individual, or organization. The penalty should depend more on the seriousness of the damage than the status of the owner.

7.2.3 THE LAW

When teenagers started hacking for the challenge to get into computers where they were not authorized, there was disagreement not only about whether the activity was a crime under existing law, but also whether it should be. Gradually, state governments passed laws that specifically addressed computer crimes. Intentional access to and use of a computer without authorization are now criminal offenses under state and federal laws. Hacker activity that includes access to computers where the hacker is not an authorized user is illegal in most cases.

Congress passed the main federal computer crime law, the Computer Fraud and Abuse Act (CFAA), in 1986. There are more than a dozen other federal laws that can be used to prosecute people for crimes related to computer and telecommunications systems in specific areas. They cover electronic-funds transfer and bank fraud, interference with satellite operations, damage to government property, and a variety of other actions. Many activities are legitimate and routine when performed with authorization, but are illegal when done knowingly or intentionally without authorization or by exceeding one's authorization. They include accessing a computer system, use of computer services, accessing (reading) files, copying data, programs, or other information, modifying data or other files, and destroying data or other files. A person can interrupt the operation of a computer or cause a computer to malfunction accidentally; these actions are illegal when done while intentionally accessing a computer without authorization or by exceeding one's authorization. Other illegal actions include access to commit fraud, disclosing passwords or other access codes to unauthorized people, and interrupting or impairing government operation, public communication, transportation or other public utilities.

As a federal law, the CFAA covers areas over which the federal government has jurisdiction: government computers (or those used by government agencies), financial systems, medical systems, and activities that involve computers in more than one state (because the federal government has the power to regulate interstate commerce). Computers connected to the Internet are covered. Denial-of-service attacks and the launching of computer viruses and other malicious programs are covered by the law in sections addressing the altering, damaging, or destroying of information and the prevention of authorized use of a computer.

State and federal anti-hacking laws provide for strong penalties: depending on the particular offense, prison sentences of up to one, five, or ten years for a first offense and fines up to $250,000. (Most laws apply only if damage is above a specified amount, for example $5000. This provision, while reasonable in many ways, frustrates operators of small Web sites who cannot get help from law-enforcement agencies when hacked.)

A looser culture predated these laws, and there is ambiguity about exactly what constitutes authorization for certain acts. Computer-system operators, programmers, and consultants used to do their work without rigid policies and laws about authorization, and some activities that were common are now illegal. In Oregon, for example, a consultant, the co-author of several computer-programming books, fought an unsuccessful legal battle for six years attempting to overturn his felony conviction for activities he claimed were arguably part of his work.[20] Anti-hacking laws need to be written carefully enough so that they do not criminalize acts of poor judgment. At the same time, programmers and young people without malicious intent need to exercise good judgment in an environment where sensitivity about security is high.

In several cases, employees who used an employer's computers for the employee's own commercial business or for personal use were charged with theft. Employees argued that use of the employer's computer was analogous to using a tool, such as a hammer or typewriter, belonging to the employer for personal business and storing personal items on an empty shelf. An employer might object and possibly fire someone for such actions, but, they claimed, it was not a criminal offense. The Indiana Supreme Court agreed with this argument in an early case.[21] Now anti-hacking laws making it a crime to access a computer in ways that exceed one's authorization can be used by employers against employees.

The USA PATRIOT Act (USAPA) was passed in response to the terrorist attacks in September, 2001. It includes amendments to the Computer Fraud and Abuse Act, several that apply to hacking in general, not just to terrorism. The USAPA expanded the definition of loss to include the cost of responding to a hacking attack, assessing damage, and restoring systems. The Act raised the maximum penalty in the CFAA for a first offense from five years to 10 years. It increased penalties for hacking government computers used by the criminal justice system or the military. It allows the government to monitor online activity of suspected hackers without a court order. We have seen that hacking covers a wide range of activity, some deserving serious punishment and some comparable to minor offenses committed by kids of all generations. A large subculture of hackers hack to demonstrate security weaknesses, weaknesses that real terrorists could exploit. Definitions of the actions to which the tougher USAPA anti-terrorism provisions apply are broad and include activity few would consider terrorism.

7.2.4 CATCHING HACKERS

The people responsible for almost all the hacking incidents described in Section 7.2.1 were caught. The author of the Melissa virus was caught in one week. The FBI traced the denial-of-service attacks in 2000 to mafiaboy and had his real name within a week. The man suspected of launching the ILOVEYOU virus and four Israeli teenagers who wrote and launched the Goner worm in 2001 were identified in about the same time. How do hacker trackers do their job?

Law-enforcement agents specializing in computer crime get technical training. They and security professionals read hacker newsletters and participate in online discussions of hacking, sometimes undercover. Law-enforcement agents, some undercover, attend hacker conferences. Security specialists maintain logs of Internet Relay Chat (IRC) channels used by hackers. A police detective specializing in financial crime and hacking told me that 30% of hackers are government informers, and the majority of subscribers to *2600*, a hacker magazine, are law-enforcement personnel; he may have exaggerated, but he made the point that the sheriff has arrived on the frontier and speaks the language. Security professionals set up *honey pots*, Web sites that look attractive to hackers, but are closely monitored so that everything a hacker does at the site is recorded and studied. Law-enforcement agents use wiretaps to collect evidence and build a case against hacking suspects.

Mafiaboy was identified as a suspect, at first only by his handle, because he, like many young hackers, bragged about his exploits. Once a suspect's handle is known, hacker trackers search the vast archives of online message boards for other posts by the same person that yield clues to his real identity. Mafiaboy had posted a message including his first name and e-mail address two years earlier. A number of other hackers were identified this way. Unsophisticated hackers are sometimes easy to trace because they do not hide. Attrition.org reported that many hackers who sent e-mail reporting Web sites they defaced did not disguise their own e-mail return addresses. Two Russian hackers who demanded jobs as security consultants after stealing thousands of credit-card numbers were arrested when they arrived in the U.S. for job interviews.

The field of collecting evidence from computer files and disks is called *computer forensics*, or sometimes *digital forensics*.[22] Computer-forensics specialists can recover deleted files, often even if the disks have been erased. In Chapter 2, we saw how easy it is to collect and save information about everything we do on the Internet and to search and match records to build consumer profiles. The same tools that threaten privacy aid in catching criminals. Some viruses and hacking attacks are traced by using ISP records and the logs of routers, the machines that route messages through the Internet. David Smith, the man who released the Melissa virus, for example, used someone else's AOL account, but AOL's logs contained enough information to enable law-enforcement authorities to trace the session to Smith's telephone line. Most people are unaware that word processors, such as Microsoft Word, include a lot of "invisible information" in files—in some cases, unique identifying numbers and the author's name. Security experts used such information to trace the Melissa virus. Privacy advocates were appalled by the hidden identifying information in files—another reminder of the tension between privacy and crime fighting.

Many of the techniques we just described worked because hackers did not know about them. When such methods receive publicity in big cases, hackers learn what mistakes to avoid. Investigators of the Code Red worm, for example, said the code held no clues to its author. Hackers, as well as people seeking privacy, learn how to remove identifying numbers from documents. Hackers learn how to forge such numbers to throw suspicion elsewhere. Thus, some of the particular methods described here will be less effective when you read this. Law-enforcement and security personnel continue to update their skills and tools as hackers change theirs.

A variety of groups and individuals from law-enforcement agencies, industry, security companies, universities, and the hacker culture itself participate in the efforts to detect hacker attacks, warn victims, devise defenses, and track down the hackers responsible. The Computer Emergency Response Team (CERT), based at Carnegie Mellon University, was established in 1988 in response to the Internet Worm. For many years its experts helped system administrators investigate and protect against intrusions. It reported newly discovered security flaws to government agencies and, after a delay to allow for defenses to be developed, to the public. As the number of hacking incidents grew enormously and other organizations formed to fill CERT's early role, its name changed to CERT Coordination Center, and it shifted function. CERT offers security advice, provides immediate security warnings to business subscribers, and planned to develop a system to certify the security of business computer networks. (CERT itself was the victim of a denial-of-service attack in 2001, bogging down its Web site for 30 hours.) The Financial Services Information Sharing and Analysis Center was formed by large banks to provide early warning of computer attacks; it learned of the ILOVEYOU virus hours before the FBI. Attrition.org provides subscribers with quick information about hacking incidents; the FBI is a subscriber. Many law-enforcement agencies established special units to deal with computer crime; the FBI's National Computer Crime Squad was an early example. In 1998, the FBI formed the National Infrastructure Protection Center (NIPC) to protect against hackers. It participated in the investigations of the Melissa virus and mafiaboy's denial-of-service attack on major Web sites. However, the Center was strongly criticized by Congress' investigative agency, the General Accounting Office (GAO), industry groups, and others for failing to warn companies under attack by hackers for weeks or months after the NIPC knew of the attacks. A GAO report included other criticisms, such as lack of expertise and failure to cooperate with other agencies and private groups.[23] The problems with the NIPC reflect interagency rivalries and tensions between the FBI, which is used to controlling information, and computer professionals, who are used to a more open flow of information.

John Perry Barlow, a founder of the Electronic Frontier Foundation, colorfully described how he spent two hours explaining the basics of computing and computer networks to an FBI agent who came to question him in 1990. In Section 3.2.1 and in a nearby box, we describe cases from 1990—the Steve Jackson Games and *Phrack* cases—in which many civil libertarians and computer professionals believe law-enforcement agencies (and the news media) overreacted. In a hacking investigation called Operation Sun Devil, Secret Service agents raided homes in 1990 and reportedly held families of hackers at gunpoint.[24] The paranoia, or hysteria, about hackers came in part from ignorance and in part in reaction to the Internet Worm and to the discovery that teenagers could break into the computers of large corporations. Understanding by law-enforcement agencies of technical aspects of hacking, the hacker culture, and the laws and procedures law-enforcement agents must follow have improved since 1990.

THE *PHRACK* CASE

In 1989, an electronic hacker newsletter called *Phrack* published part of a document about the 911 emergency telephone system. The document had been downloaded by a hacker who accessed a BellSouth telephone company computer without authorization. BellSouth claimed that the document contained sensitive information and that its publication threatened the security of the emergency system. After an investigation by the Secret Service, *Phrack*'s editor and publisher, Craig Neidorf, was charged with ten felony counts (wire fraud and interstate transportation of stolen property) with a potential prison sentence of 65 years and a large fine. The Secret Service seized *Phrack*'s computer equipment, software, and list of subscribers. The indictment charged that the E911 document was worth $23,900. The document was the focus of the case, but charges were also related to other material published in *Phrack*, including hacker tutorials.[25] Many who were familiar with this case saw it as a significant threat to electronic publishers.

The trial ended in an embarrassment for the government. On the fourth day, the charges were dropped. The defense showed that the information in the E911 document was available in other published sources and in pamphlets sold by another telephone company for under $25.

Several observers compared the *Phrack* case to the Pentagon Papers case. In the 1970s, the *New York Times* and the *Washington Post* published the Pentagon Papers, documents describing government policies and activities related to the war in Vietnam. The documents were given to the newspapers without authorization. The government argued that their publication threatened national security, but the newspaper publishers were not charged with criminal offenses. Why was *Phrack* treated differently from the *Times* and the *Post*? And why did journalists and many civil libertarians not react with the concern they might normally show for a threat to freedom of the press? One reason was that *Phrack* was not published on paper; it was distributed electronically. There was no printing "press" to be protected by the First Amendment. Electronic newsletters were not seen by tradition-bound people as legitimate news publications. Another reason was the fear, encouraged by news reports about the E911 document, that the case involved dangerous hackers out to sabotage the 911 system.

THE ISSUE OF VENUE

Normally, criminal charges are filed and a trial takes place where the crime was committed. Laws differ in different states and countries, and police from one country cannot easily carry out investigations in other countries. Now, when computer crimes cross state and international borders, what laws apply and where should the trial be held?

The Russian man who stole millions of dollars from Citicorp—without entering the United States—was arrested in London. The extradition process to bring him to the U.S. for trial took more than two years. The man suspected of writing and releasing the ILOVEYOU computer virus in 2000, which jammed computers and destroyed files worldwide, was not prosecuted because he lived in the Philippines, which had no law that applied to his actions.

In cases where the suspect and victims are in the U.S., federal laws, like the Computer Fraud and Abuse Act may apply, but the question of where to file the charges and hold the trial remains. We saw (in Section 5.2.1) that, for First Amendment cases involving distribution of obscene material, the jurisdiction was a critical issue, because community standards are an essential factor in determining guilt. In cases that do not explicitly involve community standards, venue (the place where the charges are brought or where the trial is held) can still be very important. The government could choose a location where prosecutors have more expertise in computer crime, but that choice might adversely affect a defendant who must hire distant lawyers and travel a long distance to a trial.

7.2.5 PENALTIES APPROPRIATE TO THE CRIME

There are no particularly new issues about appropriate penalties for adults who hack to steal millions of dollars or corporate secrets or who vandalize computer systems of employers who fired them. Although they use computers, these are crimes that have been around for many years and can be handled with established legal principles and laws. Terrorists who kill thousands of people by hacking should face the same penalties as terrorists who kill people by crashing airplanes into buildings. Difficult penalty issues involve hackers who are young, hackers who do not intend to do damage, and hackers who, through accident, ignorance, or immaturity, do vastly more damage than they can pay for. Clearly, offenses related to unauthorized access vary in degree, and penalties should likewise vary, as they do for trespass, vandalism, invasion of privacy, fraud, and theft. Sentences for hacking, as for other crimes, should depend on the person's intent, the person's age, and the damage done.

ACTUAL SENTENCES

In many hacking cases, especially those involving young people, the hacker pleaded guilty; the evidence was clear, and the hacker and prosecutor worked out a plea bargain. Most hackers under age 18 received relatively light sentences. Typical sentences include two or three years probation, community service, possibly a fine or order to pay restitution (some, roughly $30,000), and, sometimes, an order not to use a computer during the probationary period (or not to use one without direct supervision). The teens who launched the serious attack on the Pentagon in 1998 and broke into several universities received such sentences. The 15-year-old who disabled an airport radio system got probation even though his exploits could have endangered people. In 2000, a 16-year-old was sentenced to six months detention. He was the first juvenile to be incarcerated for hacking; he had broken into NASA and Defense Department computers and was a member of a hacker group that vandalized government Web sites. Mafiaboy, the 15-year-old responsible for denial-of-service attacks in 2000, was sentenced to eight months in a juvenile detention facility. As more young people cause more disruption, there is increasing pressure for more severe penalties.

Throughout the 1990s, many hackers over 18 received jail sentences, including several members of the Legion of Doom and Masters of Deception and a 19-year-old who hacked the White House Web site. On the other hand, a 21-year-old Argentine man who hacked into Harvard University and the Pentagon in 1995 got three years' probation. Prosecutors said they believed he did not do anything "improper" with the military files he read. He got a job doing security work and teaching about computer security.

In 1999, David Smith pleaded guilty to releasing the Melissa virus and doing more than $80 million in damage, offenses that carry a 5–10 year jail sentence.*

There are several reasons why different hackers get different sentences for what seem to be very similar offenses. Over time, attitudes change about the best way to respond to hacking. The amount of damage done is increasing. Hackers and prosecutors often agree to one charge although they know the hacker has committed other offenses. Prosecutors make judgments about how dangerous a particular hacker is. State and federal laws differ. Sometimes, people—the public, victims, and prosecutors—just get fed up and decide to "crack down" on troublemakers.

DISCOURAGING AND PUNISHING YOUTHFUL HACKING

The actions of young hackers raise difficult ethical, social, and legal issues. Most of their exploits are more like pranks, trespass, and vandalism. They usually do not include financial gain for the hacker (though, in Section 6.3.4, in the context of copyright infringement, we observed that lack of financial gain is often not significant in determining whether actions are wrong). For some, the goal is adventure; some hack for thrills, respect in the hacking community, and bragging rights. But some do extensive damage by accident, or out of sheer immature irresponsibility. And some are malicious and intentionally destructive. Some steal. A challenging issue is how to deal with young people who have not yet developed a mature sense of responsibility. How can we distinguish between those who are malicious and likely to commit further crimes and those who are likely to become honest and productive professionals? What penalties are appropriate?

One of the purposes of criminal penalties is to discourage people from committing crimes. Some people advocate heavy penalties for minor hacking to "send a signal" to others who might be thinking of trying something similar. There is a temptation to do this with hacking because of the costs to the victims and because hackers can do an extreme amount of damage, including threatening people's safety, even if they do not intend to do so. On the other hand, justice requires that punishments be in proportion to the specific case of the specific person being punished, not increased dramatically because of the potential of what someone else might do.

---

*Some estimates of damage were substantially higher. This figure is the minimum for the maximum penalty in the law.

Economists David Friedman and William Sjostrom explain how overly strong punishments can encourage people to commit more serious crimes.[26] Suppose, they say, the most severe punishment in the legal system is imposed for the crime of murder. If we try to discourage another serious crime, such as armed robbery, by imposing the same punishment, then robbers will be more likely to kill victims so that they could not be identified; the murder is "free" because its penalty is no worse than for the crime of robbery. Their argument suggests that if minor hacking offenses are severely punished, we may find hackers doing worse damage because the cost to them if caught will be the same.

Many hackers are the modern analogue of other generations of young people who snooped where they did not belong or carried out clever pranks, sometimes breaking a law. In his book *The Hacker Crackdown*, Bruce Sterling describes the phone phreakers of 1878. The new American Bell Telephone company hired teenage boys as operators. They disconnected calls and crossed lines on the switchboard, connecting people to strangers. The boys were also, like many teenage hackers, rude.[27] The phone company replaced teenage boys with women operators.

We want young hackers to mature, to learn the risks of their actions, and to use their skills in better ways. Most of them do grow up and go on to successful, productive careers. We do not want to turn them into resentful, hardened criminals or wreck their chances of getting a good job by putting them in jail. This does not mean that young hackers should not be punished if they trespass or cause damage. Kids do not mature and become responsible without good direction, or if irresponsibility is rewarded. The point is that we should not overreact and overpunish. Some young hackers will become the great innovators of the next generation. Steve Wozniak created the Apple computer, co-founded Apple Computer Corporation, and, after Apple's success, donated large amounts of money to medical research and other valuable efforts. Before he was building Apples, Wozniak was building blue boxes, the devices that enabled people to make long-distance phone calls without paying for them.[28] Nobel prize winner Richard Feynman used "hacker" techniques when he was a young physicist working on the highly secret atomic bomb project at Los Alamos National Laboratory in the 1940s. He hacked safes (not computers) containing classified work on the bomb. He found or guessed the combinations and delighted in opening the safes at night and leaving messages for the authorized users informing them that security was not as good as they thought.[29]

Many hackers do very valuable work in the computer industry, some as computer-security experts. Sometimes a hacker who is caught is given a job by the company whose computers he invaded. Give a hacker a job instead of a jail sentence? Some computer professionals and law-enforcement officials are very critical of this practice of "rewarding" hackers with security jobs. We do not reduce hacking by encouraging young people to think breaking into a computer system is an acceptable alternative to sending a resume. But, in some cases, the job, and the responsibility and respect that go with it, and the threat of punishment for future offenses, are enough to turn the hacker's energy and skills toward productive uses. Decisions about penalties must depend on the character of the particular offender. With any criminal law, there is a trade-off between having fixed penalties (for fairness, to avoid favoritism) and flexibility (to consider the particular circumstances). With young people, flexibility is probably more important. Penalties can focus on using the hacker's computer skills in a productive way, for example, tutoring school children in the use of computers, and on paying victims for damage done (if possible). Deciding on what is appropriate for a particular person is delicate, one of the difficulties prosecutors and judges face in this new area of juvenile crime.

How can we dissuade young teens from breaking into computers, launching viruses, and shutting down Web sites? We need a combination of appropriate penalties, education about ethics and risks, and parental responsibility. Parents of many young hackers had no idea what their children were doing. Just as parents have the responsibility of teaching their children to avoid unsafe behavior on the Web, as we discussed in Chapter 5, they have some responsibility for preventing their children from engaging in malicious, destructive hacking.

7.2.6 SECURITY

The extent of hacking is as much a comment on the security of computers, telecommunication systems, and the Web as it is on the skills and ethics of the hackers. Hacking is a problem, but so is poor security. Vulnerability of vital computer and communications systems is a critical issue. It exposes us to the destructiveness of teenagers, criminals, hostile foreign governments, and terrorists. How weak is the security of government and business computer networks and the Internet as a whole? Why is security weak? How can it be improved without sacrificing convenient, efficient service and without sacrificing privacy and civil liberties?

We saw, in Chapter 4, that there is wide variation in how careful and responsible different companies and organizations are about reducing the risk of computer failures and preparing for them when they occur. The same is true about security. Some agencies and businesses have up-to-date, high quality security. However, the number and variety of hacker break-ins—and the fact that many are the work of teenagers—suggests that security of many critical business and government computer systems is weaker than it should be. Direct studies of security in government systems lead to the same conclusion, year after year. The Defense Information Systems Agency estimated that there were 500,000 hacker attacks on Defense Department networks in 1996, that 65% of them were successful, and that the Department detected fewer than 1%. Some security experts say that most of the computer systems targeted do not contain classified information, and the break-ins are not serious. They are the modern equivalent of a kid sneaking into a Pentagon cafeteria, according to one security analyst. These arguments have some merit; on the other hand, we should expect Pentagon security to be good enough to keep a kid out of its cafeteria. The fact that files accessed by hackers are not "classified" is not reassuring. Military officials point out that unclassified information such as payroll and personnel records can be used destructively by an enemy. Few files in business computers are "classified," but hacker attacks are damaging and expensive nonetheless.

In 1999, the GAO reported that computer security at the National Aeronautics and Space Administration (NASA) was so weak that hackers could easily disrupt such crucial functions as the tracking of spacecraft. The GAO reported, in 2000, that the Environmental Protection Agency (EPA) computers were "riddled with security weaknesses." Hackers had access to sensitive and confidential information and were able to modify files, use the EPA's system to launch hacking attacks on other agencies, and set up their own chat room on the EPA system. A judge found hackers could easily hack into and steal from the government's Indian Trust fund which manages hundreds of millions of dollars of income from land owned by American Indians. A government study in 2001 found that 155 federal computer systems had been taken over by hackers the previous year.[30] Surveys regularly report high rates of hacker intrusions on the computers of large businesses.

WHY IS SECURITY WEAK?

It's no use locking the barn door after the horse is gone.

A variety of factors contribute to security problems. They come from the history of the development of the Internet and the Web, from human nature, from the inherent complexity of computer systems (especially the software and communications systems that run the Web), from economic and business factors, and from other sources. Failures of security have many of the same causes as other computer failures discussed in Chapter 4.

In its early years, the Internet was used primarily as a communications medium for researchers. Open access, ease of use, and ease of sharing information were desirable qualities. It was not designed for security against malicious intruders or teenage explorers. Many early systems did not have passwords; few early systems were connected to telephone networks, so protection against intruders was not an issue. Security depended primarily on trust. The World Wide Web was developed as a communications tool for physics researchers. Again, security was not a primary concern.

Now that so much personal and sensitive information is stored on computers and so many critical systems depend on computer networks, the potential cost of intrusions is much greater than it was in the early days of computing. Security techniques and practices have improved dramatically in the past few decades, but there are still gaping holes. Attitudes about security in many businesses, organizations, and government agencies have not caught up with the risk. New technologies and applications are introduced with new vulnerabilities. In the rush to get products online, to develop the potential of the Web, and to use the newest gadgets, security issues are repeatedly ignored until systems are vandalized, robbed, or shut down. Security flaws were found in "shopping cart" software used by thousands of small businesses on the Web. Wireless networks are often insufficiently protected: A security consultant parked outside major Silicon Valley computer companies and followed internal network transmissions, including e-mail and file transfers, on his laptop. He reported that hundreds of companies were vulnerable to such eavesdropping, including a company that sells software to make wireless networks secure.[31]

Many computer viruses, worms, and intrusions use well-known security flaws that have not been fixed on the victims' systems. Commenting on a worm program in 2001, a security expert said "It's astonishingly easy to avoid," but many system managers had not taken the appropriate steps. Security analysts warned of the potential for denial-of-service attacks several years before the attacks against major Web sites in 2000. Even where security professionals develop defenses, many system administrators do not use them. Known corrections for known loopholes are not implemented, out of carelessness, lack of knowledge (of the problem, the risks, or the solution), or lack of management support. Computer system administrators vary quite a bit in their knowledge of the systems they use and administer. Particularly in small businesses and organizations, many do not have adequate security training. They often have other responsibilities besides administering the system, leaving insufficient time to do a good job. Forrester Research found that almost half of the Fortune 1000 companies spent less than $1 million on network security in 1998, a small amount for such large firms. In another Forrester study in 2000, more than half the companies surveyed said lack of money prevented them from implementing necessary security.[32] The companies do not actually lack the money, of course; they had other spending priorities.

It seems to be a common human trait not to take sufficient security precautions until after a serious problem has occurred. How many people do not back up their hard disks before they lose files? How many do not lose weight until after a heart attack? The reminder at the beginning of this section, about the futility of locking the barn door after the horse is gone, predates even cars, not just computers. These observations do not excuse sloppy security; instead, they remind us that we must focus our attention on awareness of the extent of the problem and acceptance of responsibility.

IMPROVING SECURITY

There are many parallels between security issues and the safety issues discussed in Chapter 4. We saw there that principles and techniques for developing safe systems exist and that responsible software designers must learn to use them. The same is true for designing systems to be secure from intruders; systems can be designed with security as a major goal. System administrators must stay up-to-date about new risks and new security measures. For both safety and security, this is often not an easy task, but it is an essential goal and a professional responsibility.

Recognizing the risk of being open to the world, many network administrators installed "firewalls"—software or separate computers that monitor incoming communications (e-mail, files, requests for services, etc.) and filter out those that are from untrusted sites or fit a profile of suspicious activity. Intrusion-detection systems monitor computer systems for activity that suggests unauthorized or inappropriate activity. Special software can monitor information leaving a protected network to check for leaks. Good system managers do not rely on users to select good passwords; they run programs that make sure that user passwords meet security specifications. Encryption and antivirus software can be used to protect a system. To protect against allowing one's system to be used by hackers to launch attacks on others, managers can install software to monitor the volume of outgoing messages (e.g., to detect denial-of-service attacks) and make it more difficult to forge return addresses on e-mail.

Some large online retailers, like Amazon.com for example, are very careful about security, but still might be victimized. The complexity of computer systems means that there will be unexpected flaws. We cannot expect perfection, but we should expect professionalism. Just as system managers must plan for computer bugs and failures, they must plan for hacking by having appropriate backups, training, emergency plans, reporting systems, and so on.

The market responded to increased security threats with the development of many security firms and consultants offering a variety of software products and services. Digital signatures, biometrics (which we discuss in Section 7.5.2), and other new tools for identification could replace or augment passwords and help reduce access by unauthorized people. Insurance companies began offering insurance for hacker attacks. Some home insurance companies give discounts for anti-theft devices and fire extinguishers in a home; similarly some companies providing hacker insurance require that their customers use high-quality computer-security technology.

DOES HACKING IMPROVE SECURITY?

Some security companies hire hackers to attack and find flaws in systems they are developing. Some issue open challenges to hackers in general, for example at hacker conferences like DefCon. Some pay consulting fees to teams of students and faculty at universities to find security weaknesses in their products. The key distinction between this kind of hacking and most of what we have been discussing is that this is done with permission.

Many hackers who hack without permission argue that they too are performing a service by exposing security weaknesses; they are doing us a favor. Most computer professionals disagree. But the hacker argument has a bit of truth to it that is worth considering.

Security people emphasize that they know many systems have security flaws; hackers are not telling them anything new by breaking in. This was true at the time of the Internet Worm. The commission at Cornell University that investigated the worm incident commented that "It is no act of genius or heroism to exploit such [known] weaknesses."[33] On the other hand, the Internet Worm undoubtedly increased awareness of the vulnerability of the Internet and encouraged steps to reduce it.

Critics of hackers argue that if a hacker discovers a security weakness in a system, he or she should inform the system manager of the flaw, not exploit it. Unfortunately, many system operators do not close loopholes, even well-publicized ones, until there is a break-in. Chris Goggins, a well-known hacker and security consultant, said he repeatedly warned America Online of a flaw that allowed hackers to create free accounts, disconnect real subscribers, and access private files. The problems were not solved until a group of hackers exploited the flaws and caused significant problems. Many hackers send e-mail to companies to tell them of security weaknesses, but are ignored. Some security professionals say that the biggest part of their job is convincing people to take the danger of break-ins seriously.[34]

Exposing security flaws is not a legitimate justification for most hacking, but, as a side effect, hacking does often prompt security improvements that should have been made earlier. Some critics of the claim that hackers help improve security argue that the extra security would not be needed if hackers did not hack in the first place. This argument is valid for some systems, but not for most large business and government systems. Small, relatively closed communities can rely on trust and get by with loose security; a few pranksters or malicious intruders would increase security costs significantly. But the general public includes thieves, criminal organizations, terrorists, disgruntled employees, and others with hostile motives. Even if all hackers whose intent is to promote security and all teenagers were to quit hacking, administrators of most computer systems would still have a responsibility to ensure a high level of security.

HOW MUCH SECURITY?

Hackers argue that, if the owners of a computer system want to keep outsiders out, it is their responsibility to provide better security. When the computer system contains valuable or sensitive data, or if many people depend on its smooth operation, the system administrators have a professional and ethical obligation, and in many cases a legal obligation, to take reasonable security precautions to protect the system. But was the 20-year-old man who released the "Anna Kournikova" virus in 2001, bogging down e-mail service around the world, correct when he claimed "after all, it's their own fault they got infected"?[35]

There are many levels of computer security, just as there are many levels of home security—from leaving the doors unlocked, to using deadbolt locks, to installing a sophisticated alarm system. Some computer-security measures reduce convenience of use and ease of access, just as increased security at homes or airports does. The trade-offs of risks and convenience for legitimate users must always be considered. The appropriate level depends on many factors, including the likelihood of an intrusion, which, sometimes, is increased by the hackers themselves.

Does weak security justify intrusion? The hacker claim is analogous to saying that if someone can pick the lock on a house—or a computer system—he or she has the right to enter. The fact that one can commit a crime does not justify the crime.

SECURITY THROUGH SECRECY?

One approach to discouraging hacking is to reduce the availability of hacking tools and information. This can be done by imposing criminal penalties for writing or possession of sniffer programs, password-cracking software, hacking tutorials and scripts, and so on. It can also be attempted by informal individual and professional decisions to restrict distribution of security information. Although the latter can sometimes be a responsible approach, both methods have flaws.

AT&T used to rely on secrecy, or obscurity, to prevent people from making long-distance calls without paying for them. The exact frequencies of the tones that made the connections were buried in technical manuals and journals. Phone phreaks found them.[36] Experience suggests that secrecy is not a good security tool.

CERT's policy of not announcing security flaws to the public as soon as they are discovered reflects a practical and ethical dilemma: How can people responsibly inform potential victims of vulnerabilities without informing hackers who would exploit them? Distribution of security tools raises a similar dilemma. A major controversy about this problem erupted over a program called SATAN, for Security Administrator Tool for Analyzing Networks. Computer security experts Dan Farmer and Wietse Venema wrote SATAN in the early 1990s. It examined computer networks and reported on potential security problems. The authors released the program on the Internet in 1995. Farmer was the target of furious criticism from security professionals who expected a wave of hacking attacks. A CERT advisory explained the problem: "SATAN was designed as a security tool for system and network administrators. However, given its wide distribution, ease of use, and ability to scan remote networks, SATAN is also likely to be used to locate vulnerable hosts for malicious reasons."[37] The security holes SATAN searched for were known, so the systems most threatened by the release were those whose administrators had not corrected them. The publicity and controversy about SATAN may have motivated such administrators to do so. However, SATAN could be modified easily to search networks for new loopholes that hackers discovered in the future. There is a value to discretion, of course, but the authors' explanation of their action makes a sound point:

> Why wasn't there a limited distribution, to only the "white hats"? History has shown that attempts to limit distribution of most security information and tools has only made things worse. The "undesirable" elements of the computer world will obtain them no matter what you do, and people that have legitimate needs for the information are denied.[38]

As it turned out, the release of SATAN did not cause significant problems; it did focus attention on network security, and it began a serious discussion of the dilemma of how to treat security information. The problem is intrinsic; there is no perfect solution. Many researchers who discover security loopholes publish their findings after informing the companies responsible for the software so that they can prepare patches (corrections). Such publication encourages improvement and informs the public.

CRIMINALIZE VIRUS WRITING AND HACKER TOOLS?

Intentionally or recklessly initiating execution of computer virus software on other people's computers is destructive, wrong, illegal, and punishable by heavy penalties. Hacking scripts and computer code for thousands of computer viruses can be found on the Internet. Intentionally or recklessly making such programs available in a context that encourages their destructive use is irresponsible. Some law enforcement personnel, members of Congress, and security professionals proposed making it a crime to write or post computer viruses and other hacking software. We saw in Chapter 5 that writing about how to make illegal or destructive devices, such as bombs, is not illegal. On the other hand, as a security professional commented "With a computer virus, the words are the bomb."[39] A federal court ruled that software is a form of speech (see Section 3.4.1), so a law against hacking or virus software might conflict with the First Amendment. Some kinds of speech, such as inciting a riot, are not protected by the First Amendment. Would the Supreme Court consider virus code in the same category?

A law against writing viruses and hacking software could make security work and research more difficult. In 1998, security researchers at the University of California at Berkeley discovered a flaw in cellular phone technology that unscrupulous hackers could exploit. The researchers planned to demonstrate the software they developed to expose the flaw, but they were warned by their attorney that mere possession of the software might be a federal crime. Security personnel and researchers must be able to possess security and hacker software to effectively do their job. Legal restrictions on software that might be useful to hackers have problems similar to those we discussed in Chapters 3, 5, and 6 about restricting or banning strong encryption, anonymity software, and technologies to circumvent copyright protections.

7.3 Online Scams

Con artists and crooks of many sorts have found ample opportunity on the Web to cheat unsuspecting people. Some scams are almost unchanged from their pre-Web forms: pyramid schemes, chain letters, sales of counterfeit luxury goods, phony business investment opportunities, and so forth. Each generation of people, whatever level of technology it uses, needs to be reminded that, if an investment or bargain looks too good to be true, it probably is. Other scams on the Web are new, or evolved to take advantage of characteristics of the Web, and have a bigger impact than individual pre-Web crimes. In a particularly offensive example, people set up Web sites after the terrorist attacks in 2001 to fraudulently collect credit card numbers from people who thought they were contributing to the Red Cross or funds for World Trade Center victims.

We examine two areas of online crime, auction fraud and stock fraud, to see how they work and what solutions have emerged. The point is not the particular details, but the patterns. Fraud often invades new markets, then levels off or declines as people learn the risks, businesses and individuals respond with new protection mechanisms, and law-enforcement agencies combine new skills and existing law to catch and convict the crooks and discourage their activity.

7.3.1 AUCTIONS

Auction sites on the Web are extremely popular. Sellers list anything they want to sell, from collector baseball cards to clothing to art. Buyers bid, and the auction site gets a percentage. Auction sites illustrate the basic benefits of the Web: convenient compilation of a large amount of information and a way for strangers all over the world to communicate and make trades. EBay, founded in 1995, is the largest and best-known auction site. Approximately $400 million in goods was sold on eBay in 2000. In one month in 2001, 24 million people visited the site.

PROBLEMS

Quickly, problems arose. Some sellers do not send the items people paid for, or they send inferior goods that do not meet the online description. Dishonest sellers engage in *shill bidding*, that is, bidding on one's own goods to drive up the price. Some products offered for sale were illegal or were sold in illegal ways, for example prescription drugs sold without a prescription and unauthorized copies of copyrighted material such as music. Some products, though legal, are dangerous, for example drugs that can be misused. In 1999, the Federal Trade Commission (FTC) received about 10,000 complaints about fraud in online auctions. Initially, eBay had an "anything goes" attitude about its site; the company merely served to put sellers and buyers together. The company argued that it was analogous to a common carrier or to a newspaper that publishes classified ads and that it was not responsible for fraud or illegal sales.

SOLUTIONS

In the offline world, consumers know that it might be safer to buy from an established store like Macy's or Home Depot than from someone at a swap meet. Online auctions, where one interacts with invisible strangers all over the world, became, like some swap meets, places to find both bargains and rip-offs. Thus one of the first solutions was for customers to learn to be cautious. Later, online auction companies made improvements. Recognizing that their success, like e-commerce in general, depends on customer confidence and a good reputation, eBay and other auction sites adopted several practices and policies to address the problems and complaints. Before sending a check or a product, users can consider the reputation of the seller or buyer by reviewing comments posted by other users of the site. EBay insures items under $200. Escrow services, where a trusted third party holds the payment until the buyer receives and approves the product, are available for more expensive items. EBay set up a fraud unit with a staff of 100 people and a system whereby intellectual property owners can alert the company if their property is being sold illegally. The user agreement prohibits shill bidding and the offering of illegal items for sale. The rules prohibit certain other items, such as alcohol, firearms, fireworks, animals, stocks, and prescription drugs. Users who break the rules are suspended.

EBay requires a credit-card number from sellers. This discourages fraud by making identifying and tracing a seller easier in case of complaints. Requiring a credit-card number from bidders as well would help reduce various scams, such as shill bidding by the same person under different names. Neither eBay's nor Yahoo's auction site do so, because it is not popular with customers. Some users implicitly weigh their desire for privacy against fraud reduction; some users do not have credit cards.

The solutions, of course, are not perfect. A group of dishonest sellers can write glowing recommendations for each other. Fake items still appear. Some users complained that eBay requires too much proof before removing a suspect item. However, rival sellers could be making false accusations, so swifter action by auction houses to remove items might not always be fair. Some users who believed eBay did not respond to complaints quickly enough found their own solution: They set up an online discussion group to voice complaints—a common, spontaneous solution that uses the power of the Web.

Fraud is illegal whether on or off the Web. In 2000, two men were indicted for selling thousands of dollars of computers but never sending the computers. Cheated buyers tracked them down. In a highly publicized case, three men were charged with shill bidding to raise prices in hundreds of art auctions, including one for a painting on which one of them forged the initials of a well-known painter. Two pleaded guilty. One of the men, a lawyer, was disbarred.[40] In 2002, an art dealer and accomplices were arrested for shill bidding on hundreds of pieces of Lalique art glass.

A FEW MORE ISSUES

Companies called aggregators use automated software "bots" or "crawlers" to scan large auction sites, cull lists of products offered, and relist them on their own Web sites for comparison shopping. EBay blocked such software (unless the aggregator had a licensing agreement with eBay) and sued Bidder's Edge for trespass, unfair business practices, and impairing the performance of eBay's site. On the other side, the Justice Department's antitrust division investigated to decide whether eBay's blocking of the bots was an illegal anti-competitive action. In 2000, a judge ruled that, because eBay's computers are eBay's property, it could deny access to Bidder's Edge; he issued an injunction ordering Bidder's Edge to stop using its automated software on eBay's site. Recall that similar issues arose when AOL first tried to block spam (see Section 5.4.2); AOL got injunctions to stop the spammers on similar grounds.

This case raises intriguing legal and social/ethical issues. Does a Web site have a right to exclude certain visitors, including software visitors? How should the concept of trespass apply to Web sites?

7.3.2 STOCK FRAUD

Old forms of stock fraud included posing as investment experts and luring victims to invest in worthless companies with promises of quick and easy big profits. This still happens, and now on the Net. More interesting perhaps are new forms of stock fraud developed to take advantage of specific characteristics of cyberspace. The Web reaches a huge audience virtually immediately. It is ideal for spreading rumors. One can buy a stock, make glowing recommendations about it in chat rooms and on Web sites, then sell when the price briefly and artificially rises. The buying and selling can be timed perfectly with the online stock trading now available to ordinary investors on the Web. We describe a few cases with variations on this theme.

In the first criminal case involving Internet stock fraud, a company gave a man 250,000 shares of its stock for promoting the company in his online stock newsletter. He sold while telling his subscribers to buy. He and officials of the company received prison terms in 1997.

An employee of PairGain Technologies created a fake Web page to look like the site of the Bloomberg financial news service with a positive but false announcement about

PairGain. He also posted a message about the "news" with a link to the fake site. People copied and e-mailed the link, spreading the false information quickly and widely, and causing PairGain stock to rise more than 30%. In a similar case, a former employee of an online news-release service forged an announcement with bad news about Emulex and inserted it into the service's system for distribution. Emulex stock dropped from $110 to $45 in an hour. Both stocks quickly returned to normal prices after the hoaxes were discovered, but investors who bought or sold at the wrong time lost money. Another similarity between the two cases is that the men responsible were caught within a week. They were traced with tools similar to those used to trace people who release viruses and other malicious programs. The 23-year-old who committed the Emulex fraud was sentenced to 44 months in prison.

A law school student created a stock-advice service on the Web, offered free trial subscriptions, and signed up 9000 people. The Securities and Exchange Commission (SEC) claimed he and several fellow law students bought stocks, then promoted them on their service. The SEC said they also sent hundreds of messages, under different names, to Yahoo! and other stock message boards. They made more than $345,000 in profits as the stocks rose on the false rumors. They were caught.

Some 15-year-olds hack, and some commit stock fraud. The first minor charged with securities fraud made more than $270,000 in profit by flooding the Net with hundreds of messages, under different names, touting stocks he had bought.[41]

The SEC used to take months to investigate suspected securities fraud. In response to fraud on the Web, it formed an Office of Internet Enforcement and now responds at the speed of the Web culture. It uses specialized search engines to scan Web sites and chat rooms for suspicious cases. The SEC reported in 2001 that the incidence of the type of frauds we described was declining already, as people saw how easily they could be traced. More sophisticated frauds might replace them.

7.4 Fraud, Embezzlement, Sabotage, Information Theft, and Forgery

7.4.1 CREDIT CARDS, IDENTITY THEFT, CELL PHONES, AND MORE

Credit cards, automated teller machines (ATMs), telephone calling cards, and cell phones use computer technology to give us convenience, but expose us (and the companies that provide them) to risks we did not take before. Most people would not casually carry around hundreds or thousands of dollars in cash, but a credit card, ATM card, or calling card gives the holder access to large sums. We describe some examples, then consider some defenses.

CREDIT-CARD FRAUD

Losses from credit-card fraud are estimated to be several billion dollars each year; some security and law-enforcement officials believe it is higher than what is reported by the industry. There are many varieties of credit-card fraud. Account numbers are stolen by store clerks and by thieves who search the trash near stores for receipts—or just call people and ask for them, with some pretext (e.g., telling the person he or she won a prize but the card number is needed). Cards are stolen by large, well-organized theft rings and by individual purse-snatchers. Several dozen people were convicted in one case where Northwest Airlines employees stole new cards from the mail transported on Northwest's airplanes. The employees used some of the cards themselves and sold others. An estimated $7.5 million was charged on the stolen cards.[42] When cards are stolen from people directly, the card owner usually closes the account quickly, so thieves use counterfeit cards—they reprogram the magnetic strip of stolen cards with a different account number.

On the Web, credit-card numbers can be stolen in transmission, if secure servers are not used, and from stored files. We charge Web purchases without providing a signature or a look at our face, so it is relatively easy for thieves to make purchases with stolen numbers. An e-commerce security service provider calls credit-card fraud on the Web "electronic shoplifting."[43] Most fraudulent charges are made with stolen cards or account numbers, but, in some cases, a customer charges expensive items on his or her own card, then claims not to have ordered or received the goods.

Credit-card issuers make trade-offs between security and customer convenience. Most customers do not want to take the time to provide other identification when they use a credit card, or to wait while merchants check it. Customers may be offended by requests for ID. The bias toward convenience and not giving offense means that simple security measures are often ignored. Most merchants do not check signatures or photos on credit cards. A college instructor signed "Elmer Fudd" on a credit-card receipt in a retail store; the clerk did not notice. In an experiment, a white man used a credit card with a picture of a black man; no one questioned him. Losses from most credit-card fraud in stores are absorbed by the credit-card issuers, not the merchant. Thus the merchant does not have much incentive to check the cards.

The total amount of credit card sales in the U.S. was roughly $1,470 billion in 2000. Although the dollar amount of credit card fraud is high, industry sources report the fraud rate is 0.07%–0.14%. The rate is much higher on the Web, where approximately 1.25% of retail credit-card charges are disputed by the customer and charged to the merchant. (Merchants usually have to pay disputed charges when they do not have a customer signature.) Merchants and credit card companies are willing to absorb some fraud losses as part of doing business. Such trade-offs are not new. Retail stores keep small, very expensive items in locked cabinets, but most goods are easily accessible to customers for convenience and efficiency; openness encourages sales. Retail stores have always accepted some amount of losses from shoplifting rather than offend and inconvenience customers by keeping everything locked up or by searching customers when they leave the store. When a company perceives the losses as being too high, it improves security.

IDENTITY THEFT

In our modern world, where most of us live in large communities, cash checks at stores where we are not personally known, and borrow money from strangers, our identity has become a series of numbers (Social Security number, driver's license number, account numbers) and computer files (credit history, driving record). *Identity theft*, where a criminal assumes the identity of the victim and runs up large credit-card charges or cashes bad checks, is a growing problem. It might cost the victim little in direct monetary losses, but much in anguish, disruption of his or her life, and legal fees. The victim might lose a good credit rating, be prevented from borrowing money or cashing checks, lose a job, be unable to rent an apartment, and be sued by creditors to whom the criminal owes money.

In one case, a man applied for numerous credit cards in the names of real people who had good credit records; the people whose names were used did not know the accounts existed. The man lived well for two years, took several trips to Europe, and fraudulently charged more than $500,000 before being caught and sent to prison. A part-time English teacher at a California junior college used the Social Security numbers of some of her students, provided on her class lists, to open fraudulent credit-card accounts. The big credit bureaus handle hundreds of cases a day where victims complain that fraudulent accounts have been opened in their names.[44]

In Chapter 2, we saw that a Social Security number is the key to numerous records containing personal information. It is the key to the information the criminal needs to impersonate the victim. The access it gives to credit records alone is enormously helpful to the criminal for choosing a victim, getting the victim's credit-card numbers, and learning enough personal details to successfully impersonate the victim.

One of the very frustrating aspects of identity theft was that victims got little help from credit bureaus, police, motor-vehicle departments, and the Social Security Administration. The motor-vehicle departments and Social Security Administration are reluctant to issue a new driver's license number or SSN to a victim, because their record systems are designed for a person to have the same number all his or her life. Their attitude seemed to be that the fact that another person was using the number to defraud merchants and credit companies was not their problem. In 1998, Congress made it a federal crime to knowingly use another person's identification with the intent to commit a felony,[45] and government agencies began providing more assistance to victims.

Reducing the incidence of fraud by identity theft—and its monetary and personal costs—requires a combination of appropriate response from government agencies whose documents are used for identification, increased security for identification numbers and personal records, better methods for verifying the identity of a person using or requesting changes in an account, and better methods for distinguishing the victim from the criminal in future transactions.

ATM FRAUD

A few cases illustrate how automated teller machine (ATM) frauds work.

The first is an "insider" case. A man who worked for a company that installed ATM machines had access to the machines, using the installer's password. He wrote software to capture the account numbers and PINs (personal identification numbers) used by customers, then made fake cards, encoded to mimic the real ones. He and a small group of friends planned to withdraw cash from the accounts on a holiday weekend, when they would have time to raid many accounts and get away. A tip from a friend who had been told of the plan led to a raid where 6000 counterfeit cards were found.[46]

Another group of thieves, lacking insider access to a real ATM system for the capture of account numbers, set up their own machine. They installed an ATM in a shopping mall in Connecticut. Initially, to gain customer confidence, the machine gave out cash. Later, after reading each customer's card and requesting the customer's PIN, it displayed a message saying that the transaction could not be processed. After about two weeks, the machine was removed. It had served its purpose, which was to read the account numbers magnetically recorded on the cards and store the PIN typed by the customer. It was not connected to any banking system. The people who installed the machine created counterfeit cards and used them at real ATMs to steal approximately $107,000 from their victims. (They were caught and convicted.)[47]

There were simpler ways for thieves to get account numbers and PINs. They used binoculars, telescopes, and video cameras to spy on customers at ATMs. Then they collected discarded receipts, which contained account numbers. The locations of the ATMs, often in public outdoor places, made the spying easy.

TELECOMMUNICATIONS FRAUD

There are several varieties of telecommunications fraud. Industry and government estimates of the value of these activities range from $1 billion to $9 billion. (As with software-piracy estimates, the actual loss to the companies is probably somewhat lower; people use more of free or low-priced stolen services than they would if they had to pay full price.)

Just as criminals spied on customers at ATMs to get their PINs, they also spy on people entering calling-card numbers and PINs at public telephones. They sell the calling-card codes outright or set up long-distance phone centers in storefronts.

Cellular phones transmit their serial number and billing information at the beginning of each call. A popular criminal technique for avoiding charges is *cloning*, that is, reprogramming the phone to transmit another customer's number. Cell-phone fraud was estimated to cost $400 million per year. To counter cell-phone cloning, a technique was developed to store each phone's unique electronic "signature" along with its serial number. The system checks that they match when a call is made. Other methods use sophisticated mathematical techniques that can identify a phone without having the phone send its serial number.

DEFENDING AGAINST FRAUD

Solutions for credit-card, ATM, and phone fraud illustrate the continual leapfrogging of increased sophistication of security techniques and increased sophistication of the techniques used by criminals. They also illustrate the use of technology itself to solve problems created by technology.

To thwart thieves who spy on customers at ATMs to get their PINs, banks redesigned ATMs so that the keyboard is not easily visible by anyone other than the person using it. One simple protection against large losses from stolen or counterfeit cards is the cash withdrawal limit at most ATMs. To get a large amount of money quickly, a thief must raid many accounts. ATM software can include checks for unusually high activity at a particular machine, indicating possible use of counterfeit cards. (The people who installed the phony ATM in Connecticut were caught because an alert bank employee noticed a large number of transactions at a location where the thieves used their counterfeit cards.)[48] Various measures reduced robberies at ATMs: better lighting, surveillance cameras, and emergency buttons connected to the 911 system, for example. ATM-industry organizations developed security policies, standards, and guidelines for member financial institutions. Many banks stopped printing the complete account number on receipts.

The use of stolen credit cards to make large purchases was fairly safe for thieves when credit cards were new. To provide merchants with a way to check on whether a particular card was stolen, credit-card companies printed books of stolen card numbers and delivered updated copies to merchants regularly. The books were thick, with small type. Looking up the card number for each large purchase was a time-consuming inconvenience, and, because the books were never quite up-to-date, there was still ample opportunity for thieves to run up large charges. Advances in telecommunications and automation eliminated the books. Now merchants (or Web software) check card numbers immediately by connecting to credit-card company computers. The thief's window of time to use the card has shrunk to the time it takes the owner to report it stolen.

Procedural changes helped protect against theft of new cards from the mail, as in the case involving Northwest Airlines employees. To verify that the card has been received by the legitimate owner, credit card issuers required the customer to call in and provide identifying information before a new card was activated. This procedure was only as good as the security of the identifying information. Several Social Security Administration employees provided the Social Security numbers and mothers' maiden names of thousands of people to a credit-card fraud ring so that they could activate stolen cards, according to federal prosecutors.[49] Now credit-card companies use caller ID to verify that the authorization call is made from the customer's home telephone. Holograms and customer photos made cards more difficult to counterfeit and stolen cards more difficult to use. Software for credit-card systems detects unusual spending activity. When this happens, a merchant can ask a customer for additional identification, or a card holder can be called to verify purchases.

With the growth of e-commerce and theft of credit-card numbers on the Web, protecting the card numbers, in addition to the physical cards, became important. To reduce fraudulent use of stolen numbers online, some credit-card companies began a program allowing consumers to use a password for extra security in online purchases. Several companies market systems that generate a unique credit-card number for each online transaction. The card issuer generates the numbers and bills all of one person's charges to one account, but an intercepted number is useless to any hacker who steals it.

PayPal and other companies that provide online payment services initially lost millions of dollars to fraud. Gradually, PayPal developed some clever solutions and sophisticated security expertise. For example, to reduce fraud by people setting up phony accounts with someone else's name, Paypal makes two small deposits in the person's checking account and requires the person to report the amounts correctly.[50]

7.4.2 SWINDLING AND SABOTAGING EMPLOYERS AND COMPETITORS

Embezzlement is "fraudulent appropriation of property by a person to whom it has been entrusted."[51] With the use of computers, trusted employees have stolen hundreds of thousands, in some cases millions, of dollars from their employers. In a few spectacular cases, losses were in the hundreds of millions. (Volkswagen is believed to have lost more than $200 million in a foreign-exchange fraud perpetrated by high-level employees.[52]) Some frauds require specialized knowledge or programming skills. Others do not; they can be committed by clerks and other employees taking advantage of poor security on the computer systems they use as part of their jobs.

The complexities of modern financial transactions increase the opportunities for embezzlement. The complexity and anonymity of computers add to the problem and help hide scams. The victims of some of the most costly scams are banks, brokerage houses, insurance companies, and other large financial institutions. Employees of insurance companies can set up phony insurance policies and make claims on them. Employees transfer large sums to Swiss bank accounts and then disappear. Employees create fake purchase orders for purchases from phony companies and cash the checks themselves. Employees also steal data from their employer's computer and sell it to competitors.

Employees who were fired, or angry at their employer for some other reason, sometimes sabotage the company computer systems. They may directly destroy files or plant *logic bombs*, software that destroys critical files, such as payroll and inventory records, after the employee leaves. An employee fired from an insurance company was convicted for destroying more than 160,000 records with a logic bomb. There have been cases where an employee secretly sabotaged a system in the hopes of earning extra money to fix it. In one odd case, an employee continued to sabotage a printing company's computer system, deleting or garbling files, jamming terminals, crashing the system, blanking screens, and generally creating havoc, over a six-month period—while he continued to work at the company unsuspected. The company lost customers, and some employees quit or were fired because of the stress. The owner said he believed the guilty employee (sentenced to five years in prison) just enjoyed making people miserable.[53]

The motivations for sabotage are not new. What is new with computer sabotage is the ease with which a great amount of damage can be done. The lack of violence or physical destruction might make the crime seem less serious both to its perpetrators and to jurors.

DEFENDING AGAINST DISHONEST EMPLOYEES

There are many practices, both technical and managerial, that can be used to reduce the likelihood of large frauds. For example, it is recommended that responsibilities of employees with access to sensitive computer systems be rotated, so suspicious activity can be noticed by someone. Each employee should have his or her own user ID and password, and, where possible, IDs should be coded to allow only the access and actions that employee needs to perform. An employee's password should be deleted immediately after he or she quits or is fired. No one person should have responsibility for enough parts of a system to build and hide elaborate scams. (For example, in an insurance company, establishing an insurance policy and authorizing payments on claims should not be done by the same employee.) We mentioned audit trails as a privacy protection; they also protect against fraud by providing a record of transactions and of the employee who authorized them. In one case, a brokerage firm turned off its audit-trail software to speed processing of orders; an employee took the opportunity to swindle the company out of an estimated $28 million.[54] In large, impersonal institutions, it is often foolish to trade security for convenience or increased efficiency.

Many people who embezzle from employers have no criminal history. Some have a gripe against the employer; some have financial problems; some just cannot resist the temptation. Careful screening and background checks on prospective employees can be helpful, although some laws make various kinds of screening more difficult (or completely illegal).

ATTACKS BY COMPETITORS

Businesses keep sensitive and valuable information on computers: plans for new products, product and market research, customer lists, pricing policies, and so on. This information is an appealing target for unethical competitors.

Industrial espionage (also called economic espionage) used to require the physical infiltration of the victim's business, theft of paper documents, physical copying of documents by hand or with a camera, or the paying off of an insider to provide critical information. Paying off an insider is still a useful technique; now the insider might be paid for passwords, and the spying can be accomplished from a remote location through a computer network. Large quantities of digital information can be copied quickly. There might be no clues to indicate that a theft took place; nothing is missing.

A few examples from one industry: British Airways agreed to pay a competing airline $4 million for hacking the smaller company's computers and stealing passenger lists. American Airlines complained that an ex-employee hired by Northwest copied American's proprietary fare-setting information and sent it to Northwest. An American Airlines employee guessed a password and accessed sensitive pricing and scheduling data of a rival airline.[55]

Voice-mail systems are a frequent target in industrial espionage; they seem to be quite vulnerable to break-ins. Customer names, business plans, and details of contract negotiations are among the prizes. Forging e-mail, pretending to be someone in the company and asking for sensitive information, is another tactic.

7.4.3 SWINDLING THE CUSTOMER

When Blaise Pascal (for whom the programming language Pascal was named) invented a calculating machine in the 1640s, he had trouble selling them. One reason was that people suspected that such machines could be rigged to give incorrect results. It is easy to modify a computer program to do so. How do you know, when your groceries are scanned at the supermarket checkout counter, that the prices charged are the same as the ones posted on the supermarket shelves? How do you know that your computer-generated credit-card bill is accurate? How do you know you are not being robbed?

Hertz Corporation allegedly programmed its computers to do two calculations of the cost of repairs to cars damaged by renters: the actual cost to the company and a higher cost charged to the customer.[56] On the other hand, a large drugstore chain delayed implementation of a new inventory system because the check-out software sometimes generated the wrong price. Some people trust the computer and assume that the computer-printed statements and bills are correct. Others are more skeptical; they are suspicious of anything that comes out of a machine. Both miss an important point: It is not the computer that one should trust or not trust; it is the company that is using it. Some businesses have high ethical standards and exercise care to avoid mistakes. Some businesses are complete scams, and others are unethical or sloppy. The reputation and character of the business are more important than the computer.

Computer-generated bills could be impressive and daunting to some people, but the cheating of customers is not a new phenomenon. A rigged program is the computer analogue of rigged gas station pumps and taxi meters. Low-tech cheaters of customers included the old-time butcher who put his thumb on the scale while weighing a customer's meat. Someone summed up this observation as "Computers don't steal—people do." It is worth remembering that the intent is not in the machine. However, computers can make cheating harder to identify and correct.

7.4.4 DIGITAL FORGERY

Seeing is believing may soon become an anachronism of the precomputer era.

—Sanford Sherizen[57]

THE PROBLEM

A photograph shows Marilyn Monroe arm in arm with Abraham Lincoln. Forrest Gump chats with John F. Kennedy in a movie. These impossible images were produced by digital manipulation of photographs and video. We know that Marilyn Monroe and Abraham

Lincoln lived a hundred years apart, that the movie *Forrest Gump* used computerized special effects. Where is the crime? The same technology that is used for entertainment is also used for fraud.

Desktop publishing systems, color printers and copiers, and image scanners enable crooks to make fakes with relative ease—fake checks, currency, passports, visas, stock and bond certificates, purchase orders, birth certificates, identification cards, and corporate stationery, to name a few examples. A group of counterfeiters made off with $750,000 from one counterfeit check. They produced it by scanning a real check from a corporation, changing the amount and payee, then printing it on a laser printer. Forgers and counterfeiters used to need specialized skills; computer software and hardware have dramatically reduced the requirements. The equipment has improved in quality while prices have tumbled. By 1995, about 10% of counterfeit U.S. currency was produced by desktop forgery (rather than by the old method of printing from engraved plates).[58]

Cybercitizens might argue that paper documents will become unimportant as they are replaced with digital cash, electronic transactions, and digital documents, but that replacement will be gradual, and forgery will continue to be a problem. Cyberspace will have its own new digital forgery problems. A company developed an animation system that manipulates prerecorded video images of a real person to produce a video in which the person is speaking whatever words the user of the system provides. Another system analyzes recordings of a person's voice and synthesizes speech with the voice, inflections, and tones of that person. Combined, these systems will likely have many uses, including entertainment and advertising, but they can clearly also be used to deceive.[59] Photographs and video are used as evidence in legal proceedings (e.g., crime-scene photos and surveillance-camera video). A trusted and reliable means of authentication will be essential for the justice system.

DEFENSES

Defenses against forgery of printed documents include the usual array of approaches: technical tricks that make copying more difficult, education (increased training of clerks who process documents that are likely targets), business practices to reduce risk, and changes in laws.

Anti-fraud techniques, such as microprinting and the use of paper with watermarks, have been employed in the past. The U.S. government redesigned its currency in the 1990s to include many anti-counterfeiting features. For example, currency contains a "security thread" that is not reproduced by a copier or scanner, but can be seen when a bright light shines through the bill. The paper used for checks, money orders, and identification documents can have embedded fibers or use special inks that glow under ultraviolet light. Some copiers contain a chip that recognizes currency and prevents the copier from making a copy.

An example of a procedural change to reduce check fraud is for a business to send its bank a list of the number and amount of all checks issued; the bank can then quickly verify incoming checks.

In the past, banks that accepted forged checks usually absorbed the loss. Changes in state laws now place some of the responsibility on the businesses whose checks are copied, thus providing more incentive for them to improve security of their checks.

FAKING PHOTOS

The ease with which digital images can be modified raises other intriguing ethical and social issues, not related to crime.

Should news organizations modify images? Is it acceptable if the purpose is artistic, or to enhance or improve the image without changing the semantic content? News organizations and individual publishers are working out their policies. The National Press Photographers Association has a policy that considers any alteration of a photo's editorial content to be a breach of ethical standards. But where is the line between editorial content and aesthetics? Some magazines treat their cover photos as advertisements for the magazine and are more likely to manipulate them than the photos inside. (*National Geographic* generated one of the first computer-era controversies about faked photos when it moved two pyramids closer together to fit them both on the cover.) Some magazine editors realize that a reputation for manipulating photos, like any form of deception, makes all of one's work suspect. The art director of *Texas Monthly* commented that "The altered photographs we had done were really hurting the integrity of the magazine's cover to the point that when we had a great photograph, nobody believed it." The editor of *Audubon*, also citing the credibility problem, announced in an editorial that *Audubon* would not print any manipulated photos.[60]

There are numerous examples of photographs that were faked before digital technology existed. The ethical issues are not new, but they now are faced by many more people because image manipulation has become so easy; it is no longer reserved to the specialist with a darkroom. The general public must become more aware of the possibility of fakery and learn to have a reasonable skepticism.

7.5 Crime Fighting Versus Privacy and Civil Liberties

In several earlier chapters, in the context of various computer technology issues, we discussed tensions between fighting crime, on the one hand, and privacy and civil liberties, on the other. We mention a few more such issues here.

7.5.1 SCANNING FOR SCAMS

Periodically, fraud investigators at the Federal Trade Commission (FTC) and the Securities and Exchange Commission (SEC) surf the Web looking for potentially illegal scams. They send warning letters and investigate further, as appropriate. In 2000, the SEC announced a plan to use automated surveillance software to crawl through chat rooms and Web sites looking for suspicious activity or phrases like "get rich quick;" the software would build a database of suspicious postings. Is there a difference between the two methods, between human and automated surveillance? Is the SEC plan consistent with the Privacy Act and the Fourth Amendment to the Constitution? Live agents manually visiting sites will undoubtedly miss some crimes. The surveillance software monitors constantly. Is having a government agent in every room too intrusive in a free society? AOL said it prohibits the use of similar software, to protect the privacy of its members. We saw that court decisions allowed AOL and eBay to ban spam and information-collecting software from their sites. Should they have the right to ban government surveillance software too? Should the government need a search warrant, which requires a specific reason for a search, before running its automated surveillance software on a site?

7.5.2 BIOMETRICS

There are many situations where it is important to identify a person accurately—for example, when someone is using a credit card in a store or online or when someone logs on to a computer system. Credit cards can be counterfeited; passwords can be guessed or stolen. Is there a "foolproof" way to identify someone?

Biometrics are biological characteristics that are unique to an individual. They include fingerprints, voice prints, the face, hand geometry, retina scans, and DNA. Biometric technology for identification applications is rapidly developing. In the past few years, DNA matching has freed numerous innocent people who had been mistakenly convicted of such serious crimes as rape and murder.

Some biometric applications provide convenience that could appeal to consumers. One device lets you open the door of your house by touching a scanner with your finger. No keys to lose, forget, or drop while carrying packages. The main applications, though, are security and fraud prevention. Some states use a face scanner and digital image matching to make sure a person does not apply for extra driver's licenses or welfare benefits (with different names). Some computer systems require a thumbprint match to log on to a computer, physically or over the Net, reducing access by hackers. To reduce the risks of terrorism, several airports use fingerprint identification systems to ensure that only employees enter restricted areas.

It appears that the use of biometrics will increase dramatically. But there are serious problems. First, practical problems: When a credit-card number is stolen, we can get a new account with a new number, but if a hacker gets a copy of the file with our digitized thumbprint or retina scan, we cannot get a new one. Identity theft might become easier to prevent, but much worse for a victim when it occurs. Given the weak security of the Web, it is likely that hackers will be able to steal files of biometrics as easily as they now steal files of credit cards. They will rig their machines to transmit a copy of the file rather than scanning their own finger or eye.

Another problem is that biometrics make it easier to build dossiers on people. Several biometrics may be used, but just one or a few will probably dominate, say thumbprints. Our activities of all sorts may become linked by the thumbprint. We saw problems generated by widespread use of Social Security numbers in Chapter 2. Biometrics would be used for many more applications than Social Security numbers, for example, all of our online purchases and Web surfing. Like the face-matching applications described in Section 2.2.3, increased use of biometrics can increase surveillance and tracking of our activities by government agencies. The potential for more loss of privacy is huge.

7.5.3 SEARCH AND SEIZURE OF COMPUTERS

Seizure of a computer presents new problems for both law enforcement and suspects because of the computer's multipurpose use. Investigators may suspect that a hard disk contains files of illegally obscene material, material that infringes copyright, stolen credit-card numbers, or evidence of other crimes. With an appropriate warrant, it is reasonable for such material to be copied or seized and removed from the suspect's premises. But the computer may also contain files belonging to many other people, business records, subscriber lists, and myriad other things that are not covered by the warrant. Their seizure by law enforcement can be a serious threat to freedom of speech and privacy. In the 1950s, when the state of Alabama tried to get the membership list of the NAACP, the Supreme Court ruled that it could not. The Court said "Privacy in group association may . . . be indispensable to preservation of freedom of association, particularly where a group espouses dissident beliefs."[61] Now, such membership lists and subscription lists are on the same computer that may be seized and searched for another reason. But, as one journalist commented, "It's not easy to seize part of a computer."[62]

In some cases, seizures of computers appeared to be intended to cause as much inconvenience as possible to the people whose property is taken, especially in cases where no charges were filed and equipment was not returned for a long time. The government can shut down a business without a trial. Without income from their business, victims often cannot afford to take legal action for the return of their property.

7.5.4 THE CYBERCRIME TREATY

The U.S. and European governments participated in drafting the Council of Europe's Treaty on Cybercrime, an attempt to assist law-enforcement agencies with investigations and foster international cooperation in fighting copyright violations, distribution of child pornography, and other online crime. The controversial treaty went through many drafts (at least 27) and generated opposition from civil liberties organizations, ISPs, and online businesses, because it gives broad powers to investigators to track online activity and imposes expensive requirements on ISPs to store logs and other potentially incriminating data for law enforcement purposes. A deputy director of Privacy International said the treaty would "turn the Internet from a great medium for free speech into a great medium for government spying."[63]

EXERCISES

Review Exercises

7.1 What did the word "hacker" mean in the early days of computing?

7.2 Give two arguments hackers use to justify their activities. Give a counterargument to each one.

7.3 Is it illegal to release a computer virus that puts a funny message on people's screens but does not damage files?

7.4 What are two techniques used to catch hackers?

7.5 What is one technique used to reduce online auction fraud?

7.6 What is one significant kind of computer crime committed by "insiders" (employees) in a company?

7.7 What is one problem with using biometrics for identification?

General Exercises

7.8 Chris logs on to your computer at night while you sleep and uses some of your software. Robin takes your car at night while you sleep and drives it around for a while. (Neither has your permission; neither does damage.) List several characteristics of the two events that are similar (characteristics related to the effects of the events, ethics, legality, risks, etc.). List several characteristics of the two events that are different. Which would offend you more? Why?

7.9 Do you agree or disagree with the following statement by Ken Thompson, one of the inventors of UNIX? Give your reasons.

> The act of breaking into a computer system has to have the same social stigma as breaking into a neighbor's house. It should not matter that the neighbor's door is unlocked.[64]

7.10 a) How many words are in a typical English dictionary? Tell what dictionary you used and how you determined (or estimated) the number of words.

b) Roughly how many six-letter character strings are there, allowing uppercase and lowercase letters? (Show your calculation.)

c) Suppose a hacker attempts to determine the password for a particular computer account by using a program that tries each letter combination in a given file. (Assume all passwords contain six letters.) If the program takes about t seconds to test all the words in a typical English dictionary, approximately how long would it take to test all six-letter combinations allowing both uppercase and lowercase letters?

d) What implications can you draw from parts a–c of this exercise concerning good password selection?

7.11 Some people argue that a hacker who defaces a Web page of a government entity such as the White House, Congress, or Parliament should be punished more harshly than a hacker who defaces a Web page of a private company or organization. Give some arguments for and against this view.

7.12 One group hacks a German government Web site to protest the ban on distribution of Nazi material in Germany; another group hacks a German government site to protest construction of multinational chain stores such as Wal-Mart, McDonald's, and Starbucks in Germany. Which would you consider an example of hacktivism? Explain.

7.13   When Dan Farmer probed 1700 Web sites for security flaws that hackers could easily exploit, some people criticized him for not asking permission of the sites first. Do you think he should have asked? Why or why not?

7.14   Some people argued that Attrition.org's Web-site archive of defaced Web pages indirectly encouraged hackers to vandalize sites by publicizing their successes. What do you think? What are the values or beneficial uses of the site? Considering the trade-offs between good uses and bad ones, do you think it was a good idea for attrition.org to maintain the public archive?

7.15   Evaluate arguments in favor of and against passage of a law making the writing and publication of computer virus software a crime. (See Section 7.2.6.) Would you support such a law? Why?

7.16   Hackers used automatic-dialing software to flood the emergency 911 telephone system with calls, knocking out 911 service. Suppose they were 16-year-olds. What penalty do you think is appropriate?

7.17   A court ruled against Napster for contributory copyright infringement (see Section 6.3.2). Compare eBay and Napster concerning their responsibility for unauthorized copyrighted material available on their sites. Do you think there should be a similar ruling against eBay for copyright-infringing material sold there? Why? What are the similarities and differences?

7.18   At gas stations, customers can pay with a credit card without signing a receipt. Compare the risk of use of stolen or counterfeit cards with the convenience of using the machines. Do you think gas stations should require a signature? Why or why not?

7.19   Some merchants and package-delivery services ask customers to sign receipts, not on paper, but on a device that digitally captures the signature. What are some risks of using this device? What protections are there? Do you think these devices are likely to cause serious problems? Why?

7.20   To track potential counterfeit currency, checks, and so on, some copying machines automatically print their serial number on all copies they make. What are some privacy implications, or possible dangers to privacy, of this technique?

7.21   Commenting on Constitutional objections to the SEC's plan to use surveillance software to monitor the Web for possible fraud (Section 7.5.1), an SEC official said "the Constitution doesn't give people the right to use the Internet to commit fraud."[65] Evaluate this response. Is it a good argument?

7.22   Suppose thumbprint readers are a standard feature of personal computers and an ISP requires a thumbprint match to log in. Would requiring a password in addition to the thumbprint be redundant and pointless, or is there a good security reason to require both? Explain.

Assignments

These exercises require some research or activity.

7.23   Find a dozen newspaper and/or magazine articles about hackers from the past few years. How are hackers described, as criminals or heroes? Give examples.

7.24   Find an article about computer forensics. Summarize the techniques described in the article.

7.25   If you have a credit card, then, over the next few weeks, count the times each of the following occurs: You use the card without providing a signature to be verified (e.g., at a gas station or on the Web). You sign a receipt, but the merchant does not compare your signature to the signature on the card. You sign a receipt, and the merchant does compare your signature to the signature on the card.

7.26   Find a use of biometrics in your city. Describe the application and its benefits and risks.

Class Discussion Exercises

These exercises are for class discussion, perhaps with short presentations prepared in advance by small groups of students.

7.27 Suppose a denial-of-service attack shuts down two dozen major Web sites, including retailers, stock brokerages, and large corporate entertainment and information sites, for several hours. The attack is traced to one of the following suspects. Do you think different penalties are appropriate, depending on which it is? Explain why. If you would impose different penalties, how would they differ?

a) A foreign terrorist who launched the attack to cause billions of dollars in damage to the U.S. economy.

b) An organization publicizing its opposition to commercialization of the Web and corporate manipulation of consumers.

c) A teenager using hacking tools he found on a Web site.

d) A hacker group showing off to another hacker group about how many sites it could shut down in one day.

7.28 Debate the following question: Do hackers do public service by finding and publicizing computer security weaknesses?

7.29 The families of two hospital patients who died as the result of a virus in a hospital computer are suing each of the people listed below and urging the government to bring criminal charges for negligence against each of them.[66]

■ A student in a course on computer security at a small college who posted a copy of the virus program on the class Web site, with a discussion of how it works.

■ The student who activated the virus program and released it onto the Internet.

■ The president of the college.

■ The president of the college's ISP.

■ The director of the hospital whose computer system was infected by the virus, causing patient medical records to be unavailable for a full day, resulting in the deaths of the two patients.

Divide the class into ten teams, five (one for each person listed above) to present arguments in favor of civil and/or criminal penalties, and five (one for each person) to present defense arguments. After the presentations, use a class vote or discussion to decide which, if any, of the characters should not be considered guilty at all, which, if any, should bear a high degree of responsibility, and which are "fuzzy" cases, hard to decide.

7.30 Suppose you, as a group of college students, have been invited to make a 20-minute presentation for a high-school computer class to discourage the students from hacking. Plan the presentation. What aspects will you emphasize?

7.31 Suppose you are on a consulting team to design a voting system for your state in which people will vote by logging on to a Web site. What are some important design considerations? Discuss some pros and cons of such a system. Overall, do you think it is a good idea?

7.32 Discuss answers to the questions in Section 7.5.1 about automated government surveillance of Web sites, chat rooms, and so forth.

NOTES

1. I have seen estimates ranging up to $500,000 for the average, some from computer security firms, which have an incentive to exaggerate. It is difficult to get precise figures, in part because victims are reluctant to report losses.

2. Eric S. Raymond, ed., *New Hacker's Dictionary*, MIT Press, 1993.

3. Quoted in J. D. Bierdorfer, "Among Code Warriors, Women, Too, Can Fight," *New York Times*, June 7, 2001, pp. 1, 9.

4. Brian Reid, "Reflection on Some Recent Widespread Computer Break-Ins," *Communications of the ACM*, Feb. 1987, 30:2, pp. 103–105; reprinted in Peter J. Denning, ed., *Computers Under Attack: Intruders, Worms, and Viruses*, Addison-Wesley, 1990, pp. 145–149.

5. "Politicians and the Net," *Wired*, Feb. 1995, p. 46. John R. Wilke, "In the Arcane Culture of Computer Hackers, Few Doors Stay Closed," *Wall Street Journal*, Aug. 22, 1990, pp. A1, A4. David L. Wilson, "'Crackers': a Serious Threat," *The Chronicle of Higher Education*, Aug. 17, 1994, pp. A23–A24. Jared Sandberg, "Security Breach at the Internet Raises Worries," *Wall Street Journal*, Feb. 7, 1994, p. B5.

6. John Simons, "How a Cyber Sleuth, Using a 'Data Tap,' Busted a Hacker Ring," *Wall Street Journal*, Oct. 1, 1999, pp. A1, A6.

7. All the quotes are from Wilke, "In the Arcane Culture of Computer Hackers, Few Doors Stay Closed."

8. "Is Computer Hacking a Crime?" *Harper's Magazine*, March 1990, pp. 45–57. The quotation is on p. 57.

9. Wilson, "'Crackers': a Serious Threat."

10. Katie Hafner and John Markoff, *Cyberpunk: Outlaws and Hackers on the Computer Frontier*, Simon & Schuster, 1991.

11. The early but widely repeated estimate of 6000 infected computers was calculated from an MIT staff member's guess of a 10% infection rate at MIT the day after the worm struck and an estimate of 60,000 Internet hosts at the time. A lower estimate, 2000–3000, was reported later. Jon A. Rochlis and Mark W. Eichin, "With Microscope and Tweezers: The Worm from MIT's Perspective," *Communications of the ACM*, 32:6, June 1989, pp. 689–698.

12. W. Wayt Gibbs, "Profile: Dan Farmer," *Scientific American*, Apr. 1997, pp. 32, 34. Attrition.org, viewed May 25, 2001. Jared Sandberg, "Holes In the Net," *Newsweek*, Feb. 21, 2000, pp. 46–49.

13. Lee Gomes and Ted Bridis, "FBI Warns of Russian Hackers Stealing U.S. Credit-Card Data," *Wall Street Journal*, Mar. 9, 2001, p. A4. Nancy McPoland, "Extortion Attempt Exposes Credit Info Online," *net4TV Voice*, Dec. 17, 2000, www.net4TV.com/voice, viewed May 17, 2001. Brad Stone, "Busting the Web Bandits," *Newsweek*, July 16, 2001, p. 55.

14. "Withdrawal Ordered for U.S. Pentagon Hackers," *San Jose Mercury News* (Reuters), Nov. 5, 1998.

15. Lev Grossman, "Attack of the Love Bug," *Time*, May 15, 2000, pp. 48–56.

16. See grc.com/dos/grcdos.htm for a first-hand report by the victim that covers technical, sociological, and social aspects of the attack, including e-mail from the boy who launched it; viewed June 3, 2001.

17. Jonathan Napack, "Cyberthreats Rising in the East," *Wired*, Mar. 2001, p. 74.

18. John J. Fialka, "The Latest Flurries At Weather Bureau: Scattered Hacking," *Wall Street Journal*, Oct. 10, 1994, pp. A1, A6.

19. Mark Manion and Abby Goodrum, "Terrorism or Civil Disobedience: Toward a Hacktivist Ethic," in Richard A. Spinello and Herman T. Tavani, eds., *Readings in CyberEthics*, Jones and Bartlett, 2001, pp. 463–473.

20. Many documents about the Randall Schwartz case are at www.lightlink.com/spacenka/fors.

21. *State v. McGraw*, 1985.

22. Some books on computer forensics are in the list at the end of the chapter. Many computer-forensics businesses can be found on the Web.

23. Ted Bridis, "FBI Unit Fails to React on Time To Electronic Threats, Report Says," *Wall Street Journal*, May 22, 2001, p. A28.

24. John Perry Barlow, "Crime and Puzzlement," *The Whole Earth Review*, Fall, 1990, pp. 44–57. (This article describes and comments on several hacker cases.) Wilke, "In the Arcane Culture of Computer Hackers, Few Doors Stay Closed."

25. Dorothy Denning, "The United States vs. Craig Neidorf," *Communications of the ACM*, March 1991, 34:3, pp. 23–32. Other published accounts of the case, including one in the *New York Times*, state that the government and/or BellSouth gave the document's value as more than $77,000. I am using the lower figure, and other factual material, from Denning's article; she participated in Neidorf's trial. Some additional information is from John Perry Barlow, "Crime and Puzzlement."

26. David Friedman and William Sjostrom, "Hanged for a Sheep: The Economics of Marginal Deterrence," *Journal of Legal Studies*, University of Chicago, June 1993.

27. Bruce Sterling, *The Hacker Crackdown: Law and Disorder on the Electronic Frontier*, Bantam Books, 1992, pp. 13–14.

28. Craig Bromberg, "In Defense of Hackers," *The New York Times Magazine*, Apr. 21, 1991, pp. 45–49. Gary Wolf, "The World According to Woz," *Wired*, Sept. 1998, pp. 118–121, 178–185.

29. Richard P. Feynman, *Surely You're Joking, Mr. Feynman: Adventures of a Curious Character*, W. W. Norton, 1984, pp. 137–155.

30. *Information Security: Computer Attacks at Department of Defense Pose Increasing Risks*, GAO/AIMD-96-84, May 22, 1996. W. Wayt Gibbs, "Profile: Dan Farmer," *Scientific American*, Apr. 1997, pp. 32, 34. Robert Fox, "News Track: NASA Computer Security Lax," *Communications of the ACM*, July 1999, p. 10. Wade Roush, "Hackers," *Technology Review*, April 1995, pp. 32–40. Wilson, "'Crackers': a Serious Threat." "Interior Department Bars Access to Internet Site," *New York Times*, Dec. 8, 2001, p. A11. Associated Press, "U.S. Review Finds Widespread Lapses In Computer Security," *Wall Street Journal*, Apr. 6, 2001, p. B6.

31. Paul Shukovsky, "Some Online Retailers Don't Protect Data," *San Diego Union–Tribune*, May 4, 1999, (ComputerLink) p. 12. Lee Gomes, "Silicon Valley's Open Secrets," *Wall Street Journal*, Apr. 27, 2001, pp. B1, B3.

32. Reported in Rachel Emma Silverman, "Intrusion Detection Systems Sniff Out Digital Attacks, Feb. 4, 1999, p. B6, and Keith Johnson, "Around the World, Hackers Are Drawn to 'Honeypots'," Dec. 19, 2000, p. A18, both *Wall Street Journal*.

33. Ted Eisenberg, David Gries, Juris Hartmanis, Don Holcomb, M. Stuart Lynn, Thomas Santoro, "The Cornell Commission: On Morris and the Worm," *Communications of the ACM*, June 1989, 32:6, pp. 706–709.

34. Larry Lange, "Corporate America: Beware Inside Job," *Electronic Engineering Times*, Jan. 15, 1996, pp. 20, 22. Jared Sandberg, "AOL Tightens Security after Hackers Foil the Service with Fake Accounts," *Wall Street Journal*, Sept. 8, 1995, p. B3.

35. Reported in *Risks Digest*, 21:24, Feb. 15, 2001; from the *New York Times*, Feb. 14, 2001.

36. Paul Wallich, "Wire Pirates," *Scientific American*, Mar. 1994, pp. 90–101.

37. CERT Advisory CA-95:06, "Security Administrator Tool for Analyzing Networks (SATAN)," Apr. 3, 1995.

38. From the SATAN documentation, quoted in Ted Doty, "Test Driving SATAN," Chapter 15 in Dorothy E. Denning and Peter J. Denning, eds., *Internet Besieged: Countering Cyberspace Scofflaws*, Addison-Wesley, 1998.

39. Peter Tippett, quoted in Kim Zetter, "Freeze! Drop That Download!" *PC World*, Nov. 16, 2000; www.pcworld.com/resource/printable/article/0,aid,34406,00.asp. The article includes pros and cons of criminalizing virus writing and a discussion of other means of reducing viruses.

40. Linda Harrison, "US Lawyer and Pals Indicted for Shill Bidding on eBay," *The Register*, Apr. 18, 2001, www.theregister.co.uk/content/6/18354.html, viewed Apr. 18, 2001.

41. Daniel Kadlec, "Crimes and Misdeminors," *Time*, Oct. 2, 2000, pp. 52–54.

42. Barbara Carton, "An Unsolved Slaying of an Airline Worker Stirs Family to Action," *Wall Street Journal*, June 20, 1995, p. A1, A8.

43. Steven Peisner, quoted in "Credit-card Scams Bedevil E-Stores," *Wall Street Journal*, Sept. 19, 2000, pp. B1, B4.

44. "'Theft of Identity' Rises to Thousands a Day," *Privacy Journal*, Feb. 1996, 22:4, pp. 1, 4. "Credit, SSN Fraud Victims," *Privacy Journal*, Apr. 1996, p. 6.

45. The Identity Theft and Assumption Deterrence Act of 1998, 18 U.S.C. §1028, www.consumer.gov/idtheft.

46. Jeffrey Rothfeder, *Privacy For Sale*, Simon & Schuster, 1992, pp. 113–116.

47. Elizabeth Attebery, "2 Suspects Held in Phony ATM Scam," *San Diego Union–Tribune*, June 30, 1993, p. C2. F. Barry Schreiber, "The Future of ATM Security," *Security Management*, March 1994, 38:3, p. 18A.

48. Matt Barthel, "Bank Worker Gets Kudos for Cracking ATM Scam," *The American Banker*, Oct. 25, 1993, p. 24.

49. Saul Hansell, "U.S. Workers Stole Data on 11,000, Agency Says," *New York Times*, Apr. 6, 1996, p. 6.

50. Steve Bodow, "The Money Shot," *Wired*, Sept. 2001, pp. 86–97.

51. *Webster's Third New International Dictionary*.

52. Tom Forester and Perry Morrison, *Computer Ethics: Cautionary Tales and Ethical Dilemmas in Computing*, 2nd ed., MIT Press, 1994, p. 34.

53. William M. Carley, "As Computers Flip, People Lose Grip In Saga of Sabotage at Printing Firm," *Wall Street Journal*, Aug. 27, 1992, p. A7.

54. Forester and Morrison, *Computer Ethics*, p. 37.

55. "Like a Virgin," *Security Insider Report*, Feb. 1993, p. 5. William M. Carley, "Did Northwest Steal American's Systems? The Court Will Decide," *Wall Street Journal*, July 7, 1994, p. A1. Scott McCartney, "System Breach Is Stirring Up Airline Rivalry," *Wall Street Journal*, June 27, 2000, p. B1.

56. Peter G. Neumann et al, "Risks to the Public in Computers and Related Systems," *Software Engineering Notes*, Apr. 1988, 13:2, pp. 7–8.

57. "Beware of a Blizzard of Fake Documents" (letter to the editor), *New York Times*, Aug 16, 1991, pg. 12.

58. Doug McClellan, "Desktop Counterfeiting," *Technology Review*, Feb./Mar. 1995, pp. 32–40.

59. Robert Fox, "News Track: Everybody Must Get Cloned," *Communications of the ACM*, Aug. 2000, 43:8, p. 9. Lisa Guernsey, "Software Is Called Capable of Copying Any Human Voice," *New York Times*, July 31, 2001, pp. A1, C2.

60. D. J. Stout, quoted in Jacques Leslie, "Digital Photo-pros and Photo(shop) Realism," *Wired*, May 1995, pp. 108–113. Michael W. Robbins, "The Apple of Visual Technology," *Audubon*, July/Aug. 1994, p. 4.

61. *NAACP v. Alabama*, 1958.

62. Andrea Gerlin, "Electronic Smut's Spread Raises Questions," *Wall Street Journal*, May 27, 1994, p. B3.

63. David Banisar, quoted in Will Rodger, "Trans-Atlantic Treaty Would Authorize Close Monitoring of Internet Usage," *Privacy Journal*, June

2001, p. 1. The text of the treaty is at conventions.coe.int/Treaty/EN/projets/FinalCybercrime.htm.

64   In Donn Seeley, "Password Cracking: A Game of Wits," *Communications of the ACM*, June 1989, 32:6, pp. 700–703, reprinted in Peter J. Denning, ed., *Computers Under Attack: Intruders, Worms, and Viruses*, Addison-Wesley, 1990, pp. 244–252.

65   George C. Brown, assistant general counsel, SEC, quoted in Michael Moss, "SEC's Plan to Snoop for Crime on Web Sparks a Debate over Privacy," *Wall Street Journal*, Mar. 28, 2000, pp. B1, B4.

66   This exercise is a simplified and modified version of a scenario used in a mock hearing presentation at the Computers, Freedom, and Privacy conference, San Francisco, 1993, in a session chaired by Don Ingraham.

BOOKS AND ARTICLES

- "Is Computer Hacking a Crime?" *Harper's Magazine*, March 1990, pp. 45–57. Transcript of an online discussion among several well-known hackers and others.

- Kenneth Brower, "Photography in the Age of Falsification," *The Atlantic Monthly*, May 1998, pp. 92–111. Explores views of well-known nature photographers on the ethics of altering photos.

- Dorothy E. Denning, *Information Warfare and Security*, ACM Press/Addison-Wesley, 1999.

- Dorothy E. Denning and Peter J. Denning, eds., *Internet Besieged: Countering Cyberspace Scofflaws*, ACM Press/Addison-Wesley, 1998. An excellent collection of articles on hacking and Internet security.

- S. Furnell and M. Warren, "Computer Hacking and Cyberterrorism: The Real Threats in the New Millennium," *Computers & Security*, 1999, v. 18, pp. 28–34.

- Katie Hafner and John Markoff, *Cyberpunk: Outlaws and Hackers on the Computer Frontier*, Simon & Schuster, 1991.

- Lance J. Hoffman, ed., *Rogue Programs: Viruses, Worms, and Trojan Horses*, Van Nostrand Reinhold, 1990.

- David Icove, Karl Seger, and William Von-Storch, *Computer Crime: A Crimefighter's Handbook*, O'Reilly & Associates, 1995.

- Warren G. Kruse II and Jay G. Heiser, *Computer Forensics: Incident Response*, Addison-Wesley, 2001.

- Steven Levy, *Hackers: Heroes of the Computer Revolution*, Doubleday, 1984.

- Mark Manion and Abby Goodrum, "Terrorism or Civil Disobedience: Toward a Hacktivist Ethic," in Richard A. Spinello and Herman T. Tavani, eds., *Readings in CyberEthics*, Jones and Bartlett, 2001, pp. 463–473. Argues for expanding the ethical justification for civil disobedience to include hacktivism.

- Doug McClellan, "Desktop Counterfeiting," *Technology Review*, Feb./Mar. 1995, pp. 32–40.

- Janet Reno *et al.*, "The Electronic Frontier: The Challenge of Unlawful Conduct Involving the Use of the Internet," www.usdoj.gov/criminal/cybercrime/unlawful.htm, March 2000.

- Kenneth S. Rosenblatt, *High-Technology Crime: Investigating Cases Involving Computers*, KSK Publications, 1995.

- Tsutomu Shimomura and John Markoff, *Take-down: The Pursuit and Capture of America's Most Wanted Computer Outlaw—By the Man Who Did It*, Hyperion, 1996.

- William Stallings, *Cryptography and Network Security: Principles and Practice*, second edition, Prentice Hall, 1999.

- Bruce Sterling, *The Hacker Crackdown: Law and Disorder on the Electronic Frontier*, Bantam Books, 1992.

- Clifford Stoll, *The Cuckoo's Egg: Tracking a Spy Through the Maze of Computer Espionage*, Doubleday, 1989.

- Martin Wasik, *Crime & the Computer*, Oxford University Press, 1991.

8

COMPUTERS AND WORK

8.1 The Changing Nature of Work

Computers, computerized information systems, and communications networks have a profound impact on work. They eliminate some jobs and create others. They free us from the repetitive, boring aspects of jobs so that we can spend more time being creative and doing the tasks for which human intelligence and problem solving are necessary. Architects learned to use computer-aided design; they still design buildings. Accountants learned to use spreadsheets and thus have more time for thinking, planning, and analysis. But will computers begin to design buildings? Will audits be automated? Does increased productivity from computerization lead to reduced working hours and more leisure, or to fewer jobs and more unemployment, or to little change in working hours, but more wealth (or less wealth)? In the short term, how will we deal with the dislocations caused by the loss of jobs and the need to retrain? In the long term, will we have masses of people out of work? Will the need for increased training and skills create wider divisions between those who can obtain the new skills and those who cannot?

"Telework" and "telecommuting" have become part of our vocabulary, describing the growing phenomenon of working at a distance from the traditional company office, connected by computers. Computers and communications networks are causing changes in the size of businesses and in the number of people who are self-employed. The physical distribution of population is likely to change: Communications networks make it possible for companies to locate in small towns and work with dispersed consultants instead of having hundreds or thousands of employees in larger population centers. As more people work at home, they can live farther from business centers.

At the same time that information technology is giving some workers more autonomy, computers are giving employers increased power to monitor the work, communications, movements, and Web activity of employees. These changes affect productivity, privacy, and morale. Should monitoring be limited? How?

Several health issues have been raised concerning the use and manufacture of computers. How significant are they?

In this chapter, we explore these issues.

8.2 The Impact on Employment

> But nowhere is there any mention of the truth about the information highway, which is mass unemployment.
>
> —David Noble, "The Truth About the Information Highway"[1]

8.2.1 JOB DESTRUCTION AND CREATION

COMPUTERS AND EMPLOYMENT

One of the first issues many people think of when considering the impact of computers on work is unemployment. Does computerization destroy jobs? Does it cause mass unemployment? The quotation above is about the information highway, but many social scientists believe it applies to computers and technology in general. Technology critics such as Jeremy Rifkin consider the reduction in the human labor and time required to produce goods and services to be one of the horrific consequences of computers and automation.

The number of bank tellers dropped by about 37% between 1983 and 1993. A study by Deloitte and Touche predicted that another 450,000 bank jobs would be lost because of automation and electronic banking services. Electronic calculators made slide rules, used by engineers since the 17th century, obsolete; the jobs involved in making and selling them are gone. The number of telephone switchboard operators dropped from 421,000 in 1970 to 164,000 in 1996. The jobs of 35,000 electric meter readers were expected to disappear as utility companies installed electronic devices that broadcast meter readings to company computers. Similar technology can be used to monitor vending machines and oil wells, reducing the number of people needed to check on them in person. A bank holding company receives 1.5 million customer inquiries by telephone each month; 80% are handled by computer. The company reduced the number of customer service employees by 40%. Railroads computerized their dispatch operations and eliminated hundreds of employees. The New York Stock Exchange eliminated the last 150 of its floor couriers who carried messages between brokers. "What was once done by our people is now done by technology," said an Exchange official. Travel agencies closed as more consumers made airplane reservations online. As the prices of digital cameras decline, more film processors will go out of business.[2] During the early 1990s, newspapers were full of headlines about layoffs and corporate "downsizing." IBM, General Motors, Sears, and other large companies laid off tens of thousands of workers. In fact, we can go through the discussion of benefits of computers in Chapter 1 and see that many of them, by making tasks more efficient, reduce the number of workers required to carry out the tasks.

There is no doubt that technology in general and computers in particular eliminate some jobs. Human labor is a resource. The goals of technology include a reduction in the resources needed to accomplish a result and an increase in productivity and standard of living. If we look back at the examples of lost jobs described above, we see that many of them accompanied increased productivity. While the number of telephone operators was dropping by more than 60% between 1970 and 1996, the number of long-distance calls increased from 9.8 billion to 94.9 billion. The bank handles 1.5 million customer inquiries with fewer service representatives. The railroad ships more tons per worker with its new computer system. Stock brokerages and insurance companies process more orders with fewer people. The Federal Reserve reported that in 1998, U.S. factories produced 3.5 times as much as in 1960 but had only 10% more workers; productivity per worker more than tripled.[3] During the recession of 2001, overall productivity continued to increase at a much higher rate than in previous recessions; economists credited faster microprocessors and increased investment in technology.

If a technology is successful, it eliminates some jobs, but it is likely to create others. What jobs have been created by computers? People design, build, and program the electronic calculators and computers that replaced slide rules and the networks that replaced telephone operators. People build palm computers and write software for them; people make pocket telephones and routers and servers and other high-tech devices that run the Internet. The Web created new jobs in software, Web page design, and security.

In 1995, an estimated 36,000 new Internet-related jobs were created; in 1996, about 100,000 more. By 1997, more than 109,000 people worked in the cellular communications industry in the United States. In 1998, the Semiconductor Industry Association reported that chip makers employed 242,000 workers directly in the U.S. and 1.3 million workers indirectly. The chip industry, which did not exist before the microprocessor was invented in the 1970s, ranked fourth among U.S. industries by annual revenue. According to the Department of Commerce, in 1996, there were 506,000 computer scientists and engineers, 427,000 computer systems analysts, and 568,000 computer programmers. The Department expected these figures to grow to 1,026,000, 912,000, and 697,000, respectively, by 2006. In 1998, 7.4 million people worked in information technology jobs in the United States. These are high-paying jobs; salaries in high-tech companies averaged 73% higher than those for all private sector employment in the U.S. New technical jobs also create jobs for such support staff as receptionists, janitors, and stock clerks.[4] There are countless new products that use computer technology: VCRs and DVD players, computer games, fax machines, cell phones, medical devices, and so on. New products create new jobs in design, marketing, manufacture, sales, customer service, repair, and maintenance.

What is the overall effect? Do computers destroy more jobs than they create? This is a complicated question because measuring the effects of computers is difficult, and other factors also influence employment trends.

How many more people buy a microwave oven (generating more jobs in the microwave-oven industry) because microprocessors have made them more convenient to use? How many more watches or clocks are sold because they are now so cheap? When a package-delivery service installs computer systems to make its operations more efficient, fewer counter clerks, drivers, and managers can process the same number of packages. Does this eliminate jobs, or do the lower rates resulting from increased efficiency encourage more people to send packages, ultimately increasing business and jobs? A few hundred years ago, listening to professional-quality music was a rare luxury for most people; only the wealthy could hire professional musicians to perform for them. Technology, including electricity, radio, and now CDs, DVDs, and the Web, brought the cost of an individual "performance" in a private home down so low that music is available to almost anyone. The effect on employment? Thousands of musicians make a living, many a fortune, in jazz, country, classical, zydeco, new age, rock, and rap music. In the long term, if technology brings the cost of a product or service down far enough to expand the market, more people will work in that field. Other new jobs created by technology are ones not imagined or possible before.

In the late 1990s, a generation after the microprocessor was invented, the economy was booming because of computer and network technology. New companies formed and new products appeared at an astonishing pace. The unemployment rate was, at times, lower than it had been for about 30 years. Technology stocks soared. In 2000, overvalued stocks tumbled, and many "dot com" companies closed—a natural event in a tumultuous, new, fast-changing area—but mass unemployment did not follow; the unemployment rate remained low. In 2001, many high-tech companies laid off thousands of workers, but the lay-offs resulted not from technology itself, but from exaggerated expectations in the late 1990s. An industry organization reported that the number of new information technology workers needed that year was down from an extremely high earlier estimate to a very high estimate: 900,000. (In late 2001, the unemployment rate rose sharply from the impact of the terrorist attacks on the World Trade Center and the Pentagon.)

Unemployment rates fluctuate. They might be high or low when you read this, but it seems clear that computer technology did not cause significant unemployment in the last decades of the 20th century. The discussion above, and some of the discussion of other factors below, suggest that the net effect of computers on employment will be a gain. Will computers be the most important factor in determining future employment levels? We get some insight into this question by considering other factors that affect employment and the historic impact of technology in general.

TECHNOLOGY, ECONOMIC FACTORS, AND EMPLOYMENT

Since the beginning of the Industrial Revolution, technology has been blamed for massive unemployment. In the early 1800s, the Luddites (of whom we will say more in Chapter 9) burned weaving looms because they feared the looms would eliminate their jobs. A few decades later, a mob of seamstresses and tailors destroyed sewing machines because of the same fears. But, with a sewing machine, a seamstress could make more than two shirts a day. Rather than loss of jobs, the sewing machine meant a reduction in the price of clothes, more demand, and ultimately hundreds of thousands of new jobs.[5]* More than 150 years ago, the French economist Frederic Bastiat poked fun at the idea that we should oppose labor-saving technologies. He proposed a law criticizing the sun and requiring people to close their shutters during the day to provide more jobs for candle makers.

We saw that new technology reduces employment in specific areas and in the short term. What other factors affect employment levels? Consider the times of significant unemployment in the U.S. in the past century. The Great Depression in the 1930s was not caused by technology (and certainly not by computers). Economists and historians attribute the depression to a variety of factors, including "business cycles," the then-new Federal Reserve Bank's inept manipulation of interest rates, and that old standby, "greed." Unemployment was very low during the Vietnam War, then high during a recession in the early 1980s and another in the early 1990s. But growth in use of computers has

---

*Sewing machines were first marketed to factory owners, just as computers were first used by large companies. Isaac Singer had the insight to sell them directly to women, in a parallel to the eventual shift from corporation-owned mainframes to personal computers for consumers.

been dramatic and continuous, especially after the mid-1970s, when personal computers began to appear. When most of the country had recovered from the recession of the early 1990s, the California economy remained depressed. Was it because California was "computerizing" faster than the rest of the country? No; California suffered from loss of jobs in the defense and aerospace industries, as federal funding in these areas declined, and from the large number of businesses fleeing the state because California's tax and regulatory policies were more costly than those of other states. Demographics also have an impact on growth and decline of various job sectors; the Bureau of Labor Statistics predicts increases in a whole range of medical jobs because of the aging Baby Boomers and the increase in the elderly population.

The Organisation for Economic Co-operation and Development (OECD), an international organization whose members include most of Western Europe, North America, Japan, Australia, and New Zealand, studied employment trends in 25 countries from 1950 to 1995. OECD concluded that unemployment stems from "policies . . . [that] have made economies rigid, and stalled the ability . . . to adapt." The study suggested that "unemployment should be addressed not by seeking to slow the pace of change, but rather by restoring economies' and societies' capacity to adapt to it."[6] During the 1990s, unemployment in the European Community was about 11%, generally twice or more the rate in the United States. About 11% of unemployed people in the U.S. were without jobs for more than a year, compared to 40% in Europe.[7] But Europe is not more technologically advanced or computerized than the United States. The differences have more to do with flexibility in their economies and other political, social, and economic factors.

Although it is difficult to separate the effects of technology from other factors, the view that technology causes mass unemployment can be seen to be weak by examining the 20th century. Airplanes, automobiles, radio, television, computers, much medical technology, and so on did not exist before the 20th century. The use of telephones and electricity was minimal. There was an enormous increase in technology and a decrease in jobs in such areas as agriculture and saddle making, while the population of the U.S. approximately quadrupled. If technology destroyed jobs, there should be fewer people working now than in 1900. But, with four times as many people, the national unemployment rate was less than 4% in May 2000, lower than throughout most of the 20th century. (One segment of the population is working less: children. In 1870, the average age for starting work was 13; in 1990 it was 19.1.)

BUT ARE WE EARNING LESS?

Economists agree that the average hourly pay of manufacturing workers quadrupled (in constant dollars) between 1909 and the mid-1970s. They disagree about the last quarter of the century. Wages appeared to decline as much as 10% after 1970. This is sometimes cited as an indication that the value of human work is declining as computers take over tasks people used to do. Others see it as an indication that expenditures on computers have decreased, not increased, productivity. However, some economists

	1970	1997[a]
Average new home size (sq. ft.)	1500	2150
New homes with central heat and air conditioning	34%	81%
Households with 2 or more vehicles	29.3%	61.9%
Households with color TV	39.9%	97.9%
Households with VCRs	0	89%
Households with microwave oven	less than 1%	89.5%
Housing units lacking complete plumbing	6.9%	2.3%
Median household net worth	$27,938	$59,398
Shipments of recreational vehicles	30,300	281,000
Average household ownership of sporting equipment	$769	$1895
Americans taking cruises	0.5 mill.	4.7 mill.

[a] A few figures are for 1995 or 1996. All dollar figures in both columns are in 1997 dollars.

Figure 8.1 Living Standards and Leisure in the Computer Age [8]

believe the apparent decline resulted from improper computation of the Consumer Price Index. Also, fringe benefits rose significantly, increasing total compensation by about 17% according to some experts, but other experts disagree.[9] Two researchers, Michael Cox and Richard Alm, decided to avoid the problems of using income and inflation data and, instead, look at direct measures of consumption and leisure between 1970 and the late 1990s. Figure 8.1 includes a sampling of data they collected from a variety of government and industry sources. Also in this time period, attendance at operas and symphonies doubled (per person), recreation spending more than tripled (per person), and spending on toys quadrupled (per child).[10] The data indicate that, while computerization has been increasing, so have many measures of real income and quality of life. Figure 8.2 takes a longer perspective and uses a different measure. It shows how much time an average worker had to work to earn enough money to buy food and luxuries. Technology is responsible for a large share of the dramatic reductions.[11]

Since the beginning of the Industrial Revolution, working hours have declined. Most of us no longer work 10–12 hour days, six days a week. Working hours, like income data, can be counted in various ways, supporting different conclusions. Some economists report a significant decline in working hours since the 1950s; others say working hours have not declined significantly since the end of World War II. Many people continue to work more hours while income rises because they have higher expectations; many consider the lifestyle represented by the 1997 data in Figure 8.1 to be essential. Another reason, according to labor economist Ronald Ehrenberg, is that quirks in the tax and compensation structure encourage employers to have regular workers work overtime rather than hire additional employees.[12] A third reason is that taxes take a much larger percentage of income than they did in the past; thus people have to work more hours for

Product	1900	1920[a]	1970	1990–2000[b]
Milk (half-gallon)	56 min.	37 min.	10 min.	7 min.
Hershey chocolate bar	20 min.	6 min.	1.8 min.	2.1 min.
Chicken (3 pounds)	$2\frac{2}{3}$ hrs.	$2\frac{1}{2}$ hrs.	22 min.	14 min.
Electricity (100 KWH)	$107\frac{1}{4}$ hrs.	$13\frac{1}{2}$ hrs.	39 min.	38 min.
Bread (one pound)		13 min.	4 min.	3.5 min.
Oranges (one dozen)		69 min.	15 min.	9 min.
Gasoline (one gallon)		32 min.	6.4 min.	5.7 min.
Phone call (3 min., coast-to-coast)		30 hrs.	24 min.	2 min.
Air travel (100 miles)		$12\frac{3}{4}$ hrs.	102 min.	62 min.
Computing power (1 MIPS)[c]			1.2 lifetimes	9 min.

[a] The air-travel datum is for 1930.

[b] Figures in this column are from various years in the late 1990s and 2000.

[c] "MIPS" means *million instructions per second.*

Figure 8.2 Declining Cost, Measured in Working Time [13]

the same take-home pay.* Thus social, political, and economic factors mingle with the impact of computers.

A GLOBAL WORKFORCE

Manufacturing jobs moved from wealthier countries to less wealthy countries, especially in Asia, because the difference in pay rates was large enough to make up for the extra transportation costs. The Internet and the Web have reduced "transportation" costs for many kinds of information work to almost zero. U.S. companies employ programmers in India and Russia, for example. Actuaries in India process insurance claims for a British insurance company. Doctors in the U.S. dictate notes on patient visits, but there are not enough medical scribes in the United States. Digitized voice files are sent to India by satellite, transcribed, and returned by e-mail. Workers in Ireland handle customer-service calls for large businesses based in other countries.

This trend creates jobs for both low- and high-skilled workers in less wealthy countries. Lower labor costs and increased efficiency reduce prices for consumers. On the other hand, some view the globalization of the workforce as a negative result of technology. From the prospective of some higher-paid workers in developed countries, it can mean fewer jobs, accompanied by lower pay because of increased competition.

---

*Estimates vary. The Tax Foundation reported that we work, on average, two hours and 47 minutes out of each 8-hour workday to pay taxes, compared to only one hour and 57 minutes about 50 years ago.

WORKERS

In the exhibit "Workers" by Brazilian photographer Sebastião Salgado, a photograph shows dozens of laborers climbing out of a huge pit, a gold mine in Brazil. The men, packed tightly, one above another, climb 60-foot stick ladders, carrying bags of dirt on their backs. In the pit, hundreds more workers dig and fill their sacks. Another photograph shows a worker at a sulfur mine in Indonesia holding a scarf over his mouth for protection from the thick dust. A third shows the huge earth-cutting drill, perhaps 35 feet in diameter, that bored the tunnel in the English Channel; two skilled men are working on the drill.[14] Aside from the extraordinary power of the photographs themselves, one of the striking things about them is how differently someone with a positive view of technology and someone with a negative view would interpret them. To the former, the photos show dramatically how technology eliminates back-breaking, unhealthy physical labor and raises the standard of living of workers. To the latter, all three photos show the evils of technology: The mining would not be done in a nature-oriented society. The reduction of workers from a few hundred in the mine to two on the drill would be evidence of the unemployment caused by technology.

I pity the poor, and should hardly think myself innocent if any man felt more for them than I do; but the remedy for their grievances, lies not in the destruction of Machinery. They are oppressed exceedingly, but not by Machinery. Those who accuse Machinery of causing any part of the distresses of the poor, have very contracted views and narrow minds, and see but a little way. They do not seem to consider that almost every thing was new Machinery once. There was a time when corn was ground by the hand; and when Corn Mills and Wind Mills were first invented they were New Machinery; and therefore why not break and burn these as soon as any other kind of Machinery; for if they were all stopped, and corn again ground by the hand, there would be plenty of employment for many hands! Much the same observations might be made respecting every other kind of Machinery, and I have asked this question in order to show the silliness of the practice.

—George Beaumont (from *"Reflections on Luddism,"* 1812)[15]

8.2.2 CHANGING SKILLS AND JOBS

Some who are concerned about the impact of computers on employment acknowledge that, in the past, technology led to new jobs and products, but argue that the impact of computers is different—that computers will have a more negative impact. Computers differ from earlier technologies in several key ways.

Computers eliminate a much wider variety of jobs than any single new technological advance in the past. The impact of new machines or technologies tended to be concentrated in one industry or activity. Earlier automation eliminated primarily manufacturing jobs, but computers can automate services, such as those of telephone operators and receptionists, just as easily. The transition to new jobs will be more difficult because of the broad impact. Old jobs will be transformed and will require the ability to use a computer. The pace of improvement in speed, capability, and cost for computers is much faster than for any previous technology. The pace itself will cause more job disruption as people continually find their jobs being eliminated and need to retrain.

The new jobs created by computers are different from the jobs eliminated. The hundreds of thousands of new computer engineering and systems-analyst jobs require a college degree. The jobs of telephone operator, bank teller, and customer-service representative did not. Will jobs diverge into two distinct groups: high-paying jobs for the highly skilled and highly trained intellectual elite, and fewer low-paying jobs for people without computer skills and advanced education?

REASONS FOR OPTIMISM

Although it often seems that our times and problems are new and different from what came before, similar concerns were raised for other technologies. The steam engine and electricity brought enormous change in jobs, making many obsolete. When economists Claudia Goldin and Lawrence Katz researched earlier periods of rapid technological development, they found that the education system quickly adapted to train children in the necessary skills. They pointed out that a bookkeeper in 1890 had to be highly skilled, whereas a bookkeeper in 1920 was a high-school graduate using an early form of an adding machine. In the 19th century, skilled workers earned increasingly more than manual laborers, but the trend reversed in the early 20th century, because more people went to high school and the new technologies of that era reduced the skill level needed for white-collar jobs. As demand increases for new skills, people acquire them. For example, in 1900, only 0.5 people out of every 1000 in the U.S. worked as an engineer. After the huge growth in technology during the 20th century, 7.6 out of every 1000 people were engineers.[16]

Complex interactive computer systems guide workers through steps of jobs that required extensive training before. Performance-support software and training software empower lower-skilled workers and make the training process for complex jobs cheaper, faster, and easier. Such systems, for example, guide auditors through an audit of a securities firm, help employees at financial institutions carry out transactions, and train sales people. The National Association of Securities Dealers reported that its auditors were fully competent after one year using such a system, compared to two and a half years without it; they saved more than $400,000 in annual training costs.[17] Companies are more willing to hire people without specific skills when they can be trained quickly and use automated support systems.

The Bureau of Labor Statistics expects many jobs to be available that require little, if any, computer skill. It reported that 530,000 new cashier jobs would be created by 2006, and it predicted increases between 1992 and 2005 of 46–54% in jobs such as restaurant cook, bicycle repairer, and manicurist.[18]

COMPUTERS REPLACING SKILLED WORKERS

Computers eliminate more high-skilled jobs than older technologies. Software makes decisions that used to require trained, thinking human beings. There are some concerns that many white-collar, professional jobs could be taken over by computers and that human intelligence in employment will be "devalued." Computer programs analyze loan applications and decide which to approve; some programs are better than people at predicting which applicants are likely to default on their loans. Design jobs are automated. For example, software to design the electrical layout for new housing developments can do in half an hour a job that would take a high-paid employee 100 hours.[19] Even computer programming is automated; some computer programs write computer programs, reducing the need for trained programmers. Also, programming tools enable nonspecialists to do some programming, design Web pages, and so on. Look back at the Department of Commerce's projections in Section 8.2.1 for growth in computer jobs from 1996 to 2006. The numbers of computer scientists, engineers, and system analysts were expected to more than double, but the anticipated growth for computer programmers was only about 23%. Perhaps that reflects the declining relative importance of simple programming—but note that it is still a growth, not a decline.

The printing press put scribes out of work when writing was a skill possessed by only a small, "highly trained" elite. In the 17th and 18th centuries, people were shocked and disturbed by machines that did simple arithmetic, a task thought to require uniquely human intelligence. It is difficult to tell, at the current time, whether the impact of computers on jobs will be different in quality or only in degree from earlier technological changes. In the past, human imagination and desires continued to find new fields of work to replace those no longer needed or made more efficient.

TRANSITIONS

When new technologies eliminate jobs slowly, attrition (not hiring a new person when one retires, quits, or is reassigned) can reduce the number of workers without disruption. When the changes come faster and are more pervasive, as with computers, people are fired. Long-term net social gains from new jobs are not of much interest to a person who is fired. The loss of a job is immediate and personal and can be devastating. When large numbers of people lose their jobs in one small community or within a short time, difficult social problems occur. In societies that change very slowly, a person might hold the same job for all of his or her working years. This does not happen in a dynamic society where technology is developing at a fast pace. Thus, there is a need for people (individual workers, employers, and communities) and institutions (e.g., schools) to be more flexible and to plan for change.

Online training programs help people with limited hours or resources to learn new skills. Online discussion and news groups used by employees for hundreds of companies provide information about what the employees think of working conditions there. Web sites with job listings help people find good jobs in other towns if jobs at home are declining. We can learn about distant towns on the Web before spending time and money for travel to a few good prospects. Thus, computer technology, especially the Web, can help people find better jobs and can make transitions easier.

8.3 The Work Environment

Computers are changing the work environment, in some ways for the better, in some for the worse. We will look at a few of these changes: telecommuting and the impact of computer technology on business structure, in this section, and monitoring of employees' work, physical location, e-mail activity, and Web activity in Section 8.4.

8.3.1 TELEWORKING

Personal computers, modems, fax machines, and wireless communications have made it possible for millions of people to work without "going to work," that is, without going to their employer's (or their own) business offices. I will use the term "telework" and "telecommuting" for several variations of new work paradigms. The most common meaning is working for an employer at a computer-equipped office in the employee's home. Some large businesses have set up satellite "telecommuting centers" with computer and communications equipment located closer to where their employees live than to the main business office. In some jobs, such as sales, the office is mobile: The employee travels with a laptop computer and might work at a table in a coffee shop or outdoors in a park. Telework also includes running a business from one's home that relies heavily on computers and communications. By 2000, 24 million Americans telecommuted regularly or occasionally, up from about four million in 1990. Europe had approximately 10 million telecommuters in 2000.[20]

Telecommuting has a large number of benefits for teleworkers, for their employers, and for society in general, but also a number of problems.

BENEFITS

The main advantages for employers are reduced overhead and, in some cases, increased productivity. For companies that set up scattered telework centers in suburbs to replace large downtown offices where real-estate and office-rental are expensive, the savings can be significant. For those that have moved employees all the way to their homes or cars (e.g., sales people), savings include closure of dozens of branch offices. Productivity studies in areas where work is easy to measure (e.g., data entry) showed productivity gains of 15%.[21]

Telework, and telecommunications generally, make it easier to work with clients, customers, and employees in other countries. At home, one can more easily work a few hours at night that are compatible with foreign time zones.

Telecommuting reduces rush-hour traffic congestion and the associated pollution and energy use. A one-percent decrease in urban commuting could reduce gasoline usage by a few million barrels per year.[22] Telework reduces expenses for commuting and for work clothes. It saves time. It provides previously unavailable work options for some elderly or disabled people for whom commuting is physically difficult and expensive. It allows work to continue after blizzards close roads. Roughly 55% of woman-owned businesses are home-based businesses. Telework, and the flexible hours it permits, can help reduce child-care expenses and give parents more time with their children. Telework gives people increased flexibility of work location. They can live in rural areas instead of big cities and suburbs if they prefer (in "electronic cottages," to use futurist Alvin Toffler's words). Two-career couples can work for companies hundreds or thousands of miles apart.

PROBLEMS

Many early telecommuters were volunteers, people who wanted to work at home. They were more likely to be independent workers. (Many were computer programmers.) As more businesses began to require employees to move their offices to their homes, problems arose, for both employees and employers.

Some employers see resentment among employees who must work at the office and found that the corporate loyalty of telecommuters weakened. Lacking immediate supervision, some people are less productive, while others work too hard and too long. The ease of working with people around the world leads some to work odd hours to match the time zones of clients. Some employees need better direction about what work and how much work they are expected to do at home. Being at home with children could be an advantage for some telecommuters, but a distraction for others. In general, reducing the boundary between home and work causes stress for some workers and their families.

Some employees complain that the costs of office space and overhead that have been reduced for the employer have simply been shifted to the employee who must give up space at home for the office, learn how to maintain equipment that the company used to maintain, and so on.

For many people, the social interactions at work are a significant part of pleasant working conditions, so social isolation and low morale can be problems. When only some employees in a division or business work at home, their absence from informal or last-minute meetings at the office can cause problems for them and their managers. Some telecommuters fear that lack of "visibility" in the office will be a disadvantage when promotions and bonuses are awarded.

Some problems related to telecommuting can be reduced. For example, workers can use e-mail and telephone calls to help maintain visibility. Employers can address the social-isolation problem by holding regular meetings or other events where employees interact in person. Telecommuters could reduce isolation by participating in activities of professional associations and other social networks. But the problems led some companies to cut back telecommuting programs for employees. Like many of the options provided by new technologies (or social trends), telework may be very desirable for some employees and employers and of no use to others.

SIDE EFFECTS

Aside from the direct advantages and disadvantages, teleworking has several side effects that might change various business and social aspects of how we live and work.

How will telework affect our sense of community? The Industrial Revolution led to a major shift in work patterns; jobs moved to offices and factories. Working at home in the late 20th century seemed new and unusual, but, before the Industrial Revolution, most people worked at, or close to, home. Even in the past few centuries, working at home has not been uncommon. Writers traditionally work at home. Farmers worked in the fields, but the farm office was in the house. Doctors, especially in small towns, had their medical offices in their homes. Shopkeepers often had an apartment behind or above the store. Perhaps writers are closest to modern information workers who telecommute in that they tend to work in isolation. Is that why we have an image of writers spending the evenings at coffee houses or at intellectual "salons" talking with other intellectuals? Will similar activities spring up in suburbs and small towns to fill the social needs of teleworkers? In the past, social isolation was not considered a problem for people who worked in or near their homes; they lived, worked, and socialized in communities. They had the grange, the church, and the community center. Urban policy researcher Joel Kotkin observes that telecommuting might encourage a return to involvement in one's local community.[23] Is he correct? Will being there all day, doing errands locally, eating in local restaurants, and so on, generate an interest in the safety, beauty, and vitality of the community that is less likely to develop when one returns home after dark, tired from a day at the office? On the other hand, now that we can communicate with people all over the world on the Internet, will home workers stay inside, communicating with unseen business and social acquaintances, and be just as unlikely to know their neighbors as many commuters are now?

RESTRICTIONS ON TELEWORK

Telework is common now, so it might be surprising that local governments and labor unions attempted to stop it in the 1980s and that the Occupational Health and Safety Administration (OSHA) tried to regulate it in 1999. Why would they want to ban or discourage working at home?

Many communities argue that home businesses bring noise and traffic problems to residential neighborhoods. Thus local zoning laws often prohibit a home business from receiving deliveries or customers at the home. In many cities, an accountant who works in an office all day but has a tax-preparation business at home is breaking the law when clients come to the house in the evening.* These laws predate telework, but they apply to teleworkers as well. The city of Chicago ordered a couple to stop using a computer at home to write textbooks and educational software because Chicago zoning laws restricted home work that used mechanical or electrical equipment.

Some kinds of home work have been outright illegal for a long time. For example, labor laws prohibit most home sewing work, where women sew garments for clothing manufacturers and are paid by the piece. Tens of thousands of women do this work in spite of the laws. Supporters of the laws argue that the women often get less than minimum wage, and it is difficult for the government to make sure that working conditions are safe and that children are not working in violation of child-labor laws. Critics of such laws argue that they deny the women a choice, and that unions, the main supporters of the laws, are primarily concerned with the difficulty of organizing the workers. In the 1980s, various unions extended the campaign against home work to computer work. The view at the time seemed to be that most computer at-home work would be data-entry work done by low-paid women. A large union of service employees banned computer home work for its members. The AFL–CIO advocated a government ban on all computer at-home work. An AFL–CIO official warned that telecommuters might face working conditions like those of the 19th century. A 1983 article titled "Home Computer Sweatshops" in *The Nation* reflected the same worries. The AFL–CIO official also commented that "It's very difficult to organize workers dispersed over a wide geographical area."[24]

Perhaps because telecommuters tend to be independent, middle-class workers, and perhaps because their numbers grew so fast, the efforts to stop computer work at home quickly turned futile. The mistaken views about who would do computer work at home and what the working conditions would be are reminders to be cautious about banning or restricting a new phenomenon on the grounds of guesses made before its applications and benefits, as well as problems, develop.

In 1999, OSHA declared that employers must ensure that workplaces in employees' homes meet legal regulations for workplaces at work. Regulations cover electric circuits, exit signs, hazardous chemicals, clutter, extensive reporting requirements, and so on. When the OSHA statement was publicized, an immediate furor arose over the prospect of applying workplace rules to homes and the possibility of employers and government officials inspecting people's homes. OSHA quickly backed down and said it would not hold employers responsible for conditions in the homes of telecommuters.

8.3.2 CHANGING BUSINESS STRUCTURES

There is much speculation about the impact of computer and telecommunications networks on the size and structure of business. Different observers see trends going in opposite directions.

---

*Zoning laws vary in different communities; these activities are not illegal everywhere.

Some see trends toward smaller businesses and more independent consultants and contractors—"information entrepreneurs," as they are sometimes called. It can be easier for workers to work part time for different employers or clients, thus encouraging more information workers to become self-employed. Some observers project an increase in "Mom and Pop multinationals," small businesses that operate globally. On the other hand, some observers foresee computers contributing to the growth of large, multinational corporations, with mergers between giant companies—for example, communications and entertainment companies (such as AOL with Time Warner). There were many big mergers and buy-outs in the 1990s, and more are negotiated regularly. At the same time, some large companies are splitting up into smaller units. A tremendous amount of business reorganization is taking place, and it is still unclear what the eventual main trend will be.

The Economist reported that the average number of employees per firm has been declining since the late 1960s. A study of a large sample of U.S. businesses found that between 1975 and 1985, the average number of employees per firm declined by 20%. It also found a correlation between high computer use and small firm size. The reason was not that computers were putting people out of work, but rather that firms narrowed the focus of their activities, purchasing more components and services from other firms. The study argued that computers and information networks reduced the cost and uncertainties of finding and relying on suppliers and consultants; hence, businesses did more of it. The trend toward smaller companies continued. Between 1991 and 1995, companies with more than 5000 employees eliminated 3,377,000 jobs, but companies with fewer than 500 employees added almost 11 million employees.[25]

The legal, tax, and regulatory framework in which businesses operate has enormous impacts, sometimes quite indirect, sometimes unidentified, on business size, structure, and employment patterns. Such effects might prevent or slow changes that computers would otherwise cause. Complex regulatory laws, for example, tend to encourage large firms, because they can spread the cost of a large legal department over a large sales volume—and also discourage tiny firms (which are exempt from most regulations) from growing above the threshold where the regulations apply.

Two related trends, "flattening hierarchies" and "empowerment of workers," are getting notice. The availability of information technology is leading many businesses to give workers more information and more decision-making authority. Manufacturing plant workers have access to online inventory and purchasing information and make decisions about production schedules. Credit-card company service representatives, with immediate access to account information, can make decisions to cancel a late charge or finance charge, for example. The need for middle managers is decreasing, and their jobs are changing. Some say they now think of themselves as "facilitators" rather than managers; they find the information technology tools to help their workers manage their own work.[26]

8.4 Employee Monitoring

Technology now allows employers to cross the line from monitoring the work to monitoring the worker.

—Cindia Cameron, National Association of Working Women

8.4.1 BACKGROUND

Employee monitoring has become a big issue. Supervisors and managers have, of course, always monitored their employees. The degree of detail and frequency of the monitoring has varied depending on the kind of work, economic factors, and available technology. Computers have made new kinds of monitoring possible and old methods more efficient.

Before we look at the new issues raised by computers, we will briefly recall some of the past and present monitoring that does not depend on computers. Total hours worked have long been monitored by logs or time clocks. In many jobs, total output for a day can be counted (widgets produced, forms typed, sales concluded). In some jobs, such as factory assembly lines, the pace of work is implicitly monitored by the speed of the line; if a worker is not keeping up, the failure will be obvious farther down the line. Supervisors record or listen in on the work of telephone operators and customer-service representatives. Surveillance cameras have long been common in banks and convenience stores. In some of the accounts of the worst conditions in factories and clerical offices of the past two centuries, bosses patrolled the aisles watching workers, prodding them to work faster and discouraging conversation and breaks.

Electronic monitoring capabilities are the modern version of the time clock, telephone extension, and camera. Most precomputer monitoring, however, was not constant, because the supervisor had many workers to oversee and other work to do; workers usually knew when the supervisor was present to observe them. With computers, monitoring can be constant, more detailed, and unseen by the worker. Telephone systems are now so essentially combined with computer systems that telephone monitoring has become a *de facto* computer issue.

The subjects of most precomputer monitoring were so-called "blue collar" (factory) and "pink collar" (telephone and clerical) workers. New monitoring capabilities, such as reading an employee's e-mail, affect "white collar" (professional) workers, too. Supervisors of customer-service representatives can set their terminals to show exactly what the monitored worker sees and is doing on his or her screen. Some newspaper editors remotely monitor the computer screens of journalists, and some senior lawyers monitor other attorneys in their firm. Some companies install devices or software that secretly capture and store every keystroke typed at a keyboard. The vast growth of computer storage capabilities means that telephone conversations, e-mail, voice mail, Web-activity logs, and physical surveillance information can be stored longer. Such information can also be searched more easily, with the potential of making the monitored details part of the employee's permanent record.

We discuss examples and issues in three areas of electronic monitoring:

- details of performance, such as keystrokes, customer-service calls, and retail-clerk operations;

- location and performance of scattered employees;

- e-mail, voice mail, and Web surfing.

8.4.2 DATA ENTRY, PHONE WORK, AND RETAIL

Every keystroke of data-entry and data-processing clerks can be counted automatically. Some employers set keystroke quotas. Some make the records of employees' performance public in the workplace to encourage competition among workers. Terminals beep if the employee pauses in his or her work. The purposes are to evaluate individual employees and to measure and increase productivity. When the quotas are unreasonable and the pace relentless, the stress can be intense. The management style that includes constant watching, very demanding work quotas, and threats of being fired is older than computers. The modern, computerized version of such workplaces is described as an "electronic sweatshop."

Similarly, workers who answer telephone calls all day can be monitored in detail. Now the exact number and duration of each call, and the idle time between calls, can be automatically logged, analyzed, and made part of the employee's record. (We discuss the separate issue of listening in on calls below.)

Workers complain that such constant, detailed surveillance diminishes their sense of dignity and independence and destroys confidence. They are treated like machines, not people. The surveillance causes stress, boredom, and low morale. Critics point out that the stress increases health costs for the employer. Critics also raise questions about the effectiveness of such monitoring, arguing that it puts too much emphasis on quantity instead of quality. It reduces workers' commitment to doing a good job. Pressure on telephone-information operators to reduce the amount of time spent on each call, according to one critic, caused operators to cut customers off by claiming the computer was down.[27]

Telephone customer-service workers include airline and car-rental reservation clerks, catalog mail-order operators, telemarketers, credit-bureau service representatives and collections agents, and long-distance telephone service representatives—to list just a few examples. Almost anytime we call customer-service numbers, we hear an announcement that the call may be monitored or recorded. The employer has a strong interest in ensuring that customer calls be handled accurately, efficiently, and courteously. Many companies with large customer-service operations have a regular program in which supervisors listen to calls periodically to train and evaluate new workers and to check on the performance of more experienced workers. Some advocacy groups argue that monitoring customer-service calls is a privacy issue: It infringes on the privacy of the employees and customers. Employers argue that there is no privacy issue: The calls are not personal; they are the

1. Monitoring and evaluation procedures should be explained fully to employees.
2. Employees should be told, when they are hired, that business calls may be monitored.
3. Only business calls can be monitored, not personal ones. Employers should provide unmonitored telephones for personal calls.
4. Employees whose performance is criticized should have access to monitoring data and an opportunity to challenge the evaluation.
5. Problems uncovered by monitoring should lead to more training. There should be no disciplinary action unless the employee fails to improve.
6. Employees should be involved in setting up procedures for monitoring.

Figure 8.3 Guidelines for Monitoring

job the worker was hired to do, and the customer is talking to a complete stranger. (Information about an account or purchase discussed in the call would be available to the supervisor independent of the monitoring.)

Complaints about monitoring (particularly of telephone and data-entry workers) led many large firms and industries (e.g., financial services) to establish clear and detailed monitoring policies. Worker organizations propose a variety of regulations. Figure 8.3 lists a set of guidelines for monitoring. Some are included in proposed federal legislation, and some have been adopted as policy by businesses. In a Harris survey of customer-service workers, these guidelines were considered necessary by at least roughly three-quarters (in some cases, more than 90%) of respondents.[28] Unions and privacy advocates propose more restrictive regulations. Examples include maintaining statistics on productivity only for groups, not for individual workers, elimination of the monitoring of employees with more than five years' experience, and informing workers each time they are to be monitored, not just in general. These are opposed by many employers.

In retail environments, another purpose of employee monitoring (besides training and measuring or increasing productivity) is to reduce theft. Theft by retail-store employees amounts to more than losses from shoplifting ($12.85 billion versus $10.15 billion in 2000). Some stores use software that monitors transactions at the cash registers, looking for suspicious patterns—for example, a large number of refunds, voids, or sales of cheap items. (In one scam, an employee scans and charges for cheap items, but bags expensive ones for the customer who is an accomplice.)[29] Does this kind of monitoring violate employee privacy?

The controversy over monitoring laws is a good context for thinking about the distinction between policies and law. Advocates argue that regulations will benefit employers ("a blessing in disguise" for employers, according to Lewis Maltby of the ACLU[30]). Written procedures for monitoring and for use of the collected data will make monitoring more useful to the employer. Giving more freedom and respect to long-time employees will maintain their loyalty and make them more productive. Counting keystrokes is counterproductive because it increases stress, reduces worker productivity, and causes

TRACKING TRUCKERS[31]

In the late 1980s, shippers began installing tracking systems in their long-haul trucks. Now, most trucks have such devices. They communicate by satellite and can report the location and speed of the truck, as well as such other details as when the driver turns on the headlights. Drivers communicate with dispatchers or automated systems at headquarters via a keyboard.

These systems have a number of advantages. They enable more precise planning of pick-ups and deliveries, increasing efficiency and saving money. Drivers no longer waste time searching for a public telephone to check in. Dispatchers can initiate communication with drivers. Communication in general, about schedule changes, road conditions, breakdowns requiring a mechanic, and so on, improved. Data on speed and rest periods can be used to ensure that safety rules are followed. Trucks whose trailers are loaded with valuable goods are a target for thieves; more than a hundred stolen trucks were located in one year because the thieves did not know about the devices.

The main disadvantage is that many drivers see the system as an intrusion on their privacy, a Big-Brother device watching their every move. The system can be used to micro-manage the driver's actions and decisions, decreasing individual discretion. When the devices were first introduced, some truckers wrapped foil over the transmitter or parked for naps under highway bridges.

Perhaps simpler devices, like cell phones and wireless e-mail, can accomplish enough of the communications goals without monitoring location and performance detail. Do the benefits of the monitoring outweigh the privacy intrusion, or is this an example of computer technology inappropriately infringing on privacy and personal autonomy?

health problems and costs. All of these are good arguments in many cases. Employers who are convinced that the proposals are beneficial to their company can adopt them. (Many, in fact, have.) What if some employers are not convinced? If the issue is whether specific practices are "good business," rather than a question of privacy rights or safety, who should make the decisions: legislators, or the people responsible for a particular business? Which monitoring guidelines involve issues of rights that should have legal protection, and which should be matters of policy to be determined within the company?

8.4.3 LOCATION MONITORING

In the nearby box, we illustrate some issues of location surveillance with one example—long-haul truckers. Electronic identification badges that serve as door keys raise similar issues. They provide increased security for a business, but they allow monitoring of the movements of employees. Nurses in some hospitals wear badges that track their location; a supervisor at a terminal can see where each nurse is. That means the supervisor can see who someone is having lunch with and when they go to the bathroom. On the other hand, nurses can be located quickly in emergencies. Would a call on a public-address system do just as well? Is it reasonable for a person working in this kind of job to expect his or her location to be private?

8.4.4 EMPLOYEE E-MAIL, WEB SURFING, AND VOICE MAIL

> *[E-mail] combines the casualness of speech with the permanence of writing. It's got a lot of potential for embarrassing the other side.*
>
> —Allan B. Taylor, attorney[32]

The use of e-mail and access to the Web at work made a lot of work more efficient and more pleasant, benefitting both employers and employees. But new problems arose. We look at misuse of e-mail and Web access, business policies about their use and about monitoring by employers, and the issue of employee privacy. The Electronic Communications Privacy Act (ECPA) prohibits interception of e-mail and reading of stored e-mail without a court order, but the ECPA makes an exception for business systems; it does not prohibit employers from reading employee e-mail on company systems. Some privacy advocates and computer ethicists advocate a revision of the ECPA to prohibit or restrict employers from reading employee e-mail. What are the arguments for and against this view? There is no law restricting monitoring by employers of Web activity by employees at work on the company system. Should there be?

E-MAIL AND VOICE MAIL AT WORK

Billions of e-mail messages travel within and among businesses each year. At first, people thought that, because they used a password to access their e-mail or voice mail, their messages were not accessible to anyone else. This is not true. In virtually all systems, the system manager can access anything on the system. Employers can read the e-mail of employees, they can listen to voice-mail messages, and they can read computer files. How many of them do? Figures from different sources vary, because of different counting methods, but roughly half of major companies in the U.S. sometimes monitor or search the e-mail, voice mail, or computer files of their employees.

Employees who have e-mail, voice mail, and their own computer files tend to be workers with more varied job functions and responsibilities than customer-service or data-entry workers. They include, for example, computer programmers, managers, sales people, secretaries, lawyers, researchers, and college professors. Such workers commonly use e-mail and the telephone for communications with family and friends, especially where there is no clear policy against it. Their files and messages are more likely to include personal content. Thus, privacy is often an issue. Employers claim they have a right and a need to monitor the use of their facilities. The controversies stem from disagreements about the appropriate boundary between the employers' rights and the employees' privacy.

- Find needed business information in an employee's messages or files when the employee is not available.

- Protect security of proprietary information and data.

- Prevent or investigate possible criminal activities by employees. (This can be work related, such as embezzlement, or not work related, such as the selling of illegal drugs.)

- Prevent personal use of employer facilities (if prohibited by company policy).

- Check for violations of company policy against sending offensive or pornographic e-mail.

- Investigate complaints of harassment.

- Check for illegal software.

Figure 8.4 Reasons for Monitoring E-mail, Voice Mail, and Computer Files

Most companies that read employee e-mail do it infrequently, primarily when there is a complaint or some other reason to suspect a problem. At the other extreme, some employers routinely intercept all e-mail entering and leaving the company site. Some supervisors snoop to find out what employees are saying about them or the company; some snoop into personal messages.

There are legitimate reasons for employers to sometimes listen to voice-mail messages or read e-mail or files on an employee's computer. Some are listed in Figure 8.4. Some businesses install filtering software to review all outgoing messages for content that violates laws or company policy, could damage relations with customers, or could expose the company to lawsuits. The box nearby describes one application of such e-mail filtering. The most common e-mail problem reported by one company was harassment (including sexual harassment, cases with pending divorces, and love triangles). Other problems include mailing jokes to thousands of people, running a business using the company's address, personal communications, and running betting pools on football and basketball games. Several large companies, including the New York Times, Dow Chemical, Compaq, and Xerox, made headlines by firing dozens of employees for violations of company e-mail and Web-use policies, in most cases because of sexually explicit or violent content. Because businesses face increased liability for sexual harassment by employees, some companies believe the harsh penalty is necessary to protect the company from lawsuits for a "hostile workplace environment."

LAW AND CASES

There is little law controlling workplace monitoring. Monitoring for purposes listed in Figure 8.4 is generally legal. In a case where two employees were fired after a supervisor read their e-mail messages that criticized him, a judge ruled that the company could

FILTERING PROFESSIONAL E-MAIL

Most major stock brokerage companies use e-mail filters to detect illegal, unethical, and offensive e-mail sent by their brokers. Stock brokers are not supposed to exaggerate the prospects of investments, downplay the risks, or pressure clients to buy or sell. Filters search for keywords such as "risk-free," vulgarities, and sexist or racist terms. They use artificial-intelligence techniques for more sophisticated analysis of messages.[33]

Is this an example of increased monitoring made possible by new technology? Not entirely. To protect the public, the New York Stock Exchange previously required that a supervisor read all written communication from brokers to clients. When e-mail replaced mailed letters, the volume increased so much that supervisors could no longer read all the mail. E-mail filtering replaced human review of all messages with human review of only those selected by the filter. On the other hand, people tend to use e-mail for a greater variety of messages than they did printed letters—including personal messages, which are now exposed to the filters. Does routine filtering of all e-mail violate the privacy of the brokers? If it does, is it justified by the trade-offs?

read the e-mail because it owned and operated the system. In another case, monitoring discussion about a boss was accepted because the discussion could affect the business environment. Courts have made similar decisions in other cases. Courts put heavy weight on the fact that the computers, mail, and phone systems used at work are the property of the employer and are provided for business purposes.

Employers are permitted by law to monitor telephone calls for business purposes. Courts have interpreted the ban on eavesdropping on nonbusiness calls to mean that an employer must cease monitoring a call as soon as it is apparent that the call is personal.[34]

Courts have sometimes ruled against employers if there was a convincing case that monitoring was done to snoop on personal and union activities or to track down whistle-blowers. Court decisions sometimes depend on a conclusion about whether an employee had a reasonable "expectation of privacy," but this concept is not always clear. At a minimum, an employer should set clear policies and inform employees about whether personal use of employer-provided communications and computer systems is permitted and about whether, and under what circumstances, the employer will access employee messages and files. Some large companies have explicit policies that employee e-mail is private and will not be read by the employer. Others provide a notice to employees every time they log on, reminding them that the system is for business, not personal, use, and that the company reserves the right to monitor messages.[35]

A clear statement of monitoring policy by the employer removes some of the guess-work about expectations of privacy. Such a statement is essential from an ethical perspective. Respect for an employee's privacy includes warning the employee about when his or her apparently private actions or communications are being observed (except in special circumstances such as a criminal investigation). Giving or accepting a job in which an employee will use an employer's equipment carries an ethical obligation on both parties to abide by the policy established for that use (again, except perhaps in special circumstances). From a practical perspective, a clear policy can reduce disputes and abuses (both by ordinary employees and by supervisors who might have snooped in ways that violate the company policy).

Employees do not give up all privacy when they enter an employer's premises. The bathrooms belong to the employer too, but camera surveillance in bathrooms is generally not accepted. Where else is there protection for privacy at a workplace? Some courts ruled that, if employers allow employees to use their own locks on their lockers, the employee has an expectation of privacy. An employee fired by Microsoft sued the company, using the locker analogy. He claimed Microsoft invaded his privacy by accessing e-mail he had stored in personal folders, protected by a password, on his computer at work. Microsoft allowed the password-protected personal folders, so, the employee argued, the folders should have been considered private. The court ruled against him. One of the arguments was that lockers are a discreet physical space provided for storing personal items, but the computer was for work and the messages were part of the work environment. The court also commented that "the company's interest in preventing inappropriate and unprofessional comments, or even illegal activity, over its e-mail system would outweigh [the employee's] claimed privacy interest in those communications."[36]

The National Labor Relations Board (NLRB) sets rules and decides cases about worker–employer relations; it has been a focus of controversy between unions and employers since it was established more than 60 years ago. Workers have a legal right to communicate with each other about work conditions, and the NLRB ruled in some cases that they may do so on company e-mail systems. Thus, employers may not prohibit all nonbusiness e-mail. The NLRB required that a company rehire and give back pay to an employee fired for sending an e-mail message to all employees criticizing a change in the company's vacation plan.[37] In the past, the NLRB ruled that policies about use of surveillance cameras, drug testing, and lie-detector tests must be discussed with a union if a company has one. It may require that e-mail policies, likewise, be negotiated with unions.

Many of the arguments made in legal cases are relevant to ethical decisions as well. The problem, for both ethics and law, consists of defining a reasonable boundary between, on the one hand, the employer's property rights, protection of company assets, the need for access to business information, and the need to monitor for possible legal and liability problems, and, on the other hand, actions that invade personal privacy. The most reasonable policy is not always obvious, not always the same in the view of both parties, not the same for all types of businesses, and not always clear when new situations arise.

SURFING THE WEB AT WORK

For many people, their first access to the Web was at work in the late 1990s. Employees found the Web so attractive that they quickly began to use it for nonwork purposes. One study counted 12,823 visits to *Penthouse* magazine's Web site in one month in 1996 from computers at IBM, Apple, and AT&T. Various surveys found high percentages of employees at businesses and government agencies (e.g., the IRS) using the Web for nonwork purposes (e.g., 79.8%, 90%). Visits to "adult" and pornography sites were soon overtaken by visits to chat rooms and sports, shopping, gambling, and stock-investment sites. Some companies found that employees spent more than two hours a week on nonwork Web activity. One company found that 3% of its Web traffic was to an online investment site and another 4% was used by employees downloading music.[38]

As we learned in Chapter 7, computers maintain detailed logs; employers can find out where their employees go on the Web. To make sense of the huge amount of obscure data in the logs, software companies developed products to provide reports on Web use in ways useful to employers, for example, ranked by frequency of visits or reports on an individual employee's activity. Many major companies use such software. Some employers installed variants of the filtering software products developed for parents to limit Web access by their children.

Is employer monitoring of Web activity by employees an unreasonable invasion of privacy? Is nonwork Web surfing a serious problem for employers, or is it a high-tech equivalent of reading a newspaper or listening to the radio at one's desk? Employers reported a number of concerns about nonwork Web activity. The obvious one is that employees are not working the hours they are paid to work. (On the other hand, a company found that one of its top-performing employees spent more than an hour a day managing his own stocks on the Web; the company did not care because his performance was good.) Another problem is that Web sites can determine where a visitor is coming from. Some companies want to avoid the embarrassment of having their employees reported to be visiting pornographic sites, perhaps racist sites, or even job-hunting sites.

When the employer is the government, there is an additional issue: avoiding misuse of taxpayer-funded resources. On the other hand, in some environments, such as discussion and research on pending cases by judges, monitoring is clearly inappropriate. Some judges had harsh criticism for an administrator of the federal judicial system who installed Web-use monitoring software, without notice, in systems used by 30,000 employees of the judiciary, including judges. In 2001, the Judicial Conference, the board that administers the federal judicial system, proposed a policy that all employees be assumed to waive privacy in communications when using office equipment. Appeals court judge Alex Kozinski, infuriated by the proposal, argued that both confidentiality of deliberations and trust in its staff employees are essential to the judicial system. The board settled on a policy allowing limited monitoring of Internet use, rather than the proposed unlimited monitoring that included e-mail. Many privacy advocates hoped the anger of some judges at the proposed monitoring of their e-mail and the compromise policy that was adopted would lead to more verdicts in favor of employees in monitoring cases.

8.5 Health Issues

Several possible health problems are associated with manufacture and use of computers. They include radiation from computer terminals, a possible link between cell-phone use and cancer, disposal of old computers (because of potentially toxic parts), and wrist problems (repetitive strain injury) from frequent use of computer keyboards and other automated systems (such as supermarket check-out scanners). There is controversy about most of these problems, because the scientific evidence is inconclusive.

I chose to discuss one health problem, *repetitive strain injury* (which includes the perhaps better-known *carpal tunnel syndrome*), in detail rather than give a brief overview of several, in part because many of the underlying issues and uncertainties are similar.

8.5.1 REPETITIVE STRAIN INJURY

WHAT IS RSI?

You may have seen computer programmers, secretaries, or supermarket checkers wearing wrist braces, called splints—a common sign of the increase in repetitive strain injury (RSI) and carpal tunnel syndrome in the mid-1990s. By 1998, the Bureau of Labor Statistics reported that 65% of workplace injuries in the U.S. were related to RSI, up from 21% in 1982.[39] More than 1200 articles about carpal tunnel syndrome and RSI appeared in the news media in one year, many focusing on computer keyboard operators as the victims. More than 3000 lawsuits were filed against employers and equipment manufacturers because of these conditions.

RSI causes pain in the wrist, hand, and arm (and sometimes the neck and shoulders too). It is associated with frequent, repetitive, forceful and/or awkward motion and unusual hand positions, or stress on the hands and wrists. Carpal tunnel syndrome involves damage to a nerve in the wrist and can result in numbness in the fingers and eventually in permanent disability. We will use "RSI" to refer to all the various hand and wrist problems that are being attributed to computers and automation.* These injuries can make ordinary activities painful or impossible and can prevent people from working.

Some reasons for the controversy and confusion surrounding RSI are (1) RSI includes more than a dozen different conditions, each with different symptoms and treatment, (2) RSI involves soft-tissue damage for which, in many cases, there are no clear, objective physiological diagnostic tests,† and (3) symptoms can take weeks, months, or years to show up. There are uncertainties about the nature, causes, diagnosis, treatment, and prevention of RSI.

WHO GETS RSI?

RSI is not a new disease. There are references to similar problems in the 18th and 19th centuries afflicting clerks and scribes (we used to call this "writer's cramp"), women who milked cows, and others whose work required repetitive hand motions. RSI problems occur among gymnasts, sign-language interpreters for the deaf, "pushup enthusiasts,"

---

*A variety of other terminology is used. One may see "repetitive stress injury," "overuse syndrome," "repetitive motion injury," and "cumulative trauma disorder."

† There are tests for carpal tunnel syndrome.

auto workers, seamstresses, musicians, carpenters, meat processors, and workers in bakery factories. An article in the *Journal of the American Medical Association* listed 29 occupations with common RSI problems.[40]

Computer users are the newest significant group of RSI sufferers. In many professions, people use a computer all day or for many hours each day. RSI afflicts data-entry personnel (some of whom type 10,000–15,000 keystrokes per hour), airline reservations clerks, stock brokers, emergency dispatchers, journalists, computer programmers, and others, including supermarket checkers who move products quickly past a bar-code scanner.

Although RSI is not new, from the mid-1980s to the mid-1990s the number of reported cases increased tenfold. What caused the dramatic increase? Two obvious factors are the increased use of computers and increased automation (leading to a faster pace of work). Other factors are improved accuracy in reporting, coverage by the news media, and increased awareness of the problem by employees and employers. Some writers suggest that RSI received more attention because the newer sufferers are white-collar workers (including journalists!) whose complaints are taken more seriously than those of factory workers and women. Unfortunately, measuring the extent and growth of RSI is complicated by social, psychological, and legal issues, some of which are likely to exaggerate the severity of the problem, whereas others could cause undercounting. It is sometimes difficult to distinguish real and serious injuries from imagined or exaggerated ones. Some medical writers warn doctors that, for some people, RSI is an excuse to get out of boring or stressful work; for some, it is a route to monetary compensation. (Workers Compensation might cover medical expenses and lost salary, and there is the prospect of winning large awards in lawsuits against keyboard makers and/or employers.) On the other hand, before RSI received a lot of attention, company doctors might have been reluctant to diagnose such a vaguely defined injury because of the costs to the employer.

It is not clear whether the real culprit in keyboard-related RSI cases is the design of the keyboard itself, improper user technique, bad posture, bad work habits, or poor ergonomic design of chairs and work tables. All these factors seem to contribute to the problem. No one is certain why one employee performing a specific job suffers from RSI, while another person doing the same job on the same equipment does not. Scientists studied a long list of possible causes or related factors, including weight, stress, congenital defects, wrist size, varicose veins, vitamin deficiency, and whether a person is double-jointed.[41]

As with so many problems we consider in this book, there are several categories of potential solutions: technical, managerial, legal, and educational.

ERGONOMIC SOLUTIONS

Some people emphasize physical design of keyboards, furniture, and so on as the cure-all for RSI. There has been a lot of attention to proper ergonomic design of keyboards and workstations. Responding to concerns about RSI, some laptop computer makers redesigned the machines to include a wrist rest. We can now buy split, twisted, and otherwise nontraditionally shaped keyboards—each one implementing some manufacturer's idea of what will be more comfortable and less likely to cause RSI. The variety of keyboards suggests uncertainty about what is best. Or, perhaps, what is best depends on the user, and a variety of options is desirable. Modifying equipment alone does not solve the problem. One RSI expert, Dr. Emil Pascarelli, reported that virtually all the RSI patients he saw unintentionally contributed to their injuries by using poor keyboard technique. He said RSI is almost totally preventable by both improving the physical arrangement of the work area and training the user in proper technique (including the importance of rest breaks, posture, and exercises). The National Safety Council reported that 90% of companies surveyed said that redesigning workstations and jobs was successful in reducing severe RSI problems.[42]

In the future, speech input may reduce RSI caused by keyboard use. (But we may discover an increase in strain of the vocal cords.)

THE ROLE OF MANAGEMENT

Many employers resisted making changes to tackle RSI. They might have been skeptical about the reality of the problem, or perhaps they were reluctant to spend money or modify work procedures in ways they thought would reduce productivity. Gradually, more employers recognized that the problem is real and that preventive measures cost less than medical expenses and lost work time for affected employees. The Sara Lee Corporation is a good illustration of this change. The employees who suffered from RSI were bakery assembly-line workers, including those who repeatedly and quickly twisted their wrists to bend croissants into their curved shape. Although they were not keyboard operators, the solutions have general applicability. At first, Sara Lee's management did not take employee complaints seriously. Injuries, lost work time, and surgeries increased. Eventually, the company made a major effort to solve the problem. Employees and outside experts evaluated and modified work tools and procedures. The result was that the number of work days lost to RSI dropped to a small fraction of the number for the previous year.* The company estimated that its measures to prevent RSI saved $750,000 per year at one bakery employing about 600 people.[43]

The success at Sara Lee and the data from the National Safety Council may suggest that appropriate modifications to reduce or eliminate RSI are so clear and well known that there is no excuse for not having implemented them sooner. Not quite. Reduced stress among Sara Lee workers, resulting from management's show of concern about the problem, might have contributed to the improvement. Also, before problems occur, it might not be at all obvious what tools need to be changed. For example, one of the modifications made at the bakery was a redesign of an icing gun to reduce its weight and the strength needed to squeeze out the icing. Equipment manufacturers have an incentive to design their products for comfortable use and reduced injury: It makes their products

---

* Eight days in the first seven months of 1992, down from 181 days in all of 1991. At the peak, in 1987, 731 work days were lost to RSI.

sell better. But would anyone have thought to redesign the icing gun before a significant number of icers began to have RSI problems? It could be easier to solve RSI problems than to predict where they will occur.

LEGAL ISSUES

Thousands of workers suffering from RSI sued keyboard makers and employers, charging that they are at fault and should pay for medical costs and damages to the victims. The suits argued that the manufacturers should have warned the users about the potential for injury. In the first such case to reach a jury verdict, the jury took less than an hour to decide in favor of the computer maker. Many of the suits were dismissed or resulted in decisions for the defendants. A few large awards to plaintiffs (one of more than $5 million, even though the jury concluded that there was no defect in the keyboard) were overturned on appeal. The uncertainty of causation made winning such suits difficult. Defense attorneys and some judges say that RSI is too vaguely defined and that causation has not been proved. Plaintiffs, on the other hand, argue that the connection between keyboard operation and RSI is clear and that they should not have to wait the years it will take until conclusive scientific studies can be done.

Some judges and others compare the complaints to ordinary aches and pains from over-exercising or overusing a normally safe tool or device. What would we think of an RSI lawsuit against the maker of a tennis racket or a violin? It is not clear whether keyboard makers should be held legally liable for RSI injuries or for not including warnings. However, partly because of growing recognition that there is a problem, even if its exact source is not known, and partly as protection against suits, several major computer companies began providing information about proper use and arrangement of keyboards. Some put "warning labels" on keyboards, telling users to read the safety information.

The federal government's Occupational Safety and Health Administration (OSHA) imposed stiff fines on some companies where a large number of employees suffered from RSI. In one case where the fine was $1.4 million, the company (Pepperidge Farms, another bakery) argued that they should not be fined when OSHA itself did not know how to prevent the injuries. A judge partly agreed and reduced the fine. OSHA spent more than 10 years working on federal workplace rules for RSI. In 1994, it said that specific rules could not be developed because scientists did not understand the causes of the injuries or how to prevent them. Commenting on the risks of writing detailed regulations, the head of OSHA said, "Specification standards can lock you into time and technology and inhibit innovation."[44] In 2000, OSHA issued ergonomic workplace standards (for RSI and other workplace injuries) that included 1600 pages of rules. OSHA said compliance would cost almost $5 billion a year for the first 10 years but save more than twice that much by reducing lost work time. Industry groups predicted much higher costs; one think tank gave an estimate of $126 billion per year. Congress repealed the new rules in 2001.*

---

*The timing was political. The controversial rules were issued at the end of the Democratic Clinton administration and repealed during the Republican Bush administration.

THE AUSTRALIAN EPIDEMIC

In the early 1980s, Australia experienced a sudden sharp epidemic of RSI. The number of cases reported in one state of Australia more than quadrupled in a five-year period (1979–1984). Most of the people reporting problems were women in government office jobs. At the peak, in 1985, more than 50% of workers in some areas reported RSI problems. In the next few years, the number of cases declined. The Australian RSI epidemic seemed unique at the time; cases in the U.S. were comparatively rare. Several researchers, including Kiesler and Finholt of Carnegie Mellon University, studied the Australian situation. Kiesler and Finholt found that poor equipment design alone did not explain the startlingly high rate of reported RSI cases in Australia. Australia imported most of its computer equipment from other countries, which were not experiencing similar RSI increases. In fact, Australia was making ergonomic improvements at the time the epidemic occurred. The rates of injury varied in different parts of the country, even though there did not appear to be any important differences in the work or workplaces. Because of the odd characteristics of the epidemic, this study and others considered hysteria, a phenomenon where the physical symptoms are real, but the causes are psychological—what we informally call the power of suggestion. Dr. Pascarelli offered another explanation for RSI "epidemics," one that could have been a factor in Australia: When some workers in large offices begin to suffer serious pain and disability, coworkers who are having milder problems begin to worry and seek treatment sooner than they might otherwise; as the problem gets more publicity, people with very early symptoms, who might have ignored them, will seek treatment immediately; thus, the number of new cases might spike, then level off.[45]

Kiesler and Finholt found a number of factors to be relevant in the Australian epidemic. RSI became a focus for union and feminist activity in the early 80s. The medical establishment gave RSI official validation and was willing to diagnose it early. The news media covered the problem in detail. RSI was recognized as a legitimate injury by the workers' compensation system in Australia. Workers could be compensated even if they had no physical symptoms. For a six-month period in Australia, no federal worker who applied for compensation for RSI was refused. Although all these factors were relevant, a main conclusion of this study and others was that many RSI complaints resulted from generally poor job conditions and low job satisfaction. Rapid conversion to computer technology and insufficient training increased stress. One government office increased required data-entry rates to 14,000 keystrokes per hour. Keyboard operators had low status, little autonomy, and a poor physical environment. Although not denying the reality of the pain suffered by many workers and not claiming that workers intentionally defrauded employers, the study points out that "the ambiguous nature of RSI makes it the perfect candidate for many workers as they seek an approved exit from the computing pool while preserving benefits and some salary."[46] The study suggests that ergonomic changes, while important, would probably not solve RSI problems in jobs that are themselves poorly designed.

EDUCATION AND CHOICES

Users of any tool should learn the proper techniques for its use. Employers have a responsibility to provide training in proper and safe use of tools, including keyboards. We, as computer users, have some responsibility for learning good keyboard work habits. Realistic observation of human behavior suggests that, even after users are educated about proper keyboard techniques and the need for rest breaks, many ignore what they learn. We are told repeatedly by mothers and doctors that we should sit up straight, exercise often, and eat our vegetables. Many people do not follow this advice—but, once we have the information, we can choose what to do with it.

> *Balance is very important for hand comfort. You'll be surprised at how quick your wrist will ache if the knife is not balanced properly.*
>
> —George McNeill, Executive Chef, Royal York Hotel, Toronto (on an advertisement for fine cutlery)

EXERCISES

Review Exercises

8.1   List two job categories where the number of jobs declined drastically as a result of computers.

8.2   List two job categories where the number of jobs increased drastically with the increasing use of computers.

8.3   What are two advantages and two disadvantages of telecommuting?

8.4   What are two advantages or purposes of electronic monitoring of keystrokes, of the number of items scanned by supermarket checkout workers, and so on? What are two of the main problems caused by such monitoring of employees?

8.5   What types of employee monitoring most affect professional ("white collar") employees?

8.6   Name two occupations where repetitive strain injury is common, but workers are not using computers.

General Exercises

8.7   List four examples from Section 1.3 where the benefit described reduces the number of jobs needed to accomplish the task. Tell specifically what jobs are reduced or eliminated.

8.8   Why is it difficult to determine the number of jobs eliminated and created by computers?

8.9   Jeremy Rifkin argues that the ability of Japanese auto makers to produce a car in less than eight hours illustrates the threat of massive unemployment from computer technology and automation.[47] How do the data in Figures 8.1 and 8.2 help to support or refute Rifkin's point of view?

8.10   What are some ways in which computers can decrease productivity?

8.11   Measuring productivity changes resulting from computerization can be tricky. The processing cost of a deposit or withdrawal made at an automated teller machine is approximately one-fifth the cost of a transaction using a teller. On the other hand, before ATMs were available, people went to their banks less often and withdrew a larger amount of money each time. Now many people make many small withdrawals each week at ATMs.[48] Describe several factors relevant to answering this question: Did productivity go up or down?

8.12 Should there be laws banning some kinds of home-based work and not others (e.g., sewing vs. office work)? Why, or why not? If you think there should be some restrictions on home work, what principles should be used in deciding what to prohibit?

8.13 Read Exercise 2.29. In response to part (b), many of my students suggested, among other things, surveillance cameras in the workroom to make sure nothing was copied or removed. In Chapter 2, we focused on privacy of the personal information in the records being scanned. Here we focus on privacy of the workers. Do you think cameras are appropriate? Why? If you think cameras are appropriate in some workplaces and not others, give examples and formulate criteria for deciding which.

8.14 Some unions propose federal legislation to prohibit monitoring of customer-service or data-entry employees with more than five years of experience. Give reasons for monitoring experienced employees. Give reasons for not monitoring them.

8.15 Which of the monitoring guidelines listed in Figure 8.3 do you think should be enforced by law, and which should be left to company policy? Why?

8.16 A federal agency considered a law requiring all long-haul trucks to have electronic monitoring devices to ensure that laws requiring rest breaks are obeyed. Government inspectors would review the collected data instead of reviewing paper logs required previously. Give arguments for and against such a law. Do you think it should be passed? How does this question differ from the decision of a shipping company to install such devices in its trucks?

8.17 Consider the reasons given in Figure 8.4 for employers to monitor employee e-mail, voice mail, and files. For which do you think it is appropriate to have regular, ongoing monitoring for all employees, and for which do you think employee mail and files should be accessed or monitored only when a problem occurs and only for the particular employees involved? Give reasons.

8.18 In what ways is monitoring of employee use of the Web to find those employees who are violating company Web-use policies similar to and different from the use by government agencies of computer matching to find people who might be breaking laws (Section 2.2)?

8.19 Using the Freedom of Information Act and similar state laws, some people have requested the e-mail of governors, legislators, and past and current presidents. These requests raise the issue of whether the e-mail of government employees and elected officials should be treated as personal conversation or official government documents. What do you think? Why?

8.20 Consider the following scenario. An employee at an investment firm reported to a supervisor that some employees have unlicensed software on their office computers. Over a weekend, without informing the employees in advance, the company searches all computers (via its network) looking for unlicensed software.

What alternative actions could the company have taken? Give reasons why they would have been better than, or not as good as, doing the search. Do you think the search was reasonable?

8.21 Suppose an employee uses computer time, services, and storage on an employer's computer for the employee's own business. Give arguments for considering such activity a matter of employer/employee relations (analogous to using a tool belonging to the employer for personal business). Give arguments for treating such action as a theft. Then take a position on one side and defend it.

8.22 In response to the lack of scientific knowledge about whether or how computer keyboards cause RSI, a plaintiff's lawyer who handled more than 1000 RSI lawsuits commented that "The law can't wait on science."[49] Give some arguments to support this statement (as it applies to RSI lawsuits). Give some arguments against it. Do you agree with the statement? Why?

Assignments

These exercises require some research or activity.

8.23 Get a current copy of your local newspaper and review the employment ads. What kinds of jobs are most common in the ads? What percentage of the ads are for jobs that require computer skills? What percentage are for computer professionals (programmers, computer engineers, etc.)?

8.24 Collect news stories from the next few weeks (or the past few weeks, if that is more convenient) about businesses hiring or laying off workers. Write a summary including the company, the industry it is in, the number of employees hired or laid off, the reasons given. To what extent is computer technology responsible for the employment changes?

8.25 a) Interview someone who uses a computer at work, but worked at the job (or a similar job) before computers were used for it. Write up the answers to the questions below. Include the person's name, employer, and job title. (Some possible choices for an interview subject are a waiter or waitress in a restaurant where orders are entered on a computer, a supermarket checkout clerk who worked before and after checkout scanners were introduced, a secretary or clerical worker who has worked with and without computers, a librarian, a police officer, a customer-service person. Consider family members, friends, etc.)
   1. Have computers made the work easier and more enjoyable, or more stressful and unpleasant? In what ways?
   2. Were you (and others who work with you) given adequate training in the use of the computer?
   3. What seems to be the general attitude toward computers among the people you work with?
   4. Did computerizing at the job cause some people to be fired?
   b) If possible, talk to a manager or supervisor at the same place and ask what the manager thinks the employees' answers would be to the questions above. Summarize the manager's answers. Are the manager's perceptions of the employee's opinions accurate?

8.26 Was RSI "a fad or an epidemic"? Find data from the past ten years on the number of RSI cases in the U.S. or Australia (or other countries), or look for articles on RSI. What trends do you see?

8.27 Investigate health and environmental issues related to disposal of old computers. What solutions are developing? How does the scientific certainty about the problems and solutions compare to the certainty about RSI?

Class Discussion Exercises

These exercises are for class discussion, perhaps with short presentations prepared in advance by small groups of students.

8.28 Assume you work for a recently formed software company developing new computer-security products. You are on a committee to write a company policy dealing with employee use of e-mail and the Web on company computer systems and a policy dealing with the monitoring of employee e-mail and Web use. Develop your proposals for the policies.

8.29 This exercise is intended for classes consisting of mostly computer science or engineering majors. At the beginning of the 21st century, only about 28% of students earning college degrees in computer science were women. Why do you think there are so few women in computer science? Have you observed or experienced any behavior or treatment in classes, computer labs, or at work that would discourage women?[50]

8.30 Have a mock trial in class for an RSI lawsuit against a computer-keyboard manufacturer. Assign teams of students to be lawyers for the plaintiff and the defense. Assign some to be medical expert witnesses and ergonomics specialists for each side. Assign the rest of the class to be the jury.

NOTES

[1] CPU: Working in the Computer Industry (an electronic publication for workers in the computer industry), Feb. 15, 1995.

[2] Associated Press, "Electronic Dealings Will Slash Bank Jobs, Study Finds," *Wall Street Journal*, Aug. 14, 1995, p. A5D. W. Michael Cox and Richard Alm, *Myths of Rich and Poor: Why We're Better off Than We Think*, Basic Books, 1999, p. 129. G. Pascal Zachary, "Service Productivity Is Rising Fast—and So Is the Fear of Lost Jobs," *Wall Street Journal*, June 8, 1995, p. A1. The quote is from Frank Zashen, in "Big Board to Lay Off All 150 Floor Couriers" *Wall Street Journal*, July 25, 2001, p. A6.

[3] Cox and Alm, *Myths of Rich and Poor*, p. 129. Alejandro Bodipo-Memba, "Jobless Rate Skidded to 4.4% in November," *Wall Street Journal*, Dec. 7, 1998, pp. A2, A8.

[4] Robert Fox, "Newstrack," *Communications of the ACM*, Apr. 1996, p. 9. Cox and Alm, *Myths of Rich and Poor*, p. 113. The Commerce Department projections and other employment data are from several *Wall Street Journal* articles: "Chip-Industry Study Cites Sector's Impact On U.S. Economy," Mar. 17, 1998, p. A20; "High-Tech Help Wanted," Nov. 16, 1998, p. R6; Bruce Ingersoll, "High-Tech Industries, Led by Internet, Boost U.S. Growth and Rein In Inflation," Apr. 16, 1998, p. B7; "High-Tech Added 200,000 Jobs Last Year," May 19, 1998.

[5] J. M. Fenster, "Seam Stresses," *Great Inventions That Changed the World*, American Heritage, 1994.

[6] Nick Gillespie, "Change Is Good," *Reason*, April 1995, p. 15.

[7] Cox and Alm, *Myths of Rich and Poor*, p. 136.

[8] W. Michael Cox and Richard Alm, *Myths of Rich and Poor: Why We're Better off Than We Think*, Basic Books, 1999, pp. 7, 55.

[9] Theodore Caplow, Louis Hicks, and Ben J. Wattenberg, *The First Measured Century: An Illustrated Guide to Trends in America*, AEI Press, 2001, p. 160. Cox and Alm, *Myths of Rich and Poor*, pp. 18–19.

[10] Cox and Alm, *Myths of Rich and Poor*, pp. 60, 59, 10.

[11] The cost, in work time, of some products and services increased in the same time period. Increases for tax-preparation fees, Amtrak tickets, and the price of a first-class-mail stamp perhaps result from more complex tax laws and monopolies. Increases in the average cost of a new house or car are partly due to the increase in size of new homes and the increase in features of new cars.

[12] Paul Wallich, "The Analytical Economist," *Scientific American*, Aug. 1994, p. 89.

[13] Cox and Alm, *Myths of Rich and Poor*, p. 43.

[14] Salgado's powerful photographic tribute to workers, many who work in extremely harsh conditions, was published as Sebastião Salgado, *Workers: An Archaeology of the Industrial Age*, Aperture, 1993. The photos described here, and several others, also appear in Miles Orvell, "A Tribute to the World's Workers," *Technology Review*, Oct. 1995, pp. 62–69.

[15] Reprinted in *British Labour Struggles: Contemporary Pamphlets 1727–1850*, Arno Press, 1972.

[16] Phillip J. Longman, "The Janitor Stole My Job," *U.S. News & World Report*, Dec. 1, 1997, pp. 50–52. Caplow *et al.*, *The First Measured Century*, p. 31.

[17] Longman, "The Janitor Stole My Job."

[18] "Work Week," *Wall Street Journal*, Jan. 6, 1998, p. A1. "Looking Good: Where the Fast Growth Is and Will Be," *Wall Street Journal*, Feb. 27, 1995, p. R5.

[19] Zachary, "Service Productivity Is Rising Fast—and So Is the Fear of Lost Jobs."

[20] Kemba J. Dunham, "Telecommuters' Lament," *Wall Street Journal*, Oct. 31, 2000, p. B1. Definition of telework vary considerably, so estimated numbers do also.

[21] Jack Nilles, "Teleworking: Working Closer to Home," *Technology Review*, April 1982, p. 56–62.

[22] Nilles, "Teleworking: Working Closer to Home."

[23] Joel Kotkin, "Commuting Via Information Superhighway," *Wall Street Journal*, Jan. 27, 1994, p. A14.

[24] David Rubins, "Telecommuting: Will the Plug Be Pulled?" *Reason*, Oct. 1984, pp. 24–32. The quote is from Dennis Chamot.

25 "The Incredible Shrinking Company," *The Economist*, Dec. 15, 1990, pp. 65–66. Cox and Alm, *Myths of Rich and Poor*, p. 115.

26 These trends, with several examples, are described in James B. Treece, "Breaking the Chains of Command," *Business Week*, special issue on the Information Revolution, 1994, pp. 112–114.

27 David D. Redell, "Safeguard Employees' Privacy," *San Diego Union–Tribune*, Oct. 13, 1993, p. B5.

28 Louis Harris and Associates, "Privacy and Fair Employer Monitoring Practices," April, 1994.

29 Calmetta Coleman, "As Thievery by Insiders Overtakes Shoplifting, Retailers Crack Down," *Wall Street Journal*, Sept. 8, 2000, p. A1.

30 "A Conversation With Lewis Maltby" (director of the ACLU's Task Force on Civil Liberties in the Workplace), *Privacy and American Business*, Sept. 1994, pp. 9, 12.

31 Stuart F. Brown, "Trucking Gets Sophisticated," *Fortune*, July 24, 2000, pp. 270B–270R.

32 Quoted in *Connecticut Law Tribune*, Dec. 18, 1995.

33 Alex Markels, "I Spy: Wall Street Gets Sneaky Software To Keep an Eye on Broker–Client E-mail," *Wall Street Journal*, Aug. 21, 1997, pp. C1, C23.

34 Rick Raber, "When Does Surveillance Turn to Intrusion?" *Chicago Tribune*, May 2, 1995, p. 3.

35 Anne Wells Branscomb, *Who Owns Information?*, Basic Books, 1994, reports that Federal Express, American Airlines, Pacific Bell, and United Parcel Service do this, p. 94. IBM and Citicorp provide similar reminders.

36 *McLaren v. Microsoft*, Texas Court of Appeal No. 05-97-00824CV, May 28, 1999 (www.gigalaw.com/articles/gall-2000-01-p5.html).

37 *Leinweber v. Timekeeper Systems*, 323 NLRB 30 (1997), "E-Mail Law Expands." www.infowar.com/law/99/law_072099a_j.shtml.

38 Joan Rigdon, "Curbing Digital Dillydallying on the Job," *Wall Street Journal*, Nov. 25, 1996, p. B1. *Wired*, Jan. 2001, p. 80. Michael J. McCarthy, "Now the Boss Knows Where You're Clicking," *Wall Street Journal*, Oct. 21, 1999, pp. B1, B4.

39 Claudia Graziano, "'Nintendo Thumb' Points to RSI," *Wired*, Dec. 3, 1998 (www.wired.com/news/culture/0,1284,16579,00.html).

40 Edward Felsenthal, "An Epidemic or a Fad? The Debate Heats Up Over Repetitive Stress," *Wall Street Journal*, July 14, 1994, pg. A1. R. L. Linscheid and J. H. Dobyns, "Athletic Injuries of the Wrist," *Clinical Orthopedics*, Sep. 1985, pp. 141–151. *American Annals of the Deaf*. David M. Rempel, Robert J. Harrison, Scott Barnhart, "Work-Related Cumulative Trauma Disorders of the Upper Extremity," *Journal of the American Medical Association*, 267:6, Feb. 12, 1992, pp. 838–842.

41 Sara Kiesler and Tom Finholt, "The Mystery of RSI," *American Psychologist*, Dec. 1988, 43:12, pp. 1004–1015. Felsenthal, "An Epidemic or a Fad?"

42 *Investors Business Daily*, June 28, 1994.

43 Joan E. Rigdon, "How a Plant Handles Occupational Hazard With Common Sense," *Wall Street Journal*, Sept. 28, 1992, p. A1.

44 Edward Felsenthal, "Ergonomics Guidelines Lack Solutions," *Wall Street Journal*, July 19, 1994, pg. B7.

45 Mark Ragg, "Plague of RSI Suddenly 'Disappears'," *The Australian*, Sept. 7, 1987. Sara Kiesler and Tom Finholt, "The Mystery of RSI," *American Psychologist*, Dec. 1988, 43:12, pp. 1004–1015. Emil Pascarelli and Deborah Quilter, *Repetitive Strain Injury: A Computer User's Guide*, John Wiley & Sons, Inc., 1994, p. 11.

46 Kiesler and Finholt, "The Mystery of RSI," p. 1012.

47 Jeremy Rifkin, "New Technology and the End of Jobs," in Jerry Mander and Edward Goldsmith, eds., *The Case Against the Global Economy and For a Turn Toward the Local*, Sierra Club Books, 1996, pp. 108–121.

48 Bob Davis and David Wessel, *Prosperity: The Coming 20-Year Boom and What It Means to You*, Random House, 1998, p. 95.

49 Steven Philips, quoted in Felsenthal, "An Epidemic or a Fad?"

50 One can find data and speculation in popular articles, research papers, and on the Web. A few samples: Charles Piller, "The Gender Gap Goes High-Tech," *Los Angeles Times*, Aug. 25, 1998, p. A1; Paul De Palma, "Why Women Avoid Computer Science," *Communications of the ACM*, June 2001, pp. 27–29; Brandice J. Canes and Harvey S. Rosen, "Following in Her Footsteps? Women's Choices of College Majors and Faculty Gender Composition," National Bureau of Economic Research, Working Paper No. 4874, Oct. 1994; *Journal of Women and Minorities in Science and Engineering*.

BOOKS AND ARTICLES

- Michael L. Dertouzos, *Computers and Productivity*, MIT Laboratory for Computer Science, 1990.

- Ronald Kutscher, *The Impact of Technology on Employment in the United States: Past and Future*, Farmer Press, 1987.

- Thomas K. Landauer, *The Trouble With Computers: Usefulness, Usability, and Productivity*, MIT Press, 1995.

- Jack Nilles, "Teleworking: Working Closer to Home," *Technology Review*, April 1982, pp. 56–62. An early article that foresaw many of the advantages and disadvantages of telework.

- Emil Pascarelli and Deborah Quilter, *Repetitive Strain Injury: A Computer User's Guide*, John Wiley & Sons, Inc., 1994.

- Don Sellers, *Zap! How Your Computer Can Hurt You and What You Can Do About It*, (ed. Stephen F. Roth), Peachtree Press, 1994.

- Suzanne P. Weisband and Bruce A. Reinig, "Managing User Perceptions of Email Privacy," *Communications of the ACM*, Dec. 1995, 38:12, pp. 40–47.

9

BROADER ISSUES ON
THE IMPACT AND
CONTROL OF
COMPUTERS

> *In a way not seen since Gutenberg's printing press that ended the Dark Ages and ignited the Renaissance, the microchip is an epochal technology with unimaginably far-reaching economic, social, and political consequences.*
>
> —Michael Rothschild[1]

Most of the topics we considered in previous chapters focus on one subject, such as crime, copyright, or censorship of the Internet. This chapter introduces broader, perhaps fuzzier, issues. Here we consider such questions as the following: How do computers and telecommunications affect human interaction and community? Will they increase the distance between rich and poor people? What is the impact of computing on the quality of life? Is computer technology, overall, beneficial to us or harmful? How should computing technology be controlled to ensure positive uses and consequences?

Whole books have been written on these topics; the presentations here are necessarily brief, but will introduce some of the issues and arguments.

9.1 Computers and Community

> *While all this razzle-dazzle connects us electronically, it disconnects us from each other, having us "interfacing" more with computers and TV screens than looking in the face of our fellow human beings. Is this progress?*
>
> —Jim Hightower[2]

> *If children are separated from their parents by hours of TV, from their play-mates by video games, and from their teachers by teaching machines, when are they supposed to learn to be human?*
>
> —Marian Kester[3]

Many people spend hours online in chat rooms or meandering in cyberspace instead of with their families and in-person friends. Teenagers and young adults stay up all night in front of their computer screens, playing games, exploring systems, hacking, or surfing the Net. Some virtually eliminate direct contact with their families and other people. Some who are already socially awkward find the computer easier to deal with than people; the computer provides an excuse not to overcome the social awkwardness. In an extreme case, a mother was arrested for neglecting her children and leaving them in filth while she surfed the Internet.[4]

Critics of the Internet worry that computers reduce face-to-face gathering and that the Web hurts local community vibrancy. Neil Postman says that voting, shopping, banking, and getting information at home is a "catastrophe;" there are fewer opportunities for people to be "co-present," resulting in isolation from neighbors. Technology, he worries, puts a much greater emphasis on the individual and downplays the importance of community. Richard Sclove and Jeffrey Scheuer argue that electronic communication will erode family and community life to the point that people will mourn the loss of depth and meaning in their lives.[5]

How serious are these problems? Is the Internet creating a subpopulation of people who are narrow and unsocial? Is working on a computer more isolating than reading a book, an activity that is usually applauded? Is the Internet destroying communities?

Social scientists offer various theories about what makes a strong community. Robert Putnam argues that one important factor is the number of clubs and other organizations people join and are active in.[6] As Alexis de Tocqueville observed more than 150 years ago, "Americans of all ages, all stations in life, and all types of disposition are forever forming associations."[7] We join hobby clubs, religious congregations, Boy Scouts and Girl Scouts, unions, professional organizations, service clubs, hiking and running clubs, and myriad others. Such memberships create informal personal and information networks that are helpful both for economic growth and for solving social problems in a community. But participation in clubs has been declining. Critics of computers and the Internet blame them for this decline, but social scientists point to a number of other factors: modern transportation and communications (encouraging increased mobility), changes in family patterns (later marriage, more divorce, working mothers), and television. The loss of close, local community ties began before widespread use of personal computers and the Internet. Several studies found that Net users are at least as likely as demographically similar nonusers to visit with family and friends and be members of a club or organization. Some studies in the 1990s found that some Internet users spent less time with family and friends. Later studies (some by the same researchers who earlier found problems) found opposite results. Users of computers and the Internet were "voracious consumers of information," not just from online sources. They read newspapers, magazines, and books and watched serious news programs on television as much as or more than people with similar demographic characteristics who were not frequent users of computers and the Internet. A substantial number of e-mail users said e-mail brought them closer to their families. Jon Katz summarized the results of a survey by Luntz Research Companies by saying "The Internet is not a breeding ground for apathy, disconnection, and fragmentation. Instead, the online world is home to some of the most participatory citizens we are ever likely to have."[8]

The telephone was criticized as replacing true human interaction with disembodied, remote voices. It actually expanded and deepened social relationships for people who were isolated: women in general (farm wives, in particular), and the elderly, for example.[9] Today, the Internet provides communities focused on special interests or problems for which a person might not find many contacts in his or her local community. Some people who are socially awkward communicate more because of e-mail than they would without it. From its early years, according to the CEO of America Online, more people used AOL for "community" than for information retrieval. Online relationships tend to be based

WAL-MART AND E-COMMERCE VERSUS DOWNTOWN AND COMMUNITY[10]

Will electronic commerce force changes on communities that no one wants? In their article "On the Road Again? If Information Highways Are Anything like Interstate Highways—Watch Out!" Richard Sclove and Jeffrey Scheuer argue that it will.[11] They use the analogy of a Wal-Mart store draining business from downtown shops, resulting in the decline of the downtown community, a "result that no consumers wanted or intended." They generalize from the Wal-Mart scenario and warn that, as cyberspace is commercialized and we conduct more economic transactions electronically, we will lose more local stores, local professional and social services, and convivial public spaces like the downtowns of small towns. Consumers will be "compelled" to use electronic services, "like it or not." The underlying point of view in Sclove and Scheuer's article is shared by other strong critics of technology (including the Luddites, whom we discuss further in Section 9.4). Their proposed remedies are similar in spirit to others, so it is worth examining their argument.

The Wal-Mart analogy is a good one; the scenario is useful for illustrating and clarifying some issues about the impact of e-commerce on communities. Suppose, say Sclove and Scheuer, that a new Wal-Mart store has opened just outside of town and about half the town residents begin to do about a third of their shopping there, while the others continue to do all their shopping downtown. Everyone shops downtown, and everyone wants the downtown stores to remain. But downtown stores have lost about 16.5% of their sales, and many will not survive. Sclove and Scheuer describe this as an "involuntary transformation" which no consumer wanted or intended. It occurs, they say, because of a "perverse market dynamic." The changes, however, are not involuntary or perverse. The core of the problem with Sclove's and Scheuer's interpretation is their failure to make two important distinctions: the distinction between wanting something and willingness to pay for it, and the distinction between something being coerced or involuntary, on the one hand, and being unwanted, unintended, or unexpected, on the other.

Consider a simpler situation for a moment. Suppose we poll the adult residents of a small town with a population of, say, 3000, and ask if they would like to have a fine French restaurant in town. Almost everyone says yes. Will a French restaurant open in the town? Probably not. Almost everyone wants it, yet there is not enough potential business for it to survive. There is a market dynamic at work, but it is not perverse. The fact that consumers want a particular service, store, or product is irrelevant if not enough people are willing to buy it at prices that make the business viable. In Sclove's and Scheuer's Wal-Mart scenario, the downtown stores could stay in business if the people were willing to pay higher prices to make up for the 16.5% of revenue lost to Wal-Mart. But we know that if the stores raise prices, they will almost certainly lose even more customers. The town residents are not willing to pay what it costs to keep the downtown stores in business. You may object: The townspeople did not have to pay the higher prices before. Why now?

Because now the people who shop at Wal-Mart (or online) *have another choice*. Whatever price advantage or convenience lured them to Wal-Mart (or online), they were not getting that benefit before. Again there is a market dynamic at work, but not a perverse one: competition.

The second issue about the Wal-Mart/e-commerce scenario is whether the change is an "involuntary" transformation. Sclove and Scheuer say that, as local businesses decline, people will be compelled to use electronic services, like it or not. Is this accurate? No more so than Wal-Mart shoppers or cyberspace enthusiasts were compelled to shop downtown (or from other offline stores), like it or not, before they had the new option. The new status quo is no more involuntary than the previous one. Although no one wants to see the downtown decline, the actions that may lead to that result are all voluntary. When a new store opens, no one is forced to shop there. The impact on the downtown stores may not have been obvious to all the townspeople at the beginning (although now it is common enough that they might have anticipated it), but an unexpected or unintended result is not the same as a coerced result. In a free society, individuals make millions of decisions based on their knowledge and preferences. This decentralized, individualized decision-making produces a constantly changing pattern of stores, services, and investments (not to mention social and cultural patterns). No one can predict exactly what the result will be, and no one intends a particular picture of the economy or society, but (apart from government subsidies, prohibitions, and regulations), the actions of the consumers and merchants are voluntary. No one person can expect to have exactly the mix of shopping options (or other community characteristics) that he or she wants. If the result flows from the myriad decisions made by consumers and producers, it is not coerced. It is the process, not the result, that tells us whether people are being compelled.

Sclove and Scheuer propose laws and regulations to strengthen the elements they consider important to community. For example, in order to "conserve cultural space for face-to-face social engagement, traditional forms of community life, off-screen leisure activities, and time spent in nature," they give two examples of regulations they approve: adjusting charges for the Internet to discourage its use one evening a week, and using revenue from a special tax on electronic shopping to subsidize (offline) local community projects. Economists point out that tax subsidies and artificial manipulation of prices waste resources by shifting production from services consumers value more highly to those they value less. Supporters of such proposals view the individual choices as less important than the strength of the community. Coming from Sclove and Scheuer, who expressed so much concern about things "involuntary" and about people being compelled to use certain services, "like it or not," their proposals are astonishing in their casual denial of freedom and choice. Like it or not, you have to pay a higher rate for Internet access on Monday evening, even if that is the only evening you are off from your restaurant job. Like it or not, you have to subsidize community activities you do not participate in, because you prefer electronic shopping. Sclove and Scheuer do not seem to see coercion when practiced against people whose preferences differ from theirs.

Change creates new options and causes some old options to disappear. Those who prefer a new option see it as progress. Those who prefer a lost option view the change negatively. Neither side's preference is inherently or absolutely better than the other; people have different likes and dislikes, different priorities, different lifestyles. Community is important to most people. Thoughtful criticism of the impact of the Net on community can make us think about our own activities, choices, and trade-offs. Individualism and strength of community are not in opposition; coercive manipulation of people's choices and activities breeds resentment rather than community.

on similar interests rather than merely proximity in a neighborhood. We can judge from the enormous popularity of online communities that they benefit their participants.*

To the extent that computers contribute to the formation of electronic relationships with people scattered around the country and the world, they might further weaken local community bonds, but the degree of change seems small compared to the effects on communities from other technological and social changes. Automated and online services reduce the opportunities for personal interaction with neighbors and local merchants in the course of ordinary daily activities, but they free time that we can fill with activities shared with people we know well and associate with by choice.

The desire for the advantages of small community life—a slower pace, less commuting, closeness to nature, involvement with neighbors, and so on—is prompting many professionals and information workers to move to small towns. Some businesses are relocating to small towns, because telecommunications and transportation reduce the need to be in a larger city. In the 1980s, population in 20 of the 40 largest metropolitan areas declined; a study by the Office of Technology Assessment attributed the decline to advances in information technology.[12] Computer technology makes a return to small-community life easier. The Internet, satellite communications, and related technologies bring education, information, and entertainment options that were not available in small, rural towns before. Computer enthusiasts see the ability of the Net to "conquer distance" as one of its advantages, potentially allowing a reversal of the population concentration in cities. On the other hand, some people, especially young adults, prefer city life for its vibrancy and for its career and social opportunities.[13]

"Addiction" to the Internet is a real problem for some people. A study of computer "addicts" found that many had other psychological problems.[14] Without computers, computer "addicts" might be among the people who engage in other unwise or unhealthy

*This statement is not accepted by some writers who believe that people are deluded and that the technology itself forces people to use it. I take the simpler view that, when people make voluntary choices, they choose what they perceive as beneficial to them.

behavior, such as excessive gambling, alcoholism, drug abuse, eating disorders, television "addiction," and even excessive shopping. These are all problems to be addressed and treated, but they are not flaws of the substances or activities the people misuse.

9.2 Information Haves and Have-Nots: The Access Issue

The term *digital divide* appears often in headlines and articles about access to computers and information systems. It refers to the fact that some groups of people have access to and regularly use high-tech information and communication technology while others do not. There is a digital divide in the U.S. (and other developed countries) between richer and poorer people, between people of different age groups, and between people of different ethnic backgrounds. There is also a digital divide between developed countries and poor countries. Most people in the world have never made a telephone call and have little or no access to books. Lack of access to the Internet in much of the world has the same causes as lack of telephones, health care, education, and so on: poverty, isolation, and sometimes politics. These problems are beyond the scope of this book. We focus on the access issue as experienced in the U.S.; many of the ideas in the discussion are relevant in other parts of the developed and developing world.

Under the universal service guarantee in the Communications Act of 1934, telephone companies are required to provide telephone service to poor people at low rates, subsidized by other customers. Should the principle of universal service be extended to "universal access" to the Net? The focus on this issue stems from the concern that access to information might give some people such a large advantage over those without access that our society will divide sharply into the "information haves" and "information have-nots," leaving the have-nots to a lowly and unsatisfying existence. Children who do not acquire basic computer skills will be at a disadvantage when they try to find a job. The human cost in joblessness, wasted potential, and poverty could be high. Many universal access advocates see it as an issue of social equity. A variety of organizations and government committees developed principles, arguments, and proposals for universal access in the mid-1990s. Computer Professionals for Social Responsibility (CPSR) stated that "Universal access to the NII* is a necessary and basic condition of citizenship in our information-driven society. Guaranteeing such access is therefore an absolute requirement for any degree of equity."[15] CPSR listed the following as minimum requirements.

- Everyone in the country must have access to a place from which to connect to the NII.

- Hardware and software for the NII must be easy to use and must fit the needs of all users, including the disabled.

---

*"National Information Infrastructure," or NII, was a political term for the Net in the U.S. in the 1990s.

- Simple training in the effective use of these tools must be available.

- Pricing for the NII must be structured so that service is affordable by everyone.

- Access to the full range of features supported by the NII must be available to all.

CPSR noted that "access will require not merely a connection to the NII but the hardware to use that connection."[16] Other organizations defined universal access to include e-mail, Web browsers, and interactive, multimedia equipment and software. To some advocates, availability in libraries is not enough; everyone must have access from home. Universal-access advocates proposed various methods to achieve their goals, including requiring companies to provide discounted rates to poor people, taxing businesses that provide Internet services, and providing government programs to pay for computers in libraries, public schools, and community centers.[17]

It is clear that advocates of universal access see access as a right—in particular, a positive right (or claim-right, in the terminology of Section 1.2.2)—something that must be provided for everyone who cannot afford it. Ethical objections to mandatory and tax-funded programs to provide access are raised by those who emphasize negative rights (liberties) over claim rights; mandatory programs violate the liberties of business owners and taxpayers who must pay for them. Fortunately, the incredible decline in prices has quite possibly made the ethical and political disagreements less important. We consider how serious the access problem is, and what solutions are available.

TRENDS IN COMPUTER ACCESS

When personal computers first became available, they were expensive and difficult to use. The same was true of Internet access. Society went from everyone equally not having any to a small elite minority enjoying these new tools. In 1994, according to a Times Mirror survey, a family with a college graduate parent and family income over $50,000 was five times more likely to have a home computer and ten times more likely to have a modem than the family of a nongraduate earning less than $30,000. Almost half the children of college graduates used a computer at home; only 17% of children of parents with high school education or less did.[18] Poor children and children of some ethnic minorities had less access to computers both in schools and at home.

Virtually all technological innovation is first available to the rich (or others willing to pay the initially high price). The early purchases finance improvements in design and production techniques that bring the price down. Prices of many consumer products follow this pattern. Telephones and televisions were originally luxuries of the rich; now almost every household has them. When first introduced in the 1980s, compact-disk music players cost $1000. Computer prices plunged more dramatically than prices of most other products, even while the memory, speed, and variety of input/output devices

Earlier technologies		Computer-related technologies	
Television	25	Personal computers	16
Radio	27	World Wide Web	7
Telephone	35	Cell phones	13
Electricity	45		
Automobiles	55		

Figure 9.1   Number of Years (Approximately) to Reach 25% of U.S. Households [19]

and software were increasing enormously.* The vast resources of the Internet are available for about the cost of monthly telephone service.

Nearly a century ago, the electric starter for automobiles eliminated the need to crank the engine of a car, helping to make driving easier and hence popular among more people. Similarly, software innovations, such as point-and-click graphical user interfaces (GUIs) and Web browsers, made computer use significantly more comfortable for ordinary people. With lower prices, more applications, and ease of use, ownership and access spread quickly. The data I found about the extent of computer ownership and Web access differed in specific numbers (so the numbers should not be taken as exact), but all showed the same trends.[20] For example, in 1990, 22% of households owned a computer; in 2001, 63% did, and 57% had Internet access at home. 84% of homes with children in middle and high school had Internet access. This indicates that families perceive Web access to be important for their children and allocate their spending accordingly. Figure 9.1 shows that computer technology reached more households faster than earlier technologies.

Access did not spread equally among all segments of society. In the early 1990s, only about 10% of Net users were women. By 1997, the gender gap had vanished; 48% of Americans using the Net regularly were women. In 2000, Nielsen//NetRatings reported, slightly more than 50% of Net users were women.[21] Other gaps remained. In 1999, people from low-income households were about half as likely to have Internet access from home as was the general population. Black and Hispanic households were about half as likely as the general population to own a computer. Access in rural, isolated, remote regions lagged the cities, but the federal government's National Telecommunications and Information Administration reported that, in 2000, the state with the highest percentage of households with Internet access from home was Alaska.

Software that used to cost hundreds of dollars is now included in the price of a PC (and is more powerful than before). Software of all sorts, including Web browsers, is available for free. Some is provided by programmers who believe in the free-software paradigm described in Chapter 6; some is provided by companies who see it as advertising

---

*For example, the cost of disk storage fell from hundreds of dollars per megabyte in the 1980s to $5.23 per megabyte in 1991 to less than a penny a megabyte in 2001.[22] My first computer, bought in 1983, had less than a megabyte of memory, a 10-megabyte disk, a monochrome monitor, no modem or graphics, and a chip speed of perhaps a few megahertz. It cost $5000.

for other products. Several companies offer free e-mail service. Qualcomm offers two free versions of the popular Eudora e-mail program: a limited-feature version, and a full-feature version that includes ads. (They charge for the full-feature version without ads.[23]) Some cities have computer swap meets, where one can buy equipment at very low prices. The hottest, superfast personal computers of a few years ago, with their then astoundingly large disk capacity and multithousand dollar price tags, could be found on eBay a few years later for a few hundred dollars. Thus, many options are available for those on a small budget.

The phenomenon that new technologies and inventions first are expensive luxuries, then become cheaper and spread throughout the population has led some observers to conclude that it is more accurate to think of people as "haves" and "have-laters" rather than "haves" and "have-nots."[24] An unexpectedly large increase in the number of homes with personal computers in 1995 was attributed in part to increased purchases by people less affluent. In 1999, the Pew Research Center found that 40% of new adult users of the Internet had not attended college. Nielsen//NetRatings reported that, in 2000, African-Americans went online for the first time at a higher rate than any other demographic group. In 2001, the rate of increase of Internet users 65 and older was higher than the rate for the U.S. overall. Thus, groups with low access in earlier years began to catch up.

Ford Motor Company's decision in 2000 to offer home computers (for free) and Internet access (for $5 per month) to its 350,000 employees is a solution to the access problem few would have anticipated. The offer went to all workers, including factory workers and employees in other countries, not only people who use a computer at work.[25] Delta Air Lines established a similar program to give computers and Net access to its employees. Others were expected to follow. The computers are a fringe benefit to employees and a tool for improving communication between the company and employees. Apartment-building owners in New York negotiated an agreement with the union representing 55,000 maintenance and service employees to provide subsidized computers, Internet access, and training to the workers.

Why don't more families have Internet access at home? In several polls, 23–57% of the people without it said they had no need for it. In one survey, about 9% of people without Internet access cited cost as the reason. By 2001, more than 42 million people had free access to the Internet at work; many saw no reason to pay for it from home. Many retired and elderly people don't feel they need access. People set spending priorities and buy what they value most. More than 98% of American households have televisions. The Times Mirror survey, mentioned earlier, found that, although the percentage of children who had access to computers at home in the early 1990s varied significantly with socioeconomic status, there was little difference in the percentage of homes that had video games.

Most Internet-service providers require that customers have a credit card, but some low-income families do not qualify for credit cards. Thus, even if they are willing to pay, they may not be able to get Internet access at home. Flexibility in payment schemes and other solutions are needed to solve subtle problems such as this.

The market provides options for people who want to use a product but cannot afford to buy it. For example, we pay per page for photocopies at a copy store, and people who do not own a washing machine use coin-operated laundries. "Computer bars" and "Internet cafés" sprang up from Alaska to Cairo in the 1990s, when Net access from home was relatively uncommon. They provided Internet access for an hourly fee, or free with purchases of food or coffee. In 2000, a British company, easyEverything, opened an 18,300 square foot Internet café in Times Square in New York with rates as low as 25 cents an hour at off-peak times. The company operates more than a dozen such cafés in Europe.[26] By the end of the 1990s, most public libraries provided Internet access for the public for free (and reaped the headaches of the filtering debate described in Chapter 5).

Volunteers in the FreeNet movement established community networks in many cities. Community centers, and especially senior centers, offer classes in how to use computers. Individuals, businesses, and community organizations contribute equipment and services. Initially, wiring schools for the Internet was a challenge. In California, in 1996, high-tech companies sponsored NetDay, a modern "barnraising," a day on which thousands of volunteers went to schools around the state to install wire. Similar projects followed in other states. In the late 1990s, the federal government began spending about $1.5 billion a year on technology for schools. Local governments spent several billion more. By 2000, 98% of high schools had Internet access. (Disagreement continues about whether schools have enough computers; in some schools, students have to share, and to wait for, a workstation.) High-tech companies buy new computers and donate the old ones to schools. AT&T, Microsoft, Oracle, Intel, and one of Bill Gates' charitable foundations gave hundreds of millions of dollars to provide computers and Internet services for schools, universities, and libraries and to train 400,000 teachers in 20 countries how to use technology effectively in the classroom.

The market, other voluntary efforts, and libraries and schools do not provide the universality of access that some universal-access proponents consider essential. Second-hand computers do not meet their requirement of access to the full range and quality of features and services currently available. Libraries and Internet cafés do not provide access in the home. Are these goals too high, or are universal-access requirements needed?

9.3 Loss of Skills and Judgment

> *Where is the wisdom we have lost in knowledge?*
> *Where is the knowledge we have lost in information?*
>
> —T. S. Eliot, "Choruses from 'the Rock'," 1934[27] *

Computers, like other tools and technologies, encourage certain uses and consequences by making them easier. Some skills that were important before are displaced by

---

* Many have added "Where is the information that we have lost in data?"[28]

the new tools. We look at some examples of the ways computers and other technologies affect the way we do things.

WRITING, THINKING, AND MEMORY

> *I have a spelling checker.*
> *It came with my PC.*
> *It plainly marks four my revue,*
> *Miss steaks aye can knot sea.*
> *Eye ran this poem threw it,*
> *I'm sure your pleased too no.*
> *It's letter perfect in it's weigh,*
> *My checker tolled me sew.*
>
> —Jerrold H. Zar, "Candidate for a Pullet Surprise"[29]

The spelling-checker verse humorously illustrates the problem of doing what the tool makes easy and ignoring other important tasks. A computer can check the spelling of all the words in a document in less time than it takes a person to find the first one by flipping through the pages of a printed dictionary. But a spell checker looks up each word only to discover whether it is in its dictionary; it does not check on whether the word is used properly. Computers made many steps in the publishing process easier. The ease and fun of playing with layout, fonts, and graphics led many people to concentrate on those aspects of the document at the expense of thoughtful writing, correct grammar, word usage, correct information, and editing—the parts that still require hard mental effort. The convenience of using a computer can encourage mental laziness, which can sometimes have serious consequences. A newspaper editor in Pakistan received a letter to the editor by e-mail and inserted it into the newspaper without reading beyond the title. The letter was an attack on the prophet Muhammad. Angry Muslims set fires in the newspaper office; several editors were arrested and charged with blasphemy, which can be punished by death. Back when newspaper content was still being typeset and copyedited, such an accident would have been unlikely. Another example: Now that research is so easy to do online, students and scholars are less inclined to actually go to a library and look up material in older books and journals that are not on the Web.[30]

Critics of computers see the loss of skills as part of a long trend of skill losses due to technology. Taking their cue from Socrates (through Plato's *Phaedrus*), they find fault with the invention of writing. It destroyed memory and oral skill and obscured the distinction between wisdom and knowledge. With reading and writing, the complaint argues, a presentation tends to be more one-sided, more dogmatic, because there is no dialogue, no one to question arguments and conclusions.[31] Numerous critics of the Internet make similar charges against it: A vast amount of information is available, but it comes without wisdom. Computers emphasize thinking based on data, numbers, quantifiable entities. They discourage focus on judgment and values. They encourage the making of fancy charts based on complex computations, but they discourage deep thought about the purpose to which the charts will be put or the validity and meaning of the data. They encourage surfing the Net, looking for facts; they discourage discussion with others of what we found and the ability to defend a point of view in conversation.

It is valuable to observe the changes in social patterns that occur because of the invention of a new tool or technology. It helps us understand how human beings behave and how society evolves. Although it is valuable to be aware of changes in the relative importance of various skills, it is not obvious, as some critics suggest, that all the changes are bad. Some old skills are replaced by better ones. How much more poetry is available to us now in books than we could have memorized? While most of us no longer develop strong memorization skills, these skills have not been lost to those who need them, such as an actor in a one-person play that lasts two hours. Some Chinese people worry that word processors are destroying the ability to write Chinese characters by hand. A Chinese scholar, Ping Xu, reported that a similar controversy arose when pens began to replace calligraphy brushes. He argued that, if the computer is easier to use and helps people learn the Chinese language, it will prevail. Language scholar Walter Ong pointed out that the old skills are not lost; they are enhanced, but not used where the new ones function better. He argued that writing made oral communication much more effective. Certainly the Internet can be used to enhance communication. Anyone who participates in online newsgroups and discussion groups knows that dialogue and argument survive. The quality, not surprisingly, includes both thoughtful, deep analysis and insulting "flame wars." Perhaps surprisingly, as more people connected to the Internet and bought multimedia CDs and DVDs, sales of books rose steadily.[32]

This is not to say that all the criticisms are unfounded. We need to evaluate the changes carefully and identify those that truly are problems. For example, we should be alert to the tendency to overemphasize tasks that computers can do well, while ignoring other important tasks—that is, the tendency to mental laziness. We need to resist the temptation to emphasize data rather than analysis, facts rather than understanding and evaluation. We need to develop the habit of and the tools for distinguishing truth on the Web from rumor and falsehood. Some educators and parents are particularly worried that schools are contributing to these problems (and others) by emphasizing use of computers, particularly for elementary school children.

ABDICATING RESPONSIBILITY

People are often willing to let computers do their thinking for them. Abdication of responsibility to exercise judgment, and sometimes, a reasonable amount of skepticism, has serious consequences. Loan approvals, insurance approvals, and similar decisions are

IDIOTS AND DUNDERHEADS

Many losses of skills are unintended side effects of computers, but Microsoft made a conscious decision that has the effect of diminishing vocabulary and the richness and humor of language. The thesaurus in Microsoft Word 2000 lists "trick" as the only synonym for "fool." It omits "clown," "blockhead," "idiot," "ninny," "dunderhead," "ignoramus," and others—all present in earlier versions. Because of the popularity of Word and the ease of using its reference utilities, fewer people will consult standard references such as dictionaries and Roget's Thesaurus (which contain some of these and more choices: "dupe," and "simpleton," for example).

Microsoft said it eliminated words "that may have offensive uses."[33] Was this a dunderheaded decision that dulls the language and reduces literacy? Do producers of widely used reference works have an ethical responsibility to report the substance of their field accurately, or a social responsibility to remove potentially offensive words from the language?

made with the help of computerized credit and health reports. School districts make decisions about the progress of students and the careers of administrators on the basis of computer-graded and -calibrated tests. Bad decisions are sometimes made because of ignorance of the kinds of errors that can occur in the computer system, ignorance of the purpose of the system, and the mystique that anything coming from a computer must be correct. People were arrested when a check of the FBI's NCIC computer showed an arrest warrant for someone with a similar name. Does the officer think that because the warrant was displayed, the computer has decided that the person being checked is the wanted person? Or does the officer know that the system simply displays any close matches and that the responsibility for the arrest decision lies with the officer?

Sometimes reliance on a computer system rather than human judgment becomes "institutionalized" in the sense that an organization's management and the legal system can exert strong pressure on individual professionals or employees to do what the computer says. In bureaucracies, a decision-maker might feel that there is less personal risk (and less bother) in just accepting a computer report rather than doing additional checking or making a decision not supported by the computer. It is critical to remember that, in such complex fields as medicine, the computer systems might not be intended, or good enough, to substitute for an experienced professional's judgment. Complex computer programs advise doctors on treatments for patients. In environments where, when something goes wrong, "I did what the program recommended" is a stronger defense (to managers or against a lawsuit) than "I did what my professional judgment and experience recommended," there is pressure on doctors to abdicate responsibility and do whatever the program says.

9.4 Evaluations of the Impact of Computer Technology

The microchip is . . . made of silicon, or sand—a natural resource that is in great abundance and has virtually no monetary value. Yet the combination of a few grains of this sand and the infinite inventiveness of the human mind has led to the creation of a machine that will both create trillions of dollars of added wealth for the inhabitants of the earth in the next century and will do so with incomprehensibly vast savings in physical labor and natural resources.

—Stephen Moore[34]

Quite apart from the environmental and medical evils associated with them being produced and used, there are two moral judgments against computers. One is that computerization enables the large forces of our civilization to operate more swiftly and efficiently in their pernicious goals of making money and producing things. . . And secondly, in the course of using these, these forces are destroying nature with more speed and efficiency than ever before.

—Kirkpatrick Sale[35]

9.4.1 THE NEO-LUDDITE VIEW OF COMPUTERS, TECHNOLOGY, AND HUMAN NEEDS

The quotations above illustrate the extreme divergence of views about the value of computer technology. Evaluations of computers cover the spectrum from "miracle" to "catastrophe." Although most of this book has been devoted to discussing problems that arise with the use of computers, the implicit (and sometimes explicit) view has been that computers are a positive development bringing us many benefits. Our discussion of failures of computer systems warns us that some potential applications can have horrifying risks. The potential for loss of freedom and privacy via government surveillance and the building of consumer dossiers is a serious danger. Computer crime is expensive, and changes in employment are disruptive. We might urgently try to prevent some applications of computers from being implemented and urgently advocate increased protection from risks and better solutions for problems, yet not consider the threats and risks as reasons for condemning the technology as a whole. For the most part, we have looked at new risks and negative side-effects of computers as problems that occur in the natural process of change, either problems to be solved (with some combination of technology, law, education, market processes, management, and public pressure) or the price we pay for the benefits, part of a trade-off. This attitude is shared by many people with quite different political views, people who disagree about the significance of specific computer-related problems and about exactly how they should be solved.

On the other hand, there are people who utterly reject the view that computers are a positive development with many important benefits. They see the benefits as few and as overwhelmingly outweighed by the damage done by computers. The difference in perspective is illustrated by a comment made by one reviewer of this book. He objected to the "gift of fire" analogy I use to suggest that computers can be very useful and also very dangerous. The reviewer thought "Pandora's box" was more appropriate. Pandora's box held "all the ills of mankind." Kirkpatrick Sale, author of *Rebels Against the Future*, demonstrates his opinion of computers by smashing one with a sledgehammer at public appearances.

In England in 1811–1812, people burned factories and mills in efforts to stop the technologies and social changes that were eliminating their jobs. Many were weavers who had worked at home on small machines. They were called Luddites.* For almost 200 years, the violent Luddite uprising has endured as the most dramatic symbol of opposition to the Industrial Revolution. The term "Luddite" has long been used derisively to describe people who oppose technological progress. More recently, it has been adopted as an honorable term by critics of technology. Kirkpatrick Sale and many others who share his viewpoint call themselves neo-Luddites, or simply Luddites. They publish many books criticizing computers and the Internet.

LUDDITE CRITICISMS OF COMPUTER TECHNOLOGY

What do the neo-Luddites find so reprehensible about computers? Some of their criticisms are problems that also trouble people whose view of computers is generally positive; we discussed them in earlier chapters. One of the differentiating characteristics of the neo-Luddites is the depth of their criticism—their overall evaluation of computers as a terribly bad development for humankind. Among their specific criticisms are the following:

- Computers cause massive unemployment and deskilling of jobs. "Sweatshop labor is involved in their manufacture."[36]

- Computers "manufacture needs," that is, we use them just because they are there, not because they satisfy real needs.

- Computers cause social inequity.

- Computers cause social disintegration; they are dehumanizing. They weaken communities and lead to isolation of people from each other.

- Computers separate humans from nature and destroy the environment.

- Computers benefit big business and big government most.

- Use of computers in schools thwarts development of social skills, human values, and intellectual skills in children. They will create an "ominous uniformity of knowledge" consistent with corporate values.[37]

---

*The name Luddite comes from General Ned Ludd, the fictitious, symbolic leader of the movement.

- Computers do little or nothing to solve real human problems. For example, Neil Postman, in response to claims of the benefits of access to information, argues that "If families break up, children are mistreated, crime terrorizes a city, education is impotent, it does not happen because of inadequate information."[38]

Some of these criticisms might seem unfair. The conditions in computer factories hardly compare to conditions in the sweatshop factories of the early Industrial Revolution. In Chapter 8, we saw that computers eliminate some jobs and that the pace of computerization causes disruptions, but the case that computers, and technology in general, cause massive unemployment is not convincing. Blaming computers for social inequity in the world ignores thousands of years of history. Postman is right that inadequate information is not the source of most social problems. A computer in the classroom does not replace good parents in the home. But should this be a criticism of computers and information systems? Access to information and communication can assist in solving problems and is not likely to hurt. The main problem for ordinary people, Postman says, is how to find meaning in life. We need answers to questions like "Why are we here?" "How are we supposed to behave?"[39] Is it a valid criticism of computers that they do not solve fundamental social and philosophical problems that have engaged us for centuries?

To the neo-Luddites, the view that computers are fundamentally malevolent is part of a wider view that almost all of technology is malevolent. To the modern-day Luddites, the computer is just the latest, but in many ways the worst, stage in the decline of what was good in human society. Computers are worse than earlier technologies because of their enormous speed and flexibility. The negative trends caused by technology are increased by computers. Thus, if one points out that a particular problem blamed on computers already existed because of an earlier technology, Luddites consider the distinction to be a minor one.

The depth of the antipathy to technology in the Luddite view is perhaps made clearer by attitudes toward common devices most of us use daily. For example, Sale has said, "I find talking on the phone a physical pain, as well as a mental anguish." Sven Birkerts, another critic of computers, says that, if he had lived in 1900, he would probably have opposed the telephone. Speaking of the invention of the printing press, Sale laments that "literacy . . . destroys orality." He regards not only computers but civilization as a catastrophe. Some of us see modern medicine as a life-saving and life-enhancing boon to humanity; some Luddites point out that it gave us the population explosion and extended senility.[40]

Having read and listened to the arguments of technology enthusiasts and technology critics, I find it striking that different people look at the same history, the same society, the same products and services, the same jobs—and come to diametrically opposed conclusions about what they see. There is a fundamental difference between the world views of supporters and opponents of technology. It is more than the difference between seeing a glass as half full or half empty. The difference seems to be one of contrasting views of what should be in the glass. Supporters of technology see an upward trend in quality of life, beginning with people living at the mercy of nature with an empty glass that technology has been gradually filling. Neo-Luddites view the glass as originally full when people lived in small communities with little impact on nature; they see technology as draining it.

The neo-Luddite view is tied to a particular view of the appropriate way of life for human beings. For example, Sale's first point, in the quotation at the beginning of this section, makes the moral judgment that making money and producing things is pernicious. His introductory remark and his second point barely hint at the unusually high valuation he places on not disturbing nature (unusually high even in the contemporary context, where there is much awareness of the importance of protecting the environment). We explore these views further.

BUSINESS, CONSUMERS, AND WORK

Luddites generally have a negative view of capitalism, business, markets, consumer products, factories, and modern forms of work. They see the profit-seeking goals of corporations as in fundamental conflict with the well-being of workers and the natural environment. They see work in factories, large offices, and corporations in general as dehumanizing, dreary, and bad for the health of the workers. Hence, for example, the Luddite criticisms of the clock. Neil Postman describes the invention of the clock as "the technology of greatest use to men who wished to devote themselves to the accumulation of money."[41]

The difference in perspective between Luddites and non-Luddites is sometimes illustrated by choice of words, making subtle differences in a statement. What is the purpose of technology? To the Luddites, it is to eliminate jobs to reduce the costs of production. To proponents of technology, it is to reduce the effort needed to produce goods and services. The two statements say nearly the same thing, but the first suggests massive unemployment, profits for capitalists, and a poorer life for most workers. The second suggests improvements in wealth and the standard of living.

The Luddite view combines a negative attitude toward business with a high estimation of the power of corporations to manipulate and control workers and consumers. For example, Richard Sclove describes telecommuting as being "imposed by business." (Interestingly, one of the common criticisms of the Industrial Revolution was that working in factories instead of at home weakened local community bonds.)

Luddites make particularly strong criticisms of automobiles, of cities, and of the technologies involved in communications and transportation. Thus, it is worth noting that most of us get both personal and social benefits from them. Cities are centers of culture, wealth production, education, and job opportunities.[42] Modern transportation and communication reduce the price of products and increase their variety and availability. For example, we can eat fresh fruits and vegetables all year. We can drive to a large discount store instead of buying from a more expensive local shop. We can phone around town to find a store, movie theater, or restaurant that has exactly what we want. We can use the Web to shop worldwide. We can drive long distances to take a better job (without having to sell our house and move). If we move to a new city for college or a job, airplanes, telephones, and the Internet make the separations less unpleasant; we can visit or hear the voices of friends and family members, and we can send long e-mail messages for less than the price of a long-distance call.

These advantages are not highly valued by Luddites and other critics of technology. In some cases, in their point of view, the advantages are merely ameliorating other problems caused by technology. For example, Postman quotes Sigmund Freud's comment, "If there had been no railway to conquer distances, my child would never have left his native town and I should need no telephone to hear his voice."[43]

A common criticism of capitalism is that it survives by convincing us to buy products we do not need. Sale and other Luddites argue, similarly, that technology causes products to be produced that we do not need. This contrasts with the market-oriented view that sees the choices made by consumers as determining which products, services, and businesses succeed or fail (in the absence of government favoritism, subsidies, and restrictions). We examine the issue of created needs next.

DOES THE TECHNOLOGY CREATE THE NEED FOR ITSELF?

Sale argued that small, portable computers do not "meet any known or expressed need," but companies produced them simply because miniaturization of computing components made it possible. I used a laptop computer to take notes at conferences and to work while away from my home or office. I took my laptop to class and wrote a report while my students took an exam. A typewriter would have been noisy; paper would have been wasted on notes and rough drafts, to be copied later. If you have a laptop or a palm computer, you can add your own stories. So, does a small computer meet a need? It depends on what we mean by "need." Those who emphasize the value of individual action and choices argue that needs are relative to goals, and goals are held by individuals. Thus, should we ask whether "we," as a society, need laptop computers? Or should this be an individual decision with different responses? Many people demonstrate, by their purchases, that they want one. Anyone who does not feel a desire or need for one does not have to buy one. This individual-oriented approach is rejected by the Luddites, who believe buyers are manipulated by advertising, work pressure, or other forces beyond their control.

Many environmental and anti-technology groups use computers. The Web site primitivism.com is devoted to attacking the technology that supports it. (It includes an interview with Theodore Kaczynski about the development of his antitechnology views. Kaczynski is the Unabomber, whose clever bombs killed and maimed several people.) The editor of *Wild Earth*, who considers himself a neo-Luddite, said he "inclines toward the view that technology is inherently evil," but he "disseminates this view via E-mail, computer, and laser printer."[44] The question is: Is he using computer equipment because of an artificial need or because it is useful and helpful to him? Sale sees the use of computers by such groups as an uncomfortable compromise; the use of computers, he says, insidiously embeds into the user the values and thought processes of the society that makes the technology.[45]

The argument that people are manipulated by capitalists or technologies to buy things they do not really want, like the argument that use of computers has an insidiously corrupting effect on computer users, is based on a low view of the judgment and autonomy of ordinary people. It is one thing to differ with another person's values and choices. It is another to conclude that, because of the difference, the other person is weak and incapable of making his or her own decisions. The Luddite view of the appropriate way of life puts little value on modern comforts and conveniences or on the availability of a large variety of goods and services. Perhaps most people value these things more highly than the Luddites do. To get a clearer understanding of the Luddite view of a proper life style, we consider some of their comments on the relationship of humans and nature.

NATURE AND HUMAN LIFE STYLES

Luddites argue that technology has made no improvement in life, or at best improvements of little importance. Sale's list of benefits includes speed, ease, and mass access—all of which he disdains. Sale says that, although individuals might feel their lives are better because of computers, the perceived benefits are "industrial virtues that may not be virtues in another morality." He defines moral judgment as "the capacity to decide that a thing is right when it enhances the integrity, stability, and beauty of nature and is wrong when it does otherwise."[46] Jerry Mander, founder of the Center for Deep Ecology and author of books critical of technology and globalization, points out that thousands of generations of humans got along without computers, suggesting that we could do just fine without them too. Mander's objections to technology lead him to the conclusion that there can be no "good" pesticide. While many people work on technological, legal, and educational approaches to reducing pollution from automobiles, Mander says there can be no "good" automobile.[47]

What are the underlying premises behind these comments of Sale's and Mander's? We consider Sale's comment on moral judgment first. Many debates about the environment set up a humans-versus-nature dichotomy.[48] This is not the true conflict. Nature, biodiversity, forests, a hospitable climate, clean air and water, open space away from cities—these are all important and valuable to humanity. So is shelter from the rain, cold, and heat. So are life-saving medicines and medical techniques. Conflicts about the environment are not conflicts between humans and nature; they are conflicts between people with different views about how to meet human needs. In contrast to Sale's statement, moral judgment, to many people, and for many centuries, has meant the capacity to choose that which enhances human life, reduces misery, and increases freedom and happiness. Sale's comment chooses nature, not humanity, as the primary standard of moral value.

Whether an automobile is "good," by a human-centered standard, depends on whether it meets our needs, how well it does so, at what cost (to the environment and society, as well as to our bank account), and how well it compares to alternatives. Critics of modern technologies point out their weaknesses but often ignore the weaknesses of alternatives, for example, the millions of acres once needed to grow feed for horses and the hundreds of tons of horse manure dropped on the streets of cities each day, a century ago.[49] Mander's comment about automobiles again raises the issues of our standard of value and our need for a product or service. Do we need electricity and hot water on tap? Do we need movies and symphony orchestras? Or do we need nothing more than food and shelter? Do we need an average life expectancy of more than 25 years? Do we want to merely exist—do we *need* even that?—or do we want long, happy, comfortable lives filled with time for love, interesting activities, and an opportunity to use our marvelously inventive brains?

> *The Web is alive, and filled with life, nearly as complex and, well, natural as a primordial swamp.*
>
> —John Perry Barlow[50]

9.4.2 ACCOMPLISHMENTS OF TECHNOLOGY

Some aspects of the neo-Luddite anti-technology view have become part of the general public outlook: that living and working conditions are getting worse, that we are running out of natural resources, that the environment is deteriorating, that we are less healthy, for example. To a variety of scholars, this is simply false. (I mention only a few points here; the list of books at the end of the chapter includes many on both sides of this argument.) Economist Julian Simon argued that hard data, accepted by most economists, show that the prices of food are sharply down around most of the world, raw materials are more abundant (as measured by their price), and wages and salaries have been going up in rich and poor countries alike. Prices of natural resources (metals, raw materials, energy) have declined over the past 100 years (and especially in the 1980s) as a result of improvements in mining technologies and introduction of new substitutes for some minerals—for example, optical fiber for copper. (One fiber-optic cable, with about 150 pounds of silica, carries more messages than a ton of copper.) Nicholas Eberstadt, an expert on population, reported that food supplies and gross domestic product have been growing faster than population for decades in most areas of the world, in developing and developed countries. In the late 1990s, Americans spent about 12% of family income on food, compared to approximately 47% in 1901. Agronomist Norman Borlaug, who won a Nobel Peace Prize for his work in improving agricultural productivity, reported that, when new forms of wheat and crop management were introduced in India, yields rose from 12.3 million tons in 1965 to 20 million tons in 1970 and 73.5 million tons in 1999. Between 1960 and 1990, U.S. production of its 17 most important crops increased from 252 million tons to 596 million tons, but used 25 million fewer acres. Science and technology (along with other factors such as education) reduced or almost eliminated typhoid, smallpox, dysentery, plagues, and malaria in most of the world. Deaths at work, during travel, and by accidents declined dramatically. Simon summarized by saying, "just about every single measure of the quality of life shows improvement rather than the deterioration that the doomsayers claim has occurred."[51]

Technology and the Industrial Revolution have had a dramatic impact on life expectancy. A study done in 1662 estimated that only 25% of people in London lived to age 26. Records from 18th-century French villages showed that the median age of death was lower than the median age of marriage. Until recent generations, parents had to endure the deaths of most of their children. Starvation was common. Life expectancy for women was lower than for men because many women died in childbirth. (It is now several years higher for women than men, in the U.S.) In the U.S., life expectancy at birth increased from about 50 years in 1900 to about 77 in 1996 for white people and from about 33 in 1900 to about 70 in 1996 for nonwhite people. Worldwide average life expectancy increased from approximately 30 in 1900 to approximately 64 in 1990.[52]

Technology is certainly not the only factor in improving quality of life. Progress against disease, discomfort, and early death depends on the stability, freedom, and flexibility of political and economic systems as well. We have seen repeatedly that technology introduces many new problems. Measuring quality of life is subjective, and some find other measures more important than those cited above. But, for many people, these data suggest that technology has contributed much to human well-being.

9.4.3 WHO BENEFITS MOST?

Technology critics recognize that many people consider computers to be useful. Mander explains one of the reasons why, in spite of this, he still considers computers to be, overall, negative:

> People have them at home and find them empowering for themselves and their organizations. They are helpful in many ways and offer considerable personal control, unlike nonyielding technologies like television. Small social and political groups find computers valuable for information storage, networking, processing mailing lists, . . . , and so on. Yet all this begs the question. The real issue is not whether computers can benefit you or your group; the question is who benefits most from computers in society?[53]

Mander believes the answer to his question is transnational corporations and centralized corporate power. "In capitalist society, the benefits are disproportionately allotted to the people who own the machines." Our level of empowerment, he says, is pathetic by comparison. Mander says that "small businesses would actually be better off if computers had not been invented, since they are essentially one more tool that large businesses can use better."[54]

The subtitle of John Naisbitt's book *Global Paradox: The Bigger the World Economy, the More Powerful Its Smallest Players* contrasts with Mander's view that computers are bad for small businesses. Naisbitt sees telecommunications as the driving force in creating a robust global economy and reducing the size of both political and business units. A United Nations Conference on Trade and Development report projects that developing economies can make productivity gains worth billions of dollars by encouraging the

	% of **Poor** Households With Item in 1994	% of **All** Households With Item in 1971
Washing machine	71.7	71.3
Dishwasher	19.6	18.8
Refrigerator	97.9	83.3
Stove	97.7	87.0
Microwave oven	60.0	<1
Color television	92.5	43.3
Telephone	76.7	93.0
Air-conditioner	49.6	31.8
At least one car	71.8	79.5

Figure 9.2 Technology Benefits Spreading to the Poor [55]

growth of electronic commerce. The report said that "it is because the internet revolution is relevant not just to the high-tech, information-intensive sectors but also to the whole organisation of economic life that ... developing countries stand a better chance of sharing in its benefits earlier than in previous technological revolutions."[56] Mander is an extremely active opponent of globalization.

Postman acknowledges that computers are very beneficial to disabled people. He sees convenient access to online information as a tremendous advantage for scholars and scientists. But he sees the main beneficiaries of computers as government and big business. In his view, computers have little value to ordinary workers.[57] This is consistent with the Luddite view that technology in general is bad for most ordinary people, but it is in stark contrast with the views of others who see technology as most benefiting the poorest and weakest people in society. Economist Julian Simon says, "The standard of living of commoners is higher today than that of royalty only two centuries ago—especially their health and life expectancy."[58] Michael Cox and Richard Alm present data showing that the poor in the U.S. had at least the same level of many appliances and luxuries that the average American had only 23 years earlier. See Figure 9.2 for a few examples. (Luddites would probably argue that we do not need these machines.) The number of labor-saving and entertainment appliances we can buy is only one way of measuring well-being. Consider also who benefits more from a speech-activated home-environment control system: a quadriplegic, for whom it performs basic functions and provides some independence, or a rich person for whom it is a toy or convenience. Wireless communications technology makes millions of dollars for corporate executives, and a car phone is a convenience for a middle-class professional. How does the relative improvement in their quality of life compare to the impact of wireless communications on a third-world family living in a rural area that is not wired for telephones? When a drug company develops a new cancer cure and its stock goes way up, while people live 25 extra years after being cured of cancer, does it really matter who benefits "most"?

9.5 Prohibiting Bad Technologies

No one voted for this technology or any of the various machines and processes that make it up.

—Kirkpatrick Sale[59]

9.5.1 WHY AND HOW?

We saw, in Section 9.4.1, that the determination of what are true needs is dependent on our choice of values. Throughout this book, we saw controversies about specific products, services, and applications of computer technology (for example encryption, filters for Web access, music sharing systems on the Web, and surveillance cameras). How should decisions be made about the basic question of whether a whole technology, or major segments of it, will be used at all? Who would make such decisions?

Most people in science, engineering, and business accept, almost without question, the view that people can choose to use a technology for good or ill. Critics of technology disagree; they argue that computers, and technology in general, are not "neutral." Neil Postman says, "Once a technology is admitted [to our culture], it plays out its hand; it does what it is designed to do."[60] In a sense, this view sees the technologies themselves as being in control. To these critics, it is important that the decision to allow a technology be made at the beginning, on the technology as a whole.

In the view of the neo-Luddites and other strong critics of computers, decisions about technology are made by big corporations and governments without sufficient input or control by workers and other ordinary people. This view is expressed by Sale's lament at the beginning of Section 9.5: There was never a vote on whether we should have computers. Some people argue that a new technology should not be used at all until it has been studied, its consequences figured out, and a determination made that the consequences are acceptable. The idea is that if the analysis does not meet criteria set by the government, the technology would not be permitted.

A brief look at the development of communications and computer technology suggests that they do much more than they were "designed to do." The computer was designed to calculate ballistics trajectories for the military. Computers are still used by the military, but their business and consumer uses dominate. Optical scanners, speech-recognition systems, touch screens, and e-mail were developed for a variety of research, business, and consumer uses, but they are major ingredients in tools for disabled people. Postman's statement leaves little room for human responsibility and choice, innovative applications, discoveries of new uses, unexpected consequences, or social action to encourage or discourage specific applications. Computer scientist Peter Denning takes a different view: "Although a technology does not drive human beings to adopt new practices, it shapes the space of possibilities in which they can act: people are drawn to technologies that expand the space of their actions and relationships."[61] Denning says people adopt technologies that give us more choices. Note that he does not say more choices of consumer products, but more actions and relationships. Don Norman also

TELEMEDICINE: AN EXAMPLE OF RESTRICTING A TECHNOLOGY

In Chapter 1, we described long-distance medicine, or telemedicine, as a benefit of computer technology. Computer and communications networks make possible remote examinations of patients and medical test results and even of remotely controlled medical procedures. After reading Chapters 2 and 4, you should be able to think of potential privacy and safety problems with such systems. You may think of other objections as well. Should we ban telemedicine? Several states passed laws prohibiting the practice of telemedicine by doctors who are not licensed in that state. The main argument given for the laws is safety, or concern about out-of-state "quacks." The laws are designed "to keep out the charlatans and snake-oil salesmen," according to one supporter.[62] Also, telemedicine could increase the influence of large, well-financed medical centers—to the detriment of local physicians in private practice. Large hospitals could become the "Wal-Marts of medicine," says one writer.* Telemedicine could make medical care even more impersonal than it is already becoming.

Are laws against telemedicine reasonable? Was concern for patients the real reason for the laws? The arguments about charlatans and quacks seems weak, considering that the laws are targeted at doctors who are licensed, but in another state. Many doctors who support the bans see telemedicine as a significant competitive threat. As the director of one state medical board put it, "They're worried about protecting their turf."[63] The laws restrict competition and protect established special interests—a risk of any mechanism designed to prohibit a new technology or product.

suggests that society influences the role of a technology when he says, "The failure to predict the computer revolution was the failure to understand how society would modify the original notion of a computational device into a useful tool for everyday activities."[64]

Is it possible for a society to choose to have certain specific desirable modern inventions while prohibiting others or prohibiting whole technologies? How finely can decisions about acceptable and unacceptable technologies be made? In response to a criticism that the tribal life he extolled would have no pianos, no violins, no telescope, no Mozart, Sale replied, "if your clan thought that the violin was a useful and nonharmful tool, you could choose to invent that."[65] Perhaps critics of computers who recognize the value of computing technology to disabled people would permit development of such applications. The question is whether it is possible for a clan or society to choose to invent a violin or a book-reader for blind people without the technological base on which these are built, the freedom to innovate, a large enough economy to get materials from distant sources, and the large number of potential applications that make the research, development, and production of the basic ingredients of these products economically feasible.[66]

---

*This is the second time in this chapter that I have quoted someone using Wal-Mart as a negative analogy. Many ordinary people see this as an elitist attitude on the part of intellectuals who disdain their preferences.

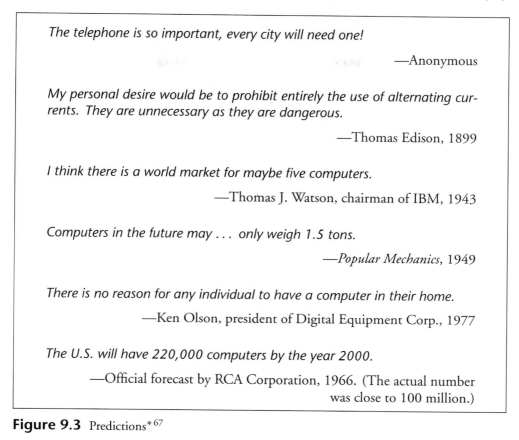

The telephone is so important, every city will need one!

—Anonymous

My personal desire would be to prohibit entirely the use of alternating currents. They are unnecessary as they are dangerous.

—Thomas Edison, 1899

I think there is a world market for maybe five computers.

—Thomas J. Watson, chairman of IBM, 1943

Computers in the future may . . . only weigh 1.5 tons.

—*Popular Mechanics*, 1949

There is no reason for any individual to have a computer in their home.

—Ken Olson, president of Digital Equipment Corp., 1977

The U.S. will have 220,000 computers by the year 2000.

—Official forecast by RCA Corporation, 1966. (The actual number was close to 100 million.)

Figure 9.3 Predictions*[67]

9.5.2 THE DIFFICULTY OF PREDICTION

How well can a government committee, a think tank, or a computer-industry executive predict the consequences of a new technology? The history of technology is full of wildly wrong predictions—some overly optimistic, some overly pessimistic. Consider the quotations in Figure 9.3. Some scientists were skeptical of air travel, space travel, and even railroads. (They believed that passengers would not be able to breathe on high-speed trains.) The quotations in Figure 9.3 reflect a lack of imagination about the myriad uses people would find for each new technology, about what the public would like, and about what they would pay for. They demonstrate humorously that many experts can be utterly wrong. We examine the prediction problem more seriously and in more depth by considering arguments made by computer scientist Joseph Weizenbaum in 1975 against

---

*Bill Gates, chairman of Microsoft, is widely reported to have said, "640K ought to be enough for anybody" in 1981, when PCs typically had 640K bytes of memory or less, but I have not found a reliable source for this remark.

development of a particular computer technology: speech-recognition systems.[68] Here are Weizenbaum's objections, accompanied by comments from our perspective today.

- *"The problem is so enormous that only the largest possible computers will ever be able to manage it."* Speech-recognition software runs on personal computers. We can buy pocket-sized personal organizers that take spoken commands.

- *"... a speech-recognition machine is bound to be enormously expensive, ... only governments and possibly a very few very large corporations will therefore be able to afford it."* Some computers come with simple speech-recognition software as a free bonus. The pocket organizers cost a few hundred dollars.

- *"What can it possibly be used for?"* Recall some of the applications described in Section 1.3: training systems (e.g., for air-traffic controllers and for foreign languages) and tools that help disabled people use computers and control appliances in their homes. People who suffer from repetitive strain injury can use speech-recognition input instead of a keyboard. IBM advertised speech-input software for poets, so they can concentrate on poetry instead of typing. People with dyslexia use speech-recognition software so they can write by dictation.

    Businesses have developed and are developing many customer-service applications. We can telephone a business, speak the name of the person we want to reach, and automatically be connected to that person's extension. Other applications include checking airline flight schedules, getting stock quotes and weather information, conducting banking transactions, and buying movie tickets on the phone by speaking naturally instead of pushing many buttons.

    A company developed a device that recognizes speech and translates it into other languages. Full translation is still a difficult problem, but tourists, business people, social-service workers, and many others will surely find many uses for limited versions. In countries like China, where the language has thousands of characters, speech recognition could be a useful alternative to a keyboard.

    Voice-activated, hands-free operation of cell phones and other appliances in automobiles eliminates some of the safety hazard of using these devices while driving.

    Industry analysts estimated that the speech-recognition market would reach $4 billion by 2001.[69]

- *The military planned to control weapons by voice command, "a long step toward a fully automated battlefield."* Some argue that we should have the best possible weapons to defend ourselves. Others argue that, if wars are easier to fight, governments fight more of them. If wars are fought by remotely controlled automated weapons with no humans on the battlefield, is that an improvement over wars in which people are slaughtered? What if only one side has the high-tech weapons? Would that cause more wars of aggression? Is there any technology that the military cannot or does not use? Should we decline to develop strong fabrics because they could be used for military uniforms? Clearly, military use of high-tech tools raises serious questions.

The passage of time since Weizenbaum expressed his objections has not produced definitive answers.

- *Governments can use speech recognition to increase the efficiency and effectiveness of wiretapping.* (Weizenbaum was concerned with abuses of wiretapping, e.g., tapping done by oppressive governments. He does not explicitly mention wiretapping of criminal suspects.) One can argue that the same tool can be used beneficially in legal wiretapping of suspected terrorists, but it is true that speech recognition, like many other technological tools, can be a danger in the hands of governments. Protection from such abuses depends in part on the recognition of the importance of strictly controlling government power and in part on the appropriate laws and enforcement mechanisms to do so.

Discussion of Weizenbaum's objections is important for several reasons. (1) Although Weizenbaum is an expert in artificial intelligence, of which speech recognition is a subfield, he was mistaken in his expectations about the costs and benefits. (2) His objections about military and government use highlight the dilemma: Should we decline to develop technologies that can be misused, or should we develop the tools because of their beneficial uses, and use other means, including our votes and our voices, to influence government and military policy? (3) Weizenbaum's argument against development of a technology because of its expected cost is similar to arguments expressed by others about current and future computer applications and other technologies. For example, a common objection to some new medical technologies is that they are so expensive that only the rich will be able to afford them. This shortsighted view can result in the denial of benefits to the whole population. We saw that for many new inventions, prices are high at first, but quickly come down. Recall that, in Section 1.3.3, we mentioned development of a computer chip to float on the retina of the eye and send visual signals to the brain. It has the potential to restore sight to some blind people. The cost was $500,000. Should it be banned because it would be available only to the very rich? The developer of the chip expected the cost to come down to $50 with mass production.

Weizenbaum was not trying to evaluate computer technology as a whole, but was focusing on one specific application area. If we are to permit the government, or experts, or the people via a majority vote, to prohibit development of certain technologies, it is essential at least that we be able to estimate the consequences—both risks and benefits—of the technology fairly accurately. We cannot do this. The experts cannot do it.

Prediction is difficult, especially about the future.[70]

9.5.3 A FEW OBSERVATIONS

We have focused, so far, on practical consequences—what might be lost by prohibiting a new technology. There is also an issue of basic liberty, the liberty to work at what one chooses, to use one's resources to invent and create, to invest in one's own ideas. Is it socially or ethically justifiable to prohibit people from pursuing the development of a new technology with their own efforts and investment? What level of certainty of dire consequences should we require before restricting the freedom of others to develop technology they believe will be beneficial?

We presented various arguments against the view that new technologies should be evaluated and perhaps banned at the start. Does this mean that no one should make decisions about whether it is good to develop a particular application of a new technology? No. The arguments and examples in this section suggest two things: (1) that decisions about development of new technology be limited in scope, perhaps limited to particular products, and (2) that the decision-making process be decentralized and noncoercive, to reduce the impact of mistakes, avoid manipulation by entrenched companies who fear competition, and prevent violations of liberty. The fundamental problem is not what decision to make about a particular technology; rather, it is to select a decision-making process that is most likely to produce what people want, to work well despite the difficulty of predicting consequences, to respect the diversity of personal opinions about what constitutes a desirable life style, and to be relatively free of political manipulation. Given the errors made by so many experts, perhaps it is fortunate for us that there was no central decision maker who could decide whether the technology of computing should be developed. The decisions were made by individual engineers, researchers, programmers, entrepreneurs, venture capitalists, customers, and teenagers who tinkered in their garages.

EXERCISES

Review Exercises

9.1   Give one of Sclove and Scheuer's objections to electronic commerce.

9.2   What is one proposal for implementing a universal-access requirement for computing and information services?

9.3   Give some examples of how people who do not own a computer can access the Internet.

9.4   What are two of the Luddite criticisms of computers?

9.5   Give an example of a mistaken prediction made about computers.

General Exercises

9.6   What are some attributes of movie theaters that are lacking when you watch a movie at home? Do you think availability of hundreds of movies at home via cable, the Internet, and DVDs will destroy the movie-theater business? Give your reasons.

9.7   Some people argue that computers reduce social contacts, especially "co-present," or in-person, interactions. How do you think the opportunities for in-person interactions today compare with those of 200–250 years ago? (If you think it is relevant, comment on the fact that Thomas Jefferson wrote approximately 18,000 letters in his lifetime and that Voltaire wrote about 21,000.[71]

9.8   The number of small neighborhood bookstores is declining, because of competition from both large chain megabookstores and online stores like Amazon.com. Should Amazon.com have been prohibited from opening? If not, should it be prohibited from selling used books, to help preserve small neighborhood used-book stores? Give reasons. Suppose you like to shop in your neighborhood bookstore and fear it might go out of business. What can you do?

9.9   Recall the discussion in the box "Wal-Mart and E-Commerce Versus Downtown and Community," and consider these questions: Do people have a right to shop in small neighborhood stores rather than in Wal-Mart and online? Do people in a small town have a right to eat in a French restaurant? Discuss the meaning and context of a "yes" answer and of a "no" answer. How does the distinction between negative and positive rights (Section 1.2.2) fit in?

9.10   Before the Web, someone who wanted to camp in a U.S. National Park could call the park headquarters or a ranger station for information and reservations (if needed). Now reservations for most National Park campgrounds are handled by one telephone center in Maryland. Information about fees, availability of showers, and so on, is accessible to the service representatives on their computer terminals. What advantages and disadvantages does the centralized system have over the old system?

9.11   A college English teacher had a policy (in the mid-1990s) that students could not turn in papers prepared on a word processor. Some students did not have computers, and the teacher considered it unfair if some could use a spelling checker and produce nice looking papers while others could not. What do you think of this policy? Give reasons.

9.12   Rewrite the spelling checker verse (in Section 9.3), correcting all the mistakes. (There are more than a dozen mistakes.)

9.13   Give an example of a bad decision or poor work that can be attributed to mental laziness encouraged by computers. (Try for one not described in the text.)

9.14   To what extent has the electronic calculator destroyed our ability to do arithmetic ourselves? What are the advantages of using a calculator? What are the disadvantages of reduced arithmetic skills? Do you think children should be allowed to use calculators in elementary school? Do you think they should be taught to use calculators in school? Why?

9.15   Many games that children used to play on boards with dice, cards, and plastic pieces are now available as computer games. Is this an example of unnecessary use of the new technology just because it is there? Describe some advantages and disadvantages of replacing a boardgame by a computer version.

9.16   When it became possible for people to make airline reservations on the Web, rather than by calling a travel agent or the airline, there was a significant increase in "no-shows" (people who made a reservation but did not show up for the flight).

a) Why do you think this happened?

b) What problems does the increase in no-shows cause?

c) Some people are promoting the idea that we could soon use the Internet to hold frequent national votes on social and political issues. What concern, if any, does the increase in no-shows for airline reservations suggest about electronic voting?

9.17   In the mid-1990s, approximately 70% of the computers connected to the Internet were in the United States. Does this suggest a growing gap between "have" and "have-not" nations? Give your reasons. (Try to find out what percentage of computers on the Net are in the U.S. now.)

9.18 In Section 1.3, we gave a few examples of how computer systems have reduced the use of paper. Overall, however, paper use worldwide increased at an average of more than 4% per year in the late 1990s. Consider the claim that laser printers and fax machines encourage use and waste of paper. Give arguments for and against this claim. Do you think the increase in paper use is a serious problem caused by computers? Give reasons.

9.19 Software developed to help parents and Internet service providers block access to material inappropriate for children was adapted for use by some governments to block access to political and religious discussions. In what way does this example illustrate the views that technology will inevitably be used for negative purposes and that, as Neil Postman said, "Once a technology is admitted, . . . it does what it is designed to do"?

9.20 Imagine a society in which the wheel has not been invented or introduced. Describe what you think the society would be like. What are the best things about the society? What are the worst? Would you prefer to live in that society or in the one you live in now? Why?

9.21 Approximately 6800 languages are spoken in the world. This number is declining rapidly, as a result of increased communication and transportation, of globalization of business and trade, and so on—all side effects of increased technology in general and of the Internet in particular. What are the advantages and disadvantages of losing languages? Overall, is it a significant problem?

9.22 a) Which of the Luddite criticisms of computers listed in Section 9.4.1 do you consider the most valid and significant? Why?

b) Overall, what do you think of the Luddite view of computer technology? Give reasons.

9.23 Describe some potentially very useful applications of a device that recognizes speech and translates it into other languages.

Assignments

These exercises require some research or activity.

9.24 Find a small, nonchain bookstore or a small travel agency. Interview the owner about the impact of the Web on his or her business. Ask if other similar stores in your city have closed because of competition from e-commerce.

9.25 Arrange to visit an elementary school where the children use computers. Report on the types of activities and exercises for which the computers were used. Evaluate them. What are the advantages and disadvantages of using a computer for each activity you observed. Were computers necessary for the activity? Do you think the computers were being used well?

9.26 We sometimes see technology described as our "national religion." On the other hand, the environmentalist viewpoint, often critical of technology, is quite strong in our society. Find two recent news or magazine articles, one that illustrates each of these points of view. Give a brief summary of each; tell how it exemplifies a view of technology. In general, which view do you think is stronger in our society? Give reasons.

9.27 UNIX is a widely used computer operating system. Find out who wrote the first UNIX system and what it was written for. Was it intended to be a commercial product?

Class Discussion Exercises

These exercises are for class discussion, perhaps with short presentations prepared in advance by small groups of students.

9.28 In developed countries and some less developed countries, computers and Internet access are available in schools. Is the "digital divide" likely to last more than one generation? What form will it take 25 years from now? How does it differ from social divisions that occurred when other information and communication technologies were introduced?

9.29 What are some skills, traditions, and/or social conventions that have been, or might soon be, lost because of computers? Include at least one that you think will be a real loss (i.e., a negative result of computers), and include at least one where you think the loss is not a problem. Give reasons.

9.30 Hold a debate in class on one variant of the following question: Does computer technology, overall, have a negative impact on
a) most people in the world?
b) poor people in a developed country (e.g., the U.S.)?
c) the middle class in a developed country (e.g., the U.S.)?

9.31 When information appeared on computer screens only as text, deaf people could read it, and programmers developed speech-synthesis programs to read the screens to blind people. The multimedia, point-and-click interfaces of the Web pose problems for disabled people. Should all business and government Web sites be required to provide full access for disabled people? Discuss arguments for both sides. Which side do you think is stronger? Why? The National Federation of the Blind sued America Online in 1999 because AOL's software was not compatible with screen-access software used by blind people. Which side do you think should win the suit? Why?[72]

9.32 Three-dimensional "printers" create a 3D structure, layer by layer, using glues and resins, under direction of a computer file. What are some likely uses for these devices? (Try to think of both good and bad uses.) Do they fill any real needs? What disadvantages do they have?

9.33 At the beginning of the 21st century, a large protest movement against "globalization" developed. Compare globalization caused by computer and telecommunications technologies to globalizations caused by significant earlier technologies. Present and evaluate some of the arguments of the current anti-globalization movement.

NOTES

[1] Michael Rothschild, "Beyond Repair: The Politics of the Machine Age Are Hopelessly Obsolete," *The New Democrat*, July/Aug. 1995, pp. 8–11.

[2] Hightower is a radio commentator, quoted in Robert Fox, "Newstrack," *Communications of the ACM*, Aug. 1995, 38:8, pp. 11–12.

[3] Quoted in Jerry Mander, *In the Absence of the Sacred: The Failure of Technology and the Survival of the Indian Nations*, Sierra Club Books, 1991, p. 62.

[4] "Net surfing mom charged with ignoring kids," CNN Interactive, June 16, 1997, www6.cnn.com/US/9706/16/briefs.pm/internet.neglect/; viewed Oct. 29, 2001.

[5] Alexandra Eyle, "No Time Like the Co-Present" (interview with Neil Postman), *NetGuide*, July 1995, pp. 121–122. Chet Bowers, another critic, also complains that computers contribute to the view of the individual as the basic social unit. Richard Sclove and Jeffrey Scheuer, "On the Road Again: If Information Highways Are Anything Like Interstate Highways—Watch Out!" in Rob Kling, ed., *Computerization and Controversy: Value Conflict and Social Choices*, 2nd ed., Academic Press, 1996, pp. 606–612.

[6] Robert D. Putnam, *Making Democracy Work*, Princeton University Press, 1993. I thank Phil Agre for bringing Putnam's work and some of the ideas in this paragraph

to my attention in his talk "Networking in the Community" at the San Diego ACM chapter meeting, Jan. 24, 1996.

[7] Alexis de Tocqueville, *Democracy in America*, Alfred A. Knopf, 1945, translated by Henry Reeves.

[8] "Technology in the American Household," Times Mirror Center for the People and the Press, May 1994, pp. 5–7. Jon Katz, "The Digital Citizen," *Wired*, Dec. 1997, pp. 68–82, 274–275. Lisa Guernsey, "Cyberspace Isn't So Lonely After All," *New York Times*, July 26, 2001, pp. D1, D5. James E. Katz and Philip Aspden, "A Nation of Strangers?" *Communications of the ACM*, December 1997, 40:12, pp. 81–86. Pew Research Center, Nov. 2000.

[9] From a study by sociologist Claude Fisher, reported in Charles Paul Freund, "The Geography of Somewhere," *Reason*, May 2001, p. 12.

[10] This is a condensed version of my article "Impacts on Community," *Computers & Society*, v. 27, n. 4, December 1997, pp. 15–17.

[11] In Rob Kling, ed., *Computerization and Controversy: Value Conflict and Social Choices*, 2nd ed., Academic Press, 1996, pp. 606–612.

[12] Office of Technology Assessment, "The Technological Reshaping of Metropolitan America," 1995.

[13] See Joel Kotkin's book in the references for an extensive discussion of the impact of computers on towns and cities.

[14] Robert Fox, "News Track: Disorderly Conduct," *Communications of the ACM*, July 1998, p. 9.

[15] CPSR, "Serving the Community: A Public Interest Vision of the National Information Infrastructure," pp. 15–16.

[16] CPSR, "Serving the Community," p. 21.

[17] National Information Infrastructure Advisory Committee, "A Nation of Opportunity: Realizing the Promise of the Information Superhighway," reported in *Telecom-Post*, Oct. 26, 1995. Robert H. Anderson, Tora K. Bikson, Sally Ann Law, Bridger M. Mitchell, *Universal Access to E-mail: Feasibility and Societal Implications*, Center for Information Revolution Analysis, RAND, 1995. Laurent Belsie, "'Universal Service' Is No Longer So Simple," *Christian Science Monitor*, Apr. 7, 1994.

[18] "Technology in the American Household," Times Mirror Center for the People and the Press, May 1994, p. 8.

[19] Most data from W. Michael Cox and Richard Alm, *Myths of Rich and Poor: Why We're Better off Than We Think*, Basic Books, 1999, pp. 161–162. Theodore Caplow, Louis Hicks, and Ben J. Wattenberg, *The First Measured Century: An Illustrated Guide to Trends in America*, AEI Press, 2001, p. 276.

[20] Most of the data in this paragraph comes from polls and studies by Pew Research Center, Forrester Research, Luntz Research Companies, Ipsos-Reid Corporation, Nielsen//NetRatings, the U.S. Commerce Department, and others, reported in various news media.

[21] Several studies mention similar figures; see, for example, Jon Katz, "The Digital Citizen."

[22] Richard Shim, "Thanks for the memory: 30GB hard drive on a platter," *ZDNet News*, Jan. 23, 2001, www.zdnet.com/zdnn/stories/news; viewed Mar. 23, 2001.

[23] www.eudora.com/products/eudora/download

[24] The term "have-lates," as a substitute for "have-nots," was first used by Marvin Minsky, to the best of my knowledge; I prefer to use "have-laters" rather than "have-lates."

[25] Ford provided computers to about 166,000 employees, then canceled the program because of financial pressures due in part to tire problems on Ford Explorers.

[26] Les Shu, "All You Can E," *Wired*, Mar. 2001, p. 76.

[27] *Collected Poems 1901–1962*, Harcourt, Brace & World, 1963, p. 147.

[28] This line appears on many Web sites that quote the two lines from Eliot's poem. The earliest source I found is Neville Fletcher (Australian Academy of Science), "A Distributed National Collection? A Science Viewpoint," July 21, 1997 (www.anu.edu.au/caul/nscf/fletcher.htm).

[29] Parts of this poem have circulated on computer networks and appeared in newspapers. The full version (36 lines), slightly different from the one I used, appeared in the *Journal of Irreproducible Results*, Jan./Feb. 1994, 39:1, p. 13. Zar attributes the title to Pamela Brown and the opening lines to Mark Eckman.

[30] Barry Bearak, "Pakistani Tale of a Drug Addict's Blasphemy," *New York Times*, Feb. 19, 2001, pp. A1, A4. Michael Lesk, "Going Digital," *Scientific American*, Mar. 1997, pp. 58–60.

[31] See, for example, Neil Postman, *Technopoly: The Surrender of Culture to Technology*, Alfred A. Knopf, 1992, pp. 3–8.

[32] *New York Times*, Feb. 1, 2001. Walter J. Ong, *Interfaces of the Word: Studies in the Evolution of Consciousness and Culture*, Cornell University Press, 1977. Americans spent $26 billion on more than two billion books in 1997 (Caplow *et al.*, *The First Measured Century*, p. 266).

[33] From Microsoft's explanation of its policy, quoted in Mark Goldblatt, "Bowdlerized by Microsoft," *New York Times*, Oct. 23, 2001, p. A23.

[34] Stephen Moore, "The Coming Age of Abundance," in Ronald Bailey, ed., *The True State of the Planet*, Free Press, 1995, p. 113.

[35] "Interview With the Luddite," *Wired*, June 1995, pp. 166–168, 211–216 (see pp. 213–214).

[36] Kirkpatrick Sale, *Rebels Against the Future: The Luddites and Their War Against the Industrial Revolution: Lessons for the Computer Age*, Addison–Wesley, 1995, p. 257.

[37] Mander, *In the Absence of the Sacred*, p. 61.

[38] Postman, *Technopoly*, p. 119.

[39] Eyle, "No Time Like the Co-Present."

40 Harvey Blume, "Digital Refusnik" (interview with Sven Birkerts), *Wired*, May 1995, pp. 178–179. "Interview With the Luddite."

41 Postman, *Technopoly*, p. 15.

42 See Jane Jacob's classic *The Economy of Cities*, Random House, 1969.

43 Postman, *Technopoly*, p. 6. The Freud quote is from *Civilization and Its Discontent* (e.g., the edition edited and translated by James Strachey, W. W. Norton, 1961, p. 35).

44 John Davis, quoted in Sale, *Rebels Against the Future*, p. 256.

45 Sale, *Rebels Against the Future*, p. 257.

46 The quotes are from "Interview With the Luddite," p. 214 and p. 213. Sale expresses this point of view also in *Rebels Against the Future*, p. 213.

47 Sale, *Rebels Against the Future*, p. 256.

48 This dichotomy has always struck me as strange, because it almost suggests that humans are alien creatures who arrived on earth from somewhere else. We evolved here. We are part of nature. A human's house is as natural as a bird's nest, though, unlike birds, we have the capacity to build both ugly and beautiful things.

49 Martin V. Melosi, *Garbage in the Cities: Refuse, Reform, and the Environment: 1880–1980*, Texas A&M University Press, 1981, p. 24–25.

50 In "George Gilder and His Critics," *Forbes ASAP*, Oct. 9, 1995, pp. 165–181.

51 Optical fiber: Ronald Bailey, ed., *Earth Report 2000: Revisiting the True State of the Planet*, McGraw Hill, 2000, p. 51. Moore, "The Coming Age of Abundance," p. 119. Nicholas Eberstadt, "Population, Food, and Income: Global Trends in the Twentieth Century," p. 34, in Bailey, *The True State of the Planet*. Family income spent on food: Stephen Moore and Julian L. Simon, *It's Getting Better All the Time: The 100 Greatest Trends of the 20th Century*, Cato Institute, 2000, p. 53. Ronald Bailey, "Billions Served" (interview with Norman Borlaug), *Reason*, Apr. 2000, pp. 30–37. Julian L. Simon, "The State of Humanity: Steadily Improving," *Cato Policy Report*, Sept./Oct. 1995, 17:5, pp. 1, 10–11, 14–15. Nonvehicular accidental deaths declined from 72 per 100,000 people in 1900 to 19 per 100,000 people in 1997 (Caplow *et al.*, *The First Measured Century*, p. 149).

52 Ian Hacking, *The Emergence of Probability*, Cambridge University Press, 1975, p. 108. Snow, *The Two Cultures*, pp. 82–83. The population data, some from the United Nations, are reported in Eberstadt, "Population, Food, and Income," p. 21, p. 23, and in Caplow *et al.*, *The First Measured Century*, pp. 4–5.

53 Mander, *In the Absence of the Sacred*, pp. 67–68.

54 Mander, *In the Absence of the Sacred*, p. 57. Comments at the Computers, Freedom, and Privacy Conference, San Francisco, 1995; Panel: "Against Computers: A Systemic Critique."

55 Cox and Alm, *Myths of Rich and Poor*, p. 15.

56 United Nations, "E-Commerce and Development Report 2001," quoted in Frances Williams, "International Economy & the Americas: Unctad spells out benefit of internet commerce," *Financial Times*, Nov. 21, 2001.

57 Eyle, "No Time Like the Co-Present." Postman, *Technopoly*, p. 10.

58 Julian L. Simon, "The State of Humanity: Steadily Improving," *Cato Policy Report*, Sept./Oct. 1995, 17:5, pp. 1, 10–11, 14–15. See the books by Cox & Alm and Moore & Simon in the references.

59 Sale, *Rebels Against the Future*, p. 210.

60 Postman, *Technopoly*, p. 7.

61 Peter J. Denning, "The Internet After 30 Years," in Dorothy E. Denning & Peter J. Denning, eds., *The Internet Besieged*, Addison–Wesley, 1998, p. 20.

62 Bill Richards, "Doctors Can Diagnose Illnesses Long Distance, To the Dismay of Some," *Wall Street Journal*, Jan. 17, 1996, pp. A1, A10.

63 Richards, "Doctors Can Diagnose Illnesses Long Distance."

64 Donald A. Norman, *Things That Make Us Smart: Defending Human Attribute In the Age of the Machine*, Addison–Wesley, 1993, p. 190.

65 "Interview with the Luddite."

66 See Jacobs, *The Economy of Cities* for a discussion of how wealth develops.

67 Telephone: Norman, *Things That Make Us Smart*, p. 191. Edison and Watson: Chris Morgan and David Langford, *Facts and Fallacies: A Book of Definitive Mistakes and Misguided Predictions*, St. Martin's Press, 1981 (Watson: p. 44). *Popular Mechanics* (March 1949, p. 258) and Olson: Christopher Cerf and Victor Navasky, *The Definitive Compendium of Authoritative Misinformation*, Pantheon Books, 1984, p. 208, 209. Olson's comment made at a convention of the World Future Society. Thomas Petzinger Jr., "Meanwhile, from the Journal's Archives," *Wall Street Journal*, Jan. 1, 2000, p. R5.

68 Joseph Weizenbaum, *Computer Power and Human Reason: From Judgment To Calculation*, W. H. Freeman and Company, 1976, pp. 270–272.

69 Simson L. Garfinkel, "Enter the Dragon," *Technology Review*, Sept./Oct. 1998, pp. 58–64.

70 This quote has been attributed to Neils Bohr and Albert Einstein; I could not find a reliable source for either.

71 Jefferson: www.princeton.edu/~tjpapers/; Voltaire: Voltaire Foundation, www.voltaire.ox.ac.uk

72 Federal rules released in December 2000 mandate that virtually all government Web sites be made fully accessible to disabled people. Some legal experts expect the rules to be applied to private commercial sites as well. Michelle Delio, "Fed Opens Web to Disabled," *WIRED News*, Dec. 21, 2000.

BOOKS AND ARTICLES

- John Attarian, "Spiritual and Cultural Perils of Technological Progress," *The Social Critic*, Winter 1998, pp. 10–18.

- Ronald Bailey, ed., *Earth Report 2000: Revisiting the True State of the Planet*, McGraw Hill, 2000. Includes much data on improvements in the environment, resource usage, food and energy production, and so on.

- Frederick Bennett, *Computers As Tutors: Solving the Crisis in Education*, Faben, 1999. Proposals for productive ways to use computers in education.

- Sven Birkerts, *The Gutenberg Elegies: The Fate of Reading in An Electronic Age*, Faber and Faber, 1994. Birkerts is a critic of computers; he writes on a typewriter.

- Theodore Caplow, Louis Hicks, and Ben J. Wattenberg, *The First Measured Century: An Illustrated Guide to Trends in America*, AEI Press, 2001.

- Benjamin M. Compaine, ed., *The Digital Divide: Facing a Crisis or Creating a Myth*, MIT Press, 2001.

- Peter J. Denning, ed., *Talking Back to the Machine: Computers and Human Aspiration*, Copernicus, 1999.

- Michael Dertouzos, *The Unfinished Revolution: Human-Centered Computers and What They Can Do For Us*, Harper–Collins, 2001.

- Michael Dertouzos, *What Will Be: How the New World of Information Will Change Our Lives*, Harper, 1997.

- Samuel C. Florman, *Blaming Technology: The Irrational Search for Scapegoats*, St. Martin's Press, 1981.

- Lawrence Gasman, *Telecompetition: The Free Market Road to the Information Highway*, Cato Institute, 1994.

- Bill Gates, *The Road Ahead*, Viking Press, 1995. How well did Gates predict what was coming?

- Steve Gibson, "Universal Disservice: The Hazards of Fretting About Info Haves and Have-Nots," *Reason*, April 1995, pp. 47–49.

- Merritt Ierley, *Wondrous Contrivances: Technology at the Threshold*, Clarkson Potter, 2002.

- Joel Kotkin, *The New Geography: How the Digital Revolution Is Reshaping the American Landscape*, Random House, 2000.

- Todd Lappin, "Déjà Vu All Over Again," *Wired*, May 1995, pp. 175–177, 218–222. A comparison of predictions of the social impact of radio 75 years ago and the predictions for the Internet.

- Peter Ludlow, ed., *Crypto Anarchy, Cyberstates, and Pirate Utopias*, MIT Press, 2001.

- Jerry Mander and Edward Goldsmith, eds., *The Case Against the Global Economy and For a Turn Toward the Local*, Sierra Club Books, 1996. Extremely critical of computer technology, automation, and technology in general. Argues that globalization should be halted and reversed.

- Jerry Mander, *In the Absence of the Sacred: The Failure of Technology and the Survival of the Indian Nations*, Sierra Club Books, 1991.

- Alan Murray, *The Wealth of Choices*, Crown Business, 2000.

- Joel Mokyr, *The Lever of Riches: Technological Creativity and Economic Progress*, Oxford University Press, 1990.

- Stephen Moore and Julian Simon, *It's Getting Better All the Time: The 100 Greatest*

Trends of the 20th Century, Cato Institute, 2000.

■ John Naisbitt, *Global Paradox: The Bigger the World Economy, the More Powerful Its Smallest Players*, William Morrow and Company, 1994.

■ Donald A. Norman, *Things That Make Us Smart: Defending Human Attributes in the Age of the Machine*, Addison–Wesley, 1993.

■ Neil Postman, *Technopoly: The Surrender of Culture to Technology*, Alfred A. Knopf, 1992.

■ Virginia Postrel, *The Future and Its Enemies*, The Free Press, 1998.

■ Robert D. Putnam, *Making Democracy Work: Civic Traditions in Modern Italy*, Princeton University Press, 1993. The observations about what makes communities work well are useful for discussions of the impact of computers on community.

■ Saul Rockman, "In School or Out: Technology, Equity, and the Future of Our Kids," *Communications of the ACM*, June 1995, 38:6, pp. 25–29.

■ Nathan Rosenberg and L. E. Birdzell Jr., *How the West Grew Rich*, Basic Books, 1987.

■ Michael Rothschild, *Bionomics: Economy As Ecosystem*, Henry Holt, 1992.

■ Kirkpatrick Sale, *Rebels Against the Future: The Luddites and Their War Against the Industrial Revolution: Lessons for the Computer Age*, Addison–Wesley, 1995.

■ Douglas Schuler, *New Community Networks: Wired for Change*, Addison–Wesley, 1996.

■ C. P. Snow, "The Two Cultures and the Scientific Revolution." In this speech, Snow argues that people in the humanities and people in the sciences have fundamentally different views of science and technology. The speech appears, with an update, in C. P. Snow, *The Two Cultures: And a Second Look*, Cambridge University Press, 1964.

■ Clifford Stoll, *Silicon Snake Oil: Second Thoughts on the Information Highway*, Doubleday, 1995.

■ William Wresch, *Disconnected: Haves and Have-Nots in the Information Age*, Rutgers University Press, 1996.

10

PROFESSIONAL ETHICS AND RESPONSIBILITIES

Honesty is the best policy.

—English proverb, pre-1600

10.1 Ethics

10.1.1 WHAT IS "COMPUTER ETHICS"?

In the previous chapters, we discussed issues and problems related to computers from a somewhat detached perspective. We saw how a new technology can create new risks and problems and how social and legal institutions must continually adapt. But technology is not an immutable force, outside of human control. People make decisions about what technologies and products to develop and how to use them. People make decisions about when a product is safe to release. People make decisions about access to and use of personal information. People make laws and set rules and standards. In this chapter, we look at those decisions and activities from an ethical perspective. We examine ethical dilemmas and guidelines related to actions and decisions of individuals and organizations who create and use computer systems.

The scope of the term "computer ethics" varies considerably. Some people include such issues as the universal-access issue discussed in Section 9.2, the environmental impact of computers, the impact of computers on employment, whether to sell computers to totalitarian governments, and use of computers by the military. These are all important issues that involve computers, but one's opinions about them usually have more to do with one's political and social views than with one's knowledge or experience as a computer professional. I believe that "computer ethics" is most usefully defined more narrowly as a category of professional ethics, similar to medical, legal, and accounting ethics, for example.* Most of the people affected by the devices, systems, and services of professionals do not understand how they work and cannot easily judge their quality and safety. This creates special responsibilities for the professional.

Thus, for our discussion, computer ethics includes ethical issues faced by a computer professional as part of the job. It includes relationships with and responsibilities toward customers, clients, coworkers, employees, employers, others who use one's products, and others whom they affect. We also include issues faced by people who are not computer professionals, but who manage, select, or use computers in a professional setting.

We look at situations where critical decisions must be made, situations where significant consequences for you and others could result from your decision. For example, what if your company is about to deliver a computer system to a customer and you believe it still has serious bugs? What if your supervisor asks you to make unauthorized copies of copyrighted software? Is it right to hire foreign programmers who work at low salaries? What if you are assigned to a job for a client whose business you find objectionable?

---

*Donald Gotterbarn presented and argued this more focused view of computer ethics well. It seems to be gaining acceptance among scholars in this field.[1]

Suppose a private company asks your software company to develop a database of information obtained from government records, perhaps to generate lists of convicted shoplifters or child molesters, perhaps marketing lists of new home buyers, affluent boat owners, or divorced parents with young children. The people who will be on the lists did not have a choice about whether the information would be open to the public; they did not give permission for its use. How will you decide whether to accept the job? You could accept on the grounds that the records are already public and available to anyone; you could decide against secondary uses of information that was not provided voluntarily by the people it concerns; you could try to determine whether the benefits of the lists outweigh the privacy invasions or inconveniences they might cause for some people; you could refuse to make marketing lists, but agree to make lists of people convicted of certain crimes, using Posner's principle (see Section 2.6.3) that negative information, such as convictions, should be in the public domain. The critical first step, however, is recognizing that you face an ethical issue.

Suppose you are a manager and discover that many of your employees are spending a lot of time visiting sports, stock, and entertainment Web sites while at work. Will you install monitoring software that records what sites each employee visits and how much time he or she spends there? Will you inform employees first? You are confronting practical and legal issues—and ethical ones.

Decisions a business or organization makes about what information to collect from visitors to its Web site and how to use that information have an ethical component. So, too, does the decision to distribute software to convert files from formats with built-in copy protection to formats that can be copied more easily. So, too, does the decision about how much money and effort to allocate to training employees in the use of a new computer system. We have seen that many of the related social and legal issues are controversial; thus many of the ethical issues are, also.

There are special aspects to making ethical decisions in a professional context, but the decisions are fundamentally based on general ethical principles and theories. In the next section, we introduce several ethical theories. We discuss some distinctions (e.g., between ethics and law) that are important to understand when tackling ethical issues. In Section 10.2, we return to computer technology and consider ethical guidelines for computer professionals. In Section 10.3, we consider some sample cases.

10.1.2 WHAT IS ETHICS, ANYWAY?

Ethics is the study of what it means to "do the right thing." It is a complex subject that has occupied philosophers for thousands of years. This presentation is necessarily simplified.

Ethical theory is based on the assumption that people are rational and make free choices. Neither of these conditions is always and absolutely true. People act emotionally, and they make mistakes. A person is not making a free choice when someone else is pointing a gun at him. Some argue that a person is not making a free choice in a situation where she might lose a job. However, free choice and use of rational judgment are capacities and characteristics of human beings, and they are reasonably assumed as the basis of ethical theory. We take the view that the individual is, in most circumstances, responsible for his or her actions.

Ethical rules are rules to follow in our interactions with other people and in our actions that affect other people. Most ethical theories attempt to achieve the same goal: to enhance human dignity, peace, happiness, and well-being. Ethical rules apply to all of us and are intended to achieve good results for people in general, and for situations in general—not just for ourselves, not just for one situation. A set of rules that does this well respects the fact that we are each unique and have our own values and goals, that we have judgment and will, and that we act according to our judgment to achieve our goals. The rules should clarify our obligations and responsibilities—and our areas of choice and personal preference. (Not all ethical theories fit this description. Ethical relativism and some types of ethical egoism do not. This chapter, however, stipulates these goals and requirements for ethical theories.)

We could view ethical rules as fundamental and universal, like laws of science, or we could view them as rules we make up, like the rules of baseball, to provide a framework in which to interact with other people in a peaceful, productive way. The titles of two books illustrate these different viewpoints. One is *Ethics: Discovering Right and Wrong*; the other is *Ethics: Inventing Right and Wrong*.[2] We do not have to decide which view is correct to find good ethical rules. In either case, our tools include reason, introspection, and observation of human nature, values, and behavior.

Behaving ethically, in a personal or professional sphere, is usually not a burden. Most of the time we are honest, we keep our promises, we do not steal, we do our jobs. This should not be surprising. If ethical rules are good ones, they work for people; that is, they make our lives better. Behaving ethically is often practical. Honesty makes interactions among people work more smoothly and reliably, for example. We might lose friends if we often lie or break promises. Also, social institutions encourage us to do right: We might be arrested if caught stealing. We might lose our jobs if we do them carelessly. In a professional context, doing good ethically often corresponds closely with doing a good job in the sense of professional quality and competence. Doing good ethically often corresponds closely with good business in the sense that ethically developed products are more likely to please consumers. Sometimes, however, it is difficult to do the right thing. It takes courage in situations where we could suffer negative consequences. Courage is often associated with heroic acts, where one risks one's life to save someone in a dangerous situation—the kind of act that makes front-page news. Most of us do not have those opportunities to display courage, but we do have many opportunities in day-to-day life. Courage in a professional setting could mean admitting to a customer that your program is faulty, declining a job for which you are not qualified, or speaking out when you see someone else doing something wrong.

10.1.3 A VARIETY OF ETHICAL VIEWS

Although there is much agreement about general ethical rules, there are many different theories about how to establish a firm justification for the rules and how to decide what is ethical in specific cases. In this section, we give very brief descriptions of a few approaches to ethics.[3] Some ethicists* make a distinction between ethical theories that view certain acts as good or bad because of some intrinsic aspect of the action and ethical theories that view acts as good or bad because of their consequences. They call these deontological (or nonconsequentialist) and consequentialist theories, respectively. The distinction is perhaps emphasized more than necessary. If the criteria used by deontologists to determine the intrinsic goodness or badness of an act did not consider its consequences for people— at least for most people, most of the time—their criteria would seem to have little ethical merit.

DEONTOLOGICAL THEORIES

Deontologists tend to emphasize duty and absolute rules, to be followed whether they lead to good or ill consequences in particular cases. One example is: Do not lie. An act is ethical if it complies with ethical rules and is chosen for that reason.

Immanuel Kant, the philosopher often presented as the prime example of a deontologist, contributed many important ideas to ethical theory. We mention three of them here. One is the principle of universality: We should follow rules of behavior that we can universally apply to everyone. This principle is so fundamental to ethical theory that we already accepted it in our explanation of ethics in Section 10.1.2. The Biblical instruction, "Do unto others as you would have them do unto you," is another statement of the same general idea.

Deontologists argue that logic or reason determines rules of ethical behavior, that actions are intrinsically good because they follow from logic. Kant believed that rationality is the standard of what is good. We can reason about what makes sense and act accordingly, or we can act irrationally, which is evil. The view that something is evil because it is illogical might seem unconvincing, but Kant's instruction to "Respect the reason in you," that is, to use your reason, rationality, and judgment, rather than emotions, when making a decision in an ethical context, is a wise one.

Third, Kant stated a principle about interacting with other people: One must never treat people as merely means to ends, but rather as ends in themselves.

Kant took an extreme position on the absolutism of ethical rules. He argued, for example, that it is always wrong to lie; for example, if a person is looking for someone he intends to murder, and he asks you where the intended victim is, it is wrong for you to lie to protect the victim. Most people would agree that there are cases in which even very good, universal rules should be broken—because of the consequences.

---

*Ethicists are philosophers (and others) who study ethics.

UTILITARIANISM

Utilitarianism is the main example of a consequentialist theory. Its guiding principle, as expressed by John Stuart Mill,[4] is to increase happiness, or "utility." A person's utility is what satisfies the person's needs and values. An action might decrease utility for some people and increase it for others. We should consider the consequences—the benefits and damages to all affected people—and "calculate" the change in aggregate utility. An act is right if it tends to increase aggregate utility and wrong if it tends to decrease it.

Utilitarianism is a very influential theory, and it has many variations. As stated above, the utilitarian principle applies to individual actions. For each action, we consider the impact on utility and judge the action by its net impact. This is sometimes called "act utilitarianism." One variant of utilitarianism, called "rule utilitarianism," applies the utility principle not to individual actions but to general ethical rules. Thus, a rule utilitarian might argue that the rule "Do not lie" will increase total utility, and for that reason is a good rule. Rule-utilitarians do not do a utility calculation for each instance where lying is considered. Generally, a utilitarian would be more comfortable than a deontologist breaking a rule in circumstances where doing so would have good consequences.

There are numerous problems with act-utilitarianism. It might be difficult or impossible to determine all the consequences of an act. If we can do so, do we increase what *we* believe will or should contribute to the happiness of the people affected, or what *they* choose themselves? How do we know what they would choose? How do we quantify happiness in order to make comparisons among many people? Should some people's utility be given more weight than others'? Should we weigh a thief's gain of utility equal to the victim's loss? Is a dollar worth the same to a person who worked for it and a person who received it as a gift? Or to a rich person and a poor person? How can we measure the utility of freedom?

A more fundamental (and ethical) objection to act-utilitarianism is that it does not recognize or respect individual rights. It has no absolute prohibitions and so could allow actions that many people consider always wrong. For example, if there is a convincing case that killing one innocent person (perhaps to distribute his or her organs to several people who will die without transplants), or taking all of a person's property and redistributing it to other community members, would maximize utility in a community, utilitarianism could justify these acts. A person has no protected domain of freedom.

Rule-utilitarianism suffers far less than does act-utilitarianism from these problems. Recognizing that widespread killing and stealing decrease the security and happiness of all, a rule utilitarian can derive rules against these acts. We can state these particular rules in terms of rights to life and property.

NATURAL RIGHTS

Suppose we wish to treat people as ends rather than merely means and we wish to increase people's happiness. These goals are somewhat vague and open to many interpretations in specific circumstances. One approach we might follow is to let people make their own decisions, to define a sphere of freedom in which people can act freely according to their own judgment, without coercive interference by others, even others (including us) who think they are doing what is best for the people involved, or for humanity in general. This approach views ethical behavior as acting in such a way that respects a set of fundamental rights of others, including the rights to life, liberty, and property.

These rights are sometimes called natural rights because, in the opinion of some philosophers, they come from nature, or can be derived from the nature of humanity. We each have an exclusive right to ourselves and our labor, and to what we produce with our labor. John Locke argued for a natural right to property that we create or obtain by mixing our labor with it. Respect for these rights implies ethical rules against killing, stealing, and deception.

Those who emphasize natural rights tend to emphasize the ethical character of the *process* by which people interact, seeing acts generally as likely to be ethical if they involve voluntary interactions and freely made exchanges, where the parties are not coerced or deceived. This contrasts with other approaches that tend to focus on the *result* or state achieved by the interaction, for example, seeing an action as likely to be unethical if it leaves some people poor.

NO SIMPLE ANSWERS

We cannot solve ethical problems by applying a formula or an algorithm. Human behavior and real human situations are complex. There are often trade-offs to consider. Ethical theories do not provide clear, incontrovertibly correct positions on most issues. We can use the approaches we described to support opposite sides of many an issue. For example, consider Kant's imperative that one must never treat people as merely means to ends, but rather as ends in themselves. We could argue that an employee who receives a very low wage, say, a wage too low to support a family, is wrongly being treated as merely a means for the employer to make money. But we could also argue that expecting the employer to pay more than he or she considers reasonable is treating the employer merely as a means to providing income for the employee. Similarly, it is easy for two utilitarians to come to different conclusions on a particular issue by measuring happiness or utility differently. A very small set of basic natural rights might provide no guidance for many situations in which you must make ethical decisions—but, if we try to define rights to cover more situations, there will be fierce disagreement about just what those rights should be. (Recall the controversies in Chapter 2 about whether there is a right to privacy, and, if so, how far it goes.)

Although ethical theories do not completely settle difficult, controversial issues, they help to identify important principles or guidelines. They remind us of things to consider, and they can help clarify reasoning and values. There is much merit in Kant's principle of universalism and his emphasis on treating people as intrinsically valuable "ends," in utilitarianism's consideration of consequences and its standard of increasing achievement of people's happiness, and in the natural-rights approach of setting minimal rules in a rights framework to guarantee people a sphere in which they can act according to their own values and judgment.

10.1.4 SOME IMPORTANT DISTINCTIONS

A number of important distinctions affect our ethical judgments, but are often not clearly expressed or understood. In this section, we identify a few of these. Just being aware of them can help clarify issues in some ethical debates.

RIGHT, WRONG, AND OKAY

In situations with ethical dilemmas, there are often many options that are ethically acceptable, with no specific one ethically required. Thus, it is misleading to divide all acts into two categories, ethically right and ethically wrong. Rather, it is better to think of acts as either ethically obligatory, ethically prohibited, or ethically acceptable.

NEGATIVE AND POSITIVE RIGHTS, OR LIBERTIES AND CLAIM-RIGHTS

In Section 1.2.2, we described two quite different kinds of rights. Recall that negative rights, or liberties, are rights to act without coercive interference. Claim-rights, or positive rights, are rights that impose an obligation on some people to provide certain things for others. We have seen that the distinction is important in debates about privacy, fair use of intellectual property, universal access to the Web, and other issues in this book. It is important in analyzing ethical scenarios, too.

DISTINGUISHING WRONG AND HARM

Carelessly and needlessly causing harm is wrong, but it is important to remember that harm alone is not a sufficient criterion to determine that an act is unethical. Many ethical, even admirable, acts can make other people worse off. For example, you may accept a job offer knowing someone else wanted the job and needed it more than you do. You may reduce the income of other programmers by writing a better program that consumers prefer. If your program is really good, you may put a competitor out of business completely and cause many people to lose their jobs. Yet there is nothing wrong with doing honest, productive work.

On the other hand, hackers argue that breaking into computer systems without authorization is not wrong because they do no harm. Lack of harm is not sufficient to conclude that an act is ethically acceptable. Aside from the fact that the hacker might do unintended harm, one can argue that hacking is a violation of property rights: A person has no right to enter your property without your permission, independent of any harm done.

SEPARATING GOALS FROM CONSTRAINTS

Economist Milton Friedman has written that the goal or responsibility of a business is to make a profit for its shareholders. This statement appalled some ethicists, as they believe it justifies, or is used to justify, irresponsible and unethical actions. It seems to me that arguments on this point miss the distinction between goals, on the one hand, and constraints on actions that may be taken to achieve the goals, on the other—or the distinction between ends and means. Our personal goals may include financial success and finding an attractive mate. Working hard, investing wisely, and being an interesting and decent person can achieve these goals. They may be achievable as well by stealing and lying. By most ethical theories, stealing and lying are unacceptable. Ethics tells us what actions are acceptable or unacceptable in our attempts to achieve the goals. There is nothing unethical about a business having the goal of maximizing profits. The ethical character of the company depends on whether the actions taken to achieve the goal are consistent with ethical constraints.[5]

PERSONAL PREFERENCE AND ETHICS

There are many issues about which we have strong feelings, some related to our ethical views. It might be difficult to draw a line between what we consider ethically wrong and what we personally disapprove of. Pick an organization that advocates some policy you deeply think ethically wrong, perhaps an abortion rights group or an anti-abortion group, or a group that advocates legalizing marriages between same-sex couples, or a group that advocates banning homosexuals from teaching in public schools. Suppose the group is solely an advocacy or educational group; it does not perform abortions or block abortion clinics, for example. Now, the organization asks you, a programmer, to write a software package, perhaps a mailing-list program. You believe in freedom of speech, but you find the job distasteful; you do not want to do anything to assist the organization.

If you decide to decline the job, are you acting on ethical grounds? In other words, can you claim that performing the job is unethical? The organization is exercising freedom of speech. Although its position is controversial and ethical issues are relevant to the social issue the organization supports, the organization is not engaged in unethical activity. Your assistance would help to further a goal you do not support. This is a matter of personal preference. There is nothing ethically wrong with declining the assignment, of course; the customer's freedom of speech does not impose an ethical obligation on you for assistance.

When discussing political or social issues, people frequently argue that their position is right in a moral or ethical sense or that an opponent's position is morally wrong or unethical. People tend to want to be on the "moral high ground" and feel the stigma of an accusation that their view is ethically wrong. Thus, arguments based on ethics can be, and often are, used to intimidate people with different views. It is a good idea to try to distinguish between actions we find distasteful, rude, or ill-advised and actions that we can argue convincingly are ethically wrong.

LAW AND ETHICS

What is the connection between law and ethics? Very little. Is it ethical to prohibit marijuana use by terminally ill people? Is it ethical for the government or a state university to give preference in contracts, hiring, or admissions to people in specific ethnic groups? Is it ethical to sell mailing lists based on customer purchasing history? Whatever the current law happens to be does not answer these questions. In addition, history provides numerous examples of laws most of us consider profoundly wrong by ethical standards; slavery is perhaps the most obvious example. Ethics precedes law in the sense that ethical principles help determine whether or not we should pass specific laws.

Some laws enforce ethical rules (e.g., against murder and theft). By definition, we are ethically obligated to obey such laws—not because they are laws, but because the laws implement the obligations and prohibitions of ethical rules.

Other laws fall into several categories; we look at the ethical character of a few of them. One category of laws establishes conventions for business or other activities. Commercial law, such as the Uniform Commercial Code, defines rules for economic transactions and contracts. Such rules provide a framework in which we can interact smoothly and confidently with strangers. They include provisions for how to interpret a contract if a court must resolve a dispute. These laws are extremely important to any society. They should be consistent with ethics; beyond basic ethical considerations, however, details could depend on historic conventions, practicality, and other nonethical criteria. In the U.S., drivers must drive on the right side of the road; in England, drivers must drive on the left side. There is obviously nothing intrinsically right or wrong about either choice. But, once the convention is established, it is ethically wrong to drive on the wrong side of the road because it endangers other people.

Unfortunately, many laws fall into a category that is not intended to implement ethical rules—or even be consistent with them. The political process is subject to pressure from special interest groups of all sorts who seek to pass laws that favor their groups or businesses. Examples include the laws that delayed the introduction of cable television (promoted by the television networks) and laws, sponsored by the dairy industry when margarine was first introduced, against coloring margarine yellow to look more like butter. Many prominent people in the financial industry reported receiving a large number of fund-raising letters from members of Congress—in the week that Congress took up new regulations for their industry. Many political, religious, or ideological organizations promote laws to require (or prohibit) certain kinds of behavior that the group considers desirable (or objectionable). Examples include prohibitions on gambling or alcohol, requirements for recycling, and requirements that stores close on Sundays. At an extreme, in some countries, this category includes restrictions on the practice of certain religions.

Copyright law has elements of all three categories we described. It defines a property right, violation of which is a form of theft. Because of the intangible nature of intellectual property, some of the rules about what constitutes infringement are more like the second category: pragmatic rules that are devised to be workable. Powerful groups (e.g., the publishing, music, and movie industries) lobby for specific rules to benefit themselves. This is why some violations of copyright law are clearly unethical (if one accepts the concept of intellectual property at all), yet others seem to be entirely acceptable, sometimes even noble.

Are we ethically obligated to obey a law just because it is a law? Some argue that we are: As members of society, we are obliged to accept the rules that are made by the legislative process so long as they are not clearly and utterly ethically wrong (e.g., slavery).

Others argue that, whereas this might often be a good policy, it is not an ethical obligation. Legislators are just a group of people, subject to errors and political influences; there is no reason to feel an ethical obligation to do something just because they say so. Indeed, some believe all laws that regulate personal behavior or voluntary economic transactions to be violations of the liberty and autonomy of the people forced to obey and, hence, to be ethically wrong.

Is it always ethically right to do something that is legal? No. Laws must be uniform and must be stated in a way that clearly indicates what actions are punishable. Ethical situations are complex and variable; relevant factors might be known to the people involved but not provable in court. There are widely accepted ethical rules that would be difficult and probably unwise to enforce absolutely with laws—for example: Do not lie. We have seen that new law lags behind new technology. This makes sense. It takes time to recognize the new problems, consider possible solutions, think and debate about the consequences and fairness of various proposals, and so on. A good law will set minimal standards that can apply to all situations, leaving a large range of voluntary choices. Ethics fills the gap between the time when technology creates new problems and the time when reasonable laws are passed, and ethics fills the gap between general legal standards that apply to all cases and the particular choices that must be made in a specific case.

While it is not ethically obligatory to obey all laws, that is not an excuse to ignore laws, nor is a law (or lack of a law) an excuse to ignore ethics.

10.2 Ethical Guidelines for Computer Professionals

In this section, we look at problems and characteristics of professional ethics, as distinct from general ethics. We look at guidelines developed by scholars and computer professionals, including the Software Engineering Code of Ethics and Professional Practice and the ACM Code of Ethics and Professional Conduct (included in Appendix A).

10.2.1 SPECIAL ASPECTS OF PROFESSIONAL ETHICS

Professional ethics have several characteristics different from general ethics. The role of the professional is special in several ways. First, the professional is an expert in a field, be it computer science or medicine, that most customers know little about. Customers rely on the knowledge, expertise, and honesty of the professional. A professional "advertises" his or her expertise and thus has an obligation to provide it. Second, the products of many professionals (e.g., bridges, investment advice, surgery protocols, and computer systems) profoundly affect large numbers of people. A computer professional's work can affect the life, health, finances, freedom, and future of a client or members of the public. A professional can cause great harm through dishonesty, carelessness, or incompetence. Often the victims have little ability to protect themselves; many are not the direct customers of the professional and have no direct control or decision-making role in choosing the product or making decisions about its quality and safety. Thus, computer professionals have special responsibilities not only to their customers, but also to the general public, to

DO ORGANIZATIONS HAVE ETHICS?

This is a relevant question here because we will be discussing decisions made in a professional context. Computer software and systems are not usually produced by one individual alone. They are produced by a company or organization, and the decisions about design, testing, and so on, are made within an organizational structure.

Some philosophers argue that it is meaningless to speak of an organization as having ethics. Individual people make all decisions and take all actions; those people must have ethical responsibility for everything they do. Others argue that an organization that acts with intention and a formal decision structure, such as a business, is a moral entity.[6] Viewing a business as a moral entity does not diminish the responsibility of the individual people. Ultimately, it is individuals who are making decisions and taking actions. We can hold both the individuals and the company or organization responsible for their acts.*

Whether one accepts or rejects the idea that a business can have moral rights and responsibilities, it is clear that organizational structure and policies lead to a pattern of actions and decisions that have ethical content. Businesses do have a "corporate culture," or a "personality," or simply a reputation for treating employees and customers in respectful and honest—or careless and deceptive—ways. A bug in a new checkout-scanner program developed for Walgreen, a drugstore chain, occasionally caused an incorrect price to be charged. Walgreen delayed introduction of a new inventory control system for six months while they solved the problem.[7] The same person working at a different company might have made the opposite decision. The policies and principles of the company influence such decisions. People in management positions shape the corporate culture or ethics of the business. Thus, decisions by managers have an impact beyond the particular product or contract the decision involves. A manager who is dishonest with customers or who cuts corners on testing, for example, is setting an example that encourages other employees to be dishonest and careless. A manager's ethical responsibility includes his or her contribution to the company's ethical personality. Principle 5 of the Software Engineering Code of Ethics and Professional Practice includes many specific guidelines for managers.

the users of their products, regardless of whether they have a direct relationship with the users. These responsibilities include thinking about potential risks to privacy and security of data, safety, reliability, and ease of use. They include taking action to diminish risks that are too high.

In Chapter 4, we saw some of the minor and major consequences of flaws in computer systems. In some of those cases, people acted in clearly unethical or irresponsible ways. In many cases, however, there was no ill intent. Software is enormously complex, and the

---

* Regardless of whether businesses and organizations are viewed as moral agents, they are treated as legal entities and can be held legally responsible for their acts.

process of developing it involves communications between many people with diverse roles and skills. Because of the complexity, risks, and impact of computer systems, a professional has an ethical responsibility not simply to avoid intentional evil, but to exercise a high degree of care and follow good professional practices, to reduce the likelihood of problems. That includes a responsibility to maintain an expected level of competence and be up-to-date on current knowledge, technology, and standards of the profession. Professional responsibility includes knowing or learning enough about the application field to do a good job. Responsibility for a noncomputer professional using a sophisticated computer system includes knowing or learning enough about the system to understand potential problems.

10.2.2 PROFESSIONAL CODES, GUIDELINES, AND RESPONSIBILITIES

PROFESSIONAL CODES OF ETHICS

Many professional organizations have codes of professional conduct. They provide a general statement of ethical values reminding people in the profession that ethical behavior is expected of them. They provide reminders about specific professional responsibilities. They provide valuable guidance for new or young members of the profession who want to behave ethically but do not know what is expected of them, people whose limited experience has not prepared them to be alert to difficult ethical situations and handle them appropriately.

There are several organizations for the range of professions included in the general term "computer professional." The main ones are the ACM and the IEEE Computer Society (IEEE CS).* They developed the Software Engineering Code of Ethics and Professional Practice (adopted jointly by the ACM and IEEE CS) and the ACM Code of Ethics and Professional Conduct (both in Appendix A). We refer to sections of the Codes in the following discussion and in the cases in Section 10.3, using the shortened names SE Code and ACM Code. The Codes emphasize the basic ethical values of honesty and fairness.† They cover many aspects of professional behavior, including the responsibility to respect confidentiality,‡ maintain professional competence,* be aware of relevant laws,° and honor contracts and agreements.° In addition, the Codes put special emphasis on areas that are particularly (but not uniquely) vulnerable from computer systems. They

---

*The somewhat outdated full names are the Association for Computing Machinery and the Institute of Electrical and Electronics Engineers.

†SE Code: 1.06, 2.01, 6.07, 7.05, 7.04; ACM Code: 1.3, 1.4

‡SE Code: 2.05; ACM Code: 1.8

*SE Code: 8.01–8.05; ACM Code: 2.2

°SE Code: 8.05; ACM Code: 2.3

°ACM Code: 2.6

stress the responsibility to respect and protect privacy,* avoid harm to others,[†] and respect property rights (with intellectual property and computer systems themselves as the most relevant examples).[‡] The Software Engineering Code covers many specific points about software development. It was translated into several languages and adopted by various organizations as their internal professional standard.

SOME GUIDELINES

We highlight a few principles for producing good systems. Most are directed at software developers. A few are for professionals in other areas who make decisions about acquiring computer systems for large organizations. Many more specific guidelines appear in the SE Code and in the ACM Code.

Understand what success means. After the utter foul-up on opening day at Kuala Lumpur's airport, blamed on clerks typing incorrect commands, an airport official said, "There's nothing wrong with the system." His statement is false, and the attitude behind the statement contributes to the development of systems that will fail. The official defined the role of the airport system narrowly: to do certain data manipulation correctly, assuming all input is correct. Its true role was to get passengers, crews, planes, luggage, and cargo to the correct gates on schedule. It did not succeed. Developers and institutional users of computer systems must view the system's role and their responsibility in a wide enough context.

Include users (such as medical staff, technicians, pilots, office workers) in the design and testing stages to provide safe and useful systems. Recall the discussion of computer controls for airplanes (Sections 4.1.4 and 4.3.2), where confusing user interfaces and system behavior increased the risk of accidents. There are numerous "horror stories" of systems developed by technical people without sufficient knowledge of what was important to users. For example, a system developed for a newborn nursery at a hospital rounded each baby's weight to the nearest pound; for premature babies, the difference of a few ounces is crucial information.[8] The responsibility of developers to talk to users is not restricted to systems that affect safety and health. A system designed to process stories in a newspaper office, to manage inventory in a toy store, or to manage a personal computer's desktop could cause frustration, might waste a client's money, and might be discarded if designed without sufficient consideration of the needs of actual users.

Do a thorough, careful job when planning and scheduling a project and when writing bids or contracts. This includes, among many other things, allocating sufficient time and budget for testing and other important steps in the development process. Inadequate planning is likely to lead to pressure to cut corners later. (See SE Code 3.02, 3.09, and 3.10.)

---

*SE Code: 1.03, 3.12; ACM Code: 1.7

[†] SE Code: 1.03; ACM Code: 1.2

[‡] SE Code: 2.02, 2.03; ACM Code: 1.5, 1.6, 2.8

WHAT SHOULD NOT BE IN A PROFESSIONAL CODE?

Professional codes of ethics are usually written by dedicated people with the goal of guiding practitioners in the field and protecting the public. It is worth noting that particular provisions are sometimes included for less worthy goals or could serve the interests of particular members of the profession rather than all practitioners and the public. For example, recall the discussion of bans on telemedicine practice by out-of-state doctors (Section 9.5.1). Would opposition to competition affect a decision about how telemedicine is treated in a professional code? One medical organization used a telemedicine ban as a bargaining chip in negotiating with a state legislature about legislation affecting doctors. Professional organizations often lobby government representatives and participate in writing laws. Deals might be made that include provisions chosen for political rather than for ethical or professional reasons. Mandatory professional licensing is an issue where economic interests can influence the position taken in a code of ethics; mandatory licensing often has the effect of reducing the number of people in the profession (particularly those who are self-taught), thereby raising the income of those who are licensed. Of course, many in the computing profession who advocate licensing are motivated by a genuine desire to improve the quality of the profession and to protect the public from dangerously incompetent practitioners.

Professional organizations tend to be large; the ACM, for example, has approximately 80,000 members, the IEEE CS approximately 100,000. In any profession, members have widely differing views on many ethical, social, and political issues. Sometimes a professional organization's code of ethics includes positions on issues where the members differ strongly; a majority of members (or a majority of members of the governing body within the organization) could use its power to endorse its favored position. For a majority to adopt its position as an ethical tenet of the profession would be dishonest. For example, it would seem inappropriate (even unethical) for the ethics code of a general organization of computer professionals to take a position on, say, working on high-tech military weaponry. It is reasonable that an organization such as Computer Professionals for Social Responsibility, members of the profession organized around shared social and political viewpoints, would adopt positions or ethical statements that might be inappropriate for the ACM or the IEEE CS.

Design for real users. We have seen several cases where computers crashed because someone typed input incorrectly. In one case, an entire pager system shut down because a technician did not press the "Enter" key (or did not hit it hard enough). Real people make typos, get confused, or are new at their job. It is the responsibility of the system designers and programmers to provide clear user interfaces and include appropriate checking of input. It is impossible for computers to detect all incorrect inputs, but there are techniques for catching many and for reducing the damage that errors cause.

Don't assume existing software is safe. If you use software from another application, verify its suitability for the current project. If the software was designed for an application where the degree of harm from a failure was small, the quality and testing standards might not have been as high as would be necessary in the new application. The software might have confusing user interfaces that were tolerable (though not admirable) in the original application but could have serious negative consequences in the new application. We saw in Chapter 4 that a complete safety evaluation is important even for software from an earlier version of the same application if a failure would have serious consequences. (Recall the Therac-25 and Ariane 5.)

Be open and honest about capabilities, safety, and limitations of software. This is important in general, and especially for *expert systems*, or decision systems—systems that use models and heuristics incorporating expert knowledge to guide decision making—for medical diagnosis or investment planning, for example. Developers must explain the limitations and uncertainties to users (doctors, financial advisors, and so forth), and users must not shirk responsibility for understanding them and using the systems properly.

In several cases, described in Chapter 4, there is a strong argument that the treatment of customers was dishonest. Honesty of salespeople is hardly a new issue. The line between emphasizing your best side and being dishonest is not always clear, but it should be clear that hiding known, serious flaws and lying to customers are on the wrong side of the line.

Honesty includes taking responsibility for damaging or injuring others. If you break a neighbor's window playing ball or smash into someone's car, you have an obligation to pay for the damage. If a business finds that its product caused injury, it should not hide that fact or attempt to put the blame on others.

Require a convincing case for safety. One of the most difficult ethical problems that arises in safety-critical applications is deciding how much risk is acceptable. In 1986, burning gases that leaked from a rocket shortly after launch destroyed the space shuttle Challenger, killing the seven people aboard.* A comment from one of the engineers who opposed the launch sheds some light on how subtle shifts in attitude can affect a decision. The night before the scheduled launch, the engineers argued for a delay; they knew the cold weather posed a severe threat to the shuttle. We cannot prove absolutely that a system is safe, nor can we usually prove absolutely that it will fail and kill someone. The engineer reported that, in the case of the Challenger, "It was up to us to prove beyond a shadow of a doubt that it was not safe to [launch]." This, he said, was the total reverse of a usual Flight Readiness Review.[9] For the ethical decision maker, the policy should be to suspend or delay use of the system in the absence of a convincing case for safety, rather than to proceed in the absence of a convincing case for disaster.

---

*The computer system was not at fault.

REINFORCING EXCLUSION

A voice-recognition system is a system (consisting of hardware and software) that identifies the person speaking. (This is different from speech recognition, discussed in Section 9.5.2, which identifies the words spoken.) One application of voice recognition is teleconferencing for business meetings, where the computer system identifies who is speaking and displays that person on everyone's screens. Some voice-recognition systems recognize male voices much more easily than female voices. Sometimes, when the system fails to recognize female speakers and focus attention on them, they are effectively cut out of the discussion.[10] Did the designers of voice recognition systems intentionally discriminate against women? Probably not. Are women's voices inherently more difficult to recognize? Probably not. What happened? There are many more male programmers than female programmers. There are many more men than women in high-level business meetings. Men were the primary developers and testers of the systems; they optimized the algorithms for the lower range of male voices.

In his book *The Road Ahead*, Bill Gates tells us that a team of Microsoft programmers developed and tested a handwriting-recognition system. When they thought it was working fine, they brought it to him to try. It failed. All the team members were right-handed. Gates is left-handed.[11]

In some applications, it makes sense to focus on a niche audience, but that choice should be conscious (and reasonable). These examples show how easy it is to develop systems that unintentionally exclude people—and how important it is to think beyond one's own group when designing and testing a system. Besides women and left-handed people, other groups to consider are nontechnical users, different ethnic groups, disabled people, older people (who might, for example, need a large-font option), and children.

In these examples, doing "good" or "right" in a social sense—taking care not to reinforce exclusion of specific groups of people—coincides with producing a good product and expanding its potential market.

10.3 Cases

10.3.1 INTRODUCTION AND METHODOLOGY

The cases presented here, some based on real incidents, are just a few samples of the kinds that can occur. They vary in seriousness and difficulty, and they include situations that illustrate professional responsibilities to potential users of computer systems in the general public, customers or clients, the employer, coworkers, and others. Many more cases appear in the exercises at the end of the chapter.

In most of this book, I have tried to give arguments on both sides of controversial issues without taking a position. Ethical issues are often even more difficult than some of the others we have covered, and there could well be disagreement among computer ethics specialists on some points in the cases considered here. In any real case, there are many other relevant facts and details that affect the conclusion. In spite of the difficulty of drawing ethical conclusions, especially for brief fictional scenarios, for some of these cases I give conclusions. You might face cases like these where you have to make a decision. I do not want to leave the impression that, because a decision is difficult or because some people benefit or lose either way, there is no ethical basis for making the decision. (It seems ethically irresponsible to do so.)

How shall we analyze specific scenarios? We now have a number of tools. We can try to apply our favorite ethical theory, or some combination of the theories. We can ask questions that reflect basic ethical values: Is it honest? Is it responsible? Does it violate an agreement we made? We can consult a code of professional ethics. But ethical theories and guidelines might conflict, or we might find no clause in the Codes specifically applicable. The Preamble of the Software Engineering Code of Ethics and Professional Practice, in Appendix A.1, recognizes this problem and emphasizes the need for good judgment and concern for the safety, health, and welfare of the public.

Although we will not follow the outline below step by step, our discussions of the cases will usually include most of these elements:

1. *Brainstorming phase*

   - List risks, issues, problems, consequences.

   - List all the people and organizations affected. (They are generally referred to as the *stakeholders*.)

   - In cases where there is not a simple yes-or-no decision, but rather one has to choose some action, list possible actions.

2. *Analysis phase*

   - Identify responsibilities of the decision maker. (Consider responsibilities of both general ethics and professional ethics.)

   - Identify rights of stakeholders. (It might be helpful to clarify whether they are negative or positive rights.)

   - Consider the impact of the action options on the stakeholders. Analyze consequences, risks, benefits, harms, costs for each action considered.

   - Find sections of the Software Engineering Code or the ACM Code that apply. Consider the guidelines in Section 10.2.2. Consider Kant's and Mill's approaches. Then, categorize each potential action or response as ethically obligatory, ethically prohibited, or ethically acceptable.

■ If there are several ethically acceptable options, select an option, considering the ethical merits of each, courtesy to others, practicality, self-interest, personal preferences, and so on. (In some cases, plan a sequence of actions, depending on the response to each.)

The brainstorming phase can generate a long discussion with humorous and obviously wrong options. In the analysis phase, we might reject some options or decide that the claims of some stakeholders are irrelevant or minor. The brainstorming effort in generating these ideas was not wasted. It could bring out ethical and practical considerations and other useful ideas that one would not immediately think of. And it is as helpful to know why some factors do not carry heavy ethical weight as it is to know which ones do.

10.3.2 COPYING AN EMPLOYEE'S FILES

You are a computer system manager. An employee is out sick and another employee requests that you copy all files from the sick person's computer to his so he can do some work.

One risk here is invasion of privacy; the sick employee might have personal files stored on the computer. Also, the sick employee could have files related to secret or proprietary company information to which other employees are not supposed to have access. There is a small risk to you and the company from a complaint or suit for invasion of privacy if you copy personal files. On the other hand, the employee making the request and the company might suffer if important work is not completed on time.

The obvious stakeholders include the sick employee, the employee making the request, and you (the system manager). There are others. Other people working on the same project might suffer negative consequences if lack of access to needed files delays its completion. Your action could set a precedent affecting privacy of the files of all employees who use the computers you manage. In any business scenario, if the revenue and success of the business as a whole could be seriously affected, the owners (perhaps thousands of stockholders) and other employees are stakeholders. In this case, we will assume the impact on this group is minor.

There might be a very simple solution to this problem: Call the sick employee, and ask permission to copy the files. But he or she may not be reachable. Another option would be to request authorization from the manager of the project on which the employees are working.

The right thing to do depends in large part on the policies, practices, and expectations at the particular company. If there is a strong policy against personal use of the computer system, if it is routine practice for employees to share files while working on a project, and if it is reasonable to believe that all the files to be copied are related to the project the employees are working on, there might be no ethical problem with copying the files. (Note SE Code 5.03.) In the actual case, the system manager refused to transfer all the files, but agreed to transfer specific files if given the filenames. This solution might work in some contexts, but not others.

If you do agree to transfer files, it is a good idea to make a list of the files copied and give it to the sick employee later. Informing the employee acknowledges that copying files may have some privacy implications and alerts the employee in case you copy anything inappropriately.

10.3.3 INSUFFICIENT PRIVACY PROTECTION

> *Your customer is a community clinic that works with families that have problems of family violence. The clinic has three sites in the same city, including a shelter for battered women and children. Currently, the clinic uses no computers. The director wants a computerized record system, networked for the three sites, with the ability to transfer files among sites and make appointments at any site for any other. She wants to have an Internet connection for e-mail communication with other social-service agencies about client needs. She wants a few notebook computers capable of storing copies of records that staffers can carry when they visit clients at home. At the shelter, staffers use only first names, but the records contain last names and forwarding addresses of women who have recently left. The director's description of the system makes no mention of passwords or encryption. The clinic's budget is small, and she wants to keep the cost as low as possible.*

The clinic director is likely to be aware of the sensitivity of the information in the records and to know that inappropriate release of information can result in embarrassment for families using the clinic and physical harm to women who use the shelter. But she is less likely to be aware of the risks of a computer system. You, as the computer professional, have specialized knowledge in this area. It is as much your obligation to warn the director of the risks as it is that of a physician to warn a patient of side-effects of a drug he or she prescribes. (See, for example, ACM Code 1.7 and SE Code 2.07 and 3.12.)

The most vulnerable stakeholders here are the clients of the clinic and their family members, and they are not involved in your negotiations with the director. You, the director, the clinic employees, and the donors or agencies that fund the clinic are also stakeholders.

Suppose you warn the director about unauthorized access to sensitive information by staff members and hackers and the potential for interception of records and e-mail transmitted without encryption. You suggest a list of measures to protect client privacy, including, for example, a unique user ID and password for each staff member, coded to allow access only to information that the particular worker needs, an audit-trail function that keeps track of who accessed and modified the records, an ID code system (not Social Security number) that can be used when discussing clients with other agencies that do not need their names, and encryption for transmission of records. (Note that your ability to provide appropriate suggestions is dependent on your professional competence and currency in the field.) You tell the director that carrying records on notebook computers has risks of unauthorized leakage, both accidental and via a bribe to a staffer. (Suppose a client is a candidate for the city council or a party in a child-custody case.) You suggest procedures to reduce such leaks. The features you recommend will make the system more expensive.

If you convince the director of the importance of your recommendations, and she agrees to pay the extra cost, your professional/ethical behavior has helped improve the security of the system and protect client privacy.

What if the director says she cannot afford the additional features and is willing to have the system developed without them? You have several options. You can develop the cheaper, but more vulnerable, system. You can refuse and perhaps lose the job (although your refusal may convince the director of the importance of the security measures and change her mind). You can add security features and not charge for them. You can work out a compromise that includes the protections you consider essential. All but the first option are pretty clearly ethically acceptable. What about the first? Should you agree to provide the system without the security you believe it should have? Is it now up to the director alone to make an informed choice, weighing the risks and costs? In a case where only the customer would take the risk, some would say yes, it is your job to inform, no more. Others would say that the customer lacks the professional expertise to evaluate the risks. In this scenario, however, the director is not the only person at risk, nor is the risk to her the most significant risk of an insecure system. You have an ethical responsibility to consider the potential harm to clients from exposure of sensitive information and not to build a system without adequate privacy protection.

The most difficult decision may be deciding what is adequate. There is not always a sharp, clear line between sufficient and insufficient protection. You will have to rely on your professional knowledge, on being up-to-date about current risks and security measures, good judgment, and perhaps on consulting others who develop systems for similar applications (SE Code 7.08).*

10.3.4 RISKY SYSTEMS

> *Your team is working on a computer-controlled laser device for treating cancerous tumors. The computer controls direction, intensity, and timing of the beam that destroys the tumor. Various delays have put the project behind schedule, and the deadline is approaching. There will not be time to complete all the planned testing. The system has been functioning properly in the routine treatment scenarios that have been tested so far. You are the project manager, and you are considering whether to deliver the system on time, while continuing testing, and to make patches if bugs are found.*

---

*Note that, although we have focused on the need for privacy protection here, such protection can be overdone. You also have a professional ethical responsibility not to scare a customer into paying for security measures that are expensive but protect against very unlikely risks.

The central issue here is safety. Your company is building a machine that is designed to save lives, but if it malfunctions, it can kill or injure patients. Perhaps the situation seems obvious: Delivering the system on time benefits the company but could endanger the patients—a case of profits versus safety. But we will defer a conclusion until after we analyze the case further.

Who are the people affected (the stakeholders)? First, the patients to be treated with the machine. A malfunction could cause injury or death. On the other hand, if release of the machine is delayed, some patients it might have cured could undergo surgery instead. We will assume treatment with the laser machine is preferable because it is less invasive, requires less hospitalization and recovery time, and overall is less expensive. For some patients, surgery might be impossible, and they could die from their cancer if the laser is not used. Second, the hospitals and clinics who will purchase the machine are affected. Delay could cause financial losses if they have planned on having the machine at a particular time. However, it is reasonable for them to expect that the machine has been professionally designed and fully tested. You are deceiving the customers if you do not tell them that testing was not completed. Third, your decision affects you and your company (including its stockholders and employees). Negative consequences of delaying delivery could include damage to your reputation for managing a project (with possible impact on salary and advancement), loss of reputation, a possible fall in stock price for the company, and loss of other contracts, resulting in reduction of jobs for the company's programmers and other employees. As a project manager, you have an obligation to help the company do well. On the other hand, if the system is delivered and injures a patient, the same negative consequences are likely to occur (in addition to the human feelings of guilt and remorse and significant monetary losses from lawsuits).

This brief examination shows that delivering the system without complete testing could have both negative and positive impacts on patients and could have both negative and positive impacts on the manager and the company. The issue is not simply profits versus safety. We assume you are honestly trying to weigh the risks of delivering the system against the costs of delay. However, we must consider a few aspects of human nature that can influence the decision. One is to put more weight on short term and/or highly likely effects. Many of the costs of delay are fairly certain and immediate, and the risk of malfunction is uncertain and in the future. Also, people tend to use the inherent uncertainties of a situation and the genuine arguments for one side to rationalize making the wrong decision, that is, for taking the easy way out. It might take experience (with both professional and ethical issues), knowledge of cases like the Therac-25, and courage to resist the temptation to put short-term effects ahead of longer-term risks.

Now that we have seen that arguments can be made on both sides, we must decide how to weigh them and how to avoid rationalization. First, the machine works well in the routine tests performed so far. The Therac-25 case illustrates that a complex system can function correctly hundreds of times, but fail with fatal consequences in unusual circumstances. Your customer might not know this. You, as a computer professional, have more understanding about the complexity of computer programs and the potential for errors, especially in programs that interact with such real-world events as operator input and control of machinery. We assume that the original test plan for the laser machine was devised for good reasons. The tests should be completed before delivery. (See SE Code 1.03 and 3.10 and ACM Code 1.2.)

Some patients will benefit from on-time delivery. Should they be weighted equally against the patients whom a malfunction may harm? Not necessarily. The machine represents an improvement in medical treatment, but there is no ethical obligation that it be available to the public on a certain date. You are not responsible for the disease of people who rely on existing treatments. Your machine is being offered as an improvement. Your obligation to the people who will use the machine is to be sure that it is as safe as good professional practice can make it, and that includes proper testing. You do not have an ethical obligation to cure people of cancer; you do have an ethical obligation to use your professional judgment in a way that does not expose people, without their knowledge, to additional harm.*

What about your responsibility to your company? Even if we weigh the short-term effects of the delay more highly than the risks of losses that would result from a malfunction, the ethical arguments are on the side of fully testing the machine. Yes, you have a responsibility to help your company be successful, but that is not an absolute obligation. (Recall the discussion of goals and constraints in Section 10.1.4.) Perhaps the distinction would be more obvious if the issue were stealing (from a competitor or a customer perhaps). Your responsibility to the financial success of the company is secondary to ethical constraints. In the present case, avoiding unreasonable risk of harm to patients is the ethical constraint (SE Code 1.02).

10.3.5 GOING PUBLIC

Suppose you are a member of a team working on a computer-controlled crash-avoidance system for automobiles. You think the system has a flaw that could endanger people. The project manager does not seem concerned and expects to announce completion of the project soon. Are you ethically obligated to do something?

Given the potential consequences, yes (see SE Code 1.04; ACM Code 1.2, 2.5). We consider a variety of options. First, at a minimum, discuss your concerns with the project manager. Voicing your concerns is admirable and obligatory. It is also good for your company. Internal "whistle blowing" can help protect the company, as well as the public, from all the negative consequences of releasing a dangerous product. If the manager decides to proceed as planned with no examination of the problem, your next option is to go to someone higher up in the company.

---

*There are many situations where patients knowingly try risky drugs or treatments. Here, we are assuming that the laser device is not being described as risky or experimental, but as a new, presumably safe, treatment device.

If no one with authority in the company is willing to investigate your concerns, you have a more difficult dilemma. You now have the option of going outside the company (to the customer, to the news media, or to a government agency). There is personal risk of course: You might lose your job. There is also the ethical issue of the damage you might do to your company, and ultimately to the people who would benefit from the system if negative publicity kills the project altogether. As the ACM Code (1.2) says, "misguided reporting of violations can, itself, be harmful." At this point it is a good idea to consider whether you are confident that you have the expertise to assess the risk. It could help to discuss the problem with other professionals. If you conclude that the management decision was an acceptable one (and that you are not letting your concern for keeping your job sway your conclusion), this might be the point at which to drop the issue. If you are convinced that the risk is real, or if you are aware of a careless, irresponsible attitude among the company management, then you are obligated to go further (SE Code 6.13). You are not an uninvolved bystander, for whom the question of ethical obligation may be more fuzzy. The project pays your salary. You are part of the team; you are a participant. (Note that this is the kind of situation suggested in the Software Engineering Code, Section 2.05, where you may violate a confidentiality agreement.)

There have been several dramatic cases where professionals faced this difficult situation. The engineers who worked on the rockets for the space shuttle Challenger knew that it was not safe to launch the shuttle in cold weather. They argued for a delay and tried to convince their managers and NASA officials of the danger. When the decision was made to approve the launch, the engineers faced the issue we are confronting here. Should they have done more, perhaps gone to others in their company or NASA, or to the news media, to stop the launch? In another example, computer engineers who worked on the San Francisco Bay Area Rapid Transit system (BART) were concerned about the safety of the software designed to control the trains. Although they tried for many months, they were not successful in their attempts to convince their managers that changes were needed. Eventually, some of their critical memos and reports were published in a newspaper. The engineers were fired. During the next few years, while several crashes occurred, there were public investigations and numerous recommendations made for improving safety of the system.[12]

One of the BART engineers made these comments about the process:

> If there is something that ought to be corrected inside an organization, the most effective way to do it is to do it within the organization and exhaust all possibilities there . . . you might have to go to the extreme of publishing these things, but you should never start that way.[13]

It is important, for practical and ethical reasons, to keep a complete and accurate record of your attempts to bring attention to the problem and the responses from the people you approach. The record protects you and others who behave responsibly and could help avoid baseless accusations later.

10.3.6 RELEASE OF PERSONAL INFORMATION

We will look at two related scenarios. Here is the first:

> *You work for the IRS, the Social Security Administration, a medical clinic, or a large credit bureau. Someone asks you to get a copy of a person's file. He will pay you $500.*

Who are the stakeholders? You: You have an opportunity to make some extra money. The person seeking the file: Presumably he has something to gain from it. The person whose file is requested: His or her privacy will be invaded. All people about whom the company or agency has personal files: If you sell one file, chances are you will sell others if asked in the future. Your employer (if a private company): If the sale becomes known, the victim might sue the company; if such sales of files become common, the company will acquire a reputation for carelessness and will potentially lose business and lawsuits.

There are many alternative actions open to you: Sell the file. Refuse and say nothing about the incident. Refuse and report the incident to your supervisor. Refuse and report to the police. Contact the person whose file was requested and tell him or her of the incident. Agree to sell the file, but actually work with the police to collect evidence to convict the person trying to buy it.

Are any of these alternatives ethically prohibited or obligatory? The first option, selling the file, is wrong. It almost certainly violates rules and policies you have agreed to abide by in accepting your job. As an employee, you are bound by the guarantees of confidentiality the company or agency has promised its customers or the public. Depending on how the information in the file is to be used, you could be helping to cause serious harm to the victim. (See ACM Code: 1.2, 1.3, 1.7, 2.6; SE Code: 2.03, 2.05, 2.09, 4.04, 6.05.)

Some would argue that selling the file is wrong because it violates the privacy of the victim, but recall that the boundaries of privacy are unclear because they can conflict with freedom of speech and reasonable flow of information. If you happened to know the victim, and knew some of the same information in the file, you might not be under an ethical obligation to keep it secret. The essential element that makes selling the file wrong in this scenario is your position of trust as an employee in a company or agency that maintains sensitive files.

None of the other actions we listed are ethically wrong. Are any ethically required? Depending on policies of the employer (and laws related to certain government agencies; see SE Code 6.06 and ACM Code 2.3), you might be obligated to report any attempt to gain access to the records. There are other good reasons for reporting the incident. Reporting could lead to the capture of someone making a business of buying sensitive information without the knowledge or consent of the person the information concerns and without the knowledge and consent of the companies and agencies responsible for the information. It could protect you if it is discovered later that files were sold and the guilty person is not known. (Some ethicists, e.g., deontologists, argue that taking an action because it benefits you is not ethically meritorious. However, one can argue that taking an action that protects an innocent person is meritorious, even if the person is yourself.)

ACM Code 1.2 and 1.7 suggest an obligation to report, but it is not explicit. There might be disagreement about whether you are ethically required to do more than refuse to sell the file. It is difficult to decide how much you are obligated to do to prevent a wrong thing from happening if you are not participating in the wrong act. A recluse who ignores evils and pains around him might not be doing anything unethical, but he is not what we would consider a good neighbor. Acting to prevent a wrong is part of being a good neighbor, good employee, or good citizen—it is ethically admirable—even in situations where it is not ethically obligatory.

Now consider a variation of this scenario:

> *You know another employee sells files with people's personal information.*

Your options include doing nothing, talking to the other employee and trying to get him or her to stop selling files (by threats of exposure or ethical arguments), reporting to your supervisor (perhaps anonymously), or reporting to an appropriate law-enforcement agency. The question here is whether you have an obligation to do anything. This scenario differs from the previous one in two ways. First, you are not directly involved; no one has approached you. This difference might seem to argue for no obligation. On the other hand, in the first scenario, if you refused to sell the file, the buyer might give up, and the victim's information would not be disclosed. In this case, you know that sensitive information is being sold. Thus the argument in favor of an obligation to take action is stronger (see SE Code 6.13 and 7.01).

10.3.7 CONFLICT OF INTEREST

> *You have a small consulting business. The CyberStuff company plans to acquire a new Web-site hosting system and it wants to hire you to evaluate bids from vendors. Your spouse works for NetWorkx and did most of the work in writing the bid that NetWorkx plans to submit. You read the bid while your spouse was working on it, and you think it is excellent. Do you tell CyberStuff about your spouse's connection with NetWorkx?*

Conflict-of-interest situations occur in many professions. Sometimes the ethical course of action is clear; sometimes, depending on how small your connection is with the people or organizations affected by your action, it can be more difficult to determine.

I have seen two immediate reactions to scenarios similar to this one (in discussions among professionals and among students). One is that it is a simple case of profits versus honesty, and ethics requires that you inform the company about your connection to the software vendor. The other is that if you honestly believe you can be objective and fairly consider all bids, you have no ethical obligation to say anything. Which is right? Is this a simple choice between saying nothing and benefiting from the contract or disclosing your connection and losing the contract?

The affected parties are the CyberStuff company, yourself, your spouse, your spouse's company, and the other companies whose bids you will be reviewing. A key factor in considering consequences is that we do not know whether CyberStuff will later discover your connection to one of the bidders. If you say nothing about the conflict of interest, you benefit, because you get the consulting job. If you recommend NetWorkx, it benefits from a sale. However, if the conflict of interest is discovered later, your reputation for honesty—important to a consultant—will be damaged. The reputation of your spouse's company could also suffer. Note that, even if you conclude that you are truly unbiased and do not have an ethical obligation to tell CyberStuff about your connection to your spouse's company, your decision might put NetWorkx's reputation for honesty at risk.

What are the consequences of disclosing the conflict of interest to the client now? You will probably lose this particular job, but your honesty might be valued and might get you more business in the future. Thus, there could be benefits, even to you, from disclosing the conflict of interest.

Suppose your connection to NetWorkx is unlikely to be discovered. What are your responsibilities to your potential client as a professional consultant? When you are hired as a consultant, you are being hired to offer unbiased, honest, impartial professional advice. There is an implicit assumption that you do not have a personal interest in the outcome or a personal reason to favor one of the bids you will review. The conclusion in this case hangs on this point. In spite of your belief in your impartiality, you could be unintentionally biased. It is not up to you to make the decision about whether you can be fair. The client should make that decision. Your ethical obligation in this case is to inform CyberStuff of the conflict of interest. (See SE Code Principle 4, 4.05, and 4.06, and ACM Code 2.5.)

Exercise 10.24 considers a slightly different scenario.

10.3.8 A TEST PLAN

> *A team of programmers is developing a communications system for firefighters to use when fighting a fire. Firefighters will be able to communicate with each other, with supervisors near the scene, and with other emergency personnel. The programmers will test the system in a field near the company office.*

Where is the ethical issue? The test plan is insufficient, and this is an application where lives could be at risk. Testing should involve real firefighters inside buildings or in varied terrain, perhaps in an actual fire (perhaps a controlled burn). The programmers who work on the system know how it behaves; they are experienced users with a specific set of expectations. They are not the right people to test the system. Testing must address issues such as: Will the devices withstand heat, water, and soot? Can someone manipulate the controls wearing heavy gloves? Are the controls clear and easy to use in poor light conditions? Will a building's structure interfere with the signal?

The New York City Fire Commissioner halted use of a $33 million digital communications system after a fireman's call for help on his radio was not heard. Firefighters reported other problems during simulation tests. The commissioner commented "We tested the quality, durability, and reliability of the product, but we didn't spend enough time testing them in the field or familiarizing the firefighters with their use."[14]

10.3.9 COPYRIGHT VIOLATION

> *Your company has about 25 licenses for a computer program, but you discover that it has been copied onto 80 computers.*

The first step here is to inform your supervisor that the copies violate the license agreement. Suppose the supervisor is not willing to take any action? What next? What if you bring the problem to the attention of higher level people in the company and no one cares? There are several possible actions: Give up; you did your best to correct the problem. Call the software vendor or the Software and Information Industry Association and report the offense. Quit your job.

Is giving up at this point ethically acceptable? My students thought it depended in part on whether you are the person who signed the license agreements. If so, you have made an agreement about the use of the software, and you are obligated to honor it. Because you did not make the copies, you have not broken the agreement directly, but you have responsibility for the software. As a practical matter, your name on the license could expose you to legal risk or to being made a scapegoat by unethical managers in your company. Thus, you might prefer to report the violation or quit your job and have your name removed from the licenses to protect yourself. If you are not the person who signed the licenses, then you observed a wrong being done and brought it to the attention of appropriate people in the company. Is that enough? What do Sections 2.02, 6.13, and 7.01 of the SE Code and 1.5 and 2.6 of the ACM Code suggest?

10.3.10 HIRING FOREIGN PROGRAMMERS

> *You are a manager at a software company about to begin a large software project. You will need to hire dozens of new programmers. Using the Internet for communication and software delivery, you can hire programmers in another country at lower salary than programmers in your country. Should you do this?*[15]

This case differs from the others we considered in that it involves wider social and economic issues. I include it for several reasons. It is a real, current controversy. Hiring of foreign programmers who work in their home country has been increasing, with potentially significant implications for the economies and the programmers in the countries involved. This is a good example for trying to distinguish economic advantage from ethical arguments. We explicitly consider Kantian and utility approaches in the analysis. Also, in other industries, several countries have passed legislation to restrict the hiring of foreign workers. The discussion here might provide insight into the ethics of such legislation. For simplicity, I use the U.S. as the country where the software company is based. U.S. companies hire programmers in India, Russia, and elsewhere. I use India in the discussion.

The people most obviously affected by the decision in this case are the Indian programmers and the U.S. programmers you might hire. Before we consider other stakeholders, we will use utilitarianism and Kant's principle about treating people as ends in themselves to generate some ideas, questions, and observations about these two groups. How can we compare the impact on utility from the two choices? The number of people hired will be about the same in either case. There does not appear to be any reason, from an ethical point of view, for placing a higher weight on the utility of one group of programmers merely because of their nationality. Shall we weigh the utilities of the programmers according to the number of dollars they will receive? That favors hiring the U.S. programmers. Or should we weigh utility by comparing the pay to the average salary in each country? That favors hiring the Indians. The utility obtained from a job for an individual programmer depends on the availability of other jobs. Are there more opportunities to earn a comparable income in the U.S. or in India? We see that a calculation of net utility for the programmers depends on how one evaluates the utility of the job for each group of programmers.

What happens when we apply Kant's principle? When we hire people for a job, we are interacting with them in a limited role. We are making a trade, money for work. The programmers are a means to an end: producing a marketable product at a reasonable price. Kant does not say that people must not be treated as a means to an end, but rather that they should not be treated merely as such. Kant does not seem helpful here, especially if we observe that the hiring decision does not treat the potential programmers differently in a way that has to do with ends and means.

Are you taking advantage of the Indian programmers, perhaps "exploiting" them by paying them less than you would have to pay the U.S. programmers? Some people believe it is unfair to both the U.S. and Indian programmers that the Indians get the jobs by charging less money. It is equally logical, however, to argue that paying the higher rate for U.S. programmers is wasteful, or charity, or simply overpayment. What makes either pay level more "right" than the other? Buyers would like to pay less for what they buy, and sellers would like to get a higher price for their goods and services. There is nothing automatically unethical about choosing the cheaper of two products, services, or employees.

We can argue that treating the Indian programmers as ends in themselves includes respecting the choices and trade-offs they make to better their lives according to their own judgment, in particular in offering to work for lower wages than U.S. programmers. But there are special cases in which we might decide otherwise. First, suppose your company is doing something to limit the other options of the Indian programmers. If your company is lobbying for import restrictions on software produced by Indian firms, for example, thus decreasing the availability of other programming jobs in India, then you are manipulating the programmers into a situation where they have few or no other choices. In that case, you are not respecting their freedom and allowing them to compete fairly; you are, then, not treating them as ends in themselves. We will assume for the rest of the discussion that your company is not doing anything like this.

Another reason we might decide that the Indian programmers are not being treated as ends in themselves, or with respect for their human dignity, is that their working conditions would be worse than the working conditions expected by U.S. workers (or required by law in the U.S.). The programmers might not get medical insurance. They might work in rundown, crowded offices, lacking air-conditioning. Is hiring them to work in such conditions unethical, or does it give them an opportunity to improve conditions in their country? Whether or not it is ethically required, there are several reasons why you might pay more (or provide better working conditions) than market conditions in India require: a sense of shared humanity that motivates you to want to provide conditions you consider desirable, a sense of generosity (i.e., willingness to contribute to the improvement of the standard of living of people in a country less rich than your own) and economic benefit: paying more than expected may get you high morale, productivity, and company loyalty.

Many laws have been passed to require that the same salary be paid to all workers when a large group of potential workers (foreigners, ethnic minorities, low-skilled workers, teenagers) is willing to work for lower pay. The main argument is that such laws will prevent the less advantaged workers from being exploited. Historically, one of the effects of these laws is that the traditionally higher-paid group gets most of the jobs. (Often that has been the intent of the law.) In this case, the almost certain result would be that the U.S. programmers would be hired. The law, or an ethical requirement that the Indian programmers be paid the same as the U.S. programmers, would protect the high incomes of programmers in the U.S. and the profits of companies that pay higher salaries. New workers or businesses that are trying to compete by lowering prices generally oppose such requirements.

So far, we have been discussing the impact of your decision on the programmers only. Other people are affected, too: your customers, the owners or stockholders of your company, and, indirectly and to a smaller degree, many people in other businesses. Hiring the Indian programmers increases the utility of your company and customers. The customers benefit from the lower price of the product, and the owners of the company benefit from the profits. If the product is successful, the company might pay for advertising, distribution, and so on, providing jobs for others in the United States. On the other hand, if you hire U.S. programmers, they will spend more of their earnings in the U.S. than the Indian programmers, generating jobs and income for others. If the product is not profitable because of higher programming costs, the company could go out of business, with a negative impact on all its employees and suppliers. To which of all these people do you have responsibilities or obligations? As a manager of the company, you have an obligation to help make the product and the company successful, to manage the project to maximize profit (not in a manner independent of ethical considerations, as we have noted, but in one consistent with them). Unless the owners of the company have a policy to improve the standard of living of people in other countries or to "Buy American," your obligation to them includes hiring competent workers at the best price. You have some responsibility for the fate of other company employees who might lose their jobs if you do a poor job of managing the project. You do not have any special obligation to other service providers you could hire, nor to people seeking jobs as programmers in either country.

Although hiring cheaper workers in other countries is often described as ethically suspect, this discussion suggests that there is no strong ethical argument for that view.

EXERCISES

Review Exercises

10.1   What are two of Kant's important ideas about ethics?

10.2   What is the difference between act-utilitarianism and rule-utilitarianism?

10.3   Give an example of a law that implements an ethical principle. Give an example of a law that enforces a particular group's idea of how people should behave.

10.4   What are two ways professional ethics differ from ethics in general?

General Exercises

10.5   Give arguments in support of "Do not lie" as a good general ethical rule. Identify which of your arguments are utilitarian and which are deontological.

10.6   Which kind of ethical theory, deontologist or consequentialist, works better for arguing that it is wrong to drive one's car on the left side of a road in a country where people normally drive on the right? Explain.

10.7   Describe a case at work or in school where you were asked or pressured to do something you thought unethical.

10.8   A computer science professor in a computer-security class assigned students to break into a computer system and bring back specific files to prove that they had. The owner of the system was unaware of the assignment. Analyze this case from an ethical perspective, using the methodology of Section 10.3.1. Consider both the ethics of the professor in making this assignment and your response as a student in the class. Are there noncomputer analogies that can help in the analysis?

10.9   In Section 2.3.1, we mentioned an incident in which a woman who filled out a detailed consumer-profile questionnaire received an offensive and threatening letter from a convicted rapist. Prison inmates had been hired to enter the questionnaire data into a computer database. What are the ethical issues involved in a direct marketing company's decision about whether to contract with a prison system or use a more expensive commercial data-entry service? In hindsight, we know that the decision in this case had serious negative consequences. Do you think the company should have foreseen such a problem, or was the decision to use prisoners for the data-entry task a reasonable one?

10.10 Review the description of the airplane crash near Cali, Columbia in Section 4.3.2. Find specific guidelines in Section 10.2.2 and the ethics codes in Appendix A that, if followed carefully, might have avoided problems in the flight-management software that contributed to the crash.

10.11 You are setting up a small business with a Web site and considering which privacy policy to adopt for the information you will collect about your customers. You will choose either informed consent, opt-in, or opt-out (as described in Section 2.3.4). Whichever you choose will be clearly and fully explained to visitors to your site. Are any of the policies ethically obligatory or ethically prohibited, or are all ethically acceptable? Justify your answers.

10.12 Your company has been hired to develop and install a surveillance system in a factory. The system includes digital cameras small enough not to be noticed. The images can be viewed in real time on monitors in a control room and will be stored. The factory manager says the purposes are to watch for safety problems and for theft of materials by workers. What issues, specifications, and policies will you discuss with the manager? Would you set any conditions on taking the job? Explain.

10.13 You are a manager at a health maintenance organization. You find that one of your employees has been reading people's medical records without authorization. What is your response? Analyze this scenario, using the methods in Section 10.3.1.

10.14 You are designing a database to keep track of patients while they are in a hospital. The record for each patient will include special diet requirements. Describe some approaches to deciding how to design the list of diet options from which a nurse will select when entering patient data. Evaluate different approaches.

10.15 You are offered a job with a company that is developing software for a new generation of space shuttles. You do not have any training in the specific techniques that will be used in the programs you will be working on. You can tell from the job interview that the interviewer thinks your college program included this material. Should you take the job? Should you tell the interviewer that you have no training or experience in this area? Analyze this scenario, using the methods in Section 10.3.1.

10.16 You are the traffic manager for a small city. The City Council has directed you to buy and install a computer system to control the traffic lights so that the timing of the lights can be adjusted to improve traffic flow at rush hours and for special events.

   a) List some potential risks of the system.

   b) List some technical requirements and/or specifications you would put in the proposal for safety.

   c) Indicate how the guidelines in Section 10.2.2 apply to this project.

10.17 You are a programmer for a company that manages large investment portfolios. You have been working on a project to develop a program to decide how to invest a large amount of money according to criteria that balance risk and potential gain according to the client's preferences. The program is complete and has performed well in preliminary testing, but the planned full-scale testing has not yet been done. It is Friday afternoon, and one of the investment managers has just received a large amount of money from a client to invest. The investment manager wants to get the money into the stock market before the weekend. He tells you that there is not enough time to use the old investment-planning method. He wants a copy of your program to run. Your supervisor, the software manager, has gone away for the weekend. What do you do? Analyze this scenario, using the methods in Section 10.3.1.

10.18 A small company offers you a programming job. You are to work on new versions of its software product to disable copy-protection and other access controls on electronic books. The company's program enables buyers of e-books to read their e-books on a variety of hardware devices (fair uses). Customers could also use the program to make many unauthorized copies of copyrighted books. The company's Web page implicitly encourages this practice. Analyze the ethics of accepting the job. Find relevant sections from the ethics codes in Appendix A.

10.19 Find at least two examples described in this book where Clause 3.09 of the Software Engineering Code of Ethics and Professional Practice was violated.

10.20 Throughout this book, we saw that many issues include trade-offs between benefits and costs. We also saw that new technologies introduce new problems, but that they are often solved or reduced by improvements or other new technologies. Clause 1.03 of the Software Engineering Code says "Approve software only if" it does not "diminish privacy or harm the environment." Should this clause say something about trade-offs, or should it be interpreted as an absolute rule? The concluding sentence of Clause 1.03 says, "The ultimate effect of the work should be to the public good." Does this suggest trade-offs? Give an example of a scenario in which the dilemma in this exercise would be relevant.

10.21 Clause 8.07 in the Software Engineering Code of Ethics says we should "not give unfair treatment to anyone because of any irrelevant prejudices." The guidelines for Section 1.4 of the ACM Code of Ethics and Professional Conduct say "Discrimination on the basis of . . . national origin . . . is an explicit violation of ACM policy and will not be tolerated." Analyze the ethical issues in the following scenario. Do you think the decision in the scenario is ethically acceptable? How do the relevant sections from the two ethics Codes apply? Which Code has a better statement about discrimination? Why?

> *Suppose you came to the U.S. from Kosovo 15 years ago. You now have a small software company. You will need to hire six programmers this year. Because of the devastation by the war in your homeland, you have decided to seek out and hire only programmers who are refugees from Kosovo.*

10.22 Consider the following statements.

1. In addition to a safe social environment, human well-being includes a safe natural environment. Therefore, computing professionals who design and develop systems must be alert to, and make others aware of, any potential damage to the local or global environment.[16]

2. We cannot assume that a computer-based economy automatically will provide enough jobs for everyone in the future. Computer professionals should be aware of this pressure on employment when designing and implementing systems that will reduce job opportunities for those most in need of them.[17]

Compare the two statements from the perspective of how relevant and appropriate they are for an ethical code for computer professionals. Do you think both should be in such a code? Neither? Just one? (Which one?) Give your reasons.

10.23 You are the president of a small computer-game company. Your company has just bought another small game company that was developing three new games. You look them over and find that one is complete, ready to reproduce and sell. It is very violent and demeaning to women. It would probably sell 200,000–400,000 copies. You have to decide what to do with the game. Give some options, and give arguments for and against them. What will you do? Why?

10.24 Suppose there are two large competing telecommunications firms in your city. The companies are hostile to each other; there have been unproven claims of industrial espionage by each company. Your spouse works for one of the companies. You are now interviewing for a job with the other. Do you have an ethical obligation to tell the interviewer about your spouse's job? How is this case similar to and different from the conflict-of-interest case in Section 10.3.7?

10.25 In 1990, the campaign of a gubernatorial candidate in Massachusetts distorted a digital image of his opponent in a television interview to make the opponent appear more menacing.[18] Do you think this was an ethical action? Why? How does it differ from using a caricature (often done in cartoons, and protected by the First Amendment)?

10.26 A Dutch hacker who copied patient files from a University of Washington medical center (and was not caught) said in an online interview that he did it to publicize the system's vulnerability, not to use the information. He disclosed portions of the files to a journalist after the medical center said that no patient files had been copied.[19] Analyze the ethics of his actions using the methodology of Section 10.3.1. Was this honorable whistle-blowing? Irresponsible hacking?

10.27 Consider the case in Section 10.3.4. Suppose that the company has decided to deliver the laser device before completing the testing and that you have decided you must inform the hospitals that are purchasing it. Discuss ethical arguments about whether to send information to the hospitals openly or anonymously.

10.28 The cases in Sections 10.3.4 and 10.3.5 concern safety-critical systems. Suppose the system is an accounting system, or a consumer tax-preparation system, or a game. Should the analysis of the scenarios differ? If so, in what way? If not, why not?

10.29 You run a small company that developed and markets a filter program that enables parents to block access to Internet sites they do not want their children to visit. A large corporation has asked you to customize the program to install on its machines to block access by employees to various game sites, sites containing pornography, and other entertainment sites not related to the employees' work. A foreign government has asked you to customize the program to install on its Internet gateways to block access by people in the country to sites containing pornography and sites containing political discussion critical of the government.

Will you accept either or both jobs? If one but not the other, make clear the reasons for the distinction.

10.30 Several professional associations of engineers opposed increased immigration of skilled high-tech workers. Was this ethical? Give arguments for both sides; then give your view and defend it.

10.31 The faculty at a large university requested that the campus store sell an electronic device, Auto-Grader, that students would use when taking machine-scorable tests. Students would enter test answers into this personal electronic device and then send the answers via infrared signal to the instructor's computer in the classroom. Once all the answers are received, the instructor's computer immediately grades the test and sends the students' scores back to their devices.

Suppose you are a university dean who must decide whether to allow use of this system. Analyze the decision as both an ethical and practical problem. Discuss potential benefits and problems or risks of using the system. Discuss all the issues (of the kind relevant to the topics of this book) that are relevant to making the decision. Mention any warnings or policies you might include if you approve use of the system.

Class Discussion Exercises

These exercises are for class discussion, perhaps with short presentations prepared in advance by small groups of students.

10.32 Many people, including Sun Microsystems cofounder Bill Joy, fear that development of intelligent robots could have devastating consequences for the human race.[20] Is it ethical to do research in artificial intelligence?

10.33 Almost all the exercises in this chapter are suitable for Class Discussion Exercises.

NOTES

1 Donald Gotterbarn, "Computer Ethics: Responsibility Regained," *National Forum: The Phi Kappa Phi Forum*, Summer 1991, 71:3; reprinted in Deborah G. Johnson and Helen Nissenbaum, eds., *Computers, Ethics & Social Values*, Prentice Hall, 1995, pp. 18–24.

2 By Louis P. Pojman (Wadsworth, 1990) and J. L. Mackie (Penguin Books, 1977), respectively.

3 Sources used in the preparation of this section include the following: Joseph Ellin, *Morality and the Meaning of Life: An Introduction to Ethical Theory*, Harcourt Brace Jovanovich, 1995; Deborah G. Johnson, Computer Ethics, Prentice Hall, 2nd ed., 1994; Louis Pojman, *Ethical Theory: Classical and Contemporary Readings*, 2nd ed., Wadsworth, 1995 (which includes John Stuart Mill's "Utilitarianism," Kant's "The Foundations of the Metaphysic of Morals," and John Locke's "Natural Rights"); and James Rachels, *The Elements of Moral Philosophy*, McGraw Hill, 1993.

4 John Stuart Mill, *Utilitarianism*, 1863.

5 Some goals appear to be ethically wrong in themselves, for example genocide, although often it is because the only way to achieve the goal is by methods that are ethically unacceptable (killing innocent people).

6 Kenneth C. Laudon, "Ethical Concepts and Information Technology," *Communications of the ACM*, Dec. 1995, 38:12, p. 38.

7 Philip E. Ross, "The Day the Software Crashed," *Forbes*, April 25, 1994, 153:9, pp. 142–156; see p. 146.

8 Bob Davis and David Wessel, *Prosperity: The Coming 20-Year Boom and What It Means to You*, Random House, 1998, p. 97.

9 Roger Boisjoly, quoted in Diane Vaughan, *The Challenger Launch Decision: Risky Technology, Culture, and Deviance at NASA*, University of Chicago Press, 1996, p. 41.

10 Charles Piller, "The Gender Gap Goes High-Tech," *Los Angeles Times*, Aug. 25, 1998, p. A1.

11 Bill Gates, *The Road Ahead*, Viking, 1995, p. 78.

12 See Diane Vaughan, *The Challenger Launch Decision: Risky Technology, Culture, and Deviance at NASA*, University of Chicago Press, 1996, for an analysis of the institutional practices that contributed to the Challenger tragedy. See Robert M. Anderson *et al.*, *Divided Loyalties: Whistle-Blowing at BART*, Purdue University, 1980, for the BART case.

13 Holger Hjorstvang, quoted in Anderson *et al.*, *Divided Loyalties*, p. 140.

14 Fire Commissioner Admits Fault Over Radios," Apr. 10, 2001, www.cbsnewyork.com/topstories/StoryFolder/story_1483538055_html; viewed Aug. 15, 2001. The inability of supervisors to communicate with fire fighters inside the World Trade Center (to tell them to leave, because the buildings were going to collapse) was a major factor in the large number of fire-fighter deaths on September 11, 2001. The new digital system had been taken out of service months earlier. Reports said it was unlikely that the digital system would have worked better than the system in use on Sept. 11; an antenna it needed was disabled by debris before the collapse. (Kevin Flynn, "A Focus on Communication Failures," *New York Times*, Jan. 30, 2002, p. A13.)

15 My thanks to my student Anthony Biag, whose questions in class on this issue prompted me to include it in this book.

16 Guidelines of the ACM Code of Ethics and Professional Conduct (Section 1.1).

17 Tom Forester and Perry Morrison, *Computer Ethics: Cautionary Tales and Ethical Dilemmas in Computing*, second edition, MIT Press, 1994, p. 202.

18 Anne Branscomb, *Who Owns Information?*, Basic Books, 1994, pp. 73–75.

19 Marc L. Songini, "Hospital Confirms Copying of Patient Files by Hacker," *Security Informer*, Dec. 14, 2000, www.security-informer.com/english/crd_hospital_316005.html; viewed June 4, 2001.

20 Bill Joy, "Why the Future Doesn't Need Us," *Wired*, Apr. 2000; www.wired.com/wired/archive/8.04/

BOOKS AND ARTICLES

Some of the books listed at the end of Chapter 1 also cover ethical issues.

■ Robert M. Anderson, Robert Perrucci, Dan E. Schendel, and Leon E. Trachtman, *Divided Loyalties: Whistle-Blowing at BART*, Purdue University, 1980.

■ Ronald E. Anderson, Deborah G. Johnson, Donald Gotterbarn, and Judith Perrolle,

"Using the New ACM Code of Ethics in Decision Making," *Communications of the ACM*, Feb. 1993, 36:2, pp. 98–107.

■ Michael D. Bayles, *Professional Ethics*, Wadsworth, 1981.

- Vint Cerf, "Ethics and the Internet," *Communications of the ACM*, June 1989, 32:6, p. 710. An early attempt to establish a standard of ethics for the Internet.

- W. Robert Collins, Keith W. Miller, Bethany J. Spielman, and Phillip Wherry, "How Good Is Good Enough?" *Communications of the ACM*, Jan. 1994, pp. 81–91.

- Joseph Ellin, *Morality and the Meaning of Life: An Introduction to Ethical Theory*, Harcourt Brace Jovanovich, 1995.

- M. David Ermann *et al.*, eds., *Computers, Ethics and Society*, 2nd. ed., Oxford University Press, 1997.

- Donald Gotterbarn, Keith Miller, and Simon Rogerson, "Software Engineering Code of Ethics Is Approved," *Communications of the ACM*, Oct. 1999, 42:10, pp. 102–107.

- Deborah G. Johnson, *Computer Ethics*, Prentice Hall, 3rd ed., 2001.

- Kenneth C. Laudon, "Ethical Concepts and Information Technology," *Communications of the ACM*, Dec. 1995, 38:12, pp. 33–39.

- Jan Narveson, *Moral Matters*, Broadview Press, 1993. The first chapter gives a good, very readable introduction to moral issues.

- Effy Oz, *Ethics for the Information Age*, William C. Brown, 1994.

- David Lorge Parnas, "Computing and the Citizen: SDI: A Violation of Professional Responsibility," *Abacus*, Winter 1987, 4:2, pp. 46–52.

- Louis Pojman, *Ethical Theory: Classical and Contemporary Readings*, 2nd ed., Wadsworth, 1995. Includes John Stuart Mill's "Utilitarianism," Kant's "The Foundations of the Metaphysic of Morals," John Locke's "Natural Rights," and other classical essays on various ethical theories.

- James Rachels, *The Elements of Moral Philosophy*, McGraw Hill, 1993.

- Richard Spinello, *CyberEthics: Morality and Law in Cyberspace*, Jones and Bartlett, 2000.

- Diane Vaughan, *The Challenger Launch Decision: Risky Technology, Culture, and Deviance at NASA*, University of Chicago Press, 1996.

ORGANIZATIONS AND WEBSITES

- Association for Computing Machinery: www.acm.org

- Computer Professionals for Social Responsibility: cpsr.org

- IEEE Computer Society: www.computer.org

- Herman Tavani, ed., "The Tavani Bibliography of Computing, Ethics, and Social Responsibility": cyberethics.cbi.msstate.edu/biblio

EPILOGUE

Certain themes or observations have come up repeatedly throughout this book.

Computer technology has brought us enormous benefits. We described a small sample in Chapter 1. Even though other chapters focus mostly on problems and controversial issues, many benefits inevitably appeared in them, too.

The human mind, and hence technology, do not stand still. Change always disrupts the status quo. Technology is always shifting the balance of power: for example, between governments and citizens; between cryptographers, who create codes, and cryptanalysts, who break them; between hackers and security experts; between people who want to protect their privacy and businesses that want to collect personal information. Entrenched powers such as governments or dominant companies in an industry will fight to maintain their prior position. We can look to governments for solutions to some problems caused by technology, but we should remember that governments are major abusers of personal information and privacy. They are institutions, like businesses and other organizations, with their own interests and incentives.

Because technology brings change, it often brings new problems. With time, we solve or reduce many of the problems, using more or better technology, the market, innovative services and business arrangements, laws, education, and so on. We cannot eliminate all negative effects of computer technology. We have to accept some. We always make trade-offs in life; few situations are exactly as we might choose.

In some areas, such as personal data collection and surveillance, computer technology has brought profound changes that could fundamentally alter our interactions with the people around us and with our governments. It is essential to think about appropriate guidelines and restrictions early so that we can design them into the standards for the technology and implement them before changes are irreversible. On the other hand, we must be careful not to regulate too soon in ways that would stifle innovation and prevent new benefits.

Virtually any new technology is guaranteed to have many beneficial uses and also destructive uses. The issue of banning a tool or technology arose in several contexts. These included encryption, anonymity on the Web, Sony's Betamax VCR, DeCSS software and other methods to circumvent copyright protection, and so on. The difficulty of predicting future beneficial uses of technologies is a strong argument against such bans. Freedom of speech and privacy protection are relevant arguments against some proposed bans.

We learn from experience. System failures, even disasters, lead to better systems. The observation that perfection is not possible does not absolve us of responsibility for sloppy or unethical work.

There are many opportunities for computer professionals to develop wonderful new products and to use their skills and creativity to build solutions to some of the problems we have discussed. I hope that this book has sparked some ideas. I hope also that the discussion of risks and failures encourages you to exercise the highest degree of professional and personal responsibility.

APPENDIX A

THE SOFTWARE ENGINEERING CODE AND THE ACM CODE

A.1 The Software Engineering Code of Ethics and Professional Practice*

Preamble

Computers have a central and growing role in commerce, industry, government, medicine, education, entertainment and society at large. Software engineers are those who contribute by direct participation or by teaching, to the analysis, specification, design, development, certification, maintenance and testing of software systems. Because of their roles in developing software systems, software engineers have significant opportunities to do good or cause harm, to enable others to do good or cause harm, or to influence others to do good or cause harm. To ensure, as much as possible, that their efforts will be used for good, software engineers must commit themselves to making software engineering a beneficial and respected profession. In accordance with that commitment, software engineers shall adhere to the following Code of Ethics and Professional Practice.

The Code contains eight Principles related to the behavior of and decisions made by professional software engineers, including practitioners, educators, managers, supervisors and policy makers, as well as trainees and students of the profession. The Principles identify the ethically responsible relationships in which individuals, groups, and organizations participate and the primary obligations within these relationships. The Clauses of each Principle are illustrations of some of the obligations included in these relationships. These obligations are founded in the software engineer's humanity, in special care owed to people affected by the work of software engineers, and the unique elements of the practice

---

*Version 5.2, prepared by the ACM/IEEE-CS Joint Task Force on Software Engineering Ethics and Professional Practices, Executive Committee: Donald Gotterbarn (Chair), Keith Miller and Simon Rogerson. Jointly approved by the ACM and the IEEE-CS as the standard for teaching and practicing software engineering. ©1999 by the Institute of Electrical Engineers, Inc., and the Association for Computing Machinery, Inc.

of software engineering. The Code prescribes these as obligations of anyone claiming to be or aspiring to be a software engineer.

It is not intended that the individual parts of the Code be used in isolation to justify errors of omission or commission. The list of Principles and Clauses is not exhaustive. The Clauses should not be read as separating the acceptable from the unacceptable in professional conduct in all practical situations. The Code is not a simple ethical algorithm that generates ethical decisions. In some situations standards may be in tension with each other or with standards from other sources. These situations require the software engineer to use ethical judgment to act in a manner which is most consistent with the spirit of the Code of Ethics and Professional Practice, given the circumstances.

Ethical tensions can best be addressed by thoughtful consideration of fundamental principles, rather than blind reliance on detailed regulations. These Principles should influence software engineers to consider broadly who is affected by their work; to examine if they and their colleagues are treating other human beings with due respect; to consider how the public, if reasonably well informed, would view their decisions; to analyze how the least empowered will be affected by their decisions; and to consider whether their acts would be judged worthy of the ideal professional working as a software engineer. In all these judgments concern for the health, safety and welfare of the public is primary; that is, the "Public Interest" is central to this Code.

The dynamic and demanding context of software engineering requires a code that is adaptable and relevant to new situations as they occur. However, even in this generality, the Code provides support for software engineers and managers of software engineers who need to take positive action in a specific case by documenting the ethical stance of the profession. The Code provides an ethical foundation to which individuals within teams and the team as a whole can appeal. The Code helps to define those actions that are ethically improper to request of a software engineer or teams of software engineers.

The Code is not simply for adjudicating the nature of questionable acts; it also has an important educational function. As this Code expresses the consensus of the profession on ethical issues, it is a means to educate both the public and aspiring professionals about the ethical obligations of all software engineers.

Principles

PRINCIPLE 1: PUBLIC

Software engineers shall act consistently with the public interest. In particular, software engineers shall, as appropriate:

1.01. Accept full responsibility for their own work.

1.02. Moderate the interests of the software engineer, the employer, the client and the users with the public good.

1.03. Approve software only if they have a well-founded belief that it is safe, meets specifications, passes appropriate tests, and does not diminish quality of life, diminish privacy or harm the environment. The ultimate effect of the work should be to the public good.

1.04. Disclose to appropriate persons or authorities any actual or potential danger to the user, the public, or the environment, that they reasonably believe to be associated with software or related documents.

1.05. Cooperate in efforts to address matters of grave public concern caused by software, its installation, maintenance, support or documentation.

1.06. Be fair and avoid deception in all statements, particularly public ones, concerning software or related documents, methods and tools.

1.07. Consider issues of physical disabilities, allocation of resources, economic disadvantage and other factors that can diminish access to the benefits of software.

1.08. Be encouraged to volunteer professional skills to good causes and contribute to public education concerning the discipline.

PRINCIPLE 2: CLIENT AND EMPLOYER

Software engineers shall act in a manner that is in the best interests of their client and employer, consistent with the public interest. In particular, software engineers shall, as appropriate:

2.01. Provide service in their areas of competence, being honest and forthright about any limitations of their experience and education.

2.02. Not knowingly use software that is obtained or retained either illegally or unethically.

2.03. Use the property of a client or employer only in ways properly authorized, and with the client's or employer's knowledge and consent.

2.04. Ensure that any document upon which they rely has been approved, when required, by someone authorized to approve it.

2.05. Keep private any confidential information gained in their professional work, where such confidentiality is consistent with the public interest and consistent with the law.

2.06. Identify, document, collect evidence and report to the client or the employer promptly if, in their opinion, a project is likely to fail, to prove too expensive, to violate intellectual property law, or otherwise to be problematic.

2.07. Identify, document, and report significant issues of social concern, of which they are aware, in software or related documents, to the employer or the client.

2.08. Accept no outside work detrimental to the work they perform for their primary employer.

2.09. Promote no interest adverse to their employer or client, unless a higher ethical concern is being compromised; in that case, inform the employer or another appropriate authority of the ethical concern.

PRINCIPLE 3: PRODUCT

Software engineers shall ensure that their products and related modifications meet the highest professional standards possible. In particular, software engineers shall, as appropriate:

3.01. Strive for high quality, acceptable cost and a reasonable schedule, ensuring significant tradeoffs are clear to and accepted by the employer and the client, and are available for consideration by the user and the public.

3.02. Ensure proper and achievable goals and objectives for any project on which they work or propose.

3.03. Identify, define and address ethical, economic, cultural, legal and environmental issues related to work projects.

3.04. Ensure that they are qualified for any project on which they work or propose to work by an appropriate combination of education and training, and experience.

3.05. Ensure an appropriate method is used for any project on which they work or propose to work.

3.06. Work to follow professional standards, when available, that are most appropriate for the task at hand, departing from these only when ethically or technically justified.

3.07. Strive to fully understand the specifications for software on which they work.

3.08. Ensure that specifications for software on which they work have been well documented, satisfy the users' requirements and have the appropriate approvals.

3.09. Ensure realistic quantitative estimates of cost, scheduling, personnel, quality and outcomes on any project on which they work or propose to work and provide an uncertainty assessment of these estimates.

3.10. Ensure adequate testing, debugging, and review of software and related documents on which they work.

3.11. Ensure adequate documentation, including significant problems discovered and solutions adopted, for any project on which they work.

3.12. Work to develop software and related documents that respect the privacy of those who will be affected by that software.

3.13. Be careful to use only accurate data derived by ethical and lawful means, and use it only in ways properly authorized.

3.14. Maintain the integrity of data, being sensitive to outdated or flawed occurrences.

3.15. Treat all forms of software maintenance with the same professionalism as new development.

PRINCIPLE 4: JUDGMENT

Software engineers shall maintain integrity and independence in their professional judgment. In particular, software engineers shall, as appropriate:

4.01. Temper all technical judgments by the need to support and maintain human values.

4.02. Only endorse documents either prepared under their supervision or within their areas of competence and with which they are in agreement.

4.03. Maintain professional objectivity with respect to any software or related documents they are asked to evaluate.

4.04. Not engage in deceptive financial practices such as bribery, double billing, or other improper financial practices.

4.05. Disclose to all concerned parties those conflicts of interest that cannot reasonably be avoided or escaped.

4.06. Refuse to participate, as members or advisors, in a private, governmental or professional body concerned with software related issues, in which they, their employers or their clients have undisclosed potential conflicts of interest.

PRINCIPLE 5: MANAGEMENT

Software engineering managers and leaders shall subscribe to and promote an ethical approach to the management of software development and maintenance. In particular, those managing or leading software engineers shall, as appropriate:

5.01. Ensure good management for any project on which they work, including effective procedures for promotion of quality and reduction of risk.

5.02. Ensure that software engineers are informed of standards before being held to them.

5.03. Ensure that software engineers know the employer's policies and procedures for protecting passwords, files and information that is confidential to the employer or confidential to others.

5.04. Assign work only after taking into account appropriate contributions of education and experience tempered with a desire to further that education and experience.

5.05. Ensure realistic quantitative estimates of cost, scheduling, personnel, quality and outcomes on any project on which they work or propose to work, and provide an uncertainty assessment of these estimates.

5.06. Attract potential software engineers only by full and accurate description of the conditions of employment.

5.07. Offer fair and just remuneration.

5.08. Not unjustly prevent someone from taking a position for which that person is suitably qualified.

5.09. Ensure that there is a fair agreement concerning ownership of any software, processes, research, writing, or other intellectual property to which a software engineer has contributed.

5.10. Provide for due process in hearing charges of violation of an employer's policy or of this Code.

5.11. Not ask a software engineer to do anything inconsistent with this Code.

5.12. Not punish anyone for expressing ethical concerns about a project.

PRINCIPLE 6: PROFESSION

Software engineers shall advance the integrity and reputation of the profession consistent with the public interest. In particular, software engineers shall, as appropriate:

6.01. Help develop an organizational environment favorable to acting ethically.

6.02. Promote public knowledge of software engineering.

6.03. Extend software engineering knowledge by appropriate participation in professional organizations, meetings and publications.

6.04. Support, as members of a profession, other software engineers striving to follow this Code.

6.05. Not promote their own interest at the expense of the profession, client or employer.

6.06. Obey all laws governing their work, unless, in exceptional circumstances, such compliance is inconsistent with the public interest.

6.07. Be accurate in stating the characteristics of software on which they work, avoiding not only false claims but also claims that might reasonably be supposed to be speculative, vacuous, deceptive, misleading, or doubtful.

6.08. Take responsibility for detecting, correcting, and reporting errors in software and associated documents on which they work.

6.09. Ensure that clients, employers, and supervisors know of the software engineer's commitment to this Code of ethics, and the subsequent ramifications of such commitment.

6.10. Avoid associations with businesses and organizations which are in conflict with this Code.

6.11. Recognize that violations of this Code are inconsistent with being a professional software engineer.

6.12. Express concerns to the people involved when significant violations of this Code are detected unless this is impossible, counter-productive, or dangerous.

6.13. Report significant violations of this Code to appropriate authorities when it is clear that consultation with people involved in these significant violations is impossible, counter-productive or dangerous.

PRINCIPLE 7: COLLEAGUES

Software engineers shall be fair to and supportive of their colleagues. In particular, software engineers shall, as appropriate:

7.01. Encourage colleagues to adhere to this Code.

7.02. Assist colleagues in professional development.

7.03. Credit fully the work of others and refrain from taking undue credit.

7.04. Review the work of others in an objective, candid, and properly-documented way.

7.05. Give a fair hearing to the opinions, concerns, or complaints of a colleague.

7.06. Assist colleagues in being fully aware of current standard work practices including policies and procedures for protecting passwords, files and other confidential information, and security measures in general.

7.07. Not unfairly intervene in the career of any colleague; however, concern for the employer, the client or public interest may compel software engineers, in good faith, to question the competence of a colleague.

7.08. In situations outside of their own areas of competence, call upon the opinions of other professionals who have competence in that area.

PRINCIPLE 8: SELF

Software engineers shall participate in lifelong learning regarding the practice of their profession and shall promote an ethical approach to the practice of the profession. In particular, software engineers shall continually endeavor to:

8.01. Further their knowledge of developments in the analysis, specification, design, development, maintenance and testing of software and related documents, together with the management of the development process.

8.02. Improve their ability to create safe, reliable, and useful quality software at reasonable cost and within a reasonable time.

8.03. Improve their ability to produce accurate, informative, and well-written documentation.

8.04. Improve their understanding of the software and related documents on which they work and of the environment in which they will be used.

8.05. Improve their knowledge of relevant standards and the law governing the software and related documents on which they work.

8.06. Improve their knowledge of this Code, its interpretation, and its application to their work.

8.07. Not give unfair treatment to anyone because of any irrelevant prejudices.

8.08. Not influence others to undertake any action that involves a breach of this Code.

8.09. Recognize that personal violations of this Code are inconsistent with being a professional software engineer.

A.2   The ACM Code of Ethics and Professional Conduct*

Preamble

Commitment to ethical professional conduct is expected of every member (voting members, associate members, and student members) of the Association for Computing Machinery (ACM).

This Code, consisting of 24 imperatives formulated as statements of personal responsibility, identifies the elements of such a commitment. It contains many, but not all, issues professionals are likely to face. Section 1 outlines fundamental ethical considerations, while Section 2 addresses additional, more specific considerations of professional conduct. Statements in Section 3 pertain more specifically to individuals who have a leadership role, whether in the workplace or in a volunteer capacity such as with organizations like ACM. Principles involving compliance with this Code are given in Section 4.

The Code shall be supplemented by a set of Guidelines, which provide explanation to assist members in dealing with the various issues contained in the Code. It is expected that the Guidelines will be changed more frequently than the Code.

The Code and its supplemented Guidelines are intended to serve as a basis for ethical decision making in the conduct of professional work. Secondarily, they may serve as a basis for judging the merit of a formal complaint pertaining to violation of professional ethical standards.

It should be noted that although computing is not mentioned in the imperatives of Section 1, the Code is concerned with how these fundamental imperatives apply to one's conduct as a computing professional. These imperatives are expressed in a general form to emphasize that ethical principles which apply to computer ethics are derived from more general ethical principles.

It is understood that some words and phrases in a code of ethics are subject to varying interpretations, and that any ethical principle may conflict with other ethical principles in specific situations. Questions related to ethical conflicts can best be answered by thoughtful consideration of fundamental principles, rather than reliance on detailed regulations.

Contents and Guidelines

1.   GENERAL MORAL IMPERATIVES. AS AN ACM MEMBER I WILL . . .

*This Code and the supplemental Guidelines were developed by the Task Force for the Revision of the ACM Code of Ethics and Professional Conduct: Ronald E. Anderson, Chair, Gerald Engel, Donald Gotterbarn, Grace C. Hertlein, Alex Hoffman, Bruce Jawer, Deborah G. Johnson, Doris K. Lidtke, Joyce Currie Little, Dianne Martin, Donn B. Parker, Judith A. Perrolle, and Richard S. Rosenberg. The Task Force was organized by ACM/SIGCAS and funding was provided by the ACM SIG Discretionary Fund. This Code and the supplemental Guidelines were adopted by the ACM Council on October 16, 1992. It was updated Jan. 16, 1998. Reprinted with the permission of the Association for Computing Machinery.

1.1 Contribute to society and human well-being.

This principle concerning the quality of life of all people affirms an obligation to protect fundamental human rights and to respect the diversity of all cultures. An essential aim of computing professionals is to minimize negative consequences of computing systems, including threats to health and safety. When designing or implementing systems, computing professionals must attempt to ensure that the products of their efforts will be used in socially responsible ways, will meet social needs, and will avoid harmful effects to health and welfare.

In addition to a safe social environment, human well-being includes a safe natural environment. Therefore, computing professionals who design and develop systems must be alert to, and make others aware of, any potential damage to the local or global environment.

1.2 Avoid harm to others.

"Harm" means injury or negative consequences, such as undesirable loss of information, loss of property, property damage, or unwanted environmental impacts. This principle prohibits use of computing technology in ways that result in harm to any of the following: users, the general public, employees, employers. Harmful actions include intentional destruction or modification of files and programs leading to serious loss of resources or unnecessary expenditure of human resources such as the time and effort required to purge systems of "computer viruses."

Well-intended actions, including those that accomplish assigned duties, may lead to harm unexpectedly. In such an event the responsible person or persons are obligated to undo or mitigate the negative consequences as much as possible. One way to avoid unintentional harm is to carefully consider potential impacts on all those affected by decisions made during design and implementation.

To minimize the possibility of indirectly harming others, computing professionals must minimize malfunctions by following generally accepted standards for system design and testing. Furthermore, it is often necessary to assess the social consequences of systems to project the likelihood of any serious harm to others. If system features are misrepresented to users, coworkers, or supervisors, the individual computing professional is responsible for any resulting injury.

In the work environment the computing professional has the additional obligation to report any signs of system dangers that might result in serious personal or social damage. If one's superiors do not act to curtail or mitigate such dangers, it may be necessary to "blow the whistle" to help correct the problem or reduce the risk. However, capricious or misguided reporting of violations can, itself, be harmful. Before reporting violations, all relevant aspects of the incident must be thoroughly assessed. In particular, the assessment of risk and responsibility must be credible. It is suggested that advice be sought from other computing professionals. See principle 2.5 regarding thorough evaluations.

1.3 Be honest and trustworthy.

Honesty is an essential component of trust. Without trust an organization cannot function effectively. The honest computing professional will not make deliberately false or deceptive claims about a system or system design, but will instead provide full disclosure of all pertinent system limitations and problems.

A computer professional has a duty to be honest about his or her own qualifications, and about any circumstances that might lead to conflicts of interest.

Membership in volunteer organizations such as ACM may at times place individuals in situations where their statements or actions could be interpreted as carrying the "weight" of a larger group of professionals. An ACM member will exercise care to not misrepresent ACM or positions and policies of ACM or any ACM units.

1.4 Be fair and take action not to discriminate.

The values of equality, tolerance, respect for others, and the principles of equal justice govern this imperative. Discrimination on the basis of race, sex, religion, age, disability, national origin, or other such factors is an explicit violation of ACM policy and will not be tolerated.

Inequities between different groups of people may result from the use or misuse of information and technology. In a fair society, all individuals would have equal opportunity to participate in, or benefit from, the use of computer resources regardless of race, sex, religion, age, disability, national origin or other such similar factors. However, these ideals do not justify unauthorized use of computer resources nor do they provide an adequate basis for violation of any other ethical imperatives of this code.

1.5 Honor property rights including copyrights and patent.

Violation of copyrights, patents, trade secrets and the terms of license agreements is prohibited by law in most circumstances. Even when software is not so protected, such violations are contrary to professional behavior. Copies of software should be made only with proper authorization. Unauthorized duplication of materials must not be condoned.

1.6 Give proper credit for intellectual property.

Computing professionals are obligated to protect the integrity of intellectual property. Specifically, one must not take credit for other's ideas or work, even in cases where the work has not been explicitly protected by copyright, patent, etc.

1.7 Respect the privacy of others.

Computing and communication technology enables the collection and exchange of personal information on a scale unprecedented in the history of civilization. Thus there is increased potential for violating the privacy of individuals and groups. It is the responsibility of professionals to maintain the privacy and integrity of data describing individuals. This includes taking precautions to ensure the accuracy of data, as well as protecting it from unauthorized access or accidental disclosure to inappropriate individuals. Furthermore, procedures must be established to allow individuals to review their records and correct inaccuracies.

This imperative implies that only the necessary amount of personal information be collected in a system, that retention and disposal periods for that information be clearly defined and enforced, and that personal information gathered for a specific purpose not be used for other purposes without consent of the individual(s). These principles apply to electronic communications, including electronic mail, and prohibit procedures that capture or monitor electronic user data, including messages, without the permission of users or bona fide authorization related to system operation and maintenance. User data observed during the normal duties of system operation and maintenance must be treated with strictest confidentiality, except in cases where it is evidence for the violation of law, organizational regulations, or this Code. In these cases, the nature or contents of that information must be disclosed only to proper authorities.

1.8 Honor confidentiality.

The principle of honesty extends to issues of confidentiality of information whenever one has made an explicit promise to honor confidentiality or, implicitly, when private information not directly related to the performance of one's duties becomes available. The ethical concern is to respect all obligations of confidentiality to employers, clients, and users unless discharged from such obligations by requirements of the law or other principles of this Code.

2. MORE SPECIFIC PROFESSIONAL RESPONSIBILITIES. AS AN ACM COMPUTING PROFESSIONAL I WILL . . .

2.1 Strive to achieve the highest quality, effectiveness and dignity in both the process and products of professional work.

Excellence is perhaps the most important obligation of a professional. The computing professional must strive to achieve quality and to be cognizant of the serious negative consequences that may result from poor quality in a system.

2.2 Acquire and maintain professional competence.

Excellence depends on individuals who take responsibility for acquiring and maintaining professional competence. A professional must participate in setting standards for appropriate levels of competence, and strive to achieve those standards. Upgrading technical knowledge and competence can be achieved in several ways: doing independent study; attending seminars, conferences, or courses; and being involved in professional organizations.

2.3 Know and respect existing laws pertaining to professional work.

ACM members must obey existing local, state, province, national, and international laws unless there is a compelling ethical basis not to do so. Policies and procedures of the organizations in which one participates must also be obeyed. But compliance must be balanced with the recognition that sometimes existing laws and rules may be immoral or inappropriate and, therefore, must be challenged. Violation of a law or regulation may be ethical when that law or rule has inadequate moral basis or when it conflicts with another law judged to be more important. If one decides to violate a law or rule because it is viewed as unethical, or for any other reason, one must fully accept responsibility for one's actions and for the consequences.

2.4 Accept and provide appropriate professional review.

Quality professional work, especially in the computing profession, depends on professional reviewing and critiquing. Whenever appropriate, individual members should seek and utilize peer review as well as provide critical review of the work of others.

2.5 Give comprehensive and thorough evaluations of computer systems and their impacts, including analysis of possible risks.

Computer professionals must strive to be perceptive, thorough, and objective when evaluating, recommending, and presenting system descriptions and alternatives. Computer professionals are in a position of special trust, and therefore have a special responsibility to provide objective, credible evaluations to employers, clients, users, and the public. When providing evaluations the professional must also identify any relevant conflicts of interest, as stated in imperative 1.3.

As noted in the discussion of principle 1.2 on avoiding harm, any signs of danger from systems must be reported to those who have opportunity and/or responsibility to resolve them. See the guidelines for imperative 1.2 for more details concerning harm, including the reporting of professional violations.

2.6 Honor contracts, agreements, and assigned responsibilities.

Honoring one's commitments is a matter of integrity and honesty. For the computer professional this includes ensuring that system elements perform as intended. Also, when one contracts for work with another party, one has an obligation to keep that party properly informed about progress toward completing that work.

A computing professional has a responsibility to request a change in any assignment that he or she feels cannot be completed as defined. Only after serious consideration and with full disclosure of risks and concerns to the employer or client, should one accept the assignment. The major underlying principle here is the obligation to accept personal accountability for professional work. On some occasions other ethical principles may take greater priority.

A judgment that a specific assignment should not be performed may not be accepted. Having clearly identified one's concerns and reasons for that judgment, but failing to procure a change in that assignment, one may yet be obligated, by contract or by law, to proceed as directed. The computing professional's ethical judgment should be the final guide in deciding whether or not to proceed. Regardless of the decision, one must accept the responsibility for the consequences.

However, performing assignments "against one's own judgment" does not relieve the professional of responsibility for any negative consequences.

2.7 Improve public understanding of computing and its consequences.

Computing professionals have a responsibility to share technical knowledge with the public by encouraging understanding of computing, including the impacts of computer systems and their limitations. This imperative implies an obligation to counter any false views related to computing.

2.8 Access computing and communication resources only when authorized
    to do so.

Theft or destruction of tangible and electronic property is prohibited by imperative 1.2–"Avoid harm to others." Trespassing and unauthorized use of a computer or communication system is addressed by this imperative. Trespassing includes accessing communication networks and computer systems, or accounts and/or files associated with those systems, without explicit authorization to do so. Individuals and organizations have the right to restrict access to their systems so long as they do not violate the discrimination principle (see 1.4). No one should enter or use another's computer system, software, or data files without permission. One must always have appropriate approval before using system resources, including communication ports, file space, other system peripherals, and computer time.

3. ORGANIZATIONAL LEADERSHIP IMPERATIVES. AS AN ACM MEMBER AND AN ORGANIZATIONAL LEADER, I WILL . . .

BACKGROUND NOTE: This section draws extensively from the draft IFIP Code of Ethics, especially its sections on organizational ethics and international concerns. The ethical obligations of organizations tend to be neglected in most codes of professional conduct, perhaps because these codes are written from the perspective of the individual member. This dilemma is addressed by stating these imperatives from the perspective of the organizational leader. In this context "leader" is viewed as any organizational member who has leadership or educational responsibilities. These imperatives generally may apply to organizations as well as their leaders. In this context "organizations" are corporations, government agencies, and other "employers," as well as volunteer professional organizations.

3.1 Articulate social responsibilities of members of an organizational unit
    and encourage full acceptance of those responsibilities.

Because organizations of all kinds have impacts on the public, they must accept responsibilities to society. Organizational procedures and attitudes oriented toward quality and the welfare of society will reduce harm to members of the public, thereby serving public interest and fulfilling social responsibility. Therefore, organizational leaders must encourage full participation in meeting social responsibilities as well as quality performance.

3.2 Manage personnel and resources to design and build information
    systems that enhance the quality of working life.

Organizational leaders are responsible for ensuring that computer systems enhance, not degrade, the quality of working life. When implementing a computer system, organizations must consider the personal and professional development, physical safety, and human dignity of all workers. Appropriate human–computer ergonomic standards should be considered in system design and in the workplace.

3.3 Acknowledge and support proper and authorized uses of an organization's computing and communication resources.

Because computer systems can become tools to harm as well as to benefit an organization, the leadership has the responsibility to clearly define appropriate and inappropriate uses of organizational computing resources. While the number and scope of such rules should be minimal, they should be fully enforced when established.

3.4 Ensure that users and those who will be affected by a system have their needs clearly articulated during the assessment and design of requirements; later the system must be validated to meet requirements.

Current system users, potential users and other persons whose lives may be affected by a system must have their needs assessed and incorporated in the statement of requirements. System validation should ensure compliance with those requirements.

3.5 Articulate and support policies that protect the dignity of users and others affected by a computing system.

Designing or implementing systems that deliberately or inadvertently demean individuals or groups is ethically unacceptable. Computer professionals who are in decision making positions should verify that systems are designed and implemented to protect personal privacy and enhance personal dignity.

3.6 Create opportunities for members of the organization to learn the principles and limitations of computer systems.

This complements the imperative on public understanding (2.7). Educational opportunities are essential to facilitate optimal participation of all organizational members. Opportunities must be available to all members to help them improve their knowledge and skills in computing, including courses that familiarize them with the consequences and limitations of particular types of systems. In particular, professionals must be made aware of the dangers of building systems around oversimplified models, the improbability of anticipating and designing for every possible operating condition, and other issues related to the complexity of this profession.

4. COMPLIANCE WITH THE CODE. AS AN ACM MEMBER I WILL . . .

4.1 Uphold and promote the principles of this Code.

The future of the computing profession depends on both technical and ethical excellence. Not only is it important for ACM computing professionals to adhere to the principles expressed in this Code, each member should encourage and support adherence by other members.

4.2 Treat violations of this Code as inconsistent with membership in the ACM.

Adherence of professionals to a code of ethics is largely a voluntary matter. However, if a member does not follow this code by engaging in gross misconduct, membership in ACM may be terminated.

Index